PLAY THERAPY THEORY AND PRACTICE
A Comparative Presentation

Edited by
Kevin O'Connor
and
Lisa Mages Braverman

JOHN WILEY & SONS, INC.

New York • Chichester • Brisbane • Toronto • Singapore • Weinheim

Copyright © 1997 by John Wiley & Sons, Inc.
Published by John Wiley & Sons, Inc.

This publication is designed to provide accurate and
authoritative information in regard to the subject
matter covered. It is sold with the understanding that
the publisher is not engaged in rendering legal,
accounting, or other professional services. If legal,
accounting, medical, or psychological advice or other
expert assistance is required, the services of a competent
professional person should be sought.

Library of Congress Cataloging-in-Publication Data

Play therapy theory and practice : a comparative presentation / edited
   by Kevin O'Connor and Lisa Mages Braverman.
       p.   cm.
   Includes indexes.
   ISBN 0-471-10638-0 (cloth : alk. paper)
   1. Play therapy. I. O'Connor, Kevin J. II. Braverman, Lisa Mages.
RJ505.P6P547   1997
615.8'5153—dc20   96-21257
                                          CIP

Preface

Recently there has been a dramatic increase in the number of publications on the topic of play therapy. These include works describing both numerous theoretical models and intervention techniques. This proliferation has resulted in a body of literature so large that it is difficult for either students or practitioners to evaluate or compare the information presented. The goal of this text is to provide a forum for the direct comparison of the major theoretical models of play therapy and their implications for treatment.

In order to present information in this book that is accurate and current, we have asked leading authorities on various theoretical models of play therapy to write original chapters that both describe their theoretical model of play therapy treatment and demonstrate the application of that model. Each author will apply their model to the same case, thus providing the reader with a basis for direct comparison. By virtue of being interdisciplinary in its approach, diverse in theoretical orientation and comparative in nature, this book will prove to be a landmark reference source for years to come.

Play Therapy Theory and Practice: A Comparative Presentation begins with an overall presentation of the case history that will be used in each of the following chapters. The remaining chapters present the following theoretical models of play therapy: Client-Centered, Psychoanalytic, Cognitive-Behavioral, Jungian, Filial, Developmental, Gestalt, Family Theraplay, Ecosystemic, Ericksonian, Adlerian, Dynamic, and Strategic Family.

Psychiatrists, psychologists, social workers, nurses, and counselors at all levels of training and experience will find *Play Therapy Theory and Application: A Comparative Presentation* informative, thought provoking, and clinically useful.

KEVIN O'CONNOR
LISA MAGES BRAVERMAN

Contributors

Garry Landreth, Ed.D.

Garry L. Landreth, Ed.D. is a Regents Professor in the Department of Counseling, Development, and Higher Education. He is a licensed professional counselor and psychologist, a Registered Play Therapist-Supervisor, and Chair of the Board of Directors of the Association for Play Therapy. He is also founding Director of the Center for Play Therapy at the University of North Texas. The Center has become the definitive leader in process and outcome research on both child-centered and filial play therapy. Dr. Landreth received the prestigious Virginia Axline Distinguished Professional Award for his work in conceptualizing and promoting the child-centered approach to play therapy. He has conducted training seminars focusing on child centered play therapy throughout the United States, and in Canada, China, and Europe.

Dr. Landreth's more than seventy publications include the books *Play Therapy: Dynamics of the Process of Counseling with Children; Group Counseling: Concepts and Procedures; Play Therapy Interventions with Children's Problems;* and *Play Therapy: The Art of the Relationship.* He is also on the editorial board of the *International Journal of Play Therapy.*

Daniel Sweeney, Ph.D., LPC, MFCC, RPT-S

Dr. Sweeney is an Assistant Professor of Counseling at George Fox University in Portland, Oregon. He is the former Assistant Director of the *Center for Play Therapy* at the University of North Texas and a psychotherapist in private practice. He is a licensed counselor in several states and a Registered Play Therapist-Supervisor. Dr. Sweeney has extensive experience in working with children and adolescents in a variety of settings, including therapeutic foster care, community mental health, and pastoral counseling. Daniel has presented at numerous state and national conferences on the topics of play therapy, filial therapy, and sandplay. He has authored several articles on play therapy issues, is the co-author of *Play Therapy Interventions With Children's Problems,* and the author of *Counseling Children Through the World of Play.*

v

Anna C. Lee, Ph.D.

Dr. Anna Lee is currently a Professor of Psychology at the European University/Portugal and an instructor-lecturer with the University of Maryland, European Extension. She received her certificate in psychoanalysis from New York University Postdoctoral Program in Psychotherapy and Psychoanalysis and has been involved in the practice of psychoanalysis for the past decade. Dr. Lee also conducts psychoanalytic psychotherapy with children and their families, currently specializing in the treatment of bicultural and multicultural children. She also is a consultant to the American Embassy in Lisbon and international schools in the Lisbon metropolitan area. Her other contributions to the area of child psychoanalysis include the following book chapters: "Child Analysis and Psychotherapy," in *The Clinical Psychology Handbook* (H. Herzen, A.E. Kazdin, and A.S. Bellack, Eds., both the 1983 and 1989 editions) and "Normal and Pathological Gender-Role Development in Children," in *From Research to Clinical Practice* (G. Stricker and R. Keisner, Eds., 1985). Dr. Lee now lives and practices in Cascais, Portugal, where she lectures frequently to an international community on the issues of parenting as well as child and adolescent development.

Susan M. Knell, Ph.D.

Dr. Susan M. Knell is a licensed psychologist, and the author of *Cognitive-Behavioral Play Therapy*, as well as numerous articles and chapters describing the cognitive-behavioral approach to play therapy, which she developed. Dr. Knell's approach to play therapy provides a theoretical framework based on cognitive-behavioral principles and integrates these in a developmentally sensitive way. This framework provides a specific problem-solving approach that helps the child develop more adaptive thoughts and behaviors. Prior to the development of cognitive-behavioral play therapy, young children were considered unable to understand or correct distortions in their thinking, thus negating the possibility of using such interventions with this population. Dr. Knell's work demonstrates that the methods of cognitive-behavioral therapy can be modeled for children indirectly through play, by using puppets and stuffed animals, leading to effective change. She conducts seminars and workshops throughout the country on this innovative approach. Dr. Knell holds appointments at Case Western Reserve and Cleveland State Universities, where she supervises and teaches graduate students.

John Allan, Ph.D.

Dr. Allan has had a 35-year interest in the psychology of C.G. Jung. This started with his own Jungian analysis with Dr. Thomas Parker, a past president of the C.J. Jung Institute of San Francisco, and later led to his supervision of child play therapy clients from a Jungian perspective. Jung's approach, focusing on the self-healing ability of the psyche, provides a rich understanding of the child's symbols and images while at the same time allowing the unconscious of the child to lead and direct the play. Dr. Allan is Professor of Child Counseling in the Department of Counseling Psychology at the University of British Columbia and author of *Inscapes of the Child's World and Jungian Counseling in Schools and Clinics*; and co-author, with Judi Bertoia, of *Written Paths to Healing: Education and Jungian Child Counseling*. He also works as a Jungian analyst in private practice and as a senior training analyst with the Pacific Northwest Society of Jungian Analysts.

Louise Guerney, Ph.D.

Louise Guerney received a Ph.D. in Clinical Psychology from Pennsylvania State University, with a specialty in child psychology. As a part-time research associate at Rutgers University she worked with her husband, Bernard Guerney, and their colleagues on development and research of filial therapy. For nearly 25 years she taught and was director of the Filial Therapy Program at the Pennsylvania State University, from which she is now retired as a Professor Emerita of Human Development and Counseling Psychology. Currently, she is associated with the National Institute of Relationship Enhancement through which she offers workshops in play therapy, filial therapy, and parent education training.

Dr. Guerney is a licensed psychologist, and a Registered Play Therapist-Supervisor. She serves on the Association for Play Therapy Board of Directors and the editorial boards of the *International Journal of Play Therapy, The Family Journal*, and the *American Journal of Family Therapy*. She is the author of a series of parenting manuals for parents, foster parents, and parent educators, as well as co-author of *Helping Your Child*, many articles, and book chapters including "Client-Centered Play Therapy," in the *Handbook of Play Therapy*.

Viola A. Brody, Ph.D.

Viola Brody, a psychologist in private practice in St. Petersburg, Florida, is currently involved in training and supervising a core group of Pre-K teachers in the Orlando public schools in Developmental Play Therapy, an approach based on psychoanalytic theory. Developmental Play Therapy had its beginning over forty years ago in a research grant from the Chicago Institute for Psychoanalysis to study the hospitalized psychosomatically ill. Her training includes work with Carl Rogers, a four-year course in Child Analysis at the Chicago Institute for Psychoanalysis, and five years with Austin Des Lauriers. This was followed by a long and varied clinical career in both Chicago and Florida. For the past twenty years, Developmental Play therapy has been offered in St. Petersburg, as well as in other parts of the United States, in Canada, Ireland, and London. She has been an adjunct professor at the University of South Florida and Eckerd College and is a Registered Play Therapist-Supervisor. Her book, *The Dialogue of Touch: Developmental Play Therapy* (1993), about Developmental Play Therapy training, is available on request.

Violet Oaklander, Ph.D.

Dr. Violet Oaklander is the author of the book *Windows to our Children: A Gestalt Therapy Approach to Children and Adolescents* and several articles, as well as video and audiotapes, on psychotherapeutic work with children. She has a Ph.D. in Clinical Psychology; a Master of Arts in Marriage, Family, and Child Counseling; and a Master of Science in Special Education. She trained with the Los Angeles Gestalt Therapy Institute for three years and has been certified as a Gestalt therapist since 1973. She is also a Registered Play Therapist-Supervisor through the Association for Play Therapy.

Dr. Oaklander travels extensively throughout the world giving training seminars on her approach to working with children and adolescents, and is presently living in Santa Barbara, California, where she maintains a private practice and is the Director of the Violet Oaklander Institute—devoted to the supervision and training of professionals who work with children. Her unique approach to working with children, which combines Gestalt Therapy theory, philosophy, and practice with a variety of expressive techniques, has won international recognition.

Felicia Carroll, M.Ed., M.A.

For fifteen years, Felicia Carroll has studied with, and been a training co-leader with, Violet Oaklander. She has credentials in educational psychology, child development, and counseling psychology. She is a Registered Play Therapist-Supervisor. Ms. Carroll has her private practice in Santa Barbara, California, and is a Director of the Counseling Center for Children, Adolescents, and Their Families. She is also the Program Coordinator for the Violet Oaklander Institute and is on the adjunct faculty of Antioch University. She has conducted training in child psychotherapy at Gestalt institutes in Europe, and at numerous counseling centers in the United States.

Terrence J. Koller, Ph.D.

Terrence J. Koller, Ph.D. is a Licensed Clinical Psychologist in Illinois. He is currently in independent practice, which includes the evaluation and treatment of mental and emotional disorders with a specialty in working with children. He also has contracts to provide administrative and legislative services to the Illinois Psychological Association. Dr. Koller is Clinical Assistant Professor of Psychology in the Department of Psychiatry at the University of Illinois Medical School in Chicago. His research interests include parent-child interaction and infant temperament.

Dr. Koller first became involved with Theraplay in 1972. He is a certified Theraplay Trainer and has conducted Theraplay workshops around the country. He has also supervised numerous individuals working to obtain their certification as a Theraplay therapist. His writings about Theraplay range from the treatment of adolescents to the evaluation and treatment of adoptive and foster-care children. His work contributed to the expansion of the use of the Marshak Interaction Method (MIM), which is currently one of the primary evaluation steps in the Theraplay treatment planning process.

Phyllis B. Booth, M.A.

Phyllis B. Booth, M.A. is a Licensed Marriage and Family Therapist, a Licensed Clinical Professional Counselor, and a Registered Play Therapist-Supervisor. For the past thirty years she collaborated with Dr. Ann Jernberg, the founder of the

Theraplay Institute, in the development of Theraplay. She is Director of Training at the Theraplay Institute in Chicago and, in that capacity, continues to supervise individuals seeking Theraplay therapist certification. Ms. Booth has presented Theraplay seminars throughout the United States and Canada. She was trained in clinical psychology at the University of Chicago. She studied with John Bowlby and D.W. Winnicott at the Tavistock Centre in London and completed a two-year training program in family therapy at the Family Institute of Chicago. She recently spent a year studying at the Anna Freud Centre in London.

Kevin O'Connor, Ph.D.

Dr. O'Connor is Professor and Director of Ecosystemic Clinical Child Psychology at the California School of Professional Psychology–Fresno. He is a licensed clinical psychologist and a Registered Play Therapist-Supervisor. Dr. O'Connor developed ecosystemic play therapy (EPT) as a way of focusing on understanding the nature of the child's difficulties in an environmental context and designing interventions that will ensure that the child's needs are consistently and appropriately met in that context. EPT promotes active, developmentally focused interventions that engage children in working to solve their problems.

Dr. O'Connor is the Executive Director of the Association for Play Therapy (APT) which he co-founded with Dr. Charles Schaefer in 1982. The APT is an international organization for mental health professionals interested in the practice of play therapy.

Dr. O'Connor maintains a small independent practice in Fresno, California, and travels extensively lecturing on play therapy. His presentations focus on the ecosystemic approach and the value of incorporating a cognitive approach into play therapy by using interpretation to promoting problem solving.

Dr. O'Connor is the author of *The Play Therapy Primer* and the co-editor of the *Handbook of Play Therapy, Volumes I and II*. He edits the *APT Newsletter* and serves on the editorial board of the *International Journal of Play Therapy*.

Jamshid A. Marvasti, M.D.

Dr. Marvasti is an attending psychiatrist at Manchester Memorial Hospital, Manchester, Connecticut. He developed Ericksonian play therapy after years of doing psychoanalytically oriented play therapy. Two elements influenced this transition. The first was his Middle Eastern background, a culture with an Ericksonian/ storytelling orientation. The second element was his belief that the psychotherapy of traumatized children overemphasized abreaction of trauma and exploration of the past, which he viewed as not always beneficial or necessary and potentially even detrimental for some children. Erickson's solution-oriented psychotherapy, which focused on the present and the client's potential, seemed made to order. Dr. Marvasti worked to extend Ericksonian child psychotherapy beyond storytelling to actual play therapy.

Dr. Marvasti has written many chapters on play therapy including: "Play therapy with Sexually Abused Children" (*Vulnerable Population, Volume II*, S. Sgroi, 1989); "Play Diagnosis and Play Therapy with Child Victims of Incest" (*Handbook of Play Therapy, Volume II*, K. O'Connor and C. Schaefer, 1994); "Play Group Therapy with Sexually Abused Children" (*Handbook of Clinical Intervention in Child Sexual Abuse: Revised edition*, S. Sgroi, 1997); and "Metaphors, Fairytales and Storytelling in Psychotherapy with Children" (*101 Play Therapy Techniques*, H. Kaduson and C. Schaefer, 1997).

Terry Kottman, Ph.D.

Dr. Terry Kottman is Associate Professor of Counselor Education in the Department of Educational Administration and Counseling at the University of Northern Iowa in Cedar Falls, Iowa. She is a Registered Play Therapist-Supervisor, with a small private practice, specializing in counseling children and families. Dr. Kottman developed Adlerian play therapy, an approach to working with children that combines the concepts and strategies of Adlerian psychology with the techniques of play therapy. She has presented many workshops on Adlerian play therapy and other topics related to working with children and families. She co-edited *Play Therapy in Action: A Casebook for Practitioners* with Dr. Charles Schaefer and co-authored *Guidance and Counseling in the Elementary and Middle School: A Practical Approach* with Dr. Jim Muro. Dr. Kottman recently wrote *Partners in Play: An Adlerian Approach to Play Therapy.*

Steve Harvey, Ph.D.

Steve Harvey, PH.D. is a licensed psychologist and is also registered by the national dance, drama, and play therapy associations. Currently Dr. Harvey is working with The Exceptional Family Member Service with the U.S. Army, treating military children and their parents in Germany. In the early 1970s, Dr. Harvey began working with groups of young, emotionally disturbed children using expressive and athletic activities in educational boys' clubs and mental health settings. He continued his education, receiving graduate degrees in creative arts therapy and educational psychology. In addition to developing several training and research projects involving family play therapy, Dr. Harvey has maintained a full-time family therapy practice, in which he performs client evaluations using integrated expressive play.

Shlomo Ariel, Ph.D.

Dr. Ariel is a lecturer at the Program for Advanced Studies in Integrative Psychotherapy of the Hebrew University of Jerusalem, and a co-director of the Center for Integrative Psychotherapy in Ramat Gan, Israel. He is the founder and president of the Israeli Association for Psychotherapy Integration. He created the Multi-Systematic Child Therapy Training Program of Tel Aviv University and the Israeli Ministry of Social Welfare, where he was director from 1984 to 1992.

Dr. Ariel has been active in research, theory development, teaching, writing, and clinical practice in the areas of play therapy since 1973. He has been developing his own model and method of multisystemic psychotherapy, involving the family and wider ecological systems in the treatment of children. His current efforts concentrate on incorporating the cross-cultural perspective into this model.

Contents

Orientation to the Text:
The Case of Jason L.

KEVIN O'CONNOR AND LISA MAGES BRAVERMAN

In planning this text, the goal of the editors was to provide a way for those interested in the practice of play therapy to directly compare both the major existing theories and the newly evolving ones with one another. Aside from the academic value of making such comparisons, it is our belief that to become a competent play therapist one must find a theoretical model that meshes well with both one's personality and the needs of one's particular client base. A problem inherent in most texts that include a variety of theories presented by different authors is that the authors select case material specifically to illustrate their own theories. The reader is usually left with the sense that no other theoretical model could have addressed the needs of the client better than the one being presented. Further, the cases are often so disparate that comparison of either the theory or the methods used is difficult if not impossible. In this text, the editors sought to overcome this problem and to enhance the reader's ability to compare the theories and applications presented by requiring all of the authors to use the same case material.

Both the theories selected for inclusion in this text and the authors selected to present them were carefully chosen from the rapidly growing body of theoretical literature on play therapy. A few of the theories have substantial histories in the field of psychology, if not in the field of play therapy per se. Several are widely used in the United States and Canada. A number were selected because they represent significant innovations in the field of play therapy. And several were selected because they are designed for use with families. In all cases, the models selected included both a substantial body of theoretical work as well as a delineated set of practices or techniques. Wherever possible, the creators of the theoretical model were recruited to write chapters on their respective theories. For those theories where that was not possible, the editors sought out individuals who are widely recognized for their expertise with respect to the theory and practice of that form of play therapy. Finally, many well-known authors were not included because their work focuses more on a particular technique or the treatment of a specific disorder rather than on a theoretical model.

The sequence of the chapters is as follows: The first four chapters represent the major psychological theories of psychotherapy as they have been adapted to the practice of play therapy. The next cluster (Chapters 5–7) also includes historically significant, although not as widely practiced, theoretical models. The third cluster

(Chapters 8–11) includes newly developed theoretical models conceptualized primarily for use with individual children. The last two chapters focus on specialized techniques developed for use with families.

The chapters are also structured so as to be as comparable as possible. A fairly detailed outline for the chapters was developed by the editors and submitted to the authors for review. They were encouraged to add to, delete from, or alter the outline so that it would best facilitate the presentation of their theory and practice. Once the outline was finalized, all of the authors were required to adhere strictly to the use of the first- and second-order headings. This requirement forced a parallel structure for each chapter. Although the editors insisted on the comparability of the structure, they did not control for the style of presentation or the content of the chapters. The result is that the chapters vary considerably in the amount of detail presented and the degree to which the theories are internally consistent or organized. This variability is indicative of two things. On the one hand, even the most established theories of play therapy are constantly evolving as psychological theory grows and develops. On the other, some of the theories are so new that they have not yet achieved the level of stability and organization that the older theories have achieved. In many ways, this text is a report on exciting and dynamic work in progress that is sure to contribute to the richness of every practitioner's thinking and technical repertoire.

The case of Jason L. was used by each author in this text as the foundation on which to present both a specific theoretical model of play therapy and the application of that model. This is an entirely fictional case, representing a composite of many of the editors' clinical experiences. The goal was the creation of a case that included both many of the problems commonly seen in outpatient treatment settings and the types of problems common to children in the late twentieth century. Once the original case was developed, we sent it to each of the authors for review. They were encouraged to suggest additions, deletions, or alterations so that the case would best facilitate their presentation. Several authors requested the addition of some material, most of which focused on a more complete description of the family dynamics. One author suggested removing an item because it seemed to make the case somewhat implausible. Interestingly, in spite of the enormous diversity of theories they represented, none of the authors said that they would be unable to address this case from their theoretical orientation. Where possible, all of the requested changes were incorporated into the final case, which follows.

INTAKE

Identifying Information

Jason is a seven-year-old male, the oldest of two children. His younger sister, Carla, is three and a half years old. There was a third sibling, a male, born when Jason was 18 months old. This child died within hours after his birth. Jason's mother, Mary, is 30 years old, of Anglo descent, and employed as a clerical worker in a small law office. His father, Emilio, is 31 years old, of Mexican-American descent, and works as a factory supervisor. The parents share traditional Catholic beliefs and attend church regularly. In spite of their belief that it was wrong, they were divorced when Jason was five years old. Both Jason and Carla live with their mother but spend alternate weekends and every Thursday night with their father.

All of the following data were obtained through Child Protective Services (CPS) reports, and from Mary L., Emilio L., and Jason. The source of the information is Mary L. unless otherwise indicated.

Logistics

Mary called to schedule the initial appointment, saying that she had some concerns about the behavior of her son, Jason. She did not describe the problem in any detail nor did she impart any sense of urgency. She did not mention that she had been referred to treatment by Child Protective Services. Although she did state that she and her husband were divorced, she readily agreed to scheduling a joint intake session. The initial interview was, therefore, completed with Mary and Emilio. Mary brought Carla to the interview in spite of the interviewer's suggestion that she not do so. During this session, information regarding the Presenting Problem, Developmental History, and Family History and Dynamics was gathered. The Developmental Teaching Objectives Rating Form–Revised (DTORF–R) (1992a,b,c) was also completed over the course of the interview. This session lasted approximately one and one-half hours. At the end of this session, each parent was given the Child Behavior Checklist (CBCL) (Achenbach & Edelbrock, 1982) to complete and return the following week.

The second session consisted of an intake interview with Jason and the administration of a complete individual test battery. This session also lasted almost two hours, including short breaks between tests.

The third and fourth sessions were scheduled several days apart during the third week. At the third session Mary completed the Marschak Interaction Method (MIM) with the children. At the fourth session, Emilio completed the same MIM tasks with the children. Each of these sessions lasted about one-half hour.

The last session prior to the initiation of treatment was a feedback and treatment contracting session attended by both Mary and Emilio. This session lasted one hour.*

Presenting Problem

Jason was brought to therapy by his mother following a referral by Child Protective Services. Mary was reported to CPS by Jason's teacher when Jason told her that bruises on his face were the result of having been smacked by his mother. Mary reports that Jason is difficult to manage. He is often angry and unresponsive to the directions or punishments she imposes. For example, he will come home from school and throw down his books as he enters the house. When Mary tells him to pick the

---

*Note: This amount of information gathering is not necessarily consistent with all of the play therapy models to be discussed in the following chapters. However, in order to obtain a comprehensive picture of Jason and his family that would allow for the application of many different play therapy approaches, a comprehensive assessment was completed.

books up, he acts as if he did not hear her. If she persists, he picks up the books and then throws them across his own room, making as much noise as he can. His negative mood and behavior alternates with episodes of withdrawal and sulking.

Emilio reports no difficulties with Jason. He is a little concerned that Jason is too clingy for a child his age. When asked to elaborate, Emilio said he worries that Jason is sometimes not as bold as he would like. He said that Jason will not assert himself when he, Emilio, is present. For example, Jason refused to return a defective toy to the store on his own and insisted that Emilio come with him and do most of the talking.

Jason was initially unable to describe any problems. He interpreted the word "problems" to mean things he was doing wrong and adamantly denied that any of his behavior was problematic. In fact, he made it very clear that he did not think he would even be in the office if it were not for the fact that his mother hit him. When the concept of problems was reframed to mean things about his current life situation that he did not like, he became more forthcoming. With encouragement, he reported that he dislikes the fact that his mother is always yelling at him and that the teachers at school seem to be following her lead. He also reported that he just does not seem to be as happy as he used to be before his parents' divorce.

Both parents reported that Jason's behavior seems to be the most difficult during the first hour or so after he gets home from school. Mary said the book throwing, just described, was typical of his after-school moods. She said that she usually leaves Jason alone for an hour or more, after which he usually approaches her asking for a snack or help with his homework. Emilio said that he responds to Jason's negative moods more actively. He usually tries to engage Jason in something physical like playing catch or wrestling. He said that Jason usually starts out quite aggressive but that "when he blows off some steam he settles right down." Jason denied being moody after school, although he did admit that school can "be a real pain sometimes."

Both parents reported that mealtimes generally went well. Mary says that she lets the children play until suppertime and only calls them when the food is on the table. She says dinner usually goes by pretty quickly as both children rush to talk about things they have done during the day. Emilio reported that he generally involves the children in meal preparation as much as possible. Each child has tasks to complete before dinner. Jason sets the table and Carla adds the napkins. Both children help measure ingredients or peel vegetables as they are able. When the meal itself is served, the conversation tends to focus on the food and the preparation more than other events that occurred during the course of the day. Jason says he likes dinner at both houses, but for different reasons. He says that he likes not having to set the table at his mother's house but that his father is a better cook. He could not report any aspect of the dinner conversation at either house.

Both Mary and Emilio reported that Jason generally gets along well with his sister. Both reported that he tends to be very directive when they play together but that, as he seems quite sensitive to her developmental abilities, he finds things she can do so as to participate in joint play. The only time things do not go well is when Carla does not seem to be in the mood to take directions or has an idea of her own.

If Jason cannot get compliance, he becomes frustrated and walks off to play on his own. Jason says playing with his sister is just okay. He likes it when they engage in pretend play of any sort but says he would rather play with his remote-control car or play catch with his dad.

Developmental History

Jason was the result of a planned pregnancy two years after Mary and Emilio were married. There were some complications with the pregnancy that required Mary to remain in bed from her 26th week until the delivery. Mary denies any alcohol or substance use (including cigarettes) during her pregnancy. The labor and delivery were attended by Emilio and Mary's mother. After a 12-hour labor, Jason was born weighing 5.0 lbs. The delivery was generally uncomplicated, although Mary reports having had difficulty pushing during her contractions due to weakness that was the result of having been bedridden for so long. Jason was quite healthy in spite of his small size. He was observed in neonatal intensive care for about 12 hours and then moved to the general newborn unit. He was treated for jaundice on the second and third days following the delivery and responded well. Mary's contact with him was sporadic during these first few days, although she was able to hold him for at least three hours out of every 12. Mother and child were discharged on the third day after delivery.

Mary reports that Jason was an irritable baby when he was awake but that he slept a lot for the first few months. She says she held him often and worried constantly about his health because she was afraid that the complications of the pregnancy might cause him to be sickly or even to die. Jason was less irritable when held and would sleep soundly for several hours at a time if carried or rocked. Jason was breastfed until he was about 11 months old, when Mary became pregnant with her second child. Because of her concerns about Jason's well-being, Mary stayed at home and took care of him. She was his primary caretaker from his birth until he began school, except for a period of about six months as described below. She did send him to preschool when he was four years old because she was having difficulty caring for both him and his baby sister, Carla. Mary reports that Jason cried a great deal when it was time to go to preschool but then seemed to enjoy it a great deal once she left. In fact, she noted that Jason seemed distant when she would come to pick him up and it would take several hours before he would warm to her again. In spite of her concerns, Jason has been a healthy child who only suffers from moderate, intermittent asthma.

Jason walked at 14 months and talked at 15 months. He was toilet trained at 30 months. Mary reports that he was a difficult toddler who tended to be quite noncompliant, although he had very few temper tantrums. For example, Jason liked to explore the environment to the point of occasionally endangering himself. If his mother attempted to contain him in any way, he would cry but not rage. Instead, he would soon become very focused on finding his way to his original destination or around any barriers Mary had erected. She disciplined him somewhat inconsistently, occasionally using time-outs and sometimes resorting to spanking.

As previously stated, Jason entered preschool at age four. At age five he entered kindergarten and an after-school program so that Mary could return to work.

Other significant events in Jason's early development are reported in the section Family History and Dynamics.

Mental Status

Jason presents as an average-size male who appears distinctly Hispanic, with dark hair, skin, and eyes. During the interview he was slightly more active than would be expected for his age, but not significantly so. He appeared indifferent to both the CPS report and to his own difficulties. He initially denied that anything was wrong and tended to minimize the impact of both past and current events. In spite of this, he related very well to the interviewer as long as he did not have to discuss himself or focus on anything he considered potentially serious or problematic. He was easily engaged, verbal, and active; his speech productivity was in the normal range. When the interviewer focused on Jason's history or current difficulties, Jason became virtually nonverbal. His affect tended to be positive, though somewhat labile. His affect seemed grounded in reality but often exceeded what would be expected, given the stimulus. His control of both his positive and negative affect seemed poor. His three wishes were for: (1) lots of money; (2) mom and dad to be remarried; and, (3) lots of baseball cards. His thought processes and content were within normal limits.

Jason was oriented times three. His long- and short-term memory were intact, as was his concentration. He appeared to be of average intellect but tended to be overly concrete when discussing his experiences. His judgment seemed moderately impaired and his insight was very limited. He reported no suicidal ideation, though Mary reported that he sometimes says that he wishes he were dead. He reports no homicidal ideation and, other than the abuse by his mother, there is no history of family violence.

A significant portion of the intake interview with Jason focused on obtaining a sense of how much of the intake information obtained from his parents Jason was aware of or could verify. When asked to describe his parents, his family, and his interactions with his sister, he reported material that was almost entirely consistent with that given by his parents. The primary difference between his descriptions and those of his parents was that he avoided mentioning experiencing any negative affect. He tended to say that everything was "fine."

Jason is currently in second grade in a public school. Academically, he does very well without exerting a great deal of effort. Behaviorally, he has always been somewhat of a problem. In kindergarten and first grade, his behavior was simply labeled "all boy." Over the past few months, however, his teacher Mrs. J. has found him to be increasingly noncompliant and disruptive. Although he rarely plays with his peers for any length of time and tends to be rather bossy when he does, he is admired by the other boys, who see him as independent and self-assured. Additionally, his teacher reported that Jason seems to do very well on tasks that he is allowed to complete individually with the help of her student aide, a 20-year-old, male college student.

Jason's most problematic behavior was involvement in a recent episode of fire setting. On his way home from school, he and another boy from his class lit the contents of a trash can on fire. A neighbor called the police. Jason's initial reaction to the police was one of general indifference. When they separated him from the other boy and became more confrontational, he broke down and sobbed for nearly 15 minutes—repeatedly promising that he would never do the same kind of thing ever again. As the investigation proceeded, it became apparent that the fire setting had been initiated by the other boy. The police decided to release Jason without any additional consequences. Subsequently, attempts by adults to talk to Jason about this incident have been met with apparent indifference, and he reports that he was not ever really frightened by the police. When asked about the incident during the intake, Jason dismissed it saying it had been no big deal.

Family History and Dynamics

Mary indicated that she is the oldest of three girls born to a fairly traditional Catholic couple. Mary's parents divorced when she was in grade school. She became quite depressed at the time but did not receive any mental health treatment. Her father died of a sudden coronary when she was an adolescent. Mary had not had much contact with him after the divorce and says she grieved only moderately. Her mother continues to live nearby and helps Mary when she can. Mary likes the practical assistance she gets from her mother but says she prefers not to interact with her much socially. She says her mother can be depressing by constantly reminding her about the difficulties she (Mary's mother) had as a single parent, seemingly minimizing the difficulties Mary is having. Mary does not have much contact with her sisters. Both married very upwardly mobile men and now live in other states. Her family of origin was generally middle class, although money was often tight.

Emilio's parents are first-generation Mexican-Americans who are still married. Emilio's father and brother have a history of moderate alcoholism, but the family history is otherwise unremarkable. Emilio has dinner with his extended family every Sunday. He says he loves his mother very much but describes her as fairly invisible in the family. "She cooks and cleans and takes care of everybody." He and his father and brother watch sports together on television or occasionally go fishing together.

No immediate or extended-family members are known to have received mental health services. Mary, however, has a history of fairly serious depressive episodes. At these times she reports decreased motor activity, decreased appetite, increased time spent in bed, and intermittent teariness. She has not sought treatment and says that the episodes usually spontaneously remit after a few weeks.

Mary and Emilio were married after having dated for several years. Both had solid jobs and took the responsibility of marriage very seriously. Both report that they were very much in love for the first few years of the marriage. They saved money and eagerly planned for their first child. Jason's birth made both parents extremely happy, and their marriage seemed to grow better and more solid. Both were very involved in child rearing.

Both were surprised but happy when Mary became pregnant for the second time. Mary's second pregnancy went very badly, again requiring bed rest to prevent premature labor. During this time, Emilio's and Mary's mothers both took over the responsibility of caring for Jason. The second child was born two months early, when Jason was 18 months old. The baby boy died within hours. Mary and Emilio were devastated. Emilio reports that Mary became very depressed at that time. In fact, she withdrew completely for a period of several months, during which time she was unable to care for Jason. Emilio reports that this was the beginning of the end for their marriage. They drifted apart, and after about 18 months Emilio began a long-term affair with a female coworker.

Mary began to realize that her marriage was collapsing and decided that another child might bring Emilio back into the family. Unfortunately, her third pregnancy was also somewhat complicated, although it went better than the second. No extended bed rest was required. Both parents were happy when Carla was born healthy. Initially, Emilio was involved with the baby, but as his relationship with Mary did not improve he soon drifted away again. Left to care for both children, Mary began to feel overwhelmed, and it was at this point that she sent Jason to preschool. Although Emilio's affair had ended, he and Mary were divorced when Jason was five years old.

After the divorce, Mary had to return to work. Jason attended kindergarten and then an after-school program while his mother worked. Carla entered full-time day care. Mary was angered by the divorce and rapidly became overwhelmed by the burdens of being a single parent. Her mother helped with child care when she could, but Mary still tended to be exhausted at the end of each day and to be short with the children. During the weekends that the children are with Mary things tend to go much better and they all report being happy and relaxed. On those days, Mary tries to avoid making any demands of the children. Instead, they go to the park or the zoo or some other minimally structured place. Mary reports that Jason becomes both verbally and physically affectionate toward her as the weekend progresses. Mary reports that the children only rarely fight with each other.

Emilio became more interested in his children after the divorce and has been very devoted to them during their visits. Although he does not spoil them with gifts or trips, he spends virtually all of each visit directly interacting with them. He plays board games with Jason, which they modify to include Carla if at all possible. He also plays a fairly unstructured version of football with them both, where everyone runs after the person who has the ball. He builds models with Jason when Carla is napping.

Mary stated that she does not like her current job very much. She is a secretary in a small law office. She feels that it is a rather mechanical job with few prospects for advancement. She would like to return to school and get a business degree. She does not see this as much of a possibility, however, as she can barely afford daily necessities—much less college tuition.

Emilio reports that he is quite happy with his current position. He has worked his way up to being a supervisor after having started on an evening cleaning crew in the factory. He is happy with his salary, benefits, and job security. He does not even seem to see the concept of enjoying the content of his work as particularly relevant. He works to make a living. He gets enjoyment from interacting with friends outside work and from doing things with his children.

Both parents report that Carla is a very easy and compliant child. Mary describes Carla as the most warm and loving child a mother could hope for. At the intake, the interviewer noted that Carla was dressed in a very pretty and frilly pink dress. She wore tiny gold earrings and a gold chain bracelet (both presents from her mother). Mary and Carla were almost constantly within arms reach of one another during the intake process. Emilio seemed enamored with Carla, but she tended to be more independent around him. When both children were in the room with Emilio, it tended to be Jason who was physically closer to his father.

PRE-TREATMENT ASSESSMENT DATA

Individual Assessment

Jason was given a full battery of psychological tests to determine his present level of developmental functioning in all spheres. The specific tests administered are described in the following section.

Tests Administered

Thematic Apperception Test (TAT). This test is a standard projective instrument (Murray et. al., 1938; Anastasi, 1982). The child is presented with a series of pictures and asked to tell a story about each one in turn. The child is instructed to tell a story that has a beginning, middle, and end and includes what each of the characters is thinking and feeling. Both the style and the content of the child's response are usually interpreted according to one of a variety of primarily psychoanalytic strategies.

RORSCHACH.   This is another standardized projective instrument (Rorschach, 1921). The child is shown 10 cards depicting abstract, nonrepresentational designs. The child is instructed to report what he or she thinks the designs might look like. The most common method for interpreting the results is the use of the Exner (1986) scoring system.

HUMAN FIGURE DRAWING (HFD).   This projective technique is described in Koppitz (1968). The child is asked to draw a picture of a person. The drawing is interpreted as a reflection of the child's sense of self, usually in a manner consistent with psychoanalytic theory.

KINETIC FAMILY DRAWING (KFD).   This projective technique is described in *Self-Growth in Families* (Burns, 1982). The child is asked to draw a picture of a (or his or her) family doing something. The method for interpreting the resulting drawing is also described in the text.

WECHSLER INTELLIGENCE SCALE FOR CHILDREN-III (WISC-III).   The original version of this standardized measure of intelligence was developed by David Wechsler in 1949. The WISC-III was first published in 1991. The test requires the child to answer questions and/or complete tasks on five verbal subtests (Information, Similarities, Arithmetic, Vocabulary, and Comprehension) and five performance subtests (Picture Arrangement, Picture Completion, Block Design, Object Assembly, and Coding). The method for scoring and interpreting the test is described in the test manual (Wechsler, 1991). The average score is 100, with a standard deviation of 15.

THE DEVELOPMENTAL TEACHING OBJECTIVES RATING FORM–REVISED (DTORF–R). "This is a developmental assessment. It consists of 171 hierarchically arranged, operationally defined objectives that encompass a developmental age span from birth to the age of 16. The rater simply begins at the earliest developmental level in each area (Behavior, Communication, Social, and Academic) to be rated. Each criterion behavior that is judged to be evident in the child's repertoire at least 80 percent of the time is checked in sequence. The rater proceeds down the list until he or she reaches a behavior in which the child does not engage regularly; this behavior becomes a treatment goal" (O'Connor, 1991, p. 151). Data on Jason were obtained from interviews with Mary, Emilio, and Jason's teacher.

Mary and Emilio each completed a Child Behavior Checklist (CBCL) (Achenbach & Edelbrock, 1983). The portion of that measure reported on here consists of a checklist of 118 items describing various behavior problems. Each item is rated as being between not true (0) and very true (2) of the child's behavior over the past six months. The resulting scores are plotted on the revised Child Behavior Profile, yielding nine scale scores: Schizoid/Anxious, Depressed, Uncommunicative, Obsessive/Compulsive, Somatic Complaints, Social Withdrawal, Hyperactive, Aggressive, and Delinquent.

Test Results and Interpretation

Emotionally, Jason appears to be struggling with issues of control. Many of his TAT stories revolved around power struggles with various authority figures. A typical example follows.

TAT, Card 7BM: These two guys are lawyers. The old guy is the boss. He is always telling the younger lawyer what to do and how to do it. The younger guy gets really mad because he knows just as much as the older lawyer but isn't given a chance. One day he goes to court and does the exact opposite of what the boss told him to do just because he is sick of being told what to do. The lady he was supposed to be defending got convicted. Now he doesn't know what to do. He feels bad that he lost the case and afraid of what the boss will do. He really wants the boss to like him but he wants to be trusted more.

When power struggles were not the dominant theme, then themes of self-control loomed large, as in the following story.

TAT, Card 2: This girl really doesn't want to go to school but she knows she has to if she is ever going to get an okay job when she grows up. She never even tells her mother or father how much she hates school because they will just say that it is important for her to go. She tries to do her best but it never seems to be good enough. Something is always going wrong and she gets in trouble. She wishes she could sneak off and do what she wants but she knows she can't. She just has to keep going to school no matter how much she hates it.

The Rorschach results indicated that Jason's reality testing was generally intact, although his impulse control was rather limited. He gave 23 responses, most of which involved the use of pure Form (F). His X+% was 75. His F+% was 90. His Lambda score was .98. His D and Adjusted D scores were −1 and 1. He received no Special Scores.

Jason's HFD was relatively meager, given his IQ as measured by other tests. The drawing was first scored using the Goodenough (Goodenough 1926, 1928; Goodenough & Harris, 1950) system, resulting in an IQ score of 90. There was very little detail, and the overall drawing was small (less than 2"). He drew a picture of a boy wearing jeans and a T-shirt and holding a football. The boy had a neutral facial expression and a rather stiff, full face-forward stance.

Jason included Mary, Emilio, Carla, and himself in his KFD. None of the family members were engaged in any activity; rather they stood in a row facing front. Mary was on the far left and was drawn first. Carla was drawn next, just to the right of Mary. Jason drew himself next, somewhat separated from Carla. Emilio was drawn last, next to Jason and to the far right of the page.

Cognitively, Jason is of above-average intelligence, having obtained a Verbal IQ score of 112, a Performance IQ of 119, and a Full Scale IQ of 116. All of his subtest scaled scores were within several points of one another except for two. Coding was five scaled score points lower than all of his other subtest scores. Picture Arrangement was three scaled score points lower than all of his scores except Coding and was five scaled score points below Comprehension. On the Communication scale of the DTORF–R, Jason was rated as being in the middle of Stage III (age 6–9), which is consistent with his chronological age. He ceilinged on items C18 and C19. He is not consistently able to use words or nonverbal gestures to show pride in his own work or to make positive statements about himself. He also tends not to be able to describe his own characteristic attributes, strengths, and problems.

Jason's social and behavioral functioning were somewhat below developmental expectations. On the Behavior scale of the DTORF–R he was rated as being at mid Stage II (age 2–6). He was reported to ceiling on items B11 and B12. Specifically, he is not regularly able to participate verbally and physically in sitting activities such as work time and snack time without physical intervention by an adult. He also does not regularly participate in movement activities such as play time, mat time, games, and music without physical intervention by an adult. On the Social scale he was rated as being late Stage II. He ceilinged on items S17 and S18. He does not regularly participate in interactive play with a peer. He also has difficulty independently cooperating with a peer during organized activity and play.

The differences in Mary's and Emilio's perceptions of Jason's problems were reflected in the CBCLs each completed. Only one of the T-scores was above the 70th percentile on either parent's CBCL, reflecting both parents' tendency to minimize the problems Jason was exhibiting. The elevated score was on the Social Withdrawal scale on the CBCL completed by Mary. The actual T-scores are listed below:

Parent	Schizoid/ Anxious	Depressed	Uncommu- nicative	Obsessive/ Compulsive	Somatic Complaints
Mary	55	67	58	55	67
Emilio	59	63	63	55	55

	Parent	Social Withdrawal	Hyperactive	Aggressive	Delinquent
CBCL Scores (*cont.*)	Mary	73	55	63	61
	Emilio	62	55	55	57

The problems Mary reported to be most serious (scored as 2—very often a problem) were that Jason is lonely, feels unloved, feels persecuted, sulks, is stubborn, likes to be alone, prefers younger children, is withdrawn, argues, demands attention, disobeys at home, is moody, swears, has a temper, and disobeys at school. The problems Emilio reported to be most serious (scored as 2—very often a problem) were that Jason is shy, is timid, sulks, and swears.

Dyadic and Family Assessment

The interactions of the family members were assessed using the Marschak Interaction Method (MIM) (Marschak, 1960; Jernberg, 1979). In this method, specific tasks are chosen by the examiner in order to elicit typical parent-child interactions. The parent is given written instructions and any needed materials, in coded envelopes, and is left alone to complete the tasks with the child. The examiner either observes or tapes the interactions and then assesses the style and quality of the interaction. The ratings are primarily based on clinical judgment rather than on a specific scoring system. The degree to which the parent is able to keep the child optimally aroused, to give the child affection, to give directions, to alert the child to the environment, and to be playful are all assessed.

During the first assessment session, Mary was asked to complete four tasks with Jason alone and then to complete four additional tasks with Jason and Carla together. The following week, Emilio was asked to perform the same tasks that Mary had completed, first with Jason and then with the children together.

Only two of the tasks that each parent was asked to perform with Jason alone and one of the tasks each was asked to complete with the children together are reported here. Each parent's performance on these two tasks seemed characteristic of his or her interaction style.

MIM task: Adult has child "draw our house," completed with Jason alone.

Mary read the card out loud and then directly instructed Jason to "draw our house."

Jason responded, "That's too hard."

"Well, that is what the card says to do, so just give it a try. I'm sure you can do it."

At this point, Jason sat silently for two minutes before starting to draw. He worked quietly for about five minutes before saying, "That is the best I can do. It isn't very good."

Mary looked at the picture and said, "I think it is quite good but I'll bet if you worked a little longer you could make it even better."

Jason sighed, "What else should I add?"

"Think about our house. What color are the shutters? What color are the flowers out front? Do we have a sidewalk in front of our house?"

Jason worked quietly for another few minutes, then handed the drawing to his mother. "Here. What do we do next?"

"Now I can see you really did your best. This picture looks a lot like our house. I can even see where your room is."

Jason smiled and briefly looked at the picture.

When Emilio did the same task with Jason a few days later, it went as follows:

Emilio began by saying, "Well, it says here that you need to draw a picture of our house. That seems like an awfully hard job. They don't know how complicated our house is."

"It's okay, I had to do the same thing with Mom last week."

"Okay, well why don't you start and then let me know if you need any help." Jason began to draw.

As Jason completed the outline of the house Emilio said, "That's pretty good. I think you are doing a better job than I could."

Jason smiled and continued drawing. As Jason added each element, Emilio commented on Jason's eye for detail and his ability to remember the various colors of the objects he was drawing. At no time was either of them quiet for more than 30 to 45 seconds. When he was finished, Jason handed the picture to Emilio, "Okay, I'm done. What's next?"

"Wow, this is a great picture."

Jason grinned, "Yeah, I know."

"You know, huh?" At this point, Jason looked shy and Emilio leaned over and tickled him. Jason laughed out loud. After about 30 seconds they proceeded to the next MIM task.

Jason spent a total of about eight minutes on the drawing he completed with his mother. He spent nearly 10 minutes on the one completed with Emilio. Jason's second drawing was much better than the first. The proportions were better and there was considerably more detail in evidence.

MIM task: Adult and child take turns rubbing hand lotion on each other, completed with Jason alone.

Mary read the card to Jason and then took the lotion out of the envelope and put some in her hands. "Jason, roll up your sleeves so I can put this on your elbows. I noticed they were pretty dry when you were in the kitchen getting dressed this morning."

"Mo-o-om," replied Jason as he rolled his eyes and looked exasperated but complied.

Mary applied the lotion, then said, "There. Now your elbows look much better."

"Oh, yuk. Now my arms are all sticky. I can't roll my sleeves back down," complained Jason.

"Here let me rub it in some more." Noticing that Jason still looked perturbed, Mary got a paper towel from next to the sink and rubbed it over his elbows. "Better?"

"Yeah. It's okay. Now it's my turn to put some on you."

Mary handed Jason the lotion and then said, "Why don't you put some on my knees since they are even drier than your elbows."

"No. I think I'll put it on your . . . neck. Lift up your hair."

"Okay, but please keep the lotion out of my hair." Mary then held her hair on top of her head. "Oooh, that's cold." Jason giggled and proceeded to give Mary a fairly effective neckrub, causing Mary to relax visibly. "You're pretty good at that. It feels great."

Jason finished. He got a paper towel to wipe off his hands. Smiling, he walked around and stood in front of his mother.

Emilio read the card, made a mildly disgusted face, and then started to laugh. "Who do you think thought these things up?"

Jason laughed, "I have no idea. And I already know this stuff feels sticky and kind of gross."

"Well, how should we do this?" Jason shrugged his shoulders. Emilio said, "I know! How about modified mud wrestling?" Jason looked at his father as if he were crazy. "We'll do thumb wrestling, but first we'll get our hands all greased up with this stuff," said Emilio.

"Cool." Jason rolled up his sleeve and put lotion on his hands. Emilio put lotion on his hands and then they gripped fingers and proceeded trying to thumb wrestle. Neither one could hold the other's thumb down as their hands were so slippery. Both began to laugh. Jason said, "This is really gross."

"I know, but you have to admit it's pretty funny." They continued to wrestle for a while. "Okay. That seems like about enough. Let's clean up."

"No. I don't want to. This is fun."

"No, it's time to stop." Emilio headed for the sink, picked up a couple of paper towels, and handed a few to Jason. Both of them wiped off their hands.

MIM task: Adult has the children share a single small bag of M&Ms®, completed with Jason and Carla in the room together.

Mary read the card and the children immediately lunged for the unopened envelopes, trying to locate the one with the M&Ms. Mary pulled the envelopes away and, in a very firm voice, told the children to sit down. The children sat.

"Can I have more M&Ms cause I'm bigger and I'm really hungry?" whined Jason.

"No. I want more cause I'm being good," replied Carla.

"Stop arguing. I will give each of you the exact same amount and I don't want you to have them all anyway because it is too close to dinner time," said Mary.

Both children started to complain that dinner was still a long way off, but Mary brought their protests to a halt by glaring at them without saying anything. She counted out 10 M&Ms apiece and gave them to the children.

Jason recounted his to make sure there were 10. Both children ate their M&Ms very quickly.

"OK mom, what is next?" asked Jason; apparently as a way of ending the task.

Emilio also read the card out loud, and again the children reached for the unopened envelopes.

Emilio beat them to the envelopes, grabbed them, and said, "Hold on you little oinkers. We have to figure out the best way to share them. Who has an idea?"

Jason replied, "Well, Mom just counted out 10 for each of us."

"We could do that. Any other ideas?" asked Emilio.

"I want to have the bag because I'm not very hungry so I want to save some of mine," said Carla.

"Before we decide who gets the bag we need to figure out how we are going to share the M&Ms," posed Emilio.

Jason thought a minute, then said, "We could count them and then divide them in half."

"What if there are an odd number of them?" queried Emilio.

"Well, you could eat the leftover one." said Jason.

Emilio laughed, "Boy, are you generous. Okay. I'll count them but I had another idea first. What if I tear the bag across the middle instead of the end so that you can each have a minibag to hold your M&Ms?"

Both children grinned and waited quietly as Emilio counted the M&Ms into two piles. Emilio then placed each child's M&Ms in a half of the bag and handed them over. The children ate a few while they talked about the tasks they had completed so far. At Emilio's suggestion, they closed up the remainder and moved on to the next task.

BIBLIOGRAPHY

Achenbach, T., & Edelbrock, C. (1982). *Manual for the child behavior checklist and child behavior profile*. Burlington, VT: Child Psychiatry, University of Vermont.

Anastasi, A. (1982). *Psychological testing*. New York: Macmillan.

Burns, C. (1982). *Self-Growth in Families: Kinetic family drawings Research and applications*. New York: Brunner/Mazel, Inc.

Developmental Therapy Institute. (1992a). *Developmental Teaching Objectives for the Developmental Teaching Objectives Rating Form-Revised: Assessment and Teaching of Social Emotional Competence* (4th ed.). Athens, GA: Developmental Therapy Institute.

Goodenough, F. (1926). *Measurement of intelligence by drawings*. New York: Harcourt, Brace and World, Inc.

Goodenough, F. (1928). Studies in the psychology of children's drawings. *Psychological Bulletin, 25*, pp. 272–283.

Goodenough, F., & Harris, D. (1950). Studies in the psychology of children's drawings II:1928–1949. *Psychological Bulletin, 47*, pp. 369–433.

Jernberg, A. (1979). *Theraplay*. San Francisco: Jossey-Bass.

Koppitz, E.M. (1968). *Psychological evaluation of children's human figure drawings*. Boston: Allyn and Bacon.

Marschak, M. (1960). A method for evaluating child-parent interaction under controlled conditions. *Journal of Genetic Psychology, 97*, pp. 3–22.

Murray, et al. (1938). *Explorations in personality*. New York: Oxford University Press.

O'Connor, K. (1991). *The play therapy primer*. New York: Wiley.

Rorschach, H. (1942). *Psychodiagnostics: A diagnostic test based on perception*. Berne: Huber. (Translation by P. Lembau & B. Kronenburg).

Wechsler, D. (1991). *Wechsler Intelligence Scale for children (3rd ed.)*. San Antonio: Psychological Corp., Harcourt Brace Jovanovich.

Wood, M.M. (1992b). *Developmental Teaching Objectives Rating Form-Revised Technical Report*. Athens, GA: Developmental Therapy Institute.

Wood, M.M. (1992c). *Developmental Teaching Objectives Rating Form-Revised User's Manual*. Athens, GA: Develpmental Therapy Institute.

CHAPTER 1

Child-Centered Play Therapy

GARRY L. LANDRETH
DANIEL S. SWEENEY

INTRODUCTION

Child-centered play therapy is not a cloak the play therapist puts on when entering the playroom and takes off when leaving; rather it is a philosophy resulting in attitudes and behaviors for living one's life in relationships with children. It is both a basic philosophy of the innate human capacity of the child to strive toward growth and maturity and an attitude of deep and abiding belief in the child's ability to be constructively self-directing. Child-centered play therapy is a complete therapeutic system, not just the application of a few rapport-building techniques.

The child-centered play therapist believes deeply in and trusts explicitly the inner person of the child. Therefore, the play therapist's objective is to relate to the child in ways that will release the child's inner directional, constructive, forward-moving, creative, self-healing power. When this philosophical belief is lived out with children in the playroom, they are empowered and their developmental capabilities are released for self-exploration and self-discovery, resulting in constructive change. The impact of living out this kind of relationship was described by a child as, "Who would have thought there was a place like this in the whole world! In here you can just be your own little ol' self."

Personality Theory

Child-centered play therapy follows the theoretical constructs of client-centered therapy, now referred to as person-centered therapy, formulated by Carl Rogers (1951). Virginia Axline, a student and later a colleague of Rogers, applied these principles to children and created what is commonly known as child-centered play therapy—a way of being with children rather than doing something to or for children. The theoretical constructs of the child-centered approach to play therapy are related not to age and physical development but rather to the inner dynamics of the individual's process of relating to and discovering the self the individual is capable of becoming. Individual development is viewed as a flowing, fluid, maturing process of becoming. The child-centered theory of personality structure is based on three central constructs: (1) the person, (2) the phenomenal field, and (3) the self (Rogers, 1951).

Person

The person is all that a child is: thoughts, behaviors, feelings, and physical being. This total person is always in the process of developing. A basic proposition is that every child "exists in a continually changing world of experience of which he is the center" (Rogers, 1951, p. 483). As the child interacts with and responds to this changing, very personal world of experience, the child does so as an organized whole so that a change in any one part of the person of the child results in changes in other parts. Therefore, a continuous dynamic intrapersonal interaction occurs in which the child (person), as a total system, is striving toward actualizing the self. This dynamic, active process is an inner-directed movement toward becoming a more positively functioning person, toward positive growth, toward improvement, independence, maturity, and enhancement of self as a person. The child's behavior in this process is goal-directed in an effort to satisfy personal needs as experienced in the unique phenomenal field which for that child constitutes reality (Landreth, 1991).

Phenomenal Field

The second central construct of the child-centered theory of personality structure is the phenomenal field—which is everything the child experiences, whether or not at a conscious level, internal as well as external. It is this internal reference that is the basis for viewing life. Whatever the child perceives to be occurring is reality for the child. Therefore, the child's perception of reality is what must be understood if the child and behaviors exhibited by the child are to be understood. Rogers (1951) proposed that "behavior is basically the goal-directed attempt of the organism to satisfy its needs as experienced in the field as perceived" (p. 491). This concept is central to child-centered play therapy.

The child's behavior must always be understood by looking through the child's eyes. Thus, the therapist religiously avoids judging or evaluating even the simplest of the child's behaviors (i.e., a picture, stacked blocks, a scene in the sand) and works hard to try to understand the internal frame of reference of the child. If contact is to be made with the person of the child, the child's phenomenal world must be the point of focus and must be understood. The child is not expected to meet predetermined criteria or fit a set of preconceived categories (Landreth, 1991).

Self

The third central construct of the child-centered theory of personality structure is the self. A portion of the child's total experiences, that is the interactions with significant others and experiences from the total phenomenal field, are gradually differentiated by the child as the self. This can be described as a part of the developing infant's private world gradually becoming recognized as "me" in the course of interacting with the environment, which results in the development of concepts about self, about the environment, and about self in relation to the environment. The self, then, is the totality of those perceptions of the child (Rogers, 1951).

According to Rogers (1951), even very young infants engage in a process of "direct organismic valuing" beginning with such experiences as "I am cold, and don't like it," even though they may lack descriptive words or symbols that match the experience. This is the beginning of a natural process in which the child positively values those experiences that are perceived as self-enhancing and places a negative value on those that threaten or do not maintain or enhance the self.

As children develop, they may experience being evaluated, first by parents and then by others. In such cases, the love they receive and the symbolization of themselves as lovable become dependent on behavior. These experiences become a part of the phenomenal field and contribute to the structure of the self. Four-year-old Robert smacks his two-year-old brother in anger for taking a toy and experiences the behavior to be very satisfying, but mom's message is that the behavior is bad and he is bad. In order to preserve a positive self-concept, the child may distort such experiences and deny to awareness the satisfaction of the experience (Rogers, 1951). "It is in this way . . . that parental attitudes are not only introjected, but . . . are experienced . . . in distorted fashion, as if based on the evidence of one's own sensory and visceral equipment. Thus, through distorted symbolization, expression of anger comes to be 'experienced' as bad, even though the more accurate symbolization would be that the expression of anger is often experienced as satisfying or enhancing" (Rogers, 1951, p. 500).

Such interactions may result in the child having confused feelings about self, doubts about self, even disapproval of self, as well as the very likely possibility of reliance on the evaluation of others rather than reliance on self-evaluation. This denial of experience to awareness may contribute to later psychological maladjustment.

Rogers (1951) hypothesized that the self grows and changes as a result of continuing interaction with the phenomenal field. He described the structure of the self-concept as "an organized configuration of perceptions of the self which are admissible to awareness. It is composed of such elements as the perceptions of one's characteristics and abilities; the percepts and concepts of the self in relation to others and to the environment; the value qualities which are perceived as associated with experiences and objects; and the goals and ideals which are perceived as having positive or negative valence" (p. 501). The child's behavior, therefore, is generally consistent with the child's concept of self.

A Child-Centered View of Personality and Behavior

Rogers (1951) articulated nineteen propositions regarding personality and behavior that provide a conceptual framework for understanding human behavior and motivation and reflect the philosophical core of child-centered play therapy. These propositions, summarized as follows, describe a child-centered view of the person and behavior of the child and provide a basis for relating to children in play therapy.

Every child exists in a continually changing world of experience of which he or she is the center. The child reacts as an organized whole to this field as it is experienced and perceived, which for the child is reality. As the child develops and interacts with the environment, a portion of the child's total private world (perceptual field) gradually becomes recognized as "me" (differentiated as the self) and concepts are formed about himself or herself, about the environment, and about himself or herself in relation to the environment. The child has a basic tendency to strive to actualize, maintain, and enhance the experiencing self. The resulting behavior is basically the goal-directed, emotionally influenced attempt of the child to satisfy his or her needs as experienced, in the field as perceived. Therefore, the best vantage point for understanding the child's behavior is from the internal frame of reference of the child.

Most of a child's behavior is consistent with the child's concept of self, and behaviors inconsistent with the self-concept are not owned. Psychological freedom or adjustment exists when the self-concept is congruent with all the child's experiences. When this is not the case, tension or maladjustment is experienced by the child. Experiences that are inconsistent with the self-concept may be perceived as a threat resulting in the child's becoming behaviorally rigid in an effort to defend the existing self-concept. When there is a complete absence of any threat to the perception of self, the child is free to revise his or her self-concept to assimilate and include experiences previously inconsistent with the self-concept. The resulting well-integrated or positive self-concept enables the child to be more understanding of others and thus to have better interpersonal relationships (Rogers, 1951, pp. 483–524).

Model of Psychopathology

Before attempting to distinguish maladjustment from adjustment, it is first important to reiterate the child-centered philosophical position that there is an inherent tendency within children to move in subtle directedness toward adjustment, mental health, developmental growth, independence, autonomy of personhood, and what can be generally described as self-actualization. It is children's natural striving toward inner balance that takes them to where they need to be. Axline (1947) described this process:

> The behavior of the individual at all times seems to be caused by one drive, the drive for complete self-realization. When an individual reaches a barrier which makes it more difficult for him to achieve the complete realization of the self, there is set up an area of resistance and friction and tension. The drive toward self-realization continues, and the individual's behavior demonstrates that he is satisfying this inner drive by outwardly fighting to establish his self-concept in the world of reality, or that he is satisfying it vicariously by confining it to his inner world where he can build it up with less struggle. (p. 10)

Therefore, the focus of the play therapist is on the inner person of the child—what the child is capable of becoming—not on the child's ways of being in the past. In this approach, the child and not the problem is the point of focus. Knowing about the causes or extent of the child's maladjustment is not a prerequisite for establishing a therapeutic relationship with the child. When the focus of the therapist is on the problem, the person of the child will likely get lost, and in the process it will be communicated to the child that his or her problem is more important. Diagnosis of maladjustment is not necessary because this is not a prescriptive approach. What the play therapist does is not based on a specific problem the child may be experiencing (Landreth, 1991). With this point established, a child-centered view of maladjustment can now be discussed.

The child's inner drive toward self-realization and affirmation of the worthwhileness of self are basic needs, and each child is striving continually to satisfy these needs. "An adjusted person seems to be an individual who does not encounter too many obstacles in his path—and who has been given the opportunity to become free and independent in his own right. The maladjusted person seems to be the one who, by some means or other, is denied the right to achieve this without a struggle" (Axline, 1947, p. 21).

Axline (1947) explained the difference between well-adjusted behavior and maladjusted behavior:

> When the individual develops sufficient self-confidence . . . consciously and purposefully to direct his behavior by evaluation, selectivity, and application to achieve his ultimate goal in life—self-realization—then he seems to be well adjusted.
>
> On the other hand, when the individual lacks sufficient self-confidence to chart his course of actions openly, seems content to grow in self-realization vicariously rather than directly, and does little or nothing about channeling this drive in more constructive and productive directions, then he is said to be maladjusted . . . The individual's behavior is not consistent with the inner concept of the self which the individual has created in his attempt to achieve complete self-realization. The further apart the behavior and the concept, the greater the degree of maladjustment. (pp. 13–14)

All maladjustments are viewed as resulting from an incongruence between what the child actually experienced and the child's concept of self. "The need for self-regard leads to selective perception of experiences in terms of conditions of worth, so that experiences in accord with the individual's conditions of worth are perceived and symbolized accurately in awareness, but experiences contrary to the conditions of worth are perceived selectively or distortedly, or denied to awareness" (Patterson, 1980, p. 482). If a child's perception of an experience is distorted or denied, a state of incongruence between the self-concept and experience exists, resulting in psychological maladjustment. Incongruence between the child's self-concept and experience results in incongruence in behavior.

Goal/Cure

Terms such as *goal* and *cure* are inconsistent with the child-centered philosophy and are avoided because they generally are evaluative and imply specific accomplishments needed by the client as determined by some external person. In the child-centered approach, the child is related to as a person to be understood rather than someone to be cured or changed.

Since the individual is in a state of continuous development and is considered to be the best determiner of changes within self, a discussion of change and growth must proceed from the internal frame of reference of the developing individual. Rogers (1951) described the process of self-actualization as increased congruence between the child's very personal phenomenal field of experience and the child's self-concept. These changes in emotionalized attitudes can be described as the child being less defensive and more open to a wider range of experiences, including being more open to and accepting of others. The child feels less vulnerable, experiences less threat, and, therefore, has more realistic and objective expectations of self and others. The child's feelings of liking and acceptance of self are no longer dependent on the attitudes of other people, and the child feels more confident and capable of self-direction—that he is adequate, valuing what he thinks and feels rather than depending on the opinions of others. The child is able to "own" his own behavior and feels more in control, empowered, and congruent.

Basic Principles of the Child-Centered Relationship

Axline (1947) succinctly clarified the basic principles that provide guidelines for establishing a therapeutic relationship and making contact with the inner person of the child in the play therapy experience. Landreth (1991) revised and extended these eight basic principles as follows:

1. The therapist is genuinely interested in the child and develops a warm, caring relationship.
2. The therapist experiences unqualified acceptance of the child and does not wish that the child were different in some way.
3. The therapist creates a feeling of safety and permissiveness in the relationship so the child feels free to explore and express self completely.
4. The therapist is always sensitive to the child's feelings and gently reflects those feelings in such a manner that the child develops self-understanding.
5. The therapist believes deeply in the child's capacity to act responsibly, unwaveringly respects the child's ability to solve personal problems, and allows the child to do so.
6. The therapist trusts the child's inner direction, allows the child to lead in all areas of the relationship and resists any urge to direct the child's play or conversation.
7. The therapist appreciates the gradual nature of the therapeutic process and does not attempt to hurry the process.
8. The therapist establishes only those therapeutic limits which help the child accept personal and appropriate relationship responsibility. (pp. 77–78)

Axline (1947) stated that it is the permissive, nonjudgmental, warm, and caring relationship that gives the child the courage to delve deeply into his or her innermost world and thus to bring out the real self. The child gains self-confidence as his or her true self is accepted by the therapist. This relationship is so powerful that it is the factor that decides whether therapy is a success or failure. Moustakas (1959) believed that "through the process of self-expression and exploration within a significant relationship, through realization of the value within, the child comes to be a positive, self-determining, and self-actualizing individual" (p. 5).

Children begin to recognize their value within when the play therapist responds sensitively to that part of their person by accepting and reflecting unverbalized but nonverbally expressed feelings. The child-centered play therapist rarely asks any questions because questions structure the relationship in the direction of the therapist's interest, place the focus on the therapist, and thus interfere with the process of the child's play. For example, asking a child to explain the meaning of a picture the child has painted implies that there is a meaning and the child should know what it is. If the child does not know, his or her self-esteem suffers. The play therapist does not question the child about play or make guesses about the meaning of the child's play. Asking "Do you ever wish you could do that to your father?" anchors the child too closely to reality, interferes with the safety of symbolic expression, and may be much too threatening to the child. Tracking the child's play—"You're squishing that man's [assuming the child has identified the doll as a man] head right between those blocks"— is much more facilitative of the child's possible inner expression, which may follow if the child feels understood. As indicated in this example, the play therapist does not label items because that would structure the child's play.

Evaluation of any kind is steadfastly avoided. The child-centered play therapist would consider it unthinkable, for example, to evaluate a child's picture, even though the child might insist on knowing "Do you think my picture is pretty?" Instead, the play therapist would describe what he or she sees. "You put some green all the way across the bottom (pointing), some blue up here, and this color over here. You made it just the way you wanted it to be." Evaluative statements deprive the child of inner motivation.

The child-centered play therapist avoids interfering with the child's play, does not offer solutions or suggestions, and above all does not allow himself or herself to be manipulated into becoming the child's teacher or doing things for the child. Assistance is provided only in rare circumstances when the child has tried and truly cannot do something by himself or herself.

Therapeutic Limit Setting

A discussion of the child-centered approach to play therapy would not be complete without an exploration of the role of therapeutic limit setting as a facilitative dimension in the process. Children do not feel safe, valued, or accepted in a completely permissive relationship. Moustakas (1959) summarized the importance of limits as a vital and necessary part of relationships:

Limits exist in every relationship. The human organism is free to grow and develop within the limits of its own potentialities, talents, and structure. In psychotherapy, there must be an integration of freedom and order if the individuals involved are to actualize their potentialities. The limit is one aspect of an alive experience, the aspect which identifies, characterizes, and distinguishes the dimensions of a therapeutic relationship. The limit is the form or structure of an immediate relationship. It refers not only to a unique form but also to the possibility for life, growth and direction rather than merely to a limitation . . . In a therapeutic relationship, limits provide the boundary or structure in which growth can occur. (pp. 8–9)

An examination of the purpose for limits readily reveals the child-centered play therapist's concern for the process rather than specific behaviors. The child's desire to break the limit is always of greater importance than the actual breaking of a limit. The purpose for setting limits can be summarized as follows: (1) Limits define the boundaries of the therapeutic relationship; (2) limits provide security and safety for the child, both physically and emotionally; (3) limits demonstrate the therapist's intent to provide safety for the child; (4) limits anchor the session to reality; (5) limits allow the therapist to maintain a positive and accepting attitude toward the child; (6) limits allow the child to express negative feelings without causing harm, and the subsequent fear of retaliation; (7) limits offer stability and consistency; (8) limits promote and enhance the child's sense of self-responsibility and self-control; (9) limits protect the play therapy room; and (10) limits provide for the maintenance of legal, ethical, and professional standards (Axline, 1947; Bixler, 1949; Ginott, 1961; Landreth, 1991; Moustakas, 1959).

This is not a completely permissive relationship. The child is not allowed to do just anything the child may want to do. There is a prescribed structure that provides boundaries for the relationship that the play therapist has already determined are necessary. Limits need to be set on (1) harmful or dangerous behavior to the child and therapist, (2) behavior that disrupts the therapeutic routine or process (continually leaving playroom, wanting to play after time is up), (3) destruction of room or materials, (4) taking toys from playroom, (5) socially unacceptable behavior, and (6) inappropriate displays of affection.

Limits are not set until they are needed. Providing a long list of prohibited activities at the beginning of the first session would certainly not encourage or facilitate exploration and expression by the child. At the point that children are emotionally involved, there is greater opportunity for significant learning. When limits are needed, the therapist should be firm and matter-of-fact so the child will not feel punished. The limits set should be minimal, specific, total rather than conditional, and enforceable.

Since boundaries have previously been determined, the play therapist can be consistent and thus predictable in setting limits. This consistency and predictability help the child to feel safe. It is within this structure that the *feeling* of permissiveness is more important than actual permissiveness. When limit setting becomes necessary, the child's desire to break the limit is always the primary focus of attention because the child-centered play therapist is dealing with intrinsic variables related to motivation, perception of self, independence, need for acceptance, and the working out of a relationship with a significant person.

Limits are worded in a way that allows the child to bring himself or herself under control. The command "Don't paint on the wall" places the therapist in an enforcer role and does not facilitate the development of the child's self-control. The objective is to respond in such a way that the child is allowed to say "No" to self. The response "You would like to paint on the wall, but the wall is not for painting on; the paper on the table is for painting on" recognizes the child's feeling, communicates what the wall is not for, and provides an acceptable alternative. The child is thus allowed to stop himself or herself. The child-centered play therapist has an unwavering belief that children will choose positive cooperative behavior when provided with conditions of acceptance of self.

Applicability for Age, Ethnic Status

Although child-centered play therapy is most widely used with children below ten years of age, positive results have been obtained with ten- to fourteen-year-old children, adults, and with specific cases of adults who have a child alter personality. Generally speaking, children's ability to think and reason abstractly prior to age ten is limited. Therefore, they need toys and play materials to communicate their thoughts and emotions adequately. For children above age ten, the guiding principle for inclusion in play therapy seems to be the child's intellectual, emotional, and social developmental level. The self-directed nature of the child-centered approach is especially appropriate for children who are developmentally delayed. Although many positive experiences have resulted from allowing children above age ten to choose whether they want to be in the standard playroom, the activity room, or the therapist's office, most children in the ten-to-fourteen age range seem to profit most from an activity therapy approach that is consistent with their developmental needs. It is important to point out that the utilization of different materials does not change the child-centered nature of the approach; the child continues to lead.

The child-centered approach is uniquely suited for working with children from different socioeconomic strata and ethnic backgrounds since these facts do not change the therapist's beliefs, philosophy, theory, or approach to the child. Empathy, acceptance, understanding, and genuineness on the part of the therapist are provided to children equally, irrespective of their color, condition, circumstance, concern, or complaint. The child is free to communicate through play in a manner that is comfortable and typical for the child, including cultural adaptations of play and expression.

Research on Child-Centered Play Therapy

The purpose of this section is not to review the myriad of research studies on client-centered (person-centered) therapy but to address the issue of required length of time commitment. The popular myth that child-centered play therapy is a slow process requiring a long-term commitment is not supported by fact. Raskin and Rogers (1989) reported that significant positive changes in self-acceptance and the individual's ability to move toward an internal locus-of-evaluation have been demonstrated in single sessions and short-term experiences. Over 45 years ago, Bills (1950) investigated the effects of nondirective (child-centered) play therapy with children identified as slow readers and found that, after six individual and three group play therapy sessions, students who had received play therapy showed significant gains in their reading ability when compared to a control group. Crow (1989), an elementary school counselor, had ten 30-minute individual child-centered play therapy sessions with 12 first-grade students who had been retained because of low achievement in reading and found that their self-concepts were significantly improved as compared to a matched control group. Based on what is known about the impact of a positive self-concept on academic learning, this study has tremendous significance, especially in view of the short-term nature of the study.

Barlow, Strother, and Landreth (1985) reported on the case of a four-year-old child whose emotional reactions were so severe that she had, over a period of several months, pulled all her hair out and was completely bald. By the end of the eighth child-centered play therapy session, previously reported behavioral symptoms had disappeared and the child's hair had begun to grow back, a dramatic picture of the effectiveness of child-centered play therapy.

Kot (1995) investigated the effects of short-term, intensive, child-centered play therapy with children who had witnessed domestic violence and were temporarily residing in women's shelters. Eleven children each received 12 individual 45-minute play therapy sessions in a span of 14 to 21 days. A matched control group in the shelters received no treatment. The children in child-centered play therapy scored significantly higher than the control group on self-concept, reduction of externalizing behavior problems, and reduction of total behavior problems on standardized measures. These results remarkably demonstrate the healing power of the child-centered play therapy relationship and the capacity of this approach to facilitate significant changes in a very short period of time.

Landreth (Lobaugh, 1991) trained 16 fathers incarcerated in a federal prison to use child-centered play therapy procedures in filial therapy sessions with their children. The fathers had special 30-minute play sessions with their children once a week on visitation day for 10 weeks. These children's self-concepts improved significantly as compared to a control group of incarcerated fathers and their children. The fathers who received the filial therapy training also exhibited significant improvement on a variety of measuring instruments, demonstrating the therapeutic impact of the training and the child-centered play sessions under very difficult circumstances—not only on the children but also on the fathers who were learning this approach. In a related research project, Harris (1995) trained 12 mothers incarcerated in a county jail to use child-centered play therapy procedures in 30-minute filial therapy play sessions with their children twice a week for five weeks. These children demonstrated significantly fewer problem behaviors on the post-test instrument than did the children of a matched control group of incarcerated mothers. The mothers in the filial therapy training also demonstrated significant increases in their level of empathic interactions with their children and significant increases in their attitude of acceptance toward their children.

Bratton (1994) trained 22 single mothers to use child-centered play therapy procedures in filial therapy sessions with their children. The mothers had special 30-minute play sessions once a week with their children for 10 weeks. A matched control group of single parents received no treatment. Parents in the experimental group demonstrated significant increases in level of empathy in their interactions with their children and attitude of acceptance toward their children. They also reported significantly reduced levels of parental stress and significantly fewer problems with their children's behavior.

Additionally, in a text compiled to describe play therapy case study and research material in digest form (Landreth, Homeyer, Glover, & Sweeney, (1996), a large portion of the studies reporting successful results used a child-centered approach in a time-limited setting.

CASE FORMULATION

Conceptualizing Jason's case from the child-centered approach takes a very different perspective from the intake information offered in the "Orientation to the Text."* Jason, said to be unable to describe any problems, "interpreted the word 'problems' to mean things he was doing wrong and adamantly denied that any of his behavior was problematic." This very statement assumes a therapeutic position that is problem-centered. Moustakas (1959) correctly noted that most therapeutic relationships with children involve problem-centered interactions. Child-centered play therapy, however, as its title asserts, focuses on the child. As such, the development of a relationship with Jason that is "Jason focused" rather than problem or diagnosis focused is central.

Assessment and diagnosis do not play a significant role in the child-centered approach to play therapy. Person-centered therapy views diagnosis and evaluation as distracting and potentially detrimental to the client (Rogers, 1951). The psychometric and background information offered about Jason, while interesting, is not considered pertinent in the conceptualization and treatment planning of his case. It may be suggested that considerable focus on evaluation and diagnosis, as well as interpretation, serves to meet the needs of the therapist and not the child. The assessment of Jason, therefore, involves attempting to understand Jason in the here and now, as well as how Jason perceives himself. This will enable Jason to view himself and his situation differently. Cain (1991) suggested "in person-centered therapy self-assessment and self-definition are seen as part of the ongoing therapeutic process" (p. 119).

A detailed discussion of Jason's past is also not a foundational issue in formulating this case. From the child-centered perspective, a focus on the past distracts from the present. Although the therapist might want to change Jason's past, that simply is not possible. What has occurred in Jason's past is now past history. Viewing Jason's case or directing therapy in light of the past limits growth toward the future. Indeed, during the intake interview, when the interviewer "focused on Jason's history," he became nonverbal and uncooperative.

---

*See "Orientation to the Text: The Case of Jason L.," p. 1.

Axline (1955) discussed her play therapy cases within the framework of emotionalized attitudes:

In psychotherapy, we are dealing with emotionalized attitudes that have developed out of the individual's past experiencing of himself in relation to others. These emotionalized attitudes influence his perception of himself as either adequate or inadequate, secure or insecure, worthy of respect or not worthy of respect, having personal worth or deficient in this basic feeling. His perception then, in turn, determines his behavior. The individual's behavior at the moment seems to be his best efforts to maintain and defend his selfhood and so maintain a psychological identity and a resistance to threats against his personality. Consequently, the child who is emotionally deprived and who has had experiences that seem to form and reinforce feelings of inadequacy and lack of personal worth learns the kind of behavior that protects his self-esteem and lessens the impact of threats against his personality . . . He may refuse to behave certain ways that are expected or demanded by others in order to maintain a self with integrity. (p. 619)

This is essentially what is occurring for Jason. He has been trying to make sense of the profound changes that have occurred in his life, and he is being labeled a "problem" in the process. This sets up what Dorfman (1951) referred to as an alteration of his "stimulus-value," which involves a child's being differently perceived, differently responded to, and differently treated, which in turn leads the child to experience further negative change. It is the negative changes that lead children to referral for treatment. The child-centered play therapy approach involves the same dynamic, but in reverse. In therapy, the child is differently perceived, responded to, and treated, which results in positive change. Jason has experienced labeling, and his behavior has correspondingly changed, as the intake information notes: "Behaviorally, he has always been somewhat of a problem."

From a child-centered perspective, Jason is dealing with the incongruence between the child he is (including all the adult issues he has been compelled to face) and the child he wants to be (the child who has been struggling to emerge). Axline (1964) suggested that the maladjusted person is someone who, because of circumstances, has been denied the right to achieve autonomy without a struggle. Jason's circumstances amount to obstacles on his path to an unimpaired self-concept. Jason's difficult behaviors are evidence of "the inner self's attempting to approximate a full realization of this self-concept" (Axline, 1947, p. 14).

Jason is looking to be recognized as a person, not a problem, as a child worthy of respect and important in his own right. The situation of his parents' divorce, his mother's depression, the labeling of his behavior, and other related issues have put Jason in a position where he has been denied the conditions to establish this self-concept. He has, therefore, attempted to realize this self-concept through maladjusted behaviors. Jason feels out of control and has chosen to channel his efforts (manifested in his unacceptable behavior) to fight against the existing barriers that prevent him from growth and self-expression. Jason's "control for both his positive and negative affect" is reportedly poor. This should not be a surprise, as he lives in a world that feels out of control and where positive and negative emotions are at best poorly defined. He is "angry and unresponsive" to imposed directions. He withdraws and sulks when confronted, which gives him opportunity to retreat into his own world to better realize his self-concept.

While the child-centered play therapist would not define Jason's behavioral and affective condition in terms of typical or atypical labels, the unavailability of a means in which to process his circumstances and experience uninhibited growth has led to an expression of his situation in an unacceptable manner. Jason responds positively to unstructured play situations, as evidenced by his positive response to his parents when he experiences this. Jason becomes verbal and affectionate with his mother following unstructured play activities, in which his mother "tries to avoid making any demands" of Jason. The absence of many of the challenging behaviors with his father that Jason exhibits with his mother appears to be encouraged by the unstructured nature of their time spent together. When offered the opportunity to play freely and uninhibited, Jason grows. Therapeutically, Jason is in need of what Axline describes in the child-centered approach as "an opportunity that is offered to the child to experience growth under the most favorable conditions" (1964, p. 35). Therefore, Jason could be expected to respond equally positively to the unstructured nature of the child-centered play therapy approach.

TREATMENT GOALS

As had already been stated, the child-centered approach does not set treatment goals. The central hypothesis governing what the therapist does is an unwavering belief in the child's capacity for growth and *self*-direction. The establishment of specific treatment goals would be a contradiction of this belief. Goals or objectives of treatment imply that the therapist knows where the child should be and that there is a specific structure by which to get there. The play therapist is not wise enough to know where another person should be in his or her life or what that person should be working on or toward. Life is much too complex to be understood by diagnosis and controlled by a prescription for growth. Further, the child is the best determiner of what should be focused on in play therapy. How can children learn self-direction if even their play is directed? Diagnostically based treatment goals usually result in the therapist's being focused on the treatment goal. Such an approach would be much too structuring and would restrict the creative potential of the child and the relationship.

Although the child-centered play therapist does not establish individualized prescriptive therapeutic goals for children, there are broadly defined therapeutic objectives that are consistent with this theoretical and philosophical approach. According to Landreth (1991):

The general objectives of child-centered play therapy are consistent with the child's inner self-directed striving toward self-actualization. An overriding premise is to provide the child with a positive growth experience in the presence of an understanding supportive adult so the child will be able to discover internal strengths. Since child-centered play therapy focuses on the person of the child rather than the child's problem, the emphasis is on facilitating the child's efforts to become more adequate, as a person, in coping with current and future problems which may impact the child's life. To that end, the objectives of child-centered play therapy are to help the child

1. Develop a more positive self-concept
2. Assume greater self-responsibility
3. Become more self-directing
4. Become more self-accepting
5. Become more self-reliant
6. Engage in self-determined decision making
7. Experience a feeling of control
8. Become sensitive to the process of coping
9. Develop an internal source of evaluation
10. Become more trusting of self. (p. 80)

Within the framework of these general objectives, the child is free to work on specific problems, and this is often the case. It should be made clear, however, that this is the child's choice and is not a result of the therapist's having hinted at, suggested, or implied that the child should do so. In this child-centered relationship, the therapist believes in and trusts the child's capacity to set his or her own goals and direction. "In this view, no attempt is made to control a child, to have the child be a certain way, or to reach a conclusion the therapist has decided is important. The therapist is not *the* authority who decides what is best for the child, what the child should think, or how the child should feel. If this were to be the case, the child would be deprived of the opportunity to discover his/her own strengths" (Landreth, 1991, p. 81).

In the latter stages of the therapeutic process, group play therapy might be helpful in providing Jason an opportunity to develop his social skills further. The interaction of the group could provide additional experiences for clarifying his developing self. Filial therapy training would be recommended for both parents to help them provide a consistent environment for Jason that would cut across both households. The skills learned in filial therapy would be a special asset to bolstering Jason's self-esteem.

TREATMENT DESCRIPTION

The term *treatment* implies that positive change is dependent upon the application of some techniques or actions. The child who enters play therapy has not self-referred—some adult has made the determination that the child needs to be changed. However, the child-centered play therapist does not enter the treatment process with this agenda. Change is a product of the relationship, and is dependent on the child's response to the environment created by the therapist. The logistics described below, while important contributing factors, cannot replace the importance of the child-centered play therapy *relationship*.

Logistics: Playroom and Materials

The play therapy sessions with Jason took place in one of the eight playrooms in the Center for Play Therapy at the University of North Texas. Each play therapy room is approximately 12 feet by 15 feet and is equipped with the materials recommended by Landreth (1991). The playroom has a vinyl floor covering for ease of cleaning, a sink with cold running water (hot water should never be connected, for obvious reasons), a chalkboard, a sandbox, a small table, child-size chairs, shelving for toys and materials, a child-size refrigerator and stove, a painting easel, and an adjoining small bathroom with just enough space for a commode. The availability of water and a bathroom prevents interruptions in the therapeutic process resulting from the child's exiting the room and prevents many struggles such as how many times the child will be allowed to leave the room for water or to go to the bathroom.

The playroom has a two-way mirror and video equipment, which provide excellent opportunities for filial therapy training with Jason's parents as described by Guerney in Chapter 5. When the interactions of parents with their children in the playroom are videotaped and then critiqued under the supervision of the play therapist, parents gain insight into their behavior with their children much more quickly. Videotaping of the play therapist's sessions is also considered to be essential for the continuing professional development of the play therapist.

Although the sessions with Jason took place in a fully equipped play therapy room, many successful play therapy experiences have occurred in an office, the corner of a classroom, and other modified settings. Although it is not absolutely necessary, children can obviously be more creative, expressive, and emotionally expansive, and can act out with greater forcefulness and energy in a fully equipped playroom.

Since toys are considered to be children's words and play is their language, careful attention must be paid to the selection of toys and materials that allow for children's self-directed activity and facilitate a wide range of feelings and play activity. All toys and materials do not automatically encourage children's expression or exploration of their feelings, needs, and experiences. Play therapy is not used as a method to get ready to do something else. The purpose is not to engage the child in some play behavior in preparation for trying to get the child to talk, tell about something that has happened, or describe something the child wants in life. The child's play *is* the message. Play materials that are mechanical, complex, highly structured, or require the play therapist's assistance to manipulate are potentially frustrating to children and may foster dependence in children who already feel helpless or inadequate. Therefore, toys and materials should be selected that

1. Facilitate a wide range of creative expression
2. Facilitate a wide range of emotional expression

3. Engage children's interests
4. Facilitate expressive and exploratory play
5. Allow exploration and expression without verbalization
6. Allow success without prescribed structure
7. Allow for noncommittal play. (Landreth, 1991, p. 116)

In addition to the furniture items listed earlier, the materials recommended by Landreth (1991) for a "tote bag playroom" constituted the core of play materials in the playroom: crayons, newsprint, blunt scissors, clay or Play-Doh®, popsicle sticks, transparent tape, nursing bottle, doll, plastic dishes and cups, bendable Gumby® (nondescript figure), doll family figures, dollhouse furniture, dollhouse (open top type on floor), Lone Ranger® type mask, rubber knife, dart gun, handcuffs, toy soldiers, car, airplane, hand puppets, telephones (two), cotton rope, and costume jewelry. Other items such as tempera paints, punching toy, and pots and pans were included and are too numerous to mention here. Landreth's (1991) chapter on playroom and materials in his book *Play Therapy: The Art of the Relationship* has a complete listing of toys. The child-centered play therapist is always careful to select toys and materials that allow children to express their feelings, needs, and experiences through the medium of the toy. Battery-operated, hand-held games do not provide an expressive outlet for exploring what has been experienced; neither do most board games. How can a child act out feelings about an experience by spinning a spinner and moving a token to the next level? For similar reasons, books should be kept out of the playroom. Books can be helpful for input or educational purposes, but they do not meet the criteria of an expressive outlet.

Frequency and Duration of Treatment

In child-centered play therapy, the frequency and duration of treatment is established by the needs of the child. As Axline (1947) points out, the child-centered play therapist does not hurry the process along:

If the therapist feels that the child has a problem and she wants to attack the problem as soon as possible, she must remember that what she feels is not important. If the child has a problem, he will bring it out when he is ready. The problem of maladjustment is so complex that one cannot draw a simple circle around some singular experience and say, "This is it." (p. 126)

In the child-centered approach, play therapy sessions are generally held once a week, but this is not a prescribed structure. The individual needs of the child must always take precedence over the usual predetermined once-a-week schedule, which is primarily for the professional convenience of the therapist or the agency. The emotional and developmental needs of children do not always follow such a rigid prescribed structure. A week in a child's life is not equal to the same amount of time in an adult's life. A week in a preschool child's life can be a very long time, and this must be considered when scheduling children. Additionally, the intense emotional needs of the child resulting from certain life experiences must be taken into account. The child-centered play therapist may meet with the traumatized child two or three times a week in the first few weeks and then move to a schedule of once-a-week sessions. The nature of some settings as well as the severity of the presenting problem may necessitate that play therapy sessions be scheduled every day, as in the case of children in a women's shelter who may be there only a maximum of two to three weeks before moving out of town or out of state. The efficacy of this kind of intensive child-centered play therapy was demonstrated by Kot (1995) in her research with child witnesses of domestic violence.

Jason was seen in play therapy once a week for 15 weeks. This is generally typical for the child-centered play therapy process and is consistent with the research findings of Phillips and Landreth (1995) who surveyed 1,166 play therapists and reported that the median number of play therapy sessions before termination was 11 to 20. Following termination with Jason, his parents were referred for filial therapy training.

Specific Strategies

It is difficult to describe the child-centered approach to play therapy without giving specific examples. In keeping with the person-centered characteristic of illustrating principles through verbatim accounts (Raskin & Rogers, 1989), the following is a transcript of some of the therapeutic interactions with Jason in the playroom.

Session 1

Therapist: Jason, this is our playroom, and this is a place where you can play with the toys in a lot of the ways you would like to.

The child-centered approach is permission-giving. It respects the child's ability to lead the process where it needs to go.

Jason: (Looks around the playroom tentatively, but does not move toward any toy or play activity.)

We would expect Jason to be somewhat cautious. He likely has not been in a situation with an adult who has allowed him to have control and take the lead. This is a very different experience.

Therapist: Looks like you're wondering just what to do in here. This is your time, and in here you can decide.

Reflection of the child's actions and affect are key in the child-centered approach. The therapist's response is already promoting Jason's self-responsibility. Note also the use of the words "in here," specifying that this playroom is a special place in which the child is able to make such decisions.

Jason: I don't know what to do (in a quiet tone, looking in the direction of the therapist but not making eye contact).

When Jason looks in the direction of the therapist, he is beginning to make contact. He is still somewhat apprehensive about the process, but is making movement.

Therapist: (Also in a quiet tone) You're just not sure what to do. Sometimes it's hard to decide. This is a place where you can choose what to do.

Note that the therapist's voice tone matches that of Jason. Empathic reflection involves more than words; it also includes voice tone, facial expression, body language, etc. The therapist's response places with Jason the responsibility to make choices and thus the opportunity to learn self-control and self-responsibility.

Jason: (Walking over to the paints) Is it okay if I play with the paints?

Jason is still seeking permission and approval. As he makes decisions for himself, he will feel empowered and will develop an internal source of approval rather than looking for external praise.

Therapist: Sounds like you have something in mind. In here you can decide.

Actually, Jason is not asking a question. He is saying that he wants to paint. By not answering Jason's question, the therapist continues to allow Jason to lead.

Jason: I think I'll make orange by mixing up the yellow and red. (Picks up paintbrush and dips into yellow paint.)

Jason has made his own decision, and is perhaps testing the perceived permissiveness of the relationship by mixing the colors.

Therapist: Oh, so you know that yellow and red make orange. Sounds like you know a lot about colors.

By giving Jason credit for knowing his colors, the therapist is building up Jason's self-esteem. Self-esteem-building responses and tracking (communicating through reflection that the therapist is paying attention to and is invested in the child's play) are important therapeutic tools in the child-centered approach.

Jason: Yeah—it's my favorite color.

Jason acknowledges the therapist's response and adds a personal dimension.

Therapist: So you've got a plan to paint something with your favorite color.

Shows understanding.

Jason: (Suddenly puts the paintbrush back forcefully in its holder, tears the paper off the easel, and groans.) Oohh!

Jason is upset with himself. This is likely a reflection of a basic self-perception that he has.

Therapist: You didn't like how that turned out.

The response conveys understanding and acceptance of Jason's dissatisfaction with his painting.

Jason: (Angry voice) I messed up!

Therapist: You're really angry about messing that up.

The focus is not on messing up the painting but on hearing and accepting Jason's feelings.

Jason: Yeah, I guess so (pauses)—can I try another one?

The therapist's acceptance of Jason's feelings allows him to accept that part of himself and frees him to try again since he does not need to defend that part of self.

Therapist: In here, that's something you can decide.

Therapist continues to return responsibility to Jason.

Jason: I guess so (looking around the room).

Therapist: Seems like you're still not too sure about this place.

The therapist continues to look beyond Jason's action—to feelings, and to intentions. It stands to reason that the playroom would be a strange place for Jason—it is a new experience.

Jason: Uh-huh (picks up another paintbrush and dips into the blue).

Therapist: You've picked another color.

Tracking of play behaviors needs to continue throughout the session to show interest and involvement.

Jason: (Starts to paint in broad strokes across the center of the paper.)

Therapist: Using a lot of paint.

Therapeutic responses in the playroom should be short, succinct, and interactive with the child's feelings and actions.

Jason: Uh-huh (switching paint brushes).

Therapist: Hmm, another color—you're covering a lot of that paper with paint.

Note that the therapist is tracking without taking the lead away from the child. Had the therapist commented to Jason that he was painting "all" of the paper, it may have created an expectancy for him to indeed paint the entire paper, thus reinforcing Jason's already evident dependency.

Jason: Yeah, I'm gonna cover the whole page! (Sounds happy and has a big smile.)

This choice was Jason's alone. He has verbalized a decision.

Therapist: You've got a plan, and that makes you happy! (Said with enthusiasm and with a smile.)

Reflecting feelings is a challenge for many play therapists. Equally challenging is matching the child's affective state. A minimized affective response diminishes the effectiveness of the response and may communicate to the child that the emotion expressed is not appropriate. A response that exceeds the affective expression of the child may be equally leading, as it sends a message to the child that he or she should have the same emotional level as the therapist.

Jason: They'd never let me do this at school. (Continues to cover the paper with paint.)
Therapist: You've noticed that this is a different place.

The therapist responds to the activity of the playroom and not to the situation at school. This reflects the importance in the child-centered approach of remaining in the present and with the child.

Jason: You know, you talk weird.
Therapist: I sound kind of different to you.

Rather than responding to Jason's adjective ("weird"), the therapist responds to the underlying message.

Jason: Yeah—you don't talk like other grown-ups. (Paper is almost fully covered with paint; Jason looks at therapist.) Do you like my picture?
Therapist: You used lots of colors in that painting. You put some green on the bottom, blue on that side (pointing), red over there (pointing), some brown near the top—you made it just like you wanted it to be. (Shows praising in tone of voice.)

A child should notice that the therapist is not like other adults!

The play therapist does not evaluate and focuses on the effort rather than the product. This is a basic difference between encouragement and praise that is key in the child-centered play therapy relationship. By focusing on the effort, the therapist can make self-esteem building statements without creating the leading and approval-oriented dynamic that comes from statements of praise.

Jason: I sure did! (Said emphatically.)
Therapist: And you're proud of your painting!

Continued reflection of feelings. It is likely that Jason has not felt feelings of pride recently in light of his life circumstances. When he has, he has also likely not been readily affirmed, as in this time in the playroom.

Later Session

Jason: (Runs into the playroom and immediately starts attacking the bop bag—he looks angry.)

There is no tentativeness evident in Jason's response to the playroom this time. A therapeutic relationship has been established.

Therapist: You look angry. You're really hitting that Bobo®.

The therapist lets Jason know that this expression of emotion and activity is just as acceptable as any other.

Jason: Yeah—I'm a ninja cop. And this guy is gonna get it! (Hits and kicks the bop bag more intensely.)

It has not been the experience in child-centered play therapy that aggression expressed in the playroom transfers to increased aggression outside of the playroom. Once negative feelings have been expressed and accepted in the playroom, the child can go on to more positive behaviors.

Therapist: Hmmm, you're in charge and that guy's really gonna get it.

Jason lives a life that feels out of control. One of the primary benefits of the child-centered approach is the opportunity to manage the unmanageable, to control in the fantasy of the play what seems out of control in the real world.

Jason: (Noticing that one of the dinosaurs is among the puppets) Hey—who left this here? Do other kids use this room?

This is an important question that children often ask about the playroom and can indicate possessiveness.

Therapist: Looks like you found a toy that you think should be somewhere else. And yes, Jason, other children do come here.

The therapist reflects the activity without labeling the item, since Jason did not label it, and answers his questions.

Jason: Oh yeah? Well, at least they should put the toys back where they are supposed to go? (Puts dinosaur back with the other dinosaurs.)

Therapist: You know just how you'd like this room to be, and you don't like them messing it up.

This response reflects his feelings, affirms Jason, recognizes that he knows what he wants, and allows him to stay in the lead.

Jason: That's right! (Said with a pouty look and sounding a little angry.)

Therapist: Makes you mad.

Acknowledging the child's feelings communicates acceptance and helps the child learn that emotions are an acceptable part of life.

Jason: Yeah! (Sounds angry, grabs the xylophone and throws it at the bop bag.)

Therapist: You're really angry, but the xylophone is not for throwing, Jason. The ball is for throwing (pointing toward ball).

This is an example of the therapeutic limit-setting model used in child-centered play therapy discussed previously. The A.C.T. model, proposed by

Landreth (1991) is a highly effective tool in the playroom. It includes: (1) A–Acknowledging the child's feelings (it is important to begin the setting of limits by continuing reflection and acceptance); (2) C–Communicating the limit (in a neutral and nonpunitive manner); and (3) T–Targeting an acceptable alternative (which recognizes that the child still has a need to express self and can do so within acceptable boundaries). A limit that is set objectively, with acceptance, and without disapproval is most often received and responded to by the child with compliance.

Jason: Okay (goes to pick up the ball and tosses it to the therapist).

Therapist: (Catching the ball) You decided to throw this to me.

Note that the therapist did not label the ball and did not respond by saying "You've decided to play catch with me." This would have been a leading statement, presuming on the child's intent too soon.

Jason: (Moving over to the shelf of animals and dinosaurs—takes armful and puts them in the sandbox.)
Therapist: Looks like you've got a plan.
Jason: I've got a plan all right (taking another armload of animals to the sandbox).
Therapist: Uh-huh.

The response affirms the child's intent and is permission-giving.

Jason: (Going for a third armload of figures—looks at therapist with a questioning expression.)
Therapist: Looks like you might be wondering if it's okay to put all those in the sandbox. In here, that's something you can decide.
Jason: Cool! (Said with some satisfaction in his voice.)
Therapist: You like being able to do that.

This response continues permission-giving and returns responsibility to the child.

Perhaps Jason is beginning to experience the satisfaction of feeling in control. Acknowledgment of feelings as well as acknowledgment of the uniqueness of the child-centered play environment continues to be important.

Jason: (Sits down next to sandbox and begins to set up the animals in military-like formation in the sand.) Time for a war.
Therapist: You know just what you're going to do—a war.

The continued giving of credit to Jason for his planning and intentions is important. This not only communicates acceptance of the specific activity but also affirms his general ability and capability. A child who receives such affirmation builds problem-solving and coping skills through the play experience.

Jason: That's right—they're all going to die.

Jason has experienced considerable loss in his life. This should be an expected theme in his play.
Shows understanding.

Therapist: They are all going to die.
Jason: Yeah—and I'm going to kill them (going to shelf and picking up toy weapons).

The loss that has occurred in Jason's life has been out of his control, and on someone else's terms. Following the concept of managing the unmanageable, the play theme of loss will occur within Jason's control and on his terms. It is an opportunity not only for Jason to process grief and loss issues, but also to develop new ways for coping with continued losses.

Later Session

Jason: (Picks up two toy tigers, one big and the other small.)
Therapist: Looks like you've got something in mind.

Continuing to follow the lead of the child.

Jason: Uh-huh. (Seems a little quiet and melancholy.)
Therapist: Seems that you just want to be quiet today, Jason.

The therapist's acceptance must extend to all expressions of the child's emotions.

Jason: Yeah. These tigers are going to take a walk in the forest (placing animals in the sandbox). And then a big storm is gonna come up.
Therapist: A walk in the forest and a big storm.

Tracking continues to be important and to communicate "being with" the child. Jason initially referred to himself, and then quickly switched back to talking about the animals. The importance of symbolic projection is key in the child's being able to approach issues safely.

Jason: It's getting too stormy. I—I mean the little tiger can't see the big one anymore. He's going to get lost! (Still talking quietly, but with some fear in his voice.)

Therapist: Sounds a little scary to get caught in a storm, and not be able to see the big tiger.

Jason's history is filled with storms, as well as separation from his mother through her various periods of depression and withdrawal.

Jason: Yeah, it is. It's scary to be all alone.

This statement extends to issues beyond the play itself.

Therapist: You know what it's like to be all alone.

Jason does know what it's like to be all alone, and he needs acknowledgment of the issue and of his willingness to process it in the play.

Jason: The big tiger is lost and scared, too.

Jason is in touch with his mother's emotional issues as well.

Therapist: Storms can be scary for little tigers and big tigers.

Jason: Storms are just scary. Even tigers need someone to hold on to.

Therapist: So they will feel safe.

Even with his tough exterior, Jason knows that he needs someone to hold on to in the midst of the "storms" that have hit his family.

Later Session

Jason: I think I'll play over here with this house today (moving to the doll house).

Jason has long since passed by activity in the playroom marked by dependency. Once again, Jason's progress in the play process is seen in his ready willingness to disagree with and even challenge the therapist. These are skills that would be expected to transfer outside of the playroom.

Therapist: You've decided to play with the house.

Jason: (Sounding defensive) I'm not playing house—only girls play house. I'm just looking at it.

Therapist: You want to make sure I

Jason has likely internalized messages

know that you are not playing house like a girl—you're just checking it out.

from his parents and peers about what is appropriate play for boys and girls. The therapist's response does not condone or condemn Jason's socialization but rather communicates understanding. The issue of teaching about sex roles, while important, is not part of the child-centered play process.

Jason: Yeah (looking relieved).

Jason's response indicates that he feels heard and accepted by the therapist.

Therapist: Hmm-hmm.

Jason: (Picking out doll figures) This is the size of my family.

When addressing family issues in the play, children may use the doll figures, or animal families, or any other set of toys. The important concern is that they be allowed to project onto any toys whatever they wish, rather than following a prescribed agenda set by the therapist.

Therapist: So that's just like your family.

Jason: Except that my family doesn't live together anymore (said somewhat wistfully—sad voice).

Jason has been processing issues of grief and loss throughout the play therapy process. His ability to deal more directly with the issue of his broken home is a result of the acceptance he has felt for his previous symbolic approaches to the issue.

Therapist: You're sad about that.

It is very important to respond to both positive and negative emotions expressed in the playroom.

Treatment Stages

In the initial session, the child-centered play therapist is concerned with being sensitive to the child's feelings and perception, helping the child to feel safe, making emotional contact with the child, and returning responsibility for self to the child. "The building of a relationship begins with what the child sees and perceives in the therapist and is dependent on the therapist's sensitivity to the child's experiencing at the moment. Making contact with the child means responding with gentleness, kindness, and softness to the child's communication of self. Through the process of accepting the child's attitudes, feelings, and thoughts, the therapist enters the child's world. Once contact with the child has been made in this way, a trusting relationship can begin to develop" (Landreth, 1991, p. 157). The building of this kind of relationship begins with the therapist's verbal introduction of the child to the playroom.

The introduction should be brief and should convey permissiveness to the child. Now is not the time to educate the child about the limits in the room; those will be set only when they are needed. A lengthy introduction keeps the therapist in the lead and deprives the child of the opportunity to take the initiative in the relationship. It is enough for the therapist to say, "Jason, this is our playroom, and this is a place where you can play with the toys in a lot of the ways you would like." The play therapist should then sit down, thus relinquishing control and direction to the child. This statement is freeing to the child in that it conveys to the child responsibility for direction. Possible boundaries are conveyed by the words "in a lot of the ways," which in effect communicate limits on behavior. The therapist now waits for the child's initiative and begins to verbally notice whatever the child does, says, or feels. As Jason looks into the two-way mirror and smiles, the therapist might respond, "You see yourself in that mirror." A major premise is that children are always communicating, not necessarily with words but with their bodies, their play, and their total self. Unlike many other approaches to play therapy, child-centered play therapy does not require or expect the child to verbalize any stories, descriptions, thoughts, feelings, guesses, insights, issues, problems, or concerns. The child is free to talk, but only if the child takes the initiative to do so. The therapist does not try to elicit verbalization or suggest that the child should begin to play. That is the child's decision. The child is allowed to lead from the very beginning. Permissiveness implies that the child can choose to play or not to play, to talk or not to talk. The initial session sets the tone for building the relationship with the child in the following sessions. The role of the child-centered play therapist is to create the kind of relationship that enables the child to discover how he or she can function independently.

Children in this kind of freeing relationship within the therapeutic principles of the child-centered approach have been found by Moustakas (1955) to progress through the following identifiable stages of the therapeutic process:

1. Diffuse negative feelings, expressed everywhere in the child's play
2. Ambivalent feelings, generally anxious or hostile
3. Direct negative feelings, expressed toward parents, siblings, and others, or in specific forms of regression
4. Ambivalent feelings, positive and negative, toward parents, siblings, and others
5. Clear, distinct, separate, usually realistic positive and negative attitudes, with positive attitudes predominating in the child's play. (p. 84)

EXPECTED OUTCOME OR PROGNOSIS

The expected outcome or prognosis for Jason can be viewed in light of the general objectives listed earlier in this chapter as being appropriate for all children. The intake information notes that Jason is struggling with issues of control that naturally emerged in the play therapy relationship as Jason discovered how it feels to make decisions, to set his own direction, and to be responsible for himself. This inner feeling of being in control is much more important than whether or not the child is actually in control.

There can be little doubt that the perception of significant adults who react to Jason as though he "has always been somewhat of a problem" is a powerful label and has contributed to Jason's incongruent self-concept. The general objectives of becoming more self-accepting and developing a more positive self-concept are certainly appropriate for Jason and were facilitated by the play therapist's unconditional acceptance of Jason and belief in his capacity to be resourceful in taking care of his own needs in the playroom.

Jason has also been described as being bossy and directive in his play with his sister. This behavior may be a function of Jason's perception of himself as inadequate. As Jason gained self-confidence in the playroom, he was able to direct his own behavior and thus had less need to direct others.

Jason's mother reported him to be difficult to manage and unresponsive to directions. Since these behaviors are very likely a result of Jason's feelings of confusion and perception of himself as being unable to cope, they would be expected to change as Jason becomes more sensitive to the process of coping as he is empowered in the play therapy relationship. This process can also be expected to be facilitated as he becomes more self-accepting and develops greater self-control, the result of responsibility for self and decision making being returned to him.

Jason described himself as being less happy than he was prior to his parents' divorce. As he becomes more accepting of himself, develops an internal source of evaluation, and discovers his own creative coping resources, he will be more accepting of others and will no longer blame himself for his parents' poor relationship.

Considering these kinds of intrapsychic changes in Jason's life, prognosis can be viewed as continued positive growth. Jason now has a more positive view of himself and, consistent with the child-centered theory of personality that behavior is congruent with the child's concept of self, he can be expected to respond positively to his surroundings. His more integrated positive self-concept will enable him to be more understanding of others and thus to have better interpersonal relationships.

CONCLUSION

In the child-centered approach to play therapy, the same principles of psychotherapy apply to all children, regardless of their presenting problem, degree of normality, or extent of personal adjustment. All children experience a need to feel understood and accepted. All children experience issues of self-concept maintenance and enhancement, and each child will deal with these issues in his or her own unique way. The child-centered play therapist does not assume he or she knows about and should, therefore, direct the therapeutic process. The content and direction of the child's play is determined by the child. In the case of Jason, who has been struggling with being accepted as he is, the unique qualities of the therapeutic relationship in the playroom enabled him to discover his own uniqueness within the context of the therapist's communication of the four basic messages: I am here, I hear you, I understand, and I care. His feelings of anger were tempered with acceptance, frustration was replaced by self-reliance, and Jason explored more deeply the self he is capable of becoming. That is the essence of being empowered.

BIBLIOGRAPHY

Axline, V. (1947). *Play therapy: The inner dynamics of childhood.* Boston: Houghton Mifflin Company.

Axline, V. (1955). Play therapy procedures and results. *American Journal of Orthopsychiatry, 25,* 618–626.

Axline, V. (1964). Nondirective therapy. In M. Haworth (Ed.), *Child psychotherapy: Practice and theory* (pp. 34–39). New York: Basic Books.

Barlow, K., Strother, J., & Landreth, G. (1985). Child-centered play therapy: Nancy from baldness to curls. *School Counselor, 32*(5), 347–356.

Bills, R. (1950). Nondirective play therapy with retarded readers. *Journal of Consulting Psychology, 14,* 140–149.

Bixler, R. (1949). Limits are therapy. *Journal of Consulting Psychology, 13,* 1–11.

Bratton, S. (1994). *Filial therapy with single parents.* Unpublished doctoral dissertation, University of North Texas, Denton, TX.

Cain, D. (1991). Person-centered therapy. In G. Corey (Ed.), *Case approach to counseling and psychotherapy* (3rd ed., pp. 119–135). Pacific Grove, CA: Brooks/Cole Publishing Co.

Crow, J. (1989). *Play therapy with low achievers in reading.* Unpublished doctoral dissertation, University of North Texas, Denton, TX.

Dorfman, E. (1951). Play therapy. In C. Rogers (Ed.), *Client-centered therapy* (pp. 235–277). Boston: Houghton Mifflin Company.

Ginott, H. (1961). *Group psychotherapy with children: The theory and practice of play therapy.* New York: McGraw-Hill.

Harris, Z. (1995). *Filial therapy with incarcerated mothers.* Unpublished doctoral dissertation, University of North Texas, Denton, TX.

Kot, S. (1995). *Intensive play therapy with child witnesses of domestic violence.* Unpublished doctoral dissertation, University of North Texas, Denton, TX.

Landreth, G. (1991). *Play therapy: The art of the relationship.* Muncie, IN: Accelerated Development, Inc.

Landreth, G., Homeyer, L., Glover, G., & Sweeney, D. (1996). *Play therapy I: Interventions with children's problems.* Northvale, NJ: Jason Aronson Inc.

Lobaugh, A. (1991). *Filial therapy with incarcerated parents.* Unpublished doctoral dissertation, University of North Texas, Denton, TX.

Moustakas, C. (1955). Emotional adjustment and the play therapy process. *Journal of Genetic Psychology, 86,* 79–99.

Moustakas, C. (1959). *Psychotherapy with children: The living relationship*. New York: Harper & Row.

Patterson, C. (1980). *Theories of counseling and psychotherapy* (3rd ed.). New York: Harper & Row.

Phillips, R., & Landreth, G. (1995). Play therapists on play therapy I.: A report of methods, demographics and professional practices. *International Journal of Play Therapy (4)*1, 1–26.

Raskin, N., & Rogers, C. (1989). Person-centered therapy. In R. Corsini & D. Wedding (Eds.), *Current psychotherapies* (4th ed., pp. 155–194). Itasca, IL: F.E. Peacock Publishers, Inc.

Rogers, C. (1951). *Client-centered therapy*. Boston: Houghton Mifflin Company.

CHAPTER 2

Psychoanalytic Play Therapy

ANNA C. LEE

INTRODUCTION

Since its modest inception in the 1920s, psychoanalytic play therapy has played an important role in the development of child analysis. This technique for the treatment of children and adolescents evolved as an extension of adult psychoanalysis and was established by Anna Freud and her followers as a result of their work at the Hampstead Child Therapy Clinic in London. As first conceptualized by Freud, psychoanalytic theory views personality development as a dynamic, multiply-determined process based on the theory of infantile sexuality, with its sequence of libidinal phases from whence derive instinctual drives and their energies. All behavior is thus motivated by the expression of these drives and their object cathexes. Throughout the life span, psychic energy is cathected toward important object relationships, shaping and molding the individual character as well as expressing the libidinal and aggressive drives, adaptive ego functions, and superego demands. In other words, the personality develops out of the need to fulfill the pleasure principle, all the while attempting to negotiate reality demands without incurring superego strictures. At no time is this process more critically developed and honed than during the formative years between birth and latency. While the personality continues to change and adapt, the traumatic neuroses that can occur during the first six years, culminating with the resolution of the Oedipal complex, set the stage for the regressions, fixations, and exaggerated defensive maneuvers that are the work of psychoanalytic treatment. Over the years, psychoanalytic understanding has evolved, informed by perspectives from cognitive psychology, ethology, and anthropology. Moreover, current psychoanalytic thinking has diversified into such directions as ego psychology, object relations, and self psychology (Hartmann, 1950; Klein, 1932; Kohut, 1971; Winnicott, 1965). As a technique, psychoanalysis continues to aim toward restructuring the personality as a whole, doing so by way of reconstruction of repressed mental contents.

Over the years, with the need to obtain greater understanding of the effects of childhood trauma arising from knowledge gleaned from adult psychoanalyses, the direct observation of child development *in statu nascendi* (in the process of developing) has allowed for validation of theoretical developmental concepts. These observations and subsequent research have thus laid the foundation for child psychoanalysis. While several theories about child analysis have evolved, that of Anna Freud (1965) is generally considered the most solid and integrated, positing the tenets and methodology by which to access and treat child psychopathology. The methods of child analysis depend on the developmental status of each patient, whether child or adolescent. As one tool of child analysis, play therapy has emerged as a fundamental technique that has allowed child analysts to recognize and understand the internal pressures of their young patients so as to ameliorate developmental arrests and fixations.

This chapter focuses on the indications for and application of psychoanalytic play therapy to the case of Jason L. It is this author's premise that the psychoanalytic framework provides the most thorough and rigorous theory of personality development. As such, it affords well-developed techniques for working with the psychopathology of childhood toward the ultimate goal of removing the impediments to normal development.

This chapter will begin with an introduction to child psychoanalysis as a theory and technique, with specific emphasis on the role of play therapy. While other theories and methods of child analysis and therapy exist (Axline, 1969; Klein, 1932; Moustakas, 1959), that of Anna Freud is definitively associated with psychoanalytic play therapy. For that reason, this chapter will limit itself to her school and those of the Freudian perspective. Specific application to the case of Jason L.* with the pathogenic factors of the manifest symptoms will next be considered, followed by the indications for and techniques of psychoanalytic play therapy as applicable to a latency-age child such as Jason L. The effects of parental psychopathology, family dynamics, separation and divorce, and their probable effects on Jason's psychic development will be explored. Finally, the chapter will conclude with a discussion of the prognosis for Jason L. and for his family. It is the contention of the author that particular appreciation and consideration of familial factors that contribute heavily to Jason's psychological disturbances merit special clinical examination. Finally, implications for future work with children and families with similar disturbance— that is, children who are victims of separation and divorce or those with depressed parents—are addressed with an eye toward prevention of further psychopathology and encroachments on the normal developmental progress.

Personality Theory

Sigmund Freud first developed psychoanalytic theory from the analyses of patients suffering from symptoms caused by repression of forbidden mental content. These include repressed childhood wishes—fantasies and memories experienced in relation to important persons in their past that were inadmissible to conscious awareness, thereby setting up signal anxiety whenever these threatened to come to conscious recognition. These were forbidden because of their sexual and aggressive

---

*See "Orientation to the Text: The Case of Jason L.," p. 1.

content, the recognition of which would do violence to the patient's need for defensive amnesia. From Freud's observations came the basis of psychoanalytic theory, one that posits that the personality develops out of the strivings of biologically based instinctual urges to seek gratification. In the process of seeking drive gratification, conflict inevitably arises between the drives and the reality principle served by the ego, causing tension through the press of signal anxiety and depressive affect experienced in the "familiar calamities of childhood: object loss, loss of love, castration, and superego demands and prohibitions" (Brenner, 1982). Freud's concept of the infantile neurosis was revolutionary for its day, as it held that early childhood set the scene for libidinal strivings that the child directed toward primary objects, specifically his or her parental figures.

Freud viewed human development as an ontogeny in which all individuals progressed in predictable, albeit dynamic, phases that he termed the psychosexual stages of libidinal development—namely the oral, anal, phallic, and genital stages. He proposed five models of the functions of the mental apparatus: the structural (the id, ego, and superego), the economic (urge of instinctual energy to seek discharge and return to homeostasis), the dynamic (moving from unconscious to preconscious to conscious levels of awareness), the genetic (tracing back the origin of symptoms to the earliest years), and the hydraulic (psychic energy, considered a closed system whereby it is either directed at an object or retracted, according to the needs of the system). While the personality is affected and modified by experiences lived throughout the life cycle, classic psychoanalytic theory holds that the major components of the personality are developed by the end of the oedipal phase. The stage of latency is thus a stage of quiescence of the instinctual urges following the generally tumultuous oedipal phase. It is a period for consolidating the gains achieved, during which time the child normally directs his or her energies toward adaptive functioning in the world, that is, toward school, peers, and social community. At the end of latency, a resurgence of libido occurs to signal the onset of the genital stage of adult sexuality, coinciding with biological maturation of sexuality in adolescence.

As a clinical method, psychoanalysis strives to help its patients understand the nature and origins of their unconscious conflicts, whether they be warded-off drive derivatives, anxiety or depressive affect, defense maneuvers, or superego determinants. Through the use of free association and the analyst's function of interpreting resistance and transference, analysis proceeds from defense and character analysis to that of repressed wishes, memories, and fantasies. Treatment aims at increasing the patient's self-awareness and capacity for problem solving, all of which eventually lead to a higher level of psychic organization (Ritvo, 1978).

Though it grew out of the reconstructions of adult psychoanalysis, child analysis differs significantly in many ways, as it is dictated by the very nature of childhood, specifically the immature state of such psychic structures as the ego and superego. The child differs from the adult, for example in four major ways: in his or her basic egocentrism, the immaturity of the infantile sexual apparatus, the relative weakness of secondary process thinking, and immature evaluation of time at various stages of development (A. Freud, 1965). Like biological pressures, psychic development also proceeds progressively toward maturation—greater integration and consolidation with the gains acquired in an earlier stage serving as the basis for learning and mastery at the next level. As Anna Freud notes: "the urge to complete development is immeasurably stronger in the immature than it can ever be in later life . . . The child's unfinished personality is in a fluid state. Symptoms which serve as conflict solutions on one level of development prove useless on the next and are discarded. Libido and aggression are in constant motion and more ready than in adults to flow into the new channels which are opened up by analytic therapy" (A. Freud, 1965, p. 28). She has advocated identifying the normal versus the abnormal, as the child analyst sees progressive development as the most essential function of the immature. She has furthermore proposed the concept of developmental lines along which normality proceeds, taking into account the intertwining of drive and ego development. Examples of such developmental lines include (1) from dependency to emotional self-reliance and adult object relationships; (2) toward body independence; (3) from egocentricity to companionship; and (4) from the body to the toy and from play to work. Anna Freud (1982) summarized the normal developmental process as consisting of the interaction of three factors: *endowment, environment, and rate of structuralization and maturation within the personality.* "Provided that all three are within the expectable norm, the child will arrive in every crucial developmental phase with the right inner equipment and meet the right environmental response, i.e., have a chance or normal growth. If, however, any of the three deviates too far from the average, the developmental result will become distorted in one direction or another" (A. Freud, 1982, p. 90).

Psychoanalytic writers such as Winnicott (1965), Mahler (1968, 1979, 1980), and others have written more extensively on the theory of object relations, extending and deepening the theoretical understanding of the intrapsychic life to that of pre-oedipal stages experienced by the infant and young child. Each emphasizes different facets of the child's progress, first in symbiotic union with the mother and later toward differentiating the self from the other in the process of establishing his or her own identity. Mahler, for example, developed the theoretical concept of separation-individuation, a process by which the infant initially melds in identity with the mother in a symbiotic bond and, through a series of phases, emerges at roughly the end of the third year as a separate entity. She writes that this achievement of the "psychological birth of the infant" is a gradual, unfolding process in the intrapsychic world of the infant and that actually all human life concerns an emotional bond with the mother, although the intensity of that bond is finally lessened in adulthood. Failure to negotiate successfully these subphases has ramifications for developmental deviance and pathology. For example, the toddler in the practicing subphase (approximate ages 10 to 18 months) experiences a "love affair with the world" because he is the center of his world as he narcissistically invests his own functions, his body, and the important objects of his world. In contrast, the toddler of the next phase, the period of rapprochement (ages 15 to 22 months), no longer feels the world to be his oyster. No longer does he believe in parental omnipotence or availability as he observes the mother's activities in life beyond satisfying his needs exclusively. He must woo back her attention, seeks to come back to her often for refueling, and demands that she be interested in whatever he requires of her. Mahler writes that "likewise, at the other end of the erstwhile dual unity, the mother must recognize a separate individual, her child, in his own autonomous right. Verbal communication has now become more and more necessary; gestural coercion on the part of the child will no longer suffice to attain the child's goal of satisfaction. Similarly, the mother can no longer make the child subservient to her own predilections and wishes" (Mahler, 1980, p. 10).

During rapprochement, the junior toddler must recognize that love objects (parents) are separate individuals with their own interests, and must give up his delusion of his own grandeur, often through dramatic fights with his mother, less so with father. This is a crossroad called the "rapprochement crisis." If the mother remains emotionally available for the toddler during this period, if she shares his exploits and helps his attempts at imitation, at externalization and internalization, then the relationship between mother and child can progress to the point at which verbal communication takes over. It is at this time that "shadowing" of the mother by the toddler takes place. "In normal cases, a slight shadowing by the toddler after the hatching process gives way to some degree of object constancy in the third year. However, the less emotionally available the mother has become at the time of rapprochement, the more insistently and even desperately does the toddler attempt to woo her. In some cases, this process drains so much of the child's available developmental energy that, as a result, not enough may be left for the evolution of the many ascending functions of his ego" (Mahler, 1980, p. 11).

Model of Psychopathology

As the infantile neurosis forms the nucleus of the psychoanalytic view of psychopathology, child analysis is indicated when there exist

> *conflicts* raging between the different agencies of [the child's] internal structure, i.e., processes which consume the energy at the disposal of the person instead of leaving it available for the various tasks of life; unsuitable *defenses* against drive activity which cripple the efficiency of the ego and restrict its sphere of influence; *anxieties* which at their height create an inner atmosphere unfavorable for the smooth unfolding of important ego functions; *fixations* of large quantities of libido on early developmental stages which impoverish further psychosexual advance; regressive moves in the area of either drives or ego which undo development; severe *repression of aggression* which limits any kind of productivity activity. (A. Freud, 1968, p. 37)

Child analysis is indicated for those situations of neurotic compromise, wherein exists imbalance in the aggression–lack of aggression continuum, imbalance between id and ego pressures and between ego and reality pressures.

In recent decades, child analysis has sought to expand and widen its scope, as more and more patients and their families have sought it out for treating children who did not present with clear-cut symptoms of neurotic disorders. Thus, during the past two decades, child analysis has turned its attention to children with ego disturbances, developmental deficiencies or deviations, or borderline conditions (Abrams, 1991; Kennedy & Moran, 1991; Weil, 1973). Weil suggests, for example, that examination of the intersystemic and intrasystemic imbalances of psychic structures may prove useful in deciding when and how child analysis is indicated. These include, for example, imbalances between the ego and drives, imbalance within the ego, imbalance between libido and aggression with aggression prevailing, and imbalance between nonhostile and hostile aggression (Weil, 1973, p. 288). She suggests that for children in whom ego imbalances and ego deficits prevail, child analysis may often not be as effective as other measures at that time. For instance, preparatory therapeutic educational help from a good new object—for instance, an empathic teacher—might provide the child a period of educative support prior to commencing analysis. Kennedy and Moran (1991) advocate a period of "developmental help" prior to participating in the rigors of the analysis as a way of offering support to the child. In their view, developmental help consists of ego-supportive elements that assist the child in making adaptations to his developmental deficits or ego immaturity:

Where the disturbance is due not only to internal conflict but also to developmental psychopathology deriving from a mixture of early neglect and damage, lost opportunities for development, unavailable or inconsistent objects, and other sorts of adverse environmental influences, the analyst will have to recognize that a purely interpretative approach may not have achieved the desired aim. It is difficult to *restore* something to the child that was missed in his early development. At best, the therapist can help him to make adaptations to such deficits and the consequent distortion of development. This work is based on the psychoanalytic knowledge of developmental needs and involves *an admixture of interpretation and ego-supportive elements within the context of a one-to-one relationship.* (Kennedy & Moran, 1991, pp. 184–185)

A major tool of child analysis is the use of play therapy, capitalizing on the child's natural proclivity to play to provide a setting for the task of "restoring the child on the path to normal development." As first described by Freud (1908), play is an integral part of human activity. The capacity to play exists throughout life, as it is an instinctual derivative that gives pleasure and relief from internal pressures. Freud linked play to the creative function, for in play, the child is the creator of his or her world, enacting indirectly the pleasures and conflicts of his or her unconscious life. He writes:

The child's best-loved and most intense occupation is with his play or games. Might we not say that every child at play behaves like a creative writer, in that he creates a world of his own, or rather, re-arranges the things of his world in a new way which pleases him? It would be wrong to think that he does not take that world seriously; on the contrary, he takes his play very seriously and he expends large amounts of emotion on it. The opposite of play is not what is serious but what is real. In spite of all the emotion with which he cathects his world of play, the child distinguishes it quite well from reality; and he likes to link his imagined objects and situations to the tangible and visible things of the real world. This linkage is all that differentiates the child's "play" from "phantasizing." (Freud, 1908, 143–144)

Play has been recognized by many other authors as an important function of childhood. Writing about requisite cognitive capacities for play, Piaget (1951) placed the onset of the child's capacity to create an imaginary situation at the age of symbolic play—around two years of age. He also viewed it as the precursor of adult dreams. In addition to its intrinsically pleasurable and creative aspects, play also contributes to the gradual assimilation of anxiety caused by traumatic overwhelming of the ego by an experience too large to be assimilated in its entirety (Waelder, 1932). Ostow (1987) maintained, first of all, that it also "provides a mechanism for disengaging from frustration and disappointment in the real world by providing illusory gratification, thereby reducing tension and stress. Second, it provides relief from intrapsychic conflict by offering pleasurable alternatives. Third, and perhaps most importantly, play allows for "not the unrestrained pursuit of pleasure . . . but rather for the exposure to realistic or unrealistic challenges, the overcoming of which relaxes tension and replaces it with pleasure . . . Play is a simulated, attenuated, and controllable reality. When the pain becomes too great, or the threat too formidable, the play can be terminated" (Ostow, p. 200). Winnicott (1971) saw play as the creation of an intermediate area of experience between subjectivity and objectivity. This originates in the transitional object relationship that stands halfway between the infant's subjective relationship with the mother and later object relationships. Play can promote the engagement and mastery of phase-specific developmental tasks and is a mode of coping with conflicts, developmental demands, deprivations, loss, and yearnings throughout the life cycle (Solnit, 1987, p. 214). Peller (1954) and Plaut (1979) have stressed that play is vital for adult development as well. In fact, Plaut underscores it as the third vital human activity that should be included in the definition of mental health, extending Freud's more puritanical dictum of love and work.

As for the content of play, Freud maintained that in play, the child expresses a most cherished wish, to be big and grown up, and in games the child imitates what he or she knows of the lives of surrounding adults. While play for the child is commonplace, it is not renounced in adulthood. It merely undergoes a transformation to other objects.

But whoever understands the human mind knows that hardly anything is harder for a man than to give up a pleasure which he has once experienced. Actually, we can never give anything up; we can only exchange it for another. What appears to be a renunciation is really the formation of a substitute or surrogate. In the same way, the growing child, when he stops playing, gives up nothing but the link with real objects; instead of *playing,* he now *phantasies.* He builds castles in the air and creates what are called *daydreams.* I believe that most people construct phantasies at times in their lives. This is a fact which has long been overlooked and whose importance has therefore not been sufficiently appreciated." (Freud, 1908, p. 145)

Play as a diagnostic and therapeutic tool has proved most valuable in child analysis. Neubauer (1987) has delineated several primary and interlocking characteristics of play and how these impact upon child analysis. First, it involves a mental act that contains a conscious or unconscious fantasy and wish. Second, it has a physical component that carries these into observable enactment. And third, play must have the quality of exploration or "trying on," that is, an awareness that what is enacted is *not real* (p. 3). If the child's play meets these criteria, play therapy may be the mode of choice by which the analyst attempts to engage the child in the therapeutic process, especially for children younger than latency age. Loss of any one of these criteria would preclude calling it play, as for instance when the play becomes obsessive and routinized rather than free and spontaneously created. Arlow (1987) suggests, for example, that children who are inhibited and compulsive—as in the stereotypic, incessant rocking and twirling of autistic children—are not playing since their play lacks symbolic capacity. Similarly, when the play loses the quality of the "pretend" or when it goes out of control, as when it becomes real in terms of consequences, then it is no longer play. The play of children who are severely deprived, or those with developmental deviations or deficits, is often poorly elaborated and tends to represent a narrow or small repertoire in terms of links to fantasies. They often fail to achieve elaboration and structure in play, which are characteristic of progressive development (Solnit, 1987, p. 212). Lewis (1993) reminds us that the role of play in therapy has been debated at length, the issue resting on whether play is inherently therapeutic or requires interpretation in order to have therapeutic impact. He concludes that it is perhaps more important to consider the child's degree of psychological health or pathology in discerning the mutative action of play: "Healthier children's play may serve an adaptive function because it provides an opportunity to process, master and work through the stresses of childhood and the pressures of development. But more troubled children's difficulties may overwhelm their ability to resolve them through their own adaptive mechanisms—including play" (Lewis, 1993, p. 13). For the latter group, "their play should be expected to have pathological elements, and its correction is likely to require interpretation of defenses, underlying conflicts, transference, and core anxieties, as well as the working through of these issues through play and talk" (Lewis, 1993, pp. 13–14).

In therapy, the analyst joins the child, entering into the child's fantasy life, and attempts to encourage the analysand's pleasurable elaboration of the fantasy-dramatization-free play by going along with the child's make-believe. The analyst's role is to establish and maintain the therapeutic alliance partly by interpreting within the medium of the play, thereby attempting to foster the sense of empathy and understanding for the young patient. The analyst must take special care not to interpret directly from the material to the reality situation, since doing so may disrupt the play before it is fully elaborated, thus limiting what can be understood from the play as well as putting into jeopardy the development-promoting aspects of the play

(Solnit, 1987, p. 210). When set in motion, the play therapy may meet with a number of different resistances, especially for the very young child for whom verbalizations might still be difficult to obtain. This is also dependent on the child's ego development, whether or not cognition, language, and reasoning are developed sufficiently to allow the analyst understanding of the underpinnings of the play itself.

Goal/Cure of Treatment

The ultimate goal of child analysis is to explore, understand, and resolve the etiology of the arrests, fixations, regressions, defensive operations, and so forth that bind up important sources of psychic energy, in order to aid the resumption of normal development. Unlike adult analytic patients, however, the child is essentially a work in progress, for whom powerful maturational trends will proceed despite whatever neurotic compromises have developed. Of course, the strength of the compromises will definitely affect the extent to which these normal processes will hold sway. At certain times, they may be completely overwhelmed and overshadowed by the ongoing battle between id and ego strivings. Developmental lines such as the line toward work, toward body integration, and toward emotional self-reliance must be evident to qualify as cure in the classical sense. Unlike adult analysis, the goal of child analysis is not a regressive reencounter with the past of stored, repressed memories, although at times regression in the service of the ego can be adaptive and development promoting. Rather, as the child is still creating these experiences for remembering, the goal of treatment here is to aid development so that growth and maturation can take place at a normal pace, more or less in keeping with the child's chronological and mental age.

Numerous pitfalls, of course, exist within the treatment. Even when play therapy is used, the analyst can hardly expect the child patient to use it in the same way that adults might utilize the analytic task of free association. This is so simply because of the cognitive limitations specific to the child's particular phase in development. Ritvo (1978) reminds us,

> What contributes so much to the importance of the transference in the analytic process is not only what makes possible terms of understanding, interpretation, and reconstruction: it also restores the feelings of immediacy, reality, and conviction to psychological phenomena arising out of the past. This is part of the process of ego becoming where id was. . . . For this part of the process to occur and progress requires the existence and functioning of an ego which can observe the self and set in motion the recognition of distinctions between past and present, between objective danger and neurotic anxiety, which arises out of the interplay of wish, fantasy, and inadequate understanding due to the immature thinking of the child . . . Though we can argue that the analytic process and the therapeutic action of analysis depend in children, as in adults, on the analysis of the transference, defense and resistance, the process in children not only must be adapted to the development of the child, but is in many instances limited by his developmental status as well. (Ritvo, 1978, p. 300)

Second, interpretation of transference continues to be the essential tool by which the analysis derives its mutative effect. "The basic transference, unless it is interfered with by a powerful dynamic force such as the ambivalence of the parents toward the analysis, is a major determinant in the child's portraying his discomfort, anxiety, and symptoms in the fantasy play in the analysis. . . . Even if the analyst cannot count on the child's active conscious participation in the analytic process, the basic transference provides a directional force for the child to present his conflicts and symptoms via play, fantasy, verbal communications, and behavioral interaction with the analyst" (Ritvo, 301). The analyst must always keep in mind, however, that as they still have their primary objects with them, there is less motivation for child analysands to experience transference manifestations or partial transferential reactions. "Analysts have repeatedly emphasized that the child has less of a tendency or need to make transferences to the analyst because he still has his primary love objects in his daily life for instinctual drive gratification or for symptom formation, which lessens the involvement of the analyst in the transference or the transference neurosis" (Ritvo, p. 297). Abreaction of affects in child analysis is useful only to the extent that it permits opportunities for interpretative work by the analyst (Esman, 1983).

Failure to experience the analyst as an object of transference does not necessarily detract from the importance that a validating, new, *real* object can play in helping the child understand internal conflicts and/or overcome developmental deviations. For example, Cohen and Solnit (1993) describe poignantly the role of the child analyst as a real object in their case material of analyses of developmentally impaired youngsters, stating

it is not a matter of either/or but how the predominance of the former (analyst as a new or real object) has a shaping influence on technique as a pathway to therapeutic leverage and action, . . . The child identifies with the analyst in tolerating change and in forgoing the familiar stickiness of the deviant developmental views and expectations associated with learning disabilities and distorted self-esteem representations. In turn, this analytic work, including the interpretation and working through of neurotic conflicts and defenses, enabled these children to use their differentiations in object relationships to promote capacities for object constancy, friendship, and identifications that can be elaborated and liberating. (Cohen and Solnit, 1993, p. 62)

Third, there are any number of resistances that the child analysand can present, chief among them being brought to treatment by parents or other authority figures rather than coming of his or her own volition:

With children, the analysis is rarely undertaken upon the request of the child, especially in the case of children under 9 or 10. The active and informed consent of the child analysand is likewise rarely obtainable at the outset of the analysis and at best is only gradually attained in the course of the analytic work. The attainment depends on the child's developmental progress in abstract thinking, language, cognition, the capacities for self-observation and self-evaluation, and the ability to project present conditions into the future. The child's active participation in the process is perforce more sporadic and less reliable than that of the adult." (Ritvo, 1978, p. 297)

Fourth, it is vital to stress that in addition to offering interpretations of conflict–defense in the idiom of the play, the analyst must choose carefully the time and setting when interpretations are offered directly because the child is so intolerant of them. "If confronted with too much interpretation in reality when defensively still resistant, the child can be prone to become anxious, uncomfortable, and uncomprehending in response to a direct interpretation, and to break off the communication by fantasy play" (p. 301).

Last, one note of caution should be struck in the case of latency-age children (as is Jason) with regard to their capacity to gain insight in treatment. The force of repression creates amnesia, as it were, for the dangers and anxieties of id and ego conflicts of the pre-oedipal and oedipal years. Such defensive forgetting is most apparent in latency children despite the relative quiescence of this period:

> There is no spontaneous move toward dismantling the defenses and of taking a closer look at themselves. Even in analytic treatment, (latency children) display the most extraordinary resistance against this possibility. They get furious with the analyst's interpretations which they consider unfair. According to their own belief, they have done the right thing to deflect or close their eyes to their drive derivatives and even under the reassuring guidance of the analyst, they are reluctant to believe that a clearer view of internal happenings would increase, not lessen the chances of moral control. (A. Freud, 1982, p. 146)

CASE FORMULATION

The case of Jason L. illustrates in bold relief many of the fixations, distortions, and arrests that Anna Freud stressed can arise when the three factors of normal development go awry: endowment, environment, and rate of structuralization and maturation within the personality. While the course of even normal development does not always proceed smoothly, the interaction of endowment, environment, and rate of structuralization and maturation within the individual is an absolute prerequisite for normal development. Jason will be viewed through the lens of these three factors, first considering together his endowment and rate of structuralization and maturity. A separate examination will then occur with regard to the psychopathology inherent in the family constellation, especially the symptoms manifested by his mother. Last, the ecosystem pressures with which this family, really two single-parent families now, struggles on a daily basis will be described.

From the prenatal period on, Jason manifested physical disturbances that raise the possibility of later constitutional vulnerability and temperament disturbances (Chess, Thomas & Birch, 1965). Specifically, the physical issues are his mother's prenatal complications requiring bedrest from the 26th week on, his low birth weight despite full gestation and mother's denial of substance abuse, and his constant irritability. These circumstances are likely to raise the question of constitutional variables operating to disturb the psychic equilibrium of the infant in the earliest months, creating a psychic sense of the body being out of control. As his mother already felt guilty about the difficult pregnancy, she worried about his survival, holding him constantly. An infant held so much would also likely suffer some reaction once this period has passed, an inevitable fact of life once the mother resumes her life and the demands of the infant are crowded out by competing factors, such as the birth of siblings, mother's return to other responsibilities, and the like. Jason walked and acquired toilet training within normal limits, suggesting adequate motoric and neurologic development. Psychologically, however, he was a difficult toddler, reportedly, who complied poorly with his mother's demands. This can be interpreted as Jason experiencing phase-appropriate autonomy strivings that abraded against the needs of his mother. Her inconsistent limit setting and spanking hardly set the stage for a consistent and just view of authority on his part, creating also a feeling of violation of body boundaries and personal space through the physical punishment that Jason experienced. This is later evident in the mother's hitting and bruising him, much of which was reported in an objectively ego-syntonic way without notable evidence of shame or guilt on her part.

Though he was endowed with sufficient cognitive resources, Jason seems remarkably impulsive, immature, and lacking in good judgment. In fact, his impulse control and frustration tolerance seem to decompensate quickly in the face of emotional distress, resulting in the maladaptive, acting out behaviors that comprise his conduct disorder. Several of these provocative episodes also eventuated in physical abuse by his mother. More significantly, however, he shows significant attachment and separation–individuation disturbance vis-à-vis his mother, a likely result of maternal withdrawal and depression during the latter part of the second year of his life. These traumas suffered by Jason occurred during the period of Mahler's rapprochement subphase. We are reminded of the requisite role of mother during this crucial period of "hatching," that the toddler requires her emotional availability as a secure base to which to return, even as he is grappling with the end of illusory parental omnipotence and omniscience. Unfortunately, in this case, Jason's mother can be considered to be largely unavailable for him as she herself was experiencing yet another difficult pregnancy, the period of depression following the death of her second child, and, soon thereafter, the pregnancy of his sister Carla. Matters could not have gone worse for him inasmuch as his mother experienced a much easier time raising his sister, causing her to treat his sister with more outright affection. To add insult to injury, he was ousted still further from his favored position as the first and only child when sent to nursery school at age four, perhaps causing him to fantasize about how mother and sister were managing without him. This might have been experienced as further rejection of him, as evidenced by his protest on leaving and his distance when reunited with his mother. Indeed, Jason's resistance toward school continues to this day. It is reported, for instance, that his worst behavior is usually the hour after school; he arrives furious and raging, requiring time to cool down before he can communicate with his mother. It can be speculated that school is also difficult because he must share the teacher's attention with peers. His more tractable and compliant behavior with his mother during weekends further raise the question of his anger and protest about separating from her during the week. When there is more time for both parent and children to relax from the pressures of school and work, the entire family system appears more tranquil.

Jason's unresolved dependency, autonomy, and oedipal needs in relation to his mother all coexist simultaneously and are infused with his anger and hostility, rendering him rebellious and defiant where his mother is concerned. While he longs for a more loving relationship with her, as noted in the observations made during MIM tasks, his disappointment over her perceived betrayals may defensively create the need to maintain distance from her, even at the expense of ungratified dependency needs. His oedipal longings are full of envy, and he appears to have turned away from her toward his father for emotional supplies.

Symptomatically, Jason's conduct disturbance can be somewhat described as an enactment of frustration and rage felt toward his mother. While his warmer and more nurturant relationship with his father compensates to some extent for the contentiousness of his relationship with his mother, it hardly approximates his disappointment over this primary relationship. Moreover, the basic premise of this writer is that the early, pre-oedipal disturbances of attachment and bonding that existed early on between Jason and his mother set the stage for their conflictual relationship, which has been exacerbated by maternal depression (postpartum and long-term), his mother's seeming preference for his younger sister, and the loss of his father's constant presence following parental separation and divorce. Jason has had to grapple with developing his own identity at a time when the primary caretaker of his life was in the grips of her own ongoing depression, rendering her psychologically unavailable to her toddler son. Structurally, his maturation could have developed more normally had these factors not intervened to cause his fixations in the phase of anal-sadism. Thus, his marked rebelliousness and hostility illustrate the enormous disappointment and rage he feels toward having emotional supplies withheld from him. This is actualized later in development by his destructive, antisocial behavior.

Perhaps a word about Jason's manifest affect is appropriate here. Pine (1987) notes that in the period of rapprochement, sadness is centered around the (child's) awareness of his separateness from the specific provider of gratification and relief (i.e., his mother) as a result of the cognitive specification resulting from the self–other differentiation. Longing occurs when satisfaction/relief can only come through the constant/specific love object who is now absent at the time of need. What is longed for in nostalgia is the nonspecific past . . . while mourning requires a cognitive acquisition of object constancy (the permanence of attachment) but also the cognitive awareness of the permanence of loss (a concept of death) (Pine, 1980, pp. 226–227). Apropos to Jason, we may say that while he principally evidences a good deal of anger toward his mother and society at large (burning the trash can, for example) he is also sad and nostalgic for the past, perhaps for the period before his family fell apart, as suggested in his wish to have his parents reunite. He also seems in mourning for the loss of his father's presence in their lives, especially since this parent is spared the rage he associates with his mother. Defensively, he reveals a tendency toward splitting vis-à-vis different objects: With females (i.e., his mother and teachers) he experiences persistent rage and defiance. With males, however, he evidences a greater capacity for more integrated object relations. In the relationship with his father, for example, he allows his dependency needs to emerge, and his father appears a willing partner to provide the nurturance he seeks. An example of this is the differential reaction to his female teachers versus his male student aide. Males are felt to be more benign, while females irritate him because they withhold nurturance from him. Toward the latter he evidences boldly his lability, variable impulse control, immature judgment, and lack of even age- and phase-specific insight. Thus, he evidences part-object relationships, split off by the presence of undigestible anger. Females who have disappointed him in the past are tainted malevolent, while males are perceived as more empathic and approachable.

Jason continues to mourn the loss of each parent in different ways, with the actual abandonment by his father and psychic abandonment by his mother. Though his tie with his father seems relatively unambivalently loving, it rests on a foundation of hostile dependency toward his mother, thereby setting the stage for poor object ties with all subsequent object relationships. One must also remember that Emilio was relatively late in assuming greater responsibility for his children. Until the separation, Mary assumed most of the child care responsibility, although Emilio was physically present. Further complicating the picture are each parent's distinct ways of parenting each child in the family, due as much to their ethnic and socio economic differences as to their individual personality characteristics. For example, Mary came from a Caucasian, middle-class background while her husband came from a Mexican one. While Mary's parents were divorced and she herself was alienated from her mother and sisters, Emilio hailed from a closely knit, first-generation Mexican family that seemed fairly functional despite the alcoholism of his father and brother. Mary and Emilio differ enormously in their own achievement strivings. Employed as a secretary in a law firm, Mary harbors greater ambitions to further her education even as she is aware of the impediments toward this goal, reflecting her middle-class origins. On the other hand, Emilio is content with his position as a supervisor in a blue-collar job.

The diagnostic protocol is revealing of several important basic components of Jason's ego structure, defenses, and resources. An intelligent child, he nevertheless seems more immature than his measured intelligence would suggest. He relates, also, in pseudo-stupid or remarkably naïve, immature ways that appear motivated by a regressive need to be a younger child, perhaps reflecting his envy of his younger sister, and as a way of satisfying age-appropriate but thwarted dependency needs. Such can be seen at one end in his clingy behavior toward his father and, at the other extreme, in his strident defense against showing vulnerability and neediness to his mother. He lacks a well-developed, observing ego and cannot comprehend the effect of his behavior on others. While this is certainly age-appropriate, given the egocentrism of this age, Jason appears to have little insight into his difficulties. Indeed, he avidly seeks to avoid all mention or discussion of his conduct disorder, as noted in his early silence during the initial interview and during confrontation after setting the trash can on fire. Nor does he assume much responsibility for his own behavior, even when confronted. His sobbing and crying when admitting his culpability are more suggestive of the shame and fear of punishment he felt rather than any well-organized remorse or sense of guilt for having destroyed property. Indeed, superego deficits are strongly suspected from this vignette, raising the specter of more antisocial acts in the future should his hostility take ascendance. While they can be seen as isolated acts of rage, they are fundamentally acts of defiance and attempts to humiliate in displacement, almost always at internalized authority figures who are experienced negatively. At this juncture of his psychic life—that is, in the beginning of the latency phase—Jason could be expected to be maturing out of the narcissistic egocentrism of this phase to a more advanced level of conscience development. His oedipal conflicts are negative, however, and show fixations with the unavailable, hostile maternal introject, thereby slowing the progress of this crucial phase. Defensively, Jason's chief ways of coping against overwhelming anxiety appear to be habitual avoidance and externalization. Occasionally, such avoidance can decompensate to outright denial and projection in the face of extreme threat. Such renders him, thereby, a child who resists fiercely admission of culpability of his pervasive acting out behavior. He also utilizes splitting and projective identification as major coping mechanisms against his anger. Thus, he is more capable of investing one object with love while hating the other, showing thereby a great difficulty in integrating the two polar opposite affects within a singular identity. Furthermore, his mood is such that he can alternate between contentment and anger in short order. Jason generally remains reality-bound, however. Despite the pervasiveness of his anger and his capacity to dissociate aspects of his thinking when rageful, at no time does he lapse into psychosis or delusional thought disorder, despite the abundance of anger he experiences. More possible, however, is his vulnerability toward psychopathy should his anger and sense of helpless rage go unaddressed.

While diffuse and labile in affect, Jason evidenced generally appropriate mood when observed with both parents in the MIM. Apparently, his mood alternates with the presence of the particular adult with whom he has well differentiated. Thus, his object relatedness appears intact even if taxed to the extreme by his resentment of his mother's distance and coldness. Such prolonged oedipal fixation for his mother rests on a template of frustrated pre-oedipal wishes to have an exclusive, dyadic relationship with her. With his sister about, the possibility for this is virtually nonexistent.

Hartmann's (1950) concept of an "average expectable environment" for each child appears poorly realized for Jason despite each parent's obvious intent on providing it for both children. In the case of Jason's mother, her psychopathology based on early deprivations is impressive. Her own depression appears to stem from an early history of familial disturbance and losses. For this reason, she reacted with anxiety to possibly losing Jason immediately after his birth. This anxiety, normal for first-time mothers, has dynamic roots in her anger toward her father and men in general. She may have distanced herself defensively from Jason in order to stave off feelings of loss were he truly ill. Later on, she experienced more losses—in the form of the death of her second infant and, eventually, the end of her marriage. Certainly, it is safe to characterize her childhood as deprived and burdened, permeated with a sense of loneliness and isolation. This is evident in her dysphoric description of her relationships with her mother and sisters. It also motivates her to avoid her mother, who is prone toward offering depressing reminders of their family's past, in addition to the mother's perceived lack of empathy for Mary's marital and family difficulties. Mary appears to have little contact with her sisters, perhaps seeking to avoid any envy she might feel over their supposed success in marrying upwardly mobile men. Was she disappointed that she married someone who was not equally accomplishing?

Throughout, Mary has minimized and denied the extent of her own depression and neediness, despite the occurrence of several fairly serious depressive episodes in her life. The question is raised, here, of the neglect she may have suffered from her own family as she endured these episodes. The cycles and vicissitudes of depression certainly suggest a long-standing need for intervention early in her life; the depression did not seem to be noticed and intervention was not offered. As an adult, Mary appears quite narcissistically concerned with her own conflicts and seems unreflective about the extent to which she was inflicting Jason psychic and physical harm. Her own impulse control seems poor in that she hit him several times, sufficient to cause bruises. While there is no reported history of Mary's being physically abused as a child, the question is raised as to the type of discipline she received during childhood. Her lack of urgency when reporting her abuse of Jason is worrisome in that she may feel justified in delivering such punishment in response to his misbehavior. In any case, her abuse seems ego-syntonic—a poor diagnostic indicator. Though overwhelmed with the pressures of single parenting, she seemed immature herself in her ability to control her rage when confronted with his defiance. To be sure, avoidance and denial appear a favored defense against anxiety in this family. As both parents seem to minimize the seriousness and implication of Jason's conduct disorder, they seem to view their own personal issues in the same way.

Devastated by her parents' divorce during latency, Mary apparently felt unresolved oedipal longings for her father, which were traumatically unresolved by his untimely death. Experiencing her mother as depressive (and perhaps even narcissistically absorbed in her own troubles), she may have longed for some comfort from this parent but this need remained unrequited. Mary's difficulty in relating to males repeats itself now with her own son: Jason's need to identify himself as a male is something that she can poorly tolerate, having been raised in an all-female household. She may also unconsciously view Jason as a reflection of his father, given his many similarities to him, and respond with hostility accordingly out of possible resentment she may harbor toward Emilio for his betrayals. Her own difficulties in maintaining an intimate heterosexual relationship are seen in her failed marriage, as she could not abandon her self-absorption to care for the needs of her husband and children during depressive episodes.

As for Emilo, he appears a man who did not have the emotional strength to confront her depression in order to help her or the family. Rather, he withdrew from his wife and sought comfort in another relationship. To his credit, however, he appears a warmer, less remote parent than Mary, able to engage his children's compliance in a more pleasurable and gentle way. He seems entirely more patient and interested in engaging their interest in the tasks of daily living, as in meal preparation, and he appears generous with praise and affection. His own report of relations with his family seems unilaterally favorable, despite the question of the effect of his father's alcoholism on his own development. His view of his mother as being nurturant but almost invisible hardly bodes well, however, for his understanding of the female gender. Perhaps this attitude and expectation of maternal abundance was reflected in his feeling of disappointment with his wife. Holding the expectation that she should nurture the family against all odds (without needs of her own), he was no doubt distressed to help with child care responsibilities whenever she experienced depressive episodes. Rather than pressing her to seek psychiatric care, however, he withdrew from her and his children. Only later, after divorce, did he assert himself in the paternal role more fully, and one speculates how much of Jason's early development he missed in so doing.

The results of the dyadic and family assessment illustrate sharply the different parental-child interactions. Mary, for example, let Jason struggle with his house drawing and intervened only after a while. Lacking much support, Jason produced little and sought to stop the activity as soon as he could. With his father, however, he felt a greater sense of parental interest and involvement. His father also employed less criticism and judgment in helping him. Thus, Jason's interest in the task was captivated, and he created a drawing that was longer and more elaborate. With this encouragement, his drawing indicated more clearly his above-average intellectual potential. There is more evidence of playfulness and humor on the part of Jason's father than his mother. The latter showed little empathic understanding for what he felt, indulged little in his need for face-saving measures, and was mindless of the shame he felt when confronted with possible failure. His father showed far greater sensitivity to this fact in his play with both children, cajoling them to do tasks even as they were protesting. Eventually he elicited far greater cooperation from them. They even viewed the task as fun and pleasurable, when before it had been irksome when supervised by their mother. Such an episode highlights clearly Moran's (1987) view of the role parents have in integrating play into their interactions with their children. "We believe that loving parents who are in tune with their children playfully react to the child's anxieties with highly specific, well-timed interventions. . . . Such parental responses aim to ease the child's dilemma by introducing a modicum of enjoyment and thereby increasing the child's options for mediating or solving conflict" (Moran, 1987, p. 17). Likewise, Plaut (1979) notes that parents' ability to enjoy playing with their children is a significant indicator of the quality of functioning of the family as a unit.

Divorce is an ever-increasing, disruptive phenomenon in our modern times, resulting in broken homes where single parents must fulfill several roles vis-à-vis their offspring. The case of Jason highlights the external pressures on both parents, especially his mother, who must give doubly to her two young children while maintaining a job outside the home as well. Her own frustrations about unfulfilled ambition, financial pressures, and related issues all impact on her capacity to parent in a consistent and positive way. Obviously, as the case unfolds, this has been impossible for her for a number of different reasons, the most profound of which is her own lack of nurturance and consequent self-esteem. Now she is faced with the sequelae of the broken marriage as a possible cause of her son's behavioral difficulties. The literature is rich with material regarding the effects of divorce on the development of children involved (Block & Gjerde, 1990; Blum, Boyle & Offord, 1989; Gavshon, 1990; Wallerstein & Kelly, 1980), a survey of which is beyond the scope of this chapter. For our purposes here, however, the reader is reminded that divorce poses serious challenges to the developing psyche, depending on the psychic strength or vulnerability of the child. Jason's expressed longing for his parents' reunion is common enough among children with divorced parents. Unfortunately they separated at a time when he was in the throes of negotiating a difficult oedipal situation, which left him little hope for comfort from the parent with whom he lives most of the time. Doubtless, he felt helpless to effect this, a blow to childish omnipotence so typical around age five, and had to come to terms with its reality in two short years. The fact that he struggles with it still echoes research data suggesting that children from single-parent families are at a small but statistically significant increased risk of psychiatric disorder, especially conduct disorder, in comparison to two-parent families (Blum, Boyle & Offord, 1990).

Finally, consideration of environmental pathogens for psychopathology causes one to reflect on the cautionary words of Anna Freud:

> What needs emphasis, though, is the fact that there is no one-to-one, invariable relationship between the fact of parents being absent, neglecting, indifferent, punitive, cruel, seductive, overprotective, delinquent, or psychotic and the resultant distortions in the personality picture of the child. Cruel treatment can produce either an aggressive, violent, or a timid, crushed, passive being; parental seduction can result either in complete inability to control sexual impulses ever after, or in severe inhibition and abhorrence of any form of sexuality. In short, the developmental outcome is determined not by the environmental influence per se, but by its interaction with the inborn and acquired resources of the child. (A. Freud, 1982, p. 93)

Diagnostically, Jason does not manifest autoplastic (inward directed) resolutions to internal conflicts sufficient to qualify for classic neurotic disturbances. He does not, for example, evidence capacity for the overflooding of ego versus superego pressures. If anything, he is more prone toward release of, and acting out of, the more primitive instinctual pressures, seeking alloplastic (outward directed) resolutions that are antisocial and even nascently psychopathic. He does not manifest impressive phase-appropriate indications of guilt and remorse sufficient to allow for assessment of normal conscience development. Only when faced with punishment does he even admit that he has acted on his destructive impulses. Thus, Jason does not fit well the criteria for child analysis and should be considered a child with a diagnosis more consistent with character pathology or borderline personality organization. His marginal defensive structure renders his thinking prone to defensive decompensation and impulsive acting up. His self-esteem appears wholly depressed, and his prevailing mood is that of disappointed rage. Diagnosis of children should be undertaken with some caution, given the developmental factors that are still operative. Perhaps Jason is most prudently considered a child with unresolved separation-individuation issues who cannot yet internalize and integrate the fury he feels vis-à-vis his maternal introject. Psychoanalytic play therapy, not child analysis, appears more suitable and is thereby recommended.

TREATMENT GOALS

Psychoanalytic play therapy aims at resolving the fixations, regressions, and, where possible, developmental deficiencies and deviations that derail the child's normal development. This theoretical model's position holds that, once these impediments are removed—at least to the extent of obtaining sufficient relief from crippling anxieties and neurotic compromises—or the individual has established sufficient trust in the goodness of his environment of objects and arenas of functioning, normal developmental trends can resume. Keeping in mind the foregoing case discussion of Jason and his family, the writer proposes the following objectives for treatment.

In the first place, short-term goals will include Jason's ceasing his most rageful forms of protest against his environment. That is, his conduct behavior will cease altogether, especially in the acting up demonstrated by his fire setting and frequent bouts of fury after returning home from school. In addition, therapy will address the areas of daily life wherein his poor self-esteem can be improved. He will be asked to consider, for example, ways in which he could cooperate more willingly with certain individuals (namely female authority figures) whom he must obey despite his constant resentment and resistance. Therapy will need to teach him ways both to check and modulate his anger in order to tolerate limits and to verbalize his negative thoughts and wishes rather than to act on them outright; therapy will need to assist him in taking responsibility for his role in creating or maintaining the interpersonal conflicts in which he is embroiled. Therapy will necessarily engage Jason's cooperation to aid in developing the therapeutic alliance. This is essential for later working through and resolving important dynamic issues.

Jason's progress in achieving this goal will be reflected in his enthusiasm for the therapy once it has begun, despite whatever initial resistance he may pose. If therapy begins to work, a dramatic decline will be evident in his antisocial behavior in approximately four to six weeks—about the length of time it takes for a child his age to gain a sense of trust in the helpfulness of this new relationship in his life, as he now has a willing and understanding adult who will devote time and energy toward sorting out his inner turmoil. On a more negative side, his resistance may be initially high and thereby pose some countertransferential difficulty for the therapist, given Jason's very real capacity to annoy and irritate. Children who externalize the responsibility for their actions onto everyone else often cause significant countertransferential annoyance or even despair for therapists unaccustomed to the hostility of borderline children. Once disappointed by absent or abusive objects, they are indeed hard-pressed to trust in themselves or others.

Second, long-term goals should first address the long-term issues of poor attachment, bonding, and separation–individuation vis-à-vis his mother, which Jason experiences profoundly. Therapy should thereby assist him in verbalizing his need and longing for his mother and his disappointment that she can parent his sister with more enthusiasm than she displays for him. In working through these feelings, he should hopefully recognize his anger as a result of disappointed longing rather than of her own inadequacies in parenting him more lovingly. As he comes to recognize his mother as a person rather than an omnipotent, idealized parent, he may come to terms with her efforts, however strained and ambivalent, rather than railing against her for withholding nurturance. He may thus come to see her in a more integrated fashion, thereby resolving the splitting of good-mother, bad-mother introjects.

Achieving this goal will be the heart of the therapy with Jason, as he will have to overcome his distrust of his mother and her abiding attachment to him. This goal is reached when Jason is able to integrate these disparate views of her into a single entity, a flawed parent who nevertheless loves him in her own way, even if this love falls short of many expectations.

Third, individual psychotherapy for Mary is absolutely crucial in order to assist with her obvious depression and poor control of her own rage. It remains to be seen whether she is a candidate for psychoanalysis; psychoanalytic psychotherapy seems more likely, given her defensive denial and poor ego resources. At the very least, she should be seen on a fairly constant basis, at least twice per week. Issues of concern in her therapy include the mourning of her multiple losses (father, second infant, and marriage), her poor control of anger, her resentment of parenting two children while working full-time, her frustrated ambition to improve her lot in life to approximate her middle-class origins, and her ambivalent relationship with her mother and sisters. One specific treatment goal for her would be to help her recognize the extent to which her own past disappointments, losses, and deficits have rendered her compromised and insufficiently prepared to provide a good enough environment for her son. Hopefully, therapy will help her gain insights into her own neediness and easier connection with females, as reflected in her entangled, tight relationship with Carla, to the detriment of that with Jason. Having grown up in a fatherless, all-female family, she was now unconsciously creating a similar one for her son. Psychotherapy for Mary will likely be long and intense, given the degree of her psychopathology and her primitive defenses utilized to keep anxieties at bay. As with Jason, the success of her therapy will depend in large part on her capacity to engage in it, her receptivity and willingness to explore exceptionally painful aspects of her past, and her sense of futility about changing the direction of her life.

In similar manner, psychotherapy for Emilio is also recommended to explore his own difficulties in raising Jason and Carla alone. It may identify his own frustrations and sense of guilt over the failure of his marriage, whether or not he could have been more supportive of Mary during her depressive episodes. His therapy should also explore the differences between them, which also contributed to the demise of the marriage. More intrapsychically, his treatment should focus on his relationship with his family of origin, his coping with his father's and brother's alcoholism, and his ways of relating to women based on the relationship with his mother. Finally, it should aim at Emilio's basic defense of avoidance, as evidenced by his lack of effort in obtaining mental health services for Mary when she was in the throes of depressive episodes. Such an avoidance approach hardly suggests the presence of sufficient ego strength to confront emotional conflicts as they occur. Rather than dealing with conflicts, he quit the field; thus, Emilio's object relatedness can be seen as fragile at best.

Fourth, collateral family therapy is strongly recommended for Jason and his parents initially. Carla can be included when she is older, if necessary. These sessions can be conducted by Jason's individual therapist or by a separate family therapist—with the latter option more optimal, to preserve the special quality of the individual work. Jason should be seen separately with each parent and later with them together. Principally, the most difficult dyadic work will occur between Jason and his mother: His need for her approval conflicts strongly with his sense of her detachment, coldness, and controlling attitude, these doubtlessly affecting their relationship deleteriously if unresolved. The therapist will need to be aware also of two very different parental approaches to raising the same child, being careful not to give in to the countertransferential temptation to align himself or herself with one parent against the other. One might be tempted, for example, to emphasize Mary's glaring inadequacies as contrasted with Emilio's warmer and softer touch with Jason.

In the fifth place, counseling for parents together is recommended on a monthly basis to ameliorate and modulate further familial contribution to the evident symptoms and to gain their cooperation with treatment goals. These parents will need to learn to work together as divorced parents in their ongoing support of each other for the benefit of their children. Their capacity to negotiate all the issues, minor and major, that affect their children will ultimately set the tone for the children's adjustment to the divorce. They will also benefit by resolving lingering issues of the marriage that exist and exacerbate their present circumstance as divorced individuals with children in common. Again, this is most likely addressed by a separate family therapist who is sensitive to the complexity of issues arising from divorce.

Sixth and last, contact with appropriate personnel in Jason's school would be helpful in order to obtain occasional reports of his conduct, the fluctuations of his daily behavior, and the sources of stress that result in his hostile, angry reactions after returning home each day. As school is often the first important place for a child outside his or her immediate family, the effect of behavior on teachers and peers can also provide valuable information as therapy continues. In Jason's case, his differential behavior with male and female teachers is quite revealing of the state of his capacity for splitting. Thus, obtaining information from his school may provide important clues for the therapy about his self-esteem, his sense of worth when with his teachers and peers, and his capacity to work in what should be the neutral arena of cognition and learning. As school seems especially frustrating for Jason presently, his therapist would do well to explore the sources of the frustration. Engaging his teachers' cooperation, even in a general way, could yield valuable information about the pressure points that elicit his most maladaptive and disturbing behaviors.

TREATMENT DESCRIPTION

Logistics

Psychoanalytic play therapy provides a setting where the child may play out and hopefully express the intrapsychic concerns that bring him or her to therapy. The setting can vary from therapist to therapist, from an office with a designated play area to an office with toys, work stations, closets full of toys, and the like. It is usually an area created with a child's needs in mind, a protected space where dramas can be acted or reenacted without dreaded consequence (Loewald, 1987). If space permits, designated areas can be arranged for the creations of different children—a shelf on a bookcase, a file drawer, or another special place where the child may store things he or she made; thereby providing an actual "holding environment" as well as a psychic one that fosters the feeling of intimacy and ongoing connection between patient and therapist. The child is reminded and encouraged from time to time to review those materials to obtain a sense of individual progress through the items accumulated.

The child patient may choose from the variety of paraphernalia available: drawing materials, dolls and doll clothing, blankets, toys, games, and balls for playing baseball and basketball. Toys may include doll families and houses, animal and human puppets, soldiers, guns, current action figures, cowboys and Indians, and so on. Materials may include the usual art supplies of finger paints and pencils, Play-Doh, markers, crayons, papers; with very young children, often a sandbox is also useful for practicing fine-motor control without having commitment and finality to errors made. While organized games such as checkers, Battleship, and the like have been less favored because they have structured rules of engagement, they are often preferred by latency-aged children (such as Jason), and they can be played with as much passion expressive of unconscious motivation as any of the variety of less structured activities. The difference is that latency children often attempt to obscure and hide the passion stirred up by the playing of the game; the empathic observer can, nonetheless, tap into the undercurrent of the conflicts, defenses, anxieties, and motivations that drive the play. Indeed, analysts (Colarusso, 1993; Eifermann, 1987; Peller, 1954; Plaut, 1979) have posed that games have their own rhyme and reason in the play of this age population and are ultimately useful as well for acting out mental content.

Regardless of the toy or game chosen, play therapy aims to elicit the child's thoughts, feelings, and wishes in indirect, nonintrusive ways. The therapist allows the child maximal freedom to play with the materials offered as long as the people and property are safe within the treatment room. In other words, limits are imposed only on furniture destruction and homicidal or suicidal acts; all else is tolerated. This process can thus give the analyst a window into the child's unconscious mental life, with all the dreams, wishes, tensions, and pressures he or she experiences. The therapist can be either observing or participating with the play constructed by the child, depending on intent. In either case, the role of the analyst is to clarify and reflect on the ongoing events of the play, occasionally commenting on its action and the needs of the individual characters, and to offer interpretations, taking care to clarify underlying issues for the child within the idiom of the play. The analyst should take care not to disrupt the flow of the material offered by the child by premature interpretations or by interpretations too close to real life. (This would be especially critical for a child like Jason, who recoils with any mention that the root cause of any problem in his life might be his own behavior. Interpretations too close to real life before he is ready for them would almost certainly reinforce his defensive need to avoid and deny.) Modern video games, a fact of life for many children today, are not recommended because they are manufactured with rules already created in the software program and do not lend themselves easily to individual creativity. Thus, playing them is a solitary venture that excludes the role of the therapist altogether. Utilizing them in play therapy is discouraged. Regardless of the medium of play chosen, it is vital to remember that the action of the therapy is in the interpretive work, not in the toy or game activity. The latter serve merely as tools by which the action of the therapy take place. With regard to type of toys used, the words of Anna Freud are instructive here:

> The role of the toy as an instrument for analysis is greatly overrated. Whatever is provided is really only an adjunct to the treatment situation, and what is really important is what the patient and analyst say and how they relate to each other, what the child reveals, and so on. . . . Play as an analytic tool concerns what is learned about the child by observing his behavior and then translating that behavior into its unconscious roots, and gathering analytic material which is produced easily because it is disguised in free associations, in dreams, in fantasy, and in fantasy play. . . . The analyst as a behaviorist can use pieces of behavior to extract unconscious meaning from them, for example to infer how the child deals with anxiety or frustration. But this is quite different from free association or from the expression of a fantasy which results from an upsurge from the depths of the mind toward the surface because different conditions have been created which facilitate the emergence of the unconscious material." (Sandler, Kennedy, & Tyson, 1980, p. 127)

With regard to the frequency of meetings, a frequency rate of two or three times per week seems minimal, given the symptom picture and urgency of further acting up potential in Jason. This frequency may also depend on other factors that impact on the particular case in hand: availability of parental support, other developmentally appropriate activities in which he may engage, and so forth. Within this context, his parents should be interviewed at least once per week to elicit their support of treatment efforts and to attenuate ongoing family dynamics that may be contributing still to the symptom picture. The collateral treatment is considered vital in this case, as much of Jason's pathology is intertwined around the issues with his parents, both intrapsychically and in reality. As in most child cases where parents are seen on a fairly regular basis, it is suggested that different therapists be utilized for each modality if at all possible. Jason's mother, to be sure, is entitled to a therapist of her own to deal with the enormity of depressive issues she manifests.

Moreover, the therapists should have ongoing consultation with each other. The separation of therapist/family specialist is advocated here to forestall contamination of the child treatment in cases where issues of trust would complicate the child's already existing difficulty in establishing the therapeutic alliance. Such a strategy might be informed by the program developed by Bearslee and MacMillan (1993) for working with children of depressed parents. These authors note that a structured approach to this problem can provide useful support for families in coping with the ramifications of parent affective disorder.

Specific Strategies

Through whatever medium selected by the child, the play therapist would attempt to engage Jason in the task of revealing himself while in the act of playing. Various scenarios are possible, of course, although one remains uncertain whether he would easily lose himself in enacting the unconscious issues he has in this way. Latency children also tend to ignore the regressive pulls signified by certain activities—dolls and such figures as toy soldiers and action heroes, for example, avoiding them for more organized games instead. The therapist plays a relatively nondirective role in the choosing and playing of activities during the session, allowing the young patient to guide and steer the direction of the play. It appears highly likely, given Jason's difficulty with managing internal pressures in modulated ways, that he would choose to hide behind more rigorous and structured activities, as provided by board games or organized play.

Having said this, should Jason choose role playing with dolls, games, or whatever, the therapist allows him to "enact these conflicts through motor means" (Sandler, Kennedy, Tyson, 1980, p. 137). One may hypothesize that many of these will deal with his issues with his parents, especially his anger and disappointment toward his mother. His feelings toward his father may be more dangerous to articulate because the likelihood of being abandoned by this parent is greater, given the reality of the divorce.

Given the foregoing, basic techniques and strategies for Jason will begin by introducing him to the therapy situation, the reasons for the referral, and the necessity of his participation in the process. Prior to this, an initial interview will have occurred between the parents and the therapist to outline the reasons for therapy, the modality utilized, the logistics (already explained in the previous section), as well as ways to present the necessity for treatment to Jason. The therapist can be presented to the child as "worry doctor," one who is concerned with the child's preoccupations and worries and has been very helpful to others with his kind of therapy. Reasons given to Jason for the necessity of therapy should include the facts of his misbehavior, the fact that he seems unhappy with the divorce, and the fact that he and his mother have fought to the point of her hitting him in the face. All these suggest significant unhappiness, from which he suffers greatly.

In individual sessions with the therapist, Jason will be introduced to the treatment situation, the play activities, materials, games, and so on and encouraged to utilize them in play without restriction. The only request made is that Jason consider telling the therapist his thoughts as they come up while playing, a request similar to the dictum to freely associate in adult analysis. With Jason, it is likely that he will gladly chat and talk as long as more touchy issues, such as his own maladaptive behaviors, do not surface immediately. In time, however, it is predicted that Jason will present fewer and fewer resistances and warm to the therapeutic situation. After all, his object hunger is quite strong, and he longs for the approval of important adults in his life even when they demand difficult things of him. It is expected that he will pick one or two of the play materials, perhaps guns, other weapons, soldiers, and the like in which to express his barely repressed hostility and create a dramatic play around them. As sessions proceed, he will likely develop a routine of play and talk, initially favoring the former over the latter. The therapist can do one of a number of therapeutic activities, whether participating in the play, as invited by the child, or hanging back and merely observing the play, commenting occasionally on the theme of the play itself. In extreme cases, the therapist may choose to remain silent if the child expresses the need for him or her to keep quiet. Some children may prefer that the therapist take the lead in the play, a signal that they feel unsure of the direction their play should go. Others will insist that the therapist remain outside the play *but* maintain absolute attention to them. Each child differs in the capacity to understand and tolerate the therapist's interventions. By persistent, neutral verbalization of the themes observed, the therapist will model for the child the act of verbalizing as an acceptable, desired activity to communicate inner thoughts and feelings. The child will reflect back to the therapist if interventions hit the mark or not; in this way, the therapist can gauge more carefully what is the empathic response to the play at hand. Jason will likely talk when he feels the security of verbalizing his negative affects without reprisal. As he comes to accept the therapeutic task, he will find it most gratifying to have the undivided attention of an adult who is devoted to understanding his inner turmoil. Even then, dropping the defensive armoring he has erected may be a slow, gradual process that accompanies the unfolding of the treatment.

Therapeutic change can be measured by the proportion of playing to talking, as well as by the quantity and quality of the verbalizations. By the latter, the therapist can also gauge the correctness of his or her interpretations, made cautiously at all times, but particularly so in the initial stages of therapy. The therapist can also note development and developmental changes that occur by the child's articulation of his thoughts.

Apropos of Jason, one may speculate that he will hold on to his misgivings for a long time, given the duration of his conflict with his mother. The therapist should therefore give him wide berth to open up only when he feels ready to discuss his problems. Eventually, the therapist will encounter the force of the mechanism of splitting, which so prominently marks his defensive structure. It would be pointless, therefore, to argue why Jason should view his mother in a more positive light despite her failings. Instead, the therapist should assist Jason with the task of exploring what he requires of her, whether it is fantastic or realistic to expect her to provide it, whether he could obtain needed satisfaction elsewhere (e.g., his father, teachers or his own ego resources), or what in reality he still requires to feel satisfied. Coming to terms with what he can realistically expect from both his parents will eventually help Jason to integrate the disparate parts of his reality and object relations into a more coherent whole. His anger toward his mother will be another indicator of the effectiveness of therapy: As it subsides and he comes to own his responses and feelings, Jason may feel less and less the need to idealize her and experience grave disappointment in the process. Learning to forgive and accept some of this reality will assist him toward greater a more mature and complex level of development.

Treatment Stages

Introduction/Orientation

This period of orientation sets the stage for what the goals are and should be explicated in terms that the child patient can clearly understand. It is here that details of the schedule of appointments and the need for attendance are specified, usually with the parent. Policies for missed sessions are outlined here. In child treatment, one must take into account the importance of reality events on a patient's life as well as on the life of his parents and adopt a stance about attendance that is less rigorous than that of adult therapy. Reasons for missing therapy might include, for example, various activities in the school or community, scheduled or unexpected holidays, illness, lessons for music or sports, or social contact with friends. A reason should be given to the child, regardless of age, out of respect for his intelligence as well as to answer questions about why he must visit the therapist in the first place, what the child can and cannot do, as well as what the analyst will and won't do. This may also include a period of education wherein the child is introduced to the language of therapy. This might include naming his emotions, if required, giving him a vocabulary by which to express his internal states. An educative period along the lines described by Weil (1973) may even prove necessary in order to provide him a period of time whereby he is initiated into the demands of treatment in a gradual, subtle way.

Based on his reaction to the initial interview, Jason will not doubt have some difficulty warming up to the situation if it suggests in any way having him accept responsibility for misconduct. He may question forcefully the necessity of having therapy in the first place, thereby refusing to verbalize his difficulties by playing instead. Eventually, however, he may shift into the mode of playing and verbalizing, a combination that will permit him to enact the conflicts experienced and have their meanings made clear.

During the opening stages of therapy the therapeutic alliance is initiated. This is a phase when many elements come together: the child's wish, conscious or unconscious, to obtain relief from his internal difficulties, his need to gain the help and support of an interested adult who is concerned about his worries, or the need to please this new object in his life who might offer new understanding of his problems. The child patient must acknowledge in some way the existence of his internal conflicts and allow the therapist to help him articulate them and work with them toward resolution. The success of the therapy depends in large part on the child's attitude toward the treatment itself and toward the therapist. Even if he is resistant, he must somehow accept the fact that he needs help and allow the therapist to provide it. He must accept the therapist's lead and have sufficient confidence and trust in the person and the work itself to permit the therapy to occur. The child may also be motivated by the presence of a new adult in his life, one with particular skills for helping him to surpass the difficulties of his life at the moment, whether they be with school or with home. While Jason shows no insight about himself or his own behavior being problematic, he yet admitted that he felt unhappy and wished for his parents' reconciliation. During the initial interview, he warmed to the interviewer as long as emotionally charged subjects were avoided, thereby showing some enthusiasm for the attention of an interested adult.

From this portion of the intake interview with Jason, it can be hypothesized that he would be open and even enthusiastic about the prospect of therapy, thus rendering the opening moves of the therapy and therapeutic alliance in an optimistic light. Though he is obviously resistant to certain aspects of the therapy—principally admission of his own dysphoria, anxiety, and culpability—he nonetheless seems open toward relating to adults if they relate to him without too many demands. Given the potential for transference reactions to females, a male therapist might prove less threatening to Jason. It may also provide yet another figure of identification, a developmental dynamic greatly appropriate for a latency-aged boy. This is not to preclude the effectiveness of a female therapist as long as this potential is always kept in mind. The tenuousness of an alliance of this kind is always a factor to consider when doing the interpretive work.

Negative Reactions

These usually occur in the context of entire transference reaction or partial transferential reactions. They occur when the negative aspects of the relationships to primary, internalized objects are stirred up in the course of treatment, and they can potentially threaten the therapeutic alliance if unrecognized or unacknowledged. Even under the best of circumstances, their power to disrupt the therapy cannot be ignored. With Jason, possible sources of negative therapeutic reactions can occur with the presence of a female therapist who is seen as controlling and critical, resonating with his complaints about his mother, and drawing on the conclusions of the projective data about his struggle with issues of control. Negative reactions can also be anticipated during the interpretation of Jason's defensiveness and denial of his misbehavior, especially around the issues for which he shows immense shame: the setting of the fire and the disruptive behavior in school. He may come to view the therapist as yet another adult trying to wrest compliance from him unwittingly. Negative reactions may be noted in his resistance to verbal expression, in his general silence or avoidance of "hot topics," or perhaps even in his refusal to play. Jason has shown in real life his defiance of certain rules and his tendency to enact his protest through action rather than verbalization. In therapy with him one can expect behavior along the same lines until such time as he feels sufficiently comfortable and secure to articulate his negative feelings, especially those of anger, envy, and fear of abandonment—these being the central affects that he cannot and dare not articulate to his significant, primary figures. A word about countertransference may be helpful here. As Jason may indeed manifest strong, virulent negative trans-ferential reactions to the therapy, this could potentially pose a countertransference challenge for the therapist. He or she must negotiate this conflict, as it may arouse feelings of rejection and boredom for the resistance a child like Jason can engen-der, especially if he engages in any kind of acting out of his transferential hostility toward the therapist. Last, one might be vigilant about observing Jason around other patients treated by the therapist, given his possible sibling rivalry and competitive-ness with his sister.

Working Through

This process is an elaboration and extension of the relevant interpretation in differ-ent contexts, situations, and directions, whether it be the tracing of a particular con-flict or partial solutions to a conflict, or the interpretation over and again of the same conflict or situation in its many guises. The end result is that the patient progres-sively withdraws his investment in a particular pattern of mental activity or behav-ior in favor of a more ego-adaptive solution. Working through depends on the ther-apist's awareness that the interpretation is not the end goal. Rather, it is the consolidation and integration of the progress made following the right interpreta-tion. As Anna Freud (Sandler, Kennedy, & Tyson, 1980) states: "To a greater ex-tent with children than with adults, more of what the therapist has interpreted tends to slip away and to reappear in a new form, when it has to be interpreted again. It is really the constant reiteration of the interpretation that serves the working-through process, especially with the child . . . Working through seems to be as much a task for the therapist as for the patient. In fact, a technical aspect of the therapist's work is to be aware of the working through needed in regard to further extensions of pre-viously interpreted material" (p. 183). Sufficient working through has occurred when the child moves on to the next level of development and is well established there.

For Jason, one can clearly see that the major issues to be worked through would include those of fear of abandonment by his parents, envy of his sister, and a gen-eral need for control of his environment. Other defenses and coping strategies need to be considered over and over again, especially to control his impulsivity and need for action when emotionally stirred up. His masochistic need to "fight the good fight with female figures" as a way of warding off his dependency on them needs to be explicated in his relationship with both mother and teachers. Perhaps this will be manifested through the relationship with the therapist as well. Issues of trust and dependency will be turbulent for Jason, especially if his therapist is female, as he has felt extremely disappointed in his mother for her psychological withdrawal, as well as for her impatience and criticality even when she is physically present.

Termination

Termination in psychoanalytic child therapy is based on several important criteria, including the achievement of the analytic goal of restoring the child to the path of normal development, the progress of the work, specifically whether or not the trans-ference has been resolved, and the child's developmentally appropriate adaptation in his or her life outside the treatment setting. For example, the level of functioning in school and at home as judged by the child, the parents, and the school, would all be important areas for ascertaining improvement. Furthermore, other important technical considerations include interruption by external circumstances, such as the patient or therapist moving away, the resistance of patient or parents rationalized into a valid external reason. Thus, whether the termination comes suddenly and whether there is some advance knowledge of it are major technical considerations as well (Sandler et al., 1980, p. 241). Elsewhere, these authors note that "the patient's experiences of being abandoned, neglected, or separated from the mother play an important part in the child's reactions in terminating. The need to work through these responses and defenses against the loss of object is an integral part of the work of termination in child analysis. It requires working on the problem of the resolution of transference ties as well as on the tie to the real object" (Sandler et al., 1980, p. 248).

In light of the foregoing, the end of the therapy can be predicted to be difficult for Jason, in view of his issues of abandonment and loss, presuming that the therapy has proceeded well with the therapeutic alliance and working through of important issues. He has shown a capacity for relating well to important objects, even when his anger has been mobilized at one time or another. He also evidences a real object hunger, longing for secure and safe objects on whom he can reliably depend. As such, he is likely to feel the loss acutely if he has come to benefit from the therapeutic relationship and if the transference has been successfully resolved. It is also likely that Jason may exhibit an upsurge of all his misbehavior as termination approaches in an unconscious effort to regain the therapy and forestall the pain of terminating. The length required for a successful termination usually hinges on the length of the treatment, shorter ones requiring four to six weeks with those of a year or longer usually taking several months.

EXPECTED OUTCOME OR PROGNOSIS

One should advocate caution in predicting the prognosis for the case of Jason. While he does not evidence grave, severe pathology at this point, the potential for further difficulty remains large. One should perhaps consider the risk factors at play here, including his poorly developed neurotic defenses against anxiety, his immature ego structure and lack of capacity for self-reflection and good judgment, his lack of superego development, and his general feeling of deprivation and parental neglect. His self-esteem regulation thus appears vulnerable to decompensation as long as he is without sufficient self-regard, at this point a difficult thing to acquire. His early deprivation of both maternal attention and investment in him during the rapprochement stage has left him feeling shaky and unprotected when in the throes of challenge to his self-esteem. He will remain vulnerable to other influences, such as peers, who pull him along in their escapades because he hardly feels confident about asserting his own thoughts and wishes.

As for his family, his mother's long-standing and, as yet, untreated tendency toward depression bodes poorly for his developing a sufficiently healthy sense of attachment to her so as to make him feel secure and loved. The one note of optimism for improving her parenting would be her acknowledgment of her own constriction of affection and deficient parenting skills, as well as her willingness to engage in her own therapy. Only when she has resolved her own issues of abandonment, loss, and neglect can she be liberated from the sense of having to parent when she herself has been bereft for so long. She is presently unable to appreciate the support of her mother very much, because her feelings about this parent are tinged with anger and ambivalence. Instead, she continues to focus on the parent who abandoned her physically and psychically, namely her father, as evidenced by her reactive depression following her parents' divorce and her constricted grieving when he died. As these conflicts and torments are resolved, more psychic energy may be available to her to parent her own children. Jason should eventually experience a greater sense of relief once his mother's psychopathology is addressed and ameliorated. Moderate in severity, his anger and rebellion are nevertheless not so heavily entrenched that his developmental path cannot be regained. His mother's tendency toward abusive behavior may be prognostically more difficult to resolve inasmuch as she seems to have reached the end of her limited capacity to nurture him with patience and tolerance. To her credit, she is able to nurture her daughter and thus may have greater capacity for him once her resistance toward parenting him is addressed in her own therapy.

It must be emphasized that Jason is not without strengths and resources. He is endowed with bright-average intelligence and a good sense of reality testing. He understands cause-and-effect relationships, as well as the extent to which he will be held accountable even if he should deny his culpability when caught. In addition, he has a strong, unambivalent bond with his father, a figure who seems more empathic and tolerant of Jason's developmental needs than his mother. These would thus serve as protective factors against further manifestation of psychopathology, especially if his parents can be counseled about their children's developmental needs for at least an "average expectable environment." One can draw on their expressed, conscious wishes to parent well and their attachment to their children, such providing a motive even in the moments of profound self-absorption in their adult dilemmas of life.

CONCLUSION

Jason's aggression and behavioral disturbance, though very much reflective of his individual character style and armoring, are multifaceted and multiply determined. On the intrapsychic level, he struggles with losses and his sense of abandonment by both mother and father at different points in his life. His aggression and behavioral disturbance also seem intimately related to his mother's feeling state and psychopathology. As the events of her life unfold, they are most deficient and depressing, given her losses, and she cannot give that which she has not received.

Support and nurturance for her will ultimately allow her to parent more effectively. Jason requires a greater sense of security with the bond toward her. Without this, he will continue to see only his father as a nurturer and sufficient parent, thus coloring his general experience with female figures as cold, critical, and abusive. If not addressed in the present, this will surely eventuate in greater pathology and fury toward women in general. His one, unambivalent source of support, his father, does not obviate the need for a less ambivalent relationship with the primary caretaker, his mother. Establishing future object relationships on that kind of a shaky foundation can only predispose him to conflictual, ambivalent relationships with female figures in the future.

Though not emphasized in traditional psychoanalytic play therapy, the work with mother is all important here. This author wishes to underscore the need to consider the mother's psychopathology as the key toward ameliorating the pathology shown in Jason. The exploration of the real-life object relationship between mother and son is dramatically different from that involving work with the child patient alone. It is critical to consider the addition of the parents' and family therapies, given the sad state of affairs between Jason and his mother. His father's role is also critical as he represents the good side of the parent split, but the integration of the disparate parts of the relationship toward his mother will ultimately assist Jason in resolving the full realm of his anger and frustration with her. Jason and his family are hardly atypical in terms of the psychopathology they evidence. He is surely a child of the 1990s in terms of the types of misbehavior he evidences and the kind of family pathology evident. As a society and ecosystem, we would do well to consider the proliferation of disorders that now confront us as a result of the gradual dissolution of the family and institutions that have before provided structure and a benign ecosystem in which for individuals to develop. A lasting contribution of the field of child therapy would be the finely tuned delineation and implementation of the protective factors that allow children and their families to survive and even thrive.

BIBLIOGRAPHY

Abrams, S. (Interviewer). (1991). A conversation with Peter B. Neubauer. *American Psychoanalyst, 25,* 10.

Arlow, J.A. (1987). Trauma, play and perversion. *Psychoanalytic Study of the Child, 42,* 31–44.

Axline, V.A. (1969). *Play therapy.* New York: Ballantine Books.

Bearslee, W.R., & MacMillan, H.L. (1993). Preventive intervention with the children of depressed parents. *Psychoanalytic Study of the Child, 48,* 249–276.

Beren, P. (1992). Narcissistic disorders in children. *Psychoanalytic Study of the Child, 47,* 265–278.

Block, J., Block, J., & Gjerde, P. (1990). Parental functioning and the home environment in families of divorce: Prospective and concurrent analysis. In S. Chess & M.E. Hertzig (Eds.), *Annual Progress in Child Psychiatry and Child Development (1989)* (pp. 192–207). New York: Brunner/Mazel.

Blum, H.M., Boyle, M.H., & Offord, D.R. (1989). Single-parent families: Child psychiatric disorder and school performance. In S. Chess & M.E. Hertzig (Eds.), *Annual Progress in Child Psychiatry and Child Development (1989)* (pp. 179–191) New York: Brunner/Mazel.

Brenner, C. (1982). *The mind in conflict.* New York: International Universities Press.

Chess, S., Thomas, A., & Birch, H.G. (1965). *Your child is a person.* New York: The Viking Press.

Cohen, P.M., & Solnit, A.J. (1993). Play and therapeutic action. *Psychoanalytic Study of the Child, 48,* 49–63.

Colarusso, C.A. (1993). Play in adulthood. *Psychoanalytic Study of the Child, 42,* 225–245.

Downey, T.W. (1987). Notes on play and guilt in child analysis. *Psychoanalytic Study of the Child, 42,* 105–125.

Eifermann, R. (1987). Children's games, observed and experienced. *Psychoanalytic Study of the Child, 42,* 127–144.

Esman, A. (1983). Psychoanalytic play therapy. In C. Schaefer & K. O'Connor (Eds.), *Handbook of play therapy* (pp. 00). New York: Norton.

Freud, A. (1965). *Normality and pathology in childhood: Assessments of development.* New York: International Universities Press.

Freud, A. (1968). Indications and contraindications for child analysis. *Psychoanalytic Study of the Child, 23,* 37–46.

Freud, A. (1982). *Psychoanalytic psychology of normal development (1970–1980).* London: Hogarth Press.

Freud, S. (1908). Creative writers and day-dreaming. *Standard Edition,* Vol. 9 (pp. 141–153). London: Hogarth Press.

Gavshon, A. (1990). The analysis of a latency boy. *Psychoanalytic Study of the Child, 45,* 217–233.

Hartmann, H. (1950) Comments on the psychoanalytic theory of the ego. *Psychoanalytic Study of the Child, 5,* 74–96.

Kapsch, L.A. (1991). A culture of one: Case study of play therapy with an abused child. *Journal of Pediatric Nursing, 6,* 368–373.

Kennedy, H., & Moran, G. (1991). Reflections on the aim of child analysis. *Psychoanalytic Study of the Child, 46,* 181–198.

Klein, M. (1932). *The psycho-analysis of children.* London: Hogarth Press.

Kohut, H. (1971). *The analysis of the self.* New York: International Universities Press.

Lax, R.F., Bach, S., & Burland, J. (Eds.). (1980). *Rapprochement: The critical subphase of separation-individuation.* Northvale, NJ: Jason Aronson Inc.

Lewis, J.M. (1993). Childhood play in normality, pathology, and therapy. *American Journal of Orthopsychiatry, 63,* 6–15.

Loewald, E.L. (1987). Therapeutic play in space and time. *Psychoanalytic Study of the Child, 42,* 173–192.

Mahler, M.S. (1968). *On human symbiosis and the vicissitudes of individuation.* New York: International Universities Press.

Mahler, M.S. (1979). Separation-individuation. *The selected papers of Margaret S. Mahler,* Vol. II. Northvale, NJ: Jason Aronson Inc.

Mahler, M.S. (1980). Rapprochement subphase of the separation-individuation process. In R.F. Lax, S. Bach, & J. Burland, (Eds.), *Rapprochement: The critical subphase of separation-individuation* (pp. 3–19). Northvale, NJ: Jason Aronson Inc.

Moran, G. (1987). Some functions of play and playfulness: A developmental perspective. *Psychoanalytic Study of the Child, 42,* 11–29.

Moustakas, C. (1959). *Psychotherapy with children.* New York: Harper & Row.

Neubauer, P. (1987). The many meanings of play. *Psychoanalytic Study of the Child, 42,* 3–9.

Neubauer, P.B. (1993). Playing: Technical implications. In A.J. Solnit, D.J. Cohen, & P.B. Neubauer (Eds.), *The many meanings of play* (pp. 44–53). New Haven: Yale University Press.

Ostow, M. (1987). Play and reality. *Psychoanalytic Study of the Child, 42,* 193–203.

Peller, L.E. (1954). Libidinal phase, ego development, and play. *Psychoanalytic Study of the Child, 9,* 178–198.

Piaget, J. (1951). *Play, dreams and imitation in childhood.* New York: Norton.

Pine, F. (1987). *Development Theory & Clinical Practice.* New Haven, CT, Yale University Press, No. 12, p. 23.

Plaut, E.A. (1979). Play and adaptation. *Psychoanalytic Study of the Child, 34,* 217–232.

Ritvo, S. (1978). The psychoanalytic process. *Psychoanalytic Study of the Child, 33,* 295–305.

Sandler, J., Kennedy, S., & Tyson, R.L. (1980). *The technique of child psychoanalysis: Discussions with Anna Freud* Cambridge: Harvard University Press.

Solnit, A.J. (1987). A psychoanalytic view of play. *Psychoanalytic Study of the Child, 42,* 205–219.

Waelder, R. (1932). The Psychoanalytic Theory of Play. In F.A. Guttmon (ed.), *Psychoanalysis* pp. 84–100, New York, International University Press, 1976.

Wallerstein, J., & Kelly, J. (1980). *Surviving the breakup.* New York: Basic Books.

Weil, A.P. (1973). Ego strengthening prior to analysis. *Psychoanalytic Study of the Child, 28,* 287–301.

Winnicott, D.W. (1953). Transitional objects and transitional phenomenon. In D.W. Winnicott, (Ed.) *Collected papers* (pp. 229–242). New York: Basic Books (1958).

Winnicott, D.W. (1965). *The maturational processes and the facilitating environment.* New York: International Universities Press.

Winnicott, D.W. (1971). *Playing and reality.* New York: Penguin (1980).

CHAPTER 3

Cognitive-Behavioral Play Therapy

SUSAN M. KNELL

INTRODUCTION

Cognitive-behavioral play therapy (CBPT) is based on behavioral and cognitive theories of emotional development and psychopathology and on the interventions derived from these theories. Cognitive-behavioral play therapy (CBPT) incorporates cognitive and behavioral interventions within a play therapy paradigm. Play activities, as well as verbal and nonverbal communication, are used. Cognitive-behavioral play therapy provides a theoretical framework based on cognitive-behavioral principles, and it integrates these in a developmentally sensitive way.

Personality Theory

Mischel (1968) argued that one should focus more on traits and habits, and less on personality types. He also emphasized the importance of situational factors in understanding behavior. His work provided a foundation for the cognitive-behaviorists. As originally conceptualized, the cognitive-behavioral approaches were insight oriented and used introspective techniques to change overt personality (e.g., Beck, 1967; Ellis, 1962). These approaches emphasized the changing of cognitive schemas (controlling beliefs) as well as behavioral symptoms. However, there is no personality theory, per se, that underlies cognitive-behavioral theory. Rather, the focus has been more on psychopathology, and the factors that contribute to psychological development gone awry, rather than on personality development and theory.

Cognitive therapy is based on the cognitive model of emotional disorders, which involves the interplay among cognition, emotion, behavior, and physiology (Beck & Emery, 1985). This model states that behavior is mediated through verbal processes. Disturbances in emotions and behavior are considered to be expressions of irrational thinking. There are three major premises of cognitive therapy: (1) Thoughts influence the individual's emotions and behaviors in response to events, (2) perceptions and interpretations of events are shaped by the individual's beliefs and assumptions, and (3) errors in logic or cognitive distortions are prevalent in individuals who experience psychological difficulties (Beck, 1976). These cognitions are unspoken, often unrecognized assumptions made by the individual.

While this model is not specifically a personality theory, it does address cognitive distortions as the basis of human behavior and thought, particularly as related to psychopathological development. For children, these distortions are often considered maladaptive, but not necessarily irrational. This is particularly true for very young children, whose thinking is, by definition, often illogical, egocentric, and concrete.

Model of Psychopathology

Cognitive therapy is based on the assumption that people's affect and behavior are determined in large part by the way they construe the world (Beck, 1967, 1972, 1976). Thus, it is one's perceptions of events—not the circumstances themselves—that determine how a person understands events. Cognitions can be in the form of covert verbal statements or images and are based on the attitudes or assumptions (schemas) developed from earlier experiences. Cognitive theory asserts that these cognitions will determine to a large extent the individual's emotional experiences.

According to the cognitive model, by knowing the meaning that a person attaches to particular situations, we can predict his or her emotional reaction. The range of cognitive distortions is infinite, but certain types of errors in thinking seem to occur with regularity. A great deal of the cognitive literature has been focused on depressed individuals, who often exhibit automatic thoughts reflecting a negative view of present, past, and future experiences (Beck, 1976). In summary, cognitive therapy is concerned with both how individuals perceive events and the cognitions based on these perceptions.

Basic Concepts of Cognitive-Behavioral Play Therapy

Cognitive therapy is based on a broad theory of psychopathology which details the intricate reciprocal interaction among cognitions, emotions, behavior, and environment. Cognitive therapy consists of a set of treatment techniques that aim to relieve symptoms of psychological distress through the "direct modification of the dysfunctional ideation that accompanies them" (Bedrosian & Beck, 1980, p. 128).

The cognitive therapist uses a phenomenological approach. Rather than considering the patient's experiences as a "screen" behind which more significant unconscious meaning resides (as the psychoanalysts do), the cognitive therapist uses the patient's report as basic data for the development of a treatment plan. The cognitive therapist's conceptualizations are based on configurations in the patient's phenomenal field, without reference to defense mechanisms or unconscious conflicts. The patient's thoughts are revealed through focused questions and careful introspection. The cognitive therapist seeks not only to produce symptom reduction, but to modify attitudes, beliefs, and expectations.

A primary goal of cognitive therapy is to identify and modify maladaptive thoughts associated with the patient's symptoms (Bedrosian & Beck, 1980). Beck (1976) uses the term *maladaptive thoughts* for ideations that interfere with the individual's ability to cope with experiences. Such thoughts may disrupt internal harmony and produce painful emotional reactions that are inappropriate or excessive.

Cognitive-behavioral play therapy is a developmentally sensitive adaptation of cognitive and behavior therapies. Through the use of play activities, therapy can be communicated to children indirectly. For example, puppets and stuffed animals can be used to model cognitive strategies such as countering maladaptive beliefs and making positive self-statements. Cognitive-behavioral play therapy has been used to treat children presenting with specific diagnoses such as selective mutism (Knell, 1993a, 1993b), encopresis (Knell & Moore, 1990; Knell, 1993a), and phobias (Knell, 1993a), as well as children who have experienced life events/traumas such as divorce (Knell, 1993a) and sexual abuse (Ruma, 1993; Knell & Ruma, 1996).

Cognitive-behavioral play therapy places a strong emphasis on the child's involvement in treatment and on a framework for the child's participation by addressing issues of control, mastery, and responsibility for one's own behavior change. By incorporating the cognitive components, the child may become an active participant in change. For example, by helping children identify and modify potentially maladaptive beliefs, a sense of personal understanding and empowerment may be experienced. Integrating cognitive and behavioral interventions may offer effects of the combined properties of all approaches, which might not be available otherwise (Knell, 1993a).

The principles of cognitive therapy for adults (Beck & Emery, 1985) can be applied with some modifications to children. CBPT is based on the cognitive model of emotional disorders. It is brief, time-limited, structured, directive, and problem-oriented, and it depends on a sound therapeutic relationship in which one role of therapy is educational. It is a collaborative process, although the nature of collaboration between child and therapist is different than with an adult. Both the inductive method and Socratic method are important, but they play a different role in CBPT with children than in work with adults (see Knell, 1993a, for a more detailed description of the adaption of these principles).

Although CBPT is unique, it is similar to other play therapies in its reliance on a positive therapeutic relationship that is based on rapport and trust; the use of play activities as a means of communicating between therapist and child; and the message that therapy is a safe place. It differs from other play therapies regarding philosophy about the establishment of goals; selection of play materials and activities; use of therapy to educate; and the use of praise and interpretations. CBPT is an active intervention in which the therapist and child work together in establishing goals and choosing play materials and activities. In contrast with other play therapies, the cognitive-behavioral play therapist may be part "educator," in that new skills are taught to the child. Finally, praise and interpretations are used to help the child acquire new skills and behaviors and gain understanding (see Knell, 1993a, for more detail regarding similarities and differences among play therapy orientations).

Goal/Cure

Beck explains cognitive change in the following way: First, therapy produces a "quieting down of the hyperactive organization" (Rachman, 1968), which can be the result of the therapist's empathy and acceptance (Truax & Carkhuff, 1967), specific relaxation instructions (Wolpe & Lazarus, 1966), or verbal approval (Wagner & Cauthen, 1968). Second, therapy sessions give patients the opportunity to experience and to test the reality of verbal or pictorial cognitions that are causally connected to their affect. Patients examine distorted ideas and are trained to discriminate between rational and irrational ideas, between objective reality and "internal embroidery" (Beck, 1970, p. 196). Through this process, the individual comes to realize that his or her ideas are irrational. Thus, one critical mechanism of cognitive therapy is the modification or shift of the patient's ideational system. As irrational concepts are deactivated, psychopathology may recede (Beck, 1970).

CASE FORMULATION

Overall, we come to see Jason* as a child with some behavior problems who seems to behave differently in different settings with different people. The history leads us to wonder what effects the life stressors that he has experienced have had on him. Among those of most concern are his parents' divorce, the constant movement back and forth between the two households, his mother's depression, and sibling issues with Carla.

The parents' subjective impressions are captured in the CBCL, which compared standardized, age-normed data. The CBCL profiles, as completed by each parent separately, shed some interesting light on this picture. First, Jason's parents' verbal descriptions present a much more problematic picture of him than the CBCL captures; this is particularly true for the mother's report. Second, the discrepancies between the mother's and father's perceptions of Jason on the CBCL confirm much of the differences in their verbal perceptions of his difficulties. Finally, the specific differences in their perceptions are important. That is, mother sees Jason as more depressed, socially withdrawn, and with more somatic complaints. Such perceptions may be, in part, reflective of her own struggles with depression and withdrawal and are supported by studies that indicate that maternal psychopathology colors parental perceptions of child problems as reported on the CBCL (e.g., Johnston, 1991). The fact that she sees him as more aggressive than his father sees him may also reflect her greater difficulty in dealing with him, particularly when his behavior is more externalized, or acting out, in nature.

Cognitive-behaviorists typically do not rely on projective techniques, in part because the theoretical rationale of such techniques is questionable, as are their psychometric properties (Anastasi, 1982). However, projective techniques, based on the hypothesis that an individual's perceptions and interpretations of unstructured materials are a projection of the child's personality (Frank, 1939), can be a valuable tool for the cognitive-behavioral play therapist. These measures may offer information about the child's conflicts, coping styles, style of organizing information, and view of the world. These measures are usually considered ambiguous and unstructured; however Knell (1993a, 1994) argued that certain projective tests may

---

*See "Orientation to the Text: The Case of Jason L.," p. 1.

provide structure for the very young child that is not available in verbal interviews. This structure is often in the form of more concrete, pictorial representations to which the child can respond. Additionally, the projective measures take some of the focus off the child and allow him or her to provide information in a format that does not appear to be specifically related to the child. Jason's responses on projective measures provide more information than is obtained in a clinical interview alone. This supports the notion that the structure, as well as the nonpersonal nature of the required tasks, makes projective techniques less threatening for him.

Jason is clearly a bright child with good verbal skills who cannot seem to use these abilities in understanding his own emotional experiences of the world, or in modulating his own behaviors, both verbal and nonverbal. He is concrete in discussing his own experiences and tends to describe his reaction to all emotionally loaded situations as "fine." Acknowledging negative affect also seems to be problematic for him. Evidence of maladaptive thoughts comes from a number of sources. First, we see many examples of how his thinking may be interfering with more adaptive functioning on the projective tests. Low self-esteem and the typically negative self-statements that accompany this lowered sense of self are evident in his TAT stories. For example, the girl "tries to do her best, but never seems to be good enough." The young lawyer in one story isn't given a chance, even though he knows as much as the older man. On the MIM, he makes self-statements referring to how difficult tasks are, and, despite trying his hardest, his perceived inadequate results are always "the best I can do."

The extremely small size and the stiff flat facial expression of the person in Jason's HFD might suggest a sense of sadness, or lack of positive affect in regard to how Jason sees himself. More information might have been obtained if the examiner had asked Jason who the picture depicted and if Jason could tell a story about the person in the picture. Such descriptive information often conveys more about the child's sense of self and how much of the picture is a reflection of his own sense of self or idealized self.

In Jason's KFD, he conveys a sense that he either continues to see his parents, sister, and himself as a family unit, or wishes that they could all be back together. The positioning of his figures suggests that he sees himself as more allied with his father than with his mother and sister. These impressions are supported by other test data, his expressed wish that mom and dad would be remarried, as well as his behavior toward his parents during the assessment.

The MIM provides information that supports some of the parent-child interactional patterns gleaned from interview and CBCL data. Mary's frustration level and difficulty handling Jason are clearly demonstrated. Despite the fact that she uses verbal reinforcement of his efforts (e.g., "I think it is quite good. . . ."), she did so only after Jason spoke with her first, and only after five minutes of complete silence while Jason worked. Emilio, on the other hand, maintains verbal interaction with Jason throughout the "draw-our-house" task, encouraging his efforts. Additionally, he used more creative forms of encouragement, such as that reflected in his comment, "I think you are doing a better job than I could," and tickling. Similarly, on the lotion-rubbing task, Mary's efforts seem somewhat mechanical and rigid, whereas the father makes more of a game out of the task (e.g., suggesting modified mud wrestling) and elicits Jason's ideas before proceeding. Emilio's creativity is seen again on the M&M® task, where he cuts the bag in two and gives each child his or her own bag of candy, as contrasted with the mother who firmly and seemingly angrily counts out the exact number of pieces for each child.

Further assessment data from the school might be useful (e.g., interview of teacher, Achenbach teacher report form). The fact that Jason responds better to the male teacher's aide might be better understood if we knew more about the aide's style and interactions with him as well as how this differs from Jason's teacher's style. It seems clear that something happens at school, or in the transition from home to school. Jason's behavior when he comes home needs to be better understood in terms of both his school and home behaviors. The fact that he does better when he is with his father after school supports a hypothesis that Jason responds better to males (e.g., father, teacher's aide). It also suggests that some of the difficulty may be in the way in which his behavior is handled by his mother, but one would also want a clearer sense of what the stressors are at school that may be contributing to this difficult transition between home and school. Further support of this may come from the mom's report of Jason's improved behavior on weekends. Certainly, one explanation might be the relative lack of stress in the mother's life on weekends. There may also be specific stressors that impinge on Jason during the transitioning period when he arrives home from school.

Parenting and marital issues seem to be important for this family. There are a number of issues that may be affecting Mary's parenting. These include, but are not limited to, the burdens of being a single parent, her feelings about working, and a sense that she is "stuck" (i.e., wishing that she could go back to school and/or gain some career advancement, but feeling that she has no opportunities to do so). There is evidence that when the pressures of the work/school week are off, she does better. Certainly, her bouts of depression may have an effect on Jason, and these should be further explored, with Mary encouraged to seek treatment. The differences between the parents' perceptions of Jason, as well as their divergent styles of handling him, seem to be contributing to his current confusion about the family situation and his behavioral difficulties. Continued marital issues may be affecting their handling of Jason. For example, there was no mention of how they handle their interpersonal difficulties in front of the children. This information would be quite important to the overall assessment and treatment planning.

In summary, Jason appears to be a child who has been negatively affected by specific stressors in his life. Key among these are his parents' divorce, disruptions of moving back and forth between parents, differences in parenting styles, his mother's depression, and sibling issues with his younger sister. Although he is a bright child with good verbal skills, Jason's understanding of his situation and his ability to acknowledge negative affect are limited. His self-esteem seems to be impaired, he appears to be sad much of the time, and his acting out behaviors can be seen within the context of a child who may be getting more attention for misbehaving than for acting appropriately.

TREATMENT GOALS

Goals for Jason

1. Increase his ability to express his feelings, use words to describe how he is feeling, and replace maladaptive acting out behaviors with more appropriate verbal expressions. The specific situations that he may need to express feelings about include:
   a. Parents' divorce, and the current living arrangements with each parent (i.e., splitting time between mother/father)
   b. Mother's different relationship with both children, and sibling issues with Carla
   c. Mother's lack of availability when depressed.
2. Explore maladaptive perceptions (e.g., causal role that he may feel he plays in divorce) and facilitate development of more adaptive thoughts and more realistic view of the situation (e.g., that parents are not getting back together). Part of this goal would be to normalize the experience of divorce for Jason.
3. Develop and increase his use of positive, adaptive self-statements to increase his self-esteem, self-control, and impulse control.
4. Increase appropriate peer activities.
5. Increase problem-solving skills, including resolution of situations that make his angry.

Goals for Parents

1. Discuss the inconsistencies between each parent's handling of Jason, establish a clearer set of rules at each home, and promote understanding and respect by each parent of the rules at the other parent's home.
2. Explore the parents' interaction with each other and facilitate open communication and positive interactions in front of the children. Decrease parents' use of the children as go-betweens in their relationship.
3. Increase mother's ability to cope on daily basis, and explore the option of individual psychotherapy for her.

TREATMENT DESCRIPTION

Logistics

Setting/Materials

CBPT can be conducted in a play therapy room with the wide assortment of materials usually available. In general, the more directive techniques found in CBPT require planning and forethought regarding the choice of materials. Among those frequently used are dolls, puppets, action figures, art materials, and other toys. It is usually best that options are available, so that a child has choices rather than feeling that only certain materials are accessible. It may be possible to buy materials to fit every possible therapeutic situation, but it may be neither necessary nor desirable. Through the therapist's flexibility, the child is encouraged to be creative, and the therapist need not buy specific toys for each child.

For Jason, the play-oriented, as opposed to verbally oriented, materials were necessary, particularly when he was dealing with more emotionally loaded topics. The assessment suggested that he became virtually nonverbal when the interviewer focused on problems, therefore it was critical—particularly related to expectations about how Jason *responds* in therapy—that he was encouraged to express himself through play, drawings, and other more nonverbal means. The therapist needed to be prepared to provide much structure for Jason in testing hypotheses and playing out alternative methods of coping through play materials.

Play materials, including art supplies and toys, were all accessible to Jason, and those chosen by the therapist closely followed Jason's lead. For example, when Jason responded negatively to drawings, but gravitated to the puppets as the therapist used them, then the therapist moved toward more extensive use of the puppets, and de-emphasized communication through drawing.

Frequency and Duration of Treatment

Ideally, scheduling for Jason was set for one session per week, with his parents scheduled to see the therapist at a separate session. Parents often find it easier to have their session before or after the child's session. This is usually not the best arrangement, however, because, in divorce situations, this often communicates to the child that the parents are together again and that it is the child's behavior that is responsible for reunification on a regular basis at the therapist's office. For many children of divorce, this message may contribute to their problematic behavior, for they construe their acting out as a means of reuniting their parents. Therefore, it would be best to encourage the parents to schedule their session at a different time than Jason's appointment. As treatment progressed, these weekly sessions might gradually be scheduled twice a month and then, monthly, as movement toward termination was established.

Specific Strategies

Play Therapy

Following Jason's lead, the therapist would structure sessions in an effort to introduce vignettes that deal with the issues that Jason is currently facing. Role-playing these scenarios exposes him to situations similar to his own, while allowing him to see reactions that are potentially more adaptive and positive than his normal behavior. For example, a puppet can demonstrate problem-solving skills as it learns to respond in adaptive ways. While problem-solving, the puppet model can talk and act out various cues (e.g., visual, auditory) to help him see how someone else might approach the problem. While the puppet attempts to deal with the issue at hand, the therapist can positively reinforce the behaviors in a way that models the appropriateness of the puppet's action for the child. This could include behaviors, as well as "thoughts," such as positive self-statements that the puppet states out loud. The goal here is to provide the child with a coping, rather than a mastery, model (Bandura, 1969; Meichenbaum, 1971). The coping model struggles, falters, and problem-solves along the way to mastering a problem, as opposed to a mastery model that exhibits a flawless performance every time. Observation of a coping model demonstrates for the child how problems can be solved and supports the notion that no one is perfect.

A wide array of behavioral and cognitive techniques can be used in the therapy. Common behavioral techniques include forms of contingency management, such as positive reinforcement, shaping, and differential reinforcement of other behavior. In Jason's case, the therapist would provide many positive verbal and social reinforcers for appropriate behaviors, both in the therapy session and in other settings. For example, when Jason reports patterns of appropriate behavior at home and school, the therapist would want to praise him and reward him in other nonverbal ways (e.g., making a "thumbs up" sign). Either within the therapy setting or at home, Jason could work toward more material reinforcers. Adding to his baseball card collection might be one positive reward system that could be explored. Shaping his behavior by encouraging closer and closer approximations to appropriate behavior can be pursued by both therapist and parents. One example is the shaping of socially appropriate expression of feelings. A puppet could model for Jason ways that one can learn to express feelings, rather than act them out.

Common cognitive techniques include cognitive change strategies such as identifying and changing maladaptive beliefs, developing coping self-statements, and utilizing bibliotherapy materials that convey cognitive change techniques through stories. However, cognitive change strategies designed for use with adults must often be significantly modified for use with children. Whereas many adults may be able to generate alternative explanations for faulty cognitions, test them, and alter beliefs (Emery, Bedrosian, & Garber, 1983), children will need much help in order to do so. The experiments can be provided as play experiences, with puppets modeling various problem-solving strategies and problem solutions. Bibliotherapy materials could include books read within the play therapy sessions, either directly to the child or to a puppet. They could also include books that the therapist suggests the parents read at home to the child.

As the therapist begins to prepare for the beginning of play therapy with this child, a number of scenarios come to mind. These include:

1. A puppet comes home from school. He throws his books and, when asked to pick them up, he flings them across the room. He frequently responds with sulking and withdrawal after being asked to pick up his things. The more he is asked to do something, the more problematic his behavior becomes.

2. A puppet goes from mom's to dad's house, and faces the frustrations of different routines and different expectations. This experience, which is often perceived as chaotic, and lacking stability, is played out by the puppet.

3. A puppet faces his mom who at times is depressed, withdrawn, and largely unavailable to him.
4. A puppet has difficulty with his younger sister, who seems to get what she wants and be very attached to the mother, who is frequently yelling and angry with the puppet.
5. A puppet has peer difficulties, often acting very bossy and then being teased and criticized by other children for his behavior.
6. A puppet faces situations that test his ability to control his impulses, such as being convinced to go along with some inappropriate actions of a group of older boys.

These scenarios are examples of specific situations that can be set up as part of the interaction between child, therapist, and puppets. The therapist must be flexible, creating dialogues with the puppets that are focused on treatment goals, but which also take into account the child's spontaneous verbalizations and behaviors. In this way, the child experiences coping models, dealing with concerns similar to those the child faces. However, rather than offering vignettes presented from a written script, the therapist creates scenarios that evolve, based in part on the child's responses and interaction with the puppet characters.

Parent Therapy

Parents are usually involved from the beginning of CBPT, when the therapist meets with them to gather assessment data. After the parents are interviewed, and the initial evaluation of the child is completed, it is usually best to meet with the parents to present the evaluation findings and agree on a treatment plan. The treatment plan may primarily involve individual CBPT with the child, work with the parent(s), or a combination of CBPT and parent work. Decisions are made based on the therapist's assessment of whether the parents will need help in modifying their interaction with the child or if the child will need assistance in implementing a treatment program outside of therapy.

When the primary work is with the child, it is still important to meet with the parents regularly. During these parent sessions the therapist will obtain information about the child, continue to monitor the parents' interaction with the child, and work on areas of concern. The therapist may also provide support for the parents as well as information on issues related to child development, as needed. Although the nature of the work with parents will vary, parents are usually seen regularly when their child is in CBPT.

For Jason's family, there are some issues that will need to be resolved if change is to occur. First and foremost, the parents will need to learn some basic child management skills in order to more effectively deal with Jason's problematic behaviors. The inconsistencies between them seem to be contributing to Jason's behavior. Following a fairly standard protocol (e.g., Forehand & McMahon, 1981), they should both be taught to use positive reinforcement more consistently and appropriately with Jason. The mother, especially, will need to "catch him being good," and learn to identify, label, and reward positive behavior. The establishment of appropriate and logical consequences for Jason's behavior will also be critical. For example, rather than yelling when Jason throws his books, mom might find a way of establishing an after-school routine for Jason. When the routine is followed, Jason could earn a privilege, rather than constantly feeling punished for his behavior before he has barely even walked in the door from school.

Mary's depression may need to be dealt with fairly directly. This would probably take place in a session without the father present in order to respect the mother's privacy and enhance the chances that she is honest and open to the possibility of individual treatment.

Treatment Stages

Introduction/Orientation

The very first part of treatment is the preparation of the child for therapy; this sets the stage for the entire therapy experience. What the parent tells the child about treatment is important. Since Jason has completed an assessment, his questions/concerns may be somewhat different than those of the child who is brought to therapy after an initial intake appointment with the parents alone. In general, it is important that the parents be encouraged to be straightforward with the child. This may include the parents' explanation to the child about their concerns. The problem should be described to the child in a simple, concrete, nonjudgmental manner. Further, the parents should indicate that they are all going to talk to someone who "helps kids by talking and playing with them." It is important not to lie (e.g., "We are going shopping"); threaten (e.g., "You need to behave or the doctor won't talk to you"); or bribe ("If you talk to the doctor, I will buy you a treat") the child (Dodds, 1985).

Bibliotherapy is one useful source for preparing a child for treatment. The picture book, A Child's First Book About Play Therapy (Nemiroff & Annunziata, 1990), provides an introduction to play therapy for four- to seven-year-old children. This and other related books can be used by the parent to help the child begin to understand the experience of play therapy. Therapists can also use the book in early therapy sessions.

For Jason, this preparation took place collaboratively between the parents and clinician. With the parents in the room, the therapist and parents explained to Jason that they were concerned about some of the things that seemed to be bothering him, and they wanted to find someone who could talk with him and help him. The picture book was used by the parents at home to reinforce what had been told to Jason to prepare him for treatment.

In addition to the specific assessment measures given, much of the early stages of play therapy can be construed as evaluative. The spontaneous play and verbalizations that the child brings to therapy must be considered in light of, and in addition to, the testing materials. Continued observations, interaction, interview, and play assessment are all important. For example, children's reactions to divorce differ from those attributed to them by parents, and parents' views are influenced by their own level of stress (Wallerstein & Kelly, 1980). Therefore, it was important to continue to assess Jason's perceptions of the divorce. What does Jason perceive of as his causal role in the divorce? Does he blame himself for the breakdown of the family? Does he believe that if he acts better his parents will get back together? Is he afraid of being abandoned by his father? A modified sentence-completion task (described below) is often seen as fun by the child and can provide valuable information for the therapist. Directive questioning of the puppets, with Jason responding for them, provided information that Jason was not able to offer more directly.

A commonly used projective technique, the sentence completion task, can be modified for use with young children. This task is designed to elicit information about the individual's thoughts, perceptions, assumptions, and underlying beliefs. The modified task, referred to as The Puppet Sentence Completion Test (Knell, 1993a), was developed to make the traditional sentence completion task more accessible for young children. Using puppets, the therapist models the sentence completion activity and then elicits responses from the child, who either speaks for himself or herself or uses a puppet to speak. Using the puppet as a prompt helps some children complete a task either that they might not understand or that they might find too emotionally threatening. Because any sentence stems can be used, items specifically geared to elicit information about Jason's particular situation were added. For example, stems such as "When my mommy and daddy divorced . . ." seemed useful, given his reluctance to discuss these painful experiences directly. *Sample responses from Jason's puppet sentence completion:*

I'd like to pretend to be *a baseball player.*

If I were bigger, I would *rule the world.*

Mommy is nice when *she doesn't hit me.*

Daddy is nice when *he plays with me.*

I am the maddest when *my mom hits me.*

When mommy and daddy got divorced I *cried.*

I wish *mom and dad would get remarried.*

School is *fine.*

Therapist-created drawings and pictures can be used to elicit feelings about the child's situations (e.g., Bierman, 1983; Harter, 1977, 1983; Hughes & Baker, 1990). Through the use of concrete referents, such as pictures depicting people with various facial expressions, children may be able to provide information about their own feelings. Pictures of parents arguing could be offered and the child asked to respond, either verbally or by pointing to feeling faces that might describe his feelings. In helping children deal with the difficulty of understanding the existence of contradictory feelings, their all-or-nothing thinking offers a very limited view of their own emotions. Harter (1977) uses drawings depicting conflicting views (e.g., smart/dumb; happy/sad; good/bad) to show that sometimes an individual can feel two seemingly conflicting feelings. The use of pictures to help describe feelings seems to be particularly useful for the child with limited verbal abilities. For Jason, pictures of a father and two children, and the mother and the same two children, were used to elicit statements. When this appeared to be too threatening for Jason, the pictures were incorporated into puppet play scenarios.

The following are selected vignettes from the early stages of play therapy. These vignettes were selected to highlight specific interventions used to help Jason meet expected goals. The appropriate goal(s), related to each intervention, is listed.

[Key: P = puppet; T = Therapist; J = Jason]

P: Wow! It's Thursday. That must mean that I am going to my dad's house tonight.

J: Hey, I go to my dad's house on Thursdays, too.

P: Oh yeah?

J: Yeah.

P: Look at this picture of a dad and his kids. Makes me think about me and my dad.

J: That's a stupid picture (pushes it away).

P: Well, I don't know about you, but boy, do I get mixed up sometimes. Going back and forth between mom and dad's house. I bet the boy in this picture feels that way sometimes.

[Goal 1a: Increase expression of feelings related to parent's divorce.]

P: Boy, school is a real pain sometimes [using Jason's actual words from the assessment].

J: You think so? Me too.

P: Yeah, I sure wish that I didn't have to go.

J: I hate school.

P: Well, I don't like it much, but I know that I have to go.

J: School is stupid.

P: Sometimes I think that too, but I am learning to like it.

J: Yuck.

P: Want to know what I do? I try really hard to be good and listen to the teacher and do my work. Then she tells me what a good job I am doing, and I like that!

[Goal 3: Increase use of positive self-statements to increase self-control; Goal 5: Increase problem-solving skills.]

P1: (To his sister) I told you to play with the truck this way. Why won't you listen to me?

P2: I want to do it like this.

J: (Observing, but not saying anything.)

P1: You never listen to me.

P2: The truck should be going this way.

P1: Forget it. (Puppet walks away to play by himself.)

T: Boy, sometimes it's really hard to play with your sister, huh?

P1: Yeah, she wants to do everything her own way. (Acts out starting to hit sister.)

T: I bet that makes you so angry, sometimes, that you want to hit her.

P1: Yeah, I'm gonna hit her.

T: Well, sometimes you are so mad that you want to hit her. But, maybe you could tell her that you are angry at her.

J: Aw, she won't listen.

P: Hey, that's what I thought, want to give it a try?

[Goal 1b: Increase expression of feelings related to mother's relationship with self and sibling; Goal 3: Increase use of positive self-statements to increase self-control.]

Middle Stages

As treatment progresses into the middle stages, therapy is focused on assisting the child in learning adaptive responses in dealing with individual situations, problems, or stressors. By the middle stages of treatment, the therapist will have a much clearer idea about which types of toys and activities the child seems to respond to, and which ones seem to be uninteresting or ineffective. Some children tend to respond more positively to drawing and other art materials than others. Similarly, puppets and puppet play seem to hold more appeal for some children, whereas others seem to feel that the puppet play is silly. In trying many different play modalities, the therapist must be aware of the child's responses to different materials and activities and respond accordingly.

As gains are noted, and treatment goals are reached in the therapy setting, the therapist will also need to focus on two key concerns. First are efforts to help the child generalize what is learned in therapy so that it may be applied in other settings. Second, efforts should be made to help the child maintain gains and avoid relapses after the therapy is terminated.

Teaching the child to master, and then maintain, adaptive behaviors learned in therapy in the natural environment is important. Despite a successful outcome in many studies of cognitive-behavioral therapy with children, an overall lack of generalization of treatment effects and a lack of maintenance of gains is often noted (Braswell & Kendall, 1988). For children, the maintenance of newly acquired skills may depend in part on the attitudes and behaviors of significant adults in the child's life. Additionally, therapy should be designed to promote and facilitate generalization, rather than assuming that it will occur naturally.

In order for generalization to occur, specific training may be required. There is no reason to expect that children will generalize from one setting to another, or from reactions from one caretaker to another. The therapist needs to build in mechanisms for this. As noted previously, generalization may be enhanced by interventions that deal with it directly and resemble real-life situations as much as possible; significant individuals in the child's natural environment should be involved in treatment and should be a source of reinforcement of the child's adaptive behavior; procedures that promote self-control of behavior should be utilized; and interventions should continue past the initial acquisition of the skill to ensure that adequate learning has taken place.

In addition to generalization, one must prepare the child and family for the possibility of later problems, which need not be construed of as failure by the family. If parents and child are prepared for setbacks, they can avoid being terribly discouraged by them. Part of the original treatment must be geared toward the possibility of setbacks, as well as accepting the belief that setbacks are part of the learning process. This may involve preparing the parent and child for what to expect, as well as for what to do if the child or family has a setback. In so doing, the therapist and family identify high-risk situations as those that might present a threat to the child's sense of control and ability to manage situations. Some authors (e.g., Marlatt and Gordon, 1985; Meichenbaum, 1985) describe "inoculating" individuals against failure, so that when there are roadblocks, the individual does not panic. Although some of this inoculation will occur in CBPT, much work will take place between parent and child outside of therapy.

Jason needed much help translating what he learned in therapy to his two homes and school environment. This involved creating scenarios that showed how the puppets translated these skills to other places and having Jason practice some of his newly acquired skills when he was willing to do so. It also involved his parents' willingness to try out different ways of dealing with him, and to continue to fine-tune these methods as it became clearer what worked with Jason and what did not. *Selected vignettes from the middle stages of play therapy:*

J: (Pointing to character he made from clay) This guy is so bad! Whap! (hits him with a hammer). Look at him! He keeps getting smacked cause he is so bad! Here come the good guys to rescue him.

T: The good guys are going to help him out, huh?

J: Yeah. Look, here's the fortress to protect all the good guys.

T: Sometimes it feels like you're the bad guy because you get hit.

J: Yeah (pretends to hit himself), I am bad.

T: I bet you wish you could hide in the fortress sometimes.

J: Yeah, keep all the bad guys away.

P: You know, I used to feel that way.

J: Yeah, what did you do?

P: Well, my mom would get mad and hit me.

J: Yeah, my mom too.

P: Well, my mom learned some new ways of helping me, and I learned how to have better behavior, too.

[Goal 2: Explore maladaptive perceptions and develop more realistic view of situation; Goal 3: Increase use of positive self-statements to increase self-esteem; Goal 5: Increase problem-solving skills.]

P1: (Pushing aside another puppet's toy) Give that to me.

P2: Hey, that's mine, leave it alone.

P1: No.

P2: That's mine, you doodoo brain.

P1: Hey, don't call me a doodoo brain.

J: (Watching, but not saying anything.)

T: Jason, look at the way that guy is shoving everyone around and taking his friend's things.

J: Yeah, they're not real happy with him.

T: Well, maybe the other puppets are tired of the way he bosses them around. Maybe they are calling him names because they don't like being treated that way.

J: Yeah, maybe. Lots of times the kids call me names.
T: Do you think it might be because sometimes you are bossy?
J: I'm not bossy.
T: Well, remember how you told me about how you told Mark what to do and took his toy?
J: Yeah.
P2: Well, I for one sure don't like it when someone bosses me around.
T: I would think you wouldn't like it. It sure is nice when all the kids treat you nicely, right?

[Goal 4: Increase appropriate peer activities.]

T: This is the mad face, this is the happy face, and this is the sad face. I wonder how you feel when you go back and forth from your mom to your dad's house?
J: Oh, it's ok.
T: (To puppet) How does it make you feel?
P: Well, I sure don't like it (pointing to the mad and sad faces).
T: Seems like it makes you both mad and sad.
P: Yeah, mad and sad.
T: I wonder if Jason feels the same way.
J: (Starts to throw things around the playroom.)
T: Seems like sometimes Jason throws things when he is feeling upset.
P: Yeah, I sometimes throw things too, but I am learning to say in words how I feel.
J: Aw, shut up puppet.
T: Seems like you are pretty angry at the puppet for telling you how he feels.
J: Yeah, well, he's a dumb puppet.
T: Sometimes kids have a lot of confusing feelings and they throw things and do stuff because it is hard to say how they feel.
J: That puppet makes me mad.
T: Yes, he makes you mad sometimes because he says some things that are hard to hear.
J: Yeah.
T: But it's good you could tell him he makes you mad
J: Yeah, puppet. You make me mad.

[Goal 1a: Increase expression of feelings related to parent's divorce; Goal 5: Increase problem-solving skills.]

T: Here is a book about kids whose parents get divorced that I want to read (starts reading the book).
J: (Walks across the room and picks up some toys to play, but seems to be listening intently as the therapist reads.)
T: (To puppet) This boy gets upset when his mom spends time with his sister and doesn't seem to pay any attention to him.
J: (From across the room) Yeah, she always gets her way.
T: Seems like Jason feels that his sister, Carla, always gets her way.

J: Yeah, she does. It makes me mad at her and at my mom.

[Goal 1a: Increase expression of feelings related to parents' divorce.]

P: Hey, I sometimes think that it is my fault that my parents got divorced.

T: Lots of kids think that; don't you sometimes think that, Jason?

J: Yeah.

P: Well, how did you learn not to think that?

J: Oh, I don't know, I just learned it.

P: Like maybe realizing that they are adults and they decided they needed to be apart?

J: Yeah, and remembering what my dad said about how he and my mom were fighting all the time.

P: Yeah, and how they are both happier now.

J: And my dad loves me, even though I can't live with him all the time.

P: And I bet your mom loves you a lot too.

J: She does.

[Goal 2: Explore maladaptive perceptions and development of more realistic view.]

Termination procedures and/or issues

Preparation for termination is usually a gradual process, where the therapist and child are talking, over several sessions, about the end of therapy. Children and parents (and therapists too) often approach termination with mixed feelings. It is often helpful to remind the child of the number of sessions remaining until the final appointment. With younger children, the therapist may need to provide a very concrete reference to the number (e.g., a piece of paper with marks for the number of appointments remaining). Termination may mean intermittent appointments until the therapy is eventually ended. These appointments may be scheduled over a period of time with a particular event in mind (e.g., beginning of school year). Thus, for example, a child who appears to be ready to terminate in the spring, but who has concerns about the new school year, may be seen sporadically throughout the summer so that the final appointment can take place *after* school begins. By spacing the final appointments several weeks apart, the therapist begins to communicate a message that the child can manage without the therapist. This can also be conveyed by positive reinforcement from the therapist for how well the child has been doing between appointments.

Selected vignette from the termination stages of play therapy:

T: It sounds like you've been working really hard at home and school. Your good behavior has been really awesome!

J: Yeah, well, I got really mad at Carla yesterday. I took her doll away from her, and she was crying.

T: Well, sometimes kids do things they know they shouldn't do. Sometimes, they get a little worried about stopping to come to therapy.

J: (No response.)

T: I wonder if you feel a little bit sad that you won't be coming to see me anymore?

J: Nah, . . . well maybe.

T: Sometimes it's hard to be here, but I think you like having a place to talk about stuff. I think you are going to miss talking to me. I will miss you!

J: Really?

T: Yes, I will, but I will be happy to know that you are doing well. You can call me or send me a letter if you want. And, I asked your mom and dad to let me know how you're doing.

It may be difficult for young children to think about therapy as finished. Many children are upset by the thought of never seeing the therapist again. For this reason, it is important that children not believe that "bad" behavior will ensure that they will return to the therapist. Some reassurance may be felt by children if they are told that it is all right to send a card to the therapist. Alternatively, they may appreciate knowing that the parent will call periodically to let the therapist know how the child is doing. It is important in CBPT to have an open door policy. For children, knowing that one can return to treatment can be very important regardless of whether they ever actually come back to the therapist.

It appeared that Jason, like other children of divorced parents, perceived the impending termination as a rejection by the therapist. As discussion of termination began, Jason's mother noted that his behavior worsened slightly, at home. It was important to continue to frame the final sessions as a positive experience, based on the positive gains that Jason and his family had been making in treatment. Efforts were made to taper sessions so that the ending was not too abrupt, and to help Jason understand that the therapist would be accessible to him, should he experience a need to return. In preparation for the final session, Jason and the therapist planned a termination celebration. The main purpose of the event was to focus on the positive aspects of the ending of treatment and his relationship with the therapist. Critical to this was emphasizing Jason's sense of self-control and acknowledging mastery of his adaptive behaviors.

EXPECTED OUTCOME OR PROGNOSIS

Jason seemed to respond to the situations modeled for him, and his responses suggest that he was integrating much of what he was learning into his own problem-solving and behaviors. As therapy was tailored to match Jason's own experiences, the efforts at changing some of his maladaptive thoughts and behaviors seemed to be effective. Given that much of his response style may have developed in reaction to his current family situation, it would be critical to note changes in the parents as well. In order for Jason to change, and to maintain these changes, his parents will need to face the role that they are playing and make changes in their efforts to deal with Jason on a daily basis. If the parents can look at their own behaviors, decrease conflicts between each other, and learn alternative ways of parenting Jason, the prognosis may be quite good. Additionally, it will probably be important that the mother face her own bouts with depression and seek treatment to alleviate her depressive episodes. On the other hand, if the parents are unable or unwilling to step past their current level of interacting with Jason, and with each other, the prognosis is much more guarded.

CONCLUSION

The present case provides an example of the successful use of CBPT in treating a seven-year-old boy. By involving Jason very directly in his own treatment, the CBPT provided a critical component of the therapy for this child and family. Clearly, his parents' involvement in their son's treatment was also an important part of the expected treatment success. However, Jason's participation in treatment provided a structured setting in which he could learn, in part, to exercise some control over his behavior and thoughts. Jason was actively involved in this process as he observed and interacted with the puppets and other play materials in some specific, directive, individualized dialogues related to his own life circumstances. In creating such individually specific scenarios, the therapist not only conveyed a sense of understanding and acceptance but also modeled problem-solving skills for Jason.

For CBPT to be effective, it should provide structured, goal-directed activities while, at the same time, allowing the child to bring spontaneous material to the sessions. Unstructured, spontaneously generated material from the child brings to therapy a part of the child that would be lost if the sessions were completely structured, and directed by the therapist. For example, when Jason says, "He keeps getting smacked cause he is so bad," he is bringing to therapy a clear statement about his own thoughts and perceptions of himself, and about how he feels when his mother hits him. On the other hand, when therapy is completely unstructured and nondirective, teaching of adaptive behaviors, such as problem-solving, cannot take place.

By presenting developmentally appropriate interventions, the therapist increased the chances that Jason would be able to participate and benefit from the treatment. Despite Jason's good intellectual skills, he has difficulty with emotionally loaded materials. Given this, much of the therapeutic interventions were structured to be concrete and to rely on nonverbal, as well as verbal, communication. A wide array of techniques and approaches can be incorporated into CBPT in order to provide this range of developmentally appropriate interventions. In addition to modeling, which is the core of CBPT, Jason's treatment included behavioral techniques, such as positive reinforcement and shaping, as well as cognitive techniques, such as identifying/changing maladaptive beliefs, learning positive self-statements, and bibliotherapy.

The importance of generalization and response prevention is highlighted in Jason's case by the therapist's efforts to help him make the connections between his thoughts, feelings, and behavior in therapy and in his natural environment. An example of this is the therapist's helping Jason see that his throwing things may be a reflection of his angry feelings. Similarly, the therapist identifies high-risk situations for Jason, such as his feelings when his mother pays more attention to his sister. The termination party might help Jason reinforce his sense of self-control and mastery related to his achievements in therapy.

BIBLIOGRAPHY

Anastasi, A. (1982). *Psychological testing* (5th ed). New York, New York: Macmillan.

Bandura, A. (1969). *Principles of behavior modification.* New York: Holt, Rinehart and Winston.

Beck, A.T. (1967). *Depression: Clinical, experimental, and theoretical aspects.* New York: Harper & Row.

Beck, A.T. (1970). Cognitive therapy: Nature and relation to behavior therapy. *Behavior Therapy, 1,* 184–200.

Beck, A.T. (1972). *Depression: Causes and treatment.* Philadelphia: University of Pennsylvania Press.

Beck, A.T. (1976). *Cognitive therapy and the emotional disorders.* New York: International Universities Press.

Beck, A.T., & Emery, G. (1985). *Anxiety disorders and phobias: A Cognitive perspective.* New York: Basic Books.

Bedrosian, R., & Beck, A.T. (1980). Principles of cognitive therapy. In M.J. Mahoney (Ed.), *Psychotherapy process: Current issues and future directions* (p. 128). New York: Plenum.

Bierman, K.L. (1983). Cognitive development and clinical interviews with children. In B.B. Lahey & A. Kazdin (Eds.), *Advances in clinical child psychology* (Vol. 6, pp. 217–250). New York: Plenum.

Braswell, L., & Kendall, P.C. (1988). K.S. Dobson (Eds.), *Cognitive-behavioral methods with children.* In *Handbook of Cognitive Behavior Therapy* (pp. 167–213). New York: Guilford.

Dodds, J.B. (1985). *A child psychotherapy primer.* New York: Human Sciences Press.

Ellis, A. (1962). *Reason and emotion in psychotherapy.* New York: Lyle Stuart.

Emery, G., Bedrosian, R., & Garber, J. (1983). Cognitive therapy with depressed children and adolescents. In D.P. Cantwell & G.A. Carlson (Eds.), *Affective disorders in childhood and adolescence—An update* (pp. 445–471). New York: Wiley.

Forehand, R., & McMahon, R.J. (1981). *Helping the noncompliant child: A Clinician's guide to parent training.* New York: Guilford.

Frank, L.K. (1939). Projective methods for the study of personality. *Journal of Consulting Psychology, 8,* 389–413.

Harrison, R., & Beck, A.T. (1982). Cognitive therapy for depression: Historical development, basic concepts and procedures. In P. Keller & L. Ritt (Eds.), *Innovations in clinical practice: A source book* (Vol. 1, pp. 37–52). Sarasota, FL: Professional Resource Exchange.

Harter, S. (1977). A cognitive-developmental approach to children's expression of conflicting feelings and a technique to facilitate such expression in play therapy. *Journal of Consulting and Clinical Psychology, 45,* 417–432.

Harter, S. (1983). Cognitive-developmental considerations in the conduct of play therapy. In C. Schaefer & K.J. O'Connor (Eds.), *Handbook of play therapy* (pp. 95–127). New York: Wiley.

Hughes, J.N., & Baker, D.B. (1990). *The clinical child interview.* New York: Guilford.

Johnston, C. (1991). Predicting mothers' and fathers' perceptions of child behaviour problems. *Canadian Journal of Behavioural Science, 23*, 349–358.

Knell, S.M. (1993a). *Cognitive-behavioral play therapy.* Northvale, NJ: Jason Aronson Inc.

Knell, S.M. (1993b). To show and not tell: Cognitive-behavioral play therapy in the treatment of Elective Mutism. In T. Kottman & C.E. Schaefer (Eds.), *Play therapy in action: A casebook for practitioners* (pp. 169–208). Northvale, NJ: Jason Aronson Inc.

Knell, S.M. (1994). Cognitive-behavioral play therapy. In K.J. O'Connor & C.E. Schaefer (Eds.)., *Handbook of play therapy: Vol. 2. Advances and innovations* (pp. 111–142). New York: Wiley.

Knell, S.M. & Moore, D.J. (1990). Cognitive-behavioral play therapy in the treatment of encopresis. *Journal of Child Clinical Psychology, 19*, 55–60.

Knell, S.M., & Ruma, C.D. (1996). Play therapy with a sexually abused child. In M. Reinecke, F.M. Dattilio, & A. Freeman (Eds.), *Cognitive therapy with children and adolescents: A Casebook for clinical practice* (pp. 367–393). New York: Guilford.

Marlatt, G.A., & Gordon, J.R. (1985). *Relapse prevention: Maintenance strategies in the treatment of addictive behaviors.* New York: Guilford.

Meichenbaum, D. (1971). Examination of model characteristics in reducing avoidance behavior. *Journal of Personality and Social Psychology, 17*, 298–307.

Meichenbaum, D. (1985). *Stress inoculation training.* New York: Pergamon.

Mischel, W. (1968). *Personality and assessment.* New York: Wiley.

Nemiroff, M.A., & Annunziata, J. (1990). *A child's first book about play therapy.* Washington, DC: APA.

Rachman, S. (1968). The role of muscular relaxation in desensitization therapy. *Behavior Research and Therapy, 6*, 159–166.

Ruma, C.D. (1993). Cognitive-behavioral play therapy with sexually abused children. In S.M. Knell (Ed.) *Cognitive-behavioral play therapy* (pp. 199–230). Northvale, NJ: Jason Aronson Inc.

Truax, C.B., & Carkhuff, R.R. (1967). *Toward effective counseling and psychotherapy: Training and practice.* Chicago: Aldine.

Wagner, M.K., & Cauthen, N.R. (1968). Case histories and shorter communications. *Behaviour Research and Therapy, 6*, 225–227.

Wallerstein, J.S., & Kelly, J.B. (1980). *Surviving the breakup.* New York: Basic Books.

Wolpe, J., & Lazarus, A.A. (1966). *Behavior therapy techniques: A guide to the treatment of neurosis.* New York: Pergamon.

CHAPTER 4

Jungian Play Psychotherapy

JOHN ALLAN

C.G. Jung (1875–1961) was a Swiss psychiatrist who collaborated with Freud from 1902 to 1912, when he broke contact because of fundamental disagreements over the nature of libido. The central human drive to Freud was sexual, and the main psychological task was the resolution of the oedipal complex. To Jung (1966), the central drive was the individuation process—the drive to separate from parental figures and to develop one's own unique personality and identity. To Jungians, the libido is fueled by the "struggle of opposites" (the desire to grow versus the desire to regress) but will change depending on a person's developmental stage; that is, the search for growth and meaning will be different for a teenager than for individuals in their eighties.

Though Jung never worked directly with children, his theory and treatment methods have a lot to offer child psychotherapists because of his belief in the self-healing potential of the psyche, the role of the archetypes in organizing human behavior, and the importance of the creative process (play, art, drama, writing) in healing and transformation. In 1902, Jung (1970) analyzed a child's dreams and indicated that the content reflected the unresolved struggles of the parents. Often children act out the unfinished and undeveloped sides of their parents. It is because of this that most Jungian child therapists will encourage the parents of the identified patient to seek their own therapy, thus enabling the child to become free of parental projections and to be able to develop and live out their own unique individuation process.

INTRODUCTION: THEORY

Structure of the Psyche

Jung's structure of the psyche is essentially tripartite: ego, personal unconscious, and collective unconscious. By ego he means an individual's conscious awareness—everything that a person is aware of about himself or herself and the surrounding world, including thoughts, feelings, fantasies, sensations and emotions. The ego is the center of consciousness and plays a critically important role in mediating between the demands of the "inner" (the personal and collective unconscious) and "outer" world (demands of parents, teachers, peers, and cultural norms). The personal unconscious is similar and yet different from Freud's concept of the id. The personal unconscious is the repository of both suppressed and repressed material—that is thoughts, feelings that are too painful for ego to look at or deal with (i.e., loss, grief, sadness, rage, hatred, envy, hopelessness, and lust) as well as undeveloped potentials, new and different sides of one's personality (i.e., typology). For example, if a child like Jason were genetically an extroverted, thinking, sensing, judging type (Jung, 1971), then his personal unconscious would contain the potential for introversion, feeling, intuition, and perception. One would expect that these are attributes that would develop in play therapy (because of the "free and protected space") and the opportunity to enact various roles with play therapy materials.

Below the personal unconscious is the area of the psyche that Jung (1968) termed the "collective unconscious" that he saw as containing the archetypes and especially the central organizing archetype of the self. By archetype, Jung meant instincts coupled with images that direct and influence behavior and emotions. Archetypes are biological forces and drives in the unconscious that often transcend culture, are found universally, and bring a certain similarity to the human experience. Archetypes center around such images of birth, death, love, the divine child, the great mother, the trickster, God, and the Devil; they have both positive and negative attributes; and they are seen in the world's great religions, myths, dreams, and folklore as well as on television and in advertising.

The drawing of a hand can be used to illustrate this tripartite construction, where the separate fingers represent an individual's consciousness and unique personal unconscious and the palm and wrist the archetypal communality we share with each other (Figure 4.1). The line drawn across the fingers is purposely varied to represent different levels of consciousness: Some people have little awareness of themselves or life, while others may have considerable awareness, verging on wisdom.

Personality Theory: Development of the Ego

A central tenet in analytical psychology (Jung's term for his theory) is the ego–self axis. This concept refers to the nature of the relationship between the conscious (ego) and unconscious mind (self). In healthy people there is a fluid yet regulated connection between the two zones. Ego is able to express thoughts and feeling in an appropriate and balanced way while holding in check various inappropriate actions.

At birth, the ego (Neumann, 1973) is embedded in the archetype of the self (i.e., in the unconscious). The ego develops during infancy and early childhood by a process of "de-integration and re-integration" (Fordham, 1994); that is, the ego fragments under the normal pressures of hunger, discomfort, and pain and re-integrates when comforting is provided. This pattern happens repeatedly in infancy, but a critical ingredient is how well the caretakers (mother/father) mediate the infant's distress and bring about calming and comforting in human contact. If this happens sufficiently well and frequently enough, then the infant develops positive parental introjects (*mother/father imagoes,* in Jungian terms) as well as good enough feelings about self and becomes securely attached. Concomitant with this is the devel-

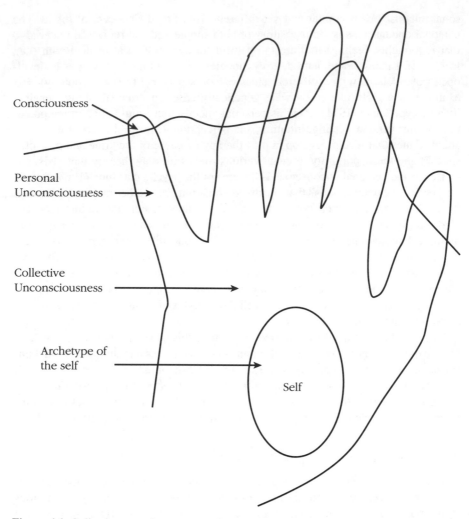

Consciousness

Personal
Unconsciousness

Collective
Unconsciousness

Archetype of
the self

Self

Figure 4.1 Collective consciousness.

opment of effective coping skills and ego defenses that later allow children (then adults) to handle their emotional life effectively. This involves the ability to integrate into awareness both good and bad feelings without resorting to an excessive amount of denial, repression, splitting, and projective identification. Healthy children laugh, sob, get angry, love, and enjoy their bodies at play.

Where the de-integration process is not met with quality interpersonal calming and comforting, then negative or attacking mother and father imagoes are introjected and ego defenses become either overly rigid or minimally functioned (Allan & Bertoia, 1992). Children growing up under such conditions are often seen as (1) overly controlled, (2) lacking in controls, or (3) prone to snapping when ego defenses suddenly break down under extreme pressure. (An example of this would be when the police became confrontational with Jason and he "broke down and sobbed for nearly 15 minutes.") Emotionally wounded children use primitive defense mechanisms, blame others for their problems, separate thinking and feeling, and hence, like Jason, are unconscious of their painful feelings and deny that there are any problems.

Development of the Personality

As the growing child moves out of the home into the community and the world of other children and adults, there is a strong pressure to conform to the norms and standards of the local culture (collective consciousness). Jung (1968) argues that even a young child's psyche is equipped to handle this. His belief is that just as the human body has evolved so has the psyche, and it has embedded in it structures that facilitate both adaptation and survival. One of the first archetypal structures to be formed is the "persona"—the social mask. The persona, like all archetypes, has both positive and negative aspects. A flexible persona allows the person to interact effectively with other members of his or her community while maintaining his or her unique identity and emotional spontaneity. However, an overly rigid persona implies that a person's ego has become fused with the persona and the individual becomes a shell of a person, never developing a true identity and hiding behind a socially acceptable role or mask. The converse is also true: Some children fail to develop a persona and remain unsocialized, developing no healthy defenses against their unconscious impulses and no skills at relating to others or adapting to social norms.

Directly related to the persona and ego is the "shadow," as it contains and reflects the underside of both. What is not acceptable to ego and persona is relegated into the shadow, as it contains repressed, unacceptable, and undeveloped aspects of the conscious personality. The shadow typically splits off from consciousness and manifests itself in destructive or disturbing behavior, which is often denied by the client. It is hard to face and own one's dark and destructive side. People would be seen as being possessed by the archetypal component of the shadow when they believe they are the Devil or evil incarnate. However, the shadow, in Jungian terms, is not all negative inasmuch as it is often the center of artistic ability where creative impulses and those impulses that challenge the status quo arise. In children, this is the area of the psyche that produces images of monsters and night terrors.

Underneath the shadow is the "syzergy"—the contra sexual aspects, the images of the feminine in males ("the anima") and the images of the masculine in females ("animus"). These images exert a powerful force in the human psyche leading to idealization (and denigration) of the opposite sex and resulting in mate selection and "falling in love." Equally important to Jung is the energy source that these archetypes provide and the opportunity for both sexes to develop what we call the "male" and "female" sides—to psychologically balance the opposite side to their dominant genetic structure. This would manifest itself in a person's ability to be both assertive and receptive, firm and caring at the same time.

Below the syzergy is the central organizing archetype, the archetype of the "self." This is the engine of the psyche. The self orchestrates the unconscious and its dream and play process. It strives toward balance and wholeness. Its energy tries to lead the psyche forward toward growth and unfolding. It is the inner voice of the psyche: It is a person's soul and it speaks a different language than the language of the ego. Rather than using words as such, the self speaks in the language of image, symbol, and metaphor. Because of this the self often feels a little alien to the ego, especially when manifested in dreams.

The energy that drives the self, the "libido," comes from the struggle of opposites, the struggle between the desire to grow and the desire to regress. The strength of these drives will vary from person to person, depending on the combination of genetic and environmental factors. How libido manifests itself in consciousness will depend on a person's typology. Different cultures value different typological structures at different times in their evolution; extroverted, thinking, sensation, judging types tend to do well in American educational institutions and in social situations. Libido can be discharged successfully into activities that are valued by the culture. Despite this advantage, psychological growth and health are seen as the maintenance of a balance between the inner and outer world—that is having the ability to function in the outer world, to successfully complete the various developmental stages and tasks while at the same time maintaining contact with one's unique inner identity.

Model of Psychopathology

Psychopathology occurs in the Jungian system when the ego defenses become maladaptive and block the flow of energy through the ego–self axis. Defenses become rigidified when the ego cannot handle emotional pain and resorts to an overabundant use of repression, splitting, and projection and projective identification. (Jung's disagreements with Freud stemmed from the nature of libido and the nature of treatment, not around the ego's mechanisms of defense.) Rigid defense mechanisms become activated when there is a repeated failure on the part of the caretakers to mediate successfully between the infant's inner needs and the outer world. This would involve a failure or inability to provide sufficient cycles of tension to calming and distress to comforting in human contact, or failure to mirror the child in accordance with the child's innate typological structure. This lack of mirroring or attunement results in the child's erecting defensive postures to protect himself or herself from feeling the pain of rejection. The postures would center around erecting a persona (or false self) that would mirror the caretaker's demands or expectations rather than expressing one's true self. Splitting would occur, resulting in images of the "bad mother or father" being repressed into the personal unconscious while idealized images of the parental images might be found in ego consciousness. The child would tend to feel deflated and inadequate, trying to live up to idealized expectations while at the same time repressing and projecting his or her hostility onto adult authority figures (such as parents and teachers) and experiencing them as acting in a persecutory fashion. Young infants and toddlers are so emotionally sensitive (as ego boundaries are weak) that they will absorb the tension and emotional affects of the parent and strive (unconsciously) to adapt to or resolve them.

Trauma also affects the psyche in a negative way by increasing defensiveness in order to protect ego from being overwhelmed by pain. Reaction to trauma will vary depending on the trauma and the intensity of it. Physical and sexual abuse will often result in dissociated states, while breaks of attachment will result in anger and despair. Energy will then be taken away from (i.e., will not be available for) healthy ego development, positive human interactions, and learning. The repressed anger results in negative motivational patterns that reveal themselves in resistance to learning (daydreaming), negativism, and anger outbursts. In Jungian terms, the repression, splitting, and dissociated states result in "autonomous complexes" (Jacobi, 1959). These are areas embedded in the unconscious that seem to take on a life of their own and result in acting out behaviors over which an individual seems to have little or no control. Complex-driven behavior is compulsive, and a person's ego is often unable to understand or control it (i.e., it seems like an "alien force").

In the case of psychosis, the ego decompensates and/or fragments under the duress of psychological pain, which results in the emergence of archetypal energies or symbols in an unchecked way. The archetype of the self dominates the ego, and a person may believe he or she is Christ or the Devil, or in the case of a child that the author treated, a seagull (Allan & MacDonald, 1975).

Goal of Treatment

The goal of treatment from a Jungian perspective is the activation of the individuation process. Basically this means helping the child to develop his or her unique identity, to overcome or come to terms with his or her losses or traumas while accepting and adapting to the healthy demands of family, school, and society at large. This encompasses Jung's concept of the "struggle or opposites"—the psychological task for all of us is to be our unique self while living in society as long as this does not involve harming self, harming others, or being harmed.

The therapeutic goals are to (1) activate the self-healing potential in the child's psyche, (2) strengthen the ego self (i.e., the connection and flow between the child's conscious and unconscious parts), (3) stimulate and develop creativity and imagination, (4) heal and transcend wounds, (5) develop an interior life, (6) develop a sense of competency and mastery, (7) develop the skills to cope with future problems, and (8) understand the complexity of life and be open to change. In summary, the goal of Jungian psychotherapy is to activate the individuation process so the client can live in relationship with himself or herself and the outer world.

CASE FORMULATION

The Rhythm of Play Therapy

Jungians see therapy as occurring in "a safe and protected space," the playroom, in a time "out of ordinary time." Jungians play particular attention to the entrance and exit phases of treatment—that is, how the child transitions into the playroom and back out of the playroom at the end of the session, as he or she reenters ordinary time. Therapy is like a ritualized experience as a child moves from the profane to "sacred time" (i.e., the therapy) and back into the profane. There is a shift, then, from the predominance of the ego (conscious reality to, in the actual therapy, a predominance of the self (i.e., the archetypal patterns and dramas of the play themes). Between the entrance and exit phase is the "working phase", where the child is deeply engrossed in the activity of play psychotherapy—sometimes so deeply it seems as if he or she is in a trance. Allan and Berry (1987) have noticed that the working phase often goes through three distinct stages: chaos, struggle (between "good and bad forces"—hero versus villain), and reparation and resolution. Some children who have been very wounded never drop down into the healing depths of play therapy and remain stuck in avoidance behavior. This fear of relationship often reflects violations of trust and needs to be interpreted for growth to occur. This rhythm or flow of the play therapy process is shown in Figure 4.2

While the diagram illustrates a typical pattern of treatment, over time the actual flow will vary from child to child. Some may enter treatment directly in the struggle phase (as with Jason*) while a few may start with reparative motifs before regressing into chaos and struggle.

Jungians are clinically trained, and most have a standard background in the mental health disciplines—psychiatry, psychology, and social work. Case formulation is based on case history notes and family of origin issues, sometimes including genograms, psychological assessment, and assessment in the first few sessions of play therapy. Often the first play therapy session or sand world gives a glimpse of some of the core wounds (Allan & Lawton-Speert, 1993). More attention tends to be given to projective material—play, art, sand world, fantasy stories—than to standard IQ tests, as the former reveal conflicts and struggles in the unconscious of the child, illuminating natural strengths as well as struggles. Often very early on the child may pick one or two symbolic figures or a particular medium that acts as the main vehicle for growth—similar to a transitional object (Winnicott, 1971).

Through examining the intake protocol, various situations would stand out for a Jungian. As Jung noted, children tend to act out the unfinished psychological struggles of the parents. Being more immature biological organisms (i.e., with fewer defenses), they would be sensitive to what is repressed in the parents and act that out in order to help the parents look at and resolve what is troubling them. However, children need to be treated in their own right (Fordham, 1994) in order to help them differentiate their own struggles from those of their parents, to externalize painful introjects and to develop their own unique style and life.

Based on his family of origin, one would expect that Jason would be struggling with his pain and anger over his parents' divorce. In addition, there would probably be racial identity issues ("to which culture do I belong?"), possible guilt over his parents' divorce ("Did I cause it?"), and additional spiritual guilt because his parents have both broken a vow of their religion and absorbed depression (and maybe guilt) over the death of baby brother. If the mother and father are shocked and de-

---

*See "Orientation to the Text: The Case of Jason L.," p. 1.

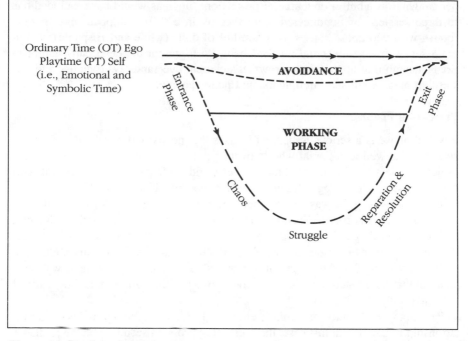

Figure 4.2 Rhythm of play therapy.

pressed, it would be expected that Jason would feel their pain and might be somewhat neglected due to their natural self-absorption with their hurts. One would imagine, too, that he would be struggling with normal love-hate ambivalence toward his sister, Carla. The physical splitting of the family can psychologically painful for both children, but, because of identity issues, it may be excruciatingly painful for Jason. This may result in uncontrolled aggression and fiery feelings, especially toward his mother.

All of these are "soft hypotheses"—to be either borne out or dropped as the case unfolds. Jungians live and work with uncertainty; nothing is known for sure. What is missing from the identifying information is the multigenerational genogram of the parents, the reasons why they married, what they hoped for and what went wrong in their relationship, and whether they received any help when their child died. The play therapist also considers that much of the source of information is from the mother. In any reporting, one bears in mind the role of projection even with "scientific data."

Logistics

The play therapist noted that the mother made the initial contact, which shows both some ego strength and concern, but also noted that she did not mention her referral source. The fact that she brought Carla to the initial appointment when encouraged not to may mean a number of different things—she could not afford a sitter, she may not have friends or family members to take care of the child, or she needed her daughter as a buffer or source of protection. Jungians would have included one to three sessions of nondirective play therapy in a fully equipped play therapy room—with two dolls' houses, two families of dolls (white and Hispanic) including a set of grandparents and a naked baby (to represent the dead baby and/or to act as a symbol of hope or new growth), a church, two sandtrays (one dry and one wet), art area, telephone, firefighters, and police people.

Presenting Problem

Physical abuse is a serious issue, and bruises that persist indicate hard and excessive force as well as a parent who is overwhelmed and out of control. There was projective identification on both the mother's and son's part—they acted out their own and each other's rage. Jason showed oppositional behavior. However, with skillful interviewing he was able to open up, to report on his world, and to identify some pain over his parents' divorce. This reflected some ego strength on his part and was seen as a good prognosis: He can identify and talk about some of his feeling directly. The aggression does not seem to be activated with the father, although he has unrealistic "macho" expectations of his son. Jason's ego strength was seen again in that he insisted that his father come to the testing with him and do most of the initial talking.

To Jung (1973), much of a child's emotional life is determined by his or her relationship to parents. In this case, the presenting problem seems to be the mother's relationship to Jason and her own emotional wounds. However, it is not yet clear what role the father played or did not play in this. Despite these facts, Jungians are insistent that children need to be seen as individuals and treated in their own right (Allan, 1988).

Both parents demonstrated some sensitivity and strength in their handling of Jason: The mother sensed his need for space and a transition time from school to home, and father engaged him in aggressive release play. Mother was the provider but fostered undue dependency, while father encouraged developmental involvement in tasks and food preparation. Jason indicated a parental preference (identification) for his father. The fact that Jason played with his sister and showed empathy for her reflects, once again, some real ego strength.

Developmental History

The issue of Mary's health and anxiety stand out here, which led to a type of anxious-ambivalent attachment. "Irritable" babies are often hard to calm, but Jason seems to have responded well to holding and rocking. However, babies who sleep a lot tend to have control problems later on (Allan, 1976) because of the lack of contact and stimulation, especially in terms of initiation and termination sequences of interaction. However, Jason showed some emotional constancy (Mahler, Pine, & Bergman, 1975) in that he functioned in preschool and demonstrated determination, curiosity, and a high exploratory drive. As Mary was the primary caretaker she received the brunt of his hostility. It is interesting that the interviewer did not ask the mother about her feelings about the death of her baby and how her feelings and behavior toward Jason might have changed as a consequence. Nor did the interviewer try to ascertain the degree of the father's involvement in the first three years of parenting.

Mental Status

This examination indicated an intact persona (Jason could relate well with the interviewer) but a guarded personality that resorted to the use of splitting defense mechanisms (i.e., was unable to talk about anything negative). He seemed in touch with reality without suicidal or homicidal impulses. Because of his distinct Hispanic appearance Jason was assigned an Hispanic male Jungian child analyst intern, as this was deemed beneficial for his identity formation and role-modeling. It was positive that he could verbalize his wish for mom and dad to be remarried. His wish for "lots of money and baseball cards" was seen as compensating transitional objects based on the failure to introject the "good breast" experience. In other words, his interior psychological life was at a disadvantage because he had not yet introjected the "good enough" mothering experience. (The playroom included both an Anglo and Hispanic mother doll to provide an opportunity to work through themes of splitting and reparation.) Jason's "mother complex" (Jacobi, 1959) activated "hatred of all women" and was seen in his negativism to his female teacher, Mrs. J., while such a projection was not activated with the male student teacher.

From a Jungian perspective, the fire setting was a major issue and reflected the "calcination" process, the intense heating of his emotions (Edinger, 1985) and the repression and projection of his inflammatory rage. Jungians include fire engines, firefighters, and "pretend" matches in the playroom. Real matches, like real food, were not included in the playroom because play therapy is not about gratification, but rather about activating the imagination to solve complex emotional issues. (The safe use of matches was something that could be practiced with the mother or father at home.) In the examination by the police, one sees the process that Jungians (Fordham, 1994) would call de-integration (i.e., sobbing), which would be seen as a positive sign that ego defenses were not that rigidly entrenched.

Family History and Dynamics

Of the two families, the mother's revealed more serious losses—the divorce of her parents and the sudden death of her father. It seemed that Mary was not getting the emotional support she needed from her own mother and that at times she would be incapacitated by her depression and hence unavailable to her children. In regards to Emilio, it seemed that his cultural conditioning and archetypal projection prevented him from seeking the person behind the roles of mother or wife. As a result, he was "unable" to see his wife's pain and to respond to it in a caring way. Through the modeling process this would have negatively impacted on Jason, who in turn had a tendency to devalue the feminine in others and in himself.

The loss of a baby often has devastating long-term effects on mothers and fathers, especially when coupled with prior losses. It is interesting to note that as the mother became sexually unavailable due to her depression, Emilio was unable to help her or them seek couple counseling and acted out sexually, thus adding another devastating loss to the mother. Jungians would see this as an anima problem in the father, and when Jason came in for individual play therapy they recommended that both the parents see their own therapists before having joint sessions to talk about parenting and family of origin issues.

Pretreatment Assessment Data

Psychological tests were useful because they give a picture of the child's internal working model of self—in relation to others and intellectual ability. Jason's test scores indicated both strengths and areas of concern. The projective tests indicated issues of power struggles with bosses, concerns over justice (i.e., what is fair or unfair) and an inability to contain his anger, which emerged in a self-destructive pattern. Like the girl in the TAT, he did not feel good about himself. One saw him making rudimentary attempts to handle these feelings and also admitting that he wanted to be liked and trusted. The Rorschach findings once again supported his adequate perceptual processing abilities but indicated his defensiveness and the fact that his responses were not enlivened by feeling. This is supported in both the HFD and the KFD. The HFD reflected his male identity but also his persona, through which he controlled his feelings and hid his real self. The KFD revealed the split in the family, the physical separation of masculine and feminine, his emotional distancing from the mother, and his identification with the father. The fact that they were not "doing anything" reflected an affectless and impaired family life. The WISC-III, while indicating above-average intelligence, also suggested difficulty in transferring from perception into psychomotor activity and in understanding social transactions. DTORF-R suggested again the introjection of a negative self-concept, as well as difficulties controlling his body and with peer interactions. These could be worked on by introducing into the playroom a punching bag and soft throwing balls so that the therapist could help Jason couple action (hitting, throwing) with words ("I'm mad at you . . . I'm mad at you for. . . ."). If his peer-friendship patterns did not change or improve after play therapy, he could be referred to an activity group therapy.

The CBCL captures an essential element that other forms of enquiry missed—both parents tended to minimize Jason's problems and hence, by the mechanism of projection, deny or minimize their own issues. He was seen as the "identified patient", and one task of the therapist would be to get the parents into their own treatment so, in a systemic way, Jason was not carrying or acting out what Jungians would term the parents' shadow sides (i.e., their unfinished business and/or underdeveloped potentials).

Marschak Interaction Method

On the "draw our house" task, the comparison between mother and father was a little unfair because the mother was faced with working through the initial resistance. So, because Jason had already successfully completed the task once, it would be easier to do it the second time with father. In view of that, this first task showed that mother's style was a bit mechanical (i.e., emotionally flat) but that she was able to work through his resistance by the use of persistence and praise to help him achieve a satisfactory end point. The father, on the other hand, was able to form a strong alliance with his son by bringing emotion into his voice and by verbalizing how difficult the task could be. Jason rose to the challenge and father continued to praise him and boost his ego. This had a positive effect on Jason, which in turn improved his performance.

With the body lotion, both parents demonstrated a "good enough" relationship with Jason, but once again the father's style—with the use of humor, creativity, and an understanding of "boys"—brought out the best results. However, mother and Jason worked through difficulties to end with a good connection.

The sharing M&Ms task showed the father with superior problem-solving skills. Though the mother was able to set limits and have the children respond to those limits, she acted in an autocratic way, whereas the father brought the children into the problem-solving tasks and came up with a solution that incorporated both of their inputs. The feeling tone at the end was one of pleasure and relaxed communication.

Summary of Case Formulation

When he told his teacher that the bruises on his face were the result of having been smacked by his mother, Jason was referred for assessment and treatment to Child Protective Services. The primary identified patient was not Jason but the mother, and she needed a referral for treatment. Knowing this frees the Jungian child therapist to concentrate on the work with the child in the playroom to help the child externalize inner struggles, then re-introject new feelings and learn new behaviors. Later, after the inner work has been done by both mother and child, the therapy would end with both of them in the playroom for three to five sessions. Ideally it would be the mother and father doing their therapy work together, followed by mother and father in the playroom with Jason, and ending with mother, father, Carla, and Jason.

Jason's current problems are a function of the ambivalent insecure-anxious pattern of attachment to his mother, his physical abuse by the mother, and the adjustment reaction to his parents' divorce. The tension from the mother's unresolved emotional issues are felt and absorbed by Jason's sensory-motor and emotional systems, resulting in frustration and anger at her and the failure to internalize the "satisfied, good enough feeling". Instead of experiencing and internalizing the belief "the world is okay, I am okay, and I can get some of my needs met" he is left with an internal working model that says "the world is a frustrating place, I'm not okay (especially around women), and I experience a lot of frustration and failure." Typically, the origins of play start on the mother's body around the breast, nipple, and/or baby bottle (or with the feminine side of the father) and, as Jason's early experiences were characterized by irritability, loss of sleep, and the mother's worry, it seemed the mother and father were not able to transform his bodily tensions into relaxation, trust, intimacy, and playfulness. His current problems reflected this damage by introjected early experiences, and because he did not feel internally satisfied he resorted to control in an attempt to get what he thought he needed. This, of course, was added to by the divorce and his rage over the parents' physical separation and his living away from his dad. This pain was compounded because he was in the latency stage of development, where he was working on issues around his male identity.

From a Jungian perspective, Jason would be seen as having a mother complex—a wound in the area of mother-child relationship that would leave him feeling internally dissatisfied and probably reactive and controlling of women in the outer world. He would handle his pain by resorting to such defense mechanisms as denial, repression, projection, and projective identification. This made him manipulative and controlling of others. He forced them to try to be a particular way in order to (1) get his needs met, and (2) have them act out his pain, frustration, and anger so he could feel he was in the right and they were wrong. These defensive patterns blocked his ego–self axis, resulting in emotionally flattened behavior and a lack of spontaneity and creativity. A Jungian would expect a rigid persona (mask) and a hidden shadow side (i.e., his aggression would be buried and would break out in secret manipulative behavior). The counterpart of this would be the absence of the healthy archetypal trickster—or the playful naughty boy who is teasing and cracking jokes. In Jungian psychology the trickster is the carrier of play and creativity and is a very healthy sign. The trickster takes on the rigidity of the status quo (the "senex" functions) and can bring about beneficial changes in rigid and boring adults and repressive educational institutions.

One always has to differentiate with children whether their problems and behaviors are normal developmental struggles or indicative of deeper wounds. Playing with matches and fire is a common stage; however, in Jason's situation, because of the failure of positive mother-son interactions and the effects of the divorce, the therapist was concerned about his repressed feelings of incendiary rage. This repressed rage had a detrimental effect on Jason's motivation and resulted in oppositional and negative behaviors that hindered both his psychological and cognitive growth and peer relations.

Jason's Strengths

Jason does have real psychological problems that need treatment, but his strengths and those of his parents were real, too. His defenses were not so entrenched that he was unable to show genuine feeling; he was able to break down and sob when questioned by the police, and both mother and father were able to elicit smiles, laughter, and overcome his resistances. He had good reality testing ability and was of above-average intelligence.

TREATMENT GOALS

Jason was seen as part of a psychological system, so for treatment to be successful, key players in the system were also treated.

Engagement with the Parents

Though the parents were divorced, it was still critical to get both of them to see the need for therapy—especially play psychotherapy—for Jason. This was crucial because the case study suggested that they both tended to minimize the seriousness of his problems. Once they believed it was helpful for Jason, they were informed that research at the Jungian Family and Children's Clinic has shown that improvement with the child is greatly enhanced when the parents meet with a therapist to talk over their own issues and the struggles and difficulties they are having with their child. As they were divorced, they wanted to meet separately with a therapist, but later they decided to have a few joint sessions.

Engagement with the Mother

As some of Jason's problems stem from his relationship with his mother and because of her early trauma (parents' divorce and her father's death), it was important for Mary to enter Jungian analysis. This gave her an opportunity to understand the effects of her own losses, fears, and anxieties as well as the chance to mourn the loss of her second baby. As the mother became more differentiated, she was in a better position to understand her typological structure as well as that of Jason and Emilio, thus improving the chances of better relationships. Her own psychotherapy helped her become psychologically stronger and also less enmeshed with Carla.

Engagement with the Father

From a Jungian frame, Emilio needed help with his depressed anima side. On one level, his unconscious attraction to his ex-wife enabled him to project his depression onto her so he would feel "fine" as long as she carried it for him. His analysis focused on helping him share and work on his own pain so he could heal his inner feminine (his anima) and develop a better relationship with himself and women. Some of this therapeutic work centered around helping him understand the devaluating and/or idealization of women in his own family, religion, and culture.

Play Psychotherapy of Jason

The goal of treatment was to (1) establish rapport and a therapeutic alliance, (2) provide a safe and protected space (the playroom) where attachment, regression, and working through of psychological problems can occur, (3) deal with issues of failure of attunement, emotional deprivation, rage, mourning, and loss, (4) activate creativity, imagination, and play, and (5) provide symbolic opportunities for healing. It is through play that children are able to externalize their wounds and struggles, develop a sense of well-being, competency, and mastery, and introject new "good enough" feelings.

Intervention with the School

Jung was always concerned with linking the inner and outer worlds and achieving a balance between the two. The Jungian child psychotherapist informed the parents and the child that he would maintain contact with the school, the principal, and the teacher. In this way, the therapist got to hear the concerns of the school personnel, built an ongoing relationship with them, and monitored the child's progress. Sometimes themes emerge in the playroom that the teacher can build on in the classroom (Allan & Brown, 1993) and sometimes things happen at school that need to be discussed in the playroom.

Successful Termination

Good treatment approaches termination consciously. Children need to be prepared for the end of individual therapy. In long-term cases (over a year), children will need at least six weeks' preparation time, whereas in short-term cases probably a month will suffice. Cases are slowly reduced from once a week to twice a month and eventually monthly. Another way to approach termination is to move from individual therapy to filial therapy, and then to end with a few sessions of family therapy. Jungians prefer a model of separate treatment sessions (six months to a year) at first in order to facilitate separation and the emergence of one's own identity (i.e., the activation of the individuation process).

TREATMENT DESCRIPTION

Logistics

Setting

Jason and his family members were seen in the Jungian Family and Children's Clinic. This clinic had staff trained to do individual play psychotherapy, adult analysis, and couple, family, and filial therapy. It has a reception area with a family-style waiting room, four individual play therapy rooms with one-way mirrors into observation rooms, and video recording devices plus a children's washroom off each play therapy room. The clinic also contains six adult offices and four group or family therapy rooms, also with video equipment. The parents were told that the center is a research and training facility and were encouraged to sign consent forms for videotaping, with their concern for confidentiality and privacy being honored. The rooms are well soundproofed. Jason, his mother, and father were assigned different therapists—Jason, a Hispanic male intern, the mother an experienced female analyst, and the father a male analyst with a well-developed anima (or strong feeling function). The male and female analysts also saw the couple together and had Jason's therapist sit in every now and again to hear the parents' view on Jason and to comment globally on his progress. The Hispanic male intern was important for Jason's identity, and an intern was judged suitable for the case because Jason's wounds were not deemed that profound or difficult to ameliorate.

Picking the play media is an important part of play therapy because toys have to be selected that provide for discharge of tension, for externalization of specific struggles and traumas, and for healing and reparation. The Jungian therapist looks for wounds in the child's life and for personal and cultural symbols that may have specific and unique meaning for the child. Intake assessment and psychological testing often reveal this information.

Jason had been hit and physically abused, so he needed outlets for his physical aggression—just as some physically abused children often need to hit out to equal the score before they can let go of their anger and experience their hurt and sad feelings. Jason needed a punching Bobo clown, big pillows and cushions so that he could throw or hit, nerf balls, bataca fighting sticks (cloth ones), crocodile puppets, and boxing gloves. These toys provided outlets for his narcissistic rage over his emotional loss of mother during her depression, his displacement over the birth of his sister, and his feelings about the divorce and separation.

In order to get relief from his "monstrous feelings," stirred up by these experiences, he needed a combination of snakes, monsters, dinosaurs, "evil" characters, witches, devils, robots, spiders, and cobwebs (particularly useful for enmeshed and insecure ambivalently attached children with mother complexes). He also required superhero men and women to develop the ego functions of the heroic struggle against all odds and to activate the belief that women are strong, competent, and capable.

As Jason was involved with a fire-setting incident and subsequently the police and the legal system, it was important to have fire trucks, firefighters, police cars, handcuffs, rope, and police—as well as a jail, judges, and lawyers, especially as these themes came up in the TAT. Jason had to learn to deal with, understand, and channel his incendiary rage and issues of fairness and justice. Board games and card games were useful for dealing with rules. Card 2 on the TAT told about his hatred of school, so a schoolhouse, chalkboard, and some children's books with the theme "I hate school" were placed in the playroom.

Because of difficulties with mother and tension in the family, a large dolls' house was selected with bedrooms, bathrooms, kitchen and living area, and a family of small dolls with detachable clothes. Two other doll families— one Caucasian and the other Hispanic—and Catholic artifacts were added to the room to help Jason deal with issues of cultural identity and religion. Also added was a "crying baby" to represent both Jason's infantile pain and the dead baby.

In order for healing and reparation to occur, there needed to be a baby bottle, a small comfortable bed (2 × 3 feet) with pillows and blankets, hospital, ambulance, doctors and nurses, medication including Band-Aids®, two telephones, kitchen area, tea set, and pretend food. Building toys like Legos® wood blocks, and cardboard boxes were also part of the reconstructive activities. As creativity and imagination are important to Jungians for psychological health, there was an arts and craft area for painting, drawing, crayoning, collage, and plastercine.

A central area of the playroom for a Jungian would be the child's sink, two sand-trays (one wet and one dry), and shelves (child height) with groupings of miniature toys (Allan & Berry, 1987; Mitchell & Friedman, 1994). Water is very important for healing (i.e., washing away dirt or "dirty feelings"), and the sand world is where children can externalize their inner struggles, can get a handle on complex and difficult feelings by manipulating and moving the miniature toys and by creating their own worlds or life spaces. From a Jungian perspective the miniature figures represent different emotions and different feeling tones: The child projects these feelings into the figures and the feeling tone changes and grows. Emotions that were stuck, blocked, or trapped become free, are experienced in consciousness and integrated into the total personality. In doing so, libido that was used to maintain defenses is now freed for expansion, curiosity, exploration, growth, and learning. Humor and a healthy emotional vitality is often seen. Jason was given his own box, with his name on it, in which he put his special toys or projects and which was brought in at the start of each session and taken out at the end.

Frequency and Duration of Treatment

Jason was seen once a week for probably ten months, and his mother was seen separately at the same time. This helped in terms of logistics. The session lasted 40 to 50 minutes, which gave the play therapist time to clean the room, make a few notes, and relax briefly before the next session. The therapeutic frame was securely established—same time each week in the same playroom. The therapist underlay the importance of this right at the start of treatment and explained the reason to the mother. Holiday times, including the therapist's attending play therapy conferences, were spelled out well ahead of the time. Jung (1967), borrowing a term from alchemy, called this the *vas bene clausam*—the well-sealed container or vessel. Jungian psychotherapy is about the expression and transformation of emotion. In order for psychological growth to occur, the therapist must provide the *temenos*— the safe and protected space, the sacred space that can hold the tension of opposites so that the transcendent functions can be activated. In other words, out of a seemingly impossible conflict a new symbol or attitude can emerge from the client that is experienced as a resolution of a problem or a shift in identity.

Specific Strategies

Rapport

The strategies that a Jungian therapist will use will depend on the stage of therapy that the child is in and the stage of the child's ego development. Basically, the therapist starts with empathy, rapport, and relationship building. The therapist tries to help the child feel safe and at ease and to create an atmosphere that the room is a safe and protected space where the child can play, more or less as he or she wants.

Treatment Philosophy

The Jungian approach is to "stay at the level of feeling of the child" and to follow the child's dramas and plays as they unfold. The therapist *witnesses* the child's play, reflects feelings, and comments on them. The therapist takes his or her lead from the child. The therapist is essentially developing a feeling-toned relationship with the child, while mirroring and being attuned, and giving words to the range of feelings and thoughts that are being expressed or enacted.

Limits

Limits are not specifically set; rather the therapist waits until they are needed. For example, when Jason started pushing sand over the edge of the sandbox, the therapist would say "Jason, the sand has to stay in the sandbox." When Jason persisted with the behavior, the therapist reflected the intent of the behavior and gave the consequence to breaking the limit: "Jason, I wonder if you're trying to let me know that you believe you're the boss here and you set the rules and it kind of makes you mad when I say what they are? . . . If the sand goes on the floor again I'll have to put the lid on the sandtray for the rest of today's session."

JUNGIAN PLAY PSYCHOTHERAPY

Therapist as a Player

Jung differed from Freud in that he believed therapy was an existential encounter between two people and that if the therapy was going to be any good both parties changed. Some Jungian child therapists take on and enact the roles assigned to them by the child as, for example, when the child says, "You be the bad guy and I'll be the cop." At the start, it is important that the child constructs the therapist's role as the bad guy (Th: "Okay, but what do I do? Where am I? What do I say? What happens next? Where do I end up? How do I feel? etc.). A "time-out" signal and procedure is put in place beforehand: "Okay, if we get lost or stuck, either of us can call: Time-out (demonstrate T hand sign), then we can talk about what happens next." This enables both the child and the therapist to step out of the role. It is an important strategy because it gives the child's ego an opportunity to be involved in very strong feelings and at the same time to disengage and reflect on the experience. Usually children are overwhelmed by feelings and have poor controls, and this approach tries to rectify that by modeling and giving them a control mechanism.

The beauty of play is that it lets one say things that one normally would not say. For example, if the therapist is enacting a role prescribed by the child and starts to feel painful and unpleasant feelings in that role, the therapist can voice these as an aside in the form of soliloquy. In this way, through the transference, the therapist is making conscious the painful unconscious feelings of the child. He or she is giving words to experiences that the child cannot verbalize because they are so painful. For example, when playing the role of the "bad boy in the class" and if the therapist starts to feel like a failure, he can verbalize those feelings as an aside: "I feel stupid . . . I feel like a failure . . . I can't do the work . . . I feel hopeless . . . I'll never be able to do this . . . Life will never change . . . No one will ever like me. . . ."

The Analytical Attitude

During play therapy the therapist is essentially an observer-participant, both attached and detached at the same time. What makes play into therapy is the ability of the therapist to think analytically about everything that is going on in the room—what is happening verbally, nonverbally, and symbolically in the play and art work. Jungians see the analytical attitude as essential to the successful outcome. The therapist's thinking about the play and the child and understanding in-depth "what all this means" seem to have a beneficial effect on the child's growth and ego development. The therapist, so to speak, takes on some of the child's feelings and struggles, chews them over, digests them, and makes them acceptable or more easily digestible (handled or understood) for the child.

Transference–Counter-Transference

The successful outcome of psychotherapy to Jung was the nature of the unconscious of the therapist. Jungian therapists tend to have a minimum of six to eight years of their own analysis. One function of this is an attempt to understand their own internal processes so these can be used to analyze the transference–counter-transference that inevitably develops in the therapy room, and to differentiate what emotions are the child's issues (transference) and what emotions stem from the unresolved issues of the therapist (counter-transference). The therapist uses his or her ego to assess his or her internal feeling states, thoughts, and fleeting fantasies, to analyze the play, and to use these insights to understand the unconscious processes in the child. Based on this, the therapist will select an intervention and may either (1) continue to observe, (2) reflect feelings and thoughts, (3) ask for clarification or amplification of the symbol or, (4) use interpretation to link feelings and thoughts, past to present, to help an issue become clearer or more understandable, or to shed light on relationships.

Teleological Point of View

Jung was interested in how the psyche evolves. He believed that direction and growth came from the archetype of the self, which activates images, fantasies, dreams, and play themes. If the therapist follows such internal productions (images, symbols) they will lead to core psychological issues and wounds and out the other side into growth. It is not so much the uncovering and analysis of the wound that brings about change as it is the acts of making and doing and creating the symbols. Internally the child knows where he or she needs to go, and the therapist follows. Play themes and symbols evolve and change in the course of therapy, and the child's ego becomes stronger and more flexible. Jung calls this process of working with an image "the amplification of the symbol," and the therapist does this by asking for clarification: "Can you tell me more about it? What does it remind you of? What happens next? If we followed it where would it lead? Can you draw or make it?"

Treatment Stages

Introduction

Once the parents discussed and agreed to the treatment plan (their own as well as Jason's), the question remained as to how to introduce the concept of play psychotherapy to Jason. In order to get away from the idea of the child as the "identified patient" the therapist encouraged the parents to own their part in the family dynamics. For example, the mother said:

> **Mom:** Jason, our family has been through some tough times over the past few years—our baby died, your dad and I got divorced, I hit you on the face, and you tell me that you hate school. Your dad and I have talked and realize we need

help. As you know we've all gone to the Family Counseling Clinic, met with the staff, done some tests, and talked a lot. Your dad and I are now going to see separate counselors and they suggest that you go to play therapy with Dr. Lopez. You'll see him once a week in the playroom where you can play and talk. Your dad and I both feel this is a good plan, and every once in a while we'll get together in the Clinic as a family and talk together. Do you have any questions?

Jason: Well, I do like to play, but why me and not my sister?

Mom: That's a good question. We think your sister is a little too young, but she will come into the family sessions later.

Jason: Okay then. When do we go?

Mom: Next Tuesday at 3:30.

Later, the therapist met Jason in the waiting room, introduced himself, and brought him down to the playroom.

Therapist: Jason, this is the play therapy room where we will meet every Tuesday from 3:30 to 4:20 P.M. It is a special safe place where children come and play and talk about things that are bugging them, share their dreams or nightmares, or ask questions about things that puzzle them or that they don't quite understand. What you do or talk about in here is confidential—it's private—it's between you and me. I don't tell your parents or teachers about it. The only time I'd talk to them about what happens in here is if you say I can. There are two exceptions however: If someone breaks the law and harms you or if you try to harm yourself or someone else then I have to report it. Is that clear?

Jason: Yeah, our teacher talks about that kind of stuff in school.

Therapist: Okay we have 50 minutes together. I'll tell you when there are 10 minutes left, and in the last five minutes I'd like to tidy up. You can help me if you like.

Jason: No—that's what women do—I like to play.

Therapist: You feel guys shouldn't clean up their mess. I clean up mine. I'd like you to help, but I won't make you. Okay, so let's start—you can play in here more or less as you wish. This is a special room and the rules are slightly different than at home or school.

Jason: Wow! What a room! I knew God had a place like this for kids somewhere in the world. Look at the dumb (Bobo) clown. He needs a good smack around the face (whack, whack) . . . oh, you came back for more, eh? Well get that stupid smile off your face (whack, whack). (The clown pops back up and hits Jason in the face. Jason explodes, falls on top of him, pounding away with his fists, screaming at him "Dummy, stupid!" Jason slips off him, bangs his own head slightly on the carpet. Bobo pops back up. Jason, lying on the carpet, starts kicking him, gets up, jumps on him again, rolls onto the carpet while holding onto him, and tries to bite his painted ear.)

Therapist (Moving in quickly): Hold on, Jason. I can't let you bite him because that would wreck him and then we couldn't play with him anymore. It's okay to be really mad at him and to want to bite him.

Jason: Yeah, I hate him—stupid, dumb, dorkhead (starts to kick and punch him and then tries to bite him again).

Therapist (Moving in quickly again. Puts one hand on Jason's shoulder and one hand on the clown, moving him away from Jason's mouth.): Jason it's okay to want to bite Bobo and nip his ear off with your teeth, but I can't let you. If you try to bite him again, I'll have to put him outside of the room until the next session. Okay? Do you understand? If you want to bite something, there's a baby bottle on the shelf and you can bite the nipple as hard as you like.

Jason: Err. Are you dumb or something? I'd never suck on that. Bottles are just for girls. (Whack, slap, and punch as he continued to flay into Bobo for the rest of the session, tossing him around and punching him. When he left, he backhanded him across the face.) Thanks, stupid. I'll beat you up next time.

Commentary

Some children come into the first session, move quickly through orientation, ignore the therapist, and jump right into their inner dramas. The transference is to the room and the toys. If the emotional feeling tone from the therapist is good enough, children go where they need to go and the work (the therapy) gets underway. The clown provided the stimulus to unleash Jason's aggression, and there was enough of it to last the whole session. It was important that the therapist felt comfortable with this expression and embraced it fully, for in doing so Jason is allowed the safe discharge of repressed affect, which in turn helped restore psychic equilibrium and set the ground for deeper work, including meaning and understanding of where this pain originally came from and how better to handle violent and hurt feelings. The discharge of rage is only the first step.

The Jungian therapist first established the *frame of therapy* (i.e., time-place variables), and then the *purpose of therapy* (i.e., play, talking about problems and dreams, and asking questions). Questions of meaning and purpose of life are central to Jungian work. Finally the *conditions of therapy* were outlined (i.e., confidentiality, reporting, and "You can play more or less as you wish"). Therapy is an attempt to provide a safe and protected space. It is not totally free. Limits are not announced at the start, as the therapist does not know ahead of time what a child might or might not do. Limits are set as the need arises.

Jason got to work right away. This scenario is quite common in some children who have been physically abused. In order to rectify the power imbalance and to externalize their heightened sense of aggression and violence, they need to inflict physical punishment on someone else. What differentiates this from acting out is that (1) it occurs in the therapy room with the therapist so that the libido can be integrated with the ego, and (2) insight and understanding can be provided. In the early stages of therapy and with so much intense activity, the therapist witnessed the aggression, reflected the intensity of the anger ("You really hit him hard" . . . "you're really angry at him" . . . "you want to hit him for a long, long time"), used his words ("You think he looks dumb and stupid" . . . "Dumb and stupid looks make you angry"), and provided physical protection for both parties (Bobo and Jason). The therapist was aware that Jason was projecting his own "dumb and stupid" introjected feelings onto Bobo. These feelings hurt him and he wanted to get rid of them. Beating up those parts of himself will not change those feelings, but it does prepare the way for verbally processing the pain later on in treatment.

Limits were set when there was a potential for damage, but the therapist was interested in more than just the limits. The source of Jason's violence seemed more than just physical abuse, his parents' divorce, and/or shame over feeling "dumb and stupid." With the biting incidence the violence had dropped down to oral rage over the "depriving breast" and not feeling well enough satisfied by his mother. This was seen as a primary wound. The therapist acknowledged the biting rage and gave permission for the wish to hurt ("it's okay to be mad at him and to want to hurt him") and then redirected the desire to bite to the nipple on the baby bottle. The fact that the redirection was rejected and led to revealing Jason's negative stereotyping of girls was heard and stored by the therapist. However the seed was placed and the therapist predicted that at some point in the future the bottle would be used for (1) biting and pulling, and (2) sucking and taking in. The baby bottle is a very important toy for children who have been orally deprived and those with learning problems, as it lets them take in and receive "nourishment" as well as practice the assertive activities of biting and chewing. The negative stereotyping against girls and women would, Dr. Lopez believed, drop off as Jason's anima feelings were allowed into consciousness.

Establishing Rapport and Building the Therapeutic Alliance

Over the next four to six weeks the pattern of intense physical expression continued but slowly began to diminish. By using empathy and reflection of feeling, the therapist took his lead from Jason and followed his drama as they unfolded. This strengthened the therapeutic bond prior to working through the negative transference and confronting and working through the resistances.

Second and Third Sessions

Jason continued to attack Bobo at the start of each session, then lay exhausted on the carpet with his arms and legs wrapped around Bobo and his head resting on the carpet. After a while he looked at the therapist and said:

Jason: Okay, let's play Cops and Bad Guys. You be the Bad Guy and I start shooting you. Do you have any guns in here? Bang . . . bang!

Therapist: Hold on, Jason. I'll play with you, but let's talk about it first. Let's set the scene; what do I do as the Bad Guy? . . . Where are you as the Cop? . . . Is there a chase? . . . How do you shoot me? . . . What happens next? Do I die or go to jail? What happens at the end? By the way, I don't have any guns or knives in here. You can make some out of wood, or use a bowling pin or your fingers.

Jason: Bowling pins are good. They are like machine guns. You broke into my mum's house and took her jewelry. My mom called 911 and I come and shoot you and you died in pain. Bang . . . bang . . . bang!

Therapist: Aghh . . . aghh . . . (falls onto carpet). Aghh . . . Don't shoot . . . I'm in great pain.
Jason: No, scumbag. Die. Bang, bang. . . .
Therapist: I'm dead. (Silence.)
Jason: Okay let's play it again, but this time you run away and I tie you up with this rope and then I shoot you.

Fourth, Fifth, and Sixth Sessions

As the game continued, the violence became less and the plot more complicated. The Bad Guy was shot less, manhandled less when tied up, taken to jail, taken to hospital to "get his wounds fixed," then taken to court, fined, and told to "get a job and work."

The therapist took on the roles assigned to him by Jason. All during playtime the therapist was acutely aware of the space between himself and Jason. He made sure that Jason did not actually physically hurt him and monitored his own feelings as he took on the emotional content of the Bad Guy as described by Jason. So when Jason told him to "steal the jewels," the therapist talked with excitement about "I want those jewels . . . I love jewels . . . they sparkle . . . they are worth a lot of money." When he got shot or tied up, he complained about the pain: "I'm hurting . . . I've been shot so badly, there's blood everywhere . . . I'm in pain . . . I don't like being tied up . . . bound up . . . controlled by the police." Initially Jason would tell him to "Shut up," put a few more bullets in him, and tighten the rope. The therapist responded in kind by deepening his painful cries, pleading for mercy, and entering hopelessness: "I'm in so much pain . . . it will never go away . . . I'll always be hurting." By taking on the role and using the transference, the therapist gave voice to the unconscious feelings embedded in Jason's psyche. Emotions that were experienced but amorphous now became identified and named—feelings of pain, hurt, and hopelessness.

When he went to jail, the Bad Guy (therapist) talked about how ashamed he felt, when in hospital how he "feels better now that [his] wounds are cared for and are healing." When the judge fined him and told him to "quit stealing and get a job," he agreed he would.

By this enactment and role-playing technique there was a teleological movement in Jason's psyche: Aggression gave way to hurt, hurt led to shame, shame led to "being taken care of" (the hospital), which led to healing, then to justice (the judge), and to the development of superego functions—"I'll quit stealing and work." It was not that Jason was a "stealer" in reality, but in play he set up a dramatic sequence that followed a typical flow in unconscious development. It was important that the therapist stayed true to the child's images and his development. Understanding the symbolic meaning of each scenario was important and helped to free the child from the compulsion of an unconscious complex. Talking about "hurt" or "hopelessness" in the role released the trapped power of these feelings. It was the repression of these emotions that led to negative motivational sets and disturbing behavior on the part of Jason.

Working Phase

Children often need to test the therapist by setting up intense dramas to see if the therapist can handle the material. If this is worked through acceptably, the child feels he or she can trust the therapist and moves to deeper material. Many children, after involving the therapist in a direct way, often move away from joint action dramas into more symbolic play with toys and into disclosure of specific traumas. Obviously, not all children engage the therapist as Jason did, or need to, and some move quite directly into their specific struggles.

Sessions 9 through 15

Jason made a dramatic shift into playing with the toys in the room. He was noticeably calmer than he had been, and at the start of each session he went over to the toy shelves and selected a variety of toys. Though it looked random, there was a definite pattern to his selection, often two opposing sides, like the army versus the invaders or superheroes versus the dinosaurs.

Then he developed a game that continued for five sessions: Superheroes versus the Spiders. The problem was that the Spiders kept winning, crawling up on the Superheroes when they were asleep, throwing their webs over them, eating their babies, and tangling up their tanks. Not even their sharp knives could get through the webs. Jason played both sides but clearly preferred the Spiders. Every once in a while he would throw a cobweb into the therapist's face and put the toy spiders on his body. The therapist started to feel frustrated because it seemed as if there was no movement or growth. In fact, in his eyes things started to get worse—the Spiders were all over the room weaving their webs over the soldiers, the dinosaurs, and the police.

> **Therapist** (Feeling uncomfortable inside): Those Spiders, they just get everywhere, wrap everyone up, and make them feel pretty useless and lousy—like they cannot do anything to get away.
>
> **Jason:** You're darn right. One's landed on your face—covered your eyes and mouth and you can't see or say anything.
>
> **Therapist** (Feeling more uncomfortable and totally controlled): You don't want me to see anything or to say anything.
>
> **Jason** (Very agitated now, screams): DON'T YOU UNDERSTAND ENGLISH? I TOLD YOU TO SHUT UP AND I MEAN IT (as he throws a cobweb in the therapist's face.
>
> **Therapist** (Now confused and overwhelmed, tries to make sense of what was occurring and offers a tentative interpretation): You get real mad at me when I don't listen to you and you want to control me and mess me up. I wonder if you feel that way when your mother and teachers ask you to do something. . . .
>
> **Jason** (Loses control and starts throwing spiders and toys at the therapist): SHUT UP! SHUT YOUR DUMB MOUTH. I HATE YOU. I HATE MY MOM. I HATE MY TEACHER. I HATE SCHOOL! (He hits out at the therapist and starts to sob.)

Therapist (Surprised by the outburst and a little frightened about whether he has done the right thing, tries to reflect the key emotions): That's okay, Jason. It's frightening to have so much anger. I'm glad you told me. I'm not frightened by your anger or your hatred. It's scary when your mom and teacher ask you to do things—I guess it feels like they are trying to control you and part of you gets mad and doesn't want to be controlled.

Jason (Continues sobbing but after a while says): I hate her. I don't want to do anything she asks. I want to hurt her. (He continues sobbing.)

Therapist: You feel really hurt by your mom.

Jason: Yeah . . . Is it time to go now?

Therapist: Yes it will be in a few minutes. Let's wait till you feel better and then we can tidy up the room together.

Jason: Okay.

Commentary

Play therapy is a frightening profession at times. Intense feelings erupt in both child and therapist, and the therapist is concerned about doing the right thing or fearing that he or she might do damage. Jung said there was no effective therapy without the therapist's changing as much as the client. After this session, the therapist called up his supervisor and asked for an appointment to go over his transference and counter-transference feelings. Despite being stirred up by Jason, the therapist handled the situation appropriately. He reflected both content and feeling and made an interpretation to an underlying dynamic of enmeshment and control. Archetypically the Spider would be seen as a symbol of enmeshment with the mother; if a child has not had enough "goodness" from the mother he can remain trapped in an ambivalent state of both wanting her (love, affection, and/or attention) and hating her at the same time. This problem often manifests itself consciously in battles around power and control. From a Jungian perspective, the task of childhood is to differentiate oneself out of the unconscious matrix of one's parents and to forge one's own independent life.

If there is an underlying depression and emotional need in the parent figures, they often cannot handle it and disintegrate under the explosive rage of the child. In the above incidence the therapist held his own ground and verbalized to Jason that it was okay to have such strong feelings and that he was not frightened by them and still cared about him. This experience often has a paradoxical effect on children: Releasing their rage at the therapist lets their ego handle it effectively in the future, as there is no longer the same degree of repression and terror. Jason discharged his rage at the therapist and the therapist did not disintegrate. Jason experienced this with a sense of relief. Rather than setting limits, the therapist focused on the use of interpretation to both help Jason control and understand his behavior.

It was interesting to note that in the middle of his anger Jason yelled out "Don't you understand English?" There was a question here about his own identity. Because of his dark skin he felt more Hispanic than American. Also, at the end of the session the therapist invited Jason to "tidy up the room together." This was an attempt to offer an act of mutual reparation and joining and one to which Jason was able to respond affirmatively.

Sessions 16 through 26

Jason was noticeably different when he returned to the playroom the next week. The mother even gave the therapist a thumbs up sign when he picked up Jason. Once in the room, Jason looked around slowly as if taking the whole room in for the first time. He noticed the dolls' house and spent the next 10 sessions playing in and around it.

Jason: Oh, look—a house. Wow! What a house! Is it new?
Therapist: You're surprised. You're wondering if I just brought the house in.
Jason: Yeah, you must have. It's so big. I would have seen it before.
Therapist: Well actually, Jason, it has been here all along but you were so busy playing with the other toys. . . .
Jason: Well now I want to play with this house. It's so big it has two families living in it: one white and one Mexican. Let's see . . . (and he spends the rest of the session in quiet, absorbed play organizing and arranging the furniture and the people).

In subsequent sessions Jason moved through themes of (1) verbal and physical fighting between the parents and adult figures, (2) divorce, with mother and father setting up different houses, (3) children being physically abused by the mother, and (4) the house being destroyed by a fire. Though the first few sessions with the dolls' house seemed to progress and move, Jason appeared to get stuck with repetitive play around the theme of physical abuse and fire. The boy "Victor" and his mother would get into a huge fistfight because Victor sassed his mom when she made him clean his room. The fight would wreck the house, and the dad would come home, make everyone clean up, and put everyone to bed. Then, in the middle of the night, a fire would break out, burning the kids and sometimes the parents. Ambulances and firefighters would come. After four sessions of this theme, without any real change in the plotline, the therapist began to get bored and frustrated. All the empathy, witnessing, and reflection of feeling did not seem to affect the evolution of play. The therapist decided to use a "stop technique" in order to slow the frantic play down and to use interpretation to make links between the conscious and unconscious personalities.

Therapist: Jason, hold on a minute. Let me try to get this straight. Victor sasses his mom, she punches him in the face, dad breaks the fight up and then a fire breaks out.
Jason: Yeah then the ambulance and firefighters come. . . .
Therapist: Okay, hold it. What's going on in Victor's head when his mom asks him to clean up.
Jason: Oh he's thinking, 'no one tells me what to do. I'm the boss of this house.'

Therapist: So he's already mad . . . Jason, I wonder if you're really angry that your mom and dad got divorced and that you're so mad that you're going to bug your mom and hurt her . . . like you feel she's hurt you.

Jason: Yeah, I'm mad at her. I'm so mad at her I could burn up the house and her in it too!

Therapist: So you are full of fiery feelings.

Jason: Yeah, I hate her for hitting me.

Therapist: Right, but I'm wondering (and here the therapist made an interpretive leap) if part of you wants her to hit you as that's the only way you can get close to her?

Jason: What?

Therapist: I think you feel both mad and sad with your mom and part of you would like her to hold you, but you're so mad at her you won't let her do it.

Jason: Yeah—she used to hold me before Carla was born.

Therapist: And you like that a lot.

Jason: Yeah (and he started to sob). . . . Dad made me put clean jeans on to go to see them in the hospital but I didn't want to go.

Therapist: It really hurt when Carla was born . . . you felt your mom and dad would love her more than you.

Jason: Yeah . . . I thought there was something wrong with me—like I wasn't good enough for them (sobbing deeply).

Therapist: That somehow you weren't okay.

Jason: Yeah . . . (the sobbing ceased and he started to feel better). But now I know that's not true. They do love me—even my mom tells me so now.

Therapist: You're feeling better about yourself and you've seen a change in your mom recently.

Commentary

The therapist followed the play of the child and monitored his own process. When he felt the emotions were stuck or blocked and the play was not evolving, he made an attempt at interpreting what was occurring on the unconscious level. If the interpretations are acceptable to the child's ego, the child will move deeper into the process. In this incidence, Victor became Jason, and Jason moved through anger into hurt and through hurt into the painful disclosure of his sister's birth and back up into commenting on his improved feelings about self and mother.

Sessions 27 through 36

Following the dolls' house work, Jason moved to the sandtable, spending the next 15 sessions working with the dry sand and the miniature toys. After each sandtray session the therapist took a Polaroid® picture to place in Jason's file. At first, Jason's mood was noticeably subdued, and in fact he seemed quite depressed. He spent a long time moving the sand around with his hands, flattening the surface down before adding a few people, houses, cars, trees, and fences. He started by saying:

Jason: I had a dream that the fire burnt up the whole Earth. Everything was destroyed, nothing lived—even the soil was burnt and became sand. Nothing grew and never would grow again. (He lay all of the toys down on top of the sand.) Can we turn out the light?

Therapist: You want to know whether you can turn out the light?

Jason: Yeah—it's dark and death is everywhere (he turned out the light). There is no light in the world—death is everywhere—nothing can grow—just like the dinosaurs became extinct, so will we.

Therapist (entering the feeling tone, reflected and restated the mood): The fire has destroyed the world . . . all life has been burnt and destroyed . . . blackness and darkness is everywhere . . . mankind has been wiped out and will not recover.

Jason: Yes—we are going to die too so let's not speak, and pretend we are dead.

Therapist: Okay. . . .

Jason remained silent until the end of the session and then left quietly. The therapist sensed something deep was happening but made no intervention, so that Jason could live in feelings without having them interpreted. At times the Jungian therapist does not attempt to move the child away from painful feelings but rather just allow him or her to be or to deepen them. The belief behind this is that emotions will change naturally if allowed full expression in a safe and protected space (such as the playroom). This phase of depression continued for four weeks until Jason came in with the following dream, which he enacted in the sandtable.

Reparation and Restitution Phase

Jason: I dreamt a baby died and we went to church and buried her. I thought I killed her because I didn't like her and that my mom was mad at me and would never forgive me (builds a village in the sand with a church at the center and a graveyard) but you know that's not true . . . I didn't like her but I didn't kill her and my mom's not mad at me anymore (puts a baby in the matchbox and buries the matchbox in the graveyard).

Therapist: That was quite a dream. . . .

Jason: Yeah, but it did happen to me though. My mom told me. She's been talking about it in her counseling and she really did have a baby boy who died when I was real young. She said it made her worry about me and my sister because she was afraid we might die.

Therapist: Your mom telling you that helped you understand her better.

Jason: Yeah and now I know my mom loves me. She wasn't mad at me all the time. She just worried about me.

Therapist: I'm a bit confused—in real life or in the dream?

Jason: Both. She loved me in the dream and in real life. I used to think she was mad at me all the time but some of the time she was just worried I was going to die.

Therapist: Knowing that helped you see that she actually loves you.

Jason: Yeah—she's different since she's been in counseling. I like her and my dad now.

Therapist: You used to like your dad more.

Jason: Yeah, but now I love'em both. Maybe I'll live with my dad when I'm in high school.

Therapist: So you're quite happy living most of your time with your mom right now?

Jason: Yeah. My mom and my sister.

Commentary

This represented a major turning point in therapy. Progress in therapy is often cyclical—regression leading to progression leading to more regression followed by progression. By staying in the depressive phase and waiting for a dream or a spontaneous change in play themes, the child's self-healing ability will lead the child and the therapist into critical material. Psychotherapy is about the transformation of affect, and often one sees themes of death followed by those of rebirth. Jason shared his fearful fantasies, disclosed his worries, and developed a new understanding and a new attitude to his mother. This was both an inner and outer phenomenon: The negative mother introject was dissolved and replaced by a positive mother introject ("she loves me"), which in turn led to a better relationship with his mother and to other women in general (i.e., his hostility to women, which was based in part on negative and frustrating experiences with his mother, disappeared).

Termination Stage

Sessions 37 through 41

Jason continued to work in the sandtray for the last four sessions. All themes of disorganization and hostility had disappeared, and he concentrated on building an elaborate and complex town surrounded by farms, a forest, and a lake. At the center of the town and was a circle, and in the circle he placed the town hall, law courts and police station. He populated the town with both white and colored people he called Mexicans:

Jason: These two peoples get on well together in this town.

Therapist: Two peoples.

Jason: Yeah—the Americans and Mexicans. They don't fight a lot and they like each other. The mayor is a white guy but the head of the police is a Mexican. The mayor teaches him English and the police chief teaches him Spanish. (He puts an American flag on the town hall and a Mexican flag on the police station.)

Therapist: So these guys are different. They are from different cultures. They are in positions of power but they share power and teach each other their own language. I guess that's a bit like you. You're both American and Mexican.

Jason: Yeah, but I didn't use to like my Mexican side—I tried washing myself to make myself white. Now I like my Mexican side and my dad is teaching me Spanish. I'm going to take it in school next year. Hasta luego!

Commentary

Jason's Jungian play psychotherapy was a long process that involved following his emotional and symbolic process as it unfolded. Split-off parts of the psyche were expressed and eventually integrated into a whole personality. The termination stage was quite short—four sessions—and the play tended to be integrative in nature. Once the personal issues were resolved, Jason was faced with finding his place in the world and coming to terms with the morality and laws of that culture. Jason had to come to terms with his dual cultural identity. He did this by disclosing his struggle, by giving each part equal status, and by deciding to learn Spanish.

Jason terminated therapy soon after this by coming in and announcing that he didn't "need to come here any more." The therapist (and family and school personnel) agreed with this, but arranged one more visit in a month's time. Sometimes termination needs to be staggered—once every two weeks, leading to once a month, then finishing. Often, with children, termination happens during a natural break like school or summer holidays. At times the therapist might sense that it will soon be time to terminate and needs to prepare the child four to six weeks ahead of time in order to work through some of the rage and hurt that comes with separation. Sometimes children announce that they wish to terminate when the therapist feels it is not appropriate, and the therapist needs to state this to the child ("You feel you are ready to end play therapy but I believe that we need to see each other a while longer. Your parents and teachers tell me that life is still difficult for you at times at home and school.").

PROGNOSIS

The prognosis for this type of child in this family is excellent. Having the mother and father come into therapy to work on their own issues, and then the couple issues, freed Jason to do his own work. The pretreatment testing indicated that, though angry and depressed, he had good reality testing, ego strength, and both a desire and an ability to relate to his parents. As he played out his issues in the playroom and resolved many of them, it would be anticipated that Jason would learn to play with other children, be able to concentrate and learn in school, as well as respond appropriately to limits set by his parents and teachers. As he came to accept himself and his family life, he would become more accepting of others.

BIBLIOGRAPHY

Allan, J. (1976). The identification and treatment of "difficult babies." *Canadian Nurse,* 72(12), 111–16.

Allan, J. (1988). *Inscapes of the child's world: Jungian counseling in schools and clinics.* Dallas, TX: Spring Publications.

Allan, J., & Berry, P. (1987). Sandplay. *Elementary School Guidance and Counseling, 21,* 300–306.

Allan, J., & Bertoia, J. (1992). *Written paths to healing: Education and Jungian child counseling.* Dallas, TX: Spring Publications.

Allan, J., & Brown, K. (1993). Jungian play therapy in the elementary schools. *Elementary School Guidance and Counseling, 28,* 30–41.

Allan, J., & Lawton-Speert, S. (1993). Play psychotherapy of a profoundly incest abused preschooler. *International Journal of Play Therapy, 2,* 33–48.

Allan, J., & MacDonald, R. (1975). The use of fantasy enactment in the treatment of an emerging autistic child. *Journal of Analytical Psychology, 20,* 57–68.

Ammann, R. (1991). *Healing and transformation in sandplay: Creative processes becoming visible* (W.P. Rainer, Trans.), La Salle, IL: Open Court Publishing.

Edinger, E. (1972). *Ego and archetype.* New York: Putnam.

Edminger, E. (1985). *Anatomy of the psyche: Alchemical symbolism in psychotherapy.* LaSalle, IL: Open Court Publishing.

Fordham, M. (1994). *Children as individuals.* London: Karnac Books.

Jacobi, J. (1959). *Complex/archetype/symbol in the psychology of C.G. Jung* (R. Manheim, Trans.). Princeton: Princeton University Press.

Jung, C.G. (1961). *Memories, dreams, reflections.* New York: Random House.

Jung, C.G. (1966). *Two essays on analytical psychology.* Princeton: Princeton University Press.

Jung, C.G. (1967). *Alchemical studies.* Princeton: Princeton University Press.

Jung, C.G. (1968). *Archetypes and the collective unconscious.* Princeton: Princeton University Press.

Jung, C.G. (1970). *Development of the personality.* Princeton: Princeton University Press.

Jung, C.G. (1971). *Psychological types.* Princeton: Princeton University Press.

Jung, C.G. (1973). *Experimental researches.* Princeton: Princeton University Press.

Kalff, D. (1980). *Sandplay A psychotherapeutic approach to the psyche* (W. Ackerman, Trans.). Santa Monica, CA: Sigo Press.

Mahler, M., Pine, F., & Bergman, A. (1975). *The psychological birth of the human infant.* New York: Basic Books.

Martin, C., & Allan, J. (1995). *Children as storytellers.* Toronto, ON: Lugus Publications.

Mitchell, R., & Friedman, H. (1994). *Sandplay: Past, present and future.* London: Routledge & Kegan Paul.

Neumann, E. (1973). *The child.* New York: G.P. Putnam's Sons.

Proner, B.C. (1988). Attacks on analysis. In M. Sidoli & M. Davies (Eds.), *Jungian child psychotherapy: Individuation in childhood* (pp. 141–164). London: Karnac Books.

Winnicott, D. (1971). *Playing and reality.* London: Tavistock Publications.

CHAPTER 5

Filial Therapy

LOUISE GUERNEY

INTRODUCTION

Filial therapy (FT) is a play therapy method that involves parents directly in the play process. Developed and researched primarily in the 1960s and 1970s by its innovators, Bernard and Louise Guerney and colleagues at Rutgers University, it was at first conceptualized as a method that would enable parents to serve, under the supervision and instruction of an experienced play therapist, as the primary change agents for their behaviorally and emotionally disordered children. Currently, FT is used most often for this purpose but has been expanded over the years to offer a variety of therapeutic formats, to employ parents as secondary change agents, and also for a means of adding a practicum component to parenting skills training aimed more directly toward parents, and indirectly for the benefit of their children. In this chapter, a brief discussion will be presented about the development of the method, its goals, and its theoretical base, along with its application in one of its therapeutic formats to the case of Jason.*

The play therapy model taught to the parents is based on the client-centered theory of Carl Rogers (1951) as translated to play therapy by Virginia Axline (1947). The instruction to parents in play therapy skills is based on learning and reinforcement principles, but the instruction is affectively oriented with an emphasis on the client-centered principles of empathy and acceptance. Since its inception, the method has always been described as "Didactic and Dynamic" (Andronico, Fidler, Guerney, and Guerney, L., 1967)—the authors' term for the duel commitment to the forthright teaching of play sessions and simultaneous focus on the parents' feelings as players and on parents as parents.

Rogers's empathy was integrated with learning principles because of an awareness that, in teaching parents to emulate the play therapist, one is not teaching computation or spelling—subjects that would not usually elicit a lot of emotional response (unless they are one's nemesis). In involving parents in this process, one is entering the potentially emotionally threatening world of the parent-child relation-

---

*See "Orientation to the Text: The Case of Jason L.," p. 1.

ship—a world of feelings and attitudes and family dynamics that would require the same respect and understanding that parents were asked to provide for their children. It should be understood, however, that the task of working with the children is always given top priority and the parents' feelings and personal concerns never dominate. FT is not a circuitous route to providing client-centered personal or parental therapy to parents. The perspectives of parents are critical and require acceptance and understanding on the way to learning how to develop the competence to conduct an appropriate child-centered play session for the benefit of their children and their relationships with their children.

Personality Theory

Rogers's Theory of Personality and Behavior was presented in the last chapter of his now classic book *Client-Centered Therapy* (Rogers, 1951) in a set of 19 theoretical propositions. His theory was built in the ideal theory-building way—that is, derived from countless empirical observations that were tested as hypotheses, then confirmed by empirical research. For the sake of brevity, only those that are most pertinent to FT and play therapy are selected and condensed here.

"The organism has one basic tendency and striving—to actualize, maintain, and enhance the experiencing organism." . . . . [the] "organism actualizes itself in the direction of greater differentiation of organs and of function." . . . "Its movement is in the direction of increasing self-government, self-regulation and autonomy, and away from . . . control by outside forces. . . . Self-actualization of the organism appears to be in the direction of socialization, broadly defined" (Rogers, 1951, Proposition II, p. 488). The therapist relies on this tendency of the human organism most deeply and fundamentally (p. 489).

Rogers explains that even though all humans are endowed with this drive to self-actualize, "this operation toward growth and enhancement is not smooth—rather the process involves struggle and pain" (1951, p. 488). He illustrates this with a description of a toddler trying to master walking: The toddler falls and bumps himself but still, except for perhaps a short lapse into the easier crawling, will continue doggedly to try to walk when he is ready to acquire this critical skill. Given normal capacities, the child is "programmed" to pursue the path of normal development despite obstacles. In the course of these experiences, a concept of the self develops.

In his propositions, Rogers refers frequently to self-structure or self-concept, which he uses interchangeably. His definition of the self-structure is "an organized configuration of perceptions of the self which are admissible to awareness" (Rogers, 1951, p. 501). Positive experiences are consistent with the concept of self as a lovable person. When the child is given negative evaluations of his experiences, for example, desperately wanting parent approval and being told that he doesn't deserve it, he is forced to deny or distort the symbolization of these experiences in order to protect the concept of self from threat. Rogers sees the self-concept as the organizing force of the personality and maintaining its integrity as one of its functions.

However, he cautions that perceptions are excluded because they are contradictory (to the self-concept), *not* because they are derogatory (Rogers, 1951, p. 506).

Thus, attempting to change the individual by telling her that she should accept a more positive view in relation to some part of her self can be met with rejections, for example, "You're only saying that because you don't know what I'm really like." Such an individual cannot accept information that is not consistent with her negative self-concept.

Rogers explains his phenomenological position as follows: The organism reacts to the field as it is experienced and perceived. This perceptual field is for the individual, "reality" (Rogers, 1951, p. 484). This is "frequently evident [in therapy]; when the perception changes, the *reaction* of the individual changes." (p. 486).

Model of Psychopathology

Rogers was well aware of the many ways the journey to self-actualization—that is, a coherent concept of self that is not distorted by unrealistic perceptions that prevent living up to one's desired potential—can be derailed and provides many illustrations of its happening as one reacts to life's experiences. He proposes that

> Psychological maladjustment exists when the organism denies to awareness significant sensory and visceral experiences, which consequently are not symbolized and organized into the gestalt of the self-structure. When this situation exists, there is a basic or potential psychological tension. (Rogers, 1951 p. 510) This tension is experienced as anxiety. The fluid but consistent organization of the structure or concept of the self does not permit the intrusion of a perception at variance with it . . . (p. 505). As an example of how denial and distortion operate in response to threat to the self, Rogers reports on a pilot whose self-image included bravery and courage. When instead he experienced fear about an impending air battle, he could not admit this to consciousness but the feelings were there and had to be reacted to in some way. The pilot reacted to his visceral fear by unconsciously creating an illness which permitted him to avoid conscious facing of the fear. (Rogers, 1951)

"Anxiety is the affective response to threat to the self and defense is a sequence of behavior in response to threat, the goal of which is the maintenance of the structure of the self. Defense involves a denial or distortion of experience to reduce the incongruity between the experience and the structure of the self" (Rogers, 1951, p. 516). However, the defensive behavior decreases only the awareness of threat, not the threat itself. Thus, as long as these threat-reducing defenses work, one can go on living maladaptively indefinitely.

Goal of Client-Centered Therapy

The overarching goal is to achieve psychological adjustment, which exists when the concept of the self has become such that all the sensory and visceral experiences of the organism are or may be assimilated on a symbolic level into a consistent relationship with the concept of the self." (Rogers, 1951, p. 513) As the individual perceives and accepts into his self-structure all of his sensory and visceral experiences and [accurately symbolizes them] he is necessarily more understanding of others and is more accepting of others as separate individuals. (Rogers, 1951, p. 520)

The concept of acceptance of all parts of one's self into the self-structure and the feeling that one is accepted by others (Rogers speaks of the latter as "other acceptance") are both innate needs (Rogers, 1951, p. 524) and central to adjustment. Thus attaining these two kinds of acceptance—self and other—become therapeutic goals. Acceptance of the client's perceptions and unconditional positive regard by the therapist are also necessary to reach the goals of client self and other acceptance. In order to achieve these goals,

the counselor's function is to assume, in so far as possible, the internal frame of reference of the client, to perceive the world as the client sees it, to perceive the client himself as he is seen by himself, to lay aside all perceptions *from the external frame of reference* while doing so, and to communicate something of this to the client. (Rogers, 1951, p. 495)

Further, Rogers states: "The best vantage point for understanding behavior is from the internal frame of reference of the individual himself." This is spoken of in the psychotherapy world as "empathic understanding" and expressing this understanding to the client as "empathic or reflective" responding (Rogers, 1951, p. 494).

The pivotal feature of Rogerian therapy is self-acceptance by the client. Accurate incorporation into the self-concept of experiences and sensations, explorations of the consequences of rejection or distortion of some perceptions, and correcting these acceptance problems through acceptance by the therapist are the work of therapy. Because the "self" is constructed through the individual's perceptions of reality it is the individual's perceptions of reality that must be the focus of the therapy. In the more directive therapies, the therapist's perception is the standard of reality and is used to direct the client toward modification of false perceptions (Rogers, 1951).

The foregoing is only a fraction of what Rogers includes in his theories of behavior, development, and therapeutic change and cannot do them justice. It is I hoped that it will be sufficient, though, to provide a base of understanding for the client-centered play therapy model and the training of parents to use it in therapeutic play applications.

It is the emphasis on understanding behavior from the vantage point of the client that makes it possible to train nonprofessionals in the method. If FT required a background in psychodynamic theory, as would be the case with many other theoretical models, it would be virtually impossible to train parents to play therapeutically. It is quite feasible to teach them and other nonprofessionals to "assume the internal frame of reference of the [child] and lay aside perceptions from the external frame of reference" (Rogers, 1951, p. 494). Carkhuff (1969) demonstrated that this kind of empathic ability was possible to acquire by relatively unsophisticated individuals, when trained appropriately.

Axline was a student of Rogers and accepted his theory and therapeutic methods in their entirety. She translated them into a play therapy method that would allow children to benefit from an accepting, nondirective approach to play. She believed that children also had the self-actualization drive and that the same accepting atmosphere would allow them to direct themselves to the most important items on a healing agenda appropriate to the individual child (Axline, 1947).

To this end, she developed a list of "Eight Basic Principles" (Axline, 1947), that are primarily operational principles for the therapist to follow as opposed to theoretical ones. However, it is clear that the prescribed therapist behaviors are derived from the Rogerian theoretical positions. In Axline's method of play therapy, the therapist is guided to use acceptance and empathic understanding, and to let the child "lead the way." In true Rogerian tradition, she calls for the therapist to avoid the use of criticism, judgment, advice giving, questioning, and interpreting, or in other ways inserting anything that would be derived from the therapist's frame of reference. The therapist should try to perceive the child's world as the child sees it and to communicate that to the child, with understanding and communicating about feelings being the highest form of response. Axline also included, in her basic principles, one relating to limits on child behavior—an element unique to child therapy (Axline, 1947).

Originally labeled nondirective play therapy, Axline's method is now also called client-centered or child-centered play therapy, to be referred to in this chapter as CC. Axline's book was reissued in paperback in 1969 (Axline, 1969) and in spite of its age remains the leading play therapy book. Starting as early as 1947, a solid body of empirical outcome research has been built supporting the efficacy of the method. Early process research revealed the therapeutic effect on children of various therapist responses with empathic (reflective) responses, the most therapeutic (e.g., Finke, 1947; Fleming & Snyder, 1947).

More recently research on parenting behavior indicates that the prescribed behaviors of the CC therapist embody the same behaviors used by parents whose children are socially competent (Baumrind, 1971). In a study of toddler compliance with parental directives, Parpel and Maccoby (1985) found that parents who were asked not to direct the children in a free-play situation and to make comments that were supportive (empathic), had children who were more compliant in their laboratory observations than did parents who were not so instructed and simply followed their own ideas of how to relate to their children. In this group, parents who were more directly controlling and intrusive elicited the least compliance. These results speak to the value of parents mastering the play session behaviors, not only for potential gains for their children but for achieving their own child compliance goals as well.

In regard to FT, there are additional elements beyond the theory and therapies of the client-centered approach. One of these was the belief on the part of Bernard Guerney (1964), that adjustment problems experienced by children were not typically a result of parental pathology, as was the prevailing view among psychotherapists at that time. He thought that they were the product of parent failure to learn how to understand their children and to respect the children's perspectives and also of parents not knowing how to exercise reasonable nonviolent control over their children. He defined parental problems as essentially learning problems. Since he and his colleagues practiced CC and valued its contributions toward reduction of child problems, he hypothesized that teaching parents to conduct CC play sessions might be the way to overcome these parental shortcomings and to bring about therapeutic change in the children—just as professional therapists do after being trained. In addition, he believed that parents were so important in their children's lives that acceptance from them might be even more meaningful for the children (Guerney, B., 1964).

The goals of filial therapy were defined in the following terms:

1. To reduce problem behaviors in the children.
2. To help parents acquire the skills of the play therapist for application in the playroom and ultimately to use as applicable in everyday life when relating to their children.
3. To improve the parent-child relationship. As children experience their parents in the role of play therapist, they and their parents will feel more positive toward each other.

Goal one typically would be expected to be achieved in CC when it is conducted by a professional. Goal three, to some extent, should also result from professionally conducted play sessions. Children usually do relate better to others after CC, regardless of who the therapist is. However, added gains were anticipated for parents and the parent-child relationship as an outcome of parent involvement.

A considerable number of empirical studies have been conducted over the years by the original Rutgers group (Guerney, L. 1975; Oxman, 1971; Guerney, B. and Stover, 1971) and others elsewhere (e.g., Glassner, 1986; Sensue, 1981; Sywulak, 1978) that do, in fact, demonstrate that these goals can be attained and that other benefits result for parents as well.

While developing the methodology for accomplishing these tasks, Guerney and colleagues recognized that the didactic piece of the approach would need to make utmost use of learning theory and behavioral principles. The details of the didactic component will be described in the section, Treatment Goals.

CASE FORMULATION

Rogerian theoretical principles explain Jason's and his mother's individual problems and their interaction problems at a macro level. For more micro-level analyses, other theoretical positions will be drawn upon in this case formulation, as indicated below.

A Word about Diagnosis

Jason's problems might be given a number of diagnostic labels, but since he is a young child and the psychotherapeutic treatment of choice, in this case CC play therapy, would not differ whatever the label, the most conservative label—that of childhood adjustment disorder—would be given. The etiology of the disorder would be the traumatic "psychological loss" of his mother at age 18 months, when she became extremely depressed and could not care for him after having been his primary caregiver until that time. There are also elements of depression in Jason himself in his statements about wishing he were dead, his flattened affect, and his low self-esteem, possibly masked in disruptive behavior in school and in the community (fire setting).

While apparently not at a clinical level, there are elements of ADHD in Jason's behavior—his impulsivity, poor impulse control, delayed social development, and his problems with transitions, at least from school to home. His scores on the CBCL support the behavioral accounts given of Jason at home and at school. However, none of the deviations appear to be of such magnitude that nonbehavioral interventions (e.g., medication) would be required. Whether ADHD has a psychological or neurological etiology or a combination of both is an open question in the fields of child psychiatry and psychology. With Jason's mother's threatened pregnancy and his low birth weight, the issue of neurological components cannot be totally ruled out. Both of the lower scores on the otherwise unremarkable WISC (Picture Arrangement and Coding) would be consistent with attention deficit difficulties and the poor social development noted on the DTORF-R. In his KFD, Jason depicted all family members as separated from each other—even his father, with whom he appeared to be closest.

Another important feature of Jason's dynamics are his conflicted attitudes toward authority figures and institutional authority, specifically against the school, so tellingly revealed in his TAT responses. Such conflict could keep him in constant internal turmoil between his desire to be compliant and accepted by others and a push to be rebellious and indulgent of his impulses to go his own nonsocial way. Rogerian personality development theory would suggest that Jason is generating much anxiety and perhaps some resultant aggression. There is an underlying theme of low self-esteem as seen on the TAT, where no matter how much the story figures with whom he appears to identify wish to do their best, they do not succeed. They wind up sentenced to being controlled by forces that violate their psychological needs—the need to feel trusted and to be appreciated. There is evidence of some superego development in that the figures feel bad about doing or wanting to do the "wrong things." In the story of the girl hating school, she goes to school anyway, accepting the authority position over her own feelings.

Parent-Child Relationships

For FT, a prognosis about the restoration of minimal parent-child relationships is important. On the basis of the following observations, the prognosis for Jason and his parents being able to modify their relationships would appear to be good. His mother is the more troubled parent but is not beyond relationship building under therapeutic conditions. The most revealing information about Jason and his parents was the observations on the MIM tasks. The differences observed in Jason when he was with his father and mother were striking. Both Jason and his mother each appear to assume that the other will not be responsive to him or her. Distorted perceptions interfere with their being able to acknowledge the realistic responses of the other. Expecting only the negative, they exude impatience and weariness about having to do the tasks together. However, Jason is able to comply, and his mother is in turn able to support his efforts when he does comply with the requirements of the tasks. In fact, she permitted herself to actually appreciate Jason's nurturing behavior of rubbing her neck. Since he chose to rub her neck in opposition to her suggestion that he rub her knees, there was a certain need on his part to have the ultimate control of that outcome. However, it turned out to be a gratifying experience for both of them when Mary was able to accept his choice instead of insisting on hers. This exchange seems to represent stirrings of a mutually satisfying relationship outcome if FT were to be undertaken.

The same episode suggests also that some of the home conflict between them may result from Mary's inability to tolerate Jason's wishes to exercise some personal control over outcomes that affect him. She may try to force compliance to personal and precise demands of hers. Insistence on this type of compliance tends to lead to child resistance to adult demands on a nondiscriminating basis.

This would likely be particularly true of children who are insecurely attached, another factor that would appear to be related to Jason's dynamics. Signs of a very early insecure attachment are presented in the history of his relationship to Mary. Jason was a difficult baby, which places great demand on a parent (Thomas & Chess, 1977). Mary must have found their relationship very unsatisfying since he was irritable during his waking moments. She was also hypervigilant about his health. Mary's anxiety about him plus his hard-to-interpret irritable behavior must have made it difficult for her to be appropriately responsive to him. This in turn might have bred an anxious, insecure attachment in Jason (Ainsworth, 1982). His insecure attachment would have made him more vulnerable to his mother's depressive episode during his infancy.

Mother

Mary herself suffers from low self-esteem, probably for a multitude of reasons. Likely contributing factors known from her history are her relatively low socioeconomic status compared to her sisters, Emilio's separation from her, and her feeling that she should be advancing herself on the job front—with no current prospects for doing so.

In all likelihood, she has suffered from low self-esteem since at least adolescence. Her depressive episode when her father died could certainly suggest that, as might the second depression when her newborn son died. Also, her esteem as a parent must have been damaged by Jason's antisocial behaviors and the report about her to Children's Protective Services.

Counter to her internalizing style, Mary suggests that she has another side as well—in her failure to comply with the intake worker's request that Carla should not accompany Mary and Jason to the intake interview. Whether this represents a compliance problem of Mary's, an inability to take Jason without Carla because of her favoritism toward her daughter, a desire to show off Carla to prove that she has parented one child well, or a simple logistical problem such as no baby-sitter is left to speculation. It was not mentioned that she was apologetic about it. If she were not, it would seem that it represented something more than a mere inability to solve a child care problem. A mother of her delicate psychological make-up who was under the suspicion of authorities would have been expected to be more concerned about compliance.

Emilio

There is insufficient information to try to analyze Emilo's dynamics, but on the surface he appears to be a concerned, responsible father. Currently, Jason appears to be most comfortable with his father, as the father seems to be with Jason.

Summary and Recommendations

Jason and his family are ideal candidates for FT. Their problems are quite typical of the kinds regularly treated via FT by clinicians in all settings and even across cultures (Ginsberg, 1976; Levinger, 1990). Jason's major problems have their origin in his relationship with his mother. In FT, this relationship can be explored under the "microscope" of the play session and problematic elements can be played out, bringing healing to Jason and to a more limited extent his mother. Certainly, their relationship can be expected to improve.

This relationship was probably at risk even before Jason was born. Mary, having already suffered one depressive episode at the death of her father, lived for months with the threat of losing her unborn child. Finally, his low birth weight generated more anxiety about him, making him a serious challenge for her. Further, although not mentioned, it is also quite possible that Mary might have experienced another painful loss when Jason turned out to be difficult—resulting in the loss of a dream of a lovable and loving child (Thomas & Chess, 1977).

Losses seem to be a major piece of Mary's experiences—her father, an infant, and a husband, with perhaps the loss of a "son ideal." With the mutual loss of her spouse and a live-in father for the children, losses were being experienced throughout the family, with little apparent external support except from Mary's mother. With all of this, Mary would have had to, to quote Rogers, "deny to awareness sensory and visual experiences" (anger at Jason and Emilio, and perhaps her father as well) and "deny and distort the symbolization of these experiences" (Rogers, 1951, p. 510) in a way that resulted in (at the loss of her father and baby) an inability to function, the final consequence of prolonged and gross denial and distortion of experience or its accurate symbolization.

The early emotional and partial physical abandonment of Jason by his mother, with whom he shared an insecure attachment, led to a further deterioration of security on each of their parts. Moreover, Carla's role in the family as "the perfect child" certainly did not help Jason's security status with his mother. Carla provided support for Mary's misperception of her own responsibility in relation to Jason's problems, and she exacerbated Mary's projections of all problems onto Jason. Carla's perceived desirable behavior would allow Mary to tell herself that she can love a "good, deserving" child and competently parent one as well. "It is only that Jason is so impossible that we have all of these troubles."

Both Jason and Mary protect themselves against facing their desired feelings about each other—for Jason, a desire to feel lovable and loved by his mother, and for Mary, a need to face her negative feelings toward him (and others in all likelihood) and to see her contributions to the development and maintenance of problems. The final result is that Mary and Emilio, to a lesser extent, project the family's problems onto Jason. Since Emilio perceives the problems as much less serious than does Mary, he has less need for this defense.

TREATMENT GOALS

Generic treatment goals for FT were previously described. The goals applied to Jason's family can be put in more specific terms for each family member and the family as a whole.

Goals for Mary

At this point, dynamics are so convoluted that it would be a long and costly process to try to employ individual counseling for Mary as a way to resolve her problems with Jason. Further, there is a real question as to whether she'd be personally committed to counseling, since she perceives the problem as solely Jason's. It would be more productive to use the behavioral approach of teaching Mary the skills of CC play sessions in order to achieve the desired goal of her learning how to relate appropriately yet genuinely to Jason.

There is another goal for Mary—that of helping her explore and accept feelings that are not in her awareness. FT provides a good vehicle for doing this because, when parents conduct play sessions, their feelings seem to surface and become available to them and the therapist for mutual examination. The importance of the dynamic component of FT is exemplified clearly with Mary. To simply teach her the skills of relating to Jason, without an opportunity for relationship dynamics and, also, to some extent intrapsychic, exploration would fall short of what she requires to relate comfortably and effectively to Jason. Structuring for FT with Mary would emphasize that parents feel better about themselves as parents when they learn to relate more effectively to their children through the play. She would also be told that her own personal feelings are important to progress and that she can introduce them when and if she wishes as they come up. Finally, Mary's improved expressed self-esteem would be desirable, particularly in the area of herself as an effective parent.

Operationally, the goals for Mary would become

1. To learn to be at least minimally competent at conducting CC play sessions with Jason and with Carla. In so doing she would be expected to develop true empathy for Jason to the point that extensive decoding of his feeling messages would not be necessary in order for her to be understanding of him.

2. To improve her parenting skills through learning how to transfer and generalize the skills of the play session for use in daily life. Playroom skills can be employed in communicating with children on a daily basis. The limits have to differ, but the same limit-setting process can be used to help her learn that she can set limits and enforce consequences without the use of inappropriate control tactics. Additional skills would need to be added later so that Mary could meet the teaching and socializing requirements of real-life parenting. (These skills will be described in a later section.)

3. To learn to identify nondefensively her genuine feelings for Jason and others. The opportunity to have these feelings accepted by the therapist as Mary catharted would be expected to lead to less anxiety and resolution of ambivalence and conflict.

Goals for Jason

The overarching goal would be to have a satisfactory CC play therapy experience via his mother. This experience should provide the opportunity he needs to accurately perceive his ambivalence toward his mother (and probably his sister as well, since she is to some degree an extension of his mother). The acceptance by his mother of these feelings should be doubly meaningful. Jason would be expected to indicate both inside and outside of the play sessions that he is feeling less conflicted about his mother, is becoming more securely attached to her and more cooperative at home. Jason likes to pretend play with his sister, and it is a reasonable certainty that he will be able to resolve his internal conflicts, also, through the metaphors of play.

Operationally, expected results would be

1. Scores on post tests that are higher than scores on pre-tests. The post-KFD should demonstrate greater family closeness and less static stances for the family members.

2. A significant drop in complaints about his behavior in school.

3. Advancement through the usual stages of CC play therapy. We describe the stages in the following order: (1) Warming up or learning to feel safe; (2) aggression; (3) exploration of feelings of dependence and independence (including regression frequently); and (4) mastery play and evidence of mastery of feelings (indicators of improved emotional and behavioral controls). This process would be expected to take about 10 sessions for Jason, as it typically does for other children in CC treatment (Guerney, 1983b).

Goals for Emilio

Emilio would learn how to conduct CC play sessions with the children, perhaps using games if he is not comfortable with pretend play. He would also try to set up realistic expectations for Jason (and Carla) and to develop some insight into the family dynamics.

While any emotional content that Emilio offered would be responded to with empathy, no goals would be set for resolving conflict, gaining insight into his intrapsychic dynamics, or building self-esteem. If the FT brought something relevant and of this nature to the surface, however, it would be explored with him.

Goals for Carla

In FT, both parents and all of the children of the family of playing age are involved in the play sessions, if at all possible. The rationale is that the target child should not be the only focus and should not be singled out for treatment. In time, most children recognize the sessions as a special gift from their parents and are glad that the whole family is involved. Sibling rivalry problems are frequently addressed in the play sessions. Moreover, the parents have an opportunity to affirm their interest in and care for each child as an individual, which tends to reduce sibling rivalry. The siblings also benefit from the therapy either because they have problems that are obvious or unrecognized by the family, or they are enhanced by the special kind of attention that the child receives from the parent in this time devoted exclusively to him or her. When all members participate, a family therapy approach actually results (Guerney, L., & Guerney, B., 1985).

It should be noted however, *that play sessions are always conducted on a one-parent-to-one-child basis.* It is felt that to put a parent with more than one child or both parents together with a child or children would reduce the unique message of the session for the child—that he or she is very special to the individual parent as an *individual.*

Carla's involvement would be as a sibling. However, it is likely that Carla would have some anger and insecurity to work through also. The family's "perfect child" frequently reveals issues that benefit from therapeutic attention as much as do those of the target child.

Filial therapists join more traditional family therapists in assuming that family problems tend to involve all family members to some degree and that a whole-family approach is the most productive. When both parents and all of the children participate, the conducting and analysis of the play sessions with the therapist provide a structured, systematic method of involving children and parents in a therapeutic experience. While this method does not have everyone sitting around a room reacting together, it provides a forum for dealing with family relationships that is age-appropriate for the children (Guerney, L., & Guerney, B., 1987). If any of the family's children are older than those usually included in the CC play session model, games and other more age-appropriate play can be substituted for the pretend play props. Or if the child and/or parent do not relate to fantasy play, other play materials are used. There is no limitation inherent in the method that would exclude any family members. Only logistical reasons or inability to cooperate would result in any family members not being included (Guerney, L., 1983a).

TREATMENT DESCRIPTION

Generic FT

As mentioned previously in the early development, Guerney and colleagues drew upon learning theory and behavioral therapy for deriving parent training principles and procedures for FT. Condensed, they are as follows:

1. Introduce parents to the task of learning how to conduct CC in a pleasant, supportive environment.
2. Consider the learning context for the parent; take into account the other demands in their lives. Assure parents that the only time we expect them to try to behave differently is during the play sessions. The other hours of the week are theirs to live as they wish with their children—within reason, of course. Abusing parents would be expected to stop abuse as a concurrent therapy goal. (We do not classify Mary as a chronic abuser.) This limited expectation for change seems to help parents feel less anxious and more optimistic that change is possible.
3. First model the CC behaviors to be learned as a whole, by using tapes and live demonstrations of play sessions.
4. Next, reduce each of the tasks included in the whole to small, separate components. Practice each component out of the play session context.
5. Reassemble the whole and provide practice in carrying out a very short play session that involves no children but only role-plays.
6. Encourage parents to conduct short, whole sessions with their own children while observed by the therapist, or, when feasible, held in the home and reported to the therapist later.
7. Increase the length of the play sessions at the treatment site and, if there is home play, increase those sessions to 30 to 45 minutes, according to the age of the child and parent endurance. Treatment site sessions may be as long as home sessions for nongroup FT when no home sessions are held. Otherwise, since they are for demonstrating to the therapist the quality of the sessions rather than for therapeutic purpose, they are generally 15 to 20 minutes long.

Progression to more advanced stages of those principles and procedures just outlined depends on success at the previous steps. Parents are reinforced heavily for every move in the right direction. Very specific feedback is given is relation to the observed play sessions, as well as intense supervision of play sessions held at home. Corrective feedback is given in terms of what might be "the thing to do when that happens again." Parents report that they don't feel that they are told that they "do the wrong thing." They seem to perceive, as intended, that the learning is positive and respectful.

In addition, as previously discussed, parents' feelings about each component of the learning experience are discussed and responded to empathically. When the therapist detects that parents' feelings are impeding their learning, or parents recognize it, every effort is made to find a way to teach that skill more effectively. Behavior theory would predict that a better behavior should replace a less desirable one, so in FT, learning the better behavior is the goal. If creative and repeated efforts on the part of the therapist do not result in desired learning, the therapist then focuses solely on the feelings. For example, a parent reports that it's hard for her to be empathic with her child because he is uncaring about her feelings. The therapist would use learning approaches and empathy to try to help the parent overcome this difficulty. If no amount of teaching helped her, the therapist would turn full attention to the feelings that seemed to be acting as a barrier (Andronico, Fidler, Guerney B., & Guerney L., 1967; Guerney B., 1964).

Logistics

FT typically has four stages, and if there is sufficient time, a desirable fifth stage can be scheduled. The stages are: (1) training, (2) practice by parents, (3) therapy sessions by parents, (4) transfer and generalization to life outside the play sessions, and, if there is time, (5) formal evaluation of progress involving the discussion of changes on parent responses to items on questionnaires that are read-ministered post-therapy, more discussion on how to preserve positive changes noted, and guidance for any areas where parents are not fully satisfied with changes—for example, improved academic progress or investigation of possible medication for ADHD. As often as not, it is the therapist who suggests that even greater change might be possible with the addition of some other service. Parents themselves might be content with less in many instances. A target number of sessions is designated at the outset. When working with a group of parents, it will typically take much longer to reach the three stated goals of FT. However, there is a great return for this extra time with a group since each participating family is addressed as a family in the group context and each experiences the support and sharing provided by other group members. Recently, Bratton and Landreth (1995) have used a 10-session format with groups and have reported significant changes on several empirical measures despite the brevity of the format. This suggests that further research on reducing the required time to accomplish FT goals might prove it possible to do so.

When a divorced couple participates in FT, each one could be placed in a separate group; one could be seen in a group and the other seen as an individual; or both could be seen individually. (Married couples participate as a pair.) For a single parent or couple, 10 to 12 sessions are usually designated, with the option of adding an extra one to three follow-up sessions. In a nongroup FT format, parents may or may not conduct play sessions at home as well as at the treatment site on having reached a level of competence to play without instant feedback. This choice would be primarily the therapist's, although the parents' wishes and circumstances would be factors in the therapist's decision. For example, parents attempting to regain custody of their children would not usually be requested to play at home.

Logistics as Applied to Jason's Family

Though divorced, Emilio and Mary are cooperative in relation to the children. Therefore, the recommendation was that each of them attend separately and bring the children with them to their respective sessions, for a series of 10 to 12 sessions— the exact number to be decided based on how much work remained to be done by about the seventh or eighth session. It was also recommended that they plan to schedule two follow-up sessions—one month and two months after the last regular parent session. Mary and Emilio will each have one and one-half hour weekly parent sessions with the therapist, at which time they will conduct play sessions with their children as soon as they are ready to do so. For logistical reasons, Emilio will be seen on alternate Thursday nights when he has visitation with the children (play sessions are a delightful form of visitation). Emilio will play with both children at his appointments. Mary will be seen every Tuesday night and will conduct only one play session a week, alternating the children, until she gains confidence in what she believes will be difficult for her to do. When she feels more confident, she will begin to play with both children at each session. She will play first with Carla, since she is not worried about controlling her. Neither Mary nor Emilio will conduct play sessions at home until the 10 to 12 sessions at the center have been completed because the therapist believed that Mary required close supervision and support, possible only with on-site sessions. While Emilio probably could have handled home sessions, it was felt that it would not be wise to have different arrangements for them—to prevent Mary from feeling that she was being treated as a "second class citizen."

Strategies

The 10 to 12 parent sessions will be divided among the four essential stages of FT roughly as follows:

1. Stage One—Training (two or three sessions). This stage includes therapist demonstrations of play therapy with the family's own children as well as other instructional activities to teach how conduct CC play sessions. The rationale for the method and the particular behaviors of the adult are explained fully.

2. Stage Two—Practice play; parents practice play sessions without the children (one or two sessions).

3. Stage Three—Parents conduct play sessions with their children (six to eight sessions). The play sessions are followed by feedback from the therapist. Feedback includes the parents' feelings about the process as well as instruction and information-gathering about the children's behavior outside of the playroom. The number of sessions is determined by the children's progress through the expected stages of CC (Guerney, L., 1983b). Described is the most typical format.

4. Stage Four—Transfer and generalization (a total of two sessions in the form of four or five partial sessions included in the feedback times following the parents playing with the children, starting usually about the fourth such session).

The reader should realize that the length and order of the stages are sometimes modified by clinicians to meet parent and (recently) health plan demands. However, the basic features of training, supervising, and feedback involving both dynamic and didactic elements, as well as guidance for transfer and generalization, must be included.

The play area is usually equipped with a collection of toys appropriate for the expression of aggression, regression, and mastery. For Jason's family included were weapons, bop bags, dolls and animals, kitchen equipment including water, playing cards, clay, crayons and other craft items, and games and mastery toys, for example, ring toss, bowling, and Battleship®. (For older children standard games such as checkers, Parcheesi®, and Clue®, would be added.)

Treatment Stages

The treatment stages will be organized in terms of the parent sessions or meetings to distinguish them from the child play sessions.

Parent Session 1

Following a short review of the goals of FT and the logistics involved, Mary and Emilio were each shown a videotape of a professional therapist conducting a play session with an unidentified child who played in an innocuous way. The therapist pointed out how the play therapist on the tape behaved in response to the child and how the child in turn reacted. The goal was to familiarize the parents with the behaviors of the therapist and their effects on children. The purpose of these behaviors was explained in detailed but simple terms, emphasizing the benefits to children.

The parents were encouraged to express their concerns about the method and their feelings about trying it. Positive expectations were provided, as well as much empathy for parental doubts, antipathy, and resistance. Reinforcement for participation was generously given. Since the family's own children were to play with the therapist the next week, logistics of bringing and supervising the children were detailed at the end of this session.

Mary and Emilio were each given copies of the Filial Problem Checklist (FPCL) (Horner, 1974) to complete before the next session. They were to fill out one for Jason and one for Carla. The FPCL is a standard list of 139 problems children experience; parents are to indicate the presence of each problem that pertains and its severity. The checklist is given again at the end of the therapy for pre–post comparisons. Empirical data on parents over the years have shown very significant decreases in parent reports of child problems (e.g., Guerney & Stover, 1971; Horner, 1974; Sensué, 1981; Sywulak, 1978).

Emilio checked 39 problems for Jason and 10 for Carla. (Emilio had no severe level checks.) Mary checked 56 problems for Jason, most at the most severe level, and 6 for Carla. Most of the problems centered on noncompliance, moodiness, and inability to get along with others.

Parent Sessions 2 and 3

Demonstration play sessions were conducted by the therapist and observed by each parent. Carla was selected for the first demonstration since she was less problematic, allowing her parents to be more relaxed and thus better able to observe the therapist's behavior more readily—their primary task.

Following this session, Mary and Emilio had a chance to talk about how Carla's play compared to her play outside the session. Since Carla was eager to demonstrate her abilities to the therapist while testing to see how the therapist reacted, neither parent observed anything notable. However, they were both proud of how well she drew and recited poems.

In the time left after the 20-minute demonstration, each of the parents participated in an empathy-training exercise to identify feelings and compose statements that demonstrated understanding. Empathy-training exercises involve the therapist reading "with feeling" statements made by children. The parents are to identify the child's feelings. After correctly identifying several feelings, parents are then asked to try to compose a "feeling statement" that reflects the child's meaning. The therapist gives prompts throughout the exercise to prevent practicing inappropriate responses and also provides the reasons for the preferred responses. For example, the therapist reads the child's statement, "I don't want to do that now," with intonations that indicate weariness and distaste. Parents in training might identify the feeling incorrectly, for example, "he is feeling lazy." The therapist would point out that this response is their evaluation of the child's feeling as opposed to what the child was really trying to communicate. The therapist suggests an alternative that more accurately reflects the child's feeling. In this example, it might be "he is not feeling up to it right now." No interpretation or motive for the feeling is included—simply a label for the feeling state. Parents are then helped to shape a response that includes the identified feeling, for example, "Right now, it is just too much." Parents are guided away from adding judgments, advice, or suggestions, for example, "Wait awhile, then do it." They are told that stopping with the empathic response leaves the action up to the child (the child leads the way in the play session) and demonstrates parental acceptance of the child's feelings and perspectives. And this acceptance will help the child overcome her problems.

Emilio and Mary had some problems confining their statements to the child's feelings or thoughts because of wanting to add their own views. This is quite typical of beginning learners of CC, both parents and professionals. Asking questions and making suggestions are difficult to extinguish in mastering CC.

In the next session, the therapist conducted a demonstration session with Jason. Things were uneventful in the session that Emilio observed. Emilio was proud of Jason's abilities and got a kick out of Jason's beating the therapist in a board game. In the session Mary observed, Jason again recognized that the therapist was an appreciative audience and took the opportunity to show off some tricks with Pog® cards he had brought with him. However, Mary had told him to leave the Pogs at home so she was upset that he had disobeyed. Jason made no effort to break limits after he was given one statement of the rule that he could not throw objects at the observation mirror. Jason saw the camera and wanted to know who could see him besides his mother; he had been informed that she was watching to learn how to play in this special way with him too.

In her parent session, Mary vented about Jason's disobedience and how she intended to punish him when he got home. The therapist explained that whatever happens in the play session is not to be carried outside, meaning no punishments outside the session or questioning about it later. However, if Jason were to play with the Pogs in the car or anywhere else outside the play session, she was free to discipline him as she would otherwise, short of physical punishment. Mary was reminded that physical punishment was frowned upon, as she had been informed when she first was seen at the center.

Mary had to learn what all parents and their children must learn when participating in FT. The play session is separate and different from the rest of the world: It starts and stops at the play site after the scheduled time, and what happens there is not carried over. She was told also that the session was not to be used as a bribe or a threat. Some parents, recognizing the importance of the session to the child, try to manipulate child behavior by threatening to withhold, or to add, a play session to attain their goals. Since Mary feels so incompetent in getting Jason's cooperation, it is quite possible that she would have wanted to seize upon play session manipulation to increase her power.

Because Mary was distressed with Jason, more time than usual was spent on her feelings of helplessness and her frustration about his troublesome ways. Mary cried because she was worried about how he will turn out. She had received another complaint from the school. Her anguish about Jason and herself as a mother was met with empathy. Little time was left for instruction but Mary was told that the limits and consequences exercised in the play session, as she would be taught to employ them, would clarify to Jason that she was in charge and that she would feel empowered when she played with him. She was also told that, in due time, this generally carries over to real life, reducing disobedient behaviors. Mary left with the wish that it would work that way for her and the thought that she felt better having a chance to talk about all of this.

Parent Session 4

In their respective sessions, Emilio and Mary conducted a complete session in short form, with the therapist acting as the child. This exercise is called "mock play sessions" and most parents, especially in groups, have a wonderful time with them. The therapist attempts to behave in ways similar to what their children might do: An acting out child would dictate mock limit-breaking play; a shy child mock withdrawn behavior. However, the therapist does not attempt to extend these behaviors beyond the capacity of the parent to respond at least minimally, according to the rules. If the parent "loses it," much laughter usually ensues and the therapist provides second or third opportunities. In addition to behaviors their own children might demonstrate, the therapist will role-play or cheat or play games or engage in other behaviors that come up in play sessions that parents might find challenging. The reader should know that all of these kinds of situations have been observed and discussed or practiced before the parent does the mock playing. If a parent cannot carry out this task, more instruction and additional mock play sessions are conducted until the parents and therapist are comfortable that the parents will be able to carry out a 10-minute session with their own children as the next step.

In the mock play sessions, parents practice the opening statement: "This is a special time (or room, depending on the circumstances). In here you may say anything you want and DO ALMOST ANYTHING YOU WANT. If there is something you may not do, I will tell you." The reason for the wording is explained word by word to the parents so that they understand the importance of stating it accurately. Much emphasis is made of stressing the "almost" anything so that there is an entree into setting limits. Children would have valid reason for protesting rules if they were told they could do anything they want instead of "almost anything."

How to use the session limit and consequence sequence is also taught. This consists of three steps. When a child breaks or is about a break a limit—for example, hitting the parent with a nerf ball, step one of the sequence would be voiced. The parent would say "Remember I told you that if there were something you should not do I would tell you. One of the things you may not do is hit me with things." Should the child continue to hit or threaten to hit, the parent should move to step two, the warning step. Here the child is told, "Remember you may not hit me with the ball. If you do that again (or start to do it), we will have to end the play session for today." Should the child continue in this same behavior, the parent moves on to step three of the sequence, which is, "Remember I told you that, if you did that again, that we would have to end the play session for today; well, now we will have to stop for today." If the child protests, the parent is to be very empathic to the child's objections but nonetheless end the session and leave the room (preferably with the child, of course). Parents worry that their acting out children will refuse to leave. Methods such as the parent leaving, turning out lights, carrying out small children, and so forth are offered. Of course, no parental hitting, pinching, yanking, or pushing is permitted. The value of parental acceptance of the desire not to leave is emphasized. This is a response that is rarely used in other limit-enforcing situations. It generally has the effect of diffusing the negative part of the situation and permits the child to comply while protesting verbally. This is a powerful moment in the play session process, especially for the acting out child. It is a message to the child that the adult can accept the feelings but will not tolerate the behaviors. For some acting out children, only a few such experiences can turn around a noncompliant lifestyle.

Parents themselves sometimes protest the step three consequence, believing it is too harsh or that the child may not have meant to do what he or she did. The therapist emphasizes that limits are not negotiable because it is impossible 95 percent of the time to know whether the child accidentally did something. Many manipulating children will stage "accidents," and, in passing over these, unwitting adults reinforce the manipulating behaviors. With professional therapists, consequences can be more varied, for example, removing the offending object, but extensive experience over the years indicates that it is best with parents to have the ending of the session consequence, only. This spares the parent from having to make decisions as to which consequence to use. Parents have trouble with those decisions, and the controlling effect of the consequence on the child can be lost or weakened while they struggle with it. However, even with parents, it is rare that a child does not comply by step two of the limit sequence, so the consequence step is almost never an issue.

The therapist tries to play the role of child as realistically as possible, offering challenges (asking a lot of questions, making demands, conducting puppet role-plays, giving orders, etc.) so that the parents will have an opportunity to actually respond as prescribed by the model. This means that the parent always strives to make an empathic statement (for example, providing necessary information or assistance) before moving on to other responses. In the case of imminent limit breaking of a dangerous nature—for example, standing on a pile of stacked chairs or trying to eat a noneatable—the empathic remark can be delayed until necessary action is taken. The safety of the child, parent, and valuable property (for example, video cameras) would be the goal. If a prescribed behavior would delay a safety measure then it would, of course, be common sense to modify the form. Parents catch on to that and have little trouble seeing the basis for prescribed limit-setting responses. Empathic statements do not come as easily for them as limits, but they recognize the importance of expressing understanding in building the relationship and helping children label their reactions appropriately. Their difficulty stems from lack of experience in responding empathically in the course of routine living. Whether done appropriately or not, there are few parents who have not practiced setting limits on their children's behavior long before they ever attempt a play session.

Mary and Emilio had the usual reactions to the mock play sessions. They obviously enjoyed the role-playing with the therapist but had difficulties in remembering to express understanding before moving on to other responses. Mary had to work on a tendency to provide corrective feedback for efforts made by the "therapist-child" that were not efficient—for example, pouring water from larger containers to smaller ones. She recognized that part of her problem was a mild concern over water mess, even though permitted in the playroom. Emilio had to restrain himself from offering unsolicited instruction with games.

Each parent had two 10-minute mock play sessions. Feedback and discussion of their feelings took place after each session so that they had guidance from the therapist on correcting problems from session one. Each of them did better in session two. These role-plays with the therapist are lighthearted, and the therapist is empathic with parents' feelings and very reinforcing of their efforts as well as their successes. In addition to developing skills, the goal is to have parents *feel* reasonably competent about their ability to play with their child.

The "therapist-child" conducted puppet plays with Emilio and Mary and assigned each of them various roles, as children commonly do. In these roles, the parents are instructed to play out the role as assigned—asking only a question or two to be sure they are playing the role as the child intended. For example, when playing teacher and pupil, one could ask, "Do you want me to do what the teacher says or disobey?" The therapist tries to help parents understand that the role-plays are an extension of the child's feeling and thought expressions and therefore deserve full support from the adult. Mary was more inhibited than Emilio in playing the roles but not inappropriate. Parents can become inappropriate in this piece of their playing by either resisting playing a role, following a path that does not further the child, or becoming such vigorous role-players that the child loses control of the direction. Parents recognize and practice in the mock sessions that the child takes the leadership in directing all session content.

Parent Session 5

This was the big session for both Emilio and Mary, when they each had play sessions with the children. Emilio admitted that he was a little worried about remembering the opening statement but otherwise was comfortable. Emilio had a 10-minute play session with both children since he attends only every two weeks. The first sessions are kept short in the event that the parents or children have a problem.

Prior to the play sessions, the therapist discussed how the structuring went at home with the children for the parent/child sessions. Each parent had been instructed about telling the children that they were now going to try to play like Dr. for a short time until they all got used to it. Mary was extremely nervous and was glad she was playing with Carla and not Jason. Jason was told about it in order to diminish possible feelings that Carla was being favored.

However, Jason wanted Mary to buy him a toy to make up for his not having a session. Mary stood firm and said that he would have a turn next week and Carla would not have a turn then. She even managed to empathize a bit with his disappointment but wished he were more patient and less competitive. The therapist empathized with Mary's frustration for a short time, but then reminded her that the major job tonight was to play with Carla. Mary was asked if there was anything she needed to review or rehearse before the session. She practiced the closing statement, which she feared she was confused about. With a 10-minute session there would be a two-minute closing warning, rather than the usual five-minute warning.

Both Emilio and Mary made few technical errors. Mary, however, was mechanical and stiff and sometimes repeated Carla's statements. At this point, Carla expressed no complaints about this. She seemed excited to have her mother in her world with her. Both parents professed to have to think first, on most occasions, about what would be the appropriate response. Emilio really had to restrain himself not to jump in and take over for Carla when she was struggling to assemble the ring toss game. Nonetheless, both felt good about their first play sessions, and Mary was a little less worried about playing with Jason in the next session.

Parent Session 6

Mary was self-primed to play with Jason. She wanted to do a little role-playing around the limit and consequence sequence so that she would really sound like an authority if she used it. However, Jason did not press her on limits; rather he introduced her to all of the toys and games in the room and showed her what he could do with them. This is typical "warm-up" stage behavior. Mary was very relieved afterward. She and the therapist discussed Mary's positive points and places where she needed improvement—primarily in ease of making tracking and empathic statements. As is the custom of the filial therapist, she finished the session by giving Mary much reinforcement and encouragement for playing with Jason and for letting him direct the session. The value of his being able to control the agenda in the presence of his mother was discussed in terms of reducing the need for him to resist her. Mary seemed to be emotionally moved by this. She wanted to try playing a full session with Jason next time he was scheduled.

Parent Session 7

In this session, both parents played with both of their children. At this point, the total number of play sessions for each child was three with Emilio and two with Mary. Jason was a little more aggressive in the play sessions with both parents. However, he responded well to the authoritative statements of his parents and refrained from testing further. But at the five-minute warning, Jason wanted his mother to let him borrow a new space-ray gun from the playroom. Mary knew that was not permitted and told that to Jason in correct "limit language." He picked it up and ran around the room and then out of the door. He was laughing vigorously and then turned and threw it back into the room. The session was ended even though theoretically there were three minutes left. (If children run out of the room, they may not return that day.) Jason made no effort to return, but he could be heard telling Carla how he tricked Mary. This behavior signals a move into the aggressive stage of the therapy—the next expected stage in CC.

   In the parent session, Mary focused entirely on the last incident. The therapist empathized with Mary's disappointment. Mary thought Jason appreciated how special the play session was for them, and she had hoped Jason would not behave like that. As usual, he "had to spoil it." She perceived him as determined to make her unhappy. After a thorough venting of these feelings, the therapist systematically analyzed the session with Mary, pointing out first many positive behaviors on Mary's and Jason's part. Since no technical errors were made, the therapist rehearsed some sample tracking and feeling responses with Mary to improve the ease with which she could respond. Her performance here was the best it had ever been. Feedback finished with much encouragement and praise for Mary for not running out after Jason or in any way trying to make that "escape" a post-session issue. Mary had really wanted to do that but felt obliged to honor the rule about play session sanctity. When finished, Mary was able to accept that the session had basically been a very good one and seemed to have put the "escape" into perspective.

Parent Session 8

Emilio's sessions with the children went smoothly. Jason battered the bop bag furiously but Emilio was able to handle this well. Carla tried to persuade her father that he should not play with Jason—only with her. At first, Emilio asked her why and started to tell her that he couldn't do that but quickly recovered to make minimally skilled empathic responses. Carla responded well to those and explained that (as she saw it) Emilio played better with Jason than he did with her at his house, so Jason didn't need a special time. She wanted her dad to be more in tune with her and more sincerely involved in things she liked to play. Emilio did not attempt to defend himself but listened and commented until she moved on to something else. She wound up sitting on his lap after that. While not unusual for Carla to lap sit, it was the first time she had done so after an emotional confrontation.

The therapist debriefed with Emilio, who was surprised at Carla's perception because he saw himself as in no way less interested in Carla's life. However, after many empathic remarks from the therapist about his confusion and hurt, he thought that perhaps Carla resented the time he and Jason spent on throwing practice and talking about baseball and basketball together.

Carla provoked Mary for the first time in her play session when she wanted Mary to take off her glasses, jewelry, shoes, and belt so that Carla could put them on a doll. This was a personal limit for Mary and she remained firm, but she didn't like that Carla continued both to whine about it and to tell Mary she wasn't nice.

In the debriefing, Mary poured out that Carla also tries to manipulate her sometimes and how that really hurts because she had always been there for Carla—unlike Jason—and has given her everything, and why wasn't she contented? Following empathic responses, the therapist talked about all of the signs in the play session that Carla was very attached and devoted to her mother and that this episode was much more of a control issue, not one of not caring about Mary's feelings.

A discussion followed, with some examples of control versus feeling issues that might occur outside of the play session given to Mary to label, to help her to distinguish feeling issues from control issues and to respond accordingly. A suggested hypothetical example, which could be mislabeled and thus inappropriately handled, was Carla's wanting something that is impossible for Mary to provide. Since there is no action that can or should be taken in such a situation, the issue to be dealt with is Carla's feelings about it. (In due time Mary will be taught how to introduce her feelings into such a situation after being appropriately accepting of Carla's.) It was explained that an issue would be labeled a control issue when action is required, for example, Carla's taking Jason's possessions. Some parental control must be exercised then. Of course, as in the play sessions, feelings must be addressed at some point, as well as exercising control, but the primary need is to control the undesirable behavior. The principle here is that children's feelings should be understood and respected but they cannot control the outcome. Therefore, when only expressions—not actions—are put forth, the parent's responsibility is to respond appropriately to the feelings and not make a control issue out of it. Parents will, as did Mary, frequently respond to a request for the impossible by telling the child that she shouldn't ask or want such things; sometimes they will go further by saying the child is selfish or unreasonable to want them. These are control strategies. In FT, parents learn more appropriate control strategies for use with control issues in play sessions and real life as well, and they learn not to use control strategies for feeling issues. This exercise was the first instruction for real life that Mary and the therapist covered.

Jason was aggressive in Mary's session but not so physical as with Emilio. He was knocking down animals, puppets, and toys in the room with a toy broom while wearing a scary mask. Mary flinched a few times when things came somewhat in her direction but set no limits and managed to comment on how Jason wanted "to get" these objects and that it felt good when he did.

In the feedback session, the therapist was pleased to hear that Mary was not really scared and could see that such play meant a lot to Jason, although she didn't know why. She knew that she should let him be more physical at home and wondered if she should get him a bop bag for home use. The therapist suggested that would be a great idea once they stop playing at the treatment center and hoped that Mary would be able to continue to give Jason a one-half-hour special time a week at home for many weeks to come; the therapist suggested that they definitely continue doing so until after the second follow-up meeting two months after they finished the current sessions.

Since Jason had had only two really aggressive sessions with Mary and more would probably be necessary for Jason to work through his aggression, it was suggested to Mary that she continue to attend the center for 12 sessions. Mary readily accepted this recommendation. This would amount to eight play sessions with her for each child. She felt that, after the play sessions, Jason was much easier to handle, even after last week when he had teased her and run out. Emilio agreed to continue until he had attended twelve times as well.

Parent Sessions 9 and 10

Jason aggressed extensively in both Mary and Emilio's sessions for one more session. Again, he was much more physical in Emilio's sessions but his anger was visible in both. He continued in the aggressive stage as would be expected in CC for a child with his history. With the support of the feedback sessions, both parents were accepting of this behavior with the expectation that it would permit Jason to be less angry in real life. Carla began to be nurturing and, in very detailed instructions, gave a Koolaid® party for her father and shared baby care with her mother using playroom dolls. She herself went no further than to talk baby talk *for* the dolls. Carla seemed to have dealt with the aggressive stage in short order and to have progressed to the nurturing (dependence exploration) stage.

Beginning with session 9, transfer and generalization became a regular part of the post-play session meetings with both Mary and Emilio. With improved skills, less time was required for session feedback, and time was devoted to thinking about ways to use play session skills at home. In preparation for inserting additional skills for real life in the last three sessions, both parents were given copies of the book, *Parenting: A Skills Training Manual* (Guerney, 1995), and assigned to do the exercises there for the next meeting. The parenting course is derived from therapist play session behaviors, augmented by the needed skills for "real life," of reinforcement, "personal messages," and an examination of realistic expectations.

Parent Sessions 11 and 12

In these last sessions of the series, play sessions took less time to review because both Mary and Emilio had no technical difficulties and the children were engaged primarily in mastery play—making the sessions quite smooth and uneventful. This permitted time for discussion of the exercises in the parenting skills book and discussion about realistic expectations. Both Mary and Emilio were surprised to realize that they expected too much of Jason in some areas. They had previously believed that they were usually too easy on him. Emilio really spent very little time on the assigned exercises but did catch on to the notion that the use of the parenting skills was a logical extension of the playroom skills. He and Mary reported in their respective sessions examples of use of empathic responding, limit setting, and reinforcement with the children in their daily lives, one of the original treatment goals.

In their play sessions, both Mary and Emilio demonstrated the most critical ability of the CC therapist—to be accepting of the children without needing to control them, even though their empathic responses were not as skilled as those of some parents. The children continued to really love the play times. Both Jason and Carla began playing more real-life games with Emilio. Such activities begin to increase in the last stage of CC, the mastery stage. Children seem to want to increase challenges to their skills and abilities to exercise control over their emotions and impulses. However, Jason lingered a little longer in the nurturing stage with his mother, probably because of the deprivation of her nurturing that he experienced as a baby.

With Mary, both children played in nurturing ways but were very much in control and not dependent on Mary. Jason's session was remarkable in that he not only took care of Mary but designed scenarios in which she took care of him when he was wounded rescuing people from a fire. He used virtually the same scenario both weeks but played for a shorter time on this theme the last week.

In the debriefing, Mary cried again because she said that she felt tenderness toward Jason as they played out these nurturing themes, and she could see that the feeling was mutual. She could not remember when she had felt warmth and tenderness toward Jason in many years. If she had such feelings, they were usually mixed with some feeling that she needed to stop him or get him to do something. In the playroom, she had no such compunctions and actually enjoyed these exchanges.

The therapist went through the usual reinforcement with Mary and shared her own delight with the positive tone of the sessions for Mary and Jason. She pointed out that Jason exhibited the beginnings of this behavior in the MIM when he rubbed oil on her. Mary had seemed ambivalent about that experience then, and the therapist asked what made it seem different now. The dialogue follows:

Therapist: You seemed to thoroughly enjoy this mutual taking care of each other this time. It was harder for you the first time you came here to let Jason rub you with oil. What do you think has made it easier?
Mary: I don't feel like I have to control Jason so much now. I can relax more. It started in the play sessions when I could see that, with the loose rules, he could have done many things that he knew would make me mad but he rarely did. I could see that he really wanted me to be with him, so he wasn't so testy. I didn't worry that he was going to drive me crazy. He's been easier to handle at home as well. Like we talked about in the parent lessons, I have cut back on getting after him about every little thing and have realized that I can't expect him to be like a grown-up. But when I do want him to stop or to do something, I really follow through and he does it usually. I don't need to yell so much and

threaten to punish him. Carla was never difficult like Jason but she is easier too, less whiny and demanding of my attention or love. I didn't think that this could work so well when we came here but I really had no choice. The child protective services have closed our case now and I am really happy about that.

Therapist: You can see how the playing has made things better for you in a number of ways—in and out of the play session.

The children had been told before the tenth session that they would be coming to play only three more times, including the tenth session, making a total of eight play sessions per child for Emilio and seven for Mary. Both children expressed regret and Jason went into a pout, which the parents handled by dealing with his feelings empathically. However, both were pleased to learn that they would continue to play at home and would even get a bop bag in Mary's home play.

Arrangements were made for two follow-up sessions at the center in the same format—play sessions, feedback about them, and discussion of real-life issues and progress. Parent feeling issues continue to be part of these post-play session meetings, consuming more or less of the time depending on how concerned the parents are.

By the second follow-up session, Jason had had no reported school difficulties for three months. He told his mother that his teacher was nicer, some of the kids were also nicer, and he didn't mind going to school as much. His home play sessions were active but demonstrated controlled expression. At the center, the same pattern was seen. For example, in follow-up session one, Jason claimed that he was going to pour water on Emilio's head but stopped and said, "I wouldn't do that." While aggressive in tone, this act appeared to be a demonstration to himself and his dad that he had control of his aggressive impulses. At the mastery stage, children frequently create opportunities to get to the brink of an action and then pull back. If they don't actually verbalize what they are demonstrating, they make it clear enough to the trained observer.

EXPECTED OUTCOME OR PROGNOSIS

As cited earlier in treatment goals, the following were anticipated: to achieve positive changes at post treatment on pre-tests, to see Jason's school problems significantly decreased, and to see Mary and Jason relating more positively. Much of the information about their relationship would be apparent from observing their play sessions, but anecdotal reports from home and school were also needed. These reports supported the changes seen in the play sessions. Because Mary and Emilio met their goals of learning to conduct acceptable play sessions, the further therapeutic goals were met.

On the post-FPCL, both parents cited many fewer problems for Jason, with the decreases primarily around cooperation and obedience. They also rated Jason higher on the other parent measures they had filled out prior to beginning treatment.

Since there seems to have been a genuine turnaround in the Mary/Jason relationship, it is expected that it will continue on a smooth course at least until adolescence, at which time old issues may surface again, as sometimes happens. The therapist expects that Mary and Emilio will continue to be more realistic in their expectations of Jason and Carla, more accepting of their perspectives, and more able to be appropriately assertive in making demands of and in directing Jason. Further, they will probably continue some form of play session at home for some time to come. It was recommended that they seek another follow-up session or two in another two months, and Mary probably will. She is very receptive to the concept of empathic understanding and seemed to gain some genuine insights into her conflicted feelings about Jason and to resolve many of these. She indicated that, when the children are older and she can make time to go to school, perhaps she'd like to become some kind of counselor herself.

CONCLUSION

This case is an excellent example of the route to positive change when a psychoeducational approach is applied to family-based psychological problems. Because of the obvious psychological issues of the mother, it would have been reasonable to target her for individual therapy. Individual therapies or a standard form of family therapy might well have been considered. These alternative approaches to FT, with a skilled therapist, would certainly have held promise for improved functioning. However, the author feels strongly that FT results were just as solid and even more comprehensive in a shorter time than might have been achieved through another approach.

As with all psychoeducationally based approaches, the FT strategy was to make an assumption that learning new positive ways to behave would by-pass the need for analysis and focus on current problems. However, FT adds what strictly behaviorally oriented psychoeducational training programs do not have—the nesting of the training in new behaviors within a humanistic approach to change. The author maintains that both components are necessary to make therapy complete. A study by Eardley (1978) empirically compared standard FT with a variation that had only the didactic component. The group with both components reached more change goals for both parents and children. With these key components of empathy and acceptance, resistance to change and to learning new behaviors is reduced. Blame and delegation of responsibility are absent, so the individual has only internal resistance to change to overcome—not perceptions and insights imposed by the therapist. Parents who are accepted and respected seem to be willing to learn in the contained and relatively safe atmosphere of the playroom. The more typical therapeutic task of mastering new behaviors 24 hours a day poses greater difficulty to parents than trying to do so in short, manageable play sessions.

The acceptance offered Jason and Carla by their parents, most importantly Mary, permitted the children to lower encumbering defenses and deal with their real feelings and accept them. Parental acceptance led to self-acceptance, which resulted in reduced symptomatology for Jason. Acceptance and respect for the parents by the therapist, along with the *in situ* training and empathically oriented feedback, paralleled the parents' acceptance of their children. This parallel strategy is powerful and, as with Jason's family, can lead to better adjustment for both children and their parents.

BIBLIOGRAPHY

Ainsworth, M.D. (1982). Attachment: Retrospect and prospect. In C.M. Parkes & J. Stevenson-Hinde (Eds.), *The place of attachment in human behavior* (pp. 3–30). New York: Basic Books.

Andronico, M.P., Fidler, J., Guerney, B.G., Jr., & Guerney, L. (1967). The combination of didactic and dynamic elements in Filial therapy. *International Journal of Group Psychotherapy, 17,* 10–17.

Axline, V. (1947). *Play therapy.* Cambridge, MA: Houghton Mifflin Company.

Axline, V. (1969). *Play therapy* (rev. ed.). New York: Ballantine Books.

Baumrind, D. (1971). Current patterns of parental authority. *Developmental Psychology Monograph, 2,* 1–103.

Bratton, S., & Landreth, G. (1995). Filial therapy with single parents: Effects on parental acceptance, empathy, and stress. *International Journal of Play Therapy, 4*(1), 61–80.

Carkhuff, R.R. (1969). *Helping and human relations* (Vol. 1–2). New York: Holt, Rinehart and Winston.

Eardley, D. (1978). *An initial investigation of a didactic version of Filial therapy dealing with self-concept increase and problematic behavior decrease.* Unpublished doctoral dissertation, The Pennsylvania State University, University Park, PA.

Finke, H. (1947). *Changes in the expression of emotionalized attitudes in six cases of play therapy.* Unpublished master's thesis, University of Chicago, Chicago, IL.

Fleming, L., & Snyder, W. (1947). Social and personal changes following non-directive group play therapy. *American Journal of Orthopsychiatry, 17,* 101–116.

Ginsberg, B.G. (1976). Parents as therapeutic agents: The usefulness of Filial therapy in a community mental health center. *American Journal of Community Psychology, 4*(1), 47–54.

Glasser, N. (1986). *Parents as therapeutic agents: A study of the effect of Filial therapy.* Unpublished doctoral dissertation, North Texas State University, Denton, TX.

Guerney, B. and Stover, L. (1971). *Filial therapy.* Final report, No. MH 1826401, 1–156.

Guerney, B.G., Jr. (1964). Filial therapy: Description and rationale. *Journal of Consulting Psychology, 28*(4), 303–310.

Guerney, B.G., Jr. (1976). Filial therapy used as a treatment method for disturbed children. *Evaluation, 3,* 34–35.

Guerney, L. (1975, April). *A follow-up study on filial therapy.* Paper presented at the annual convention of the Eastern Psychological Association, New York.

Guerney, L. (1983a). Introduction to Filial therapy. In P. Keller & L. Ritt (Eds.), *Innovations in clinical practice: A sourcebook* (Vol. II, pp. 26–39). Sarasota, FL: Professional Resource Exchange.

Guerney, L. (1983b). Client centered (non-directive) play therapy. In C. Schaefer & K. O'Connor (Eds.), *Handbook of Play Therapy* (pp. 21–64). New York: Wiley.

Guerney, L. (1991). Parents as partners in treating behavior problems in early childhood settings. *Topics in Early Childhood Special Education, 11*(2), 74–90.

Guerney, L. (1995). *Parenting: A skills training manual* (5th ed.). State College, PA: The Institute for the Development of Emotional and Life Skills (IDEALS).

Guerney, L., & Guerney, B.G., Jr. (1985). The relationship enhancement family of family therapies. In L. L'Abate & M. Milan (Eds.), *Handbook of social skills training and research* (pp. 506–524). New York: Wiley.

Guerney, L., & Guerney, B.G., Jr. (1987). Integrating child and family therapy. *Psychotherapy, 24*(3S), 609–614.

Guerney, L., & Welsh, A.D. (1994). Two parents as change agents for their two children: A Filial therapy case study. In T. Kottman & C. Schaefer (Eds.), *Play therapy in action: A case Book for practitioners.* Northvale, NJ: Jason Aaronson Publishing Company.

Horner, P. (1974). *Dimensions of child behavior as described by parents: A monotonicity analysis.* Unpublished master's thesis, The Pennsylvania State University, University Park, PA.

Levinger, A.C. (1990, November) Filial therapy combines parent education with play therapy. *Communiqué, 16,* entire issue.

Oxman, L. (1971). *The effectiveness of filial therapy: a controlled study.* Unpublished doctoral dissertation, Rutgers University, New Brunswick, NJ.

Patterson, G.R. (1976). Parents and teachers as change agents: A social learning approach. In H.L. David (Ed.), *Treating relationships.* Lake Mills, IA: Graphic Publishing Company.

Rogers, C.R. (1951). *Client centered therapy.* Boston: Houghton Mifflin Company.

Sensué, M.E (1982). Filial therapy follow-up study: Effects on parental acceptance and child adjustment. (Doctoral dissertation, The Pennsylvania State University). *Dissertation Abstracts International, 42,* 148A.

Stover, L., Guerney, B.G., Jr., & O'Connell, M. (1971). Measurements of acceptance, allowing self-direction, involvement and empathy in adult-child interaction. *The Journal of Psychology, 77,* 261–269.

Sywulak, A.E. (1978). The effect of Filial therapy on parental acceptance and child adjustment. (Doctoral dissertation, The Pennsylvania State University, 1977). *Dissertation Abstracts International, 38,* 6180B.

Thomas, A., & Chess, S. (1977). *Temperament and development.* New York: Brunner/Mazel.

CHAPTER 6

Developmental Play Therapy

VIOLA A. BRODY

INTRODUCTION

Personality Theory

The theory of personality that provides the framework for the developmental play therapy approach is the object relations and attachment theory of Mary Ainsworth, M.C. Blehar, E. Walters, and S. Wall (1978) and John Bowlby (1969). Research on touch by Barnard and Brazelton (1990), Des Lauriers (1962), Harlow (1958), Montagu (1986), and Spitz (1946) also supports the conceptual focus of developmental play therapy.

Attachment is the name of the first mother-child relationship outside of the womb. In this relationship the mother provides the condition the child needs to develop an inner or core self. That condition is touch. Through the mother's caring touch the child experiences his physical body, his mother's physical body, and the pleasure of feeling his own living body. The first self is a body self (Freud, 1923).

The pleasurable experience of the mother-child contact provides the condition the child needs to experience himself as "real, separated, and differentiated from a mother, who is also experienced as real, and providing him with satisfactions and gratifications" (Des Lauriers, 1962, p. 37).

Des Lauriers (1962) continues:

> The child can relate to the mother only if he experiences her as a mother, that is, separate from him. The libidinal energies striving for satisfaction find the possibility of ultimate pleasure only when conditions for reality experience are given, that is, when an ego exists that can experience pleasure, and when an object exists that can be related to in the experience of pleasure. (p. 39)*

In the attachment theory model, touch is an ongoing body-contact dialogue between one specific adult, usually the mother, and a child—one as the adult who pro-

---

*Printed with permission from International Universities Press.

vides and one as the child who receives and seeks contact. It is the pleasure element in this touching relationship that enables the child to feel his body. Through his felt body the child becomes aware of himself. This bodily felt awareness "carries" the "consciousness" of the self (Merleau-Ponty, 1962).

This bodily felt awareness furnishes the drive toward relating through verbal language in order to keep the mother doing what she is doing ("Do it again."). In other words, the child starts to talk because he's aware that he feels something fun and pleasurable, that he wants more of this feeling, and that there is someone really listening to whom he can talk and with whom he can share. The child has something to say because he feels something. Out of the repeated felt experiences of one's body comes the ability to talk, to image, to fantasize, and to think abstractly.

A child who has experienced this repeated body contact with an adult who is fully present for him and with him will always have a solid sense of his body—a "home" or "centering place" within himself. He will know how to ground himself. He will know how to ask for what he needs because he knows what that is.

Developmental play therapy is based upon this model. Like the mother in the model, the developmental play therapist (DPT) initiates the dialogue of touch. The touch dialogue is creative, playful, and intimate—the basic way an adult and a child get to know each other. Developmental play therapy is the first play therapy because it provides the basics needed for symbolic play.

The basics include experiencing the awareness of the body when touched. This awareness creates an inner self that enables the child to deal with the world from the inside out. Self-esteem begins here—feeling good about one's body. To feel good about his body, however, requires the presence of someone who is able to see the child as he is, without judgment, and who knows how to provide the kind of contact that the child needs in order to feel seen.

Touching, then, is a communication between the one touching and the one touched. Through her hands—body parts almost miraculously capable of an infinite variety of pressures, delicate to strong—the toucher communicates the quality of her presence. Her touches tell the one touched how the toucher feels about him. In response, the one touched—all without words, and moment by moment—expresses his experience of being touched. Expressive touch is the first mode of communication, the first give and take in the life of the human individual. It is the foundation on which all later verbal and nonverbal communication must build. It provides the rationale for what every DPT does: bring about therapeutic communication by touching the child. Every DPT strives to be aware at all times during developmental play therapy of the messages her touch sends to the child and aware, as sensitively, of the child's bodily responses to the touching she initiates.

The recent past has made us starkly aware of the tragedy of child abuse. We know that many adults have touched children roughly and violently and that some have touched children for their own sexual gratification. Much effort has been directed toward exploring what life experiences motivate child abuse. We have learned that many child abusers have been subject to abuse in their own childhood. But we have learned, also, that those who have experienced themselves touched often with loving care as children do *not,* as adults, abuse children. Or, if they start to harm a child, they catch themselves immediately and stop. Those who have experienced consistent loving care through touch develop an inner voice that does not allow them to harm a child.

In developmental play therapy, the touching experience includes hands, fingers, face, feet, toes, and the body as a whole when the child is cradled or when playing some of the DPT games (Brody, 1993, p. 358). The genital area of a child is not touched or identified by the DPT. However, some young boys, and occasionally some girls, have a need to be identified as sexual beings. To a boy who exhibits his sexual organ, the DPT says, "You want me to know that you are a boy and that you have a penis. That's nice that you have it, and now you can put it back in your pants." If a sexually abused child invites sexual contact from the therapist, the DPT says, "That is something you and I are not going to be doing. That part of your body is private and belongs to you. No one should touch it but you." If a physically abused child asks to be spanked, the DPT says, "I do not spank children, so I would never spank you."

Teachers today report an ever increasing number of young children who cannot relate even on a nonverbal level. These children are attached to no one. Therefore, more and more, training is provided for teachers in the use of touch as a DPT uses it. These teachers are told that touch is the essential starting place for reaching children who need this very basic "mothering," in order to relate, first, to one other person, and then to relate with awareness and lovingly to all the others who will be significant to their lives. To forbid all teachers to touch young children who lack all attachments would deprive these children of their most basic need.

As you follow Jason's therapy sessions in this article, you will experience and come to understand the meaning of touch as well as the quality and kind of touch expressed in developmental play therapy.

Model of Psychopathology

The developmental play therapy model views psychopathology as a reflection of the child's lack of awareness and appreciation of his physical body. Hence, he is not well grounded. He has no center or inner self that takes charge and organizes his behavior *from the inside out*. This description fits children who have been abused, children with behavior problems, and those with autism, psychosis, and ADD (attention deficit disorder)—in short, all children with attachment-related problems. Most of these children are unaware of feeling anything.

In addition to those just described, many bright, highly verbal children also show a lack of awareness and appreciation of their physical bodies—expressed in low self-esteem, difficulty in relating to others, and a lack of interest and joy in what they are doing. That is, they are unable to benefit from their intelligence and creative ability because they don't experience their energy, motivation, and belief in themselves.

Goal

The goal of developmental play therapy is to provide the child with the condition needed to develop his core self—the inner self that guides and controls him from the inside out. The condition that initiates this process is touch provided by an adult who knows what it means to touch.

Cure

The child is "cured" in developmental play therapy when he demonstrates, in his interactions with the therapist, that he is an organized, goal-directed child who enjoys doing what he does. The child especially shows his inner organization in the way he handles the termination of therapy.

Provided the child has had the needed amount of time in therapy, the child responds to the termination of therapy in the following stages:

1. The child experiences and expresses some kind of pain—sadness, anger, sometimes tears.
2. In the following session, the child experiences and expresses love, empowerment, or joy through some form of a drawing, or a poem. The form he creates defines for him the relationship he had with the therapist.
3. In the final session, children in developmental play therapy tend to do two things initiated by them: They play once more the games they played with the therapist and they ask to be held or "carried" by the therapist (in order to create a memory of being held that they can take with them).

When asked what they liked best during the time they were in therapy, the children typically say either the "cradling and the lullaby" or that they could do something the therapist could not do. These responses to the termination come from children who have learned that they have an "I" inside themselves and who are able to give form to their feelings.

CASE FORMULATION

Jason's Core Self*

Jason does not have a core self in the sense that he is in charge of himself *from the inside out*. Instead, he is busy reacting to and trying to deal with an outside world in which others appraise him negatively, offer him no support, and reject his unique personhood. The negative world that Jason experiences is portrayed in his responses to the Thematic Apperception Test, TAT cards 2 & 7BM.

Jason's inner self has incorporated and internalized the negative attitudes that have been thrust upon him. His inner voice echoes them as he judges himself. His own inner voice says, "You're no good. You never do anything right no matter how hard you try. When you do things you want to do, you make a mess of it. Talking to your mother or father doesn't do any good because they don't listen."

Yet, in spite of all this, Jason feels a longing to be "liked" and to be "trusted." He sees that there is such a thing as love in his family—between his mother and his three-year-old sister, Carla. Awareness of his longing for love and trust begins the development of his core self—an inner self that is his and is for him.

---

*See "Orientation to the Text: The Case of Jason L.," p. 1.

Because he has not felt seen, understood, and loved by his parents Jason has intense feelings of frustration, anger, fear, and sadness. Sometimes he wishes he were dead (reported by Mary). He can't deal with these feelings because there is no one with whom he can share them.

What Jason does is to act out his feelings—"swearing, arguing, demanding, disobeying, throwing his books, sulking, withdrawing," and even being involved in a fire-setting act with another boy. Jason says that he doesn't like his mother yelling at him but he doesn't tell her that. Jason plays down the incident of mother slapping him.

Jason has a lot of energy and he has to use it some way. It is as if he's going to make somebody pay attention to him one way or another. He succeeds in this unconscious aim when his behavior at school is disturbing enough that it gets him into therapy.

The Behavior Scale shows that Jason cannot participate in school activities whether "sitting activities or play activities with peers without adult intervention." His teacher reports that Jason has become "more noncompliant and disruptive." To do his schoolwork well Jason has to have the attention and help of one adult staying with him throughout his task. Mary reports that Jason prefers to play with younger children. The Behavior Scale rated him at mid Stage II (age 2 to 6).

Clearly, Jason's behavior is that of a younger child. Jason is trying to be a seven-year-old but fails because he does not have the inner resources he needs to function at his age level.

During the testing (MIM task—"draw our house") Jason does experience Mary as seeing him and supporting him when *she was told* to do something specific with him. Jason's responses in this mother–child interaction show the qualities of his core self: He has no confidence in that self and no positive appreciation of that self. Yet, with Mary's continued support, Jason was able to experience his inner self, for one moment, as positive toward him. In other words, when his mother is present *with* him and *for* him, she feels real to him and he feels real and present.

This interaction between Mary and Jason demonstrates that this developmentally three-to-four-year-old Jason needs a relationship with one person who is there solely for him—a person who structures, supports, and enjoys being with him and watching him sense himself as competent. In this situation, his mother did not reinforce Jason's negative view of himself. Instead, she gave him a different voice to internalize—"Try, you *can* do it."

This interaction also reveals that both Mary and Jason need someone to provide structure and focus if their meetings are to promote Jason's development. When someone provided his mother with a focus then she could provide a focus for Jason.

Jason's Experience of His Body

This model states that the awareness of one's body comes about through caring touch from another who knows how to convey caring through touching. What touching experiences does Jason experience with his parents? Jason's physical contact with his mother includes being "smacked" on his cheek so hard that he had a bruise. He also gets spanked occasionally. This is not the kind of touch that creates an attachment relationship and a core self in the child.

When his mother *was told* to put lotion on Jason's elbow in the MIM task, he allowed it with reservations. He much preferred to put the lotion on mother, who really enjoyed it, saying, "It feels great!" Jason spent a long time on her because she was inviting this touching.

When his father was asked to do the same exercise with the lotion with Jason, Emilio created a thumb-wrestling game with lotion all over their hands. Jason said, "This is fun" and didn't want to stop. Emilio told him he had to stop and had to wash his hands. Jason said, "No, I don't want to." Emilio said, "It's time to stop."

Emilio's attitude differs from Mary's in that the mood was lighter and he created a game in which the lotion could be experienced as fun. And Jason told his father what he wanted: "I don't want to stop. This is fun." Emilio showed that he could set limits. However, since this seems to be the only time Jason really had fun and had asked for something he wanted, it would have been nice for Emilio to have recognized Jason's enjoyment by saying, "Since you liked it so much, we'll do it one more time and then we have to stop."

Jason's Mother

As stated before, the beginning of everything a child learns begins with an awareness of his physical body brought about through touch by someone who knows how. Jason's mother does notice and touch him but only when he does something that irritates her, such as throws his books, disobeys, or sulks (Parent Report DTORF-R). Mary's touch consists of an occasional "smacking" and "spanking."

As far as noticing and seeing Jason, she doesn't do that. When he comes home from school, she doesn't see him. Only his books are noticed and they are in the wrong place. She doesn't notice his anger, only his actions. She doesn't see his unhappiness as he walks in the door. Thus, she doesn't say, "What happened in school today? What's the matter? I haven't seen you all day. Sit down and tell me about it."

Jason's mother cannot see his unhappiness because she is experiencing and involved with her own anger. Perhaps, she, like Jason, needs to be seen and appreciated at the end of the day. She experiences not being seen and understood by Jason instead of his appreciation and understanding of her. Both are in the same boat.

Jason's mother presents the picture of a woman whose basic needs to be seen, understood, and touched have not been met. Therefore, she cannot give Jason what she herself has rarely, or never, experienced.

Mary's history supports this assessment (Family History). As the oldest child, "she took care of everybody." Thus, like Jason, she was deprived of her early childhood. She was depressed much of her life and never sought therapy.

Although Mary looked forward to having her first child, the pregnancy was complicated. From the beginning, she experienced Jason as a difficult child—irritable as an infant and "noncompliant" as a toddler. She said, "I disciplined him inconsistently, occasionally using time-outs and sometimes resorting to spanking." Even when Jason was a sick infant and she held him, her touching was not coming from her heart. Her touch had worries and fears in it. She never enjoyed him. She viewed him as sick or about to become sick. He aroused a lot of anger in her.

Jason and his mother did not have time to get to know each other. Their contact with each other was constantly interrupted during the first five years of Jason's life. When Jason was 11 months old, she became pregnant again. This child was premature and died. Mary became depressed and could not care for Jason. Emilio began seeing another woman. A third child, also a complicated pregnancy, was born when Jason was three—his sister Carla. Mary could not take care of both Jason and Carla, so she sent Jason to preschool when he was four. His parents divorced when Jason was five.

Mary experienced her two children, Jason, age seven and Carla, age three and a half very differently. She described Carla as the "most warm and loving child a mother could have." During the intake, she and Carla were always touching each other.

Mary's history supports the conclusion that Jason's deficiency goes back to the first four years of his life. Jason cannot use his above-average intelligence because the foundation—the relationship with his mother and the bodily felt experiences—has not been laid. She could not provide the necessary touching relationship.

What we have in Jason is a boy who is developmentally three or four years old, being forced to act like a seven-year-old (his chronological age). That makes everyone frustrated—parents, teachers, schoolmates, and Jason. He spends his energy trying to control the outer world because he has no inner world of his own. He needs to go back to the earlier period of his life, experience what he has missed, and bring it forward in order to be a typical seven-year-old. His mother also needs the fundamental experiences she has lacked in order to be a giving, happier, and more mature person.

TREATMENT GOALS

Jason

The first and primary goal is to help Jason experience his body. To do this the therapist looks at him, sees what she sees, and then touches him. She initiates the contact. By doing this she aims to spur Jason to invest energy in himself. He will demonstrate this by showing interest in how he looks, expressing how he likes his body, and experimenting to see what he can do with his body.

The second goal is to support Jason as he shifts toward providing his own structure—saying what he wants or showing off what he can do. The therapist does this by stepping back and becoming more of a listener and a receiver. She follows his instructions and allows him to struggle with whatever he tries to create.

The third goal is to be available and present when he experiences painful feelings, especially those stirred up by the termination of therapy and when he himself creates what he needs to say goodbye.

Jason's Mother

Mary would be seen on a weekly basis for herself. The goal for her would be the same primary goal as for Jason; namely, to focus her attention on her physical body as the first stage in helping her become aware of herself. She would continue in treatment after Jason terminates.

The School

The school would be asked to report any changes they saw during Jason's therapy and to write a final report at the end of his treatment.

TREATMENT DESCRIPTION

Logistics

Setting

The office is approximately 11.5 feet square. It contains a couch, at the end of which is a low metal file (sometimes children sit or stand on it), a window with a ledge on which children can sit, a desk (used for drawing) with a swivel chair (sometimes children like to spin in that chair), a bookcase, a closet with large folding doors used by some children as a hiding place or to play hide-and-seek games, and in the middle of the room a rocking chair used by the therapist to sit in and cradle a child.

Materials

A tape recorder, a plastic bottle of hand lotion, paper, pencils, and crayons.

Frequency and Duration of Treatment Stages

One-hour weekly sessions for three months or 12 sessions.

Specific Strategies and Treatment Stages

Introduction/Orientation

Developmental play therapy, as with any therapy, begins with a "Hello"—a get-acquainted time for child and therapist, a time for the therapist to let the child know what he will be doing here and what the therapist will be doing.

The quality and essence of developmental play therapy is conveyed to the child from the beginning of the "Hello" phase. For example, looking at Jason, the developmental play therapist (DPT) might say, "Hello," as she shakes his hand. "You don't know me and I don't know you and already our hands are saying "Hello" to each other." The DPT waits for Jason's response. Thus, the dialogue begins.

The DPT does not begin the Hello part by telling Jason why he is here and what he might be doing. Instead, she begins by focusing his attention on experiencing her and on experiencing his body. Thus, in the very first contact Jason gets a sense of who she is and who he is.

The first contact between child and therapist sets the stage for the developmental play approach. It focuses on experience of his body as the avenue that leads the child to know who he is. Put another way, the Hello phase begins the essential process of the child becoming interested in himself, invested in himself, and liking himself. The child accomplishes this through his attention on his body—the home of his core self.

In the Hello phase the DPT initiates what goes on in therapy. She notices and touches the child (e.g., "Your eyes are blue; you brought your hands with you today," touching them). At this stage, the child is not responsible for providing structure. It is the therapist's function to provide and the child's function to receive. The child responds in whatever way he does. The DPT does not control the child's behavior. The child is free to do what he needs to do with a few exceptions. The child is stopped at once if he tries to hurt himself or the therapist, or tries to destroy the contents of the room.

In summary, what the DPT provides is touch and presence. Touch, presence, intimacy between child and therapist in a here-and-now relationship—these are the therapy. They begin in the Hello part.

Session 1

Mother and Jason come up the stairs and ring the doorbell. The DPT greets them and tells Mary when to return to pick Jason up. She says Goodbye to Jason and leaves. The DPT leads Jason to the office and closes the door. She invites Jason to sit down on the couch and the DPT sits on the swivel chair facing him.

DPT: (Quietly, looking at Jason) Hello. Let's say Hello with our hands (offering her hand to Jason).
Jason: (Holds out his hand and takes therapist's hand.)
DPT: (Shaking his hand gently) I bet you didn't know that hands could say Hello, did you?
Jason: (Looks at therapist and smiles.)
DPT: Does your other hand want to say Hello too?
Jason: No . . . Okay (nodding, yes).
DPT: (Repeats the hand-shaking with Jason's left hand.)
Jason: When is my mother coming back?
DPT: She will be here at the end of our play time to get you. Tell me your name. I do know your name but I want to hear how *you* say it.
Jason: Jason
DPT: I like the way you say it. Can you say it higher?
Jason: Jason (at a higher pitch).
DPT: Wonderful! Can you say it down low?
Jason: (Says it lower and deeper, begins to get into it.)
DPT: Do it again and this time put your hands on your Adam's apple (shows him) and tell me what you feel.
Jason: (Puts his hand on his throat and nods his head yes.)
DPT: You can feel something there when you talk, right?

Jason: Uh-huh (yes).

DPT: Your name is Jason. My name is Vi. You may call me Vi. Do you know why your mother brought you here to see me?

Jason: I don't know.

DPT: You're here to have some play time with me. I'll see you every Monday afternoon at this time.

Jason: (Looking around) Where are the toys?

DPT: We won't be playing with toys but I will play some games with you. I will show you one right now. (Taking one of his hands) Did you know that your hands have hills and valleys in them? (Running her fingers between each finger on Jason's hand, outlining each finger from top to bottom) You go up a hill and down in a valley.

Jason: (Looks at the hand touched in the game) When is my mother coming?

DPT: Your playtime isn't up yet. She will be here when it's time. You don't know me yet and I don't know you yet. (Looking at Jason) You're quite a big boy. Stand up and let's see how tall you are. Stand next to me here.

Jason: (Stands next to therapist.)

DPT: You come to here on me (placing her hand on his head and on herself). Come over here by the wall and let's measure you. (Measures him with a yardstick, asking him to help hold it and makes a mark on the wall with his initials.)

Jason: (Allows this without saying anything; then walks over to the rocking chair, sits down in it, and starts rocking.)

DPT: (Walks over to the rocking chair, sits down on the floor in front of the rocker and Jason. Puts her hands on the rocking chair and guides the rocking and sings, to the tune of "Rock-A-Bye-Baby", Rock-A-Bye Jason in the rocking chair.) I see Jason and here are his two feet (touching them), here are his knees (touching them), and here are his two hands (touching them).

Jason: (Allows this for a brief time, then gets up out of the rocking chair) Now it's my turn to do it to you.

DPT: That's very nice of you but you know I am the mother and you are the child. So can I be the mother?

Jason: Okay (with a reluctant tone).

DPT: (Sits in the rocking chair, reaches over and lifts Jason on to her lap, chants, to the tune of "*Frere Jacques*") Here is Jason, here is Jason, here is his hair (touching it), here are his eyes (touching them), here is his nose and here is his mouth (touching them).

Jason: (Begins to get restless, starts to get off DPT's lap.)

DPT: Wait a minute before you get up. I have to say Hello to your feet. They have on these nice shoes.

Jason: (Gets up, looks around the room, points) What are those pictures on the wall?

DPT: It's time to get ready to say Goodbye. You know when you first walked into this room, we had to say Hello because you didn't know me and I didn't know you. Remember how we said Hello?

Jason: Shake hands.

DPT: What could we do to say Goodbye?

Jason: Shake hands.

DPT: Okay (shakes his hand). Goodbye. I'm going to say Goodbye by giving you a hug. (Hugs him, leads him out the door to Mary who had returned.)

Comments

This first session illustrated the developmental play approach—the use of touch to provide the child with a focus that makes him pay attention to his body. It also illustrated how the DPT took charge by keeping the focus on the experience of touch, and it showed how the relationship between child and therapist was initiated through touch in the very first session.

This first session showed Jason's reaction to having a very new experience for him—being the recipient of the sole attention of one person. At first, he just allowed the DPT to do what she did; he just let it happen. Later in the session when he began to *feel* the contact with the DPT, he became anxious. Then he began to ask about his mother and to try control by asking to take care of the therapist. When Jason returns for the second session, he will present himself from a new place.

Session 2

Jason: (Walks into the office, holds out his hand) Shake! (Said loudly with a smile.)

DPT: (Takes his hand, shakes it, looks at him) Oh, you remember we did that last week. Your hand is so warm (looking at his palm). See all these lines here— one goes this way (tracing it with her finger) and one goes this way.

Jason: (Watches intently; then opens and closes his hand as if he likes the feel of doing it.)

DPT: We could sing a song for that (chants) Open . . . Close (opens and closes her hand).

Jason: (Closes his hand) It won't open.

DPT: Can I open it?

Jason: Try.

DPT: (Takes his hand and tries to pry it open.)

Jason: (Holds his hand tightly closed—a fist.)

DPT: (Pretending to pry Jason's fist open and groaning as she tries) Well, I can't do it.

Jason: (Smiles as he opens one finger at a time) See, I can do it!

DPT: You're right. You're the only one who can open your hand. Great! (Hugs him.)

Jason: (Smiles and giggles.)

DPT: You know we could draw a picture of those wonderful hands (leading him over to the desk on which are paper, pencils, and crayons). Put your two hands on the paper and I'll draw around them . . . Now put your hands on the paper and see if they fit (after Jason had looked at the picture of his hands).

Jason: I want to draw yours.

DPT: (Allows it) You did a good job there.

Jason: (Puts his hands on the paper with the DPT's hands and compares his.)
DPT: If you sit on the couch here, I'll show you another game with hands. It's called the "Slippery Hand" game (Brody, 1993, p. 357). (Putting a small amount of lotion in her hand, she holds her hand out to Jason.) Would you put your hand in mine?
Jason: Oh, no. Yuck!
DPT: Well, do it anyway and see what happens.
Jason: (Does it gingerly.)
DPT: (Rubs the lotion into his hand and then massages his arm in a circular motion) I'm climbing up your arm (with her hand close to his shoulders). See if you can pull.
Jason: (Pulls his arm through DPT's hands.)
DPT: (Playfully) You're getting away. You're getting away.
Jason: (Finishes sliding his arm through DPT's two hands, laughs.)
DPT: (Playfully) Oh you got away!
Jason: Do it again.
DPT: Well, what about doing it with the other hand? You don't want to leave him out, do you? (Repeats with other hand.)
Jason: (Laughs) Do it again.
DPT: You liked that! We could let your feet have that fun too.
Jason: (Starts taking his shoes and socks off.)
DPT: (Initiates the same game with his feet.)
Jason: (Giggles a lot when DPT does his feet.)
DPT: (Touches toes firmly so as not to tickle.) [Developmental play therapy does not involve tickling.]
Jason: Do it again.
DPT: It's time to get ready to say Goodbye for today. I'm going to hold you while I put your shoes and socks on (picking him up and putting him in her lap, starts putting socks on).
Jason: (Pointing to a toe) This toe is sore.
DPT: (Puts lotion on the toe, then puts on his socks.)
Jason: (Pointing) This toe needs some too.
DPT: You don't want to go.
Jason: I need more.
DPT: You can get more when you come next time (puts his shoes on; stands him up). Here's a hug. (Leads him to the door and outside to meet his mother). Tell your mother you had a good time today.
Jason: (To mother) I had a good time.
DPT: On your way home you can tell your mother what you did. (Waves Goodbye to both as they go down the stairs.)

Comments

In session 2, Jason allowed himself to receive. He *felt* his body and experienced his body asking for more touches. He enjoyed the pleasure of the touch (which made him want more), and he enjoyed his power ("See, I can do it."). The negative feeling emerging in this session is his frustration over having to stop something as soon as he begins to enjoy it—a repeat of events in his early life (Family History).

The fact that Jason had such a good time in session 2 provided him with the positive feelings he needs to allow his negative reactions to surface. They can then be expressed and experienced consciously in the sessions that follow.

Working Through

Jason will relive his negative experience in his interactions with the DPT when he feels safe—certain that she won't go away no matter what he does and sure that she is strong enough to handle his anger.

Jason's anger comes from his inability to control anything; for example, he feels that when he has a good feeling something happens to take it away. He was beginning to feel this in session 2. He was having a good time and then the DPT said we have to stop.

The strategy for this stage is to be a container, a vessel to hold Jason's negative feelings. That is, they will be contained in this room with the DPT right here. No matter what he does, he cannot get rid of her. She sets limits as needed—holding and focusing Jason's attention on his body. And she acts so that he is always aware of her presence and responding to her.

Session 3

Jason: (Enters the room, sits down and covers his face with his hands.)

DPT: Hello Jason (no response). Where is Jason?

Jason: I'm not here.

DPT: Somebody is here. I can feel his hand (touching it).

Jason: Don't touch me. Leave me alone. Dummy (said softly).

DPT: Well this is the hand that I did the Slippery Hand game with last week (touching it lightly).

Jason: (Removes his hands from his face, looks at the DPT and yells) I *told* you not to touch it. That hand is poison. It will kill you! (Yells very loudly.)

DPT: We can't let that hand hurt anyone. I have some magic that will fix that hand so it won't hurt anyone (takes his hand and kisses it).

Jason: The other hand is poison too.

DPT: Oh that hand needs my magic too (kisses it). Now see if there is any other part that needs my magic.

Jason: My feet (taking off his shoes and socks). Do what you did last time.

DPT: Your feet liked that (laying her hands on the top of each foot without doing the game and looking at Jason). "I'm going to show you a new game. It's the "Gingerbread Cookie" game (Brody, 1993, p. 358). Did you ever have a gingerbread cookie? (Jason nods.) Well, I'm going to make you into one. What kind shall I make?

Jason: A chocolate one.

DPT: (Placing Jason on her lap as she sits on the couch) First, I have to put you in my mixing bowl (holding Jason tight as she moves him around while making the sound of an electric mixer, then laying him across her lap, face up). Now I take my rolling pin and smooth you out (moving her arm over him lightly from head to feet). Now I take out my cookie cutter to shape you. Here's your head (outlining his head and then each body part when named). Here are your shoulders on this side, your arm, hand, your thumb, pointer-finger (outlining each finger), big-boy finger, ring finger, and pinkie finger. (Moving from the hand to the armpit and down that side of his body, the hip, leg, feet, and every toe (going between the toes without tickling), back up the leg on the inner side as far as the knee, crossing over to the other leg and repeating the same on the left side of the body. [The genitals are not identified or touched.]

Jason: (Is relaxed; his body says "Keep doing it. I like it.")

DPT: Now I put in the eyes (very lightly touching them) your nose, mouth, ears, hair (lightly touching each as named.) Now I pour on the chocolate—you said you wanted a chocolate cookie?

Jason: Right.

DPT: (Moves her hand lightly over his head, torso, legs, and feet, going *around* the genital area) Now I put you in the oven to cook (pretending to close the oven door— makes SHHH sounds for heat, moving her hands above him for the heat). Now are you done?

Jason: No.

DPT: (Continues making "heat") This cookie is smelling so good. Are you done now?

Jason: Yes.

DPT: You know what you do with a cookie, don't you?

Jason: (Covers his face with his hands playfully.)

DPT: Oh, you don't want me to eat the face. I'll taste the hands first (kissing the outside of his two hands as they cover his face).

Jason: (Holds up one foot and then the other one for DPT to kiss.)

DPT: (Kisses them) Is there another part you want me to taste before we have to stop for today?

Jason: (Removes his hands from his face, looks at DPT, and points to his face.)

DPT: (Kisses each cheek.)

Jason: (smiles) My mother's never going to believe this.

DPT: To say Goodbye this time I'm going to hold you and rock you (moves from the couch to the rocking chair carrying Jason; sings Brahms's Lullaby.)

Jason: (Lies there with eyes closed as she sings.)

DPT: (Singing) (Lullaby and good night
Thy Mother's delight
Bright angels around
My child shall stand
They will guard you from harm
They will guard you from harm
You shall wake in my arms
You shall wake in my arms)

(Hugs Jason, carries him to the door, puts him in the arms of his mother) Here is your baby.

Mother: (Looks surprised as she takes him in her arms.)

DPT: I think he needs a little kiss to wake him up.

Mother: (Kisses Jason, who opens his eyes and looks at her; puts Jason down and takes his hand as they walk out the door.)

Comments

Nearly all attachment–problem children seen in developmental play therapy ask at sometime to be picked up and carried "like a baby." In Jason's case, he was picked up and carried because his total relaxation during cradling told the DPT that his body did not want to be disturbed. By carrying Jason to Mary without breaking the continuity, the DPT enabled Jason to return to his infancy to get what he needed. At the same time, she enabled Mary to become a mother for a few moments and to experience herself giving Jason what he needed in the present.

The Baby Stage (Sessions 4, 5, 6)

In the first three sessions, Jason experienced the Hello part of developmental play therapy. It included resistance followed by acceptance of the DPT and her touch. Now he is ready to enter the Baby Stage, a time for reliving his infancy—this time with some awareness. In this phase, Jason does not pretend to be a baby. He is a baby. He does what babies and young children do.

In the Baby Stage Jason's body tells him what to do. In every session, he wants to do the Gingerbread Cookie game and he enriches the game with his own additions. He calls this game "The Slow Gingerbread Cookie." By his instruction he shows that he wants the therapist to take a long time touching him. One time, when naming each of his toes, Jason said "the ring toe." This showed he remembered her saying "the ring finger" as she named each finger. If she leaves any part out, he tells her. His comments and instructions show that he is paying attention to each part of his body as it is touched and named. He feels very much alive. He is not just lying there letting her touch him with his attention someplace else. Thus, in the Baby Stage, therapy is not just a matter of physically touching the child through games. Rather, it is how the therapist "plays" the games, a matter of the time, energy, and presence the DPT gives to them. The DPT does them from her heart.

Following the Gingerbread Cookie game, Jason often lies down on the floor, sometimes with his eyes closed but he's not asleep. Sometimes when he does that, the DPT chants softly, naming the parts of his body, lightly touching them (here's your little head, here is your neck, here are your shoulders, etc.). Sometimes he reaches out and touches the DPT with his foot or a hand. When Jason is very quiet, sometimes the DPT says nothing and does nothing. The DPT is just there. Then they have moments of total silence.

Once when Jason lay on the floor with his legs facing the DPT he gave her a little kick. She grabbed his foot, saying "No kicking." Then she gave that foot some extra touching.

Jason showed three needs in these sessions: the need to be touched a lot; the need to experience his body itself without being touched; the need to be separate from the DPT but still in her presence, without touch and without words—in silence. In the Baby Stage, Jason is learning that he has an inside. He relates to the world now from the inside out in contrast to trying to control the outer world.

Because Jason now has inner resources, he recognizes he can provide his own structure. That change in him enabled the DPT to shift her function from that of a provider and initiator to that of a responder and supporter. It would have been a serious mistake if she had disturbed his quiet periods by presenting him with another game. If she had done that, Jason would not have experienced himself as seen and understood. From the outside it looks as if not much was going on in the Baby Stage. However, a lot was going on inside Jason. He was doing his own work on himself. The basic work of the Baby Stage leads to the later stages of therapy.

The Inter-Subjective Stage (Sessions 7, 8, 9)

In sessions 7, 8, and 9 Jason began to relate to the DPT by using verbal language. He began seeing the DPT as a person separate from him—hence, one with whom he could talk and relate. He looks at her as if seeing her for the first time: "How come you have all those wrinkles on your face?" He asks her if she can see him with her eyes closed. So the DPT and Jason practice trying to see each other with their eyes closed and their faces touching. They make a game of closing and opening their eyes and seeing each other ("The Owl" game, Brody, 1993, p. 360).

Jason likes to go to the desk, sit down, and draw, especially toward the end of a session. In session 7, Jason has a hard time stopping his drawing when told it's time to stop, put on his shoes and socks, and say goodbye for today. "You can take your drawing with you or leave it and finish it next time."

Jason: (Jumps up, marks up the wall with a crayon—very angry.)
DPT: (Grabs him, too late for the walls; sits him on the couch) I didn't like you doing that (said firmly).
Jason: You're bad. I'm going to put you in the time-out room.
DPT: You didn't like it when I told you to stop.
Jason: (Yells loudly) Yes I did! (Half laughing, half crying.)
DPT: (Finishes putting on his shoes and socks, stands him up, looks at him) Are you going to say Goodbye to me?
Jason: Goodbye. (Lets DPT hug him, leaves intact and calm.)

In session 8, Jason, as before, likes to end a session by going to the desk and drawing. When the DPT tells him it's time to get ready to stop and say Goodbye, Jason says, "No", but almost immediately he catches himself and says, "Okay." He gets up, puts his shoes and socks on, and says, Goodbye in a relaxed calm way.

NOTE: A couple of weeks after sessions 7 and 8, both the teacher and his mother reported that they saw a change in Jason. He was less defiant and more cooperative.

Session 9

Jason: (Comes in smiling.)
DPT: You're smiling, Jason.
Jason: I played soccer today (hides his face and giggles).
DPT: My goodness! Come over here and let me interview you (turning on the tape recorder). Ladies and gentlemen, we have a new member on our soccer team. (To Jason) Would you tell us your name?
Jason: Jason.
DPT: How old are you?
Jason: Seven and a half.
DPT: Tell us about yourself.
Jason: I'm Jason and I played soccer today. It was fun (his shyness disappearing).
DPT: Anything else you want to tell us?
Jason: I can stand on my head.
DPT: Would you like to show us?
Jason: (Goes to the wall and stands on his head.)
DPT: That's great! I didn't know you could do that (plays back the interview for him to hear but he is not that interested in listening to it).

In this stage, Jason occasionally tries out his verboten words on the DPT, especially in the beginning of a session when he doesn't know quite where to begin. He says, in a soft voice, "Fat lady, dummy, fart." She responds with, "You know a lot of words," and then continues with what she is doing. He was only trying to get a reaction out of her as he did with his mother.

Although Jason now relates through verbal language, he still retains the desire to communicate by touch. He begins one session by asking for The Slow Gingerbread Cookie game. He reminds the DPT of every part that she leaves out. In addition, the DPT nearly always ends a session with cradling and singing the Brahms Lullaby, which he also can sing.

Comments

In the inter-subjective stage, Jason had the kind of relationship with the therapist that allowed him to express, experience, and deal with one of his core problems—his noncompliant behavior with almost everyone. Experiencing his anger with the therapist freed him from that old behavior that kept him from relating to anyone. Now he can begin to learn through relating to others, letting them in.

Termination Procedures

The termination with Jason takes place in sessions 10, 11, and 12. In developmental play therapy, the DPT sets the date for the termination. The child does not have a part in that decision. Once the DPT decides on the child's readiness for termination, the child is given three sessions to complete the termination process. In those three sessions the child has the opportunity to express the pain at the separation, to express his positive feelings, and in the last session, to review all the things he enjoyed so that he can take them home with him—in his body and in his memory.

The most intimate and moving part for the child is the last session. He experiences an overview of the whole therapy in that one session. The child's last-time sharing takes on a special quality of intimacy and self-validation that was not there before.

The termination in development play therapy is not like a graduation where others are invited to celebrate one's growth. It is a private celebration between child and DPT, an integral part of developmental play therapy.

Session 10

Toward the beginning of this session, the DPT brings up the issue of termination with Jason. "You're doing so well here that you won't need to come here much longer."

> **Jason:** I don't want to stop.
> **DPT:** You have a little time to think about it. We will play today and two more times after today. Then we'll say Goodbye. Remember when we said Hello in the beginning? Now it's time to say Goodbye.
> **Jason:** Would you come to my house and see me?
> **DPT:** No.
> **Jason:** (Teary)
> **DPT:** Are you crying? Can you feel your tears? What do they taste like?
> **Jason:** Salty.
> **DPT:** (Sings) It's all right to cry
> Crying gets the sad out of you
> It's all right to cry
> It might make you feel better
> **Jason:** (Cries harder for a few moments) I didn't do good, did I?
> **DPT:** You did very well. I'm going to put a gold star on your hand (putting star on his hand). You did good.
> **Jason:** My toes are going to miss you.
> **DPT:** You could ask your mother to do your toes.
> **Jason:** She won't do it.
> **DPT:** You could say Hello to your toes yourself then.
> **Jason:** Cradle me and sing to me like you do.
> **DPT:** (Picks him up, sits in the rocking chair, sings the Brahms lullaby (Jason sings with her); then carries him to the door.
> To Mary: I'm going to play a game of "Pass It On" and this is what I am passing on to you—your beautiful son, Jason (hands him over to mother who holds him in her arms a few moments before leaving, looks at the therapist, and says, "thank you").

Session 11

Jason enters the room smiling. He sits on the DPT's lap and hugs her (new behavior). He says he's going to sing a song for her. He makes it up as he goes along.

> **Jason:** The flowers are growing
>   The sun is shining
>   It is spring
>   And I love you
>
> **DPT:** Thank you. *I love you too.* You are so good with words. I am going to write what you said (goes over to the desk for some paper and prints I love you).
>
> **Jason:** I want to write it (copies it and adds a smiley face).

When it comes time to do the cradling in the Goodbye part of the session, Jason reminds the DPT how to hold him. "You're to rock me up and down," as he gestures, showing her the motion. Jason did this because he remembers how the DPT changed the way she held him during the cradling. In the Baby Stage, she held him in the nursing position. Beginning with session 7, she changed the position to one more appropriate for an older child—namely, holding him facing the DPT with her hands behind his head and back, rocking him up and down.

When Jason stands up ready to go, suddenly, without any warning, he jumps up on the DPT, putting his legs around her waist. Automatically she grabs him to hold him. He says, "Pretend I'm your baby. Carry me."

She holds him tightly as she walks to the door (he's heavy). Jason smiles and loves it. She puts him down and says, "Goodbye." He says, "Goodbye."

Session 12

Jason enters the room whining and half crying, saying that he has a stomachache and he doesn't like it. The DPT offers to hold him. He says, "That won't help." She holds him and puts her hand on his stomach, telling him to breathe. Jason does it but says, "Nothing helps. I want to get better."

Jason does seem to be in some pain. Still holding him as she sits on the couch, she asks, "What do you need to make it better?" Jason says, "I don't know. I was going to bring you something so you wouldn't be lonely but I couldn't find any flowers." "That was nice of you to think of me and I'm glad just to have you here right now. *You* are my flower. You are a handsome boy."

Jason responds with a little smile showing he could receive the compliment at least for the moment. He returns to saying, "I want to get better."

The DPT says, "Just lie here quietly with me. You don't have to do anything. Just see how nice it is to be here with me, and you don't have to do anything (Jason has been on her lap all this time). She puts her hand on his stomach and tells him to feel her hand as his stomach muscles move up and down. "While you are feeling your breathing, I want you to think about how you want to say Goodbye to me today."

Jason brightens up as he says, "Do the gingerbread game one more time. I love that game."

DPT: (Starts to outline the shape of the cookie.)

Jason: You're supposed to put me in the mixer first.

DPT: Oh, you don't want me to leave anything out. You like that when I squeeze you tightly (holding him tightly as she shakes him up in the "mixer").

Jason: (Giggles) I'm not mixed yet.

DPT: (Continues the "mixing" and then outlines his body, bakes him; he stays in the oven a long time.)

Jason: (Points to parts he wanted kissed—face, hands, toes.)

DPT: How is your stomach now?

Jason: My stomachache is gone. It was just being quiet with you (gets off the therapist's lap, goes over to the desk and starts to draw—the way he likes to end a session to give form and meaning to it).

Jason draws two houses—very solid sturdy-looking houses. They were separated by a street or an area. Pointing to his drawing, Jason says, "This is St. Petersburg," and pointing to each house, "This is where Vi lives and this is where I live. I had a good time at Vi's."

The DPT says, "That's wonderful. I like your drawing a lot. You *know* where *you* live and you *know* where *I* live. I had a good time with you too, Jason. Before we say Goodbye, tell me what you liked best out of all the things we did." Jason says, "The cradling and when you sang the lullaby." The DPT hugs him and he gives her a kiss on the cheek—new behavior for him. He leaves, taking his drawing with him.

Comments

Session 12 illustrates how the DPT accepted the way the child described his experiences. That is, she didn't give Jason her interpretation of his behavior. For example, she did not make a connection for Jason between his stomache and this being their last time together. That would not have helped him and it would only have distracted him from the work he needed to do, namely, to allow himself to feel the pain he was experiencing—and Jason had the inner resources that allowed him to feel the pain. By so doing, Jason did his own healing. That is why the DPT rarely makes interpretative statements.

Experiencing his pain freed Jason to realize his core self—demonstrated in the way Jason defined the quality of the child–therapist relationship at the end of therapy: two solid buildings, separate but in visual communication with each other, each knowing where the other is in this world.

Report on Mother's Therapy

Mary was seen in therapy for weekly sessions during the time of Jason's therapy. Over time, she became more aware of the feelings and energy in her body. This was illustrated by her initial and later responses to crying during therapy sessions. Initially she said, "I don't know why my eyes water when I come here," and later, "I don't know why I start crying every time I come here."

Mary said she was strongly moved the day that the therapist put Jason in her arms at the end of his session. She also began experiencing a feeling of love for herself. As she opened to her inner self, she also became more available to Jason. The DPT will continue seeing her for a year.

Mother's Report on Jason

Mary reported that she saw a change in Jason within the first two weeks of therapy: He wanted to be near her. When she looked at TV, for example, he would sit next to her and push himself against her. She was surprised when he got into her lap one day. She liked it—that he did that.

School Report on Jason

The teachers reported that Jason is much less disruptive. He is calmer and more attentive in class. He talks more and lets them know where he is. He participates in the school soccer games. Also Jason showed he was beginning to enjoy school.

PROGNOSIS

Jason's prognosis is excellent because, through therapy, he has made changes that will endure. These include much greater ability to take charge of himself as opposed to futile and frustrating attempts to control the world outside of himself. Also, the unconscious motivation that led to Jason's having to act out has lessened because, with the DPT, he experienced the anger behind his acting out behavior and directed his rage more appropriately. This pattern of awareness and consciously directed behavior can be expected to occur more often as he matures. During his therapy sessions he learned to relate to the DPT and, to some extent, because of the awakening influence of the therapy experience, to his mother and school fellows. The ability to relate to others, of course, has a transforming influence on any growing child, just as the lack of capacity to relate almost inconceivably narrows a human life. Finally, and most important, through therapy Jason became interested in himself, explored his inner self, came to like himself. Thus Jason is armed for ventures into life, ventures he can frame and judge on the basis of his own needs and likings.

Jason made phenomenal growth in such a short time—12 sessions. This is not unusual for children like Jason treated by the developmental play therapy approach. Once they experience this caring, touching relationship they move very fast.

Mary's increasing ability to be available to Jason supports the favorable prognosis. Since mother is continuing her therapy after his termination, she can get help with Jason if needed, and further changes in her will foster further growth in Jason.

Jason already has the intellectual equipment—verbal language and above-average IQ—available as soon as he has an inner self that feels and knows what it needs. When therapy began, he was like a wonderful car that has no engine. It can't run or make a sound. The engine that was lacking in Jason was the alive, feeling awareness of his body. In a person, it is the body that moves and makes sounds. At the end of his therapy, Jason has a body and he has hooked it up to his intellect. He has an engine and he can drive his beautiful car.

CONCLUSION

Development play therapy with Jason clearly demonstrated the healing effect of touch—as defined in the developmental play therapy approach—on children like Jason who have been deprived of this kind of touch in their early mother–child relationship.

Teachers, therapists, and psychologists usually do not see the need for this basic touch experience in children who are intelligent and have good verbal language when they reach school age. Yet, the intake, history, and pre-treatment data ("The Case of Jason L.") all pointed to the conclusion that Jason's behavior problem at age seven stemmed from and reflected the fact that Jason's mother, because of her own needs, was unable to be there for Jason in any consistent way for the first four years of his life. Hence, he could not possibly have behaved and related like a seven-year-old though he had above-average intelligence and good verbal language.

The goal of developmental play therapy with Jason was to provide him with the touch experience he must have to create a sense of self—his core self. The kind of touch he received from the DPT in his therapy was the impetus that both began the development of his core self and decided its character.

Jason's Response to Touch

In the intake exercise (MIM), Jason preferred to do the touching, thereby taking care of Mary, rather than to be touched himself. Once he became used to being the receiver of touch in therapy sessions, however, he could not get enough of the touches provided by the DPT. He began *asking* for the touching games in every session.

For the first six sessions Jason *was* a baby —not a pretend baby. He could be a baby because the DPT *was* a mother—not a pretend mother. He and the DPT were on the same wavelength; that is, he needed to be touched and played with and she met that need, or he needed to lie quietly in her arms and so she cradled him and sang to him. Whatever he did he felt her presence. His developing inner self was a body self. A child's self-esteem begins here, begins always with the awareness of the body self.

Following these sessions, Jason found words that expressed his body feelings ("Do it again." "I don't want to stop.") Further, he could organize his experiences and represent them in a drawing. He also showed his acting out, uncontrollable behavior within the later sessions and got in touch with his anger—something he had not done before. That was the beginning of his learning to control himself instead of the outer world controlling him. He could carry on a verbal dialogue and relate through words. Words now represent his experiences, images, and memories. For the first time, perhaps, he learned to accept limits (when he drew on the wall).

In the termination phase, everything came together. Jason relived and reviewed everything he had done that he liked. The terminating process showed that he could experience and handle feelings—the sadness of terminating, the joy of being with the DPT expressed in poetry and drawings, and the experience of mastering his psychosomatic reaction to the termination. The latter is especially important in light of Jason's many disruptions. In his life, as soon as he began to become attached, he had to leave. Then at that time, he could not have said Goodbye because he had not said Hello. This time he *has* said Hello and now he *can* say Goodbye.

Jason's experience of himself as separate from the DPT is reflected in his ability to empathize with another when he showed he didn't want the therapist to be lonely. Most importantly, he went away feeling good about himself. His negative inner voice (TAT 2), "I'm not good enough," has changed to a positive voice, "I can do it." He can take charge of himself.

The touching games and the cradling were a part of every session even after Jason had moved into relating through verbal language. All the children the author works with always want a touch experience to take with them at the end. In the next to the last session, Jason did what other children have done; namely, he suddenly jumped up on the DPT asking her to "Pretend I'm your baby and carry me." Now, Jason *is* a *pretend* baby—very different from before. By his action and request, he created within himself the feeling of being cared for, of being held and loved. The feeling became his to take with him, to remember, to use when an older Jason needs the magic of loving touch.

Jason's drawing of the two houses in his last session reflects him as experiencing himself as real, separate, and differentiated from the DPT, who is also experienced as real, separate, and giving.

The Role of the DPT

In every case the DPT provides the kind of touches and quality of relationship that were illustrated in Jason's therapy. To do this, the DPT must be present with the child, must be sensitive to the life energy in her own body. Only then as she touches a child can she experience the quality of this child's energy. Communication by touch is a dialogue of energies. In the beginning, the DPT initiates activity and provides energy. Later, she follows the lead of the child. She knows when to touch and how, and when not to touch. It is the *way* the DPT plays the touching games that makes the difference to the child, not the games themselves.

Children organize and express their appreciation of their growth and their close relationship with therapists in creative ways. Further, it is okay for a therapist to be moved by the work she and the child do. When she allows herself to feel moved, the child benefits because the child feels moved too. In this way, the child knows that the DPT loves him because she lets her love show. This is what best defines developmental play therapy—the presence, the intimacy that child and DPT share.

BIBLIOGRAPHY

Ainsworth, M.D., S., Blehar, M.C., Waters, E., and Wall, S. (1978). *Patterns of attachment.* Hillsdale, NJ: Erlbaum.

Barnard, K.E., & Brazelton, T.B. (1990). *Touch: the foundation of experience.* Madison, CT: International Universities Press.

Bowlby, J. (1969). *Attachment and loss:* Vol. 1, Attachment. New York: Basic Books.

Brody, V.A. (1963). Treatment of a prepubertal twin girl with psychogenic megacolon. *The American Journal of Orthopsychiatry 33*(3).

Brody, V.A. (1993). *The dialogue of touch: developmental play therapy.* (Available from Viola A. Brody, 519 Plaza Seville CT. # 38, Treasure Island, Florida 33706.)

Brody, V.A., Fenderson, C., Stephenson, S. (1976). *Sourcebook for developmental play therapy.*

Des Lauriers, A. (1962). *The experience of reality in childhood schizophrenia.* Madison, CT.: International Universities Press.

Field, T. (1993, February). Congressional staffers witness miracle of touch. *APA Monitor:* Science directorate.

Freud, S. (1923). *The ego and the id.* London: Hogarth Press, 1927.

Goleman, D. (1988, February 2). Experience of touch research points to key role in growth, *New York Times, 1,4.*

Harlow, H. (1958). The nature of love. *The American Psychologist, 3,* 673–685.

James, B. (1994). *Handbook for treatment of attachment—trauma problems in children.* New York: Lexington Books.

Levin, D.M. (1987). *The body's recollection of being.* London: Routledge & Kegan Paul.

Merleau-Ponty, M. (1962). *Phenomenolgy of Perception,* London: Routledge & Kegan Paul.

Montagu, A. (1986). *Touching: the human significance of the skin* (3rd ed.). New York: Harper & Row.

Moustakas, C.E. (1992). *Psychotherapy with children.* Greeley: CO: Caron Publishers.

Sechehaye, M. (1951). *Autobiography of a schizophrenic girl.* New York: Grune & Stratton.

Simon, S. (1976). *Caring, feeling, and touching.* Sunderland. MA: Values Press.

Spitz, R. (1946). Hospitalism: A follow-up report. *The Psychoanalytic Study of the Child* (Vol. 2). New York: International Universities Press.

Stern, D.N. (1985). *The interpersonal world of the infant.* New York: Basic Books.

Winnicott, D.W. (1953). Transitional objects and transitional phenomena. *International Journal of Psycho-Analysis, 34,* 89–97.

CHAPTER 7

Gestalt Play Therapy

FELICIA CARROLL AND VIOLET OAKLANDER

INTRODUCTION

Theory

Gestalt therapy is a humanistic, process-oriented form of therapy that is concerned with the integrated functioning of all aspects of the person: senses, body, emotions, and intellect. The fundamental principles and concepts of Gestalt therapy are rooted in psychoanalytic theory, Gestalt psychology, and humanistic perspectives, as well as phenomenology, field theory, existentialism, and Reichian analysis of physical resistance. An extensive collection of literature on Gestalt therapy that has grown from the original works by Frederick Perls, M.D., (1948, 1969) presents these theoretical assumptions and principles and describes Gestalt therapy as it is practiced today (Perls, Hefferline, & Goodman, 1951; Polster & Polster, 1973; Yontef, 1993).

All of the concepts and principles presented in the Gestalt therapy literature are relevant to an understanding of child growth and development as well as child psychopathology and psychotherapy. The previous works by the authors (Oaklander, 1978, 1982, 1985; Carroll, in press) demonstrate the process of Gestalt therapy with children and adolescents. Other authors such as Gordon Wheeler (1994) have also discussed the practice of Gestalt therapy with children. In this chapter is presented an application of the practice of Gestalt therapy to child psychotherapy developed by Violet Oaklander.

Personality Theory

Fundamental to the Gestalt theory of personality development is the principle of organismic self-regulation. This organic process allows for the needs of the child to be met and supports integration of experience, resulting in learning, growth, and fulfillment of the potentialities of the child. From the Gestalt view, the child is a total organism, including biological and psychological processes, structure, and function. The child is born as a fully functioning, integrated organism encompassing senses, body, emotions, and intellect. As the child develops according to his or her unique genetic blueprint, these processes become more differentiated and the individuality of the child evolves.

Each human being is conceived, birthed, and grows in context. Even though the child is an individual with unique biological and psychological predispositions for behavior, he or she interacts within a given context, or *field*. These interactions include finding and using resources from the environment that assure the sustenance and growth of this individual. In the ongoing maintenance of wholeness, the child is constantly faced with needs whether they be physical, emotional, or intellectual. The child experiences discomfort until he or she finds a way to satisfy each need and to assimilate the experience in order to achieve a sense of satisfaction or a new equilibrium. Thus, the process of organismic self-regulation requires awareness of an interior and exterior environment.

This awareness requires the full use of the sensorimotor system: hearing, seeing, tasting, kinaesthetic smelling, proprioception, and touch. The awareness of stimuli from within the organism, or by stimuli from without, results in excitement or arousal of the motoric system and eventual contact with the identified source of need gratification. The experience is then assessed, assimilated, "chewed up," and used by the child for growth.

This interaction with the environment is called *contact* in Gestalt theory. As the child develops, differentiation occurs through physical maturation and contact with the environment. *Contact* is the process of being aware of a need and moving into the environment to fulfill it.

In order to make contact with the environment, in order to get needs met, the child must *aggress* into the environment. To aggress means to move toward something. This is a healthy and necessary biological and psychological function. Life is not a passive matter. It is aggression that serves the life of the child and which allows distinctions to be made between the child and the environment. From the Gestalt view, it is aggression that enables the self to orient, mobilize, and organize its excitement or energy. Aggression, therefore, is essential for growth and learning.

All living things interact or exchange with the environment at the contact boundaries of the organisms. "The contact boundary is the point at which one experiences the 'me' *in relation* (italics are the authors') to that which is 'not me,' and through this contact (awareness of being in relation to), both are more clearly experienced" (Polster & Polster, 1973, pp. 102–103). As this experience of distinction (me–not me) occurs, over time a sense of self develops. For a child, this process of the emerging sense of self is affected by his or her biologically determined predisposition toward physical and psychological maturation. Likewise, the interactions with the environment must be nurturing to this organic unfolding. Through contact, the child forms self-gestalts or a relatively constant set of beliefs, values, attitudes about who she is and who she is not; who the other (animate or inanimate) object is or is not; and her capacity to relate. The boundary of the self, or I-boundary, develops and, depending on experience, it becomes permeable and flexible, or more rigid and closed, or diffuse and open. In Gestalt theory, contact and clear choice at the I-boundary is recognized as healthy functioning, which is characterized by the principle of acceptance and rejection. As the I-boundary becomes more distinct, the child develops preferences and makes choices of what to incorporate into the self and what to reject.

This process is called creative adjustment, or figure formation and destruction. Healthy functioning and growth depend on the flow of this process. The self, or a sense of who I am and who I am not within given contexts, is an animated clustering of functions, or a by-product of ongoing creative adjustments, at the contact boundary. "Given the novelty and infinite variety of the environment, no adjustment would be possible by the conservative inherited self-regulation principle alone, contact must be a creative transformation" (Perls, Hefferline, & Goodman, 1951, p. 185).

As humans, we have the capacity to symbolize and abstract our experiences. This capacity allows us to reflect, plan, communicate, and give meaning to our experiences. Without the intellectual capacity to think, symbolize, and communicate with our environment, we would merely be responding automatically or conservatively. Creative transformation or individuality would not be possible, and growth and learning would be minimal.

The child's capacity to represent experience is the essence of her mental life. Representation enables the child to experience existence in a self-reflective manner. Each child organizes her experience based on numerous variables, such as her sense of self, earlier situations, and states of differentiation. Consequently, her perspective, or her phenomenology, is distinct to her.

Healthy functioning from the Gestalt view is integrated; that is, all aspects of the child—physical, emotional, and intellectual—function in a well-coordinated, wholesome manner. The continuing well-being of the child is adequately supported internally and externally, allowing for maturation, growth, and learning. The experience of this integrated functioning, which is free of conflict or obstruction, results in a sense of aliveness and faith in her capacity to live and cope with life.

In the healthy personality, the self, which is both a style of organizing and the by-product of experiential organization, is ever changing. The self transforms novelty from contact with the environment by assimilating what nourishes its growth and rejects that which constricts or is toxic to itself. Such healthy functioning is experienced as spontaneous, graceful, effortless, joyful, and meaningful. It entails energetic relationships with self, others, and the universe.

Model of Psychopathology

As action, contact, choice, and authenticity characterize health in Gestalt therapy, so stasis, resistance, rigidity, and overcontrol characterize ill health. The illness states are seen as states of psychological discomfort, often associated with anxiety. They signal some imbalance within the individual, possibly some blocking of natural functioning. The discomfort may signal some prevention of the natural assimilation of input from the environment and, thus, inhibit learning and growth. (Korbs, Gonell, & Van de Riet, 1989, p. 53)

The child who is symptomatic or experiencing continuing discomfort is having difficulty with the natural functioning of growing up. In fact, the behavior or emotional state that causes a parent to bring a child into therapy is the child's attempt to get his or her needs met and to continue with growth when the more natural processes of contact have resulted in psychological or physical pain, such as fear of abandonment or trauma. Integration is inhibited and the contacting process is disturbed. Something in the child's life has become too much to incorporate.

When a child comes into therapy, it is assumed that her behaviors or symptoms are the result of the child's efforts to get her organismic needs met in a given environment. The therapist must help the child find a way to restore her natural functioning, which she once had but now appears lost. This natural functioning of the organismic self-regulatory process allows the child to assimilate the new situations in her life, including therapy, and to get on with living. Something in the child's life has become too much to incorporate.

Another source of ill functioning in children comes directly from the fact that a major function in the mental life of a child is introjection. Through the process of abstraction and representation of reality into mental symbols for reflection and valuing, the child constructs self gestalts based on organization of her experience of self and, very importantly, the reactions, responses, and instruction of significant others in her life. The child swallows these internal and external events whole. To the child these introjects are unquestionable. She absorbs the views *in toto* and not as one of many possible ways of being or the consideration that the view is wrong. Children do not have the cognitive or emotional maturity to discriminate what fits from what does not fit for them or the situation, and they therefore tend to accept everything they hear, or imagine they hear, about themselves. They form whole schemas or beliefs about themselves and how they are, or are to be, in the world and in relationship with others. These beliefs are generalizations about the self, such as, "I'm stupid," "I'm to be nice to everyone," "There is something bad about me," "Life is too much for me," or "I never do anything right."

The child is left believing deep down that something within herself is very wrong. The more the child absorbs both negative *and* unassimilated positive self messages, the more she tends to feel an actual loss of self. She begins to interrupt and constrict her own process of growth. She shuts down her senses, contracts her muscles, withholds expression, and limits the use of her intellect.

Such constriction results in a fragmentation within the self. The useful, healthy function that allows us to withhold responses begins overfunctioning. The child's spontaneity and natural contact functioning become inhibited, even attacked, by her controlling capacity. Such constriction and self-attack results in a diminished experience of the organizing capacities of the sensoric and motoric functions.

Consequently, contactful relating with one's self, others, and the environment is disturbed. Often, the child will despair when trying to cope with a particularly chronic or traumatic experience, such as coping with an alcoholic father or the divorce of her parents. Developmentally, the cognitive and emotional development of the child (egocentricity) may predispose her to blame herself for the failure of the family. Her capacity to organize these expressions meaningfully is naturally limited, and environmental resources to assist her are not available. In order to protect herself from psychological collapse, the organism places the experiences within the ground of her life. Here it remains as "unfinished business," draining off energy, clamoring for attention. The self support to attend to these painful experiences is not available because it has been weakened in the failure to assimilate it in the first place.

The natural needs of growth and development continue to create excitement or tension and press for gratification. Some, or all, of those needs and excitement are now "enemies" that are experienced as threats to the survival of the child. The symptomatic behavior of a child is his effort to get his needs met in an environment with standards and contingencies that necessitate that the child thwart his natural organismic functioning in favor of behaviors that are more acceptable to the environment. So, in order to avoid rejection and abandonment, and to gain approval, a child will exhibit symptomatic behaviors that keep him from engaging in healthy contact with his world—for example, other children, teachers, parents, or books. He may project his feelings as a way of denying his personal experience. He may deflect from painful feelings by hitting, punching, or kicking. He may retroflect anger and grief by constricting his body to the point of having headaches, stomachaches, or asthma attacks. He may be hyperactive or "space out" in order to avoid what he is feeling.

A child may engage in confluent behavior as a means of feeling some segment of self. He will be very good or pleasing to the adults in his life, willing to do whatever is asked of him.

These behaviors are evidence that aspects of the child's organismic process needs to be restored, and that the child's sense of self is tenuous and frail.

Goal of Treatment

Perls (1948) states, "The criterion of a successful treatment is: the achievement of that amount of integration which facilitates its own development." The disturbed child needs help to restore healthy organismic self-regulation, to reawaken an awareness of internal and external events, and to be able to use the resources available in her environment to get her needs met. Experiencing the contacting process—what I do and how I do it—leads to integration, choice, and change. This includes the child's accepting the heretofore unacceptable, alienated, and rejected parts of herself. She must become aware of her self-hatred and her aggression that is directed toward the self. She needs to learn to redirect this energy toward appropriate objects in the environment. In order for change to occur, the child must become "fully invested in his current positions" (Beisser, 1970, p. 77) and discover an understanding of himself and his way of being in the world. This acceptance allows for integration of the alienated thoughts, feelings, and beliefs.

Wheeler (1994) describes this process:

> In Gestalt therapy we . . . express the . . . idea by saying that we are always looking for lost voices of the self, that place or time where the *self process,* which we have described here as the integration of our inner and outer worlds, was still proceeding without too much inhibition of either of these two experiential poles— and then where that inner world of authentic self feelings and desires, was split off, suppressed, contained, or left too alone with itself in silence. (p. 8)

Through the course of therapy, and within the therapeutic relationship, the child's ability to support herself increases and her sense of self becomes more clear. Strengthened in this way, she is more able to experience the pain in the unfinished situations of her life, to rediscover the split-off parts of herself, and to assimilate (accept and reject) them. The child can then feel internally resolved and function wholesomely.

Another goal of treatment is to work with the various social systems with which the child interacts—interrelates—to foster their being more accepting and nourishing of the child's physical, emotional, and intellectual well-being. If the social environment remains unresponsive, refractory, or rejecting of the child, then she is faced with recurring disturbance. This may require family therapy, parent education, school consultation, and the like.

The purpose of treatment, therefore, is to restore the alive, graceful functioning that places a child once again on her rightful path of growth.

CASE FORMULATION

This case formulation* relies on the narrative information from the intake, developmental history, mental status, and family history. The more standardized assessment test results might be interesting, but the therapist would not typically have such test results available in her clinical work. She probably would have made the observations provided by the Marschak Interaction Method through clinical interviews and activities with the parents and children during regular sessions.

Jason, although underweight, was born a healthy, intelligent, fully functioning child. His prenatal care was sufficient and his parents happily greeted him into their lives. He was embraced, and his developmental needs for physical and psychological nourishment were at least minimally met for 12 to 18 months when, suddenly, his universe was ruptured by a series of catastrophic circumstances: mother's depression, mother's withdrawal due to pregnancy, death of a sibling, father's withdrawal, divorce, disruption of family life, and so on. The ongoing natural processes of organismic self-regulation require a responsive supportive environment, especially during the early years when dependency characterizes all areas of the child's life. Jason, at the dawn of his life, had to abandon his own spontaneity and organismic processes in order to deliberately control his inner life and hold on to a fragment of hope for psychological and emotional survival.

As Jason was met by the therapist at the age of seven, he was withdrawn, unhappy, and feeling at times as though his life was not worth living. The therapist knew from his history that, prior to his being 18 months old, he lost his mother to a complicated pregnancy, which forced her to spend time in bed and to withdraw from him. From that time forward, his childhood needs for emotional and psychological connection with his mother had been frustrated and unmet. The context of his life had been fraught with abandonment, and his child demands for emotional nourishment had been rejected. His mother's clinical depression, the withdrawal of his father, the entrance of

---

*See "Orientation to the Text: The Case of Jason L," p. 1.

his sister, the major reorganization of his family through divorce when he was five years old, and the actual physical loss of both his parents and the structure of his home were disruptions of unmeasurable significance. Subsequently, he was required to adjust to long periods of time at school, a chronically depressed mother, and a new family routine of visitations and inconsistent styles of child rearing.

Organismic Self-Regulation and Desensitization

Jason's development and natural functioning as a child had been impaired by these failures of his environment. These traumas had caused him, since infancy, to inhibit his ability to get his needs met through the contacting processes with his world. This meant that he was dulling his senses, was constricting the motoric functions of his body, and was unable to organize and represent his internal, affective world. Such restrictions of input about his internal and external worlds resulted in a faulty sense of security and an impaired ability to make contact with his environment in appropriate ways.

The divorce of Jason's parents reinforced the abandonment pattern he had experienced. This type of trauma reverberates deep within the affective and cognitive centers of the child's mental life. Jason was developmentally at an age when family was the major source of identity and meaning. In infancy, he lost his mother, who was that source then; and, at another vulnerable age, his family dissolved.

Children experience such dissolution as overwhelming and internalize the experience as dissolution of themselves. The pain is too great. It is overwhelming and cannot be assimilated. In order to go on psychologically and emotionally, the child must accomplish the mental feat of placing the experience within the ground of his experience. It remains there, unprocessed and unassimilated. The result for Jason was that his internal affective world became fragmented and unorganized.

His inner world became unwanted and rejected and threatened to overwhelm him if experienced fully. Jason, rather than expressing his rage and grief at the world (for which he had no self or other support), created the only meaning that he could—which was to blame himself: "I must be bad, wrong (etc.) for those whom I love and need to abandon me." The parents did not recognize the abandonment, for it was a loss experienced deep within the child. Deep inside, Jason felt, "There is something wrong with me." The "me" was the totality of himself: his senses, emotions, body, and intellect. With this, Jason lost something more—himself. If he successfully suppressed this experience into the ground of his being, he began the process of deliberate control of his own liveliness and spontaneity in the world.

Retroflection and Negative Introjects

The therapist learned about how Jason, at age seven, was beginning to show physical signs of this constriction of self. Jason found school "a real pain." Jason may have been telling the therapist about how much tension he felt as he held in his frustration, anger, and grief. The moderate and intermittent asthma (which would require a physician's supervision) may also have been an expression of his abandonment anxiety and his unmet dependency needs.

Even though Jason had desensitized and suppressed the fear and pain in his life, he still attempted to find a way to express his feelings in some way. Without awareness, Jason could not choose a healthy form of expression and thereby support his growth. His indirect attempts at expressing some of his feelings—"throwing books" after school, "being moody" as well as attempting to get protection and support, and "not being as bold as he (his father) would like" were met with disapproval and rejection. Jason ended up being blamed and identified as a problem at home and at school. He was experiencing that "his anger was not okay," that "his dependency needs and vulnerability were not okay." In these accounts we could imagine the degree of self-hatred and self-rejection that Jason must have felt.

The slap by his mother was an outward, physical expression of what Jason already did internally to himself. It was a devastating blow that coalesced his constriction of experience and withdrawal from emotional contact with others. His indifference to this treatment, which left bruises on his face, was indicative of the pervasive desensitization and resignation leading to the collapse of his affective vitality. Deep within himself he believed he deserved the slap, and he also internally raged at the pain it evoked. This rage, his emotional excitement, that had no healthy expression became retroflected into an intrapsychic attack of his own natural functioning. He suppressed his spontaneous responses toward the environment. His constricting of his natural bodily energy resulted in symptomatic behavior.

Control and Power

There were many reports of Jason's controlling behavior with his sister, classmates, and at home. His outward conduct indicated his internal need to overcontrol his emotions and behavior. He was devoting much deliberateness toward containing both his powerful feelings of rage and grief and the terrifying experience of being so vulnerable in a world that was out of his control. The fire-setting incident could be understood as a misplaced attempt to overcome his powerlessness by feeling power, though only momentarily, over chaotic forces.

Field or Contextual Issues

Other matters were of interest in reviewing the background of Jason's life prior to treatment. There was no mention in the notes about whether his mother, Mary, had been referred for treatment. This will be discussed further in the sections Treatment Goals and Treatment Description. Jason's sister, Carla, may also have been benefited from treatment. The brief description provided of her behavior and style of relating as being "very easy and compliant" may have been indicative of a poor sense of self and a redirection of her liveliness into confluence, essentially, or a failure to organize a distinct self.

Strengths

Jason was an intelligent child who was well liked by his peers. He had interests he enjoyed and he achieved well at school. His parents, in spite of their individual difficulties and inconsistent parenting, were loving and wanted to relate to him in caring ways. He showed a gentle, caring, and empathic attitude in his relationship with his sister and friends.

Jason retained a strong will to survive, to reverse the constriction of his natural functioning and his withdrawal from others. His total organism, his life force, pressed for vitality and growth. The very symptoms that others observed were his continuous attempts to get his needs met. Metaphorically, if a life is constrained, it may grow sideways, but it will nevertheless grow. This press for life as experienced in Jason's resistance, moods, and acting out was what would sustain him on the restorative path toward integration. Jason's vitality, as this seven-year-old boy who had experienced so much emotional pain, demonstrated the persistence and resiliency of the human spirit.

TREATMENT GOALS

Gestalt play therapy would require that Jason's therapist let go of expectations for him or what the course of his therapy "should" be or what "should" take place. It is essential, in each session, that the therapist disallow any form of expectation for him, for only then can she be fully available in every moment to the therapeutic interaction as it unfolds.

Nonetheless, the therapist would have treatment goals based on the Gestalt model of healthy growth and development as well as healthy functioning. Jason's therapist would use judgment about the direction of his therapy that would change as the treatment progressed, based on her assessment of his needs and growth.

The following treatment goals are based on observations provided in the case summary that indicate Jason had a faulty sense of who he was, a constricted mental life, and an impaired ability to make contact with himself and his environment.

Therapeutic Relationship

The most essential aspect of Gestalt play therapy is the therapeutic relationship. Jason's therapy depended on his having a trusting, contactful relationship with his therapist based on the experience of mutual respect. From the initial meeting, Jason must perceive that the therapist is interested in his experience and his point of view on the matters that have caused him to be brought into treatment.

Consistent with the Gestalt approach, the child therapist regarded herself and the child as being equal in entitlement. Jason's experience, expression, and phenomenology established him as the authority on himself. The therapist, regardless of her adult status or professional training, was no more important than Jason. The therapist brought all of her training, wisdom, and her full self into a contactful way of being with him, and she thereby supported Jason's development of more contactful relationships. She recognized the necessity of boundaries such as time limits, use of materials, and so forth for his sense of safety with her and the playroom. So she maintained her boundaries, never losing herself in Jason's life situation.

The therapist met Jason, as he was, in each session. Without manipulation, she worked to understand the nature of his capacity or willingness to participate in the therapeutic work. Through their caring, respectful relationship, he could become comfortable in exploring and talking about his life.

In all cases, establishing a trusting relationship is the first treatment goal. With some children, it may be the single goal of the treatment.

Restoration and Differentiation of Sensory and Motor Functioning

The foundation for a sense of self and contactful relating is in the use of the contact functions—our sensory and motoric organs. As a child constricts these functions they become progressively desensitized, dulled, and disjointed in their organization of experience. Jason's therapy needed to include experiences that awakened his senses and restored graceful movement of his body. As he became able once again to perceive his distinct senses, sensations, and actions, he could then know that he was the feeler and the doer and could be a responsible person, even at seven years of age.

Develop Self-Support

Each child is an inextricable part of family and cultural systems. Yet he is an individual. This process of being and becoming a separate self is not automatic (although the biological thrust for its unfolding is genetically determined). There is a tendency as a result of developmental characteristics (ego-centricity), processes of introjection (taking in ideas, beliefs, etc. without discrimination), enmeshed family systems, and cultural demands for conformity for the child not to discover through his experiences who *he is*. The disturbed child is fundamentally confluent with his world and sees himself through the eyes of others. This hinders his ability to know who he is and who he is not. It limits his development of mastery and responsibility for his choices. It was essential that the therapy provide Jason with activities that strengthened his knowledge of himself and his uniqueness.

In therapy, Jason could become more aware of who he was, what he felt, what he liked and did not like, what he needed, what he wanted, and what he could do and how he could do it. Jason could find that he had choices and that he could explore new behaviors.

Expression of Emotions and Organization of Aggression

Another important goal of Gestalt play therapy is for a child to become more aware of his emotions: that is, how each emotion feels in his body, what each emotion means, how he can use them, and how he can express them in direct and appropriate ways. A child in therapy usually has restricted his emotional expression, which can lead to the onset and maintenance of such symptoms as headaches, asthma, stomachaches, and tiredness.

Anger is the least understood of all the emotions. There is little tolerance for its expression in our culture. The suppression of frustration, anger, and rage is often the cause of many difficulties in a child's disturbed or inadequate sense of self. It is common for a child's expression of self, which requires aggression in service of the self, to be misinterpreted by adults as hostility. That confusion is introjected as a part of the child's view of self. Jason's therapy, therefore, needed to facilitate his understanding of his emotions, especially anger, and to find ways of getting his needs met in ways that didn't get him into trouble with others or bring harm to himself.

Integration of Organismic Functioning

This model of Gestalt play therapy stresses the need for a child to rediscover, through the assistance of the therapeutic relationship, his capabilities of self-support and emotional expression. Another goal of treatment would be to restore all of Jason's organismic resources in order for him to be fully functioning as his unique self. Therefore, he had to come to accept all aspects of himself—even those he or others might not like—before complete healthful growth would be possible. He needed to reassimilate or reconstellate those aspects of himself that he had constricted, rejected, projected, dissociated, or modified in some way.

In summary, the goals for Jason's treatment were as follows:

1. To create together with him a therapeutic relationship that was based on *mutual* trust and respect.
2. To restore and refine his sensory-motor functioning.
3. To develop his sense of who he was and his capacity to support himself.
4. To expand his awareness of his emotional experience.
5. To achieve that amount of integration of organismic functioning that would allow for his ongoing healthful development.

Forming a Therapeutic Alliance with Parents

A successful course of treatment also required a relationship with many other people in Jason's life—in particular, his parents. Our understanding of a child's behavior has to begin with, and continually include, an assessment and involvement with the child's life as a whole. All of the factors in his life are interdependent. The therapeutic work with Jason required his therapist to relate not only with his intrapsychic life, but also with most of the external elements that impressed upon his well-being.

A fundamental tenet of Gestalt therapy is that behavior is a function of the field of which it is a part. In order to understand a child's behavior or symptoms, the therapist must begin with the situation as a whole and not exclude any part of it. There were many people involved with Jason at the beginning of his treatment: family members, school personnel, legal authorities, friends. Each person or group was a significant part of Jason's life, and, thus, must be included in his therapy.

TREATMENT DESCRIPTION

Logistics

As Jason came into the therapist's office with his parents, Mary and Emilio, he realized that this was no ordinary office. He found a vast collection of miniature figures, a sandtray, an assortment of games, a dollhouse, baskets full of puppets, a sturdy table for clay, and an assortment of kitchen tools for clay work. There were other toys, such as telephones, dolls, medical kits with working stethoscopes and digital thermometer, plastic water pistols, rubber darts, books, and comfortable chairs and pillows. The therapist allowed Jason to look around and told him that he could look at the room more carefully after the therapist had a chance to talk with him and his parents. They all met together in the consultation area of the room.

This first session was extremely important for establishing relationships with Jason and his parents. Usually, the therapist has talked with both parents prior to meeting with the child. The main message that the therapist conveyed was that they must talk to her, with Jason present, about their concerns and reasons for coming into treatment. This allowed the therapist to ask Jason about his responses to— agreements or disagreements with—what his parents were telling her. She made certain that Jason knew her name and what she did, as a counselor, as well as how his parents wanted her to be of assistance to them. She talked with them about how she works, explaining that the first few sessions would be evaluative in nature. She began to assess Jason's therapeutic needs and the needs of the family. During this initial interview, the therapist talked directly to Jason about his life now that his parents were divorced; she talked openly about how Jason saw their relationship as his parents. She established respect and interest in his views as well as those of his parents.

The therapist's assessment would include conversations with teachers and child protective workers, as well as individual sessions with both parents. She would also include Jason's sister, Carla, in subsequent family sessions. During this evaluation time, the therapist continued to see Jason individually for weekly sessions to learn more from him about his life, his experience of himself, and his ability to make contact with himself and with her.

Specific Strategies

Projective Techniques

This approach to play therapy uses a variety of projective techniques—games, storytelling, and expressive modalities— to communicate with the inner world of the child. Although the techniques used with a child encourage projection, they are not for the purpose of providing the therapist with material for interpretation. The child and therapist participate together toward understanding the projections in his drawings, stories, and so forth, and for the child to own what fits with his experience with the description of the symbols in his work.

Interpretation

If an interpretation is offered, it is as a tentative possible way of viewing the child's work, or the therapist's associations or thoughts. The child can verify or reject these ideas. Through this process of mutual interpretation, Jason can feel the interest in him and encouragement of him to become interested in himself. Oaklander (1993) explains that the professional's task is to assist the child in sharing his or her wisdom with the therapist. As the doors to self-acceptance and self-ownership are very gently opened, through open and contactful sharing, the child strengthens his or her self-understanding and gains new self-support.

Treatment Stages

The Gestalt play therapy process does not prescribe a sequence of steps or stages. However, the work is guided by the goals described in the previous section. In general, unless Jason was able to make good contact with his world, he did not have internal resources available to resolve the more difficult and complex issues such as his parent's divorce and his mother's physical abuse of him. Thus, the therapeutic process began by strengthening the building blocks of his experience, his sensory functions, and a trusting relationship with another person.

In the early assessment stage of treatment, the therapist asked Jason to draw a picture that included a house, a tree, and a person. In response to this request, he drew his picture quite willingly (Figure 7.1). He took his time and was especially attentive that the door was big enough for the person to enter; he changed the size of the door several times until he had it just right.

Figure 7.1 Jason's completed drawing. See text for details.

After he told the therapist he was finished, she asked him to tell her about his picture.

J: This is a boy who lives in a big house. He lives by himself most of the time. Sometimes, though, his mom is there.
T: Are there other members of his family?
J: Yes, a father and a sister.
T: Where are they?
J: (Softly) I don't know. They live somewhere else (he added quickly).
T: This is a very big house. You were very careful in drawing the door.
J: Well, he does have to be able to get in and out.
T: What's the boy doing outside?
J: He's playing basketball. (Jason then drew a basketball hoop and a ball in the boy's hand.)
T: Jason, would you be the boy in your drawing? Give him a voice, like a puppet. (He got it right away.)
J: I'm a boy, and I'm playing basketball.
T: Are you playing alone?
J: Yes, there is no one else here.
T: I see. How do you like that?
J: It's okay.
T: What's it like for you to live in this big house?
J: It's okay. I have lots of room.

As Jason talked, his tone of voice and body posture revealed his resignation. His "It's okay" was flat and unconvincing. Everything, even the empty spaces, seemed to accentuate the smallness, aloneness of the figure. The sun was pale, small, and lacking in radiance.

The therapist pursued these thoughts with him. She asked Jason if he ever felt like the boy in the picture. He looked at her very puzzled.

T: Well, the boy seems very small and his world seems very big. Do you ever feel that way, like maybe things are bigger than you?
J: Sometimes I feel that way about my parents.
T: What do you mean?
J: They are divorced and it all seems too much.
T: Too much to think about? (Jason looked up from the picture and studied the therapist's face for a few moments. Then he slowly nodded, yes.)
T: Jason, sometimes when people draw chimneys with smoke coming out like it does in your picture, it can mean that they worry a lot about things, or maybe feel sad. (Softly, she asked) Do you ever feel that way?
J: Yes. I worry about my mom.
T: What do you worry about your mom?
J: I don't know. (He shrugged. His body language indicated that he was losing contact with this activity and the conversation.)

Resistance in Treatment

Resistance with a child is expected and respected. It is the way the child has of protecting his self from being overwhelmed by unassimilated internal experiences and emotions. When a child's energy suddenly fades, or withdraws, or deflects to another activity, these may indicate the child's way of protecting himself from what is emerging in the work.

In the theoretical literature of Gestalt therapy, these are regarded as disturbances at the contact boundary that joins the child and his environment. Psychological symptoms, problematic behaviors, or psychosomatic symptoms are indications of difficulties the child is having in maintaining healthful contact with his environment and with other people.

In working with a child, we meet resistance again and again for, as the child approaches material that is too difficult and weighty for him to deal with at that time, he will close down and break contact (Oaklander, 1992). When this resistance is respected the child feels respected, and more trust in the therapist and the therapy develops. Then he can become more responsive to working through his experiences.

This was the first session between Jason and the therapist, and they had much work to do before he could share more comfortably his concerns, fears, and problems. The therapist was encouraged by the liveliness and strength of Jason's tree. She wondered if it showed that he had internal sources of nurturance and support that would be his holdfast during this time of uncertainty. She commented about the beautiful tree. Jason smiled and became more lively. "Yes," he commented. "The boy likes to climb the tree." When she asked him if he would be willing to come back so that they could both understand more about his worries, he nodded slightly, yes.

The next several sessions with Jason involved the child and therapist in all sorts of games and clay work, which developed his sensory and physical capacities. He especially enjoyed playing with or pounding the clay.

The modality that he enjoyed most, however, was the musical instruments (Oaklander, 1990). He discovered them one day, and immediately started playing each one: drums, shakers, bells, triangles, kazoos, rattlers of all types, whistles, and the like. At first he just improvised. He played a piece and then the therapist played a piece. Sometimes she repeated a rhythm or pattern that he was playing. He liked this control and her willingness to follow his lead. The music activities allowed Jason maximum control of the therapeutic situation. As his anxiety level lessened, he became more contactful and spontaneous in his interactions with the therapist. She heightened these contactful exchanges between them by suggesting that he start a rhythm with one instrument. She would match his rhythm with another instrument. He would stop playing and pick up another instrument, and soon their instruments were "talking" to one another through rhythm and tone.

Next, the therapist introduced the idea that the instruments could express emotions. They played happy music, sad music, angry music, scared music. As they played, each of them took turns telling about a time they felt the feeling that the music described. Once, when he told about feeling sad, Jason talked about the day his father moved out of their house. The therapist only reflected his feelings as a way of letting him know that she understood how sad he must have felt when his father left.

This activity was one that allowed Jason to feel stronger within himself. He enjoyed the musical expression. The banging of drums and bashing of cymbals alleviated much tension. He could easily have control and work cooperatively at the same time. Jason was interacting by using his senses, his body, and aesthetic (cognitive and affective) judgment. Through the musical play they developed a variety of ways to communicate, and he began to explore and share his emotional world.

With this increased self-support and the foundation of the therapeutic relationship, Jason was ready to begin talking about his anger and to acknowledge that he got angry. The therapist usually starts by asking the child to assist her in making a list of things that made him mad. They drew his angry feelings, giving them shape and color. They played games such as "Splat" and the "Talking, Feeling, Doing" game, which allowed him to feel more his aggressive self and to enjoy expressing himself in a safe relationship.

This is usually a good time to bring in parents and siblings for a family session in which to talk about anger and how different members express anger. When the therapist meets with a family, she needs to be aware that she enters into the complexity of the ongoing family life and adds to that complexity. Her presence alone becomes a part of the dynamics, and every person attributes his own meaning to her participation. She needs to be aware of the tension within herself as she holds the tension of inertia and the press for change among the family members. The best resolutions come if the therapist restrains her tendencies to impose her views and support the family, rather finding a solution or resolution from within their circle.

During a family session, Jason brought up the fact that his mother had slapped him when she was angry at him. Jason looked at his mother (who had been in supportive counseling for several weeks and was on antidepressants). He told her directly that he did not like her doing that. Mary agreed that it was wrong and that she had lost control of her anger. She told Jason that she was sorry, she should not have done it, and that she would not do it again. Jason and his mother both had tears in their eyes. The family and therapist were all touched by her sincerity and candor. The therapist turned to Jason and said, "What would you like from your mother now?" Jason, to her surprise, got out of his seat, which was next to his father, went to his mother, and crawled onto her lap. They hugged each other for a long time.

As they walked out of the session, Jason was laughing. He ran ahead of Mary, Emilio, and Carla, shouting over his shoulder, "Hey, hurry up!"

As Jason's work progressed, the therapist explored more fully the negative feelings that he held toward himself. One session was particularly helpful to him.

The therapist and Jason had been playing with puppets, and one set of puppets (Jason's) was annihilating another set (the therapist's, of course). Jason was the director of these aggressive shows and liked the therapist's hammy, dramatic death scenes for each animal. After all of her animals had been destroyed, she quietly and offhandedly asked Jason if he ever got mad at himself. "Yes," he responded strongly.

"I didn't like it when I started the fire with Tony." Once again the therapist was a little surprised by his directness. "Jason, would you draw a picture for me of you and Tony starting the fire?" "Okay," he responded. He took time drawing the picture, putting in lots of details. When he had finished, she asked him to talk to that boy in the picture who was starting a fire. "Don't do that! You're going to get into trouble. It's dangerous." Jason spoke firmly.

T: Be the boy in the picture and talk back to yourself, Jason.

J: This is fun. We're not going to build a big fire. No one will know.

T: Jason, what does that boy feel as he is starting the fire?

J: Big and powerful!

(Sometimes it is amazing how much wisdom and self-knowledge children have available.)

T: I think so too, Jason. I think starting fires can be a way to feel big and powerful. That part of you, Jason, who started the fire is a younger part of yourself which feels small and scared in a big world. His mom is sad and one day his dad moves out and his mom leaves to go to work. He's worried and thinks everything is bigger than him, including his anger. He's afraid that maybe he'd have to live all by himself.

Jason was engaged, listening to this deeply familiar story.

T: Jason, let's imagine that this boy has a fairy godmother who understands that he is starting fires to make himself feel bigger inside. Let's pick out a puppet to be that fairy godmother. (He selected a puppet. The therapist asked Jason to have the godmother puppet talk to the fire-setting Jason. He hesitated, uncertain about what she was asking.) Jason, you know how godmothers are. They are wise and loving. They know who we are inside and accept us for who we are, even when we feel small and scared.

Jason was quiet. The therapist continued:

T: I can imagine his fairy godmother saying something like, "Even though you sometimes feel very little inside and sometimes start fires to feel bigger and powerful, I love you. You're a terrific kid." (His eyebrows went up and a smile spread over Jason's face.)

The therapist asked Jason if he could have his puppet say something like that to the boy in the picture.

J: You're a terrific kid. . . .

T: . . . even though you sometimes feel little.

J: Yeah (Jason repeated), even though you feel little inside.

J: But that boy is me! (Jason pointed out).

T: That's right, Jason. Can you have the fairy godmother say that to you?

Jason looked at the puppet, then spoke for it to himself:

J: I like you even though you feel little and do things that are dangerous. (Jason looked at the therapist and smiled.)

As the session closed, the therapist asked Jason if he would select a toy from his home to be the younger part of himself that felt so small and to say to that part of him each night before going to bed, "I love you." He agreed, and from that time forward, he became happier and more lively. Both his parents commented on the change. One day, toward the end of his therapy, Jason went in and told the therapist that he thought he was getting bigger—inside.

Termination

After approximately one year of weekly sessions with Jason and his family, enough integration had been achieved and enough environmental support was available for closure of treatment to begin.

It is at this point that the natural process of figure destruction occurs. In other words, the contact with the therapy and the therapist loses energy, and this relationship recedes into the ground of the family's life. Other activities and relationships become more interesting. This is the hallmark of a successful treatment.

Ending a relationship with a child and his family is a time filled with many emotions. It is a necessary loss (Viorst, 1986) that is required for life to continue and fulfill itself. Closure, therefore, is a special time in the treatment process.

Jason, his parents, and therapist designated a certain time period for closure, covering four to six sessions. These sessions were consecutive. The therapist did not find the "weaning" process to be therapeutically supportive. In fact, the experience of closure, a sense of ending, maybe even loss, is an important part of being in relationship.

During this time the therapist had sessions with Jason in which they talked about his not coming to visit her. They drew pictures about their feelings, created puppet shows in which characters said Goodbye, and went on with their activities. There were family sessions in which they reviewed what had been accomplished and anticipated what was ahead. In the final session, the therapist let Jason and his parents know that she was available if ever they wanted to call. In fact, she let them know that she would be interested in knowing about how they were doing from time to time.

Closure is not Goodbye. Children and parents frequently come in for follow-up sessions to talk out a problem or work through another milestone or transition in the family. Children, themselves, request later sessions to work on something that is troubling them, or just to say Hello or touch base with a remembered toy.

EXPECTED OUTCOME OR PROGNOSIS

Perls (1948) identified the criterion for a successful treatment as: "the achievement of that amount of integration which facilitates its own development. A small hole cut into an accumulation of snow sometimes suffices to drain off the water. Once the draining has begun, the trickle broadens its bed by itself; it facilitates its own development" (pp. 52–53). By this criterion, Jason had a successful course of therapy.

However, his ongoing development requires the support, nurturance, and guidance of his parents and family. Therefore, Jason's prognosis was dependent on the successful treatment (using Perl's definition) of his parents and their development of coordinated co-parenting skills.

In this case scenario, Mary showed much growth and recovery from her depression. She assumed responsibility for her abuse of Jason and learned constructive ways of coping with tension and frustration. She was able to reestablish an emotional connection with Jason. Within this loving bond, he could move into his life with faith in himself, others, and the ineffable nature of existence.

Jason's restored vitality, good sense, joy, and strength would free him from seeking the false security of the elusive fragments, "big and powerful."

CONCLUSION

Most children who are seen clinically have redirected their natural aggression toward making contact with their environment and others into a psychic power that attacks and controls the self and their spontaneous self-expression. Consequently, they become constricted, fragmented characters, lacking in grace and liveliness.

The symptoms that have caused a child to be brought into therapy are symptoms that indicate a lack of integration. These symptoms may be behavioral, affective, interpersonal, or, more likely, a combination of difficulties. These symptoms reveal inner conflicts or fragmentation of the child's personality that contributes to a blurred sense of self and boundaries, avoidance of contact—a woodenness or artificiality within the developmental process. Without adequate therapeutic intervention the child becomes a character in the world rather than a real, alive individual.

Even though integration takes place incrementally throughout the therapeutic process, for the child to be free of the burden of unfinished situations within himself, a more *direct* process of examining the core introjects and assimilating a new experience with the self must take place.

Gestalt play therapy is a process whereby the child's energy can find its intended direction—in the service of meeting the ongoing developmental and growth needs of the child. Such fulfillment brings the child into more nurturing interactions with all of life.

Gestalt play therapy is an effective approach to the treatment of most childhood disorders and disturbances in healthy, emotional development. This approach can be used to restore and strengthen a child's rightful path of organismic growth.

BIBLIOGRAPHY

Beisser, A. (1970). The paradoxical theory of change. In J. Fagan & L. Shepherd (Eds.), Gestalt therapy now. Palo Alto, CA: Science and Behavior Books.

Carroll, F. (1995). *The Pinocchio syndrome: Path to wholeness*. Presented at the First Annual International Therapy Conference, October 12–15, 1995, New Orleans, LA.

Carroll, F. (1995). *The Pinocchio syndrome: Path to wholeness* (Cassette Recording): Sylva, NC: Good Kind of Sound.

Clarkson, P., & McKewn, J. (1993). Fritz Perls. Newbury Park, CA: Sage Publications.

Korbs, M., Gonell, J., & Van De Riet, V. (1989). Gestalt therapy: Practice and theory (2nd ed.). New York: Peragmon Press.

Oaklander, V. (1978). Windows to our children: A Gestalt approach to children and adolescents. Moab, UT: Real People Press (New York: The Gestalt Journal Press, 1992).

Oaklander, V. (1982). The relationship of Gestalt therapy to children. The Gestalt Journal, 1:64–74.

Oaklander, V. (1982–1983). Working with anger and introjects. Institute of Guidance Counsellors Journal (Ireland), 7:3–7.

Oaklander, V. (1985). Gestalt therapy with children (Cassette Recording: 1). Seattle, WA: Max Sound.

Oaklander, V. (1985). Gestalt therapy process with children and adolescents (Cassette Recording: 3). Seattle, WA: Max Sound.

Oaklander, V. (1986). Working with the anger of children and adolescents (Cassette Recording: 2). Seattle, WA: Max Sound.

Oaklander, V. (1986). Self-Nurturing process with children and adolescents (Cassette Recording: 4). Seattle, WA: Max Sound.

Oaklander, V. (1990). Music as therapy (Audiotape). Seattle, WA: Max Sound.

Oaklander, V. (1992). Gestalt work with children: Working with anger. Gestalt therapy: Perspectives and applications (E.C. Nevis, Ed.). New York: Gardner Press.

Oaklander, V. (1993). From meek to bold: A case study of Gestalt play therapy. In T. Kottman & C. Schaefer (Eds.), Play therapy in action: A casebook for practitioners, pp. 281–299.

Perls, F. (1948). Theory and technique of personality integration. In J. Stevens (Ed.), Gestalt Is. . . . Moab, UT: Real People Press, 1975, pp. 45–55. (Originally printed in The American Journal of Psychotherapy, 2(4), October 1948:565–586.)

Perls, F., Hefferline, R., & Goodman, P. (1951). Gestalt therapy. New York: The Gestalt Journal Press, 1994. (Earlier published by Julian Press, Bantam Books, 1980.)

Perls, F. (1969). Ego, hunger, and aggression. New York: Vintage.

Polster, E., & Polster, M. (1973). Gestalt therapy integrated. New York: Brunner/Mazel.

Viorst, J. (1986). Necessary losses. New York: Simon and Schuster.

Wheeler, G. (1994). Compulsion and curiosity—A Gestalt approach to OCD. Gestalt Review, 4(2):1–8.

Yontef, G. (1993). Awareness, dialogue, and process. New York: The Gestalt Journal Press.

CHAPTER 8

Fostering Attachment through Family Theraplay

TERRENCE J. KOLLER AND PHYLLIS BOOTH

INTRODUCTION

Description of Theraplay

Theraplay is an engaging, playful treatment method that is modeled on the healthy interaction between parents and their children. It is an intensive, short-term approach that actively involves parents—first as observers and later as co-therapists. The goal is to enhance attachment, self-esteem, trust, and joyful engagement and to empower parents to continue, on their own, the health-promoting interactions of the treatment sessions.

Theraplay was developed by Ann Jernberg (1979), based on the work of Austin Des Lauriers (1962), Des Lauriers & Carlson (1969), and Viola Brody (1978, 1993). In 1968, faced with the challenge of providing treatment for several thousand preschool children in the Chicago Head Start Program, Ann Jernberg adapted Des Lauriers's and Brody's principles to form the Theraplay method. Like Brody, she geared the treatment to the child's current developmental, not chronological, level. She retained Des Lauriers's ". . . vigor; intrusiveness; body and eye contact; focus on intimacy between child and therapist . . . ; emphasis on the here-and-now;" and ignored "the bizarre, the past, and fantasy . . ." (Jernberg, 1979, p. 2).

Theraplay in its current form resembles the therapies of Des Lauriers and Brody in many respects but it differs from them in intensity, vigor, and perseverance as well as in the degree to which the therapist initiates and takes charge of the sessions.

In describing Theraplay, Jernberg (1993) says "because of its play and bonding-enhancement properties, Theraplay . . . has been found to be of particular value for children referred for problems of attachment. . . . Theraplay's bonding and attachment-enhancing properties are a function of its design" (p. 255). Jernberg (1979) says:

> The best way to understand the principles underlying the Theraplay method is to rediscover the basics of the mother-infant relationship: What are the typical daily pleasurable interactions in the nursery? What does a normal mother do to and for

her baby? How does the healthy baby respond? What characterizes the cycle they thus set in motion between them? And what are the specific effects of their reciprocal behavior on each of the partners involved? (p. 4)

Jernberg describes the many playful, loving interactions typical of a healthy parent-child relationship. For example, the mother nuzzles her baby's neck; plays peek-a-boo; spins, rocks, and bounces her baby; coos, chatters, and makes nonsense sounds; and holds him or her close and nurses. In treatment, the interactions between therapist and child and between parent and child replicate the lively, intimate give and take of this nursery scene.

In distinguishing Theraplay from other treatment methods, Jernberg (1993, p. 262) lists the following characteristics: It is playful, uses no toys and few props, asks no questions, focuses on health, is structured by the adult, encourages physical contact with the therapist, has an agenda designed to meet the child's needs, encourages regression, and is geared to enhancing parent-child attachment.

Theraplay Dimensions

Just as in the interactions between parents and their infants, Theraplay combines elements of *structure, challenge, intrusion/engagement,* and *nurture* in a setting that is playful, physical, and fun. In order to understand this better, let us look at how each dimension plays itself out, both in the parent-infant relationship and in treatment (see Jernberg, 1993).

Structure

In the parent-infant relationship, the adult provides the structure. He or she takes responsibility for the safety and comfort of the baby. The adult is attuned to the infant's needs and responds accordingly, initiating playful, stimulating contact when appropriate, and soothing, comforting contact when needed. In treatment, the therapist is in charge, for the same reasons that the parent is in charge with an infant. It is not reassuring to a frightened, unhappy, or chaotic child to experience the adult as uncertain or to feel that he or she must decide what to do. In Theraplay sessions the dimension of structure is addressed through clearly stated safety rules (e.g., "No hurts!"), through activities such as singing games that have a beginning, a middle, and an end, and through activities that define body boundaries. This dimension is important for children who are overactive, unfocused, or overstimulated, or who have an anxious need to be in control.

Challenge

In the parent-infant relationship there are many opportunities to challenge the child to extend a bit, to master tension-arousing experiences, and to enhance feelings of competence. For example, a mother might "walk" her baby on her lap, or a father might hold his baby high, saying "So big!" In treatment, challenging activities are done in playful partnership with the adult. For example, the therapist might challenge the child to balance on a pile of pillows and jump into his or her arms on the count of three. Such activities encourage the child to take a mild, age-appropriate risk in order to promote feelings of competence and confidence. This dimension is especially useful for withdrawn, timid, or anxious children.

Intrusion/Engagement

In the parent-infant relationship, many activities, such as peek-a-boo, blowing on the tummy, and playing "I'm gonna getcha," serve to draw the baby into interaction with his or her caretaker. The activities are unexpected, delightful, stimulating, and engaging. In treatment with a withdrawn or avoidant child, similar activities offer adventure, variety, stimulation, and a fresh view of life, allowing the child to learn that surprises can be fun and new experiences enjoyable.

Nurture

In the parent-infant relationship, nurturing activities abound—feeding, rocking, cuddling, and holding, to name a few. Such activities are soothing, calming, quieting, and reassuring. In order to meet the unfulfilled emotional needs of the older child in treatment, many nurturing activities—such as feeding, making lotion hand prints, or swinging the child in a blanket—are used. Such activities help make the world seem predictable, warm, and secure and reassure the child that the adult is able to provide comfort and stability. This dimension is especially useful for children who are overactive, aggressive, or pseudomature.

In Theraplay *all* activities are infused with the loving playfulness that characterizes healthy parent-infant interaction.

Personality Theory

From the beginning, the Theraplay approach shared four major assumptions and similar views of psychopathology and of the possibilities for cure with interactional theories of development, particularly those of Self Psychology (see the work of Heinz Kohut, 1971, 1977, 1984) and Object Relations Theory (especially the work of Winnicott, 1958, 1965, 1971). Over Theraplay's twenty-five years of clinical practice, an increasing body of research in the fields of child development and attachment theory has given further support to many of its tenets. (See Ainsworth, 1969; Belsky & Nezworski, 1988; Karen, 1994; Stern, 1985.)

1. The Theraplay approach assumes that the primary motivating force in human behavior is a drive toward relatedness. Personality development is essentially interpersonal. The early interaction between parent and child is the crucible in which the self and personality develop.

This view of the importance of the early parent-child relationship in personality development is shared by Self Psychology, Object Relations Theory, and most current researchers in child development. For example, Bowlby (1969) sees attachment behavior as controlled by innate mechanisms in both adult and infant that ensure the baby's survival. Under normal circumstances, the adult caretaker responds to the infant's cries, smiles, and babblings. Once the baby is mobile, he or she explores only while assured of the caretaker's presence and frequently returns to the caretaker as to a secure base (Ainsworth, 1969). Stern (1985) describes the development of the self as an interactional process between the innately social infant and its engaged, empathic mother.

2. The playful, joyful empathic, attuned responsiveness of caretakers is essential to the development of a strong sense of self, feelings of self-worth, and secure attachment.

A number of individuals stress the importance of playfulness in the parent-infant relationship. For example, Stern (1974) writes, "The more games with which a mother can interest and delight an infant, the more practice he will have in experiencing affectively positive arousal . . . in a greater number of human situations" (p. 416). Winnicott (1971) writes, *It is play that is the universal,* and that belongs to health: playing facilitates growth and therefore health; playing leads into group relationships; playing can be a form of communication in psychotherapy . . . (p. 41. Italics in original).

Empathy is important to the developmental theories of Kohut, Winnicott, Ainsworth, and Stern. For Kohut (1984) empathic responses of caretakers to the infant's affective states lead to the development of a cohesive nuclear self.

> Throughout his life a person will experience himself as a cohesive harmonious firm unit, . . . only as long as, at each stage in his life, he experiences certain representatives of his human surroundings as joyfully responding to him, as available to him as sources of idealized strength and calmness, as being silently present but in essence like him, and, at any rate, able to grasp his inner life more or less accurately so that their responses are attuned to his needs and allow him to grasp their inner life when his is in need of such sustenance. (p. 52)

Winnicott (1958) states that the basis of mental health is "laid down in earliest infancy by the techniques which come naturally to a mother who is preoccupied with the care of her own infant" (p. 219). The baby begins life as an unintegrated receiver of experience. It is the mother's response to the child which allows him or her to become integrated. For Winnicott "there is no such thing as a baby . . . [there is only] a nursing couple. . . . Without a good-enough technique of infant care the new human being has no chance whatever" (p. 99).

Stern (1984) believes that the affect attunement between a mother and her baby leads to awareness on the baby's part of its own feelings and ultimately to the capacity to empathize with others. According to Ainsworth, the securely attached child has a mother (or primary caregiver) who "is warm, sensitively attuned, consistent [and] quickly responds to her baby's cries" (see Karen, 1994, pp. 442–443).

Stages in the Development of Attachment

Attachment is an ongoing process that can be affected at each stage by many factors. When we look at Jason's development we will consider what happened to him during these early stages of attachment formation and how it affects his current behavior.

Pregnancy: Preparatory Bonding

During pregnancy, a healthy mother begins her attachment to her child through a process of thinking about, talking to, and imagining her future interactions with her baby (see Jernberg, Booth, Koller, & Allert, 1983). Winnicott (1958) uses the term *primary maternal preoccupation* to describe the biologically based state of "heightened sensitivity" that develops during the last trimester of pregnancy. It is this state that enables a mother to "adapt delicately and sensitively to her infant's needs at the very beginning" (p. 302).

0–4 Months

During the first four months, the mother's sensitivity enables her to respond to her baby's needs. The baby contributes his or her share to the process by crying, smiling, babbling, and sucking. The baby learns that the world can respond to his or her needs.

4–8 Months

The interaction becomes much more a two-way street. The mother and baby begin the give and take of interactive play. The baby learns that she or he can make a difference, can influence the mother to respond to needs. The baby's view of self as a competent attractive being is developing. The mother's view of herself as a competent, loving parent is increasing.

9–18 Months

Although it starts earlier, clear evidence of discriminated attachment appears during this period. The baby cries in the presence of strangers and clings to the primary caretaker. In the mother's presence the baby feels safe to explore the environment, returning to her side periodically as to a secure base (see Ainsworth as reported in Karen, 1994, pp. 149–150). The parent's presence acts as a source of safety, comfort, and calmness. Later, the child will be able to think about what is safe and be able to soothe and comfort himself or herself. By the time he or she is ready to start school, the child will be able to separate from his or her parents knowing that they will be available when needed or that the teacher is a good substitute for them.

The Effects of Separation and Loss

Although attachment is innately programmed to occur, problems can arise that interfere with its healthy development. Inconsistent availability of the mother as well as separation and loss can lead to insecure attachment. Bowlby (1969), in his writing, and the Robertsons (1969), in their films, documented the devastating effect on young children of separation from their primary caretakers. The children typically went through three stages of emotional reaction to their separation: protest, despair, and detachment. When reunited, the children responded with angry avoidance and took some time to warm up to the parent. Many of the children experienced long-term effects of the early separation. Karen (1994) summarizes Bowlby's interpretation of these findings:

> Separations from the mother were disastrous developmentally because they thwarted an instinctual need. It's not just a nice thing to have someone billing and cooing over you, snuggling you, and adoringly attending to your every need. It is a built-in necessity, and the baby's efforts to obtain it, like the parents' eagerness to give it, are biologically programmed. (p. 94)

3. The capacity to soothe and nurture oneself in later life depends on early experiences of being soothed and nurtured.

This is an important concept for both Kohut and Winnicott. Kohut (1984) believes that early experiences of being able to merge with the calmness and omnipotence of an idealized parental self-object are later "transmuted into self-soothing structures capable of preventing the spread of anxiety" (p. 30).

Winnicott's concept of the maternal holding environment points to the importance of the mother's being able to maintain a calm, safe, nurturing environment where the infant is free from overwhelming stimuli and able to develop a true self. Greenberg and Mitchell (1983) summarize Winnicott thus:

> The infant needs the maternal provisions which define good-enough mothering including: an initial perfectly responsive facilitation of his or her needs and gestures; a nonintrusive "holding" and mirroring environment throughout quiescent states; . . . These relational needs are a developmental imperative; if they are not met, no further meaningful growth can take place. (pp. 198–199)

4. When things go well in the relationship, the infant develops an inner representation of himself or herself as lovable, special, competent, and able to make an impact on the world, of others as loving, caring, responsive, and trustworthy, that is, as being reliably available; and of the world as a safe, exciting place to explore. In other words, within a secure attachment, the infant begins a process of learning about himself or herself and the world that is positive and hopeful and which will have a powerful influence throughout his or her life.

In order to explain the profound and lasting impact of early experience, Bowlby (1973) invoked the concept of inner working models:

> . . . each individual builds working models of the world and of himself in it, with the aid of which he perceives events, forecasts the future, and constructs his plans. In the working model of the world that anyone builds, a key feature is his notion of who his attachment figures are, where they may be found, and how they may be expected to respond. Similarly, in the working model of the self that anyone builds a key feature is his notion of how acceptable or unacceptable he himself is in the eyes of his attachment figures. (p. 203)

The key issues are: How acceptable am I in my parents' eyes, and how consistently available are my parents?

Model of Psychopathology

Psychopathology results when early and ongoing experience leads to a negative or inadequate sense of self. In the absence of positive and responsive interactions, the child learns to view himself or herself as unlovable and incompetent, to view others as uncaring and untrustworthy—as unreliably available—and the world as unsafe and full of threat. In other words, within an insecure attachment, the process of learning about oneself and the world becomes negative and hopeless. Many behavior problems of older children can be traced back to their beginnings in insecure attachment and in the consequent negative views of themselves and the world.

Both Kohut and Winnicott relate early caretaker failures to later psychopathology. Kohut (1984) says "the essence of psychopathology is the defective self (i.e., the self prone to states of fragmentation, weakness, or disharmony). . . . The pathological condition of the self is due to disturbances of the self-self object processes in early life" (p. 70). Winnicott sees mental health as "constituted by the relative integrity and spontaneity of the self. Psychopathology . . . entails corruption and constriction in the movement and expression of the self. The necessary and sufficient factor responsible for mental health is appropriate parental provisions—good-enough mothering" (see Greenberg & Mitchell, 1983, p. 200).

This emphasis on the role of caretaker failures leading to pathology runs the risk of blaming caretakers. While the Theraplay model also looks at the caretaker's role in establishing the infant's sense of self for good or ill, it takes a broader view of the causal factors. Caretaker inadequacies may be due to illness (as in Jason's case) and lack of environmental support, as well as to immaturity and lack of good caretaking experiences during the mother's own childhood (see Belsky and Nezworski, 1988; Karen, 1994). "As for the infant's contribution," Jernberg (1993) says, "there may be a difficult temperament, physical deformity, lethargy, or hyperactivity" (p. 252).

Support for the importance of infant temperament in determining security of attachment is found in a study by van den Boom (as reported in Karen, 1994). Using a sample of one hundred babies who had been classified as highly irritable at birth, she found that, in the control group for whom there was no intervention, only 28 percent became securely attached. The other group received three two-hour counseling sessions between the child's sixth and ninth months designed "to enhance the mother's sensitivity and effectiveness." Within this group the percent of securely attached babies increased dramatically to 68 percent. Karen (1994) reports that

> Because the irritable babies were less responsive to their mothers, smiled and made pleasing sounds less frequently, . . . the mothers tended to become discouraged and give up on them in various ways. . . . Other mothers, . . . fearful of disrupting a quiet infant, had stopped interacting with their babies when they were *not* crying. Van den Boom encouraged such mothers to play with the child. (p. 309–310)

The Goal of Treatment

The Theraplay approach assumes both that change is possible and that the essential ingredients of change lie in the creation of a more positive relationship between the child and parents. Because the roots of the development of the self, of self-esteem, and of trust lie in the early years, it is essential to return to the stage at which the child's emotional development was derailed and provide the experience that can restart the healthy cycle of interaction. Activities are geared to the child's current emotional level rather than to his chronological age. Parents are encouraged to respond empathically to their child's regressive needs. The goal of treatment is to change the inner representation of the self and others from a negative to a more positive one.

While there is considerable evidence that an early attachment category (i.e., secure or insecure) is both persistent and stable, there is also evidence that change, both positive and negative, is possible. Examples of positive change can be found when the child has a good adoption experience, or when family circumstances improve. As Sroufe (1988) reports "when our poverty mothers form stable relationships with a partner, child adaptation improves" (p. 23). And, of course, a child's security can be negatively affected by loss through death or divorce or through long absences due to illness.

Winnicott (1958) emphasizes the importance of regression in the process of cure. For him, the curative factor in treatment is not primarily in the verbal interpretations, but in the way that the analytic setting fills early developmental needs. The goal is to compensate for parental failures in adaptation, and to "provide a certain type of environment" that allows the patient "to do the work" (Winnicott, 1958, p. 168). Regression is important because it represents a return to the point at which the environment has failed the child. "The tendency to regression in a patient is now seen as part of the capacity of the individual to bring about self-cure" (Winnicott, 1965, p. 128).

CASE FORMULATION

Jason's current problems (including the problems in his relationship with his mother, which led to the referral by Child Protective Services) can be seen as stemming from his early insecure attachment.* His behavior might also be seen as fitting the diagnostic category of attention deficit hyperactivity disorder (ADHD): irritable baby, very active, labile, with difficulty concentrating. The assumption of this presentation, however, is that his temperament interacted with his unfortunate attachment history to produce insecure attachment and that it is the insecure attachment that must be addressed in treatment. Many factors in the assessment data support this hypothesis. These include factors in Jason's early history that have been found to be precursors of attachment problems, as well as descriptions of Jason's current

---

*See "Orientation to the Text: The Case of Jason L.," p. 1.

seven-year-old behavior which, in follow-up studies, have been found to be typical of children who were insecurely attached as toddlers.

Description of Problem by Jason's Parents

Mary and Emilio's very different views of Jason's problems reflected the different nature of Jason's attachment to each parent. Mary described him as demanding, angry, unresponsive, and difficult to manage. Her CBCL description added a more empathic view of the feelings underlying his difficult behavior: socially withdrawn, lonely, feels unloved, and feels persecuted. Emilio reported no difficulty managing Jason but he saw him as clingy, shy, timid, and less assertive than he would like.

Developmental History

Jason's was a planned pregnancy, with both parents eagerly anticipating his birth. Unfortunately, pregnancy complications kept Mary in bed from her 26th week until delivery. There is no way at this point of knowing for certain how this period of worry about the outcome of the pregnancy might have affected the process of prenatal bonding. One mother who experienced a similar threat to her pregnancy reported that she consciously withheld her attention from the baby for fear that she would be too devastated if she lost it (personal communication to Booth, 1985). Because she does not describe her feelings about this period, we can only speculate that Mary, too, might have hesitated to fully engage with her baby.

At the time of delivery, Mary was physically weak because of the long bed rest and had only sporadic contact with Jason during the first few days. Once they were home, Mary "worried constantly" about his health because she was "afraid that the complications of the pregnancy might cause him to be sickly or even to die." In addition, Jason was an irritable baby. The combination of Mary's fears for his life and Jason's irritability must have created tension during the early months of their lives together.

As time went on, Mary's fears about Jason's health could have led to an anxious hovering, which would make it difficult for Jason to negotiate the separation-individuation phase of his development. Evidence supporting this hypothesis was seen in Jason's difficulty separating when he first went to school and may also account for what Emilio described as Jason's being "too clingy for a child his age."

When Jason was 11 months old, Mary became pregnant with her second child. This was the beginning of a series of losses and separations that profoundly affected Jason's attachment history. This second pregnancy again required bed rest and led Mary to wean Jason from the breast. For more than a year, Emilio's mother and Mary's mother became Jason's primary caretakers. When Jason was 18 months old, a second baby was born and died within a few hours. Following this, Mary was very depressed and "withdrew completely for several months, during which time she was unable to care for Jason." Emilio reported that this was the beginning of the end of their marriage. For Jason, it was probably the beginning of the end of any sense that his mother might be reliably available to meet his needs.

Lieberman and Pawl (1988) report: "In our work with disturbed infants and their parents, it has often been useful to understand symptoms in the child as deviations in the ability to internalize the role of the parent as a reliable protector" (p. 334). Using the vocabulary of attachment theory, one could say that this loss of his mother as his primary caretaker would lead Jason to view the social environment as inconsistently available and unresponsive. The resulting picture of himself would be that he was inadequate or unworthy of help and comfort. Karen (1994) says "the internal models of very young children are particularly subject to distortion, because they readily misinterpret the meaning of their parents' communications. They feel hated and rejected as a result of untimely separations; they interpret outwardly rejecting behavior as proof that they are not loved" (p. 210). Such models of self and other engender chronic anxiety, as they are used to anticipate, order, and assimilate future experience. We can imagine that for Jason, any transition or separation might stir up the anxious expectation that he could not count on his mother to return.

Evidence from reports of Jason's toddler behavior supports the notion that his early attachment was not secure. He explored the environment to the point of occasionally endangering himself. This behavior contrasts with the behavior of securely attached children who explore the environment more safely. Lieberman and Pawl (1988) say that recklessness and accident proneness is one outcome of insecure attachment. It can be interpreted as a

predominance of exploration at the expense of attachment behavior. . . . Children showing this pattern may be developing counterphobic defenses against anxiety in the sense that they attempt to manage their uncertainty over the mother's availability as a protector by taking off on their own and courting danger, rather than seeking protection from a source they perceive as unreliable. (p. 333)

When Jason was three and a half years old, his sister Carla was born. Soon the relationship between Mary and Emilio deteriorated to the point of separation. Left to care for both children, Mary felt overwhelmed. Six months after Carla's birth, Jason (then four years old) was sent to preschool. He had difficulty separating from his mother, crying bitterly at her departure. This response reflects Jason's insecurity as well as Mary's anxiety about leaving him. Once she had left him, Jason was able to settle down and enjoy preschool. Upon his mother's return, he was distant and aloof for several hours. For Jason, the pattern of taking some time to warm up after a separation continues to this day—now accompanied by overt expressions of anger.

As his parents' marriage disintegrated, there were further changes. In order to allow his mother to return to work, Jason was entered into both kindergarten and an after-school program. Mary reported that, when she first went back to work, she was exhausted at the end of each day and therefore was "short" with the children. Since at the time of the referral Mary did not like her job, she may well have continued to be tired and unhappy at the end of the day. Thus, at the very times when Jason needed his mother to be emotionally available, she was often unavailable.

While one can only speculate about what specific attachment category Jason would have fit at 18 months of age, his seven-year-old behavior had many characteristics of the older avoidantly attached child as outlined by Karen (1994) in his Appendix: *"Typical Patterns of Secure and Anxious Attachment."* By age six, with his parents, the child is "abrupt, neutral, and unenthusiastic. [There is an] absence of warm physical contact." Avoidant children are sullen, oppositional, and not inclined to seek help when injured or disappointed (p. 443).

School and Peer Relationships

Jason's school behavior, from the beginning, had been somewhat problematic. Initially he was described as very active, "all boy." Then his teacher found him to be increasingly noncompliant and disruptive. According to Jason, his teachers began to yell at him just as his mother did. Teachers respond to avoidantly attached children by "becoming controlling and angry" (Karen, 1994, p. 443). Sroufe says, in order to help such a child, the adult needs to confound the child's feelings of low self-esteem by refusing to reject him, by being playful, positive, appreciative and empathic (Karen, 1990).

Jason rarely played with peers and tended to be bossy when he did, but he was admired by the other boys, who saw him as independent and self-assured. Karen (1994) reported that avoidantly attached children have "no close friends or [their] friendships [are] marked by exclusivity [and] jealousy. They are often isolated from the group" (p. 443). Jason's pattern of handling problems by denial (things are "no big deal") and by presenting a tough, unfeeling surface may have been attractive to other kids at a distance, but it did not lead to good peer relationships. Behind Jason's tough-guy mask was a very insecure little boy. His breaking down and sobbing when finally confronted on his own by the police over the fire-setting episode was clear evidence of his underlying feelings.

Jason's school experience did not increase his self-esteem or help him deal with his angry feelings. His behavior after school (the angry acting out behavior that led to Mary's hitting him in the face) was partly the aftermath of what happened in school, partly as a result of his difficulty with transitions, and partly related to Mary's exhaustion and unavailability at the end of the day. Transitions, such as coming home from school, are particularly difficult for children who are not securely attached. Mary reported that the most difficult time for Jason was the hour after school. Emilio handled this by initiating interactive games such as playing catch or wrestling, which helped Jason "blow off steam." After that, he was able to be more calm. Mary left Jason alone for an hour or more, waiting till he approached her to ask for a snack or for help with his homework. As might be expected in view of her empathy for Jason's underlying feelings, Mary assumed that he did not want her around and respected his need for distance. Her empathy in this situation, however, only prolonged the separation difficulty because it failed to address Jason's need for contact in spite of himself. It is interesting to note that Jason became more affectionate as weekends progressed. Perhaps when Mary was relaxed and available and when there was time to warm up, Jason could reconnect to her. His being able to warm up to her indicated that he was still hopeful that he could get what he needed from her.

Family History and Dynamics

Very little was known of either parent's family history. That they came from different cultures was a fact that was taken into consideration in attempting to understand their expectations for Jason as well as their views about child rearing.

Mary's pattern of responding to loss with extended periods of depression has roots in her own childhood, beginning when her parents were divorced. She saw her mother as unable to respond to her needs, asking more from her emotionally than she was able to give. Mary has a very close relationship with Carla.

Jason's relationship with his father was closer than that reported between Jason and his mother. As the noncustodial parent, Emilio was not as overwhelmed by a full-time commitment to his children's care. He seemed to be more consistently available to Jason during their times together.

Surprisingly, Jason gets along well with Carla. He tries to boss her but is able to take into account the fact that she is younger than he. It might have been expected that Carla would be seen as an intruder into his uneasy relationship with his mother and therefore be a target for his anger. But, instead, Jason seemed to identify with her needs as a younger child.

Analysis of the Marschak Interaction Method Observations

Draw our house—This is a challenging task that provides information about the parent's expectations of the child and the child's response to those expectations.

Jason's response to this task with his mother was to say, "That's too hard," and even after completing the drawing he said, "It isn't very good." While Jason drew, Mary sat silently, making no comments on his work. Once he finished, Mary said, "I think it's quite good but I'll bet if you worked a little longer you could make it even better." This was reminiscent of Jason's second TAT story in which the girl "tries to do her best but it never seems to be good enough." It was interesting to see that Mary's expectations were really quite high, in view of the fact that Emilio saw her as allowing Jason to be babyish. While Mary challenged Jason to do better, she made it possible for him to succeed by breaking the task down into smaller details: "What color are the shutters? Do we have a sidewalk?" When Jason finished, Mary was very positive in her response, "I can see you really did your best." Jason smiled briefly.

With his father, the situation was quite different. It was Emilio who voiced concern that the task was too difficult, "That's an awfully hard job," and Jason who reassured him, "It's OK. I had to do the same thing with mom." Throughout Jason's drawing, Emilio attended and commented on the various details in a positive, supportive way. "That's pretty good. I think you are doing a better job than I could." At the end, he was enthusiastic about the results—"Wow, this is a great picture." Emilio's strategy was to avoid power struggles and lower his expectations. The result was that Jason spent more time on this second drawing, and it was more detailed and better proportioned. It was apparent that Jason needed and responded well to the kind of supportive, connected interaction that his father provided. By voicing the view that the task might be difficult, Emilio set the stage for Jason to work to his own standards—"It's OK. I can do it." By continually providing a supportive voice throughout the task, he made it possible for Jason to maintain his focus, to be expansive, and attend to detail. This is a clear example of what Jason needs in order to maintain focus and feel good about himself in relation to demanding tasks.

Adult and child take turns rubbing hand lotion on each other—This is a nurturing task that shows whether the adult can provide nurture and whether the child can accept it.

Mary presented the task as if it were a necessary grooming act, intended to correct a deficiency in his appearance. "I noticed your elbows were pretty dry this morning." Jason responded with exasperated compliance. His "Oh yuk" could be simply a seven-year-old's annoyance at being babied by his mother or the response of an irritable, tactually sensitive child to the touch of lotion. In either case, he was unable to accept a nurturing activity that had the potential for enhancing their relationship and of soothing and calming him. On the basis of this one interaction it was not possible to know whether Jason could accept nurturance from his mother if it were done in a more playful, less critical or serious manner. Because of his many rejections of her approaches, Mary may have felt inadequate and may have thus resorted to a routine caretaking approach rather than venturing into more creative nurturing uses of the lotion.

When Mary suggested that Jason put lotion on her knees "which are even drier than his elbows," Jason rejected the notion, suggesting an alternative, "on your neck." Mary's concern that he would mess up her hair suggested she had little faith in Jason's impulse control and feared his aggressive impulses toward her. In spite of her concern, she praised his way of doing it, "You're good at that. It feels great." This interaction raised the possibility that there may be a pattern of Mary's needing caretaking from Jason. Mary seemed to play a similar role in her relationship with her own mother.

Adult has the children share a single bag of M&Ms—Another nurturing task with the added dimension of the interaction between the two siblings.

The candy set up an immediate competitive reaction in the two children as both rushed to find the candies: Jason said, "I'm bigger"; Carla said, "I'm better." They responded immediately to Mary's stern command to "Stop arguing!" Mary then gave ten M&Ms to each child and withheld the rest, saying, "It's too close to dinnertime." One source of the children's competitiveness may have been their sense that there was a limit to the available supplies. Both this task and the lotion task suggested that Mary was uncertain how to nurture. In this case, she worried about spoiling their appetite when she could have been increasing her attachment to them. She needed help becoming the *good* mother she struggled to be.

Emilio handled the children's eagerness and competitiveness with good humor; "Let's figure out how to share them." Again he was able to side-step conflict. After hearing each child's suggestion, Emilio offered a solution that allowed each a full share, and he provided a makeshift bag to carry them in. Emilio's handling of the problem was relaxed, good humored, and fair, but it lacked the intimacy that could have been achieved had they fed each other the candy.

Summary of Assessment Data Findings

Mother

1. As would be expected in light of his early history, Jason's relationship with his mother was more needy and conflictual than with his father. His initial insecure attachment had a lasting effect on his self-image, self-control, and expectations of others, which accounted for the anger and sullen withdrawal that characterized Jason's behavior. It was easy to see how the combination of Jason's distant, sullen, defiant behavior and Mary's exhaustion and exasperation could have produced the physical attacks that brought them to the attention of the Child Protective Services.
2. Mary had high expectations for Jason and for herself and was not consistently able to give him the support that would help him meet those expectations.
3. Mary was unable to respond in a generous, nurturing manner to meet Jason's needs. This was not surprising since, as a child, she was not given the empathy she needed.
4. In spite of her difficulty responding to Jason's needs for nurture, there was evidence that Mary understood Jason's underlying feelings better than his father did.

Father

1. Because there was no significant separation during the early years, and because Emilio had maintained consistent ongoing contact since the divorce, Jason had a more secure relationship with his father than with his mother.
2. While Emilio, like Mary, had high expectations for Jason (for example his expectation that a seven-year-old boy should be able to go by himself to return a defective toy), he avoided conflict, in the observed interactions, by lowering his standards and by democratically asking the children to suggest solutions.
3. Emilio seemed able to provide the calm, good-natured acceptance that allowed Jason to feel calm and capable.
4. Emilio found it difficult to accept Jason's regressive needs and therefore did not encourage the intimacy that would be helpful to Jason.
5. In spite of the many helpful aspects of Emilio's way of relating to Jason, his relaxed democratic approach did not provide the clear structure and control that would have been necessary to overcome the effects of Jason's early insecurity.

TREATMENT GOALS

1. Form a secure attachment between Jason and both parents, especially with his mother.
2. Change how Jason views himself and others, as well as his expectations of how they will respond to him from negative to positive.
3. Provide the soothing empathic experiences that Jason missed as an infant because of his irritability and because of Mary's worries and depression.
4. Change his parents' ways of interacting with Jason so that they can carry on the therapeutic work at home.
5. School intervention: Help Jason's teacher(s) understand his needs. Include the teacher(s) in some treatment sessions, if possible.
6. Because Mary may have missed, in her own childhood, the nurturing and empathic responsiveness that she would need to give Jason, provide nurturing experiences for her through role-playing her interactions with Jason.
7. Work on relationship issues that might get in the way of Mary's and Emilio's being able to respond to Jason's needs.
8. As a final step, include Carla in a few sessions to help both parents manage the competitiveness between the two children.

Thus, rather than focusing on controlling Jason's hyperactive and aggressive behavior and possible attention problems, treatment focused first on changing Jason's relationship with both parents so that they could understand and respond to his underlying needs and he could come to trust and value their wisdom. When the treatment was completed, Jason's activity level and ability to attend was such that an ADHD evaluation did not indicate a problem.

TREATMENT DESCRIPTION

Logistics

The Theraplay assessment procedure includes the following three elements:

1. An intake interview with both parents without the child, which covers much of the information available in the present case plus information about attachment issues, including the parents' relationship to their own parents.
2. An assessment of the child's relationship with each parent, using the Marschak Interaction Method (MIM). Standardized checklists or complete test batteries are not routinely used. If there is a question about intellectual or neurological functioning or about the child's inner conflicts, appropriate testing is arranged.
3. A feedback session with the parents in which the initial evaluation of the problem is discussed, segments of the videotaped MIM sessions are used to illustrate particular points, and a treatment plan is proposed.

Typically, two therapists are assigned to each Theraplay case. The Theraplay therapist works with the child in the playroom while the Interpreting therapist works with the parent(s) behind a one-way mirror. It is the job of the Interpreting therapist to help the parent(s) understand what is taking place in the playroom and to prepare them for their eventual participation in the sessions. The parent(s) watch the interaction during the first four sessions. In the remaining sessions, they enter the room for the second half of each session and begin to practice what has been found to work well with their child. The goal is that the parents be able to carry on at home a new, more rewarding way of relating to their child.

Theraplay sessions are designed to follow a treatment plan that is subject to change based on the child's response to each session. Therefore, the activities, playroom props, and therapeutic focus may differ from session to session, depending on the specific needs of the child and parent(s). Activities are chosen based on an assessment of the child's specific needs for structure, challenge, intrusion/engagement, or nurture (see the previous discussion of Theraplay dimensions on pages 205–206). Given Jason's need to develop a more secure attachment to his parents, there was less focus on challenging tasks and more on those that were nurturing and playful. Because Jason had demonstrated that he could become oppositional, activities were structured so that the therapists remained in charge of the sessions. This ensured that Jason did not succeed in his efforts to distract them from their task of establishing a warm, secure relationship.

A major component of Theraplay treatment is parent support. It is this support that makes Theraplay so effective with children like Jason who are incapable of giving much to their parents or of reciprocating what their parents give to them. By supporting parents, Theraplay therapists help them through difficult times. The therapists explain the child's specific treatment plan, predict how they think the child will react, and explain the Theraplay therapist's maneuvers in dealing with the behavior their child manifests. For example, Jason's parents were told, "See how the therapist handles Jason's efforts to avoid closeness."

Setting

The playroom setting for Theraplay is unique in its apparent simplicity. Although a few simple objects are used in playing with the child, the primary playroom object is the adult—first the Theraplay therapist and then the parent or caretaker. The playroom is simple, functional, and comfortable.

The ideal Theraplay playroom consists of an uncluttered space covered with gym mats with access to a sink for water and cleanup and a cupboard for storing material not needed for a particular session. Gym mats are preferred to carpeting for their ease of cleaning and resistance to water, which allows the therapist to utilize props that may create a mess. Large pillows for sitting on or for use in games can remain in the playroom. One playroom wall should contain a one-way viewing mirror with appropriate sound equipment. The playroom should also have a videotape camera for recording MIM evaluations and Theraplay sessions if desired. Many Theraplay playrooms contain a wall covered with corkboard so the child's creations can be displayed. The design of the playroom matches the philosophy of treatment, which considers the adult to be the primary playroom object, believes that healthy play can be regressive, and places the adult in charge of the action.

Materials

Creativity is encouraged in stocking the Theraplay playroom, but certain props are found in every playroom. A well-stocked playroom includes:

Large pieces of paper for drawing
Crayons and markers
Modeling clay
Bubble-blowing equipment
Large pans for water
Healthy food that can be safely stored (e.g., raisins, apples)
Drinking cups
Yardstick and measuring tape
Baby powder
Hand lotion
A mirror
Dress-up hats
Large towels
Washcloths
A blanket
Tape for hanging artwork

For each session, the therapist has available only materials needed for preselected activities. By focusing attention away from playroom props, the Theraplay therapist encourages personal interaction. This is especially important for insecurely attached children, like Jason, who often prefer to play with a toy than with another person. The use of props can lead to a focus on the materials rather than on the relationship. Props also encourage adults to move into a teaching role and thus increase the risk of measuring the child's emotional growth by intellectual achievements. Theraplay is challenging but is not geared toward helping the child master educational goals.

Frequency and Duration of Treatment

Theraplay sessions are structured and designed to include periodic evaluation of treatment goals. An initial contract with the family consists of eight to twelve Theraplay sessions following the intake interview and MIM evaluation. Additional sessions are scheduled after review by, and mutual agreement between, therapists and parent(s).

The frequency of Theraplay sessions is determined in the same manner as in other forms of psychotherapy. Theraplay therapists generally schedule one session per week unless there are other circumstances requiring more frequent sessions. These circumstances include crisis situations; time limitations because of moves, summer camp, school, and the like; and situations where the child's need for intervention requires from more frequency.

Theraplay sessions are one-half hour in length and are very intense. Each session is preplanned such that every minute is utilized. Because the Theraplay therapist is providing most of the structure and is conducting the session with the belief that he or she will give to—not receive from—the child, the work is very demanding. One must keep in mind that, while the session is only one-half hour in length, Theraplay is two simultaneous half-hour sessions—one with the child and one with the parent(s).

Specific Strategies

Jason's treatment was structured to help him feel better about himself and others, especially his parents. While one cannot always choose the sex of the therapist to meet the specific needs of a client family, Jason's Theraplay therapist was a woman, because it was with women that Jason had the greatest conflict. A male Interpreting therapist provided a model for Emilio and for Jason of a man who was both structuring and nurturing. As they watched Jason in session, his mother and father were helped to increase their empathy toward him and, ultimately, feel closer to him (e.g., "Notice how much he likes it when the therapist claps her hands when he jumps."). The Theraplay therapist approached the session in an upbeat, playful, child-centered way. The basic outline of a Theraplay session includes activities that are active and stimulating as well as calming and nurturing. Within this structure, a therapist is flexible and changes activities based upon feedback from parents or the behavior of the child. In response to Jason's efforts to distance himself, his therapist persisted in helping him experience a meaningful relationship. The therapist did not allow Jason to take charge of the sessions or dictate the pace. She was prepared to soothe Jason at some point during the therapy if Jason became particularly resistant or distressed.

Each Theraplay activity is chosen because it is fun—what any child Jason's age would enjoy—and because it encourages playful interaction. Jason's parents were told that, in spite of this, he might resist the therapist's overtures and react negatively. If such a reaction occurred, it would not be because the Theraplay activities were poorly chosen or because they had not trained him well, but because of Jason's discomfort with the unaccustomed intimacy and structure. The ongoing empathic, intrusiveness of the therapist gradually led to Jason's being able to feel more comfortable with closeness. Jason's need to act older and become a caretaker was foiled by the Theraplay therapist's insistence on remaining in the adult caretaker role. Jason was encouraged to step back for awhile and experience caretaking in a way he might have missed when younger. Throughout the sessions, his parents were reassured that they did the best job they could in rearing him. Theraplay accepted what they had done and helped them expand their repertoire of ways to meet Jason's needs. When Jason's parents became uncomfortable during the sessions, they were reminded that difficult times had been predicted. Most parents feel better when they recall that negative behavior was predicted and considered part of the treatment process.

Treatment Stages

Introduction/Orientation

PARENTS' ORIENTATION TO THERAPLAY.   Jason's parents' orientation began with the intake interview. They were encouraged to ask any questions that arose during this session. They were told that the next step in the evaluation process would be the scheduling of the Marschak Interaction Method (MIM) (Marschak, 1960, 1967, 1980; Marschak & Call, 1966). The parents were given a brief description of the MIM and asked for signed permission to videotape the session. They were told that their videotape would be used only to give them feedback. Another specific release of information form would have to be signed before the tapes could be used for any other purpose. All records generated from Theraplay evaluations and sessions are kept confidential and are not released without valid, signed releases of information.

Following the MIM evaluations, a feedback session was scheduled to include both the Interpreting and Theraplay therapists and both parents. During the feedback session, Jason's parents were shown videotaped segments of their interaction in order to demonstrate points about how Jason responded to their way of handling him. The bulk of the feedback focused on the positives of their behavior—for example, how well Mary structured the drawing task and praised Jason for his effort and how well Emilio maintained supportive contact with Jason during his drawing. They were shown how he calmed down during the nurturing (lotion) task and how much he tried to please them. Jason's pseudomature behavior was pointed out and his parents were told how this will take a toll on him in the long run. They were also shown how he attempted to gain distance from them, either by provocative behavior or noncompliance.

THE TREATMENT PLAN.   At the end of the feedback session, the treatment plan was discussed with the parents. It was hypothesized that Jason avoided disappointment and attempted to limit anxiety by distancing himself from others and acting as if he were older, while in reality he had the needs of someone younger than his years. Therefore, Jason's treatment plan was developed to include activities that are regressive and nurturing yet challenging. For example, he and his therapist might thumb-wrestle, play tug-of-war, and race through a tunnel of pillows. She will feed him raisins, cool him down with a damp washcloth, and sing him a song. She might draw an outline of Jason's feet and hands and a profile of his head. Throughout these activities, the therapist will provide Jason with lots of encouragement and praise for his efforts. The action will keep moving and will be determined by the therapist's empathic awareness of Jason's needs.

Jason's father initially reacted positively and enthusiastically to this treatment plan. He liked the challenging, fun-loving quality of the activities. He had more difficulty, however, accepting the idea of regressive, nurturing play. Jason's mother, on the other hand, was apprehensive about the plan and projected her anxiety onto Jason, saying that he would not like this type of play. She predicted that Jason would not be as cooperative as his father expected him to be. She was correct in anticipating Jason's resistance, which is a normal response in the treatment process.

Although divorced, Jason's parents were comfortable working together for Jason's best interest. Issues that arose in the relationship between the parents were dealt with by the interpreting therapist.

CHILD'S ORIENTATION TO THERAPLAY.   Parents often ask what to tell their child about psychotherapy. It is recommended that they say something like, "Our family is going to learn to have more fun together and this will help us all feel happier." Evasive answers and attempts to trick the child into coming to the sessions are strongly discouraged. Jason's parents were given concrete examples of what to say such as "You know how upset you get when you can't get your way and how hard it is for you to finish your work." It was also suggested that they take some responsibility for the problems so that Jason would not feel that he alone was being blamed. Thus, mother might say, "You know how I sometimes get so angry I've lost control and hit you." Father might add, "You know how angry I get when I think you're acting like a baby, when all you want is some attention."

Parents are encouraged to approach the day of the first Theraplay appointment like any other day. It is important that they take a matter-of-fact attitude and not communicate any anxiety to the child. Given his cooperative behavior during the MIM, it was not expected that Jason would resist returning to the clinic for the first session.

Parents generally have the ability to take a child to an appointment when they believe the appointment is absolutely necessary. For example, if a child has a high fever, the parent takes the child to the pediatrician, even if the child is fearful of doctors and fears injections. The parent communicates a nonanxious, optimistic message to the child that the doctor's appointment will help the child feel better. Parent anxiety accounts for most of the difficulty encountered in bringing a child to a therapy appointment. This pediatrician example is useful in helping parents understand the role they must play in bringing the child to therapy.

HIERARCHY OF AUTHORITY.   A hierarchy of authority and mentoring exists in Theraplay treatment. The top position in this hierarchy is temporarily occupied by the therapist, followed by the parent(s), and then by the child. Theraplay therapists demonstrate the kind of behavior they want parent(s) to show their children. These behaviors include activities that are nurturing, challenging, engaging, structuring, and playful. A weak therapist cannot encourage parents to be strong. A pessimistic therapist cannot expect parents to be optimistic. Parents cannot learn to support upset children if they do not feel supported when *they* are upset. Blaming parents for their children's problems only lowers the parent's self-esteem and has a negative impact on the child.

THE FIRST SESSION.   Jason and his family were warmly greeted by both therapists in the waiting room and escorted to the playroom. The parents and child were given a tour of the observation room behind the one-way mirror. Jason and the Theraplay therapist left the parents and the interpreting therapist in the observation room and headed for the playroom. Once in the playroom, the therapist pointed out the one-way mirror and had Jason tap on the glass, asking the parents to tap back.

The action immediately went into high gear. Jason was instructed to sit on a pillow on the gym mat and told, in a light-hearted way, "I'm going to do a check-up to make sure you brought all your parts." The therapist then proceeded to count Jason's toes, fingers, eyes, knuckles, ears, and feet—sometimes making intentional counting errors to add some humor and to encourage Jason's participation.

The next activity continued this check-up theme by having Jason stand against a wall so the therapist could mark his height with a piece of chalk. The therapist measured Jason's height with a tape measure and recorded it on a piece of paper. Jason was then asked to reach as high as he could with the chalk and mark that point on the wall. Finally, Jason was asked to hold the chalk, jump as high as he could, and mark how high he had jumped. All chalk marks were measured and recorded. Outlines of Jason's hands and feet were traced on paper and hung on the wall. Jason's efforts did not have to be record-breaking to receive praise: "What a great jump; terrific form." The Theraplay therapist models his or her optimistic statements on the way a good parent rewards a very young child for effort even if the quality of the work does not reflect an adult standard. Other tasks, such as seeing how many pillows Jason could balance on his head, were followed by cheers from the therapist, even though Jason, at that time, could balance only one pillow.

This first session, like all Theraplay sessions, alternated active games with quiet periods of feeding and with cooling down with a fan or a damp washcloth placed on Jason's face. Jason was not expected to perform to any standard and was recognized for the joy he brought to the interaction.

Since Jason was taken by surprise during the first session, he had no time to think of resisting activities introduced by the therapist. He entered in enthusiastically and left the session bragging to his parents about how high he had jumped. Jason's parents were encouraged to match his level of excitement about the session and to let him know that they, too, were impressed with his jumping ability. It was necessary to prompt his parents to praise his achievement because Jason was completing activities that were somewhat regressive in nature. In such situations, parents do not have to fear they are pushing their child too hard or expecting the child to achieve for their sake. Since his parents had viewed the entire session, Jason was spared the inevitable question often asked by parents whose children are receiving psychotherapy: "So what did you talk about?"

BEHIND THE ONE-WAY MIRROR.　Throughout this session, Jason's parents were given explanations of what they saw in the playroom. If Jason resisted an activity, the parents were encouraged to watch how the Theraplay therapist dealt with resistance. Any questions the parents had were directly answered. The parents were encouraged to do some of these activities at home with Jason during the next week. Jason's parents were uncomfortable with some of the Theraplay activities, and the source of their discomfort was explored. For example, Jason's mother was uncomfortable with regressive, nurturing activities. Her discomfort was related to her own failure to be nurtured as a child and to her fear that regression would lead to Jason's unending dependence. When she understood that her fear was unwarranted, she was able to relax during these more regressive periods of the therapy.

Negative Reaction

The negative reaction is an important step in the treatment because it signals the child's beginning hope and trust. It is as if the child is now ready to test whether an adult can be trusted to stay with him even when he shows his angry feelings. Having the therapist—and later his parents—stay with him, calmly contain his violent behavior, and not retaliate and reject him is a powerful experience (which may need to be tested many times). Following such outbursts, children often relax, sobbing into the therapist's (or parents' arms) as if, for the first time, they feel that someone can truly share their feelings and comfort them.

PARENT PREPARATION FOR THE NEGATIVE REACTION. Jason's parents were carefully prepared for his inevitable negative reaction. They were told: "This is a very important part of the treatment because it tells us the therapist is getting through to Jason. Jason acts this way because he is trying his best to avoid the anxiety caused by feeling close to someone." They were also told: "Many children throw tantrums and must be held until the tantrum is over. These children become verbally and physically abusive. Do not feel embarrassed if Jason behaves this way. If Jason does not become aggressive he may become limp and will be 'walked-through' the session's entire treatment plan by the therapist. It is not unusual for a child to keep his or her eyes tightly closed throughout a session during the negative phase. This negative stage could last for a number of sessions but not forever." Parent preparation for the negative stage is very important. Preparation and prediction immunize parents against excessive anxiety when negative behavior emerges. Then, when their child becomes negative, the parents are more relaxed and better able to watch how someone else handles this behavior.

NEGATIVE REACTION: IN THE CHILD. Negative reactions can occur within or between sessions as early as the first session or after experiencing a number of sessions. Jason's parents were warned about the possibilities and how to respond to them. If Jason's negativity were to begin between sessions (for example, he might become more oppositional at home or school or refuse to return for his next session), his parents were told they should not argue with him, that they should set appropriate limits and ensure that he comes to the next session. They were encouraged to call the Interpreting therapist between sessions for support and advice.

More typically, negative behavior occurs *during* the Theraplay sessions. Oftentimes, parents describe their child's behavior as improved at home such that they cannot understand why their child behaves so badly with the therapist. Indeed Jason became negative during a Theraplay session but not before experiencing a number of "good" sessions. This was easier for the parents to handle because they had time to internalize the Theraplay approach and to imagine how they might handle the negativity. Once the negative stage sets in, most parents worry that the child will resist coming to the next session and are surprised when the child does not object.

Initially Jason reacted to the Theraplay sessions, as he had to the MIM evaluation. He waited for the therapist to take the lead and then carefully followed. He responded positively to encouragement. He was especially interested in activities that were more challenging and performance oriented. When the activities were more nurturing and intimate, he became uncomfortable. He felt the conflict between his positive feelings when encouraged and supported and his anxiety in anticipation of a potential loss of those good feelings. Fearing rejection, he needed to test the relationship.

Jason's initial compliance was gradually replaced by subtle attempts to control the sessions. He playfully attempted to slow the action by talking about each activity or by lingering beyond the imposed time limit. He laughed when the therapist stuck to the plan and did not do what he wanted.

The therapist, skilled in recognizing resistance, did not allow Jason to take charge, nor was she intimidated when he later went beyond passive resistance and actually threw a tantrum. Slowly, Jason realized that his subtle attempts to control the session would not work, and he became increasingly more unresponsive. At the beginning of the third session, he avoided the therapist's offered hand, ran to where the props were gathered for the session, and began playing by himself. Jason sullenly ignored the therapist's efforts to gain his attention and continued to play on his own. When the therapist refused to leave him alone, Jason became angry. He attempted physically to push the therapist away and to throw things. Because the therapist wanted to maintain an intimate connection with Jason, she did not resort to putting him in time-out. Instead, since in his agitation Jason was becoming a physical threat to himself and to her, she gently, but firmly, held him and stated the Theraplay rule—"No hurts!"

Faced with his therapist's persistence, Jason became distressed and asked for his mother or father to come into the playroom as a way of distancing himself from the therapist. He acted in a provocative way in an attempt to make the therapist angry. The therapist set limits but never criticized or rejected him. The therapist's goal was to ensure that Jason was safe while maintaining intimacy.

The therapist took responsibility for soothing Jason rather than expecting him to calm down by himself. She held him until the aggressive episode was finished. Following a tantrum, children like Jason often break down into tears. After Jason stopped crying, his therapist helped him recover by wiping his face with a cool washcloth, combing his hair, and straightening his clothes. This kinesthetic soothing is more easily remembered and, after a number of episodes, is internalized by the child. If separated from a caretaker by being placed in time-out during these critical outbursts, a child will experience abandonment even though the child acts as if he or she wishes to be left alone. In spite of his apparent upset, Jason left this difficult session very relaxed and experienced a good day with his parents.

His parents had been warned to anticipate this tantrum and to watch how the therapist handled it. As the tantrum began, the Interpreting therapist, behind the one-way viewing mirror, leaned forward toward the mirror and said: "Good, now we have a chance to watch how these difficult times are handled." This kind of statement increased the parents' interest and decreased their anxiety about the emerging struggle.

NEGATIVE REACTION: IN THE PARENT(S).   Parent(s), too, experience negative reactions. Preparation for negative reactions in the child should be followed by warning the parent(s) that they also might experience a negative reaction. If two parents are involved in the treatment, it is rare that both react negatively at the same time. However, protest from just one parent can jeopardize the continuation of treatment. Typical negative reactions include complaining that activities are too young for their child, that the parent(s) can't understand how "just playing games" can possibly help, or that the therapist is being insensitive to the child's feelings and should stop being so intrusive. Some parents cannot tolerate a child's crying and want to "rescue" the child from the therapist. Parents may also experience embarrassment about and anger toward a child who is uncooperative or aggressive. The Interpreting therapist must be sensitive to these reactions and encourage the parent(s) to talk about them so they can be reassured. If parent(s) have been warned in advance that they may feel this way, a simple reminder of this prediction helps them relax. The therapist will suggest to a parent who has trouble watching a session that he or she take a break from the observation room and either get a drink of water or take a short walk.

In the extreme, some parent(s) have threatened to enter the Theraplay room and stop the therapy. The Interpreting therapist sees this as a therapeutic emergency and quickly confronts the parents by pointing out the consequences of such behavior. They are told that, without intervention, the child will continue to experience the problems that brought him or her to treatment in the first place and that they, too, must act differently to help their child. Furthermore, they are reminded that the playroom activities are games all children enjoy. They are told their child will come to enjoy this someday, but not without first experiencing some discomfort. Jason's parents were told, "Without help Jason will continue to keep distant from others. He will do things that make you feel bad. His behavior will at times be so provocative that you may again feel like you are losing control."

PARENTS' REACTION TO JASON'S BEHAVIOR IN THERAPLAY.   Jason's father enjoyed, and was very interested in, the initial sessions when Jason was playful, active, and cooperative. He found it increasingly difficult to watch sessions when Jason became negative, and the Theraplay therapist insisted on completing an activity that Jason resisted. Emilio advised cajoling, compromising, or changing activities when Jason protested. His need to avoid conflict became apparent when he reported knowing a better way of getting Jason to cooperate. For example, he said, "Jason just wants the therapist to close her eyes for a moment to play hide-and-seek. If the therapist will do this, Jason will gladly do what the therapist wants and thumb-wrestle." Jason's father found it difficult to see that Jason needed adult direction and intimacy and that successful parenting was measured not by task accomplishment but by Jason's ability to accept nurturance and adult authority.

Jason's mother, on the other hand, was relieved to see others experience the same problems she experienced. She felt less incompetent when an expert ran into opposition from Jason. She was interested to see how the therapist set limits and modeled her behavior after the therapist's. She had the opportunity to see from a distance why Jason behaved the way he did and to then feel some empathy about his reaction. Jason's mother learned to be more nurturing and better at limit setting rather than engaging in power struggles with him. Her self-esteem rose when she saw that she was not the only target of Jason's opposition.

Working Through

As Jason began to accept the therapist's authority and to enjoy being soothed, he became more regressive in his behavior. He resorted temporarily to infantile behaviors such as baby talk; he became more compliant and quiet. This behavior is typical of children who have protected themselves from their infantile needs by becoming aggressive. Parents often become very uncomfortable when their child begins to act like a baby. The Interpreting therapist prepared Jason's parents by predicting infantile behavior, but not until much of the negative stage had passed. Too much input early in the process is not meaningful to parents and is difficult for them to integrate. Jason's parents were told that this regressive behavior gives them a chance to go back in time and relate to Jason in ways that will increase their closeness to him.

Once Jason emerged from his first bout of negativity, the Interpreting therapist also prepared the parents for relapses in Jason's behavior. The therapist warned the parents that they might feel very disappointed if Jason becomes negative again. The contrast between times when Jason is compliant and comfortable with intimacy and those when he acts out will make the difficult times seem even worse. His parents were told: "Jason's behavior will be like waves after a storm. There will be rough periods but, with time, these periods will become farther apart and less intense." Theraplay working through requires adults to maintain a positive, engaging attitude. They must help the child have fun in spite of himself or herself.

THERAPLAY: PARENTS AND CHILD TOGETHER.   Part of the working-through process requires parents to gain mastery in handling their child. Jason's parents were asked to enter the Theraplay room halfway through session number five, after Jason had worked through his negativity. As is typical, Jason went through a second negative, regressed, and dependent period at this point. This gave the parents a chance to work with Jason's resistance while being coached and supported by the therapists. Because of the parents' need for support and the fact that mother and father needed different kinds of direction, the Interpreting therapist also joined the activity in the playroom. The Interpreting therapist helped the parents follow through with activities initiated by the Theraplay therapist and supported them in their efforts. Jason's father was encouraged to make use of his playful approach yet he was helped to stay in charge of the activities. When Jason became oppositional or aggressive, his father was asked to step in and set limits.

Jason's mother, on the other hand, was encouraged to engage in the more soothing and nurturing activities. She was helped to experience Jason's more needy and receptive side. She was discouraged from focusing on his performance or from fine-tuning his behavior. She was protected from his attempts to distance himself from her by the therapists and by his father. She was also trained to respond quickly to negative behavior rather than wait until she became upset. The therapists' goal with Jason and his mother was to help strengthen their bond. This was particularly helpful in reducing the possibility of abuse because Jason's mother was now better able to understand his needs and not take misbehavior personally.

Throughout the sessions with the parents, both therapists were supportive and upbeat. They showed the parents exactly how to play with Jason and had them repeat games several times until they became expert at playing them. Whenever a parent was asked to do something with Jason ("Here's a towel, Mom, play a game of tug-of-war, but make sure Jason waits while you count to three."), the therapists watched with optimistic interest and encouragement. Jason and his parents were helped throughout the sessions to make eye contact and to say only positive things to each other. Jason's parents were asked to carry on activities at home and to report their efforts to the Interpreting therapist next session. The parents were praised for their efforts to work together in spite of their marital difficulties. These family Theraplay sessions continued until the therapists felt the parents had mastered their roles.

Termination Issues and Procedures

Although Theraplay is short term in nature, and therefore transference may be less intense, termination is well planned. Since the time-limited nature of treatment is part of the initial treatment plan, the termination process is anticipated right from the start. However, because of the many unknowns that confront any therapist treating a child, the actual date of termination is not set until it is appropriate to do so. The therapists and parents will then agree upon a termination date based not only on improvement but also on potential improvement. The therapists began the termination process with Jason in the tenth session—based not on whether all of Jason's problems had been solved at the moment, but on their evaluation of the parents' ability to interact effectively. They expected the treatment to continue, with the parents as therapists, after the formal Theraplay sessions had ended. In order to monitor the process, follow-up or check-up sessions were scheduled at monthly intervals for one year.

Once a specific termination date was set, the parents and Jason were reminded of the importance of continuing their interaction after the sessions ended. They were praised for their good work and given examples of how differently they behave now than when they first entered treatment. Jason's father was praised for his ability to be playful yet firm: "Dad, you are so good at counting to three and helping Jason wait his turn." He was encouraged to support Jason's mother by setting appropriate limits on Jason's behavior when he is with him. Jason's mother was praised for her ability to react early to Jason's misbehavior and to quickly look for opportunities to nurture him: "Mom, you are the best at feeding Jason those raisins and fanning him when he is hot and tired." Jason's good qualities, many that she could take credit for, were pointed out. The therapists worked to enhance her pride in Jason and thus raise her self-esteem and attachment to him. Jason was recognized for the pleasure he brings to others: "Jason, we are going to miss all the fun of playing with you in the future. Your parents are lucky to have you."

Throughout the final stage of Theraplay, Jason's parents were supported for their good efforts both in and out of the sessions. By the time they were ready for termination, only fine-tuning of their behavior was necessary. The formal Theraplay sessions ended on the twelfth session with a termination party. This party was made as festive as possible. All in attendance were given party hats, and Jason's favorite food was provided. Jason's creations were collected and reviewed before being packed up to be sent home with him. All were congratulated for their efforts. The atmosphere of this last formal session was upbeat and optimistic.

EXPECTED OUTCOME OR PROGNOSIS

Jason's age, his parents' motivation, and the nature of his difficulties all pointed to a good prognosis. All members of Jason's family were basically healthy and capable of relating in a manner that guarantees a good therapeutic outcome. Rather than limit treatment to talking to any one family member, Theraplay intervened at a very basic level and provided a new experience for the whole family, aimed at helping increase attachment and understanding.

Since Jason was not expected to behave in any particular way, he could not do poorly during the sessions. He merely had to be present for the sessions and behave as his reactions led him to behave. As anticipated, he was initially ambivalent about allowing himself to accept nurturance and regression and reacted negatively when this type of experience was provided for him. Once he realized it was safe to experience intimacy and to allow adults to take charge of situations, Jason relaxed and behaved in a way that his parents found appealing. He was then able to enjoy life without the burden of feeling that he could only count on himself to make things safe and predictable.

Because the entire thrust of the treatment was to bring parents and child closer together, Jason's parents felt more comfortable as time passed and they engaged in more behaviors that encouraged intimacy. A reverberating system had been created whereby the positive feelings generated by one family member were reflected back to another. Although Jason's parents became experts at carrying on the treatment at home and in monitoring their own progress, they were told that future Theraplay sessions or consultation would be available if problems arose. The prognosis for this family was very good.

CONCLUSION

Jason's parents began their lives together sharing healthy, optimistic goals. They wanted to be close to each other and to share their closeness with children. The children came, but not without complications. Neither parent was prepared to deal with the death of an infant. Following a series of unfortunate disappointments, their marriage fell apart. Each, used his or her own background and culture to deal with the loss, but they were unable to use each other for consolation.

Who knows what might have happened had things not been so complicated for these parents? Although Mary had a history of depression, the closeness she could have experienced with Emilio and her children might have been enough to fill the gaps from her childhood. Emilio's cultural background provided him with a close-knit, supportive family. Mary was not so fortunate and faced her problems alone; her basic internal strength helped her survive her losses but left her vulnerable to frustration.

Both parents did the best they could to raise their children. Firstborn Jason experienced all the parents' struggles without the cognitive ability to understand what was happening. A survivor, like his mother, and a person to face a challenge, like his father, Jason coped with his fears alone. He created tests to measure the ability of others to stay close to him. He had no way of knowing that these tests would create problems in themselves. His own frustration and anger created behavior so provocative that adults lost control around him.

This family began their lives together in love and hope. By the time they sought Theraplay treatment, they had lost sight of their strengths and needed outside help to regain their confidence and return to their earlier, more optimistic view of the future. The parents were able to do this because they felt supported by the Theraplay therapists, because they learned new ways of relating to their son, and because they were no longer burdened by the loss experiences and stresses of the past. Jason could do it because he was given what he needed: a secure attachment to reliable, responsive, strong, and loving parents.

The Theraplay therapists never wavered from their hopefulness about this family. They communicated confidence and optimism and were authentic in their support. Every member of the family was nurtured and challenged when ready. The parents were made to feel their good fortune in having a child like Jason, and Jason could not help feeling special and valuable. Although they knew from the beginning that Jason would end treatment demonstrating his charming, engaging side more often, the Theraplay therapists could not help but feel the loss that paralleled the parents' gain.

BIBLIOGRAPHY

Ainsworth, M. (1969). Object relations, dependency and attachment: A theoretical review of the infant-mother relationship. *Child Development, 40*, 969–1025.

Belsky, J., & Nezworski, T. (Eds.). (1988). *Clinical implications of attachment*. Hillsdale, NJ: Erlbaum.

Bowlby, J. (1969). *Attachment and loss. Vol. I: Attachment*. London: Hogarth Press.

Bowlby, J. (1973). *Attachment and loss. Vol. II: Separation, anxiety and anger*. London: Hogarth Press.

Brody, V. (1978). Developmental play: A relationship-focused program for children. *Journal of Child Welfare, 57*(9), 591–599.

Brody, V. (1993). *The dialogue of touch: Developmental play therapy.* Treasure Island, FL.: Developmental Play Training Associates.

Des Lauriers, A. (1962). *The experience of reality in childhood schizophrenia.* New York: International Universities Press.

Des Lauriers, A., & Carlson, C.F. (1969). *Your child is asleep: Early infantile autism.* Homewood, IL: Dorsey.

Greenberg, J.R., & Mitchell, S.A. (1983). *Object relations in psychoanalytic theory.* Cambridge, MA: Harvard University Press.

Jernberg, A. (1979). *Theraplay: A new treatment using structured play for problem children and their families.* San Francisco: Jossey-Bass.

Jernberg, A. (1989). Training parents of failure-to-attach children. In C.E. Schaefer & J. Briesmeister (Eds.), *Handbook of parent training: Parents as co-therapists for children* (pp. 392–413). New York: Wiley.

Jernberg, A. (1990). Attachment enhancing for adopted children. In P.V. Grebe (Ed.), *Adoption resources for mental health professionals* (pp. 271–279). New Brunswick, NJ: Transaction Publishers.

Jernberg, A. (1993). Attachment formation. In C.E. Schaefer (Ed.), *The therapeutic powers of play* (pp. 241–265). Northvale, NJ: Jason Aronson Inc.

Jernberg, A., Booth, P., Koller, T., & Allert, A. (1983). *Reciprocity in parent-infant relationships.* Chicago: The Theraplay Institute.

Karen, R. (1990, February). Becoming attached. *The Atlantic Monthly,* pp. 35–70.

Karen, R. (1994). *Becoming attached: Unfolding the mystery of the infant-mother bond and its impact on later life.* New York: Warner Books.

Kohut, H. (1971). *The analysis of the self.* New York: International Universities Press.

Kohut, H. (1977). *The restoration of the self.* New York: International Universities Press.

Kohut, H. (1984). *How does analysis cure?* (Edited by A. Goldberg with the collaboration of P. Stepansky.) Chicago: University of Chicago Press.

Lieberman, A., & Pawl, J. (1988). Clinical applications of attachment theory. In J. Belsky & T. Nezworski (Eds.), *Clinical implications of attachment* (pp. 327–351). Hillsdale, NJ: Erlbaum.

Marschak, M. (1960). A method for evaluating child-parent interaction under controlled conditions. *Journal of Genetic Psychology, 97,* 3–22.

Marschak, M. (1967). Imitation and participation in normal and disturbed young boys in interaction with their parents. *Journal of Clinical Psychology, 23*(4), 421–427.

Marschak, M. (1980). *Parent-child interaction and youth rebellion.* New York: Gardner Press.

Marschak, M., & Call, J. (1966). Observing the disturbed child and his parents: Class demonstration of medical students. *Journal of the American Academy of Child Psychiatry, 5,* 686–692.

Robertson, J., & Robertson, J. (1969). *John, aged 17 months, for nine days in a residential nursery* (Film). Young Children in Brief Separation Film Series. University Park, PA: Penn State Audio Visual services.

Sroufe, R. (1988). The role of infant-caregiver attachment in development. In J. Belsky and T. Nezworski (Eds.), *Clinical Implications of Attachment,* pp. 18–38. Hillsdale, NJ: Erlbaum.

Stern, D. (1974). Goal and structure of mother-infant play. *Journal of the American Academy of Child Psychiatry, 13,* 402–419.

Stern, D. (1984). Affect attunement. In J. Call, E. Galenson, & R. Tyson (Eds.), *Frontiers of Infant Psychiatry* (Vol. II, pp. 3–14). New York: Basic Books.

Stern, D. (1985). *The interpersonal world of the infant: A view from psychoanalysis and developmental psychology.* New York: Basic Books.

Winnicott, D.W. (1958). *Collected papers: Through paediatrics to psychoanalysis.* London: Tavistock Publications.

Winnicott, D.W. (1965). *The maturational processes and the facilitating environment: Studies in the theory of emotional development.* London: Hogarth Press.

Winnicott, D.W. (1971). *Playing and reality.* London: Tavistock Publications.

CHAPTER 9

Ecosystemic Play Therapy

KEVIN O'CONNOR

INTRODUCTION

Ecosystemic play therapy is a hybrid model that derives from an integration of biological science concepts, multiple models of child psychotherapy, and developmental theory first formally described in 1994 (O'Connor & Schaefer). In that chapter the author described the theoretical model and discussed in substantial detail the concepts of structure versus fill in any theoretical model. Structural elements are those that define a theory and, therefore, do not change from one practitioner to another. Fill elements are those that reflect the attitudes, beliefs, and experiences of the individual practitioner. For example, the concept of psychopathology is seen as a structural element of ecosystemic play therapy in that the practitioner must have some way of conceptualizing the problem to be addressed in treatment. Whether a given ecosystemic play therapist believes psychotic behavior to be a manifestation of a biologic or a behavioral problem is an example of fill.

While the range of fills that might be considered to fall within the purview of ecosystemic play therapy is virtually endless, two elements characterize the work of the ecosystemic play therapist. One is a commitment to maintaining an ecosystemic perspective at all times: This is easier said than done. Constant focus on the impact of the various systems in which a client is embedded can lead to feelings of helplessness and hopelessness on the therapist's part. However, losing that focus generally results in less than optimal treatment at best, and treatment failure at worst. The other characteristic of an ecosystemic play therapist is the adoption of a clear and consistent personal theory. That is, ecosystemic play therapists know the fill they are using and apply it consistently. This ensures that they practice consistently over time and that they are able to convey a clear strategy for change to their clients. Both of these seem essential to the provision of effective psychotherapy.

The structural elements that form the basis of ecosystemic play therapy have been derived from many other models of psychotherapy and play therapy, child development, and an ecosystemic world view. These are reviewed in *The Play Therapy Primer* (O'Connor, 1991). "The structural elements that evolved from this integration and form the frame for the theory and practice of ecosystemic play therapy include the concepts of personality and psychopathology, the notion of treatment goals or a definition of cure, a description of the role of play in the treatment, and the technique itself" (O'Connor & Schaefer, 1994). Rather than repeat the full theoretical discussion of the nature of these structural elements and the concept of fill that is presented in the ecosystemic play therapy chapter (O'Connor & Schaefer, 1994), this chapter will assume that the reader understands and accepts the structural elements listed and will focus on the particular fill used by the author. This will allow for a clearer presentation of the application of that model to the case at hand.

The Ecosystemic Model

In order to practice ecosystemic play therapy

> one must understand the implications of the term ecosystemic and accept that this is not only a viable, but valuable base for the conceptualization of any therapeutic intervention. Ecosystem is defined as "a complex of community and environment forming a functional whole in nature" (Webster's, 1963). Most often people associate the term with biology and the study of all of the factors that impinge on any given organism. In psychology the term is often used to describe a series of nested systems in which an individual is embedded. The concept of nested systems however is not sufficiently complex to reflect the nature of any individual's real ecosystem. Similarly Figure 9.1 does not do the concept justice but will serve as a starting point for this discussion. The reader should note that neither this chart nor any element within it is meant to be an all inclusive or even necessarily stable over time. The very nature of an ecosystemic model is such that it is readily inclusive of additional points of view and that it evolves as time passes. (O'Connor & Schaefer, 1994, p. 61)

The basic unit of the model is the individual, and this immediately differentiates ecosystemic play therapy from most other systemic models, as these tend to minimize the role of the individual in favor of an emphasis on one system or another. As can be seen in Figure 9.1 the ecosystemic model used here even conceptualizes the individual as a self-contained system made up of mind-body interactions. "Depending on one's philosophy, personal beliefs and theoretical orientation one might include other elements in the description of the individual as a system. These other elements might include the soul, id, ego, superego, anima, animus, and so forth" (O'Connor & Schaefer, 1994, p. 61). When conceptualizing Jason's case* at this level from an ecosystemic perspective, one would take note of the fact that he suffers from moderate, intermittent asthma and develop some hypotheses about how this might affect his cognitive and socioemotional functioning.

Within the ecosystemic model, mental health is seen as dependent on the quality of one's interactions with others. Thus this youngster and an adult or adults in-

---

*See "Orientation to the Text: The Case of Jason L.," p. 1.

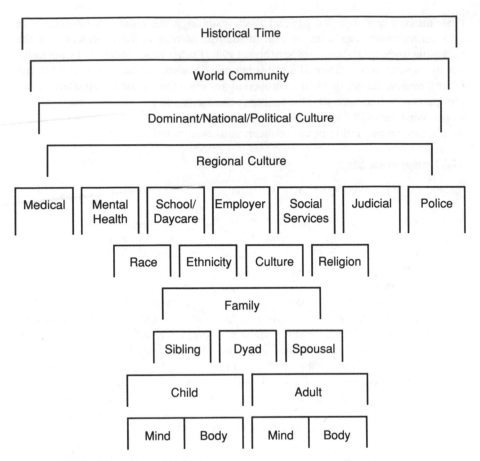

Figure 9.1 The Ecosystemic Model.

teract, forming a dyad that immediately brings with it the creation of both the child and the parent roles.

> The pair, with or without other individuals, also forms a family. The very nature of families brings at least two roles, if not actual systems, into play; those of siblings and spouses. This is to say that even if one is discussing a single parent/single child family one must understand that, within the dyad, it is acceptable for these two to interact as parent and child while it is neither acceptable for them to interact as siblings nor as spouses. These roles, as reflections of actual systems, exist even when the systems themselves do not exist. (O'Connor & Schaefer, 1994, p. 62)

In Jason's case, parental divorce has resulted in the creation of two overlapping family units. He has moved from a situation where caretaking was shared by both parents, with his mother as the primary figure, to a situation where each parent is actually the primary caretaker for a set amount of time. Now the movement of the parents in and out of the primary caretaker role is not dependent on their own availability or skills or on the child's needs but on the calendar and the clock. Not only must they bear the burden of parenthood alone when they are with the children but they must now find ways to get those needs that were being met through their spousal interactions with one another met elsewhere.

The impact of race, ethnicity, culture, and religion both within a family and between a family and the systems in which it is embedded is often very complex. Race is generally considered a relatively useless concept from a psychological point of view because the genetic, physical, and psychological variability within racial groups often exceeds the differences between the groups. Concepts such as ethnicity and culture are more meaningful because they reflect the person's self-identification. In the L family, two ethnic groups are represented, and yet they share a common religion. This suggests both a source of potential conflict and a force that would ameliorate that conflict. Often persons of Mexican-American descent adopt more traditional gender roles, and this may create conflict—especially in marriages between a Mexican-American male and an Anglo female. There is some evidence of ethnocultural difference between Mary and Emilio. Like many Anglo-Americans, she has become quite disengaged from her family of origin while he remains quite involved with his in the Mexican-American tradition. Ethnocultural or gender role differences may also account for the fact that Emilio was minimally involved in the children's care until after the divorce. The fact that Catholicism tends to support traditional gender role patterns and that this religion is shared by Mary and Emilio may reduce the impact of some of these ethnocultural differences within the family.

Besides considering the potential impact that members' ethnocultural identification may have on the interactions of the family, it is also important to note how differences between the family's ethnocultural identification and that of the dominant culture in their community manifest on a day-to-day basis. Information about the response of the community to either Mexican-Americans or Anglo-Americans is not related in the case description. Nor is there any discussion of whether or not being bi-ethnic presents any particular problems for the children. Depending on the community, these issues may be insignificant or they may prove to be sources of substantial stress and conflict.

Like many families the Ls have been or are involved with many other systems. Mary had extensive contact with the medical system as a result of her difficult pregnancies, and there is some evidence this sensitized her to the potential for medical problems with her children. Jason has also had contact with the medical system as a result of his asthma, but the impact of this is not described. Jason is in school and that is a source of stress for both him and the family. Carla is in full-time daycare. Both Mary and Emilio are employed and work in separate settings. Mary's employment seems to be a source of stress and disappointment, while Emilio seems quite happy with his employment situation. Mary and the children have become involved with social services because of Mary's abuse of Jason, and, as a result, the family is about to become involved with the mental health system. Finally, we note that Jason has also been involved with the legal system as a result of his participation in the fire-setting incident. A superficial count reveals a family involved in at least eleven different systems (Anglo-American community, Mexican-American community, Catholic Church, medical, mental health, public school, daycare, Mary's employment, Emilio's employment, social services, and law enforcement). When we stop and consider the number of people each system probably represents we see that an impressive number of individuals may have a direct and daily impact on the emotional well-being of the L family.

In addition to all of these systems that have direct and continuous contact with the family and, therefore, with Jason, one cannot ignore the potential impact that the regional culture, dominant culture, and world community may have on this family. A recent event gives us an excellent example of this. In 1995, the voters in California passed a proposition that would have severely restricted the social benefits available to illegal aliens in the state. This proposition would have had a clearly disproportionate impact on families of Mexican extraction who were living in California. One of the problems was the fact that the average person would have no way of distinguishing a 'legal' from an 'illegal' Mexican, so that all those of Hispanic origin in the state were likely to come under suspicion. This vote triggered a period of intense animosity between Anglo-Americans and Mexican-Americans. One of the unanticipated results was that some families stopped sending their children to school as this was one place where their legal status might be discovered. Obviously, immersion in such an event would prove very stressful for any family and might prove particularly so for a family of mixed ethnicity like the Ls.

The impact of historical time on a family like the Ls is not immediately evident. However, the fact that social services became involved is an example of how the experiences of a family are dependent on the historical context in which they exist. Thirty or forty years ago it would have been unthinkable for an outside agency to become involved in a family's business over an incident of corporal punishment. At that time, parental prerogative was seen as almost absolute and intervention was almost nonexistent. This means that Mary L. would have been raised in a time when her present behavior was not seen as a cause for intervention. But social norms have changed dramatically in her lifetime. In the United States in the 1990s we have come to accept such massive intrusions as the appropriate. While this family may indeed benefit from intervention, one should not ignore the degree to which community values are being imposed on the behavior of both an individual and a family.

The other factor that is affected by the passage of time is the nature of the family and the developmental level of the individuals within it. At this time, Carla is in the preoperational stage of development, while Jason is in the concrete operations stage. Before Jason leaves this stage, Carla will join him in it, making them more similar than different for a while. On another plane the family has shifted from being a two-parent, nuclear one to being two, separate, single-parent households. Given that Mary and Emilio are quite young, it is likely that one or both will remarry and new family constellations will be created. The fact that change is inevitable does not make it any less stressful. The ecosystemic play therapist keeps this in mind noting that transitions between stages are generally more stressful for individuals and families than are periods within any given stage or phase.

One issue that bears *special* consideration in a discussion of systems is the relative value placed on each of the systems when viewed from the perspective of any one system. This valuing or evaluating seems to be a somewhat inevitable result of the very interaction of these same systems. The fact that some people value medicine to the point that they think a parent should be forced to care for his or her child in a certain way in spite of the parent's religious beliefs, which place God over the desires of humankind, is an example of such relative valuing. At this time there seems to be a growing consensus that it is important for all of us to preserve, and work to value, differences on many levels. While this is not particularly threatening when it comes to preserving the cuisines of the world, it tends to be quite threatening when it comes to something like differential patterns of child rearing.

Several styles of reconciling differences are evidenced as people from one cultural group move into lands dominated by another cultural group. First, on some levels, the new group may work to preserve differences; their children may be taught the language of their culture of origin. Second, in other areas the new group may attempt to acculturate, that is to reach a compromise between their own and the surrounding cultures (Padilla, 1980). Last, the new group may assimilate (Gordon, 1964), or become like the surrounding culture as they adopt the region's style of dress, for example. Generally, the individuals who fare the best in these situations seem to be those who find a balance between self-serving (survival) instincts and their individual attachment or group affiliation needs.

This balancing occurs naturally in every system. It must be reached at the individual level, where the child must weigh attachment to his or her caretakers against independence. It happens at the dyadic level where the parent and child must find a balance that ensures that each gets his or her critical needs met. It happens at the level of the family where the family struggles to exist against those forces that push it to become a mere collection of individuals and those competing systems that would subsume one or more members. Every parent who has chosen to not attend a critical work/business function in order to go home to be with his or her child knows the reality of this struggle. It happens at the cultural level as was previously described. And, it happens between individuals and society at large. Society suffers when one of its members fails to be adequately socialized, as in the case of sociopaths, but it also suffers when its members have been so completely socialized that no variability and therefore no creativity exists. (O'Connor & Schaefer, 1994, p. 65)

To summarize, children and their behavior exist within the context of multiple interacting systems that change over time. Depending on one's perspective, some of these systems may be seen as more or less valuable than others, but this may bear little relationship to their impact on the child. The ecosystemic play therapist takes all of these systems into account when conceptualizing the presenting problem and formulating a treatment plan. At the same time that the ecosystemic play therapist works to promote growth and development on an individual level, he or she must also be committed to preserving and valuing diversity wherever and whenever possible.

Ecosystemic Play Therapy Theory

Against the general background of the nature of the ecosystemic perspective, next to be discussed are the structural elements of ecosystemic play therapy and the fill used by the author in his application of the model to clinical work.

Personality Theory

As previously stated, within ecosystemic play therapy one theory of personality is not seen as inherently better or closer to the *truth* than another. The importance of a personality theory is that it provides the therapist with a consistent model for conceptualizing the internal functioning of the individual—the mind-body interaction if you will. Included in most theories of personality are three elements: A hypothesized basic life force motivating human behavior, a way of explaining and understanding the impact of development on individual functioning over time, and a way of conceptualizing psychopathology. The way in which these structural elements have been filled by the author is described in the following.

BASIC DRIVES.   The basic life force is a biologic derivative related to the survival instinct. It is not very different from the psychoanalytic concept of libido (S. Freud, 1933). It motivates persons to do whatever it takes to get their needs met, often, in relatively egocentric ways. Further, it motivates people to avoid punishment. This drive is modified in two ways through the process of socialization. One modification results from the fact that the human infant is totally dependent on others for survival. As a result of this forced dependency, the infant learns that he or she must trust others and rely on them to meet some, if not most, of his or her needs. As the infant develops, the drive is again modified as the children come to realize that they can get more of their needs met more efficiently when they work cooperatively. As a result of these two modifications, the egocentric nature of the drive is channeled into social interaction and cooperation.

ROLE OF DEVELOPMENT.   With respect to the impact of development on the functioning of the child's personality over time, the author places cognitive development and functioning in a central role. Advances in cognitive development are believed to literally drive development in other areas. For example, a child will not achieve a high level of moral development as described in Kohlberg's model (1976) if he or she is not capable of abstract reasoning. No matter how well socialized a mentally handicapped child is, his or her social interactions will never be the same as those of a child of average intelligence. Because more human development occurs within the first two years of a child's life than occurs in the entire remainder of his or her life, it is not surprising that those early interactions the child has with the environment are herein viewed as crucial (Caplan, 1978; Caplan & Caplan, 1980). The relevance of the child's interactions with his or her early environment, including all significant others, to the conceptualization of the child's personality functioning and psychopathology and to the development of an effective ecosystemic play therapy treatment plan cannot be overstated (O'Connor & Schaefer, 1994, p. 69). The centrality afforded cognitive development means that a thorough assessment of the child's developmental functioning will be critical to conceptualizing the presenting problem and designing an intervention within ecosystemic play therapy.

PSYCHOPATHOLOGY. The term psychopathology as it is commonly used carries with it two—often significant—problems. One is the belief that the pathology or problem behavior in question always lies with or within a specific individual, the identified client. This sometimes causes therapists to overlook very real sources of life difficulty that lie in the client's relationships or environment. The other problem is that the use of psychopathology labels often causes the therapist to forget that many of these labels and categories are socially defined and subject to the whims of culture and history. For example, hallucinations were once thought to be a sign of demonic possession but are now usually attributed to biologic causes. Yet, in some cultures hallucinations continue to be seen as valuable because they show that the individual is in touch with the spirit world. Because of these inherent problems the author uses the term *psychopathology* in quite a different way. People who are unable to get their needs met at a level they consider to be satisfactory, or those who are unable to get their needs met in ways that do not substantially interfere with the ability of others to get their needs met, are said to be experiencing psychopathology. The source of their inability to get their needs met may be individual, interactional, or systemic in origin.

Individual psychopathology is diagnosed when the inability to effectively get one's needs met lies entirely within the individual. Individual psychopathology often has biologic or genetic underpinnings. Autism is probably one of the best examples of individual pathology. Interactional pathology is diagnosed when one or more persons cannot get their needs met in the context of one or more of their interpersonal interactions. Many of the problems exhibited by children who have been abused would fall into this category. These children's ability to get their needs met through social interaction has been severely damaged by their experience. Finally, systemic pathology is diagnosed when one or more persons are unable to get their needs met in one or more of the systems in which they are embedded because of the nature of those systems. Children who are moved from one foster home to another on a regular basis generally display serious symptomatic behavior that further interferes with their ability to get their needs met in future homes and in other settings as well, and yet the social service system is still more likely to move a problem child than to provide the resources necessary to avert the move. Often when one form of psychopathology is present it may trigger responses that generate other types of pathology. A mentally retarded child (individual psychopathology) is much more likely to be abused (interactional psychopathology) and more likely to end up in a care setting that is less than adequate (systemic psychopathology).

Psychopathology is not diagnosed when the individual is only occasionally or briefly unable to get his or her needs met. Rather, psychopathology is diagnosed when the person repeatedly engages in behavior that does not get his or her needs met and is unable to generate alternate behavior or to engage in effective problem solving. Once the individual becomes stuck in a pattern where his or her needs are not being met, then psychopathology is diagnosed and intervention is likely to be in order.

In Jason's case there seemed to be evidence of all three types of psychopathology operating at different levels. Given Mary's strong history of repetitive depressive episodes, it did not seem unreasonable to postulate that she may have had a biologic predisposition to depression, an individual pathology. There was certainly a long history of interactional psychopathology between Mary and Emilio that is likely to have had a negative effect on Jason and his sister. It also seemed clear that Mary and Jason were experiencing interactional psychopathology in that they were particularly stuck and unable to develop strategies that would result in their getting their needs met. There was also evidence of potential systemic pathology in the fact that Jason was doing so poorly at school in spite of his intelligence. Given this, it seemed that various individuals, dyads, and systems in this case were particularly good candidates for ecosystemic play therapy.

Goal/Cure

"The ultimate goals of play therapy are to: facilitate the child's resumption of normal development and to maximize the child's ability to get his or her needs met while interfering as little as possible with the gratification of other's needs" (O'Connor & Schaefer, 1994, p. 71). This goal is accomplished by helping children develop new strategies for getting their needs met through problem solving that recognizes all of the ecosystemic factors impinging on the problem. Effective problem solving cannot occur unless the therapist can help children become unstuck in their attempts to get their needs met.

The ecosystemic play therapist helps children problem solve and become unstuck by providing them with an alternative way of understanding their life situation or problem. The ecosystemic play therapist does this by providing the children with alternative experiences, with an alternative cognitive understanding of the problem, or, preferably, both. New experiences help the child understand on a very concrete level that things in life can be different. For an experience to be beneficial, the child need not understand why it was different than the ones before—only that it was different. This allows the child to entertain the notion that change is possible. These alternative experiences can be provided directly in session or can be provided in other settings or systems. The therapist need not have the child perform a math problem successfully in session in order to have a positive impact on the child's self-esteem. The therapist could consult with the child's teacher to ensure that such an experience occurred in the child's classroom and have an equal, if not greater, impact. Alternative cognitive understanding is usually achieved through language. Child clients are told that the problems they are experiencing are not as they appear and that solutions other than the ones they have tried may be effective. A simple example of this type of intervention is seen in a strategy used to help a child overcome fears of monsters in the dark. The child is told that nighttime monsters are very sensitive to light, so that being hit by the beam of a flashlight causes them to disintegrate. The child armed with a flashlight is then ready to battle nighttime monsters and have his or her needs for safety simply and effectively met.

Both alternative experiences and cognitions are powerful interventions. The combination is even more powerful as children both understand what is different and have experienced the more positive outcome their new understanding can bring about. The primary drawback to the provision of alternative experiences is that the therapist is limited to what can be recreated in the playroom, and all problematic life experiences are not easily recreated. Another limitation is that when problems are recreated in the playroom they often do not generalize beyond its walls. Alternative cognitive understanding is usually much easier to provide. It can be done through something as simple as a direct, educational statement or through something as complicated as a symbolic, interpretive puppet show. Situations that are not easily replicated in the playroom in the form of actual experiences can be readily discussed or described. Shifts in understanding also tend to generalize better than do experiential shifts. The primary limitation is that the language required to explain the problem may be more abstract than the child can effectively utilize. For example, trying to help children understand how catharsis will make them feel better can be a daunting task, while having them bash a Bobo doll when they are angry until they feel better is an easy experience to create.

Whether the child is helped to problem-solve and become unstuck through experience or cognitive understanding, chances are play will be a central element of the process. Play serves four general functions in children's daily lives and development:

1. Biological Functions: Play provides a medium through which children can learn basic skills, be kinesthetically stimulated, and relax.
2. Intrapersonal Functions: Play allows for the gratification of "functionlust" (Slobin, 1964) and the ability to work toward mastery of situations and conflicts.
3. Interpersonal Functions. Play serves as a medium for practicing separation/individuation and for acquiring social skills.
4. Sociocultural Functions: Play allows children to imitate desired adult roles. (Schaefer & O'Connor, 1983)

All of these functions complement the play therapy process and can be utilized to help restructure children's experience. It is the therapist's responsibility to use play and other activities to maintain the child in a level of optimal arousal so that learning and development can occur (Jernberg, 1979).

To summarize, in this portion of this chapter the author has reviewed the theoretical fill he uses in conceptualizing three of the structural elements of ecosystemic play therapy: personality, psychopathology, and the definition of goal or cure in therapy. Three components were stressed with respect to understanding personality and human behavior: One was the role of mind-body interactions. Another was the importance of primary drive(s) and their modification through the socialization process. And the third was the crucial role that development plays over the course of the life span. Psychopathology is viewed as the inability of the individual either to get his or her needs met or to get them met in ways that do not substantially interfere with the ability of others to get their needs met. It may arise as a function of individual, interactional, or systemic factors or as some combination of the three. Finally, the conceptualization of the goal of treatment or cure as establishing the individual's ability to get his or her needs met—in ways that do not interfere with the ability of others to get their needs met—and reestablishing normal development was discussed. In the next sections, we will examine the essential characteristics of the ecosystemic play therapist and the ecosystemic play therapy client.

Therapist Qualifications/Characteristics

In order to practice ecosystemic play therapy effectively, a therapist should have a minimum of a master's degree in a mental health field and specific training in the ecosystemic concepts and their application. In addition to these general requirements, the specific didactic and clinical requirements developed by the Association for Play Therapy for Registered Play Therapists should be met by the ecosystemic play therapist. These requirements include:

- A Master's degree in a medical or mental health field that includes graduate training in: child development, theories of personality, principles of psychotherapy, child and adolescent psychopathology, and legal, professional and ethical issues
- A minimum of 150 hours of instruction in play therapy
- Two years (2,000 hours) of supervised experience, including one year post-Master's
- A minimum of 500 supervised hours of play therapy experience (Association for Play Therapy, 1995)

Aside from specialized training the ecosystemic play therapist must also have certain personal characteristics in order to practice effectively. Six essential characteristics are listed here. This list is not meant to be exhaustive but rather it highlights those characteristics that are viewed as critical.

The ecosystemic play therapist is able to:

- Consciously and consistently place the child client's needs above his or her own. The ecosystemic play therapist knows that his or her needs are to be met outside of the therapy and maintains suitable personal and professional support networks to ensure that personal needs and issues never interfere with a client's progress in treatment.
- Recognize and maintain good personal and systemic boundaries. The ecosystemic play therapist recognizes the limitations of his or her role both within the client's life and within the mental health system. In that role the ecosystemic play therapist avoids bringing his or her own systemic issues into the client's life and avoids usurping the roles that others should play in the client's life.
- Work to preserve diversity in the face of his or her personal views and values so long as what is being preserved does not interfere with the fundamental goal

of ecosystemic play therapy, namely helping the child get his or her needs met and met in ways that do not substantially interfere with the ability of others to get their needs met.

- Inspires confidence in the client due to his or her faith in (1) the efficacy of ecosystemic play therapy, (2) his or her own skills and, (3) his or her ability to keep both the client and himself or herself safe.
- Tolerate ambiguity and regression in children. Because children already function at much earlier levels on the developmental continuum than do adults the therapist who works with children must be prepared to deal with very primitive and powerful thoughts, emotions and behavior if and when a child client regresses severely.
- Be flexible in both his or her thinking and behavior. Creativity and therapeutic gains do not come out of cognitive, emotional or behavioral rigidity.

Ecosystemic play therapists are a highly varied group on all dimensions. They share a high level of training and professionalism and a commitment to helping children function optimally in all of the systems in which they find themselves embedded.

Client Characteristics

Ecosystemic play therapy is seen as a treatment modality that can be readily adapted to work with any child or problem because of its developmental and broad systemic approach to the conceptualization of problems. Further, because the modality specifically emphasizes the ability of the client to get his or her needs met, there is little danger of creating pathology that is not present nor intervening in situations where no intervention is actually necessary. If the client is able to get his or her needs met effectively, then therapy is not indicated. Further, therapy should be discontinued when the client is able to get his or her needs met consistently in a manner that does not interfere with others getting their needs met.

Jason was a good candidate for ecosystemic play therapy because he was not getting his needs met consistently, and some of the strategies he was using to get his needs met seemed to interfere with others getting their needs met. He was functioning below developmental expectations, particularly in the area of his peer social interactions. Further, there was evidence of probable individual, interactional, and systemic psychopathology.

CASE FORMULATION PROCESS

The importance of a comprehensive case formulation to the effective implementation of ecosystemic play therapy cannot be overemphasized. Without it the therapist will not have hypotheses as to the type of psychopathology that is interfering with the child getting his or her needs met, nor will the therapist have a sense of the ecosystemic factors impinging on the child's functioning. Effective problem solving cannot occur in the absence of an accurate problem definition. Further, suitable interventions cannot be planned in the absence of a thorough understanding of the child's current developmental functioning.

Intake and Assessment

In order to develop a comprehensive case formulation the ecosystemic play therapist must first gather comprehensive data regarding (1) the client's developmental functioning, (2) the client's perception of the systems in which he or she is embedded and of the specific problems that have led to the referral, and (3) the organization and functioning of the systems in which the child lives. These data are usually gathered from the client, the primary caretaker(s), and relevant reporters from other systems such as teachers or physicians. The intake is usually conducted with the primary caretaker(s) and the child, although others may be included when needed. Specific assessment data may or may not be gathered, depending on the nature and complexity of the referral problem. When an assessment is performed, it may range from simply obtaining developmental ratings of the client's functioning from significant adults to a complete developmental, cognitive, emotional, and behavioral evaluation of the child. Assessments may also be carried out with the caretaker(s)/child dyad, the family, or any other group that is significantly involved in the problem. The intake process can usually be completed in two hours. The duration of the assessment process depends entirely on what needs to be completed.

Having obtained the intake and assessment data, the ecosystemic play therapist must then organize the information to reflect the functioning and impact of various systems on the client's life. While there is no prescribed way to accomplish this, the use of *Play Therapy Treatment Planning and Interventions: The Ecosystemic Model* (O'Connor & Ammen, in press) facilitates the process. The first four sections of the Workbook organize the intake and assessment data by the system under review and lead to the diagnosis. The system reviews included in the Workbook are individual, family, social, educational, legal, medical, and mental health. Rather than repeat the intake and assessment information for the case of Jason L., the following will give the reader a sense of the way the information would be organized in the completed Workbook.

PLAY THERAPY TREATMENT PLANNING WORKBOOK: SECTIONS I–IV*

SECTION I: FACE SHEET. In this section, basic information about the client, payee, family constellation, and presenting problem are gathered. Unlike many traditional approaches, the Workbook emphasizes the need to gather the child's, parents', and others' views of the presenting problem. The goal is to define the problem in behavioral terms, including its onset, history, frequency, and severity. It is important to include each reporter's affect regarding the problem, as these may give clues to their motivation for changing the problem. Particular emphasis is placed on obtaining the child's view of the

*Source: From O'Connor, K., Ammen, S. (in press). *Play therapy treatment planning and interventions: The ecosystemic model.* San Diego: Academic Press.

---

problem, as this will form the basis for the treatment contract with the child. The goal is to identify those needs the child has that are not being met. Usually, these will be related in some way to the dominant negative affect the child is experiencing.

SECTION II: INTAKE AND SYSTEMS REVIEW. In this section, the individual, family, social, educational, legal, medical, and mental health systems in which the child is embedded are reviewed. This information may be gathered from records, a wide variety of reporters, and direct observation. It is critical that enough information be gathered to allow the play therapist to develop a sense of the child's world. Specific emphasis is paid to those needs the child has that are going unmet or are being met in problematic ways. A list of the areas covered in each of the system reviews follows:

Individual System: pregnancy and delivery, the client's infancy with special attention paid to bonding and attachment, attainment of developmental milestones, early sibling and peer relationships, a mental status exam, and behavioral observations.

Family System: current family relationships and dynamics, family history, significant adults' current occupational functioning, familial ethnocultural identification, and the familial religious affiliation.

Social System: current and past social functioning and, where applicable, child's interpersonal/sexual history.

Educational System: client's school and academic history as well as his or her current school circumstances.

Legal Systems: child abuse/domestic violence, substance abuse, family history of substance abuse, and involvement in the Family Court, Criminal Court, and/or Juvenile Justice systems.

Medical System: allergies, serious accidents, head injury with loss of consciousness, serious illness, chronic illness, hospitalizations, present medications, eating and sleeping pattern, and any family history of medical problems.

Mental Health System: the client's and the family's prior contacts with the Mental Health System, including outpatient or inpatient treatment, current psychiatric treatment, current and previous medications, and any extended family psychiatric history.

SECTION III: ASSESSMENT DATA. While the previous sections of the Workbook collate all types of information, this section is reserved for data gathered through more formal assessments. These assessments may include ones described in various case records, behavioral checklists completed by any persons who know the child well, informal observation, and formal testing.

Individual Development: All data that describe the client's development along emotional, cognitive, behavioral, social, and physical lines are listed here.

Dyadic Functioning: Data that describe how various dyads within the family function are listed here. Particular attention is paid to the relationship between the identified client and the primary caretaker. In those cases where the client spends time in two or more households, this would include gathering data on the client's relationship with the primary caretaker(s) in each household.

Family Functioning: Data are gathered that illuminate the type and quality of the family's interactions.

SECTION IV: DIAGNOSIS. In this section, the client is described using the *Diagnostic and Statistical Manual for Mental Disorders IV* (American Psychiatric Association, 1994) multi-axial classification system.

Having organized the intake and assessment data in the first four sections of the Workbook, the ecosystemic play therapist must still integrate the data in a way that will make these useful for treatment planning. This process occurs in the completion of the first four sections of the Workbook Appendix A:

I. Developmental Integration of Intake Information
II. Developmental Description of the Child
III. Hypothesis Development: Etiologic Factors
IV. Hypothesis Development: Maintaining Factors.

Because these portions of the Workbook are unique to ecosystemic play therapy, their application to the case of Jason L. is included in its entirety.

Workbook Appendix A: Section I: Developmental Integration of Intake Information

In Table 9.1, the events of the child's life are matched to the developmental stage(s) at which they occurred. Age is generally a good indicator of developmental level in "normal" children, and the usual ages at which children enter into each of Piaget's (1952, 1959, 1963, 1969) developmental stages are noted in italics in the Cognitive Stage column. When there have been problems that have affected the child's developmental progress, the ages at which various developmental stages were actually reached should be indicated in this same Cognitive Stage column along, with the child's attainment of developmental milestones.

Having organized the intake and assessment data along developmental lines, the therapist is ready to proceed with generating both a developmental description of the child (Workbook Appendix A: Section II) and with formulating hypotheses regarding the child's response to these life events (Workbook Appendix A: Section III).

Workbook Appendix A: Section II: Developmental Description of the Child

In this section, the ecosystemic play therapist uses all of the data gathered during the intake and assessment process to develop a comprehensive developmental description of the child client's present functioning. Special attention is paid to developmental lags or to unevenness with respect to the child's development across various spheres.

Developmental Level

GENERAL.   Overall, Jason impressed as being just slightly older than his chronological age. While he seemed to act tough and indifferent, it seemed more like a toddler's bluster than a hardened lack of emotion. It is likely that others perceived him to be "streetwise" or "smarter than he lets on." That is, they would have judged him based on his cognitive skills and then seen his problematic behavior and social interactions as unthinking or even willful rather than attributing these to developmental difficulties.

TABLE 9.1   DEVELOPMENTAL INTEGRATION OF INTAKE INFORMATION

Age	Cognitive Stage	Individual History	Family	Social
<Birth				
Birth	*Sensorimotor*	Birth weight: 5 pounds Irritable, but slept often. Jaundice 3 hours out of every 12 hours, contact with mother	Mary very anxious about Jason's health.	
1	14 month walked 15 month talked	11 months: Jason weaned from breast.	11 months: Mary becomes pregnant. Maternal Grandma cares for Jason. 18 months: Male sibling born and dies. Mary begins depressive episode lasting several months.	
2	*Preoperational* 30 minute: toilet trained	History of oppositional behavior begins. High level of exploratory behavior.		
3			36 months: Emilio begins extramarital affair. 3.5 year: Carla born.	
4			Emilio ends extramarital affair.	
5			Mary and Emilio divorce. Mary returns to work.	
6	*Concrete Operations*			
7		fire setting with peer		Fire setting with peer

(Continued)

TABLE 9.1 (*Continued*)

Age	Educational	Legal	Medical	Mental Health
<Birth			Mother required bed rest during pregnancy	
Birth				
1				
2				
3				
4	Jason enters preschool.			
5	Jason enters kindergarten and after-school programs, where some problem behavior noted.			
6	Jason enters first grade; some problem behavior noted.			
7	Jason enters second grade. Increasing noncompliance and disruptiveness reported.	CPS report filed. Police called when Jason involved in fire setting with a peer.	Intermittent asthma. Date of onset not reported.	CPS mandates treatment.

INTERPERSONAL.   Jason's cognitive skills made it possible for him to present well in 1:1 interactions with adults. His peer social skills were below age expectancy. He seemed to do better with younger children, such as his sister, when he could be in control. Jason seemed oppositional in the style of a younger child. His judgment with respect to the appropriateness of behavior suffered when peers were present, as was seen in his classroom behavior and the fire-setting episode.

Cognitions

FUNCTIONAL LEVEL.   Jason appeared to be on target with respect to his cognitive development. Both his developmental milestones and his IQ were consistent with average to high average functioning. However, there was evidence to suggest that his emotional difficulties sometimes made it difficult for him to use his cognitive skills effectively. This was evidenced in his poor performance on the HFD and his tendency to become more concrete when discussing emotional topics during the intake interviews.

SIGNIFICANT ORGANIZING BELIEFS.   In this section, the ecosystemic play therapist develops hypotheses regarding those core beliefs the client may have that significantly color the client's world view. These may be the result of specific experiences, cognitive developmental limitations in interpreting or understanding the world, or even specific teaching the child has received. These beliefs are important because they will color the child's view of his or her life problems and of the treatment itself. These beliefs may or may not be conscious on the child's part, although the wording of the hypotheses usually makes them appear conscious.

Given the intake and assessment date, it appeared that Jason's core beliefs might include:

1. "Events in my life are beyond my control." (As a result of his experience of multiple life changes that were outside of his control.)
2. "My mother cannot or will not help with my life problems and with getting my needs met and my father expects me to take care of myself and gets angry/annoyed if I act in a dependent." (As a result of his experience of his mother's repeated bouts with depression but most especially her depression following the death of her infant son when Jason was 18 months old.)
3. "Expressing negative affect will not get me what I want and should be avoided because it may bring on consequences I do not like." (As a result of his experiences with adults' reactions to his anger both at home and at school; and as a result of his father's reactions to Jason's expressions of dependency or neediness.)
4. "When my parents do not get along, they are even less likely to be available to help me get my needs met." (As a result of his experience of his parents' divorce.)

5. "Women like girls best and men like boys best." (As a result of the fact that his mother seems most attached to Carla, while his father seems most attached to Jason.)

6. "Work drains my mother and leaves her unable to meet my needs at the end of the day."

7. "School drains me and leaves me unavailable to meet my own or anyone else's needs at the end of the day."

8. "One cannot be dependent and liked at the same time." (As a result of his father's reactions to Jason's expressions of dependency or neediness.)

9. "Neither of my parents are willing or able to respond to my needs with respect to the problems I have at school."

Emotions

TYPE.   Primarily, Jason appeared anxious and angry during the intake, resulting in defensive and mildly oppositional behavior. These responses and behaviors seem consistent with his mood most other times.

RANGE.   By report, Jason is capable of a full range of emotional intensity with respect to both negative and positive emotions—from very happy (during time spent with father), to very anxious (confrontation with police), to very angry.

REPERTOIRE.   Jason seems to be able to experience a full complement of affects within the range of what can be expected of a child at his developmental level. There is some suggestion, however, that his ability to express these affects is more limited than would be expected, given his intellectual functioning and his developmental level.

REALITY BASE.   Jason's affects seem consistent with the reality of his experience except for his anger, which often seems to exceed what would be appropriate for the situation.

Response Repertoire

The terms autoplastic and alloplastic may not be familiar to the reader. These are psychoanalytic terms that describe an individual's primary response when faced with a problem. Autoplastic individuals attempt to change themselves or their behavior when faced with a problem irrespective of the source or nature of the problem. Alloplastic individual attempt to change others or the environment when faced with a problem irrespective of the source or nature of the problem. Most individuals have a dominant style but may switch between the two under certain circumstances. Individuals who have chronic difficulty getting their needs met tend to use one style or the other reflexively and without consideration for the situation or the nature of the problem. Healthier individuals seem able to make conscious or near conscious decisions about the most appropriate type of response.

AUTOPLASTIC.   This appears to be Jason's primary response to difficulties in his environment. He withdraws rather than pushing others to change or attempting to change his situation, although he appears angry or sad.

ALLOPLASTIC.   This seems to be a secondary response strategy for Jason. When he is not allowed to escape a problem situation, then he expects others to change their behavior in order to solve the problem.

Note that, in spite of Jason's tendency to be autoplastic, he also seems to display an external locus of control. This is a very difficult combination and causes a high level of frustration. He believes that he must solve his own problems with very little help from others, and at the same time he believes that he has very little effective control or power. He sees power and control located outside of himself.

Workbook Appendix A: Section III: Hypothesis Development: Etiologic Factors

In this section of the Workbook the therapist develops hypotheses regarding the origins of the child's present level of function or dysfunction. The therapist attempts to understand how the child came to be this way. What about the child and/or his or her ecosystem resulted in a situation in which the child's needs are not being effectively met? The hypotheses should be derived from the data using the therapist's theoretical model as the template. Remember that these are hypotheses, not statements of fact. They will be used to guide the therapy but will be modified or discarded if they do not lead to effective problem solving.

Child Factors

ENDOWMENT.   Here the ecosystemic play therapist develops hypotheses as to how the client's basic endowment may have contributed to the child's present functioning.

The possibility that Jason had a low level of neurologic immaturity and subsequent attention deficit or learning problems should be ruled out, given that there were significant problems with the pregnancy and that Jason slept a lot and was irritable as an infant. Due to these problems, Mary was very worried about Jason as an infant, and this may have made it more difficult for Jason to attach securely to her. Jason's high average cognitive abilities probably contributed to his development of an autoplastic problem-solving style, as it is likely he experienced early success using this approach. This can be seen in the high level of exploratory behavior he displayed in toddlerhood, where it appears he felt he must go out and explore the world on his own to find his own supplies. Also, because of its intermittent and frightening nature, Jason's history of asthma may have exacerbated his ambivalent attachment to his parents. Asthma frequently triggers fear of dying in children which, in turn, tends to make them ambivalent about their attachments to adults. They may wish to cling because they feel safer with a competent adult around, and yet they may also resent the feelings of helplessness and dependency the disease engenders. The reality is that neither Jason nor his parents can protect him from these episodes and that even his own body acts in ways he cannot control.

DEVELOPMENTAL RESPONSE.   Here the ecosystemic play therapist develops hypotheses about the impact of various life events on the client's present functioning. It is particularly important to consider here the probable interaction of the event and the child's developmental level at the time that event occurred. For example, a child of two does not experience or react to parental divorce in the same manner that a child of five does. Use of the standard wording presented in the following hypotheses makes it easier for the therapist to keep track of the event, the child's developmental level, and the outcome.

- Because Mary was very anxious about Jason's health during his first few months of life, he may have developed an anxious rather than a secure attachment to her.
- Because Mary was required to be on bedrest during her pregnancy when Jason was only a year old, he probably developed concerns about the consistency of her availability and her caretaking, further complicating his attachment and basic trust.
- Because Jason's sibling was born and died when Jason was 18 months old, his anxious attachment to his mother probably increased, as it is not uncommon for young children to be very frightened by a sibling's death—seeing it as a form of enforced separation.
- Because Mary became severely depressed upon the death of her infant son when Jason was 18 months old, Jason probably developed concerns about the consistency of her availability and her caretaking, further complicating his attachment and basic trust. He may also have begun to question the degree to which Mary's needs would take precedence over his own in the future.
- Because of the problems that occurred when Jason was between one and two years old, a time when children are developing a sense of mastery, Jason may have begun to feel helpless.
- Because Mary gave birth to another child, a girl, when Jason was three and a half, his resolution of his Oedipal conflict seems to have been compromised. At this age, it is normal for children to generalize their attachment to their primary caretaker to include other adults, usually the other parent. It is likely that this was already occurring when Carla was born. Her birth is likely to have heightened his valuing of the relationship with his father, but at the same time would make him even less trusting of relationships. He may have felt that his mother simply replaced him as soon as he began to invest in his father.
- Because Emilio began an extramarital affair when Jason was four years old, Jason's ability to develop a secure attachment to his father may have been compromised. It is likely that Emilio's emotional and maybe even physical availability to Jason decreased during the time of the affair, just as Jason may have had hopes of taking refuge in this newly developing relationship.
- Because Jason was sent to nursery school at age four, secondary to the birth of his sister, Carla, his anxious attachment to his mother was probably exacerbated. It is important to note that, even at this time, he displays an autoplastic response style as he isolates himself from his mother when she picks him up at school. Further, the timing of this event may have actually interfered with his developing peer relationships, rather than helping. At age four, a child should be developing interests in peer social interactions. However, difficult separation from the primary caretaker can cause the child to refocus on that relationship to the detriment of any potential new relationships.

- Because his parents divorced when Jason was five years old, it is likely that Jason's attachments suffered. He may have become preoccupied with the danger of losing significant others. He may have felt that his father left and abandoned him to the care of the mother he no longer trusts. Jason would have been angry at his father but would have been unable to express it for fear of driving his father even further away, ending their highly pleasurable contact during their weekly visits. He may also have begun to resent living with his mother but would have been unable to express that resentment because she continues to be his primary caretaker.
- Because of the sequence of events in Jason's preschool and early school years, it is likely he was so preoccupied with his own emotions and with maintaining his relationships with his parents that he never had the time or the interest in developing stable peer relationships.

Ecosystemic Factors

FAMILY. The family history has greatly contributed to the development of Jason's world view as just described. He has learned not to show weakness or dependency because his father does not like it. He has learned that mother is, intermittently, a poor source of supplies and that this is worse, now, as single parenthood seems to drain her of her emotional resources. Jason seems to model his reaction to school after his mother's reaction to her work.

PEERS. Peers did not seem to play a significant role in the development of Jason's difficulties. During his early exposure to peers at preschool it is likely that he was so preoccupied with the events that led to his placement in that program that he did not invest much emotional energy in his peers or notice their ability to be reinforcing. No special friendships are reported to have developed with any of his peers since he began school.

OTHER. Educational, medical, legal, cultural, historical: School seems to be a significant and persistent stressor for Jason. It is likely that he experiences the demands of interacting with his peers to be more than he can handle and diverts their attention from his deficits by acting out and appearing to be in control. The contribution that the medical system may have made through its responses to his asthma is not mentioned. It would not be surprising to find that the medical treatment he receives tends to reinforce feelings of helplessness and dependency. No other systems seem to have contributed significantly to the development of Jason's current pattern of functioning.

Workbook Appendix A: Section IV: Hypothesis Development: Maintaining Factors

In this section of the Workbook the therapist develops hypotheses regarding those factors that maintain the child's present level of function or dysfunction. The therapist attempts to understand why the child is stuck and unable to engage in effective problem solving. The therapist also attempts to determine what persons or systems are most likely to resist or oppose change if shifts are effected in the course of play therapy. These hypotheses should be derived from the data, using the therapist's theoretical model as the template. Again, the therapist should remember that these are hypotheses, not statements of fact. They will be used to guide the therapy but will be modified or discarded if they do not lead to effective problem solving.

Child Factors

ENDOWMENT.   Jason's cognitive skills make it relatively easy for him to maintain an autoplastic response style. Asthma may make an ongoing contribution to his sense of being out of control and to fears of separation and possibly even death. If there were neurological problems at infancy, they do not appear to be having any effect at present, although attention deficit disorder should probably be ruled out as the cause of his difficulties at school.

DEVELOPMENTAL RESPONSE.   Most of the issues identified in the etiologic hypotheses seem not to have been resolved at the point of referral. Jason seemed to subconsciously perceive school as Mary's way of getting rid of him, and he thus harbored the belief that if he did not do well there he would be sent home, where he could be with her. His attachment to his father was not without complication, as he idolized Emilio to the detriment of his attachment to his mother. Last, his preoccupation with his attachment to each of his parents interfered with his desire and ability to seek out peers as potential sources of gratification and support.

Cost/Benefit Analysis of Beliefs, Emotions, and Behavior

Here the ecosystemic play therapist develops hypotheses about the gains and losses the child experiences as a result of his or her symptoms and pattern of functioning. It is important to note that even the symptoms that appear most painful probably have their benefits or it would not be maintained. For example, Jason's low-level acting out brings on negative consequences, but it also serves as his only vehicle for communicating his anger. It is also important to note that the child may have absolutely no sense of what he or she is losing. The parentified child, for example, is rarely aware that he or she is missing out on being a child, as he or she may have never experienced the joys that just being a child can bring.

COST.   Jason was losing quite a bit as a result of his pattern of functioning. He experienced persistent poor school performance. He bore the brunt of intermittent anger from both his mother and father and from his teacher at school. He was unable to develop age-appropriate peer relationships and to enjoy the related rewards. His attempts to maintain his attachment to his father inadvertently pushed him farther from his mother and from some of the supplies she could provide. His basic needs for attachment and emotional release and support were not being met on a consistent basis.

BENEFIT.   Jason's pattern of functioning did gain him a sense of power and control over his environment and his life. His tendency to try to meet his own needs rather than depend on others met with intermittent success. Given this intermittent reinforcement, the tendency became stable and highly resistant to change. Last, his behavior and pseudoindependent style gains him peer admiration, if not friendship.

Ecosystemic Factors

FAMILY.   Mary continued to be only intermittently available at the time of referral, reinforcing all of Jason's ideas about the world and the ability or desire of others to meet his needs. Emilio was able to be the perpetual good guy, further complicating Jason's problems in relating to his mother. Carla continued to be perceived as a source of competition for resources, especially in the children's interactions with their mother.

PEERS.   Although Jason got admiration for his tough behavior, he did not gain friends. It seems likely that the other children admired his spirit but stayed away from him in order to avoid trouble. Because he never had peer friends it is unlikely that Jason knew what he was missing in terms of potential resources and reinforcement.

OTHER.   Educational, medical, legal, cultural, historical: School was a chronically frustrating and punitive experience for Jason. Emilio's Mexican background may have played a part in his investment in Jason's macho independent behavior.

Having completed the data integration and the hypothesis formulation, the therapist returns to the Workbook and completes Section IV: Diagnosis and Section V: Case Formulation.

Workbook Section IV: Diagnosis

The following diagnostic formulation is based on the system described in the Diagnostic and Statistical Manual of Mental Disorders, Fourth Edition (American Psychiatric Association, 1994).

AXIS I: CLINICAL DISORDERS.   DSM-IV: 309.40: Adjustment Disorder with Mixed Disturbance of Emotions and Conduct, chronic.

AXIS II: PERSONALITY DISORDERS AND MENTAL RETARDATION.   No diagnosis.

AXIS III: GENERAL MEDICAL CONDITIONS.   ICD-9-CM (U.S. Department of Health and Human Services, 1994): 493.90: Asthma, unspecified.

AXIS IV: PSYCHOSOCIAL AND ENVIRONMENTAL PROBLEMS.   This is the axis that best reflected the majority of problems Jason was experiencing at the time of referral. There were problems between himself and his mother and, to some extent, between himself and his father. He has few if any peer friends and is acting out at school. His most recent behavior had caused him to have problems with the legal system, in addition to all the others.

AXIS V: GLOBAL ASSESSMENT OF FUNCTIONING.   60, Mild symptoms and moderate difficulty in social and school functioning.

Workbook Section V: Case Formulation

Jason was seen as a child whose developmental progress had been compromised as a result of a number of historical and familial variables. As with all cases accepted for ecosystemic play therapy, the primary problem was seen as his current inability to get his needs met effectively and in ways that did not interfere with others' getting their needs met. The fact that this problem had started when he was only a toddler and increased in severity over time was seen as causing the developmental lags he was exhibiting in the areas of attachment behavior, especially relative to his peer interactions.

Mary's anxiety regarding Jason's health during his infancy triggered the beginnings of an anxious attachment between them. Both probably came to feel that something bad might happen if they were not together. This led Jason to skewed interpretations of subsequent events in their lives. He may have unconsciously interpreted her weaning him when she became pregnant as a sign that the new baby's needs would take precedence over his own and he may have become angry or resentful. When the sibling died, Jason may have felt guilty for his anger. When Mary became severely depressed, leaving Jason in the care of his grandmother, Jason seems to have decided that his anger was, indeed, dangerous given that it had caused his mother to abandon him. Yet, at the same time, given his age, it is likely that he was very angry at her for withdrawing, further intensifying his ambivalent attachment to her. These feelings would also have initiated his belief that his mother was not always able or willing to care for him and would have reinforced his sense of needing to take care of himself. Not surprisingly, it is at this time that his oppositional behavior begins.

At the age of three, most children begin to substantially generalize their attachment to their primary caretaker to other adults in their world. This means that the basis for Jason's attachment to his father would have been the same anxious, ambivalent attachment he had with his mother. Unfortunately, Emilio was not available to help Jason resolve these issues because he had begun to withdraw from the marriage into an extramarital affair. Jason's suspicions that his own needs played second fiddle to those of his caretakers would have been reinforced.

Carla's birth and the subsequent divorce of his parents cemented Jason's view of each parent and of adults in general. Carla was seen as taking over his mother's time and attention and may even have been blamed for driving his father out of the house. As Mary became more overwhelmed by the demands of single parenthood, her unwillingness or inability to be a caretaker would have been reinforced in Jason's mind. Emilio's sporadic attention created further ambivalence in Jason's attachment to him. On the one hand, Jason must have been thrilled with the new attention he received from Emilio. On the other hand, he must have resented the fact that this attention had not been there before and that it was available only during certain days of the week after the divorce. The result of these very strong conflicts and feelings with respect to his relationship with each of his parents was that Jason's development arrested at the stage where he was attempting to generalize his primary attachment to other adults. It appears that he started this stage by becoming increasingly involved with his father but never progressed to the point where he could respond to other adults, such as teachers. Given that he never moved to attachments with other adults, Jason was unable to take the next step and attempt to generalize his attachment to peers. This was both good and bad. It is probably good that Jason never generalized his anxious and ambivalent attachment to his peers because this would have created even more problems for him. Unfortunately, not having done this means that he is several years behind his peers and will have to work hard to catch up in developing peer friendships.

All of the members of this family seem essentially capable of healthy personal and interpersonal functioning. Their difficulties seem to have arisen from their attempts to cope with an unfortunate series of circumstances that led to the development of some nonproductive strategies for getting their needs met. Given that the current difficulties manifest at the individual, dyadic, and family systems, a treatment plan that addresses all of these in sequence should be developed. In addition, consultation to the school and the medical system should be undertaken to reduce the degree to which they may be reinforcing these problems.

TREATMENT GOALS

Based on the hypotheses the therapist has developed and on the case formulation, the therapist goes on to develop specific treatment goals. These goals are comprehensive, reflecting a true ecosystemic understanding of the case. In Workbook Appendix A: Section V the therapist lists all of the case goals, determines which can be addressed in the course of therapy, the priority of each, and the context in which each goal might be best addressed. Workbook Appendix A: Section V as completed for Jason L. is presented in Table 9.2.

TREATMENT DESCRIPTION

Ecosystemic play therapy differs from some of the other play therapy models in that a specific and explicit treatment contract is entered into with the child and the parent(s) who will be participating. This contract may be verbal or written. Because children do not usually understand the purpose and nature of psychotherapy, it is critically important that the child perceive that therapy will be of direct benefit to him or her so as to foster the maintenance of the treatment alliance. The treatment contract that might be accepted by Jason L. and his parents is presented in the following as it would appear in the Workbook: Section VI.

Workbook Section VI: Treatment Contract

Contract with Child

The contract with Jason would need to be very carefully negotiated, as he seems to have a great deal invested in being seen as competent and without problems. This may be due, in part, to his need for control and his fear that if he admits to stresses or difficulties the thin veneer of confidence he is able to maintain will be eroded. It is most likely that Jason will only agree to a contract that addresses the problems he is experiencing in his interactions with others. A viable contract might be as fol-

TABLE 9.2   GOAL DEVELOPMENT/SYNTHESIS AND TREATMENT PLANNING

Part A: Develop goal statements specific to the factors identified in Section VI and VII.
Part B: Check those goals to be addressed in context of psychotherapy.
Part C: Number the psychotherapy goals in order priority.
Part D: Determine the system or context in which each of the treatment goals should be addressed.
Part E: Determine the interventions to be used in the course of the treatment.

Part A: Comprehensive Goal List	Part B: Therapy	Part C: Priority	Part D: Context	Part E: Intervention
Attachment				
Improve the quality of Jason's attachment to Mary	X	1	I, D, F	EPT
Improve Jason's perception of Mary's ability to meet his needs.	X	2	I, D, F	EPT
Decrease the frequency and intensity of Jason's experience of anger.	X	2	I, D, F	EPT
Work through Jason's grief with respect to the divorce.	X	3	I, D, F	EPT
Increase Emilio's tolerance for Jason's age-appropriate expressions of dependency.	X	1	I, D, F	EPT
Work through Jason's ongoing thoughts, feelings, and responses to his mother's repeated depressive episodes.	X	4 or >	I, D	EPT
Work through Jason's ongoing thoughts, feelings, and responses to his mother's response to his sib's death.	X	4 or >	I, D	EPT
Work through Jason's thoughts, feelings, and reactions with respect to his overly positive valuing and identification with Emilio inasmuch as it interferes with his ability to positively experience his interactions with his mother, Mary.	X	4 or >	I, D, F	EPT
Increase Mary's ability to cope with single parenthood.	X	4 or >	I	E, PT, I
Decrease Jason's toddler-like ambivalence with respect to control vs. attachment.	X	1	I, D, F	EPT
Control: Internal and External		4 or >		
Increase Jason's ability to constructively express his anger.	X	1	I, D, F	EPT
Increase J's sense of control (develop more internal locus of control).	X	4 or >	I, D, F	EPT
Increase Jason's recognition of, and tolerance for, his own needs.	X	4 or >	I, D, F	EPT
Decrease the frequency and intensity of Jason's experience of frustration.	X	4 or >	I, D, F	EPT
Increase Jason's frustration tolerance.	X	4 or >	I, D, F	EPT
Decrease Jason's use of bravado as a cover for emotional distress.	X	4 or >	I, D, F	EPT
Improve balance between Jason's use of autoplastic and alloplastic strategies.	X		I, D, F	EPT
Prevent future fire-setting episodes.	X	1	F	E, C
Increase Jason's understanding of, and ability to manage, his asthma.	X	4 or >	M	C

(*Continued*)

TABLE 9.2   (*Continued*)

Part A: Comprehensive Goal List	Part B: Therapy	Part C: Priority	Part D: Context	Part E: Intervention
Self-esteem				
*C18 Jason will use words or gestures to show pride in his own work and will make positive self statements.		4 or >	I, D, F, P	EPT, G
Increase Jason's ability to communicate his needs to others		4 or >	I, D, F, P	EPT, G
Increase Jason's level of independence		4 or >	I, D, F, P	EPT, G
*C19 Jason will learn to describe his characteristic attributes, strengths, and problems.	X	4 or >	I, D, F, P	EPT, G
		4 or >		
Peer Relations				
Help Jason problem solve how to be independent and have peer friends.	X	4 or >	P	G
Increase and improve Jason's peer relationships.	X	4 or >	P	G
*B11 Jason will verbally and physically participate in sitting activities such as work time or snack time (at both home and school) without physical intervention on the part of an adult.	X	4 or >	S	C
*B12 Jason will verbally and physically participate in movement activities such as physical education or music (at both home and school) without physical intervention on the part of an adult.	X	4 or >	S	C
*S17 Jason will engage in interactive play with his peers.		4 or >	P, S	G, C
*S18 Jason will cooperate with his peers during organized activities and play.	X	4 or >	P, S	G, C
		4 or >		
School				
Identify source of Jason's school-related problems.		4 or >	S	C
Improve Jason's school behavior.		4 or >	S	C

CODES: Part D: I = Individual, D = Dyad, F = Family, S = School, M = Medical, P = Peer
Part E: EPT = Ecosystemic play therapy, C = Consultation, PT = Parent training, I = Individual adult therapy, E = Education, G = Group.
*These are the DTORF-R goals as listed in the Orientation to the Text, p. 1.

lows. "I would guess that the thing you like least about your life right now, the part that makes you feel the worst, is how often adults tell you that you are doing something wrong or yell at you. It seems like school must be the worst of the worst. It must seem like you get in trouble for everything. Then your mother gets mad at you again for what happens at school, about getting along with your sister and about following directions at home. And, even your father wants you to do things you don't want to. In therapy, let's plan to work to see if we can find ways to keep adults from spending a lot of time yelling at you or making you feel bad."

Contract with Parents/Family

The contract with Mary L. would include helping her identify ways she can take care of herself so that she will have the energy to reorganize her approach to managing Jason's behavior. Further, she would be asked to attend a series of sessions with Jason in order to strengthen their attachment. This increased attachment will serve as the base that will see them through the difficult times they will face as Mary becomes more structured in her child management. The contract with Emilio would also specify that he attend a series of sessions aimed at increasing the attachment bond between himself and Jason. Although they appear to have a strong bond, much of it seems to be based on Jason's fear of abandonment—fear that, if he should make his father angry, Emilio will leave him in the same way he left his mother. Rather than be left, he hopes to ally with his father and gain strength out of potentially being the one who leaves, as opposed to the one who is left. Further, therapy would be aimed at helping Emilio have more developmentally realistic expectations with respect to Jason's skills and behavior.

Logistics

Setting

The specific details of how the ideal playroom should be laid out and furnished are described in the *The Play Therapy Primer* (O'Connor, 1991). Essentially, the room should be large enough to allow for gross motor play. It should have an area that is identified as being for messy activities and one that is for quiet activity. Access to a sink is good for painting and cleanup. Having a space and furnishings that are as close to indestructible as possible should be a primary concern, so that both the child and the therapist remain safe and so that the therapist will have to spend as little time and energy as possible setting limits. This would be particularly important in treating a child like Jason, who is likely to begin to act out his anger as he becomes more aware of it. Since Jason is currently overcontrolled, the therapist will want to be particularly cautious about setting limits for fear of further reinforcing his belief that any expression of anger will result in negative consequences.

Materials

In ecosystemic play therapy the therapist is the primary material, thus the use of toys and other materials is quite limited. The focus of any ecosystemic play therapy is on the interaction between the child and the therapist, not the child and the materials. The goal, as has been previously stated, is to help children get their needs met in ways that do not interfere with others getting their needs met. Whenever possible, it is desirable to have the child learn interactive or cooperative strategies for getting his or her needs met, and that is where the therapist serves an important function. The therapist is available not only to help the child develop new needs-meeting strategies but to directly meet those needs the child expresses in session that are appropriate to the child-therapist relationship.

In ecosystemic play therapy the children are not allowed free access to all of the toys that the therapist possesses. The toys are stored in either a locked cabinet or closet in the playroom, or in another room altogether. Prior to each session the therapist selects approximately three to five toys for the client and places these in the playroom. These are the only toys to which the child will have access over the course of that session. Toy selection is based on the needs of the child and the specific goals of that session. Usually three of the toys are selected based on the child's developmental functioning. One toy would be selected because it would be appropriate for slightly below the child's current developmental level, one because it is appropriate to the child's developmental level, and one because it is appropriate for children at a slightly higher developmental level. The other criterion for selection would be the degree to which the toy or material pulls for specific content related to the child's treatment goals. These two criteria may overlap so that a toy is both developmentally and symbolically useful to the goals of the session. The specific toys selected for use in each of Jason's sessions are listed in his treatment plan later in this chapter.

Frequency and Duration of Treatment

The frequency of ecosystemic play therapy sessions depends on two factors. Younger children may need to be seen for more frequent but shorter therapy sessions, which helps to match the pace of the sessions to the speed of their developmental changes and helps them to perceive the continuity between sessions. Older children's sessions may be scheduled farther apart, but most children have difficulty maintaining the momentum of the therapy if the sessions are more than a week to 10 days apart. The other factor to be considered in determining the frequency of children's sessions is the intensity of the current crisis. The more intense the crisis, the more frequent the sessions. This applies whether the crisis is internal or external to the child. Children who have developed sudden and intense symptoms are in need of intensive intervention in the same way that children who have been exposed to a specific trauma need such interventions.

The overall duration of ecosystemic play therapy depends on a number of variables. If the treatment can be conceptualized in a focused and very goal-oriented manner, it can often be completed in a very short span of time, potentially only a few sessions. The more generalized and systemic are the problems affecting the child, the longer the treatment is likely to take. Therapy will also take longer when the problems are ongoing and outside the child's or therapist's control, such as parental substance abuse. Finally, the therapy may also take longer if the child is in the middle of making significant developmental shifts so that the therapist is, in effect, having to help two different children. This type of problem is often seen in young children who experience a trauma such as sexual abuse. They enter treatment as preschoolers with one set of problems that are addressed in the course of the therapy, only to find that new problems related to the original trauma arise when they enter school. This does not mean that young children should be in therapy indefinitely—only that they may have to return to therapy intermittently as their development progresses.

Jason's therapy was conceptualized as a series of sessions that would build successively larger functional units within the family. Jason was seen for three individual sessions in order to focus on his individual issues and to prepare him for the dyadic and family work that was to come. He was then seen for two sessions with Mary followed by two sessions with Emilio. These were followed by two sessions in which he was seen with Mary and Carla and two in which he was seen with Emilio and Carla. A single termination session with each family group was then scheduled, yielding a total of 13 sessions. Following this course of treatment, Jason was moved to peer group play therapy to address his social skills deficits for an additional 12 sessions.

Specific Strategies

Therapist Behaviors in Session

The ecosystemic play therapist's primary function in session is to maintain the child at an optimal level of arousal so that learning and change can occur. The therapist accomplishes this through the use of structuring, challenging, intruding, and nurturing behaviors (Jernberg, 1979). Structuring behaviors include those things that the therapist does in order to reduce the child's level of arousal and to keep the child safe. In therapy, structuring includes everything from selecting the toys to setting limits. Challenging behaviors are those things the therapist does to increase the child's level of arousal by pushing him or her to function slightly above current developmental level. Virtually all of the problem solving the therapist does with the child falls into this category, as do most interpretations. Intruding behaviors also raise the child's level of arousal. Any time the therapist enters the child's physical space or uses language to focus the child on a specific behavior or problem, intrusion is taking place. Last, nurturing behaviors tend to maintain children at their existing level of arousal. These include everything from verbally reinforcing a child, to a pat on the hand, to a full-blown hug and kiss. However, achieving optimal arousal is not an endpoint in the therapy process but rather a means by which the therapist makes it possible for the child to engage in problem solving and change.

Once the child's arousal level is in an appropriate range, the therapist engages the child in problem solving by providing the child with either alternative/ corrective experiences or new cognitive understanding of the problems at hand. Corrective experiences may be created in the context of the play session or in the child's interactions outside of the session such as when specific homework is assigned. Corrective experiences may be either symbolic or actually experienced. Many symbolic corrective experiences are created through pretend play such as having the child engage in a puppet play in which a problem the child has experienced is recreated with a different outcome. Actual corrective experiences are usually the result of direct interaction with the therapist, such as when the child becomes enraged and is met with acceptance and encouragement by the therapist rather than the anger and intolerance he or she may have experienced outside of the session.

Alternative cognitive understanding of the problem is usually achieved either through the problem-solving process or through the therapist's use of interpretation. A five-stage model of interpretation is presented in *The Play Therapy Primer* (O'Connor, 1991). The levels of interpretation described are reflection, pattern, simple dynamic, generalized dynamic and genetic. In a reflection, the therapist conveys a thought, feeling, or motive to the child that the child has not previously expressed directly. A pattern interpretation consists of identifying similarities or consistencies in the child's behavior over time. A simple dynamic interpretation connects the first two by identifying a relationship between the child's unexpressed thoughts, feelings, or motives and patterns in his or her behavior. In a generalized dynamic interpretation, the therapist notes the degree to which this pattern is seen across the child's behavior in different settings. And, finally, in a genetic interpretation the therapist identifies the historical source of the pattern for the child, usually noting the discrepancy between the source event and the current events that trigger the same pattern of response in the child. Both corrective experiences and alternative cognitive understanding are created by the therapist in order to help the child to break set, to engage in functional problem solving, and to proceed to get his or her needs met in new and more effective ways.

One other role that the ecosystemic play therapist may need to take on is that of advocate for the child in various systems in which the child is embedded. Sometimes this role is actually mandated, such as when the therapist must report known or suspected child abuse. More often the role comes about as a function of consulting with the child's parents, teachers, physician, or social worker. The ecosystemic play therapist is much more likely than other types of child therapists to be drawn into an advocacy role because of his or her systemic view of the case. The ecosystemic play therapist knows that symptom reduction is not likely in a child who is being constantly frustrated by his or her daily experience with a problematic teacher or a disinterested foster parent. All child therapists are more likely to be drawn into advocacy roles than are those who treat adults because of the fact that children are dependent on their caretakers and can rarely initiate major changes in the systems in which they are embedded. While functioning as the child's advocate may be essential for a positive outcome to the therapy process, several cautions are in order. The therapist must be careful to become an advocate only when it is in the child's best interest and not because of his or her own needs. Second, the therapist must be careful not to usurp the role of those who can or should be serving as the child's advocate. While the therapist may be highly motivated to push for change in the child's life, taking an advocacy role may be detrimental in the long run if, for example, it results either in the parents' feeling their role has been undermined or in the withdrawal of someone who should be playing an active role in the child's life. Whenever possible, the therapist should work to have the natural advocates within the various systems do their part to support the child. Last, the therapist should be aware of the heavy burden created by becoming an advocate for the child outside of the session and of the potential for burnout.

Treatment Stages

Ecosystemic play therapy proceeds through much the same stages as any other type of therapy. Slightly modified, the six stages described in the Theraplay (Jernberg, 1979) model seem to fit the process seen in ecosystemic play therapy quite well.

Introduction/Orientation

During this stage, children familiarize themselves with the therapist, the playroom, and the materials. They are usually hypervigilant at this point and will have difficulty focusing on the problems at hand and the therapy process. For some children, this stage may last only a half an hour or so, while for others, especially those who have been abused, it may drag on for a dozen or more sessions.

Tentative Acceptance

At this point the children become less vigilant and seem to decide that being in play therapy may not be so bad after all. They will engage with both the therapist and the materials, but they still tend to avoid the work of the therapy. They may actively resist talking about specific problems but be very willing to come to session. Over the course of this phase the child tends to engage in progressively more testing of limits and to attempt to exert considerable control over the course and content of the sessions.

Negative Reaction

This stage is entered at the point that children realize that being in play therapy is not quite the fun and games escape they thought it might be. In ecosystemic play therapy, where the therapist has exerted control over the sessions and insisted on remaining problem-focused from the outset, this phase tends to begin quite early, usually manifesting by the third of fourth session. This phase ends as soon as children are convinced that the therapist will not use his or her control maliciously and that the therapist's sole focus is really to help them get their own needs met. The successful negotiation of this phase is critical to the successful outcome of the therapy.

Working Through, Growing, and Trusting

It is during this phase that the bulk of the work of the therapy takes place. Problems are identified, problem solving is applied, and potential solutions are developed. Strategies and solutions that are devised in session are rehearsed, both in the session and in the real world, and modified until they are effective in meeting the child's needs. Most of the change and the generalization of that change occurs in this phase. The duration is dependent on the child's capacity for engaging in functional problem solving, the nature and complexity of the problem, and67
the ability of the child's environment to support the gains the child makes.

Termination

This phase is initiated once the child's symptoms have abated and he or she seems to be able to effectively get the majority of his or her needs met, both in and out of the therapy sessions. This phase takes longer in proportion to the length of time the child was in therapy and when attachment problems were a significant part of the treatment focus.

The final portion of the Workbook, Section VII, provides a format for the therapist to use in developing an initial treatment plan. This section can be used in a number of ways. The therapist may decide to see only the child in treatment and complete the treatment plan accordingly. The therapist may decide to see first the child and then the child along with other family members. In this case, the therapist may plan to complete the first two or three phases of the treatment with the child individually and then to include other family members for participation in the remaining phases. Finally, the therapist may decide that three (or more) complete courses of treatment are in order—for example, a series of individual sessions, followed by a series of family sessions, followed by a series of peer group sessions. In this case the therapist would develop three different treatment plans, one for each of the series of sessions. For the sake of clarity and to reduce any potential redundancy in content, both the treatment plan and a description of a single session from each phase of Jason's treatment will be presented together in the following sections.

Workbook Section VII: Initial Treatment Plan

Stage I: Introduction and Exploration: (Anticipated number of sessions: 1.)

PARTICIPANTS: Jason.

TARGET CONTENT: The initial sessions were geared toward reducing Jason's toddler-like ambivalence with respect to attachment versus control. It appeared that he felt that he was in a forced choice situation where he had to sacrifice one for the other.

MATERIALS: Crayons or markers, sheets of 8.5 × 11" white paper, two small flexible plastic baby bottles.

EXPERIENTIAL COMPONENTS: Because Jason was likely to be somewhat defensive during the first session, a nondemanding and familiar task was presented initially. The therapist had him draw pictures of his family and an event at school. The therapist worked to make the sessions playful as soon as possible to prevent Jason from becoming too product oriented while drawing. To accomplish this, he made the transition from the independent drawings to an interactive drawing task by introducing the Squiggle Drawing Game (Claman, 1980) following the family drawing. Since this activity still tends to be somewhat goal oriented, the therapist next transitioned from it to scribble wars. The therapist and Jason each took a crayon or marker, and the therapist placed a single piece of paper between them. The goal was to complete a simple drawing while preventing the other person from completing his. This therapist focused on being silly rather than competitive, so that the result was interactive and positive. Having introduced a nonthreatening competitive activity the therapist then segued into a squirt gun fight with a pair of plastic baby bottles filled with water. On a symbolic level, the degree to which this activity embodied Jason's conflict between attachment and control is less than subtle—in that nurturing objects were used competitively. The goal was to move from this nonthreatening competitive activity to a nurturing one. After a short period of squirt gun play, the therapist recommended that they find an alternative way to use their squirt guns so that they didn't end up soaked. Shooting at targets was suggested, and the specific target was each other's open mouths. This was then structured into an activity where the therapist pretended to be a dentist. The dentist/therapist had the client/Jason sit in a chair so that he could conduct an exam while using the water bottle to squirt water on Jason's teeth. The bottle was used to touch Jason's teeth, and gradually he began to bite the nipple, using his aggression to mask his anxiety about the passive, dependent role in which he found himself. At this point the therapist worked carefully to ensure that Jason continued to see this as a light and nonthreatening activity. Jason was encouraged to take drinks from the bottle, but the tone stayed light and silly. As the session drew to a close, the therapist suggested that Jason choose a flavor of juice or soda to have the therapist put in the bottle for the following session. Without a moment's hesitation, Jason chose grape juice.

During this session, Jason was also introduced to the focused nature of the interaction and had a chance to explore the ways in which the therapist would react to his various feelings and behavior. He accepted the degree to which the therapist led the session as long as the session was kept fun. The therapeutic goal was to provide Jason with experiences in which he had little control, and yet the adult used his control in such a way that Jason's needs for attention and fun were met.

VERBAL COMPONENT(S):   There were two verbal components to the session. The therapist continuously reflected Jason's affect and the motives behind his behaviors. One important interpretation was the identification of Jason's discomfort with the idea of being pushed to have fun. That is, "Boy, I'll bet this is a little weird. Here you are playing with a grownup and it's the grownup being silly, not you. There is probably a part of you that wants to be saying this is stupid or silly and say 'we should quit', but then you'd be the one acting like a grownup and that wouldn't be very much fun at all." Often the therapist just pretended to state out loud what Jason was probably thinking. "Boy, I'll bet you're saying to yourself: 'This guy is a major nut case.' " "I'm not sure I like this, but since it is at least a little bit fun I guess I'll go along." "Just when I start to relax because I think I've figured out what is going on, this guy does something totally unexpected. It is weird but fun." "I'm not sure I like having another person be the boss in the session." The connection between having relaxed fun or being taken care and the parameters of Jason's treatment contract was also made explicit.

Stage II: Tentative Acceptance: (Anticipated Number of Sessions: 1.)

PARTICIPANTS: Jason.

TARGET CONTENT: The identification of Jason's ambivalence about control versus attachment and the degree to which his tendency to take control interfered with his actually getting his needs met.

MATERIALS: One flexible plastic baby bottle filled with the juice or soda Jason chose during the previous session. Other small food items like Cheerios®, raisins, and M&Ms. Pretend toys for caretaking: a doctor's kit, a hairbrush, and wet washcloth.

EXPERIENTIAL COMPONENT(S):   During this session, the therapist continued to focus on providing Jason with experiences during which he got his needs met without having much control over the activity. The session started out with the dentist/client activity that closed the last session. This time, however, the therapist focused more on the nurturant aspects of the play rather than on the pretending or on any potentially competitive elements that may have carried over from the previous session. The next activities continued this theme as the therapist introduced food into the play. The therapist began by pretending to fill Jason's "cavities" by pressing a raisin onto the surface of Jason's back teeth. Next, the therapist asked Jason to serve as the target for some throwing practice. Even though Jason was not thrilled with the idea, the therapist throws M&Ms at Jason's mouth from some distance—encouraging Jason to try to catch them in his mouth. Any M&Ms that Jason misses the therapist scrambled to pick up before Jason could get to them while saying "Oh no, the only way you get these is if you cooperate with my feeding them to you." At this point the therapist had introduced the idea of using cooperation to get one's needs met, helping to break the set that caused Jason to feel that he must either completely subjugate his needs to others so that they will, on occasion, want to meet his needs or that he must take control and act out in order to get his needs met. As the session progressed, the therapist moved to progressively higher contact caretaking activities by brushing Jason's hair and wiping off Jason's face with the washcloth. Jason resisted this type of intimacy and dependency more than he has resisted the initial activities, but the therapist was persistent in the face of protest while maintaining a positive and friendly tone.

VERBAL COMPONENT(S): Again, the primary interpretive points made during this session were the identification of Jason's ambivalence about giving up control in order to get nurturance. The therapist pointed out that Jason seemed to feel best when he was being the boss—as in when he kept his mouth shut and refused to catch the M&Ms—but that being the boss meant he did not get to eat any candy. The therapist also pointed out that, as the interactions became more caretaking, Jason's negative feelings seemed to increase apparently because now he was not the boss. Having done this, the therapist made a generalized dynamic interpretation. "Jason, I'll bet the same kind of thing happens at home. It is kind of like what happens when you get home from school. You've spent the whole day trying to be the boss and not let the other kids or the teachers give you any garbage. By the time you get home you're tired and would really like it if your mother would take some time just to take care of you and make you feel better. The problem is that by that point you've been boss for so many hours it is hard to let go, so you end up not saying what you want. Then you begin to get mad at your mother for not understanding how you feel, and when she says anything you blow up." This reframing of the problem Jason was having with his mother formed the basis for future problem solving with respect to how Jason could more effectively get his needs met in the context of his relationship with his mother and with others.

Stage III: Negative Reaction: (Anticipated number of sessions: 1.)

PARTICIPANTS: Jason. Mary should be available in the waiting room in case Jason's anger comes to a head and he subsequently wants to be nurtured by his mother.

TARGET CONTENT: The identification of Jason's ambivalence about control versus attachment and the degree to which his tendency to take control interfered with his actually getting his needs met.

MATERIALS: One flexible plastic baby bottle filled with Jason's choice of juice and some snack food items.

EXPERIENTIAL COMPONENT(S):   This session pushed the attachment versus control issue through highly interactive activities over which the therapist maintained control. During this session, the therapist remained in control at all times so that Jason's usual style of responding was not possible. However, the therapist took care not to pursue control simply for control's sake. Rather, the therapist also conveyed his intent to have fun. Gross motor activities like thumb, arm, or leg wrestling were used, as were ones where the therapist used Jason as an object. The latter included holding Jason upside down, spinning him, and even physically guiding him through various gymnastic moves like somersaults. During this session, Jason's initial willingness to relinquish control disappeared and he became actively resistant. The therapist recognized Jason's anxiety and subsequent desire for control, reflected it, but did not yield to it. At one point, Jason even became aggressive, but the therapist responded with support and continued control. The therapist set limits and briefly, physically restrained Jason, while remaining verbally supportive of Jason's ability to control himself in the face of anger.

After several brief power struggles where the therapist remained upbeat and goal oriented in the face of Jason's anger, Jason reluctantly began to relinquish control. He made one final attempt at usurping the therapist's control by attempting to strike the therapist, but the therapist caught his hand and deflected the move into arm wrestling. At this point, Jason attempted some passive resistance, but when the therapist continued on in his pursuit of pleasurable interactions, Jason relented. The therapist continuously reflected how difficult this shift was for Jason and focused on being very nurturant. Jason received immediate positive reinforcement for even approximating the assumption of a developmentally appropriate level of dependence.

Quite suddenly, Jason wanted to be nurtured in ways more appropriate to a toddler than to an eight-year-old boy. The therapist expected this, given that it had appeared likely that Jason had quite a backlog of unmet needs and that he would want to test adults' capacity to be nurturing to the same extent that he had tested the therapist's ability to use his control benevolently. However, given that Jason had two apparently competent parents available, the therapist engaged in a minimum of direct nurturance and instead structured the subsequent sessions so that Jason's needs were met by the parents rather than by the therapist. Jason needed to learn that his parents really wanted to meet, and were capable of meeting, his needs in developmentally appropriate ways. Therefore, once Jason's anger had dissipated, Mary was immediately brought into the session so that she could offer support and nurturance. She had been forewarned that Jason might seem unusually needy for a while, both in and out of session, and to expect that this phase would pass fairly quickly.

VERBAL COMPONENT(S): During this session, the interpretive focus continued to be Jason's ambivalence with respect to control and attachment or dependency. However, since this core conflict had been identified in the first session and expanded in the second, this session focused more on the manifestations of the conflict in Jason's behavior rather than on the simple identification of the problem. For example, Jason's initial anxiety in response to the therapist's control was reflected, and then the therapist made overt attempts to help Jason manage the anxiety without becoming aggressive or withdrawing from the interaction. The therapist said, "It sure is hard to let someone else be boss even if you are having fun; it makes you very uncomfortable and nervous. But I know you can handle it. Stick with me here. Watch my face so that you know I'm not being the boss because I'm angry or because I want you to have a bad time here. It's important for you to learn to be comfortable letting others be the boss sometimes so that you can sit back, relax, and have fun. As soon as you are able to have a good time, even if you're not the boss I'll show you how to begin taking turns being the boss with other people and planning fun things for each other to do." This type of reframing and problem focus continued and was elaborated in subsequent sessions.

Stage IV: Growing and Trusting: (Anticipated number of sessions: 1 individual session and 8 additional sessions with various participants.)

Prior to beginning of this phase, an individual feedback and planning session was scheduled with each parent separately. These sessions consisted of two parts. During the first half of the session, the therapist reviewed with the parent the MIM tape completed by that parent during the intake process. During the second half, the parent was engaged in planning the subsequent sessions to be held with Jason. The goal of these sessions was to fully engage the parents in the treatment process prior to their joint sessions with Jason so that they would not disrupt his progress as they went through their own initial treatment phases.

The focus and intensity of this type of preparatory session tends to push the parent through the first three phases of treatment all in one session. The use of the MIM as a feedback tool can often be a very effective lead-in to dyadic or family therapy because parents do not seem to find these feedback sessions particularly threatening. The review is focused on both the child's and the parent's engagement in the session and on identifying those things that each did to create positive moments in the session and those that made for unpleasant moments. Using this list of engaging and disengaging behaviors, the therapist and parent then go on to plan treatment sessions that will maximize the former while minimizing the latter. If, in the first session, the parent does not get to the point at which he or she can express at least some low-level concerns or objections relative to some aspect of the session (negative reaction), then it may be wise to schedule a second session prior to beginning work with the parent and child. If the parent cannot express concerns as the planning of the subsequent sessions proceeds, then it is likely he or she is either not fully engaged in the process or that concerns or objections will arise later once they are in the playroom with their child. One parent with whom this author worked was very anxious and read books on the treatment, as well as asking to observe the therapist conducting sessions with her child before she finally felt she was ready to come into the sessions herself. This degree of preparation seems preferable to being stuck in a session with a child who is ready to work and a parent who decides that now would be a good time to be resistant.

PARENT MEETING.　During the first half of the session, Mary and the therapist reviewed the videotape of the MIM that she completed during the initial assessment. During the session the therapist focused Mary on Jason's behavior during the MIM. He cued her to watch for signals that Jason was becoming underaroused—acting distracted, bored, or withdrawn. He also cued her to watch for when Jason was becoming overaroused and frustrated or angry. In either case, Jason would consequently either not cooperate with the task at hand or not remain fully and positively involved in the interaction between himself and his mother. As Mary became attuned to Jason's level of arousal, she and the therapist began to look at those things Mary did that seemed to keep Jason engaged and happy versus those things that tended to trigger a negative response. Throughout the review, Mary was essentially taught problem identification and problem-solving skills.

It was important for the therapist to help Mary feel that there were positive aspects to her relationship with Jason and that the changes she would be asked to make over the course of the therapy did not mean that she had been a bad parent, nor did they mean that she would have to put more energy into parenting. Without this reassurance, Mary would have felt completely overwhelmed or even depressed and, therefore, less rather than more able to cope with changes in Jason's level of neediness.

During the second half of the session, the therapist and Mary reviewed brief portions of the videotapes of each of Jason's first three individual play sessions. As with the review of the MIM, the focus was on identifying those things that the therapist did that tended to overarouse or underarouse Jason. Following the review, Mary and the therapist developed a plan for Mary to follow during her first dyadic play session with Jason. They discussed strategies for positive structuring and for providing Jason with nurturance before he could act out, so as to anticipate his needs and prevent his becoming surly or withdrawn. They also discussed ways that Mary could continue some aspects of the play sessions at home between sessions. The use of "special time" for this purpose is described in The Play Therapy Primer (O'Connor, 1991) and will not be repeated here.

Each subsequent dyadic and family session was split into two parts. The first part lasted about fifteen minutes and consisted of reviewing the preceding session with the parent and planning the current session. The review was structured in exactly the same way as the review of the MIM, with the intention of identifying those behaviors that kept the parent and Jason positively engaged. The planning portion was designed to help each parent understand the therapeutic goal to be accomplished during the session, as well as to help them preplan some strategies for solving problems that might arise during the session and to engage them fully in the process so as to maximize the generalization of their in-session behavior to their interactions with the children out-of-session.

DYADIC AND FAMILY SESSION PARTICIPANTS: Mary and Jason had two sessions in a row together (Sessions 4 & 5). These were followed by two sessions in which Emilio and Jason were seen together (Sessions 6 & 7). Next, two sessions were scheduled for Mary, Carla, and Jason (Sessions 8 & 9), followed by two sessions for Emilio, Carla, and Jason (Sessions 10 & 11).

TARGET CONTENT: The identification of Jason's ambivalence about control versus attachment and the degree to which his tendency to take control interfered with his actually getting his needs met; the specific identification of the different ways this conflict manifested itself in his interactions with each of his parents; and the identification of the degree to which Jason viewed Carla as being his competition for parental attention rather than a potential ally. Problem solving was initiated with respect to each of these areas of difficulty. The degree to which various historical events in the family had contributed to Jason's perceptions and interfered with problem solving was also identified.

Since the sessions in this phase of treatment were repeated with each parent, only one session out of each pair is described (as indicated with an *).

*Session 4: Mary and Jason. (Session 6: Emilio and Jason.)

TARGET CONTENT: The goal of the first session with each parent was to recreate the experience of benevolent control that Jason had in his first sessions with the therapist in his interactions with his parents. The therapist reflected and interpreted Jason's reactions to being the focus of each parent's attention and his lingering discomfort with having relinquished control.

MATERIALS: Baby bottles, snack foods, art materials (including very large sheets of paper), pencils, crayons, and measuring tape.

EXPERIENTIAL COMPONENT(S):   The experiences in this session were designed to merge intrusion and nurturance. The parents were to insist on continuous interaction with Jason but to do so in a way that consistently met his needs. During session 4, Mary began with an activity that celebrated Jason's uniqueness and fully focused her attention on him. She laid a large sheet of paper on the floor and had Jason lie on top of it. She then drew around him, while commenting on the size and shape of every limp and appendage. Once the outline was complete, she had Jason sit next to the paper so that she could begin to fill it in while looking at him. She attempted to notice and positively comment on every detail, the specks of color in his eyes, the length of his hair and nails. Every part was measured and notes made right on the picture. As Jason took an interest, he was allowed to help with the picture but only as directed by his mother. In order to keep Jason's attention from wandering, the whole activity was completed relatively quickly. Jason clearly delighted in the attention being paid to him and in his mother's silliness as she did things such as attempting to measure the length of his eyelashes.

During the second half of the session, Mary moved through several nurturing activities. She repeated the game the therapist had played where Jason's mouth was the target for M&M throwing. She discovered that, as she held the M&Ms, their color began to bleed, and she then used them to paint designs on Jason's face while feeding him the used-up paintbrushes. When she was done, they admired her handiwork in the mirror. Later, she had Jason lie very still while she washed his face with warm water and a washcloth. Toward the end of the session, Mary held Jason and told him stories about some of the positive and negative events in their family history. One story was about how happy she had been when he was born and how nervous she was as a new mother. The other was about how sad she was when his brother died and her recollection of how Jason had reacted at the time. During both, she made an effort to talk about specific things Jason had done and to comment on how he must have felt at the time. For example, she said, "When you were a tiny baby I checked you so often that you probably laid in your crib and thought "For crying out loud mom, how's a kid supposed to get any sleep around here with you poking at him all the time?"

Throughout this session, the therapist coached Mary when she got stuck or seemed unclear as to how to proceed. The overall tone of the session was soothing and relatively quiet. Both Jason and Mary seemed happy and relaxed when it was over.

VERBAL COMPONENT(S):   During this session the therapist reflected Jason's affect, thoughts, and motives in much the same way as he had during the first three sessions. Mary had been instructed to respond to Jason directly whenever the therapist reflected something Jason had not verbalized. In this way, if the therapist reflected that Jason was beginning to feel anxious in a particular encounter, then Mary would respond by verbally recognizing Jason's feelings and agreeing to change the activity in some way. The therapist also occasionally repeated pattern or simple dynamic interpretations of Jason's primary issues as they had been identified in the first three sessions. The primary issue for interpretation continued to be Jason's constant struggle to find a balance between his need for control and his need for attachment. Generalized dynamic interpretations drew the connection between these conflicts and their interactions outside of the sessions. "Boy you sure do make faces when your mother fusses over you, but you still kind of smile like you sort of think it's nice or at least funny. I'll bet that is what it is like sometimes when you get ready to go to church. Mom is fussing and you're getting all exasperated but still thinking that it would actually be sort of nice if only she wouldn't get so carried away." The therapist did make a genetic interpretation in response to Mary's story about Jason as a baby. He noted, "I'm sure you loved your mother a whole lot when you were a tiny baby and that it felt weird when you wanted her to go away because she was checking on you too much. Even then you wanted her to be around because you loved her but you wanted her to go away so that you could get something you needed, like sleep." As much as possible, however, the therapist stayed in the background, encouraging Jason's and Mary's interactions.

Session 5: Mary and Jason. (*Session 7: Emilio and Jason.)

TARGET CONTENT: The focus continued to be on Jason's ambivalence regarding control and attachment. Because the sessions with Emilio followed similar sessions Jason had completed with Mary, direct comparisons could be made between the two. Care was taken not to pit the parents against one another but rather to focus Jason on the ways in which comparing them tended to interfere with his enjoyment of his time with either of them.

MATERIALS: Chocolate pudding, very large sheets of paper, soap, washcloth, and towel.

EXPERIENTIAL COMPONENT(S):   The purpose of this activity was to have Jason find pleasure in an activity where he remained totally passive. As in the session with Mary, Jason was told that he was going to be a bunch of giant paintbrushes that his father and the therapist would use to paint with the chocolate pudding. Emilio and the therapist rolled up Jason's sleeves, took off his shoes, and rolled up his pant legs. They then spread chocolate pudding on his hands and used these to begin painting on the large sheet of paper that had been spread on the floor. Since this was Jason's second time at this activity, he accepted it rapidly but seemed just slightly bored. Emilio picked up on this and decided to up the ante. He immediately spread chocolate pudding on Jason's feet and used those as brushes. Again, Jason was delighted but not terribly surprised, as his mother had done the same at the therapist's urging. At this point, Emilio's tendency to be very active took over. He said that he had a great idea. He knew that Jason had on his gym shorts under his pants so, noting out loud that there were only men in the room anyway, proceeded to strip Jason down to his shorts. Jason had trouble resisting as his total disbelief was causing him to laugh too hard. Initially, Emilio put pudding on one part of Jason's body at a time and made a print on the piece of paper. They made arm prints and knee prints and face prints. Then Emilio put pudding all over Jason, from head to foot, and rolled him across the paper making a body trail. Jason verbally protested every step of the way but had to try to talk while laughing so hard he could barely breathe. At no point did he physically resist.

Because the pudding painting took up the majority of the session, the cleanup was completed fairly quickly. This portion was more business than pleasure—much in contrast to Mary and Jason's cleanup time. Mary had Jason lie down while she gently washed his hands and again told him stories about when he was younger. She even sang to him at one point. Jason had responded by virtually going off to sleep. Emilio had Jason stand in the sink and tried to get him just clean enough that he could ride in the car without sticking to the seat. While cleaning up, they talked enthusiastically about the session. Jason kept repeating, "I can't believe you put pudding on my (naming various body parts)."

VERBAL COMPONENT(S):   As in previous sessions, Jason's ambivalence regarding control and attachment was the focus of the therapist's interpretive work. However, in this session two elements were added. The therapist repeatedly interpreted how the balance of the conflict between control and attachment seemed to have swung toward the attachment side, much to Jason's benefit. He noted that he could not have imagined Jason allowing himself to be covered with chocolate pudding a few weeks ago—much less allowing himself to have fun in the process. He stressed the progress Jason had made and the obvious pleasure it brought him. The therapist also noted the differences in Mary's and Emilio's style of interaction and the specific pleasure that each style brought Jason. He compared Mary's session with Jason to snuggling down in bed when you were really tired and it was cold outside, and Emilio's session to riding a roller coaster. Both felt great, both were necessary, and you wouldn't want to give up one for the other. The therapist also noted that, when Jason compared his mother and father, he put himself in much the same place as when he tried to choose between control and attachment. It was not as if one were better than the other, nor were they mutually exclusive; rather each had its benefits and its own time and place.

*Session 8: Mary, Carla and Jason. (Session 10: Emilio, Carla, and Jason.)

TARGET CONTENT: During the family sessions, the focus shifted from Jason's conflict with respect to attachment versus control to his anxieties with respect to getting his attachment needs met in various situations. Specifically, the plan was to shift his view of Carla from one where he saw her as competing for limited parental resources to one where she could be an ally and a source of emotional supplies in her own right.

MATERIALS: Small, individually wrapped, hard candies.

EXPERIENTIAL COMPONENT(S):   This session was geared toward eliciting cooperation between Jason and Carla so that both could experience gaining parental attention and reward through positive interaction with one another. Two games were played repeatedly, with both children having an equal number of turns at each game.

The first game consisted of a version of the "hotter-colder" game. The therapist took one child out of the room while Mary and the other child hid a piece of hard candy somewhere in the playroom. The therapist then returned the other child to the room so that he or she could attempt to find the piece of candy. Mary coached the one who had hidden the candy as to when to say "You are getting hotter" or "You are getting colder" to guide the one looking for the candy. The motivation to give good directions was high, as once the child found the piece of candy he or she did not get to keep it but had to turn it over to the child who had hidden it. If the child searching for the candy resisted following directions so as to keep the one who had hidden it from getting the candy, that child could always take his or her revenge on the next turn. Both children played the game well and were able to give each other feedback about the process. Jason wanted Carla to hide the candy in more difficult spots and assured her that he would find it as long as she gave good clues. Carla wanted Jason to help her by physically guiding her as well as saying "hotter," or "colder." Both complied with the other's directions. Mary also coached each child on how to make the task developmentally appropriate for the other.

The other game played during the session was also designed to get the children focused on one another and to recognize the developmental differences between them. The therapist again took one child out of the room. Mary and the remaining child then altered something about that child's appearance. When the child outside the room returned, he or she tried to figure out what had been altered. If the child could not guess, then he or she was given clues. Rather than giving candy following each turn, the reinforcement was delayed—with each child receiving four candies apiece after they had each played a total of four rounds, whether they had been successful in identifying the alteration or not. During this game, Mary had to work harder to get each child to play at the other's developmental level rather than at their own.

VERBAL COMPONENT(S): Only interpretations that directly reinforced what the children were learning experientially were made. As the therapy had moved beyond the identification of core issues, no new genetic interpretations were made: Rather an effort was made to expand those made earlier. Considerable effort was made to identify ways that the pleasure the children were getting in the session could be obtained outside of the session. Generalized dynamic interpretations such as, "I'll bet you and Carla could do something like this while your mother was busy with an important phone call. Instead of both of you trying to get your mother's attention while she talked, you could spend the time showing Carla how to build a really tall tower out of blocks, and then your mother could come and show both of you a new block-building trick when she got off the phone. That way everyone could feel good." This type of cooperative problem solving was emphasized throughout the session.

Session 9: Mary, Jason, and Carla. (*Session 11: Emilio, Jason, and Carla.)

TARGET CONTENT: During this session, the therapist identified the potential conflicts that competition could create—especially when the siblings are at very different developmental levels. The conflict Jason might experience between his desire to be competitive and win versus being cooperative and earning a concrete reward was again compared to the conflict between attachment and control. Both were important and both brought you rewards, but it was always necessary to determine which one would work the best in any given situation.

MATERIALS: Crayons, blindfold, large sheets of paper, tape.

EXPERIENTIAL COMPONENT(S): Two activities were introduced during this session. The first was a modified version of Simon Says, and the other was the completion of a family mural. The goal of each was to attempt to balance cooperation and competition.

During the Simon Says game, the children each received an M&M if they both followed Simon's directions correctly *or* if they both missed the direction. Emilio alternated both simple and complex directions and varied the speed of his delivery. Initially, Jason focused on Emilio and the direction and tried to follow the direction every time. As Carla missed about half of the directions, they were not getting very many M&Ms. As Jason realized this, he tried to coach Carla both verbally and by getting her to watch him so as to bring her performance up to his level. This strategy meant that Jason had to attend to both Emilio and Carla. This helped, but it also slowed the game down so that, while they were getting more M&Ms, they were earning them slowly. At this point, Emilio suggested that Jason problem-solve again and see if there was a way he and Carla could improve their hit rate even more. He encouraged Jason to think about what Carla was doing. He discouraged Jason's focus on trying to correctly following Simon's directions. Suddenly, Jason caught on. He ignored Emilio's directions. He focused entirely on Carla and simply copied whatever she did. Now they earned M&Ms for every trial, and both were delighted. Carla reached over and spontaneously hugged Jason, who beamed with pride but did not turn to look at either Emilio or the therapist.

For the second part of the session, the family was given a large sheet of paper, crayons, and markers. Emilio informed the children that they could split the remaining M&Ms if they each completed a drawing on the mural, but that he would take them out for hamburgers after the session if they could figure out a way to work together and complete a single picture. He then worked with both to engage in some very active problem solving about how they could work together when their skill levels were so different. He helped Jason identify that a solution would require that he give up some of his goal orientation and allow the picture to be fairly simplistic. He helped Carla identify that she would need to slow down and let Jason work on the picture, too. They developed a plan whereby each child would take a 15-second turn at working on the identified goal of drawing a picture of their house. To get them started, Emilio drew the outline before either of them took a turn. As the children took turns, he liberally reinforced their efforts and their mutual tolerance of each other's additions and changes of the picture. This complex task was introduced both for its own therapeutic value as well as to measure the family's ability to problem-solve and work cooperatively.

VERBAL COMPONENT(S):   The targeted content was interpreted as the family played the games. Because this was the second-to-last session, no new content was introduced. The gains each of the family members had made since starting therapy were verbally reinforced. The therapist talked less during this session than in any of the previous ones and said virtually nothing as the family worked to complete the mural. The hope was that the family recognized their underlying issues at this point and could problem-solve as needed. If this had turned out not to be the case, the members would have been consulted to determine whether or not they were actually ready to terminate or if additional sessions should be scheduled.

Stage V: Termination: (Anticipated number of sessions: 2.)

PARTICIPANTS: One session was used to accomplish termination with Mary, Carla, and Jason and one was used to complete termination with Emilio, Carla, and Jason.

TARGET CONTENT: During termination, it is important that the therapist not bring up any new content, no matter how tempting. In this case, the therapist reiterated previous genetic interpretations and synthesized and summarized the contents of the previous sessions. The therapist presented an overview of the work that emphasized the positive changes that had occurred and the changes both Jason and each family had been able to accomplish. All were copiously complimented on a job well done.

MATERIALS: Selected by each family at the end of the previous sessions. Mary, Carla, and Jason chose to repeat the chocolate pudding painting and to have cookies and juice for their celebration at the end of the session. Emilio, Carla, and Jason chose to repeat playing Simon Says and to bring a board game from home. They chose to have cake and milk for their celebration at the end of the session.

EXPERIENTIAL COMPONENT(S): Mary had to work hard to manage doing the chocolate pudding painting with both children. She had been warned by the therapist about how active Emilio's and Jason's session had become, but she chose to proceed anyway. In her planning session with the therapist, she focused on ways she could complete the task simultaneously with both children rather than having them take turns, as she thought they might act out if left to their own devices for even a few minutes during this highly stimulating activity. She chose to blindfold both children and focus on making the experience very sensory. The blindfolds meant that the children could not focus on each other and were, therefore, less likely to compete.

In session, Mary rolled up each child's sleeves, blindfolded them, and had them lie on the floor on either side of the large sheet of paper. She took each one's hand and dipped it into the chocolate pudding and began to massage their hands together between hers. She asked each child to describe what it felt like and to try to differentiate her hands from each other's hands. Then she had them smell the pudding and describe the smell and to list other things they liked to smell. Next she used Carla's hand to feed Jason some pudding and his to feed Carla. Both children said this felt very weird, but both giggled throughout. Finally, Mary made an interwoven design on the paper from each child's handprints. Mary cleaned off each child's hands before taking off the blindfolds so that there would be less likelihood that the children would try to continue the activity in a way she could not manage. Both children were clearly pleased with the activity and with the design Mary had made.

The party at the end of the session was a simple celebration of their gains as a family. The therapist talked about where they had started and encouraged them to talk about the positive changes that had occurred since. Whenever any of them mentioned areas for continued improvement, the therapist provided assurance that those gains could be readily achieved.

VERBAL COMPONENT(S): No new material was introduced in this session. The initial underlying conflicts were restated. Examples of how these conflicts had been managed in the various sessions were stated by the therapist and often expanded on by either Mary or Jason. The decrease in each family member's anxiety and frustration over the course of the therapy was noted, as was the obvious increase in the pleasure they took in their interactions. Suggestions for ways to continue the types of activities begun in the sessions at home were introduced and discussed. Finally, Goodbyes were said and all were informed that they could return for "tune-up" sessions if they felt themselves getting stuck again at any point in the future.

Stage I-V: Play Therapy Group: (Anticipated number of sessions: 12.)

Following the completion of this portion of the treatment plan, Jason was moved to a play therapy group for a total of 12 sessions to bring his peer social interactions up to age level. As with the initial course of treatment, the focus of the group was on strategies for getting one's needs met effectively. In this context, however, the emphasis was on viewing peers as a potential source of social and emotional supplies as well as the effectiveness of cooperation and problem solving in meeting basic individual needs. The format of the group was exactly as described in Chapters 14 and 15 of *The Play Therapy Primer* (O'Connor, 1991). The course of that treatment will not be described here, as it was not conducted in a manner unique to ecosystemic play therapy. As is usually the case when a significant change is made in the treatment process, Jason went through each of the phases of treatment all over again. However, because of his previous therapy experience, each phase was shorter and less intense than it had been during the first series of sessions. Jason completed the series of sessions successfully and was reported to have begun making friends in his class at school. He had had one classmate spend the night during a weekend visit with his father. Jason had also expressed an interest in joining the soccer team at his school. Fortunately for this therapy, several of the children in the group came from divorced families, so this content was able to be included in some of the discussion sessions. Divorce-related problems, postdivorce adjustment, and specific problem-solving strategies were all incorporated into a group format that primarily focused on the development of peer social skills.

Parallel Intervention with Mary L.

Subsequent to the initial sessions in which Mary was engaged in planning for her involvement in Jason's play sessions, it became apparent that she was having difficulty finding ways to get her own needs met. At this point, she was referred for individual therapy so that she could address her history of depressive episodes and her unresolved feelings about her divorce, as well as to develop strategies for getting her own needs met. It was hypothesized that this work would help her function better, both as an individual and in her role as a single parent.

Consultation with School and Medical Systems

These consultations were undertaken largely to decrease the possibility that the actions of persons in either of these systems might be inadvertently reinforcing the problems that Jason and his family were experiencing. The consultation with the school targeted two issues. One was Jason's need for feeling empowered and in control. The therapist helped the teacher devise some ways of giving Jason choices and responsibility in the classroom, one of which consisted of giving Jason the choice of completing one of two equivalent assignments, whenever possible. The other issue addressed was Jason's developmental lag with respect to peer interactions. The teacher had believed that Jason was capable of peer interactions but simply chose not to interact. Shifting the teacher's focus and asking her to attempt to reinforce any effort that Jason made to interact with his peers was all that was recommended here.

The consultation with the physician also targeted Jason's desire for control and highlighted his ambivalence about having to be taken care of by his parents. A two-step plan for addressing Jason's asthma attacks was developed. For the less serious attacks, Jason was given an inhaler and told how to self-administer the medication. He was told that he could use up to two doses on his own without asking permission. (These instructions were conveyed to the school, and an inhaler was placed at Jason's disposal in the school office.) With Jason, the physician stressed his belief that Jason could manage all of his attacks himself. The second phase of the plan was introduced merely as a precaution, put in place mostly so Mary would not worry. With Jason present, Mary was supplied with additional medications and instructions on how to manage attacks of various intensities. Again, both were reassured that Jason would be able to manage his attacks on his own and that the plan for Mary's interventions was just a precaution. Both this intervention and the one with the school were designed to increase Jason's sense of control and to shift his attention to attachment issues.

EXPECTED OUTCOME OR PROGNOSIS

Given the overall health of all of the participants, it was anticipated that the problems Jason was experiencing would respond both quickly and well to a goal-oriented ecosystem play therapy intervention. Indeed, this was the case, and the treatment was completed in 13 sessions that included Jason and one individual session with each of his parents. Because conflicts between attachment and control were thought to underlie the problems Jason was experiencing, it is anticipated that there may be some reoccurrence of the problem as he enters adolescence. In adolescence, most children experience conflict between their childhood attachment to their parents and their desire to function competently on their own. This normal developmental event may revive some of Jason's anxieties, so that both parent's should be cautioned to watch for signs of withdrawal or acting out as Jason develops. A brief intervention at that time should avert the typical problems of adolescence becoming so severe that they interfere with further developmental progress.

CONCLUSION

Ecosystemic play therapy is a relatively new model of play therapy that was first described in the *Handbook of Play Therapy, Volume II: Advances and Innovations* (O'Connor & Schaefer, 1994). The model attempts to integrate concepts and strategies from many other theories of psychotherapy with developmental concepts to form a model for comprehensive case conceptualization and intervention. In the model, certain key elements are identified as essential to the integrity of the theory. While retaining those elements, the practitioner of ecosystemic play therapy is encouraged to develop the details of the theory in a way that he or she finds internally consistent. The key elements of the theory and the details of the model that the author uses are:

Key Element	Author's Fill
Use of an ecosystemic world view	Figure 9.1
Concept of basic drives	Biological survival instinct modified through socialization experiences
Concept of psychopathology	The inability to get one's needs met effectively and in ways that do not interfere with others' getting their needs met
The concept of goal or cure in therapy	Breaking the client's set approach to problems, allowing him or her to engage in creative problem solving so as to get needs met and to resume normal developmental progress
Intervention strategies	The use of multiple, overlapping interventions aimed at altering the problem, the client's view of the problem, and the client's response to the problem

In this chapter, the author has attempted to apply this model to the case of Jason L. In so doing, it was intended that the details of the author's specific way of conceptualizing and implementing ecosystemic play therapy have been made clear. The reader is reminded that this presentation is meant only as an illustration of the way in which the author applies the model, rather than illustrating the only way in which the model might be used. Another therapist, using this approach, might come up with a different and equally effective treatment plan; however, the key elements of the model would remain intact. The strength of ecosystemic play therapy lies in the degree to which it bends to suit the systems in which the client and therapist find themselves and yet retains its integrity. Hopefully, the future will see further clarification of the key elements of the model as well as attempts to measure the efficacy of the approach in clinical work.

BIBLIOGRAPHY

American Psychiatric Association. (1994). *Diagnostic and statistical manual of mental disorders (4th ed.).* Washington, DC: American Psychiatric Association.

American Psychological Association. (1991). *Guidelines for providers of psychological services to ethnic, linguistic and culturally diverse populations.* Washington, DC: American Psychological Association.

Association for Play Therapy. (1995). *Registered play therapy application.* Fresno, CA: Association for Play Therapy.

Axline, V. (1947). *Play therapy.* Boston: Houghton Mifflin.

Bettelheim, B. (1967). *The empty fortress.* New York: Free Press.

Bevan, W. (1991). Contemporary psychology: A tour inside the onion. *American Psychologist, 46(5),* 475–483.

Caplan, F. (1978). *The first twelve months of life.* New York: Bantam.

Caplan, F., & Caplan, T. (1980). *The second twelve months of life.* New York: Bantam.

Claman, L. (1980). The Squiggle Drawing Game in child psychotherapy. *American Journal of Psychotherapy, 34(3),* pp. 414–425.

Erikson, E. (1950). Childhood and society. New York: Norton.

Freud, A. (1928). Introduction to the technique of child analysis (L. P. Clark, Trans.). New York: Nervous and Mental Disease Publishing.

Freud, A. (1965). Normality and pathology in childhood. New York: International Universities Press.

Freud, S. (1905). Three essays on the theory of sexuality, standard edition (Vol. 16). London: Hogarth Press, 1957.

Freud, S. (1933). Collected papers. London: Hogarth Press.

Georgi, A. (1985). Phenomenology and psychological research. Pittsburgh, PA: Duquesne University Press.

Glasser, W. (1975). Reality therapy. New York: Harper & Row.

Gordon, M. (1964). Assimilation in American life: The role of race, religion and national origins. New York: Oxford Press.

Hammond-Newman, M. (1994). Play therapy with children of alcoholics and addicts. In K. O'Connor, & C. Schaefer, Handbook of play therapy, Vol. II: Advances and innovations. New York: Wiley.

Jernberg, A. (1979). Theraplay. San Francisco: Jossey-Bass.

Klein, M (1932). The psycho-analysis of children. London: Hogarth Press.

Kohlberg, L. (1976). Moral stages and moralization. In T. Lickona (Ed.), Moral development and behavior. New York: Holt.

Landreth, G. (1991). Play therapy: The art of the relationship. Muncie, IN: Accelerated Development, Inc.

Mahler, M. (1967). On human symbiosis and the vicissitudes of individuation. Journal of the American Psychoanalytic Association, 25, 740–763.

Mahler, M. (1972). On the first three subphases of the separation-individuation process. International Journal of Psycho-Analysis, 53, 333–338.

Maslow, A. (1987). Motivation and personality (3rd ed.). New York: Harper & Row.

Mead, J., and Westgate, D. (1982). Investigating child abuse. Canyon Lake, CA: For Kids Sake.

O'Connor, K. (1991). The play therapy primer. New York: Wiley.

O'Connor, K., & Ammen, S. (in press). Play therapy treatment planning and interventions: The ecosystemic model. San Diego: Academic Press.

O'Connor, K., Ammen, S., Schmidt, M., Anderson, S., Bantugan, C., Mouanoutoua, V. L., O'Sullivan, D., Brown, L., Davis-Russell, E., & Shibuya, P. (1993). The development of the parenting self-efficacy scale to assess at-risk parenting in ethnically diverse families: A preliminary report. Child Abuse and Neglect: The International Journal, under submission.

O'Connor, K., & Schaefer, C. (1994) The handbook of play therapy, Volume II: Advances and innovations. New York: Wiley.

Padilla, A. (1980) Acculturation: Theory, models and some new findings. Boulder, CO: Westview Press.

Piaget, J. (1952). The origins of intelligence in children. New York: International Universities Press.

Piaget, J. (1959). *The language and thought of the child.* London: Routledge & Kegan Paul.

Piaget, J. (1963). *The psychology of intelligence.* Patterson, NJ: Littlefield-Adams.

Piaget, J., & Inhelder, B. (1969). *The psychology of the child.* New York: Basic Books.

Rogers, C. (1942). *Counseling and psychotherapy.* Boston: Houghton Mifflin.

Rogers, C. (1951). *Client-centered therapy.* Boston: Houghton Mifflin.

Rogers, C. (1959). A theory of therapy, personality and interpersonal relationships as developed in the client-centered framework. In S. Koch (Ed.), *Psychology: A study on science* (Vol. 3). New York: McGraw-Hill.

Rogers, C. (1961). *On becoming a person.* Boston: Houghton Mifflin.

Schaefer, C., & O'Connor, K. (1983). *Handbook of play therapy.* New York: Wiley.

Schwartz, S., & Johnson, J. (1985). *Psychopathology of childhood.* New York: Pergamon.

Slobin, D. (1964). The fruits of the first season: A discussion of the role of play in childhood. *Journal of Humanistic Psychology, 4,* 59–79.

Sue, D. (1981). *Counseling the culturally different.* New York: Wiley.

Summit, R. (1985). Causes, consequences, treatment and prevention of sexual assault against children. In J. Meier (Ed.) *Assault against children.* San Diego: College Hill, pp. 47–97.

United States Department of Health and Human Services. (1994). *International classification of diseases, 9th revision, Clinical modification.* Washington, DC: U.S. Government Printing Office.

Webster's seventh new collegiate dictionary. (1967). Springfield, MA: Merriam.

Weiner, B. (1993). On sin versus sickness: A theory of perceived responsibility and social motivation. *American Psychologist, 48(9),* 957–965.

Wood, M., Combs, C., Gunn, A., & Weller, D. (1986). *Developmental therapy in the classroom (2nd ed.).* Austin, TX: Pro-Ed.

CHAPTER 10

Ericksonian Play Therapy

JAMSHID A. MARVASTI

INTRODUCTION

Milton Erickson, M.D., was not a play therapist, nor was he known for being a child psychiatrist. Nonetheless, he successfully treated children and adolescents with principles similar to those utilized in adult psychotherapy. Dr. Erickson was concerned that his approach and technique would be mechanically imitated by other clinicians. He advised his disciples to form their own techniques: "Don't try to imitate my voice or my cadence. Just discover your own. Be your own natural self" (Erickson, 1983). On the basis of Erickson's advice, the author has tried to use some of his patterns and principles in play therapy, integrating Ericksonian approaches and techniques with psychodynamic play diagnosis. The result is termed "Ericksonian play therapy."

The author's philosophy regarding the usage of the Ericksonian name in this type of play therapy is based upon the assumption that if something looks like a duck, walks like a duck, and sounds like a duck, it is, therefore, a duck. This type of play therapy relics on one's assets rather than liabilities, focuses on the present and future rather than on the past, utilizes the child's potential, and reframes the presenting symptoms—transforming them into their own solutions. In addition, this therapy utilizes trance without the child's awareness, communicates through metaphor and storytelling, avoids interpretation of doll-play (or child-play), and does not necessarily search for insight. In this modality of play therapy, dolls appear to the child to be entering into a natural trance, while the therapist's puppet plays the role of an older, wiser self and tells a therapeutic story interspersed with suggestions, metaphors, and happy endings (Marvasti, in press).

In this chapter, the treatment is divided into two distinct entities, play diagnosis and play therapy. The play therapy includes Ericksonian principles and a "solution-focused" orientation. However, due to the lack of any Ericksonian guidelines for diagnostic work-up, play diagnosis can be performed with virtually any technique, provided that it ultimately reaches a diagnosis. In this chapter, the play diagnosis has a psychodynamic orientation, although other techniques are acceptable. No attempt is made to reconcile the psychodynamic school and Ericksonian psychotherapy; rather the chapter illustrates the necessity of determining the diagnosis in child therapy.

The term *diagnosis* is capable of being reframed and redefined. In the present situation, the word implies only the psychopathology. It may be redefined as a process of assessment of the child's conflicts, with emphasis on problem-solving potential, coping methods and skills, and whether there is any disorder capable of being controlled with medication only.

As Erickson said, "My voice goes everywhere with you, and changes into the voice of . . . your playmates and the voices of the wind and of the rain . . . ." It is hoped that the echo of Dr. Erickson's voice extends into doll houses, puppets, and stuffed animals.

Several terms in Ericksonian psychotherapy require a brief explanation for the purpose of familiarity.

Direct suggestion: Telling the client what to do very directly (the client may or may not be in a trance).

Evoking abilities and resources: Directing clients to gain access to their own potentials and capabilities.

Indirect suggestion: Using metaphors, implications, nonverbal suggestions, and the like, in order to instruct indirectly and advise a patient.

Interspersal: Nonverbally emphasizing certain words, phrases, or sentences in order to make an indirect suggestion.

Metaphor: A figure of speech in which one thing is likened to another or spoken of as if it were another thing. A derivative of the Greek words *meta,* meaning "over," and *pherin,* meaning "to carry." It denotes the transfer of knowledge from one context to another (Pearce, 1996, p. 2).

Ordeal: Directing the client to perform some burdensome action when a symptom occurs.

Reframing: Offering a new meaning of a situation, action, or the like (O'Hanlon, 1987, p. 170).

Symptom prescription: Directing the client to perform deliberately a symptom that the client wants to get rid of.

Symptom scheduling: Directing the client to perform a symptom at specific times only, and to avoid it at other times.

Utilization: Utilizing the client's presenting symptom in order to resolve it.

Milton Erickson's Life

Milton Erickson began his career as psychiatrist in Arizona shortly after his graduation, in 1930, from medical school. Throughout his career, he was considered a highly creative, intelligent man with brilliant ideas—but at the same time, a man with many physical problems. Most debilitating were the results of the polio that he had contracted as a teenager. The disease left his extremities partially paralyzed. In fact, many of Erickson's theories and accomplishments with his patients were based upon the personal experiences of an "injured healer," as his students referred to him. For a number of years he suffered from a great deal of pain, so it is not surprising that he showed such interest in the utilization of trances and hypnosis for pain.

Erickson's psychiatric philosophies matured at a time when Freudian theory was quite popular. However, Erickson created his own ideas, and, at times, many of his techniques and principles of therapy directly opposed those of psychoanalysis. For example, he did not consider the unconscious a place for pathology, repressed rage, and perversion. Rather, he respected the unconscious as a place that contained the capacity to heal. Instead of using free association and dreams as the royal road to the unconscious, he used metaphor, stories, and anecdotes to bypass the conscious level and reach the unconscious level of the patient.

Communication Style in Ericksonian Play Therapy

One of the forms of parallel communication used by Erickson is *refraction,* the process of speaking with one person in the hopes of indirectly suggesting a message to another. In play therapy, refraction is used frequently as the therapist (or the therapist's puppet) talks to the dolls, while the child infers the hidden message. The therapist can create improvements in the doll, symbolizing changes desired in the child. Hopefully, the child will identify with the doll's characteristics or, at the very least, understand that things are changeable. Erickson also utilized "two-level communication" in order to communicate simultaneously with both the conscious and the unconscious mind (Erickson & Rossi, 1976/1980). Through this approach, the conscious mind is influenced by the literal content of a story or anecdote, while, simultaneously, the unconscious mind receives special suggestions that are interspersed during verbal communication.

Clinicians have used various sources of material for these stories such as fairy tales, the therapist's or the child's own imagination, and preordained themes. Several basic ingredients of story making offered by clinicians for the purpose of creating a metaphorical storyline include: (1) presenting a metaphorical conflict similar to the child's conflict; (2) presenting a metaphorical crisis that eventually becomes a turning point of resolution; (3) developing a new sense of identification, and (4) culminating this resolution into a celebration (Mills & Crowley, 1986, p. 138). First, a storyline including the qualities mentioned is crafted as therapeutic suggestions are communicated to the child through the process of interspersing. These interspersed messages are underscored during storytelling with the help of vocal dynamics such as changes in the tonal quality of a therapist's voice.

In Ericksonian play therapy, the puppet's storytelling also contains metaphors and interspersed suggestions, which are emphasized in a slow, rhythmic voice, with changes in nonverbal and verbal aspects.

Case Example No. 1

During play therapy with a child who was the family scapegoat and carried the burden of other family members, the child projected this image onto a little doll in the doll house. The little doll was blamed for everything bad that happened, but she tolerated it and seemed to become another Cinderella. In this circumstance, the therapist did not pathologize the life of Cinderella; on the contrary, he accepted it and gave it a positive outlook. The therapist's puppet said: "This little doll is *very strong and everyone knows it, too.* So they throw all their troubles and faults onto her. This doll is *the strongest member of the family* because she can tolerate criticism, unlike the other dolls in this family who cannot tolerate their shortcomings and faults and cannot hear about them. Therefore, they rely on this girl to take responsibility and make them feel good about themselves. The little doll is *good, strong, and powerful;* she is *a hero.*"

Then the therapist softly changed his voice and said: "Now my puppet wants to tell a story to this family in the doll house, and you, little doll, listen carefully to this story which is just like a bedtime story: many dolls, upon hearing it, may gradually fall asleep. *The name of the story is "Mountain Man"*:

In old, old times, far, far away, there was a king who lived in a palace in a beautiful village. Next to this palace, there was situated a mountain which prevented the sun from shining onto the palace. The King was very upset about not having the sun in his home. One day, he ordered everyone in the village to carry a portion of the mountain away so that the mountain would be totally removed and there would not be any shadow on his palace. So all the villagers began carrying around portions of the mountain. But one by one they grew tired, lazy, and started to complain and cry. So everyone began to look for a person who was not bothered by carrying a rock on his back. They found *a strong man* who *stood straight* while walking with the rock on his back. Eventually, one by one, the people began putting their portions on top of his rock. He accepted them all and never complained, cried or protested. Eventually, all the rock from the mountain was placed on the back of one man, *our hero, the strongest man in the world.* The man was carrying around an entire mountain on his shoulders, relieving all the other villagers from that heavy weight. The king learned what had occurred and told the Mountain Man that *he was the strongest man in the village* and that he should be the future king. The king asked the mountain man to marry his daughter, the princess, and then placed his own crown over the Mountain Man's head. He was *the hero of the village. All the villagers were very happy and they came and thanked the Mountain Man* because he took on everyone's pain and carried it without protesting or complaining. *He was the strongest man around.*" (In this story the italicized words indicated "interspersed" suggestions.)

Mills & Crowley (1986) felt that such metaphors could stimulate a child's imagination to its highest strength, consequently effecting self-knowledge and transformation. They argued that children, upon hearing a story, would not proceed to analyze it, but rather, simply would enter into it with the full force of their imaginative powers, powers that prove critical in the healing process. The justification for the utilization of metaphors relies upon the premise that metaphors may pass the conscious level and enter into the unconscious of the child. Although no scientific research and data are available to prove or disprove this theory, many case histories and anecdotal statements prove the influence of metaphors on the unconscious.

Sharpe (1980) referred to Ericksonian psychotherapy tactics as "fighting fire with fire." She explained that in this technique, the "stupid child" is confronted with an equally "stupid therapist." The child's demands and requests are graciously granted but "misunderstood." For example, the word *water* is printed on paper and placed in a glass at the request of a lazy child who asks for water, a child who is capable of getting his own water. The patient's false reality is accepted at face value, to the dismay of the patient.

Ericksonian Play Therapy

In this modality of play, the ego defense mechanisms are not neutralized. The similarity between the doll's life and the child's life will not be explained to the child (contrary to the psychodynamic technique). In this technique, neither insight nor interpretation of unconscious material is required for change, and the cause-effect relationships of symptoms are not explored. The focus is on the present, the future, and the solution: The child's potential and resources are explored, rather than the problems and conflicts. The first task of a play therapist is to develop a relationship with the child so that eventually the child may utilize the therapist's image or the therapist's puppet as a wise companion, a positive element that the child did not have prior to therapy.

Before play therapy begins, play diagnosis and assessment are required. The purpose of play diagnosis is not only to find the diagnosis, but to discover not only the family dynamics, but also the child's resources, assets, perception of self, and family and world view. In addition, such diagnosis reveals any indication of trauma and its impacts as well as the child's perception of the trauma. The diagnostic findings are for the therapist and need not be interpreted or explained to the patient. It is important that the therapist is able to see the world through the eyes of the child. In the beginning, play diagnosis may be unstructured—a form of free play with the purpose of learning about a child's perception of his or her world. At this point, the therapist follows the child's lead. The child will eventually transport the therapist to the state in which the child is currently trapped. Once the therapist acquires some knowledge of the child's perception, the play will gradually become more structured and the child will slowly begin to follow the therapist's lead. In this way, the therapist can direct the child to the desired point. This type of play therapy is a transition from pathology to normality, from the symptom as a painful phenomenon to a solution, and from weakness to potential.

In this technique, the therapist uses dolls and puppets in order to tell a story. The therapist's doll, through the use of anecdotes and metaphors, takes the child's doll into the doll house, and with the help of the child's doll, cocreates a story. The therapist's doll alters the outcome of the story and directs it toward a successful, happy, and positive ending. Storytelling may occur in the doll house, for example, as a group of dolls encircle a fire and listen to a story. The therapist's doll gradually closes the eyes of the other dolls, relaxing them to the point that they appear to be in a trance. This may aid the child in falling into a trance as well. The dolls are then left to relax and listen to the puppet's statements about good days and happy endings. The Ericksonian technique is then used inside the doll house, for instance, to find positive qualities in the character of a doll (which represents the child).

Case Example No. 2

In treating a seven-year-old girl who refused to eat, as an objection to her family's disorders, the therapist arranged a family of dolls inside a doll house and took his own puppet for storytelling. The therapist told the child, through his puppet: "I will need your help with half of the storymaking. I want you to make the first half of the story, and I will make the second half of the story. In the second part, you can be like the other dolls, and just relax and listen. This is the time that you can imagine or pretend that you are living in this doll house and pretend that you are inside watching everything."

The therapist's puppet begins to tell the following story:

Once upon a time, there was a house full of animals, called Animal House, where there lived a dog, a cat, a lion, and a monkey. There was also a guinea pig, which was very small and was constantly teased by all the other animals in the house. She was small and could not defend herself. Everyone called her "gopher" and bossed her around all the time. Sometimes they called her "ugly" and "midget."

(The therapist stopped here and asked the child: "How do you think the guinea pig feels now? Why don't you play the guinea pig's role from here on?" The child took the guinea pig doll and started to talk to the therapist puppet.)

Child's Doll: I feel upset and I want to cry.
Therapist Puppet: What's this guinea pig good at? How could she make herself happy?
Child's Doll: The guinea pig would go to her room and think.
Therapist Puppet: What does she think about?
Child's Doll: She daydreams.
Therapist Puppet: And what does daydreaming do for her?
Child's Doll: I don't know, but she thinks a lot.
Therapist Puppet: How does she feel when she daydreams or thinks?
Child's Doll: She feels good because she thinks no one can bother her.

The therapist speculated that the child's potential and coping mechanism (projected onto the guinea pig) is the power of her fantasy and imagination, and through daydreaming the child is creating a world that is fair and peaceful. The therapist continues the story:

The little guinea pig was upset and tearful, but sometimes she tried to *make herself feel better* by fantasizing a world in which *she would be the strongest, biggest* creature in the forest and would order the lion and tiger to become *her* gophers. One day the *wise bear* listened to the guinea pig's sad story and told her that, if

she ate more food, she would become *bigger* and *stronger* and no one could bully her. She started to eat a lot of food and hoped that by doing so she would grow *bigger* and *stronger* and would be able to one day boss around all the animals and not be hurt by them.

One of the therapeutic principles used in this play therapy is the holistic technique, meaning that play therapy is sometimes directive and sometimes nondirective (Marvasti, 1989). It is a very individualized treatment program, based upon the child's symptoms, potential, and ego structure. This kind of therapy is solution oriented, rather than problem oriented. The doll's problem is considered a "message" and is acknowledged and utilized for the purpose of treating or substituting the problem, or transforming it into a different one. Therapists may communicate through storytelling. For example, if a child is suffering from somatic pain and a fear of injections, the therapist's puppet may tell a story to the other dolls about a sick little doll who received a lot of injections and had to endure much pain. But the injections *made the sick doll stronger,* and the bitter syrupy medicine *made her healthier* to the point that she was *stronger in all her broken places.*

In Ericksonian play therapy, the interpretation of the patient's unconscious is avoided. Also, there is no interest in bringing the unconscious element to the conscious. Generally, transference is deliberately discouraged, or ignored, or it may be utilized in the same manner as symptoms for the purpose of resolving it. However, countertransference may develop before the therapist has any control of it, or is able to abort it. In this circumstance, the clinician may need to acknowledge it to himself or herself (and not necessarily to the client), utilizing this phenomenon as a tool in strengthening his or her character, qualities, and therapeutic skills. Countertransference is considered to be a positive development in a therapist, a gift from his or her unconscious and a vehicle for growth, rather than a cluster of pathologies and unwanted occurrences (Marvasti, 1992).

Is Play Diagnosis Necessary?

Some Ericksonian clinicians felt that Erickson did not give enough attention to formal assessments and diagnostic work-ups, per se, and as Zeig (1987) mentioned, "In Ericksonian approaches, diagnosis is as brief as possible and merely serves the forces of constructive utilization" (p. 393). However, a minority challenges this notion. For example, Otani (1989) explained that despite Erickson's deemphasis on the formal assessment of problems (Erickson & Rossi, 1979, p. 179), he was a skilled psychiatrist with more than 50 years of rich clinical experience. Also, Zeig (1985, chap. 4) referred to Dr. Erickson's rare ability to identify and detect fine details about his clients through his delicate observation and listening skills. Otani (1989) concluded that Erickson did, in fact, diagnose his clients, "But did so quickly and accurately."

Lankton and Lankton (1986), two well-known Ericksonian practitioners, emphasized the use of Leary's Interpersonal Checklist as a diagnostic tool to identify interpersonal needs. The Lanktons suggested that interpersonal areas could be rein-

forced if embedded into metaphors and therapeutic stories. So, in a way, the Lanktons explain the need for diagnosis before treatment. Play diagnosis is needed to determine the client's assets, potential, resources, favorite hero, liability, interpersonal conflicts, and family dynamics, especially. Lankton and Lankton (1986) believe that metaphors should match the client's behavior patterns so he or she will unconsciously begin to work on conflicts and problems with the new resources offered. In order to identify the client's behavior patterns, a play diagnosis phase is needed.

Haley (1973) labeled Ericksonian psychotherapy as "uncommon therapy." For example, Erickson did not look upon bedwetting as a negative pathological issue; further, he had no interest in finding the unconscious meaning of the bedwetting, if any, nor did he care to understand the cause of the bedwetting. He used his technique by instructing the patient to perform consciously what could be the unconscious behavior (e.g., to wet his bed before he fell asleep each night). Through this technique, the patient took control of his symptom; and eventually the patient got tired of wetting his bed every night (O'Hanlon & Hexum 1990). In another case, Mills and Crowley (1986) treated a bedwetter by advising a child to pick out a special night when she would like to wet her pants. This technique is an ultra-short-term therapy used to remove the symptom and could become a model for the treatment of other problems, provided that a thorough diagnostic work-up was performed initially (i.e., play diagnosis and mental status evaluation). Recent clinical literature reveals that many sexually or physically abused children have been seen by therapists, school counselors, and pediatricians with presenting symptoms such as bedwetting, somatic complaints, and behavioral problems, rather than any complaints of abuse. Many of these children did not talk about any abuse, nor did their parents. The presence of abuse was discovered only through a diagnostic interview, where the diagnostician speculated that perhaps some of the behavioral and somatic disorders were, in fact, messages communicated by the child to others, and possibly having underlying causes. Therefore, by focusing all energies on the symptoms and the solution, and not completing a thorough diagnostic work-up, one may not discover that a child was suffering from abuse.

The drama of not discovering sexual abuse in children is blamed upon psychoanalytic speculation that a client's disclosure of incest is merely his or her projection and wishful thinking. If, in fact, the abuse is real, then the Ericksonian therapist may also take the blame for not asking or exploring the underlying disorder (e.g., incest) and merely focusing on the presenting symptoms (e.g., bedwetting). Again, it should be emphasized that the diagnosis is intended for the therapist's eyes only, and not for the client.

Some of Erickson's disciples believe that the psychodynamic theory and Ericksonian principles are not fundamentally reconcilable (Matthews, 1995). They argue that psychodynamically oriented therapy has an intrapsychic view and is pathology oriented, in contrast to the Ericksonian interactional and health orientation. However, in this chapter, by dividing the treatment into two segments— diagnosis and therapy—it is emphasized that while Ericksonian play therapy is in contrast to psychodynamic orientation, assessments or diagnosis could be performed using any techniques. Another important point is the fact that the thera-

pist should treat the *person,* and not the *diagnosis.* An individual is beyond his or her diagnosis.

Personality Theory

Erickson, unlike other practitioners who believe that personalities are formulated genetically or at a very young age, seemed to take the pragmatic stance that the human personality is mutable (O'Hanlon, 1987, p. 18).

Model of Psychopathology

Erickson did not focus on cause or etiology of human pathology and abnormal behavior. He did not create any theoretical basis for psychological development. He did not believe in many theories of human development and psychopathology; it seems that he did not feel that these theories were helpful in treatment. His writings are reminiscent of a statement once made about bedwetting: "There are many hypotheses about bedwetting, but none of them hold water."

O'Hanlon & Weiner-Davis (1989) mentioned that part of the difficulty in understanding Erickson is that "he had no theory—no theory of psychopathology, that is. He speculated very little on the origin of problems" (O'Hanlon & Weiner-Davis, 1989, p. 15). For Erickson, the symptom was neither right nor wrong, but rather a message from the patient's unconscious, a message that Erickson was only too glad to observe and utilize (Mills & Crowley 1986, p 49) Erickson did not hold the view that symptoms are necessarily the expressions of underlying problems or past traumas: "I think that the vast majority of habits developed by people tend to be habits based on habitual patterns of response, and so they are not necessarily symptomatic of deep traumatic experiences" (Rossi & Ryan, 1985, p. 21).

Erickson also believed that since normal behavior and growth are to be expected, symptoms and pathology are blockages of natural healthiness. Mills & Crowley (1986) confirmed that symptoms from an Ericksonian point of view are viewed as a result of "blocked resources" (the child's natural ability and potentials) rather than as manifestations of psychological or social pathology.

Regarding the symptom as a medium and message. Heller (Heller & Steele, 1986) assumed that all presenting problems and symptoms are really metaphors and contain a story about the true identity of the problem: "It is therefore the responsibility of the therapist to create metaphors that contain a story that contains the (possible) solutions. The metaphor is the message" (Heller & Steele, 1986).

Erickson did not have a formal theory as to the process by which problems arise and how psychopathology develops. The closest he came to such theorizing was in expressing his view of rigid behavior. He observed the rigidity in patients' beliefs and behavior and considered this pathological. As O'Hanlon (1987) said, "Where rigidity has been, he seems to be saying, let there be flexibility."

Goal/Cure

One of the most important elements of Erickson's psychotherapy is its naturalistic quality, meaning that the therapy should elicit the individual's natural abilities and potentials. Erickson believed that everybody reacts differently on the basis of his or her own experiences and background (Erickson, 1966). Nothing needs to be added from the outside, as all the answers are within (O'Hanlon, 1987).

Erickson felt that people are naturally capable of supporting and maintaining their mental health if permitted to do so. The trance, for example, is one such vehicle. Erickson mentioned that a trance is a natural potential in everybody, and one may experience it on a daily basis. He felt that psychotherapy and hypnosis could be implemented in a very informal way, integrating each into ordinary conversation. Ericksonian psychotherapy assumes that natural growth and healthy behavior are to be expected. Symptoms and psychopathology are considered forms of blockage of natural healthiness (O'Hanlon, 1987, p. 7). Symptomatic behavior may be blocked by relabeling the behavior, by overpowering and manipulating it, or by providing an ordeal that makes it more difficult for a child to continue the symptomatic behavior.

As the psychotherapeutic process continues, the patient discovers his or her potential, internal healing power, and resources, and utilizes all of these for the solution of the problem. Through the usage of metaphors and storytelling, the therapy enables a child to look into an inner world and find a solution within himself or herself. There is a certain amount of responsibility that a therapist needs to bear, such as the need, at times, to make decisions for the patient.

To provide a practical example of Ericksonian therapy, one may focus on the treatment of thumb sucking. Erickson treated a child with thumb-sucking problems by explaining to the child: "Now let us get one thing straight. That left thumb of yours is your thumb, that mouth of yours is your mouth, those front teeth of yours are your front teeth. I think you are entitled to do anything you want to with your thumb, with your mouth and with your teeth" (Zeig, 1980, p. 12). Once Erickson accepted, validated, and respected the patient's symptom, he proceeded to utilize the thumb-sucking behavior, but paradoxically prescribed its increase by advising the child to give his other fingers their rightful turn, "I think you really would like to give each of your fingers a proper turn." Of course, the child attempts the laborious task of allotting equal sucking time for all ten fingers and soon gives up the entire task of sucking (O'Hanlon & Hexum, 1990).

Another example is Erickson's treatment of a young man with low self-esteem and low self-confidence who had just taken a job in a bank. Erickson asked many questions about his work, taking special interest in mistakes he had made. Erickson mentioned "every time he made a mistake in his work, what interested me always was the procedure by which it was corrected—never the details of how he made the error" (Haley, 1985, Vol. 1 p. 83).

Haley (1963), as well as others, considered Erickson's work as "directive," meaning that the therapist's job is to get the patient to "do something." The therapist ought to expect change as inevitable. In addition, according to Erickson's point of view, patients' defects can become their assets. He strongly emphasized the positive, suggesting that whatever a patient divulges ought to be accepted, including symptoms such as pessimism, resistance, rigid ideas, and even delusion.

CASE FORMULATION AND TREATMENT GOALS

Any case formulation in this family required further diagnostic work-up, such as a play diagnosis session with Jason.* During play diagnosis, the child is encouraged to play with play material. The child is encouraged to use ego defense mechanisms such as projection, displacement, and symbolization with the aid of play materials, storytelling, and picture drawing. Through this process, one obtains knowledge about the child's self-image, family dynamics, fears, assets, problem-solving capacity, and interpersonal conflicts. The doll house becomes the child's house, and the events that take place in the doll house become the projection of a child's perceptions of his home and family. The child displaces his feelings onto the monster, dinosaur, cowboy, or Indian. Hence, the play materials become the representatives of the child's emotional state. The therapist, through the study and identification of the symbolic meaning of child's play, will speculate about what the child is experiencing in real life (Marvasti, 1994).

After play diagnosis was performed, it was speculated that Jason originally communicated his pain and dissatisfaction through temper tantrums, and later on it became a habit and was perpetuated. The discovery of the root and original cause of his pain was not essential, as it was never meant to be explained to Jason or his parents; nor was such insight a necessary element in changing the symptom. However, in child psychotherapy, it may be necessary for a therapist to have some knowledge about cause/effect relationships for the purposes of detecting any maltreatment or in order to perform milieu therapy. (For example, a child's poor self-image and isolative behavior may be due to his dyslexia. In this case, milieu therapy would attempt to change his regular class to a special education class and decrease his parents' expectations of his academic accomplishments.)

Play diagnosis revealed that Jason's original symptoms developed in reaction to losing his mother's care during her second and third pregnancy and depression. He was also upset over his mother's overprotectiveness as a reaction to the loss of her second child. This was evidenced in Jason's play diagnosis, where a monster would frequently arrive at a farmhouse and kidnap a baby. The parents became very concerned about losing their other children and would not allow them to play around the farm. The parents locked their children inside their rooms for their own protection, and the children remained "bored to death" in their loneliness. The therapist speculated that Jason is resentful of his mother's overprotection of him, having lost her second child to death.

Other negative elements that Jason perceived as difficult were his feelings of abandonment by his father after his parents' divorce. Also, pressure and encouragement from his father to be "masculine" and "not clingy" opposed Jason's needs for dependency/attachment toward his mother.

In psychotherapy with all three family members, a solution-oriented approach

---

*See "Orientation to the Text: The Case of Jason L.," p. 1.

was frequently utilized. Some of the principles of solution-focused therapy could be summarized as follows:

1. Characterize present and future orientation with well-defined goals.
2. Change is considered constant and inevitable: A Greek philosopher once said, "You can't step into the same river twice." The therapist, through verbal and nonverbal means, conveys to clients his or her surprise if the problem were to persist (O'Hanlon & Weiner-Davis, 1989 p. 35). The therapist seeks a small change and enlarges upon it, as it appears that small improvements can change the whole system (Haley, 1973, p. 34). This is dubbed by clinicians to be the ripple effect.
3. Always search for exceptions: Explore the times when the problem was not present. By eliciting and constructing the exceptions to the problem and encouraging the exceptions to occur more often, "the therapist helps the client develop a sense of control over what had seemed to be an insurmountable problem" (Walter & Peller, 1992 p. 14).
4. Consider the miracle question (De Shazer, 1988, p. 5): "If during the night, a miracle occurs and your problem disappears, what would you do differently?"
5. Utilize reframing and positive connotation: Change the viewing of the situation that is perceived as problematic (O'Hanlon & Weiner-Davis, 1989, p. 126). Therapists may ascribe positive intent to activity that was previously labeled problematic.

Ericksonian psychotherapy frequently uses solution-oriented therapy. In this arena, the trend is away from explanations, problems, and pathology, and toward solutions, competence, and capabilities (O'Hanlon & Weiner-Davis, 1989 p. 6.). As Minuchin (Minuchin & Fishman, 1981) mentioned, Erickson instructed his patients to explore alternate ways of organizing their experiences without exploring the etiology or dynamics of the dysfunction (p. 268). However, in psychotherapy with Jason's family, a list of problems was identified as a result of requirements from a third-party payer (medical insurance), which would not authorize payment for treatment without a complete disclosure of problems and diagnosis.

Following is the list of problems:

1. Incomplete mourning processes by both parents concerning the loss of their second child.
2. Mary's possible biological tendency for depression.
3. Mary's loneliness and fear of having a new partner, based on her statement that "the pain of losing someone is more than the pain of loneliness."
4. Emilio's need to reject his dependency on women. He also had feelings of inferiority due to his cultural background.
5. Jason's development of a rigid habit of temper tantrums at home.

6. Jason's perception of his parents' divorce as a traumatic event.
7. Jason's conflictual message sent by his parents; he perceived that his mother looked at him as a little, helpless child in need of overprotection. From his father, he got the impression that he should act more like a "man," more "masculine," and not cling to his mother.
8. Jason's attitude of being "bossy" and his need to be "in control."

TREATMENT DESCRIPTION

Playroom/Play Material and Frequency/Duration of Treatment

The playroom is an office with closets, a soft floor, washable wallpaper, and children's furniture with no sharp corners or edges; it is ideal if the playroom can be adjacent to the waiting room, so the child may be able to see his parents through an open door or windows, should he develop any separation anxiety. Play material may include a doll house, a doll family, and several dolls or puppets that represent different characters (i.e., monster, prince).

The therapist used a special puppet or doll as an older, wiser self, and eventually the therapist led Jason to manipulate the therapist's puppet in order to direct the story toward a solution for a happy ending. In each play session with Jason, the "older, wiser" doll was given to him to take home and return the following session. In the last session, Jason received the therapist's puppet as both a gift and a wiser companion. The frequency of treatment sessions with Jason was a weekly meeting for 12 weeks.

Treatment Stages and Specific Psychotherapeutic Strategies

Generally, in this type of therapy, the duration of treatment is not predictable; nor is it divided into stages. As Walter & Peller (1992) explained, the client will reveal through his or her behavior and feedback whether or not additional sessions are necessary. "When one approaches therapy one session at a time, there are no phases or stages. Every session is the first, every session is the last" (Walter & Peller, 1992 p. 141).

Ericksonian Play Therapy with Jason

The therapist spoke with Jason about what they planned to do together during a one-hour session: "We will have fun, and if you like stories, I know a lot of them, and we can read a couple of children's books together. There is also a doll house with dolls such as Superman, cowboys and Indians, and a monkey family. If you wish, we will play together."

While it is true that play diagnosis and play therapy frequently overlap one another, for the sake of simplicity, the first two sessions with Jason were considered purely play diagnosis, as the therapist encouraged the child to create stories to be acted out by toys and puppets and to answer to the therapist puppet's questions such as: "What is going on in this family?" "Why is the monkey child upset?" "What is the best thing that could happen to this doll?" "How will this family behave if all their problems are resolved overnight?" "Let's ask this monster to tell us about his good things," "Can we ask the monster what is making him angry?" "Where are this monster's parents?" and "Why don't they feed him so he wouldn't have to eat people?" During the play diagnosis the therapist was neither directive nor suggestive and did not contaminate the child's statement or play. However, in the play therapy sessions, the therapist became active, structuring the play session and constantly reframing the negative statements or events that happened to the dolls or the protagonist of the story. The therapist actively explained the positive aspects of a painful experience and utilized the doll's symptoms for the purposes of transforming them into positives or resolutions.

In one of the sessions, Jason played with a family of monkey dolls who resided on a tree branch; but, frequently, when a storm blew and the tree became shaky, the branch broke and the monkeys fell to the ground. Eventually, everyone found one another and again congregated on one branch. On one occasion, though, the father monkey decided to leave the family and reside on a different tree, far away from the family. All of the other monkeys missed him and periodically visited him, and the kids felt sad when they returned to their mother's tree. The monkey child missed his father.

The therapist felt that the issue of divorce and separation from the father was still a traumatic event for the child (who was projecting his feelings onto the monkey child).

On the basis of this assumption, the therapist's puppet, created a story about a village of divorced families, with all of the divorced fathers living in a neighboring village, while the mothers and children resided together in another village. "During Christmas time, *both villages were beautifully decorated.* On all special days, such as birthdays and Thanksgiving, the children had two parties, one in each village. Santa brought them presents in both villages. The kids eventually realized that *conditions had improved.*" (In this section, the italicized words indicate interspersed suggestions.)

   The therapist redefined and reframed the divorce from a child's point of view. "Now I am welcomed in two houses and I can have twice as many toys to keep in daddy's and mommy's homes."

During the fifth session, now within a doll house setting, Jason played out a scenario where a doll (representing Jason) suffered from mood swings. His feelings and self-image were constantly affected by the comments and behavior of others. He had no stable self-identity and at times felt bad because the mother doll told him he was "bad." Conversely, he felt as if he was on top of the world when his babysitter complimented him on his beautiful hair and told him that the cat appreciated his feedings. The therapist puppet continually tried to uncover the positive assets of the little doll, but when asked about any interests, hobbies, and amusements, Jason answered, "Nothing."

The therapist then introduced a new doll into the house, named "Wise Doll." He sat everyone down and instructed them to "be quiet and listen."

Wise Doll told a story about a lonely leaf which fell before the mercy of the wind, a wind which blew the leaf in any direction it chose. Sometimes, a strong wind would blow it to the ground, and the leaf would smash against the ground and cry; and sometimes a nice breeze would lift the leaf to the tops of the trees, enabling it to see all the beauty around it.

After a while, the leaf grew tired of being blown around uncontrollably. The leaf thought to itself that *there must be some way to take control.* The leaf was tired of being a passive leaf, allowing for manipulation by the winds. *Thus, it wished to become a tree, a strong tree,* which could divert the wind's direction. The leaf attempted to *change its situation for the better.* Suddenly, it noticed a small stem growing at its base. The leaf thought that if it held its stem straight up and stuck it into the ground, it would grow up to become a tree. After some time, a strong wind blew by, grasping the leaf and pushing it down into the ground. But the leaf firmly held onto its stem which became embedded into the ground and remained there. Gradually, this stem began to root. Eventually, *it became a big, strong tree* with lots of branches, fruit and leaves. *Now, this big, strong trunk of a tree* was *able to direct and divert the wind.*

Wise Doll completed his story to an attentive audience of dolls in the doll house. A few even shut their eyes, so they could listen to the story better. This little doll fell asleep for a few moments, awoke and gazed into a mirror, and *found within himself strength, happiness, power* and a name. He *stood up strong and straight,* his two legs firmly pressed upon the ground and called himself "a tree." *He realized his value,* telling himself: *"I am nice, beautiful, and smart. People love me and enjoy being with me."*

(In this story, the italicized words indicate interspersed suggestions.)

Several tasks were given to Jason and his mother during different therapy sessions. One of Jason's homework assignments was to obtain an axe and some wood so that he could chop wood at home every day after school for half an hour. His mother was instructed to watch him as he chopped wood for the fireplace. The goal for the chopping of wood was to utilize Jason's energy for a constructive purpose (rather than for a temper tantrum) and to illustrate to Mary that Jason was not a baby anymore and could gather firewood for the family's winter fuel. Also, Jason learned that he was capable of holding his mother's complete attention by doing positive work, such as chopping wood for their fireplace.

In his mother's presence, Jason also was given the task that every Monday, Wednesday, and Friday, when he came home from school, between 3 and 4 P.M., he was to throw all of his books onto the floor and make a lot of noise; and the next day he would have to pick them all up and put them back on the shelves. The mother was instructed to stay in the kitchen during this time and cook food for the children. Jason was instructed that he could throw his books only on the three designated days per week, but that he should continue to do this, even when he didn't feel like it.

Jason's conflict with both parents was addressed. The message impressed upon him by his mother was that he was a little, helpless child in need of her overprotection. The message from his father was to be a "man," "masculine", and not "clinging" to his mother. In therapy, this double message was evidenced in the doll house session, where the therapist reframed it and left the doll to reach its own conclusion that it was best to be a human, and that a human being sometimes likes to cling to someone and sometimes wants to be independent and self-reliant—both are okay for human beings. Then the therapist puppet told a story to the dolls gathered in the dollhouse:

> Once upon a time, a thousand years ago in a village, there lived a couple who wished to have a child. The mother wanted a girl with long hair as beautiful as her own, and the father wanted a boy with big muscles; so they argued with each other all the time. Eventually the wife delivered a baby whose body was one-half boy and one-half girl. The baby grew up slowly and was confused about his or her identity. When the child was with the father, he pretended to be a boy and flexed his muscles so he could please his father; and when the child was with the mother, she pretended to be a girl so she could please her mother. Eventually the child became sick and tired of being forced to be a boy only some of the time and to be a girl only some of the time. So the child went to the village magician and asked him for help.

The story ended on a positive note, with the magician meeting the child's parents and convincing them that their child was a *human being* and possessed the characteristics and qualities of both males and females.

Another technique used with Jason was the utilization of his symptoms. The parents' original complaints about him were his tendencies to be "bossy" and to "want to be in control." The therapist told Jason that it was not fair that he was bossing around only his sister, because in his home there were two kids, Carla and himself. He was instructed to boss himself as well and "to be in charge of both kids," so that if one had a temper tantrum, Jason needed to help control it. In this manner, Jason was advised to utilize his control issue to boss himself and his temper tantrums.

The therapist persistently looked for "exceptions." For instance, he inquired of Jason, "Do you throw your books in anger every day or are there days that you don't?" "What happens differently on days in which you come home in a good mood?" The therapist then urged Jason to follow that same activity every day. He asked Jason what his mother did that was different on those days, and "What should you do to give your mother the impression that you can be trusted and she doesn't need to worry about you?"

In regards to Jason's reaction to his parents' divorce, it was explained to both him and his parents that it is almost universal for children to wish for their parents' reconciliation. It is also normal for a child to miss the departing parent and to be upset. Jason and his parents then were given homework—to discover the positive changes after the divorce. Jason was asked what he would do differently if his parents were not divorced. He replied that he could spend more time with his father. Hence, the therapist recommended that Emilio increase his contact with Jason.

Jason also felt that his parents were abandoning him because of his bad behavior. Although he was not able to express this verbally, he demonstrated it during a play session with a family doll. On the basis of his feelings, a story was crafted with the same metaphorical conflict:

Long, long ago, there existed a volcanic mountain called Wawa, which was located not too far off from a beautiful village. The villagers spent many happy occasions with Wawa, especially during the spring and summer, when Wawa had beautiful flowers and fruit trees. But Wawa had a problem. Sometimes it exploded and transformed into a volcano that would spit fire and hurt people. Soon, many of the villagers moved away from Wawa. Eventually, Wawa realized that many of the visitors with whom it enjoyed spending time had left because of Wawa's exploding. The volcanic mountain had found itself all alone.

Wawa grew upset and didn't know how to control its temper, its fiery volcano. One day, Wawa asked a wise bird what to do. The bird told Wawa, "Look inside yourself; the answer is there." Wawa looked inside itself and saw nothing more than the fiery blazes of the volcano.

On another occasion, a wise cloud was passing over Wawa, when Wawa stopped it and asked the same question as it did the bird. The cloud repeated the bird's reply: "The answer is within you."

Wawa began to think long and hard about what the bird and cloud had said. Eventually, this was all it could think about.

The meaning of bird's and cloud's advice dawned upon Wawa one cold winter. All around, the village was very cold, and people were unable to leave their homes because it was so cold outside.

Then, finally, Wawa realized what the bird and cloud meant by looking within itself to find the answer. Wawa discovered how it could warm up the entire village—by allowing the heated material inside it to bubble up but not spill over into the village. So as the cold wind passed over Wawa toward the village, Wawa would first heat it up, allowing the village to receive warm air.

The warm weather enabled the villagers to get out, and, gradually, they felt comfortable nearing Wawa. The closer they came to it, the warmer and more comfortable they felt.

Wawa was no longer alone. As the villagers moved closer to it, it began to smile and became happy. The wise bird reported the change in Wawa to other villages, and the other villagers soon returned home to Wawa and their own village.

Wawa thanked the wise bird and wise cloud for their advice. It realized it had the power to change the things that bothered others into the things that helped them. Wawa believed that everyone has within himself or herself the ability to solve problems.

Solution-Focused Psychotherapy with Mary

Mary was evaluated from a psychiatric point of view; her family history was obtained, and it was revealed that she suffered from depression and could respond to antidepressive medications. The therapist prescribed an antidepressive medication for Mary and explained to her its side effects. He also added that, every month, several of his patients reported to him that they had substantially improved by being on this medication. The therapist explained to Mary that the medication may give her more motivation, energy, interest, and desire to explore and discover her positive qualities, potentials, and assets.

During the initial psychotherapy session, Mary sometimes daydreamed. Rather than considering this as a kind of "resistance," the therapist utilized the daydreaming in a positive way, talking about Mary's capacity to create elaborate and rich fantasies, which the therapist considered a positive quality. He connected the capacity for imagination as a basic foundation for creative writing and innovation. Also, he suggested she use this capacity to fantasize about her success and victory over depression. In the same session, the therapist also recommended: "At every session for the first ten minutes, you will fantasize about a beautiful memory, and I will be quiet, fantasizing myself. Also, for the last five minutes of our session, you will fantasize about a beautiful memory, and I will be quiet, fantasizing myself."

Mary had remained focused on her multiple episodes of depression during the last 15 years. But the therapist attempted to direct her attention to how she was able to overcome these episodes of depression, repeatedly asking, "How did you resolve it then? Let's use the same technique now."

The therapist asked Mary about her attitudes or behavior toward Jason on days when he had neither a temper tantrum nor conflict. "What do you do differently?" the therapist asked. Mary was then instructed to maintain that same positive attitude toward Jason, even on days when he experienced behavioral problems. Mary was also asked how she had been able to stop Jason from throwing his temper tantrums before. Mary responded that, on occasion, she had been successful in keeping Jason from acting out by, for example, distracting his attention to something exciting as soon as he returned home from school. The therapist reminded her of her achievements in the past and directed her to utilize her potential and problem-solving capacity. She was directed to focus on the solutions rather than on the problem; to focus on her superiority, not her shortcomings; to focus on what she knew, rather than on what she didn't.

The individual session with Mary revealed that she was still mourning the loss of her father, and that she had fears that her children would also die and leave her. She also felt that any future partner that she might have would eventually abandon her. Apparently, the death of her newborn baby and the divorce of her husband increased Mary's preoccupation with loss and her fears of abandonment. This issue prevented Mary from finding a partner after the divorce, although she wished and fantasized about it. In one of the sessions, the therapist gave a homework assignment for Mary to participate in a church-related singles' dance party. Mary admitted her desire to go to this party, but during the next session, she informed the therapist that she was reluctant to go because of "being tired." The therapist aided Mary in overcoming this problem by planning to have Emilio pick her up at her home at a designated time and drop her off at the church door. Emilio was to then drive back to the therapist's office and inform him of the success of his mission.

In an individual session with Mary, the therapist was openly direct with her, encouraging her as well as giving her education and information, such as the time and place for the dance party. Mary mentioned that she needed to have a partner "for the sake of my children, if not for myself." The therapist confirmed that having a partner might be important for her children, as it would aid in the child-rearing process. Also, the therapist talked about his personal experience when he was in the military service in the Middle East. He was assigned to guard the border of his old country for defensive purposes. He found that his commander always put two soldiers together in one foxhole at the battlefront. These two soldiers were able to lean on each other when they were frightened. One would sleep while the other remained on guard; one would use the other's shoulder for crying on if needed; and also, the two would put their minds together. The therapist related another, metaphoric story about two slender branches of a tree that were next to each other, and when a storm came, they were very shaky and almost broken by the wind. However, when the next storm came, they started to entwine with one another. They became stronger—more resistant and stable—together under the threat of a storm.

Mary's pain and sadness, resulting from losing Emilio, were considered very normal behavior and were framed positively, "Attachment is pleasurable so detachment should be painful. If there was no pain, then you were not attached at all."

Mary gradually became less overprotective and overworrying of Jason. She was aided by the realization that there had been many days in the past in which she had trusted Jason and had even allowed him to take care of Carla. These days, Mary and Jason have a great time without conflict or temper tantrums. Mary learned during a therapy session that she was in fact capable of relating to Jason positively, considering him a healthy boy with a certain amount of potential to protect himself and to take care of himself independently.

During a session, the therapy explained to Mary that her worrying during Jason's infancy was as normal as that of any other mother with a pregnancy complication. She was reminded that every time a pediatrician had evaluated her child's health and reassured her, Mary felt delighted and believed that she had a healthy son. She was directed to reexperience that feeling, and, if needed, to consult with Jason's pediatrician. Mary was reminded about her capacity to utilize a reassuring statement and instill a delightful feeling in herself. This was labeled as a valuable psychological asset that Mary was to use more often.

Mary was encouraged to look at any small piece of improvement in Jason as if it were a kind of reassurance from her pediatrician, so that she could instill a happy, safe, and tranquilizing mood upon herself.

Psychotherapy with Emilio

The individual session with Emilio revealed that he had some feelings of inferiority regarding his ancestry, as the son of a Mexican immigrant, and therefore had difficulty considering himself an equal to the American white male. The therapist obtained information from a librarian about Hispanic heroes and their accomplishments. He gave Emilio a homework assignment to read a book about Zapata, a Mexican hero, and to study the richness of Hispanic literature, language, music, and civilization. Individual sessions also revealed that Emilio felt rejected by Mary after the death of their second child. He felt that he was "not like a man" and that Mary did not give him enough attention and was not taking care of his needs. It was obvious that Mary was very depressed after the death of her child and was unable to give enough nurturing to her husband or to her son. The pregnancy was also somewhat traumatic for Emilio, as Mary stayed in bed for several weeks due to complications. In evaluating Emilio, it became evident that the girlfriend with whom he was involved while married was a substitute for the baby that he had lost, and possibly for the wife that he had lost to depression. Emilio explained that, during that time, he needed "something or someone who could decrease the pain of losing a child. Later on, Mary ignored me totally, no attention or caring. She was in bed all day, couldn't have any eye contact with me, was crying and was very bitter." It was also clear that Emilio still had positive feelings for Mary, but he was afraid of her depression, as he felt that Mary's depression was a form of rejection. He felt that he married her to bring happiness to her, and could not comprehend how she could get depressed while he was a hard-working man, a good provider, and always very kind to her. Emilio was given important information about depression and how it can affect relationships. The therapist explained that depression is considered a consequence of biochemical changes in the brain that produce a lack of energy, motivation, and interest. The person becomes withdrawn and may have no energy to give. Many partners of depressed individuals may interpret this as a sign of rejection and lack of love.

It seemed evident that when Emilio was complaining about Jason with comments such as, "He's too clingy," he really was talking about himself. He was referring to his own clinging need, his need for dependency, which he had projected onto Jason. Also, he battled this intense need for dependency and his longing for belonging and attachment by being very masculine, in control, and somewhat bold. He attempted to control his son's clingy behavior toward Mary because his son reminded him of himself, and of his need for dependency and attachment to a female. (None of these diagnostic speculations was ever shared with Emilio or Mary.) The therapist attempted to "reframe" the definition of "being a man" and being "masculine" by defining that "a real man, a strong man, is one who becomes aware of his normal needs for dependency and affection and breaks the stereotyped fallacy of sexism and gender difference." The therapist also explained part of the training of Persian elite soldiers. These soldiers are instructed to fistfight with each other as a group in an arena-like field. At the end of any fight, white sheets are brought to the arena to dry the bleeding bodies, and all soldiers traditionally hug each other and cry for some time as they hold on to one another. "While they are crying, they soothe and cling to each other like small children to their mothers, and none of them is ashamed of it as the response is encouraged by their commanders and teachers."

Psychotherapy with Mary and Emilio

Jason's parents were seen together for three sessions. Mary related how her depression made her miserable and left her incapable of making any decisions. She felt tired all the time and blamed herself for the inability to give anything to Jason and Emilio. The therapist reframed her inability to give by explaining that the depressed brain is focusing all of it's mental energy on fighting the depression and has nothing left over for such things as decision making and caring for others, which in themselves require a good deal of mental energy. The therapist suggested that, instead, others should be caring for the depressed person so that all mental energy could be utilized to fight the depression. He gave an example of how primitive cultures dealt with illness. The entire tribe would take over the duties and responsibilities of the ill person thereby allowing him or her to concentrate his or her energies on getting well.

In one of the sessions, in a symbolic manner, both worked through their incomplete mourning processes. This occurred at a time when the family cat had died, so the therapist asked Mary to bring in a stuffed animal that resembled the cat, and he also asked Emilio to bring in something similar. Emilio chose a picture of the cat, cut it out, and brought it to the therapist's office. Both parents became tearful. The therapist, focusing on spirituality and fate, told them that since they both were practicing Catholics, they should "accept the fate" and consider the destiny of losing the child to Heaven. Both parents were in tears and held each other, hugged each other, and cried. Both then prayed and accepted that they had lost the child to Heaven. They agreed to focus the rest of their lives on the pleasure of parenting the two children who remained with them.

The therapist also attempted to utilize the healing power of *ritual and ceremony* by instructing both parents to put the stuffed animal and Emilio's picture of the cat inside the shoebox, burying it underground. Both cried, said Goodbye, held each other, and started to focus on the ways in which the lives of their children could improve.

OUTCOME

A follow-up visit after six months revealed:

1. Emilio felt that he had reached a closure regarding the loss of his second child and had completed the mourning process.
2. However, Mary's feelings of sadness and pain, in response to the loss of a second child, still remained. "Although it is a little less now, it is still very devastating to me," she commented. On the basis of her statement, the mourning process was deemed as yet incomplete. The therapist speculated that there had been multiple losses in Mary's life since her adolescence and that the grieving process may take a relatively long time to be completed. The ther-

apist also held himself responsible for any failure of therapeutic goals and began to reevaluate his technique; as Walter & Peller (1992, p. 41) observed, there is no one right way or best way to help people. "The client response is only feedback and merely means that you need to do something different."

3. Mary's depression subsided. She felt the depression was alleviated primarily by the medication.

4. Mary had never attended a singles' dance club. Apparently Emilio would give her a ride to a different dance club, where they would eat and dance together for hours, without talking about any subject except their children. This ritual has continued on a weekly basis.

5. Jason's temper tantrums and his book-throwing subsided. Mary reported that since she started to demonstrate the behavior and attitude that she had on "Jason's good days," his behavioral problem (often present when he returned home from school) substantially decreased. She also reported that after some time, Jason gradually forgot to throw his books on the floor as instructed by the therapist. "He once said he doesn't need to do it anymore because he thinks his therapist's instruction to 'throw the book for fun' was to prevent him from throwing books in anger," Mary said. "Now that he doesn't throw books in anger anymore he doesn't need to do it for fun either. He would rather spend all his time splitting wood for the fireplace."

6. Jason's bold and assertive behavior in the presence of his father and his clinging and withdrawn behavior in the presence of his mother both decreased. This happened after Emilio had grown comfortable with his own normal desires for dependency and attachment toward a woman and Mary had stopped overprotecting Jason and overworrying about him.

7. Emilio's feelings of inferiority regarding his cultural background were no longer present and he denied ever having "this kind of feeling." He began studying the Mexican culture, became very interested in Latin American art and literature, joined a Mexican-American club, and developed interest in the investigation of his roots. He eventually traced his genealogy back three generations.

8. Jason reported no incident of being hit by Mary "even when I do the worst thing in the world." Since Emilio spent more time with Jason, his feelings of abandonment by his father decreased.

9. Emilio discovered, reframed, and accepted his normal longing for an attachment to Mary. Emilio decided to return to Mary, and they remarried. Both eagerly invited their therapist to attend their wedding ceremony. The therapist participated in this event with no reservations in regard to seeing his patients in a "nonclinical" setting. (Erickson sometimes invited his patients to his home and introduced them to others who could be of help. At times, he also arranged to meet his patients at a restaurant for dinner and conversation [Haymond, 1995, p. 38].)

10. Mary's fear of abandonment did not substantially decrease ("I only trust Emilio 80 percent."). However, once her depression subsided, her self-esteem and confidence increased. She felt that, as a woman, she was "good enough," and if Emilio left her again it would be because of his problem, not hers.

CONCLUSION

Ericksonian play therapy is a technique that is very much individualized and reliant upon the therapist's flexibility and innovation. In this modality of therapy, play diagnosis is necessary. The therapist needs to discover the child's potential, resources, assets, interpersonal issues, and his or her favorite hero through play diagnosis.

Transference is discouraged but, if developed, may be utilized in the same way as symptoms. Countertransference may develop, and the therapist, without sharing it with the client, may learn something about himself or herself and may utilize it for his or her personal maturity and professional growth. The values of professional supervision, and of obtaining a second opinion in the discovery of countertransference, cannot be minimized.

The Ericksonian play therapy technique also utilizes the presenting symptoms in order to resolve them, relying upon the potential and the solution rather than on sickness and pathology. Emphasis is on the present and the future rather than the past. Insight regarding the origin of symptoms is not needed for change, and the unconscious is considered an arena of potential and creativity, rather than a dark closet full of skeletons and perverted materials.

Although play therapy can be invaluable for many young patients, not all behavioral problems of children can be corrected through this technique. Similarly, Ericksonian play therapy may not be suitable for every psychiatric patient. This is a therapeutic technique and modality that should be modified to match the client rather than attempting to mold the patient to fit the technique.

In the case of Jason L.'s family, a short-term, solution-oriented psychotherapy was conducted. Metaphors, storytelling, paradoxical intervention, and symptom description were used in helping Jason overcome his behavioral problems. Fairy tales and anecdotal material containing indirect suggestions, interspersal statements, and refraction were used. Jason was able to enter into a natural trance, and he allowed for a metaphorical story to bypass his conscious mind and touch his unconscious. The healing power of the child and his parents was relied upon, and treatment was based upon the fact that people had a capacity to overcome their conflicts.

Symptoms were utilized, and the positive aspects of behavior, assets, and potentials of all family members were tapped. Reframing, persuasion, direct suggestion, and task assignment were used with parents; they were directed to look at their potentials and assets rather than at losses and old injuries. The therapist used his self as a therapeutic tool, by explaining some of his life occurrences and relaying anecdotal examples of his personal experiences. The therapist, by being optimistic and solution oriented, became an example and a model for both parents.

As all stories and fairy tales that are used in this therapy end happily, eventually Jason L.'s family also entered into a state of success in overcoming their despair through the healing power of their minds, and they lived happily ever after. . . .

BIBLIOGRAPHY

De Shazer, S. (1988). *Clues: Investigating solutions in brief therapy.* New York: Norton.

Erickson, M.H. (1966). *Advanced psychotherapy* (audiotape). Des Plaines, IL: The American Society of Clinical Hypnosis.

Erickson, M.H., & Rossi, E.L. (1979). *Hypnotherapy: An exploratory casebook.* New York: Irvington.

Erickson, M.H. (1959/1980). Naturalistic techniques of hypnosis. In E. Rossi (Ed.), *The collected papers of Milton H. Erickson on hypnosis. Vol. I. The nature of hypnosis and suggestion* (pp. 168–176). New York: Irvington.

Erickson, M.H. (1983, February). Quotation in *NYSEPH Newsletter, 1*(2):3.

Erickson, M., & Rossi, E. (1976/1980). Two-level communication and the microdynamics of trance and suggestion. In E. Rossi (Ed.), *The collected papers of Milton H. Erickson on Hypnosis. Vol. I. The nature of hypnosis and suggestion* (pp. 430–451). New York: Irvington.

Haymond, P.J. (1995). Ericksonian approaches to curiosity in the treatment of incest and sexual abuse survivors. In S. Lankton & J. Zeig (Eds.), *Difficult contexts for therapy* (pp. 37–49). New York: Brunner/Mazel.

Haley, J. (1963). *Strategies of psychotherapy.* New York: Grune & Stratton.

Haley, J. (1973). *Uncommon therapy.* New York: Norton.

Haley, J. (1985). *Conversation with Milton H. Erickson, M.D. (3 vols.).* New York: Triangle.

Heller, S., & Steele, T. (1986). *There's no such thing as hypnosis.* Phoenix: Falcon Press.

Lankton, S., & Lankton, C. (1986). *Enchantment and intervention in family therapy,* New York: Brunner/Mazel.

Marvasti, J.A. (1989). Play therapy with sexually abused children. In S. Sgroi (Ed.), *Vulnerable population sexual abuse treatment for children, adult survivors, offenders, and persons with mental retardation (Vol. 2,* pp. 1–41). Lexington, MA: Lexington Books.

Marvasti, J.A. (1992). Psychotherapy with abused children and adolescents. In J.R. Brandell (Ed.), *Counter-transference in psychotherapy with children and adolescents* (pp. 191–214). Northvale, NJ.: Jason Aronson Inc.

Marvasti, J.A. (1994). Play diagnosis and play with child victims of incest. In C. Schaefer & K. O'Connor (Eds.), *Handbook of play therapy, Volume Two, Advances and Innovations* (pp. 319–348). New York: Wiley.

Mills, J.C., & Crowley, R. (1986). *Therapeutic metaphors for children and the child within.* New York: Brunner/Mazel.

Minuchin, S., & Fishman, C. (1981). *Family therapy techniques.* Cambridge, MA: Harvard University Press.

O'Hanlon, W.H. (1987). *Taproots: Underlying principles of Milton Erickson's therapy and hypnosis.* New York: Norton.

O'Hanlon, W.H., & Hexum, A.L. (1990). *An uncommon casebook. The complete clinical work of Milton H. Erickson, M.D.* New York: Norton.

O'Hanlon, W., & Weiner-Davis, M. (1989). *In search of solutions: A new direction in psychotherapy.* New York: Norton.

Otani, A. (1989). Integrating Milton H. Erickson's hypnotherapeutic techniques into general counseling and psychotherapy, *Journal of Counseling & Development, 68* (Nov/Dec): 203–207.

Pearce, S.S. (1986). *Flash of insight, Metaphor and narrative in therapy,* Boston: Allyn and Bacon.

Rossi, E., & Ryan, M. (1985). *Life reframing in hypnosis.* New York: Irvington.

Sharpe, F.A. (1980). Indirect hypnotic therapy. In Richie Herink (Ed.), *The psychotherapy handbook.* New York: Meridian Books.

Walter, J., & Peller, J. (1992). *Becoming solution-focused in brief therapy.* New York: Brunner/Mazel.

Zeig, J.K. (1980). *A teaching seminar with Milton H. Erickson.* New York: Brunner/Mazel.

Zeig, J.K. (1985). *Experiencing Erickson: An introduction to the man and his work.* New York: Brunner/Mazel.

Zeig, J.K. (1987). Therapeutic patterns of Ericksonian influence communication. In J.K. Zeig (Ed.), *The evolution of psychotherapy* (pp. 392–409). New York: Brunner/Mazel.

CHAPTER 11

Adlerian Play Therapy

TERRY KOTTMAN

Jason walked into my playroom, looked around, sat down on the floor, and stared at me, as if to say, "Well, what now, lady?"* I said, "This is our playroom, and in here you can do many of the things you want to." He replied, "And nothing you want me to do." He walked over to the shelves, picked up a small tiger, brandished it in my face, and said, "This is Growl. He's the tiger nobody can tell what to do. GRRRRRRR!!!"

INTRODUCTION

Adlerian play therapy is an integration of the concepts and strategies of Individual Psychology with the rationale, materials, and techniques of play therapy (Kottman, 1992, 1993, 1994, 1995; Kottman & Johnson, 1993; Kottman & Warlick, 1989, 1990). In order to understand this approach to play therapy, the counselor must have a working knowledge of the basic tenets of Individual Psychology, the psychological theory developed by Alfred Adler (Adler, 1930/1963, 1931/1958; Dinkmeyer, Dinkmeyer, & Sperry, 1987; Manaster & Corsini, 1982; Sweeney, 1989).

Personality Theory

Proponents of Individual Psychology believe that people are inherently social beings who are motivated by the need to belong (Ansbacher & Ansbacher, 1956; Dinkmeyer, Dinkmeyer, & Sperry, 1987). From this theoretical framework, all behavior has a purpose or goal (Adler, 1927/1954, 1930; Dreikurs & Soltz, 1964). People are creative, and they have the capacity to make decisions for themselves about their attitudes, feelings, and behaviors in order to move themselves toward their goals (Adler, 1930; Ansbacher & Ansbacher, 1956, Manaster & Corsini, 1982). They make these choices based on their own subjective interpretation of events and relationships, rather than on the actual facts (Ansbacher & Ansbacher, 1956; Beames, 1992).

---

*See "Orientation to the Text: The Case of Jason L.," p. 1.

Formation of the Personality

According to Adlerian theory, the following issues are essential in the formation of each individual's personality: (1) people have a need to belong; (2) people move toward goals; (3) people are creative and unique; and (4) people experience life from a subjective perspective.

People Have a Need to Belong

Adlerians believe that each person has a need to belong and to gain significance (Dinkmeyer, Dinkmeyer, & Sperry, 1987; Sweeney, 1989). Based on this desire to belong, each child examines his or her family to decide how best to fit into the family. The very young child observes family members' actions and attitudes toward him or her and toward other people and begins to make judgments about how to earn love and respect and about the rules of relationships and life. The primary foci of these observations are the family atmosphere and the family constellation (Dewey, 1971; Dinkmeyer, Dinkmeyer, & Sperry, 1989). The parents' relationship, the parents' attitudes toward discipline and parenting, and the parents' lifestyles are all factors in the family atmosphere (Dewey, 1971; Griffith & Powers, 1984).

> Family constellation consists of the personality traits of each member of the family, the emotional connections among various members, the dominance or submission of different members, the size of the family, age differences among the children, the gender of the children, sibling subsets, and the birth order (Kottman, 1995, p. 135).

From these observations of the family atmosphere and family constellation, the child comes to conclusions about self, others, and the world. By the time the child is six or seven years old, he or she has developed a lifestyle and specific goals for living based on these judgments. This lifestyle is the person's general orientation to life, a plan for gaining significance and belonging (Ansbacher & Ansbacher, 1956; Dinkmeyer, Dinkmeyer, & Sperry, 1987).

The child acts as if the convictions that make up his or her lifestyle are a true, unbiased picture of the world. Each individual bases his or her decisions about behavior on these perceptions and judgments, using a kind of private logic that may not be accessible or comprehensible to others (Manaster & Corsini, 1982; Sweeney, 1989).

If the child does not see a way to belong in the family in a positive way, he or she will find a way to belong in a negative way (Dreikurs & Soltz, 1964; Kottman, 1995). He or she can develop either a constructive, "useful" lifestyle or a destructive, "useless" one (Ansbacher & Ansbacher, 1956; Dreikurs & Soltz, 1964).

> In most families, by the time the child is 6 or 7, the entire family has a fixed idea of who the child is and how the child behaves. These expectations—by both family members and the child himself or herself—constitute a psychological "box" in which the child lives. This box can define who the child is and what

the child does, becoming boundaries of the child's lifestyle. The box can be positive or negative, but in either case, it is usually confining to the child. (Kottman, 1995, pp. 10–11)

In Adlerian play therapy, it is the therapist's job to discover children's lifestyles and explore their private logic. By coming to understand children's "boxes," the therapist can help them make conscious choices about what parts of their lifestyles are useful to them and what parts they would like to change. After they have begun to alter their perceptions of themselves, others, and the world, they can learn new ways of gaining significance and interacting with others (Kottman, 1992, 1993, 1994, 1995).

Another facet of the need for belonging, according to the tenets of Individual Psychology, is social interest (Ansbacher & Ansbacher, 1956). Social interest is a sense of solidarity with other people and a feeling of belonging in the community of human beings (Dinkmeyer, Dinkmeyer, & Sperry, 1989; Manaster & Corsini, 1982). Adler (1927/1954, 1930, 1931/1958) believed that children are born with an innate capacity to learn this feeling of connection to others. Without nurturing and education designed to enhance this innate tendency, however, children may not develop social interest. Adler (1930) suggested that the development of social interest is "the barometer of the child's normality" (p. 11).

Many of the children referred to play therapy seem to have limited social interest (Kottman, 1995). They are mainly concerned with themselves and may not be interested in or have the skills for connecting with others. Quite frequently, these children have not learned how to form positive attachments with their parents, siblings, other family members, teachers, or other children.

In Adlerian play therapy, one responsibility of the therapist is to enhance social interest (Kottman, 1995). By building a relationship with the child, the play therapist can begin to foster the child's attachment to one other human. The hope is that eventually, through playing out nurturing scenarios and playing with another child in the playroom, the child will generalize this attachment to others. In parent consultation sessions, the Adlerian play therapist teaches the parent(s) specific strategies for encouraging the child and for teaching the child how to connect with the parents and with others (Kottman, 1995).

People Move toward Goals

Adlerians believe that the primary motivating force for human beings is the movement toward goals or purposes (Dinkmeyer, Dinkmeyer, & Sperry, 1989; Manaster & Corsini, 1982). According to Adler (1930, 1931/1958), all behavior is goal directed and purposive. In order to understand the person and his or her behavior, it is necessary to understand the goal of the behavior. Many times, the person is not aware of his or her own goals or of the striving toward those goals, and by helping the client gain an enhanced awareness of the goals of his or her behavior, the counselor can increase the client's capacity for making informed decisions.

Dreikurs and Soltz (1964) classified the goals of children who are feeling discouraged and experiencing problem behaviors in four categories: attention, power, revenge, and proving inadequacy. By examining children's behaviors, their responses to correction, and other people's reactions to their behaviors, the counselor can discover the goals of discouraged children's behaviors (Dinkmeyer & McKay, 1989; Dreikurs & Soltz, 1964).

Since most of the children referred to play therapy are discouraged, the Adlerian play therapist explores these dynamics to discover children's purposes (Kottman, 1993, 1994, 1995). When the therapist understands the goals of children's behaviors, he or she can help them to examine these goals and decide if they want to continue to pursue them or not.

If children choose to strive toward other, more positive goals of behavior, the counselor can help them to learn and practice new and constructive attitudes and behaviors. Dinkmeyer and McKay (1989) defined positive goals of behavior as (1) attention, involvement, and contribution; (2) autonomy and self-responsibility; (3) justice and fairness; and (4) avoiding conflict and accepting other people's opinions and beliefs. One goal of Adlerian play therapy is to move children from the destructive, discouraged goals of behavior to these constructive, encouraged ones (Kottman, 1995).

Many of the children who come to play therapy seem to have the goal of attaining power (Kottman, 1995). These children believe that they count and are significant only when they can be in control—of themselves and of other people (Dinkmeyer & McKay, 1989). In the author's clinical experience, children whose goal is power usually come from one of three distinct backgrounds, characterized by their (1) having too little power, (2) having too much power, or (3) having families in which the children perceive everything as being out of control. Adlerian play therapists must consider these circumstances in designing play therapy interventions and parent consultation strategies (Kottman, 1995).

People Are Creative and Unique

Each person has creative abilities to facilitate movement toward the future attainment of his or her goals (Manaster & Corsini, 1982). This creativity contributes to the unique quality of each individual.

> This uniqueness is seen to be the expression of a fundamental, mysterious creativity that is innate in each person. It is this creative element that takes the givens of life (heredity, environment) and interprets them, modifies them, expresses them in purely subjective and surprisingly unpredictable personal ways. (Beames, 1992, p. 34)

The celebration of this personal creativity and uniqueness is one of the key elements in the practice of Individual Psychology. The counselor looks for ways to encourage clients—exploring their assets, lifestyles, goals, and behaviors for the special qualities that contribute to the clients' uniqueness. The counselor also tries to reframe problem areas so that clients can learn new, more hopeful ways of looking at themselves and their situations.

This encouragement process is possible due to the creative nature of people.

Personal creativity allows individuals to make new and different interpretations of events and relationships and to make new decisions about themselves, others, and the world (Kottman, 1995; Mosak, 1979). They can also learn new behaviors, attitudes, and interactional patterns, expressing their lifestyles in different, more positive ways.

Celebrating children's uniqueness and encouraging them to focus on their strengths is an essential component of Adlerian play therapy (Kottman, 1994, 1995). The Adlerian play therapist looks for the special ways that children express their uniqueness and tries to help them learn to appreciate and value themselves. In parent consultations, the Adlerian play therapist points out children's assets, reframes negative expressions of uniqueness, and teaches parents to encourage their children and their strengths.

People Experience Life from a Subjective Perspective

Adlerians believe that each individual person has his or her own interpretation of events and relationships. From the phenomenological perspective of Individual Psychology, this interpretation is more important than the actual events and relationships (Dinkmeyer, Dinkmeyer, & Sperry, 1989; Griffith & Powers, 1984). "The individual's biased mode of apperception is always present, and always unique to his [or her] lifestyle" (Beames, 1992, p. 20). This subjective perspective is a function of the person's lifestyle because he or she filters everything that happens through his or her convictions about self, others, and the world, using private logic, as if these convictions were true.

In children, the subjective perspective influences the actual formation of lifestyle. Since children are very powerful observers but may not have the insight or information needed to make reliable interpretations of their observations, they sometimes incorporate faulty convictions into their lifestyles (Dinkmeyer, Dinkmeyer, & Sperry, 1989; Kottman, 1995). "Based on these mistaken beliefs, people develop a private logic that frequently remains out of their awareness, but which is the foundation for their reasoning and for many of their assumptions, decisions, attitudes, and behaviors" (Kottman, 1995, p. 15).

From an Adlerian perspective, one important aspect of this personality formation is the development of inferiority feelings. Because of a gap between the self-ideal and the emerging apperceptions of self in the lifestyle, children develop feelings of inferiority that persist into adulthood (Ansbacher & Ansbacher, 1956; Mosak, 1979). "Inferiority feelings are those universal feelings of incompleteness, smallness, weakness, ignorance, and dependency first experienced by the infant and the small child" (Griffith & Powers, 1984, p. 19). Although everyone has these feelings of inferiority, some people react to them constructively, as a positive challenge for improvement, and some people react to them destructively, as a mark of their own inadequacy.

The job of the Adlerian play therapist is to try to understand and value the child's subjective perspective, while gently challenging his or her faulty convictions and private logic and helping to frame feelings of inferiority positively (Kottman, 1993, 1994, 1995). Since the child's emerging lifestyle is evident in the play, the play therapist can see patterns that represent the child's beliefs about self, others, and the world. In parent consultation, the Adlerian play therapist gathers information about the parents' subjective perspectives on the child and about their understanding of the child's unique perceptions. As the play therapist's insight into the child grows, he or she can also help the parent(s) better understand and value the child's perspective.

Model of Psychopathology

According to Adlerian theory, maladjustment is a form of discouragement. Based on the inability to find useful ways of belonging and being significant and on the inability to cope with feelings of inferiority, individuals who manifest psychopathology become discouraged because they cannot cope with the problems they encounter in life (Dinkmeyer, Dinkmeyer, & Sperry, 1989; Griffith & Powers, 1984; Manaster & Corsini, 1982). Those individuals who lack the courage to interpret feelings of inferiority as an inspiration may manifest their discouragement through expressions of helplessness and worthlessness or through overcompensation in the form of a superiority complex. As previously discussed, another form of maladjustment is a low level of social interest, a lack of connection with others.

Adlerian play therapists assume that children referred to play therapy are discouraged (Kottman, 1995). The circumstances of their discouragement may vary—abuse, neglect, or other form of trauma; pampering; too little or too much power; chaotic families; alcoholic, addicted, or mentally ill parents; and so forth. Discouraged children have negative convictions about themselves, others, and the world, and their destructive, self-defeating goals, behaviors, and attitudes reflect these convictions.

Goal/Cure

The goals of intervention in Individual Psychology are to help the client (1) gain an awareness of and insight into lifestyle, (2) alter faulty self-defeating apperceptions and move from private logic to common sense; (3) move toward positive goals of behavior; (4) replace negative strategies for belonging and gaining significance with positive strategies; (5) increase his or her social interest; (6) learn new ways of coping with feelings of inferiority; and (7) optimize creativity and begin to use his or her assets to develop self-enhancing decisions about attitudes, feelings, and behaviors. As the client attains these goals, he or she moves toward the ultimate objective of therapy: reduction of discouragement. In Adlerian play therapy, the play therapist combines play and conversations with the child with parent consultation to help the client achieve these goals.

Each of the four phases of Individual Psychology has its own internal goal (Dinkmeyer, Dinkmeyer, & Sperry, 1989). In the first phase, the counselor works to establish an egalitarian, empathic relationship with the client. In the second phase, the counselor explores the client's lifestyle, helping the client begin to understand his or her beliefs, attitudes, goals, emotions, and motives. By the third phase, the counselor's goal is to help the client to gain insight into his or her lifestyle, faulty convictions, and self-defeating goals and behaviors. During the fourth phase, the counselor must help the client take this insight and convert it into action, making behavioral and attitudinal changes (Dinkmeyer, Dinkmeyer, & Sperry, 1989).

Adlerian play therapy has the same four phases and goals as other applications of Individual Psychology. Because the Adlerian play therapist is working with children, he or she must look for small shifts in attitude and behavior in the process of the play in the playroom and in observations by parents and teachers to measure progress in the attainment of these goals.

Further Information

This description of Adlerian theory is necessarily sketchy, given the limited space of this presentation. Readers who are interested in pursuing Adlerian play therapy and other forms of Adlerian interventions with clients should consult the references in this chapter for further information on the concepts and strategies of Individual Psychology.

CASE FORMULATION

Since Adlerians do little formal assessment of clients, preferring to incorporate informal exploration of lifestyle, goals, private logic, and faulty assumptions in the therapy process, the therapist would not usually conduct an elaborate intake and assessment procedure such as the one presented in the initial chapter of this book. The play therapist did a much more informal gathering of information as she built the relationships with Jason and his parents and explored Jason's lifestyle. By the third phase of the play therapy process, the therapist knew much of the information contained in the intake/assessment data, but she had obtained it over a longer period of time simply as a part of the ongoing relationship.

During the first several sessions with the parents and the child, the Adlerian play therapist usually asks specific lifestyle questions (Kottman, 1995), such as those included later in this section. The author has used the information available from the intake/assessment in the first chapter to generate answers to these questions. For some of the information used in formulating the conceptualization of this child, the author simply relied on the information provided in the intake/assessment material without providing the questions she would have asked to obtain that information. Those queries would be scattered through the first ten sessions with the parents and the child and would be asked in response to situations in the playroom and in the family's life. The primary difference between the intake and assessment in the first chapter and the methods in Adlerian play therapy involves the pace and manner in which the information is gathered. The Adlerian play therapist obtains similar data over time, rather than in the concentrated form presented in that chapter, and gathers it in a less formal manner.

Gathering Information from the Parents

The therapist had an initial meeting with both of Jason's parents to begin to build a relationship with them and to start formulating a conceptualization of the family and of the child. This gave the therapist an opportunity to assess their relationship and their patterns of interacting with each other and their children.

During that initial meeting and subsequent parent consultations with them, the therapist asked Mary and Emilio a series of questions designed to help her begin to develop hypotheses about the family atmosphere and family constellation and how those affected Jason's lifestyle (Dinkmeyer & Dinkmeyer, 1977; Eckstein, Baruth, & Mehrer, 1992; Kottman, 1995.) The therapist asked them questions about their own families of origin and their relationship with one another in order to get an idea about their parenting strategies and their philosophies of discipline. Instead of being asked a series of questions in a formal interview fashion, they were asked these questions in a conversational manner during the first several sessions of parent consultation. (For each of the lifestyles questions, the author has provided an explanation of the purpose in asking that particular question and how it helped with a conceptualization of Jason from an Adlerian perspective.)

Therapist: If Jason's behavior problems were eliminated, how would things be different in your family? (This question was designed to try to get an idea of the purpose of the negative behaviors for the child and for the family. It also gave some clues about the family atmosphere, especially the parents' level of discouragement and attitudes toward the child and the presenting problem.)
Mary: Things would go more smoothly. I wouldn't have to get mad so often, and I would be able to have more peace.
Emilio: I really don't see a big problem with Jason's behavior, so I don't think things would change very much.
Therapist: Describe each person in the family. How does each person stand out in the family (both positively and negatively)? (This question was designed to explore how each person gains his or her significance in the family, hopefully highlighting each person's assets. It can also be the basis for examining the family constellation from the parents' perspective.)
Mary: I don't know whether to describe Emilio—he's not really in the family any more since we're divorced. (Encouraged to describe both herself and her ex-husband) . . . OK . . . Emilio is a good father to the children. He wasn't always a good husband to me. Sometimes he was, but he just couldn't always be there for me, and we had to divorce. Jason is a hard kid to raise. He is really moody, and he gets angry a lot and won't do what I tell him to do. I guess I could say that he has a mind of his own and that many times he won't mind me. He just doesn't like to be told what to do . . . he always needs to be the boss and he just won't let me be the boss. I . . . I am a person who just wants things to be peaceful and quiet and happy. I sometimes get very down, but I know I will always get back up again sooner or later. Carla is a happy kid. She is fun to be with. She always does what she is supposed to do, and she is really easy to raise.
Emilio: I am hard-working and hard-playing. I think I am a good dad. I wish I had been a better husband, but I couldn't, so we divorced. Mary was hard to live with. She was depressed all the time and lots of the time she is angry—at me and the kids and life. Carla is a cute little kid. She is very loving. Jason is okay—sometimes he gets into trouble with his mom and his teacher, but he's fine with

me. I just wish he would stand up for himself more. He sometimes seems like's he's a bit of a sissy. I wonder if that's because he lives with his mother.

Therapist: Which parent is Jason most like? In what ways? (This question provided one way of examining how Jason gains his sense of belonging in the family. It also gave clues about the family atmosphere by showing which parent the child emulates.)

Mary: Jason is much more like Emilio. They always want to be in charge. He's not like me at all. He never seems down or depressed. He's always moving.

Emilio: Jason is like both of us. He's like me in that he likes to take charge. He's like Mary in that, if he doesn't get his way, watch out. They both also use whining to get what they want.

Therapist: What are Jason's responsibilities? (With a child whose goal is power, the answer to this question can help establish whether the child has too much power, too little power, or comes from a chaotic family. It also gave clues about the family atmosphere.)

Mary: At my house, Jason doesn't really have any jobs, other than playing nicely with Carla. It's just easier for me to do things myself than to try to get him to do anything around the house.

Emilio: Both of the kids have jobs when they're staying at my house. Jason and Carla both help set the table and clean up after themselves. Jason gets himself ready in the morning. He's old enough to do things without any help even though sometimes he asks for help doing things that he really already knows how to do.

Therapist: What does Jason do that bothers you or other family members? How do you feel when he does this? What do you do when he does this? How does he react when you correct him? (These are standard questions that help the counselor begin to make guesses about the goals of the child's behavior. The four goals of discouraged children are characterized by specific types of problem behaviors, parental reactions, and children's responses to correction (Dinkmeyer & McKay, 1989; Dreikurs & Soltz, 1964). The information about consequences for behavior problems to this question can also reveal aspects of the family atmosphere and the parents' level of discouragement about parenting and about the child.)

Mary: Jason does lots of things that bug me. He's always getting into trouble, especially when he comes home from school. He won't pick stuff up. Lots of times he ignores me when I ask him to do things around the house or to stop behaving badly. I get really angry when he won't do what he's supposed to do, especially when he just ignores me. I bug him to get him to do the stuff, but he just pretends I'm not there. Sometimes I just blow up and hit him. That's what got us here in the first place. Nothing does any good though—he just pouts and ignores me even when I yell at him.

Emilio: Jason doesn't do anything that really gets me mad. Sometimes it bugs me when he acts grouchy when he comes home from school, but it's easy to get him out of that. I think the biggest thing that bugs me is when he won't try to do stuff that I know he can do and he won't stand up for himself when I know he can do it. I just wish he would be more of a man. Sometimes I have to make him stand up for himself. He gets kind of pouty when that happens, but sooner or later he acts like a man.

Therapist: What does Jason do well? (This type of question elicits the parents' perceptions of the child's assets.)

Mary: He's nice to his sister.

Emilio: He's a good kid. He helps around the house when he's at my house. He's good at sports, and he's a good artist. He's fun to be with.

The therapist asked the parents other questions to get more information about their parenting strategies, their own lifestyles, their families of origin, the relationships between the members of the family, and Jason's perceptions of himself and others. However, this information was provided in the intake and assessment data in the first chapter, and there are no specific standard questions designed to obtain these data, so the author did not include questions that she would have asked to obtain this information.

Gathering Information from the Child

During the first several sessions with Jason, the therapist informally began to ask him questions to help her understand his lifestyle, his private logic, and the goals of his behaviors. In order to gain an understanding of these elements of his personality, the therapist needed to explore his perceptions of the family atmosphere and family constellation. The therapist wanted to assess the level of Jason's social interest and his discouragement. She also wanted to examine how he deals with his feelings of inferiority and how he expresses his personal creativity, especially in the area of assets.

In time, the therapist got much of the same information provided in the initial intake/assessment chapter. In addition to these intake/assessment data, the therapist also wanted Jason's answers to the following questions. For each question, the author has provided an explanation of her purpose in asking that particular question and how it would help her conceptualize the child from an Adlerian perspective.

If you didn't have the problems you have now, how would things be different in your life? (The child's answer to this question helped the therapist to understand how he perceives the presenting problem and his sense of responsibility for creating and eliminating the problem. It also helped to establish the child's perspective on the family and the family atmosphere.)

Jason: (At first, he refuses to answer this question, but eventually says:) The only problems I have in my life right now are that my mom hit me and I have to come here. If that wasn't happening and people didn't always try to tell me what to do, everything would be just fine, no problem.

Therapist: Describe each of the people in your family. (The purpose in this question was to gain a picture of how the child saw each member of the family gaining significance in the family. It also provided useful information about family constellation and family atmosphere.)

Jason: My dad's cool. He pretty much lets us do what we want to. Sometimes we have to do jobs at his house, but they're not very hard. We have fun with him. My mom's a secretary. She's a grouch a lot. She's always mad at somebody, usually me, and she always bugs me to try to get me to do stuff. My sister is okay. She's little, so she doesn't always want to do cool stuff though. (He had to be reminded to describe himself, as he was also a part of the family.) I am okay. I am good at some stuff, but people like my mom and my teachers are always trying to tell me what to do. (Probed for specifics . . .) Oh, I don't know. Just things.

Therapist: Which of your parents are you most like? How are you like that parent? (This question helped to establish how the child gained a sense of belonging in the family. It provided an indication of whether the child saw himself gaining a place in the family by positive or negative means. It also supplied insight into the child's perspective on each of the parents and the family atmosphere.)

Jason: I'm most like my dad. We like to do the same kinds of things, like play ball and stuff.

Therapist: What do you get in trouble for at home? (The purpose of this question was to assess the child's willingness to "own" problems. It was also part of assessing the goals of behavior from the child's perspective.)

Jason: (Jason denied ever getting into trouble for anything. However, when he was playing with the tiger family, the therapist asked what the little boy tiger got into trouble for.) Growl's a tough tiger. At his dad's, he doesn't get in trouble for anything, and at his mom's, he gets in trouble for everything.

Therapist: What happens when you get into trouble? (This question helped assess the child's perceptions of consequences for his behavioral problems. It also contributed to an understanding of the goals of the child's behavior and the child's perceptions of the family atmosphere, especially in the area of discipline.)

Jason: (Again, Jason refused to answer this question since he contended that he never got into trouble for anything. When he answered the other question about the little boy tiger, the therapist followed up with a question about the consequences when Growl got into trouble.) Since Growl never gets into trouble at his dad's, nothing ever happens to him there. When he gets into trouble at his mom's, she always yells at him, and sometimes she hits him. She doesn't think Growl can do anything right.

Therapist: What would you change about your family? (This question gave clues about the family atmosphere, family constellation, and the child's level of discouragement.)

Jason: Nothing. (Urged to think about this question a bit more, he replied:) I'd like my parents to get back together and be happy. Other than that, everything's fine. Oh, I wish my mom would stop telling me what to do, too.

Therapist: What are you good at doing? (The answer to this question helped give the therapist an idea of the child's perceptions of his assets and methods of coping with feelings of inferiority.)

Jason: Playing ball, driving my remote-control cars.

Therapist: What do you like about yourself? (This question revealed information related to the child's perceptions of his assets and methods of dealing with inferiority feelings.)

Jason: Everything.

Therapist: What do you wish you were better at doing? (Same as the previous two questions, plus the child's level of discouragement.)

Jason: Can't think of anything. Maybe playing ball, but I'm pretty good at it now.

An Adlerian Conceptualization of Jason

An Adlerian case formulation includes hypotheses about the client's lifestyle. This may include ideas about the client's (1) core beliefs about self, others, and the world; (2) self-defeating convictions; (3) goals of behavior and the underlying conditions influencing those goals; (4) strategies for belonging and gaining significance; (5) level of social interest; (6) level of discouragement and methods of coping with inferiority feelings; and (7) personal assets. As part of this process, it may also be helpful to consider the effects the family atmosphere and family constellation have on the client. Since parent consultation is an integral component of Adlerian play therapy, when working with children using this modality, it is also important to assess the parents' parenting skills and any personal problems that may interfere with their ability to use parenting skills appropriately.

Core Beliefs about Self, Others, and the World

The following is a list of the therapist's hypotheses about Jason's core beliefs about himself, others, and the world and his conclusions about his behavior based on those beliefs:

I am . . . powerless to get what I want—especially from my mom.

I am . . . a person who likes to be the boss of myself.

I must . . . not let others tell me what to do.

I must . . . not take a risk, because I might fail.

I must . . . not let anyone know I have a problem because they might not love/respect me anymore if they knew.

I must . . . not stand up for myself.

Others are . . . always trying to tell me what to do.

Others are . . . unpredictable . . . you can't count on them.

Others are . . . not to be trusted. They will hurt me if I let them.

Others are . . . not always on my team.

Others are . . . likely to overreact.

Others are . . . probably not going to want to be friends with me.

The world is . . . unpredictable.

The world is . . . unfair.

The world is . . . an okay place, sometimes fun and sometimes not.

Based on these beliefs, I must behave . . . in ways that let me be in control, so that other people can't tell me what to do or hurt me. Especially my mom.

Based on these beliefs, I will . . . not let myself really care about what happens in my life. Even when I do care, I will act as if I don't to protect myself.

Based on these beliefs, I must behave . . . in a way that keeps people from hurting me—I will keep myself from caring about my mother and other people so they can't reject me.

Based on these beliefs, I will . . . have fun when I get the chance.

Self-Defeating Convictions

The therapist's analysis of the answers to the lifestyle questions and the information gathered in the intake/assessment indicated that Jason seemed to have several self-defeating convictions. It was apparent that he did not have very much trust in himself or in other people, especially his mother. This lack of trust tended to interfere with his ability to build a relationship with his mother and to make friends with peers at school. Jason seemed to think that he must always be in control of situations or that he would be hurt by others or that he would have no power at all. This all-or-nothing thinking also apparently influenced the level of his self-control. His pattern tended to be that he felt totally in control of himself or he felt as though he was totally out of control. He tended to believe that he could not acknowledge problems and that he must act as if everything in his life was going fine and that he had no negative feelings. Jason almost seemed afraid that, if he acknowledged difficulties, he would somehow be blamed or punished for those problems, rather than helped to work things out.

While some of these convictions might have been based on an accurate assessment of situations and relationships, they were still self-defeating for Jason. He seemed to be engaging in many behaviors and attitudes that become self-fulfilling. His mother, his teacher, and children at school might have given him some reasons to distrust them. However, by refusing to trust others or let them get close to him, Jason continued to push others away from him. As he pushed them away, his mother and other people reacted in negative ways that reinforced Jason's lack of trust in others. This self-fulfilling pattern also seemed to affect his need to be in control and his unwillingness to acknowledge problems and negative feelings.

Goals of Behavior

In order to diagnose the goal of a discouraged child's behavior, the Adlerian play therapist examines the child's behavior, the emotional responses of adults when they encounter those behaviors, and the child's reactions when he or she is corrected for those negative behaviors. Examining these three areas with Jason, based on his and his parents' answers to the lifestyle questions and watching his actions in the playroom, the therapist suggested that Jason's primary goal of behavior was power. This was evidenced by the power struggles he got into with his mother and his teacher, by his ignoring his mother when she corrected him, by his negative moods, withdrawal, and sulking, by his tendency to be directive with his sister and other children, and by his refusal to play with others when things did not go his way. Jason seemed to feel that he did not have enough age-appropriate power when he was at his mother's house. He felt controlled by her, at the bottom of the tower of power, with no power of his own. Rather than let his mother control him, he simply shut down. This was his method of gaining a modicum of power. He also seemed unwilling to own his power when he was with his father, as evidenced by his unwillingness to stand up for himself or try activities that he had not already mastered.

According to Dreikurs and Soltz (1964) and Dinkmeyer and McKay (1989), there are two forms of power seeking: passive and active. Jason seemed to be manifesting the passive form of power seeking. His tendency to be noncompliant, without having temper tantrums, his refusal to acknowledge problems and negative affect, and his tendency to cry without rage all indicated that Jason took the passive approach to maintaining control. He seemed to have a need to make sure that no one else could have power or control over him, rather than a need to control others. This was supported by the fact that the primary person Jason engaged in power struggles was his mother, who tried to control him and his behavior. He did not get into power struggles with his father, even though his father was more demanding in terms of helping around the house, because his father did not attempt to control him. His father seemed to accommodate Jason's need for independence and provided outlets for his energy and aggression rather than asking him to always stay "in control." However, Jason's unwillingness to own his power and be assertive when he was with his father indicated that he was not completely comfortable with control and power issues with his father either. Jason seemed almost afraid that Emilio might reject or punish him if he acted too powerful with his father.

Strategies for Belonging and Gaining Significance

Jason seemed to have two completely different ways of belonging and gaining significance—a negative method with his mother and a semipositive method with his father. With his mother, Jason was the bad child, especially as compared to his sister. By refusing to be compliant and continuing his passive-aggressive approach to his interactions with his mother, he had established himself as the problem in the family. This behavior kept his mother involved with him in a negative fashion, but negative attention was better than no attention at all. Jason could not possibly compete with Carla for the position of the good child since Carla had always been her mother's favorite.

With his father, Jason gained his sense of belonging by emulating his father—he was all boy. He wanted to be just like Emilio—they shared the same activities, they shared attitudes about life and work (school). Many of Jason's answers to the lifestyle questions and the queries in the intake/assessment process were echoes of the responses made by Emilio. However, the positive connection with his father was somewhat mitigated by the fact that Jason was not willing to be "a man" with his father. His continued dependency and lack of assertiveness kept his father involved with him, but in a negative fashion that obviously bothered Emilio.

The differences in the way his parents responded to him and this pattern of gaining his significance and belonging in divergent ways in the two households must have been rather confusing for Jason. At his mother's house, he was punished for trying to be too powerful, and at his father's house, he was denigrated for not trying to be more powerful. It was difficult for him to solidify his lifestyle and generalize a pattern of attitudes and behaviors because of the inconsistency in the two family atmospheres and the disparate reactions and expectations of his parents.

Level of Discouragement/Methods of Coping with Inferiority Feelings

Jason seemed to have a moderate level of discouragement, based on his self-defeating convictions and the lack of consistency in the family atmospheres in his parents' households. He lacked the confidence to try new behaviors and the courage to take the responsibility for problems and negative emotions. By denying that he and his family had any difficulties, blaming his mother for problems, and remaining somewhat dependent and unassertive with his father, Jason kept himself from experiencing his own ability to cope with problems.

Jason's relationship with his mother and the family atmosphere while he was at her house seemed to contribute significantly to his general level of discouragement. Mary was very negative about Jason and his behaviors. When her efforts to control him were unsuccessful, she got angry and punished him, sometimes resorting to physical abuse. This contributed to a rejective and disparaging family atmosphere at her house. She also tended to pamper Jason by doing things for him that he could do for himself, rather than taking the more difficult route of expecting him to do things for himself.

Jason's interactions with Emilio tended to alleviate some of his discouragement. Emilio encouraged Jason by focusing on his assets rather than his liabilities. Emilio refused to pamper the children and continued to have high expectations for Jason's contribution to the household. Emilio also contributed to Jason's feelings of courage by his democratic parenting—sharing age-appropriate power with him, rather than getting into power struggles with him. However, Jason seemed to be somewhat discouraged by Emilio's negative reaction to his refusal to "be a man."

While Jason had many feelings of inferiority, his tendency to deny them prevented him from accepting them as a positive challenge to move toward his ideal self. On the positive side, he was not completely overwhelmed by these inferiority feelings, as evidenced by the fact that he had not given up and become depressed or suicidal and he had not developed a superiority complex and tried to outdo others.

Personal Assets

Jason had many of the positive attributes of a typical oldest child. In some situations, especially at his father's house, Jason was responsible and reliable. He succeeded in his schoolwork with little effort. He exhibited above-average intelligence. His peers in school perceived him as independent and self-assured. Given encouragement, positive attention, and affirmative feedback from others, Jason reacted in an extremely appropriate and appreciative manner. He knew his own mind and was determined and persistent. Jason was accepting and loving toward his sister and willingly interacted with her. When situations were more relaxed with his mother, he became verbally and physically affectionate. He had high levels of energy and moderate athletic ability. Unlike many children referred to play therapy, Jason demonstrated moderate levels of social interest. Although he seemed to avoid verbally expressing his connection with others, his behavior with his sister, which was usually loving and supportive, and his behavior with his father, which was usually cooperative and interested, suggested relatively strong attachment to these two people. With a solid foundation like this, it was relatively easy to increase Jason's degree of social interest.

Parenting Skills and Problems

Emilio had relatively well-developed parenting skills. He seemed to have established a predominantly positive, democratic family atmosphere. He focused on assets, used encouragement to motivate the children, and had high expectations for them. He engaged the children in making decisions for themselves, at the same time that he exerted appropriate parental power and responsibility and instituted logical and natural consequences for inappropriate behaviors. He redirected rather than engaging in power struggles with the children.

While he was not without fault, Emilio seemed to have few personal problems that would interfere with his exercising adequate parenting strategies. His major weakness as a parent was his tendency to minimize problems and to underreact to negative situations, but he seemed as though he would be amenable to suggestions to improve this area of weakness. He also needed to rethink his rather denigrating reactions to Jason's lack of assertiveness and tendency toward dependency. By working on more encouraging and less sexually stereotypic reactions to this behavior, he could refocus and encourage Jason rather than discourage him. Emilio also needed to work with Mary to achieve a more consistent family atmosphere in their households.

Mary seemed to lack effective parenting strategies. One of her main difficulties with Jason was her own struggles with power and control. Mary seemed to alternate between trying to control Jason and his behavior and pampering him. She was also extremely critical of Jason. Although learning new parenting skills was invaluable for Mary, some of her personal struggles continued to interfere with her ability to apply these skills. Mary's own level of discouragement (which results in depression and anger) sometimes sabotaged her efforts at better parenting.

TREATMENT GOALS

Since, in Adlerian play therapy, the therapist worked simultaneously with the child in play therapy and the parents in parent consultation, she had treatment goals for Jason and for his parents. The therapist derived the treatment goals with Jason and his parents from the general goals of Individual Psychology. The treatment goals included changes in Jason's (1) perceptions of himself, others, and the world, (2) self-defeating beliefs, (3) goals of behavior, (4) methods of belonging and gaining significance, (5) level of social interest, (6) methods of coping with his feelings of inferiority, and (7) awareness of his own assets. The therapist also worked toward minor changes in Emilio's parenting as well as major changes in Mary's parenting strategies and her methods of dealing with her own discouragement.

More specifically, the therapist wanted to help Jason gain an awareness of his own lifestyle. This involved increasing his understanding of how he saw himself, others, and the world and how his faulty apperceptions contributed to his difficulties with others. Because of his age, Jason was not able to articulate this increased awareness, but he was able to recognize and acknowledge how his private logic was getting him into negative situations when the therapist or his parents and teachers pointed this out to him. The therapist worked on Jason—replacing some of his self-defeating beliefs about himself, others, and the world with more affirmative convictions, especially in the area of trust and power. One important element in achieving this goal was to reduce his all-or-nothing thinking and replace it with common-sense, realistic reasoning.

As a result of the shift in Jason's convictions with regard to control and power, the therapist wanted to help him to move away from the goal of power toward the more positive goals of behavior. With encouragement and support, Jason could move from striving for power in a passive-aggressive manner to striving for attention, involvement, and contribution. As he became more comfortable with letting go of the negative strategies he had been using for belonging with his mother and generalizing the positive strategies he used to gain his significance with his father, he evolved into striving for autonomy and self-responsibility.

As evidenced by his relationship with his father and his sister, Jason was capable of connecting with other people. His peers in school also had a positive perception of his ability to interact with others. These indicators suggested that Jason did not lack social interest. However, his relationships with his mother and his teacher and his own perception of his relationships with other children lent credence to the idea that he needed to enhance his social interest. This was accomplished in play therapy by building a strong egalitarian relationship between Jason and the therapist. During the final phase of play therapy, reorientation/reeducation, the therapist continued to cultivate his social interest by involving his sister in several sessions of play. It also enhanced this development to invite one or two other children of Jason's age, either other clients of the therapist or friends from his neighborhood or school, to participate with him in several sessions of play before termination.

The primary way Jason seemed to cope with feelings of inferiority was denial. While this was consistent with this father's coping strategies, this method of dealing with problems did not seem to be working well for Jason. The therapist hoped to help Jason begin to view areas of inferiority as possibilities for growth rather than weaknesses to deny or avoid. She began this process by acknowledging areas in which Jason felt less than competent and by metacommunicating about his discomfort with acknowledging his feelings of inferiority.

One of the primary goals of treatment with Jason was to use encouragement to help him become more aware of his own creativity and help him start to recognize and capitalize on his own assets. Teaching Emilio and Mary to consistently use encouragement to focus on Jason's strengths helped to make the attainment of this goal more likely. All of these changes resulted in Jason's having improved attitudes, behaviors, and relationships with other people.

With Emilio, the treatment goals included encouraging him to continue the positive elements of his parenting and to try to achieve a more consistent family atmosphere by increasing his support of Mary and her relationship with the children. The therapist also wanted to move Emilio toward spending more time with the children, especially with Jason. Emilio also needed to capitalize on his natural ability to use encouragement to stress Jason's assets and reduce his criticism of Jason's dependency and his demands that Jason "be a man."

Mary had to learn new ways of gaining cooperation from the children rather than engaging them in power struggles or pampering them. She needed to learn to communicate more clearly about her expectations and wishes. It was moderately helpful to teach her to use encouragement and methods of focusing on Jason's assets rather than his liabilities. Learning to use her own reactions to recognize the goals of behavior, especially power, helped her begin to respond to Jason's passive-aggressive behavior in a more constructive way. As she began to understand Jason's lifestyle, his self-defeating convictions, and the goals of his behavior, she was able to react with more helpful strategies, such as setting up logical consequences and letting the children experience natural consequences. In order to optimize the positive effects of the parent consultations and parenting skills on Mary and her relationship with her children, especially Jason, the therapist referred her for personal counseling.

TREATMENT DESCRIPTIONS

Logistics

A play therapist can do Adlerian play therapy just about anywhere—in a school, in an office, in a clinic, in a home, and so forth. There is not a specific setting for Adlerian play therapy as long as there is a space where the client and the counselor can have privacy so that the child can be sure of the confidentiality of the sessions.

The playroom where the therapist worked with Jason had windows that covered two of the walls and shelves that covered the other two walls. It contained a sandbox, an easel for painting, a small desk filled with art supplies, a puppet theater, a large basket filled with masks and costumes, a kitchen area with a wooden stove and refrigerator, a doll house, a barn and a farmhouse, and a cradle for dolls. The therapist sat on the floor on a pile of very big pillows, and she had several small footstools and a child-sized chair for sitting on as well. The floor was carpeted, and there was a big piece of plastic underneath the easel so that clients who wanted to paint did not have to worry about getting paint on the carpet. (Obviously, many play therapists will not have the luxury of this kind of space. A person could certainly do Adlerian play therapy without all of this "stuff.") This is the space in which Jason and the therapist played together. He would wait in the small waiting room adjacent to the playroom while she talked to his parents. The therapist had many toys and children's books and magazines in the waiting room to occupy parents and children while they waited.

In Adlerian play therapy, the playroom is equipped with many different kinds of toys, similar to the selection in a nondirective, client-centered playroom (Kottman, 1994, 1995; Landreth, 1991). There should be representative toys from each of five categories: (1) family/nurturing toys (such as dolls, a bendable doll family, an animal family, pots and pans, and a doll house); (2) scary toys (such as snakes, insects, monsters, and any other toys that children might perceive as frightening); (3) aggressive toys (such as weapons, toy soldiers, handcuffs, and a stand-up punching bag); (4) expressive toys (including paints, crayons, markers, Play Doh, finger paints, and other art supplies); (5) and pretend/fantasy toys (such as masks, a doctor kit, puppets, a telephone, hats, transportation toys, and the like). The toys are arranged according to categories, so that the scary toys are with the other scary toys, the family/nurturing toys close to the other family/nurturing toys, and so forth. This arrangement contributes to the playroom's being a consistent and predictable place where children can feel comfortable (Kottman, 1995; Landreth, 1991).

After the initial session with the parents, Adlerian play therapists divide their once-a-week sessions between the child and the parent(s). With Jason and his parents, the therapist arranged to see Jason for 45 minutes and one of his parents for 45 minutes. Adlerian play therapists design the time according to their conceptualization of the family and the needs of the members. Though it might have been interesting to have had some joint sessions with Emilio and Mary, the therapist arranged most of the parent consultation sessions with Mary, interspersed with an occasional session with Emilio.

The usual range of time spent in Adlerian play therapy is six to nine months. The therapist saw Jason and his family for about six months (about 26 sessions). The therapist suggested that Mary continue her individual sessions with another therapist after she terminated the play therapy and the parent-consultation sessions.

Specific Strategies/Treatment Stages

Adlerian play therapists typically use certain intervention strategies in each of the four phases of Adlerian play therapy. However, the phases are not completely discrete, so that there is some overlap between the techniques used in each. For instance, the author continues to use the relationship-building techniques throughout the play therapy process. Although the modality that Adlerian play therapists use to communicate is different (play with the children, talk with the parent), they frequently use similar techniques in sessions with the child and with the parent(s).

In the first phase of play therapy, the focus is on building a partnership—a caring relationship with the child. Among these techniques are: tracking behavior, restating content, reflecting feelings, encouraging, giving explanations and answering questions, asking questions, and interacting actively with the child. Other techniques used in building the relationship are metacommunicating about purposes, cleaning the playroom together, and setting limits. With a child striving for power, Adlerian play therapists custom-design their interaction with the child based on their interpretation of the background situation. If the child has too much power at home, the play therapist will immediately set the precedent that they share power in the playroom, taking turns making decisions, getting to be the boss, and so forth. This is especially true with pampered children. If the child has too little power at home or comes from a chaotic family, during the first phase of counseling, the therapist lets him or her make all the decisions and have as much control as possible in the playroom. (In subsequent phases, the therapist moves toward sharing power with these children.) With the parents during this phase, the primary intervention approach is to listen to them empathically and encourage any positive aspects of their parenting.

In the second phase of play therapy, the therapist explores the child's lifestyle by examining the goals of his or her behavior, exploring the family atmosphere and family constellation, and soliciting early recollections. Based on the information he or she gathers during this process, the therapist formulates hypotheses about the child's methods of gaining significance, self-defeating convictions, and all the other elements of his or her lifestyle. The Adlerian play therapist uses questioning strategies with the parents to help understand their perceptions of the child's lifestyle and their own lifestyles. During this phase, the therapist also begins to teach parenting skills and to assess the impact of the parents' personal issues on their ability to apply parenting skills.

In the third phase of play therapy, in order to help the child gain insight into his or her lifestyle, the therapist tentatively shares inferences about goals of behavior, self-defeating convictions, and the other lifestyle components. The therapist interprets both the play and the verbalizations in the playroom and metacommunicates about patterns in the child's behavior and his or her reactions to the interpretations. By using the child's metaphors, designing therapeutic metaphors, and telling one another stories, the therapist capitalizes on the element of play as the key factor in the child's communication. The therapist may also make overt connections between the child's behavior in the playroom and his or her interactions outside the playroom, pointing out patterns in attitudes and behavior.

With the parents in this phase of play therapy, the Adlerian play therapist continues to teach parenting skills. She may also do some minor counseling with parents on personal issues—especially those related to their families of origin, where they learned their basic parenting skills—that seem to be interfering with their application of parenting strategies. It is important during this phase to encourage all efforts and progress, no matter how small, on the part of the parents.

In the fourth phase of counseling, in order to help the client with reorientation/reeducation, the Adlerian play therapist guides the child to generate alternative behaviors for problematic situations (both in and out of the playroom); teaches new, more socially appropriate behaviors, especially in the areas of social skills and negotiation skills; practices these new behaviors with the child, using the toys and role playing; and encourages the child for shifts in attitudes, feelings, behaviors, communication patterns, methods of gaining significance, and so forth. With the parents, the therapist works on encouraging them to use their new parenting skills consistently and to generalize any personal insights into their relationship with their children.

The Adlerian play therapy does not use all of these techniques with every child. Since each child is unique, the therapist must choose specific tools from the repertoire of intervention strategies with a particular child in mind. Also, since a typical Adlerian play therapy relationship extends over a long period of time, it would be impossible to illustrate every strategy used with a child. For each of the four phases of the work with Jason, the author will provide detailed descriptions of selected representative interactions and intervention strategies.

Building an Egalitarian Relationship

In this first phase, the therapist's primary focus with Jason was to gain his trust and to communicate that she had no desire to control him. Since he believed that he did not have enough power, the therapist tried to give him as much power as possible in the beginning of the relationship. She consistently refused to make decisions for him, even when he asked her to do things for him and to take care of him, by returning responsibility for decisions to him. Because he had this pattern with his mother, Jason tried to coerce the therapist into either playing power games with him or pampering him. The following is an example of this method of building trust and a sense of power by the therapist's refusing to make decisions for Jason and giving him the power in the playroom:

Jason: What color should I paint this house?
Therapist: That is for you to decide. (Returning responsibility to the child.)
Jason: I want you to tell me. I don't want to decide.
Therapist: You want me to take care of you by telling you what to do, but I know you can make up your own mind. (Refusal to get into a power struggle. Metacommunication about his purpose—desire to be taken care of and avoidance of self-responsibility. Encouragement of his ability to make decision/be responsible/exercise age-appropriate power.)
Jason: I don't want to. What's your favorite color?
Therapist: You're getting frustrated with me because I'm not doing what you want me to do, so you're going to try to get me to decide for you in a different way. You want to show me that you're the boss. (Reflection of feelings. Metacommunication about his purposes.)

To build a relationship and increase Jason's feeling vocabulary, the therapist did a lot of reflecting of feelings during this phase. Since Jason tended to ignore or deny negative feelings, the therapist was prepared for his contradicting or ignoring her when she reflected those feelings. She watched his nonverbal reactions when she reflected feelings, especially deeper level, more intimate and vulnerable feelings like hurt and fear, so that she could see when he had a recognition reflex (an involuntary response to a guess or interpretation that indicates the client has had a strong emotional reaction). When the therapist saw him react to her reflection of feelings, she metacommunicated about what she thought his reactions meant. The following was a typical interchange between Jason and the therapist about feelings.

Jason: My dad was going to take us to the zoo this weekend, but it rained.
Therapist: You seem disappointed that you didn't get to go to the zoo with your dad. (Reflection of a feeling.)
Jason: No. I didn't care. (Denial of feeling.)
Therapist: You didn't want me to think that you were sad or disappointed about not getting to go. Sometimes when you're sad or disappointed, you would rather pretend that you're not. (Metacommunication about his reaction and pattern of behavior.)

Encouragement is a power tool for building relationships. In Adlerian play therapy, there are several key methods of encouraging children (Kottman, 1995). Jason needed a great deal of encouragement to counteract his level of discouragement, so the therapist used all of the various ways of encouraging him. She pointed out his efforts, noticed any progress or small positive changes that he made, and avoided doing things for him that he could do for himself. She acknowledged his assets, especially those demonstrated in the playroom. In modeling the courage to be imperfect by making and acknowledging mistakes, she communicated to him that it was quite acceptable not to be perfect. She avoided using evaluative words and relied on Jason to assess his own performance. By stressing the behavior, rather than the person, she began to teach him that his worth did not depend on his behavior.

During this initial phase, the therapist asked some questions every session. She limited herself to five or six questions about the child's lifestyle (Kottman, 1995), so that she did not jeopardize the relationship by appearing to interrogate the child. Since Jason did not like to answer questions directly, she used his play metaphors to frame her questions (Kottman, 1995) By asking questions about the dolls, puppets, and other toys, rather than asking Jason direct questions about himself and his family, the therapist avoided evoking his passive-aggressive refusal to let her control his behavior. The following interchange is an example of the indirect questioning strategy the therapist used with Jason.

Therapist: Which of the little tigers does the daddy tiger like the best? (A lifestyle question asked indirectly, using the toys and the play metaphor of the child.)
Jason: The boy tiger, Growl. He can do lots of stuff that the dad tiger likes to do. That little girl tiger just doesn't know how to do that kind of stuff. But the dad thinks she's nice though.
Therapist: You wanted to make sure that I knew the dad loved both of the little tigers. (Reflection of feelings, metacommunication about his purpose.)

While the therapist frequently interacts actively with children, either just playing or role-playing with them, during this first phase with Jason, she avoided doing this. This decision was based on his passive approach to power. Jason was so sensitive to nuances of power and worried about others trying to control him that she hesitated to actively interact with him for fear that he would misinterpret her behavior during play and think that she was trying to control him.

The therapist also had to be sensitive to this issue in her approach to cleaning the room. The author believes that picking up the room together can build a sense of teamwork between the play therapist and the client (Kottman, 1995), so she usually engages the child in cleaning up the room with her. With Jason, the therapist tried to approach this issue in the same manner that his father engaged him in setting the table and other household chores. Jason seemed to respond well to this, so she made cleaning the room together into a game the two of them could play. He would be in control of the process, which also could help avoid any resistance. The therapist set up cleaning the room together the first time by saying, "It is time for us to pick up the playroom together. What do you want to pick up and what do you want me to pick up?" She watched Jason's nonverbal reactions closely to catch any resentment or resistance. She did not sense any initial negativity, so she continued to use this strategy with him.

Although Jason's pattern in striving for power was passive, the therapist did have to set limits several times during the beginning phase of therapy. The author primarily limits the child hurting self or others, or purposefully damaging the playroom and the toys. She limits in a four-step process (Kottman, 1995). The first step is to set the limit by simply stating the playroom rule. This formulation keeps the rule impersonal in order to avoid power struggles. The author then reflects feelings and/or makes a guess about the child's purpose. The third step in limiting is to engage the child in generating acceptable alternatives. This usually involves a process of negotiation with the child to determine acceptable possibilities. With Jason, this was usually as far as this process had to go. Since this process both avoided the therapist's appearing to control his behavior and let him have a say in what was acceptable and what was not, he seldom went any further. The few times Jason violated the agreement by repeatedly breaking a limit, the therapist evoked the fourth step and set up logical consequences for noncompliance. The following is an example of the kind of limit setting the therapist did with Jason.

Jason: (Aiming the dart gun at the therapist) I'm going to shoot you.
Therapist: It's against the playroom rules to shoot people with the dart gun. It looks to me like you're wondering what I will do if you threaten to shoot me. I bet you can figure out something you can shoot that is not against the playroom rules. (Stating the limit, making a guess about the purpose of the behavior, engaging the child in generating alternatives.)
Jason: I could pretend that bop bag is you and shoot it.
Therapist: You figured out something you could shoot that would not be against the playroom rules. It's okay in here to pretend to shoot people. (Negotiating, affirming the child's ability to redirect himself.)

Several times Jason felt as though the therapist was trying to tell him what to do, and he shot her with the dart to prove that she could not tell him what to do. On those occasions, the therapist set up a logical consequence in case he decided to ignore the rule again. Such a sequence went something like:

Therapist: We need to figure out some consequence that will happen if you choose to break the rule about shooting people again. (Inviting the child to participate in generating the consequences.)

Jason: You can take the gun away from me. (His attempt to make the therapist be the enforcer who was going to try to make him do something he didn't want to do.)

Therapist: I think you are old enough to take care of it yourself without help from me if you make the decision to break the rules again. (Encouragement and refusal to be put into the enforcer position.)

Jason: Okay, I can put the gun away.

Therapist: Do you think that you will need to put it away for the rest of the session, or do you want to put it away for ten minutes and then try again? (Gave him power and choices; gave him a chance to behave appropriately with the problem toy.)

Jason: Ten minutes sounds good. Can I set the timer myself?

This process gave Jason a chance to practice negotiation skills and encourage responsibility for himself and his personal decisions. The therapist did not have to do this final step much in the first phase of counseling, as they got to know one another. During the second and third phase, Jason began to test limits, trying to get the therapist to react to him in a fashion consistent with the expectations incorporated in his lifestyle. Jason tried to get the therapist to react the way he expected her to react, by trying to provoke her into telling him what to do so he could demonstrate that she could not tell him what to do—this was his box.

Exploring the Child's Lifestyle

In this phase, the therapist explored Jason's goals of behavior and his perceptions of the family atmosphere and family constellation. To gather this information, she asked questions of Jason and his parents, including some of those the author described in the Case Formulation section of this chapter.

The author also finds it helpful to ask children to draw a Kinetic Family Drawing (Knoff, 1985; Kottman, 1995). In a Kinetic Family Drawing, the child draws a picture of everyone in the family; each person is *doing* something. From an Adlerian perspective, the action that each person does in the drawing can be representative of how that person gains his or her significance in the family. An interpretation of the drawing can also suggest patterns in relationships among family members. The author has adapted the questioning strategies used with the drawing to gather information about lifestyle, family atmosphere, and family constellation (Kottman, 1995). In the author's interpretations of the drawings and the answers to the questions, she tried to rely on common sense, rather than reading all sorts of symbolic meaning into the drawing.

Jason's KFD (as described in the intake/assessment data in the first chapter) provided limited information about the family atmosphere and the family constellation.

The fact that Jason's KFD did not have any of the figures engaged in activities seemed to reflect his passivity, which was one of the ways he gained significance, attention, and power in the family. The fact that none of the family members were interacting suggested that Jason saw the family members as separate entities who had very little connection with one another. The spacing of the family members seemed indicative of the distance Jason perceived in the relationship between Mary and Emilio, Mary's overinvolvement with Carla, and Jason's relative closeness with Emilio.

When Jason finished the drawing, the therapist asked him some questions about (1) the arrangement of the figures; (2) what activities the family members would do if they were doing anything; and (3) what each family member hoped for, feared, liked doing, and liked about the other family members. This was a way of gathering more information about Jason's perceptions of the family atmosphere and family constellation. However, in keeping with his usual interactional style, Jason did not give the therapist very many answers in response to direct questions. The therapist got more information by talking about "this family" and "this person" than she did talking about "your family," "Emilio," "Mary," "Carla," and "you."

Because of this pattern of discomfort with directness, the therapist shifted to an indirect approach to gathering information and making interpretations. With Jason, because of his lifestyle pattern of refusing to let anyone else control him, it was more helpful to use the dolls, the animals, and other toys as vehicles for asking questions and making interpretations. The therapist asked questions about discipline, parenting strategies, relationships, personality traits of various family members, characteristic ways of coping with difficult situations using the toys and their actions, attitudes, and feelings as metaphors for Jason and the other members of his family. Jason was especially interested in the animal families, the toy soldiers, and the animal puppets. His favorite toys, like Growl—the little boy tiger, all reflected a need for control and power.

The therapist was quite interested in the interactions of Growl's family, since Jason tended to identify with them as powerful animals—"because nobody in the jungle can tell *them* what to do." Growl was kind of bossy with other, smaller animals, and he was rather defiant with the mother tiger. Growl's mother snarled and threatened a lot, and sometimes she swatted the tiger children, making them fly across the room. Occasionally she would just disappear, leaving the tiger children with the father tiger. Growl's father would tell the children not to worry about the mom, that he could "take care of them just fine." The therapist asked many questions about the interactions of Growl's family, trying to understand Jason's perspective on the affective tone and relationships within this metaphoric representation of his family.

With some children, the author asks them to tell her about their early memories, since Adlerians believe that the memories of events and interactions from early childhood can represent how individuals see themselves, others, and the world (Dinkmeyer, Dinkmeyer, & Sperry, 1987; Kottman, 1995). Given his reluctance to reveal himself and his issues directly, the therapist was not surprised when Jason's descriptions of his early memories had such sketchy detail that it was impossible to draw any conclusions from the memories other than the fact that he felt a need to protect himself and he did not like to comply with requests from others, which she already knew.

Based on the information that the therapist gathered during this phase of the play therapy process, she formulated her conceptualization of Jason and his family. As illustrated in the Case Formulation section of this chapter, this would include guesses about Jason's (1) core beliefs about self, others, and the world; (2) self-defeating convictions; (3) goals of behavior and the underlying conditions influencing those goals; (4) strategies for belonging and gaining significance; (5) level of social interest; (6) level of discouragement and methods of coping with inferiority feelings; and (7) personal assets. In the third phase of Adlerian play therapy, the insight phase, the therapist worked to help Jason gain insight into his lifestyle and begin to make decisions about things he wanted to change in his attitudes, behavior, and patterns of interacting with others.

Helping the Child Gain Insight

Having formulated her conceptualization of Jason based on the data she gathered in the first and second phase of counseling, during the third phase the therapist began to share that conceptualization in the form of tentative hypotheses with Jason and his parents. She interpreted both the play and the verbalizations in the playroom. This way, she avoided the basic mistake of simply doing talk therapy in the playroom, which would not work with Jason, given his reluctance to talk about his problems directly. It was particularly important during this phase of the therapy to focus on Jason's play and the metaphors contained within the play. Since the therapist was revealing information that was out of Jason's awareness and this information sometimes evoked a defensive reaction, metaphors (the ones used naturally, specially designed therapeutic metaphors, and storytelling techniques) were especially useful tools during this phase of counseling. A primary focus during this phase was to help Jason generalize what he was learning about himself and about interacting with other people. The therapist metacommunicated about the underlying messages in Jason's communication and about the meaning of his reactions to her guesses and interpretations. She also made overt connections between what was happening in the playroom and what was happening in the rest of Jason's relationships.

One of the primary tools with Jason during this phase of counseling was the therapist's ability to share her understanding of his lifestyle using tentative hypotheses or guesses about goals of behavior, basic convictions, strategies for belonging, and methods of coping with feelings of inferiority. She used the animal families, the toy soldiers, and animal puppets to communicate her thoughts about how his feelings of being powerless and unconnected lead to his believing that he had to make sure that no one else could control him. Growl, the tiger, expressed his feelings that the other animals, especially his mother and the elephant, were always trying to tell him what to do. The therapist reflected his feelings and thoughts about this, while she also reflected the other characters' feelings and thoughts in order to help Jason consider alternative perspectives on his relationships. The therapist made a lot of guesses about Growl's goal of making sure that all those in the jungle knew that they could not tell him what to do. Growl sometimes expressed happy feelings about being able to keep everyone else from telling him what to do, and he sometimes talked about being lonely and wished that he had more friends. At first, he did not trust most of the other animals, with the possible exception of his father and his little sister. Gradually Growl tried to make friends with other animals, and although occasionally he got his feelings hurt because things did not work out, he usually had fun with the new friends.

The therapist also used other metaphoric techniques such as mutual storytelling (Gardner, 1971, 1986), custom-designed therapeutic metaphors (Lankton & Lankton, 1989; Mills & Crowley, 1986), and Creative Characters (Brooks, 1981, 1985). Jason resisted these strategies because he perceived her asking him to engage in these exercises as an attempt to tell him what to do. By refusing to participate, he passively asserted his own power.

When he did this and when he had other reactions to her interventions, the therapist used metacommunication to talk about his nonverbal communications, the underlying messages in his communication, and the patterns of his reaction to her tentative hypotheses and interpretations (Kottman, 1995). By acknowledging his responses and pointing out these patterns, the therapist helped Jason learn to recognize how he was feeling and thinking in various situations. The following is an example of an exchange in which the therapist used metacommunication to interpret Jason's behavior and motivation.

> **Jason:** (Walking into the playroom) I'm not doing that dumb storytelling that you wanted me to do last week, so don't even try it on me.
> **Therapist:** You wanted to let me know right up front that I couldn't tell you what to do this week. You sound kind of mad—it seems like you think I might try to trick you into doing something you don't want to do. (Reflecting his purpose, metacommunicating about a lifestyle pattern.)
> **Jason:** Yeah. My mom tries to trick me like that.
> **Therapist:** You think that your mom tries to get you to do things by tricking you and you really get mad about that. I think maybe you're afraid that's what is going to happen with me. You want to let me know that I can't get away with telling you what to do or getting you to do things by tricking you. (Reflection of feelings, metacommunicating about his purpose and his underlying message.)

Another important technique during the insight phase of Adlerian play therapy is connecting the child's patterns of attitudes and behaviors in the playroom with those he or she uses in other situations. With Jason, the therapist made guesses about how he expressed his goal of power with her in the playroom and with other people in his life. As he let go of this goal and began shifting into more positive goals with her in the playroom, the therapist pointed out that he had begun to let go of this goal in other settings as well. It seemed to be helpful to suggest various relationships and situations in which he could successfully strive for the more constructure goals of behavior. This strategy was also useful in helping Jason learn to own his assets in places other than the playroom and in encouraging him to generalize the ability to trust others and acknowledge problems and negative feelings. Verbalizing the connection between what Jason did in the play therapy environment and what happened in the real world served as a segue to the fourth phase of Adlerian play therapy, reorientation/reeducation.

Reorientation/Reeducation

In this phase of Adlerian play therapy, the therapist actively prepared Jason to transfer skills and attitudes he had learned in the play therapy process into situations and interactions in other places. She used brainstorming to help Jason generate new ways of thinking, feeling, perceiving, interpreting, and behaving for outside the playroom. When necessary, she also taught Jason new skills. In order to maximize the possibility of successful transfer of these coping mechanisms, the therapist set up practice opportunities—inside and outside the playroom. As Jason began to act on revised choices about lifestyle, goals of behavior, ways of gaining significance, and so forth, the therapist encouraged his effort and progress.

With Jason, the best approach in the reorientation/reeducation process seemed to be continuing the indirect approach. The therapist made suggestions for behavioral and attitudinal changes for Growl and his family, the toy soldiers, and the animal puppets. She asked Jason to brainstorm ideas for how the toy soldiers could settle their disputes other than hiding in the sand or shooting at one another. She taught the animal puppets negotiation skills so that they could directly ask for what they wanted and needed from each other without taking things from one another or fighting with one another. She had Growl practice various ways of keeping control of himself without getting into power struggles with other animals, especially the elephant and the mother tiger. When Growl used active and direct ways of relating to the other animals, rather than passive-aggressive methods of making sure they could not control him, the therapist noticed his new strategies and encouraged him for making those changes The therapist suggested that she and Jason role-play various situations with his mother and his teacher, hoping to get him to own problems and their solutions. By the end of their time together, Jason was occasionally willing to do this, but he still preferred less direct means of learning and practicing new behaviors and attitudes.

So that Jason could experiment with new behaviors without taking the risk of actually trying them with other children outside the playroom, the therapist asked him if he would be willing to have his sister spend part of several sessions with them in the playroom. When Carla came to sessions, the therapist suggested that Jason and Carla negotiate to decide what they would play together and how long to play with one another. When Jason gave up and deserted Carla because she was not playing exactly what he wanted her to play, the therapist asked him to try to talk to her and work it out, rather than giving up. After several joint sessions with Carla, the therapist asked Jason to choose a friend to bring with him for three or four sessions. With the friend, the therapist continued to work on Jason's sharing power, asking for what he wanted, communicating directly, and acknowledging problem situations. She encouraged him for effort and for progress, and she emphasized his strengths—both personal and interactional.

Since Jason had such a strong need for self-control, it was particularly important for him to be involved in the decision to terminate. Before the therapist made the decision to start her termination countdown, she asked Jason whether he felt that he was doing anything differently than before he came to play therapy and when he thought that he would be ready to stop coming to the playroom. She emphasized the positive changes she had seen in the playroom and changes in other relationships reported by him and his parents. The therapist had several sessions alone with Jason, without any other children, to help him consolidate the new concepts and behaviors he had learned in the play therapy process. They spent a lot of time during those sessions with Growl, the tiger whom nobody could tell what to do.

EXPECTED OUTCOME OR PROGNOSIS

In some ways, Jason was the ideal kind of client to have in Adlerian play therapy. His issues related to power and trust were amenable to the kinds of lifestyle interpretations and tentative hypotheses that are the "bread-and-jam" of Adlerian play therapy. His passivity, denial of problems, and refusal to directly communicate were somewhat of a problem, but he was very reachable through indirect, metaphoric methods of communication.

Also indicative of a positive prognosis was the fact that one of his parents (Emilio) had relatively good parenting skills, and the other (Mary) had clear-cut deficits that could be remediated. However, Mary's continuing, untreated depression and her rather obvious hostility to Jason and the inconsistency in the family atmospheres could have sabotaged the therapy process. If Mary were willing to participate actively in counseling to deal with her personal issues and to apply additional parenting skills consistently, the prognosis for Jason would have been extremely positive. Otherwise, that tiger would continue to Growl—loudly and often.

CONCLUSION

Adlerian play therapy is an approach to working with children that uses toys, play media, and art techniques to operationalize the strategies and concepts of Individual Psychology. Since Adlerians believe that each person is a unique and special individual, each application of Adlerian play therapy is also unique and special. The author finds herself constantly adapting and altering the strategies in her bag of tricks and adding new ones, depending on the child and his or her family. Because of the unique nature of the clients and the unique nature of each intervention, it was difficult to write about an imaginary (to the author) child. During the process of writing this chapter, the author found herself spending a great deal of time and energy thinking about what Jason would be like and how he would react—to the therapist, to the toys in her playroom, to various interventions. Since the author's own lifestyle has an element of needing to be right and wanting to be superior, this was a struggle for her personally. The other frustrating element of this process was that, in this short space, it was impossible to give the reader a complete and exact picture of what Adlerian play therapy would look and feel like. The author hopes that she has been able to give the reader at least an inkling of this exciting process.

BIBLIOGRAPHY

Adler, A. (1930). *The education of children*. South Bend, IN: Gateways Editions.

Adler, A. (1954). *Understanding human nature* (W.B. Wolf, Trans.). New York: Fawcett Premier. (Original work published 1927)

Adler, A. (1958). *What life should mean to you*. New York: Putnam Capricorn. (Original work published 1931)

Adler, A. (1963). *The problem child*. New York: Putnam Capricorn. (Original work published 1930)

Ansbacher, H., & Ansbacher, R. (Eds.). (1956). *The individual psychology of Alfred Adler: A systematic presentation in selections from his writings*. San Francisco: Harper & Row.

Beames, T. (1992). *A student's glossary of Adlerian terminology* (2nd ed.). Chicago: Adler School of Professional Psychology.

Brooks, R. (1981). Creative characters: A technique in child therapy. *Psychotherapy, 18*, 131–139.

Brooks, R. (1985). The beginning sessions of child therapy: Of messages and metaphors. *Psychotherapy, 22*, 761–769.

Dewey, E. (1971). Family atmosphere. In A. Nikelley (Ed.), *Techniques for behavior change* (pp. 41–47). Springfield, IL: Charles C Thomas.

Dinkmeyer, D., & Dinkmeyer, D. (1977). Concise counseling assessment: The children's lifestyle guide. *Elementary School Guidance and Counseling, 12*, 117–124.

Dinkmeyer, D., Dinkmeyer, D., & Sperry, L. (1987). *Adlerian counseling and psychotherapy* (2nd ed.). Columbus, OH: Merrill.

Dinkmeyer, D., & McKay, G. (1989). *The parent's handbook: Systematic training for effective parenting (STEP)* (3rd ed.). Circle Pines, MN: American Guidance Service.

Dreikurs, R., & Soltz, V. (1964). *Children: The challenge*. New York: Hawthorn/Dutton.

Eckstein, D., Baruth, L., & Mehrer, D. (1992). *Life-style: What it is and how to do it* (3rd ed.). Dubuque, IA: Kendall/Hunt.

Gardner, R. (1971). *Therapeutic communication with children: The mutual storytelling technique*. Northvale, NJ: Jason Aronson Inc.

Gardner, R. (1986). *The psychotherapeutic technique of Richard A. Gardner*. Northvale, NJ: Jason Aronson Inc.

Griffith, J., & Powers, R. (1984). *An Adlerian lexicon*. Chicago: Americas Institute of Adlerian Studies.

Knoff, H. (1985). *Kinetic drawing system for family and school: A handbook*. Los Angeles: Western Psychological Services.

Kottman, T. (1992). Billy, the teddy bear boy. In L. Golden & M. Norwich (Eds.), *Case studies in child counseling* (pp. 75–88). New York: Macmillan.

Kottman, T. (1993). The king of rock and roll. In T. Kottman & C. Schaefer (Eds.), *Play therapy in action: A casebook for practitioners* (pp. 133–167). Northvale, NJ: Jason Aronson Inc.

Kottman, T. (1994). Adlerian play therapy. In K. O'Connor & C. Schaefer (Eds.), *Handbook of play therapy* (Vol. 2, pp. 3–26). New York: Wiley.

Kottman, T. (1995). *Partners in play: An Adlerian approach to play therapy*. Alexandria, VA: American Counseling Association.

Kottman, T., & Johnson, V. (1993). Adlerian play therapy: A tool for school counselors. *Elementary School Guidance and Counseling, 28,* 42–51.

Kottman, T., & Warlick, J. (1989). Adlerian play therapy: Practical considerations. *Journal of Individual Psychology, 45,* 433–444.

Kottman, T., & Warlick, J. (1990). Adlerian play therapy. *Journal of Humanistic Education and Development, 28,* 69–83.

Landreth, G. (1991). *Play therapy: The art of the relationship*. Muncie, IN: Accelerated Development, Inc.

Lankton, C., & Lankton, S. (1989). *Tales of enchantment: Goal-oriented metaphors for adults and children in therapy*. New York: Brunner/Mazel.

Manaster, G., & Corsini, R. (1982). *Individual Psychology: Theory and practice*. Itasca, IL: F.E. Peacock Publishers, Inc.

Mills, J., & Crowley, R. (1986). *Therapeutic metaphors for children and the child within*. New York: Brunner/Mazel.

Mosak, H. (1979). Adlerian psychotherapy. In R. Corsini (Ed.), *Current psychotherapies* (2nd ed.). Itasca, IL: F.E. Peacock Publishers, Inc.

Sweeney, T. (1989). *Adlerian counseling: A practical approach for a new decade* (3rd ed.). Muncie, IN: Accelerated Development, Inc.

CHAPTER 12

Dynamic Family Play Therapy: A Creative Arts Approach

STEVE HARVEY

INTRODUCTION

Theory

Families play in informal and improvised moments together throughout their day. Such play has a spontaneous quality and occurs naturally. In these relaxed episodes, one can observe how an emotional quality is both reflected and created in the communicative style among the players. Such play offers catharsis, recuperation, and mastery of the emotional tension in intimate relationships. These moments of creative relationship are extremely varied and are shaped by a family's unique emotional atmosphere in accordance with the developmental issues of parents and children. Some examples include the face play of mothers/fathers and infants, toddlers' games of chase, an elementary child's more organized games with rules, and the dramatic stories and humorous exchanges between teenagers and their parents. Such natural moments of play can offer a rich avenue by which to develop family intervention.

Dynamic play therapy is an intervention style that engages family members in creative, expressive activity making use of such natural play. Whether the play is done together, in small groups of family members, or individually, the therapist's aim is primarily to help the family develop and expand their spontaneity and to generate playful metaphors that address relational difficulties. In this style of family play therapy, the therapist engages family members in various play modalities, including art, drama, movement, and video making. This intermodality approach is used to encourage family members to join together in an experience of mutual creativity rather than using play as an avenue to merely generate metaphors to be talked about. It is this experience of encouraging actual joining in creative, play moments together that is thought to provide one of the more powerful elements of change in this intervention style. As family members are able to experience this joining and to create an "expressive momentum" in their play, the therapist is then able to help guide family members into creating dramatic interactive play together in which new, emergent metaphors can help them experience a mutual catharsis, understanding, and sense of mastery in their emotional/intimate experience with each other. By both nurturing a cooperative creative spirit and helping a family develop new metaphors through this style of play, the essential goal of dynamic play therapy is to help family members "rechoreograph" the quality of their emotional relationships and intimacy.

Personality Theory

Given the emphasis on relationships between family members, creativity, and emotional intimacy, dynamic play therapy does not emphasize the more traditional personality theories that address the psychopathology and deviance of individuals. While individuals within a family may have significant psychological difficulties that clearly require individual attention, the main emphasis of dynamic play therapy is to build the creative and expressive strengths of a family together. Because of this central goal of nurturing and developing cooperation, creative mutuality, and intimacy, dynamic play therapy draws on theoretical models of creative problem solving (Getzels & Csikszentmihaly, 1976), those humanistic approaches to family therapy (Satir, 1967, 1972), attachment theory (Bowlby, 1982), and the curative powers of the play experience (Schaefer, 1993). The presentation of such theoretical models and the integration into this form of family play therapy has been presented in earlier works (Harvey, 1989, 1990, 1993, 1994a, 1994b, 1994c, Harvey & Kelly, 1993). These ideas will be reviewed only briefly here.

One of the central aspects of human relationships utilized by dynamic play therapy is the spontaneous, flexible, and mutual play that develops between parents and children from a child's earliest moments of conception and birth onward. Those researchers and clinicians (Harvey, 1994c; Stern, 1985; Tortera, 1994) interested in parent-infant play clearly observe how such playful exchanges develop a natural dance or choreography involving eye contact, smiling, and responsiveness in mutual, nonverbal exchanges. As a child grows and a parent-child relationship matures in toddlerhood, such games become more elaborate, using sound and face making, verbal exchanges and larger sensory-motor play involving running, jumping, and tumbling. Clearly, by the preschool years, mothers, fathers, and their young children engage in an extended range of dramatic role-playing in addition to a wider variety of physical, mutual exchanges. A visit to a playground or park where young children and their parents are playing reveals a wide variety of such family interchanges. Such play develops into more verbal and humorous interactions as a family matures. In observing such play, one is struck by the spontaneity and naturalness of the participants and how such play generates a spirited and emotional joining. It is characterized by an attunement or responsiveness and by the ability of parents and children to solve any mismatching of their intentions quite easily with mutual flexibility.

In these episodes, themes tend to repeat, and emotional issues become quite evident. Examples of such themes include a young toddler who has just been injured casting his willing mother or father into the role of doctor to "cure" him; a young infant who is frightened by separation initiating nonverbal communication to cue her parent's secure embrace, physical holding, and visual attention through face games; a preschooler's playful exploration with a role in which he magically transforms himself into a very powerful problem solver under his mother's watchful eye and sometimes active participation. Clearly in the best of circumstances, families' mutual play produces a healing process in which their spirited mutual creativity and imagination transform such themes in a way that the players experience affiliation, intimacy, and affirmation. Schaefer (1993) has identified several curative powers of such play. These powers appear to be generic to the experience of this mutual play itself.

This positive experience with play clearly contributes to a family's emotional growth. However, those who have observed families with children who have experienced abuse or trauma, or are in the midst of loss or divorce, are quick to see how difficult and painful such mutual play and engagement can be. From these observations it is clear that the task for the play therapist is to help families who experience difficulties discover for the first time or rediscover their own natural play that can address their emotional difficulties, thereby rebuilding their intimacy. The therapy task is to help families generate play experiences that draw on the therapeutic powers of play described by Schaefer (1993).

For such family play experiences to occur regularly, emotional security is essential. After many years of careful observation and research, Bowlby (1972, 1973, 1982) observed how important the attachment between parents and children can be. Parents who consistently and sensitively match their emotional responses to their young children's nonverbal signals of distress generate feelings of security within their families. However, parents and children who are unable to accomplish this form insecure attachments characterized by avoidance, ambivalence, and disorganization in their ongoing nonverbal communications with each other, especially in strong emotional situations. The outcome of secure attachment is the development of an emotional, bodily felt sense of trust between parents and their children. On the other hand, parents and children with insecure attachment tend to experience a basic sense of mistrust and fear. According to Bowlby, an additional concept related to secure attachment is that of secure base for exploration. Central to this tenet is the notion that there is a direct relationship between the amount of security a child feels and the amount of effective, clear exploration a child engages in as he or she grows. Conversely, insecure children's exploration is negatively affected. These concepts can also be applied to the family situation in which the entire system of emotional relationships of a family contributes to a secure base that allows the whole family to explore once a sense of security is achieved (Byng-Hall, 1991). However, if this sense of security is negatively impacted, as in the case of divorce, loss, or abusive trauma, exploration and mastery of emotional conflict are likewise negatively impacted.

These concepts are important for the dynamic play therapist when observing family members together. The mutual play of parents and children who have secure attachments generate exploration and flow, curiosity, mastery, creativity, good feeling, and intimacy among the players, whereas the play between parents and children who are insecure is characterized by a sense of fearfulness and lack of cooperation.

The playful exploration of such families' emotional as well as physical world is significantly negatively impacted. With these concepts in mind, the goals of dynamic play therapy are to help parents and children find some success in their mutual play together, however small. By using their positive emotional response to their mutual play, the therapist helps to rebuild a sense of positive feeling and security together. Such security is established when more exploration can occur, leading to longer episodes of natural play. As such natural play occurs, families begin to generate their own positive healing and regeneration of relationships.

Model of Psychopathology

Psychopathology, or the problem to be addressed in this style of intervention, is conceptualized as any expression within the system of family relationships that detracts from a sense of overall, bodily felt security experienced by family members. Clearly, Bowlby's ideas concerning a parent's, child's, or family's collective experience of unresolved separation and loss, and a parent's history with intimacy and attachment, serve as the underlying contributors to the amount of security or insecurity in a family's emotional life. In turn, insecurity in a family's attachment affects the quality and style of their natural play together. Along this line, Maine and Solomon (1993) found that one of the factors leading to disorganized attachment between mother-infant dyads was the mother's unresolved grief around the loss of her parent. These authors hypothesized that such mothers' fear of loss contributed to their inability to remain consistently sensitive to their young children, leading to the children's experience of confusion when seeking security.

Not only can an individual family member's history with attachment-related episodes and loss contribute to lack of security in a family, but an entire family's experience with such episodes of unresolved loss and separation can contribute to the development of insecurity as well. The system of emotional family relationships can become significantly guarded and defensive following significant unresolved loss, as in the death of a child or divorce. When an entire family's system of achieving security through repeated patterns of communication is significantly disrupted— as in the case of a death of a family member, abuse, or a family breakup—the entire family clearly goes through an adjustment as well. As in a parent-child dyad, if such an adjustment to loss remains unresolved, the entire family can develop an avoidant, ambivalent, or disorganized style of communication. The entire family needs to have the opportunity to express, understand, and integrate significant feelings of anger, sorrow, and pain following loss and separation. Without such an opportunity, the development of unrecognized family grieving can develop. The outcomes of such a family experience can erode the feeling of the family as a secure base.

Given a family in a situation in which defensive communication replaces intimacy, one of the things that becomes eroded quickly is the quality of mutual, intimate family play. In this state, the more spontaneous expression between family members becomes quite painful, producing problems and emotional tension. The sense of free expression and playful exploration of expression becomes limited.

Individual family members typically introduce expressions designed to defend their self-esteem and fragile feelings of closeness. Personal differences are not tolerated. Typically, interactions are characterized by strategies that include avoidance of intimacy, controlling of others, and withdrawing of basic affections. Daily interactions develop a characteristic of similar, repetitive emotional exchanges, producing a similar quality of emotional tension. When questioned, family members can even recognize the familiarity of the argumentative or withdrawn interactive patterns that occur throughout their daily life. In this state, the free spontaneity of emotional expression and play degenerates rapidly.

Goals

The overall goal of dynamic play therapy intervention is to help families reestablish a mutual, creative, playful expression and to increase the episodes of the naturally occurring play. Once parents and children can play together again, the goal of the intervention is to help guide the family to more consciously create metaphors that directly relate to and express their emotional pain. As mentioned previously, such pain is usually related to unresolved loss and separation.

After the initial stages of helping family members play together in a more free and spontaneous manner, the resulting in-office expression usually begins to reflect a single core issue that influences the thematic material of the mutual play. Usually this theme relates to the central loss of intimacy and/or the fear of developing new closeness. This theme can usually be recognized through its repetitive nature, although when presented initially it is somewhat disguised.

As the therapist and/or family begins to recognize the elements of this core episode, story, or dramatic scenario, the therapist's job becomes one of helping the family members define their emotional responses and engage in the play with more spontaneity. Usually these later play episodes are quite cathartic. During the play interactions in this stage of therapy, family members begin to generate for the first time or rediscover intimacy and attachment. The goal of the work in these stages is to help family members rechoreograph their attachments as well as resolve past experiences with separation and loss as they play together.

CASE FORMULATION

The case of Jason L. and his family fit quite well with the theory of dynamic play therapy.* In this case, Jason was clearly the identified patient or the family member identified by school authorities, social services, and his family as the problem. However, when considering the family history of mother and father and the events surrounding this family's life prior to and including divorce, it was clear that all members of this family, individually and collectively, experienced significant alien-

---

*See "Orientation to the Text: The Case of Jason L.," p. 1.

Due to the parents family history, it affected their own interaction w/ their children

ation from each other. From the material presented, it appeared that despite mother's and father's best genuine efforts at creating a successful and loving family for themselves, and the children's strong underlying feelings of love and loyalty toward their parents, Jason, Mary, and Emilio—and quite possibly Carla, the younger sister—experienced a great deal of pain, with accompanying avoidance of intimacy. Despite many positive elements in their relationships, from the information provided it appeared that the quality of their core emotional relationships contained elements of constriction of spontaneity. This put a damper on the amount of natural playfulness and creativity these family members could experience with each other. Further, there was a strong possibility that the family as a whole experienced depression and lack of fulfillment in their emotional exchanges.

Individually, each of the parents brought difficulties from the emotional histories of their nuclear families to their current family. This was seen most clearly from the events of Mary's life. She reported strong themes of loss and separation. From her description such losses were unresolved. Following the breakup of her nuclear family through her parents' divorce, her father died. In her current family, Jason's younger brother died shortly after he was born. Finally, she experienced great difficulty throughout all her pregnancies. From the descriptions of this behavior, it appeared that Mary likely felt a great amount of ambivalence and fear as she approached experiences of intimacy. Following the death of her son, she reported significant episodes of depression, which may well have been related to her general experience associated with loss. Mary's history with loss likely was transmitted to her children, especially Jason, though a general inconsistency of her sensitive and attuned responses to them. Such a maternal response during Jason's first years also likely contributed to feelings of insecurity, leading to an ambivalent attachment style on his part.

Emilio, Jason's father, also presented with some difficulties in his emotional engagement in his past as well as present family situations. He reported that his brother and father were somewhat alcoholic. Further, following the death of his second son and his wife's depression, he had a long-term affair. This suggested the presence of some general emotional withdrawal from intimacy in a family situation. On the positive side, verbal reports and observations on the Marschak Interaction Method (MIM) pointed to quite positive interactions between Emilio and his son, suggesting that Jason and his father shared moments of playful spontaneity easily. However, it was yet to be seen whether such spontaneity would develop naturally, given longer contact between them. Both Emilio and Jason needed to develop a commitment to each other to use their playful exchanges to consistently address problems, including difficulties with intimacy and withdrawal.

Like his mother and father, Jason's behaviors suggested that he may have felt very alone in his family situation and that he was unable to consistently express his deeper feelings of pain in any clear, consistent, and independent fashion. Despite being apparently very much loved and wanted, he experienced his mother's fear of loss, his mother's and father's reaction to the death of his younger brother followed by extended periods of maternal nonavailability due to depression, his father's withdrawal from the family, and the breakup of his family. The conception, birth, and death of his younger brother came at a particularly vulnerable time in Jason's psychological development. Young toddlers typically experience strong, ambivalent feelings of the want and need for independence coupled with the continuing need for dependence on their attachment figures. It is likely that events in Jason's second year, coupled with a difficult infancy, contributed to a lack of full playful enjoyment of his independent play. Such emotional fulfillment with independent play typically helps solve the developmental strivings for individuation in toddlerhood. Without this achievement of successful independent play, Jason's security in social growth would be compromised.

Finally, with the conception and birth of his sister and his parents' subsequent divorce, it is likely that Jason continued to experience an insecure family environment, leading to continued constriction of his independent emotional expression. Given his symptoms at seven years of age, Jason's social and emotional development was affected by his insecurity toward his attachment figures. Such insecurity left him unable to solve basic conflicts of wanting to approach his parents for security, yet needing to avoid them because of past disappointments in their responses to him.

Within this family context and general emotional atmosphere, Jason's behavioral problems and emotional immaturities could be seen as an interactive strategy to deal with his own fears of separation and lack of confidence in and enjoyment of his independence. Perhaps the most relevant piece of the assessment of Jason included his social/emotional developmental delays as reported by the DTORF-R, his social withdrawal supported by the CBCL, emotional constriction indicated through his projective drawings, difficulties with impulse control as indicated on the Rorschach, and strong need to engage in power struggles with authority indicated by the TAT. These testing results, coupled with an above average intellectual ability as well as presenting problems of aggression, moodiness, and general irritability around his mother after periods of separation, all suggested an ambivalent, resistant attachment strategy in which he was unable to achieve emotional security, satisfaction, and enjoyment in his own independence, but remained fearful and overwhelmed by feelings of abandonment. Without intervention, it was likely that he would continue to remain developmentally immature and emotionally constricted and would have difficulty with peer relations and the development of intimacy and appropriate self-confidence as he grew, despite his intellectual strengths. Unfortunately, separation was experienced by Jason as an overwhelming abandonment, and his fearfulness remained largely unconscious, affecting his interpersonal relationships with both his friends and past and future family.

Both Emilio's and Mary's description of Carla as a perfect, loving child further suggested Jason's isolation within the family system. Because of the lack of open and honest expression of mourning related to the family breakup, as well as the death of this couple's second child, it was likely that Carla would function in the role of a replacement child for the dead infant. While temperamentally she may have been a very easy child to parent, the emotional dynamics with Jason's family surrounding separation and loss may have cast her in the role of the perfect child. Within this family's emotional atmosphere, both Mary and Emilio liked strongly reinforced Carla's more "positive" social communication while ignoring her natural aggression and independent strivings, leading her toward being a "good girl" at all costs. Under these circumstances, she was at risk for developing a false self in order to be more fully accepted by her parents.

Given the scenarios previously described, this family as a whole can be thought of as developing interactive strategies to survive significant losses and separations. Unfortunately, the price of obtaining emotional survival through isolation and the constriction of natural play expression is that the family could well remain isolated from each other and unable to share the stronger feelings related to attachment needed to develop a sense of emotional security. This may affect their future relationships, not only with each other but with others with whom they desire closeness, such as in a remarriage and stepfamily situation, or with peers, and ultimately in Jason's and Carla's future close friendships and marriage partners.

The episodes of physical abuse between Mary and Jason can be thought of as an intensified, rigidified, and dramatic version of the general atmosphere of insecurity, mistrust, fear of loss, and unresolved grieving coupled with strong needs in these individuals to control their emotional world. However, with the addition of physical violence, a very important emotional line has been crossed in that all family members had to deal with the possibility that violence could occur again. Such expectations only further worked against the development of intimacy and mutuality needed to resolve the loss and development of natural play. Therefore, these episodes needed to be addressed honestly, with everyone in the family, by developing new agreements not to use physical assaults to solve conflicts, to respect each other's internal tensions, and to develop alternative means of expression with each other. Without such agreements, gains in any family-oriented therapy would be limited.

TREATMENT GOALS

The main treatment goal of this intervention was to help this family as a whole— and each parent with each child—experience a greater sense of emotional security. Within this goal, this family needed to address the resolution of losses and the separation of divorce. The parents needed to seek out and participate in some individual sessions, as well as in dyadic sessions separately with their son. Some sessions needed to be completed with the entire family. To accomplish these global goals, some initial stages needed to be accomplished first. Each parent needed to establish a sense of spontaneous, mutual play with the son. Such play required therapist direction in the initial stages of treatment to help them focus on mutually enjoyable activities and to help redirect them when such play became problematic or irrelevant for them. For this to occur, each parent and Jason needed some individual sessions to develop their own style of play in their favorite modality. For example, Jason enjoyed more sensory-motor or physical play, while his mother used a combination of art and verbalization. Additionally, each parent needed help in engaging Jason in his day-to-day life, such as behavior management techniques or expressive means, such as mutual drawing, during his episodes of moody behavior.

The goal of such intervention was to help both Jason and his parents (Mary in particular) establish some behavior management that addressed the presenting problem of moodiness accompanied by physical conflicts. Mary needed to learn how to identify these internal cues, as well as the interpersonal situations with Jason that led her to strike him.

As the family members collectively and individually had some success with developing alternative methods of expression and more behavioral control in the home setting, as well as generating some enjoyable play episodes together, Jason was seen individually to help him recognize, develop, and enjoy his independent, spontaneous play and subsequently develop metaphorical and more direct verbal expression concerning his sense of loss from the divorce. Further goals were to help him establish a sense of appropriate inputs as to when visitation with his father started and stopped, and what the transition between these visits looked like. Some children of divorce find it very helpful to have input into what toys or clothes they can take back and forth with them, or which activity helps them to readjust to a parent's home. The general goal of this is to help children establish a sense of appropriate control and choice making in an otherwise very adult-dictated situation (divorce and breakup of the family). In this stage of therapy, Mary and Emilio also needed to address their own issues surrounding the loss and breakup of their family.

Following these stages of therapy, a final goal was to help the entire family establish a sense of resolution concerning the major losses they had experienced together— the death of an infant and the breakup of their family. It was suggested that, during such activities, Carla could be involved, as these episodes have affected her as well. During such conjoint activity, the development of a family play ritual (Imber-Black, Roberts, & Whiting, 1988) marking the death of the second son and the end of the family were designed to include Carla's direct participation. Throughout all of these therapy stages, efforts to help the family develop episodes of natural play together occurred.

TREATMENT DESCRIPTION

Logistics

Setting and Materials

More extensive descriptions of the kind of play material and the therapy room setting have been described in earlier works (Harvey, 1989, 1990, 1993, 1994a, 1994b). Only a brief description to orient the reader on how the use of play props can facilitate family interactions will be provided. While dynamic play therapy can be accomplished in any number of settings, including inpatient, the current author has practiced this intervention style primarily in an outpatient setting.

As in other forms of play therapy, psychotherapists working with adults often complain of noise coming from play activity such as laughing, children's screams, or other sounds such as banging, gymnastic balls against the walls, and so forth. Therefore, it is recommended that the dynamic play therapy room be set far enough aside from other activities to avoid such complaints, as it is far more beneficial for the therapist to work at helping family members develop some kind of free and spontaneous expression rather than worrying about colleagues' negative reactions to the sounds that children and adults might make while playing together. It is also quite helpful to have rooms large enough so that a family can freely engage in dramatic and movement play activities. A 15' × 20' carpeted room is usually sufficient for these purposes. It is helpful to have a separate section of the playroom or separate office designated as a talking area with couch and chairs. With young children it is very difficult for a family to sit down and talk among the play props. Therefore, having a designated "talking room" and "playroom" have proven to be quite helpful in making this separation.

The props for dynamic play therapy are usually somewhat different than the smaller props used in other forms of play therapy. Rather than a dollhouse or sandtray, this intervention style makes use of large pillows, stuffed animals, scarves, stretch ropes, and gymnastic balls to encourage full body movement and dramatic enactment. The play props include stuffed animals of varying sizes, including those as large as grown adults, those the size of children, and the more usual, smaller animals. Large, 4' × 1$^1/_2$' × 6" rectangular pillows are particularly helpful for building houses, walls, and defining play areas in the room. Large, multicolored, 6', 4', and 3' scarves are very helpful for costuming and prop pieces. Long pieces of elastic sewn in a circular shape between 3' and 6' diameter are useful for tug-of-wars or having family members connect in joined activities. Large, multicolored parachutes and gymnastic balls also help encourage and organize kinetic activity. Large pieces of butcher paper, in either tablets or rolls with various forms of crayons, colored pencils, and markers are helpful to go from dramatic or movement activity to art. Other art materials that have proven to be useful are Play Doh and other sculpting clay. Immediate access to a video camera and monitor are helpful so that families can make movies for their immediate viewing or for viewing as a homework assignment. Especially in cases involving the courts, special caution needs to be taken concerning any videotaping. The therapist needs to make efforts to ensure the confidentiality of play sessions.

Frequency and Duration of Treatment

In dynamic play therapy, family members are seen on an average of once a week. The therapist helps the family members plan who will attend each session. It is expected that children will be seen alone, parents will be seen alone, or parents and children will be seen in small groups. This is sometimes accomplished by splitting up the hour. A specific series of sessions with a particular grouping of family members is expected as the treatment progresses. Typically, in the case of divorce, conjoint sessions with the identified parent occur. Sessions with both parents are expected occasionally as well, if the parents can tolerate each other's presence. If the parents agree to a treatment plan, it is best for each parent to bring the child(ren) on alternating weeks. Toward the end of therapy, sessions involving the whole nuclear family can be planned for and implemented.

Usually such sessions require preparation with the respective parents and children. Specific goals and activities are planned to decrease the amount of unresolved hostility that might occur. For example, both parents may be included with the children to produce a mural drawing of how they remember positive experiences as a family. Given this directed task, it has been this author's experience that most parents, even after they are divorced, are able to participate in a cooperative manner if properly prepared.

Depending upon the amount of loss experienced by a family, additional sessions during the week may be necessary to deal with the intensity of the feelings that a family member might begin to experience. However, these extra sessions are seen as periodic and not necessarily a regular part of the treatment process.

As in many other family therapy styles, homework assignments are given to family members. These assignments include parents using simple behavior management techniques, children drawing out conflicts, and parents and children engaging in scribble wars in a prescribed fashion. The goal of these homework assignments is to increase playful expressive activity at home, particularly between parents and children.

From this author's experience in cases such as this, it is likely that therapy will be relatively long term (approximately one year or longer). This length of time is seen as essential to adequately address the issues of loss and the development of trust. Also, additional time is needed to see the children for sequences of sessions with each parent separately.

Treatment Stages

Introduction

Jason, his mother, father, and younger sister were introduced to dynamic play therapy in an intake much as the one described at the beginning of this book. In dynamic play therapy, usually one or both parents contact the therapist with a presenting problem. At this point, the therapist briefly describes the therapy process, explaining that, although the child is seen alone occasionally, there is a family orientation in which children are seen with their parents to address home issues as well as underlying conflicted feelings. Additionally, a goal of this initial phone conversation is to communicate to both parents that a preliminary goal of the dynamic play therapist is to help their child engage in the treatment process and, most specifically, that the therapist would make every effort to find some expressive play activity that both they and their child will enjoy. In Jason's case, to accomplish this goal the parents were instructed to tell their child that during the first session there would be some play activity, particularly physical activity such as tug-of-war, pillow fights, and drawing. This activity is for fun and not used to open verbal interpretation.

During the first session, the therapist met with both parents and Jason briefly, explaining to Jason the nature of the referring phone contact. In this case, "Your mother called me about some of the problems you've had at school and at home, and I've seen many children who get angry, especially when their parents break up. Typically what happens is that I talk a little bit with your parents and then I can help you make games with your parents to try to find some other ways for you and your parents to express yourselves." Jason was then asked to complete a series of drawings on a large piece of newsprint with his choice of markers, crayons, or pencils. These drawings included a house-tree-person, his family doing something, "scribble with your eyes closed and turn it into something," and a free drawing. While Jason was drawing, a clinical interview—very similar to the one described—with the parents proceeded, including questions about presenting problems and developmental history. Separate times with each parent occurred shortly thereafter to gain a complete understanding of the divorce and their goals in therapy. Each parent was also given material to read about family play therapy and some techniques for in-office and home activities.

Importantly, the parents were informed about the process of family play therapy and told how they would become engaged in drawing, dramatic, and movement activities with their children. Descriptions of homework were given, including such examples as scribble wars. Simple behavioral charts were explained, with the idea that expectations of behavior management as well as play expression were needed. Such ideas were presented as possibilities, as families are encouraged to offer their own experiments and solutions, particularly as the therapy proceeds. This important element of dynamic play therapy is to help family members engage in their own series of creative problem solving and creative expression in an intrinsic manner, as opposed to simply following what is prescribed for them.

Following these verbal exchanges between the therapist and parents and after Jason finished his drawings, some play activity occurred between Jason and his mother and Jason and his father, as promised to him. This step was particularly important, as many children feel threatened by verbal exchanges in the beginning of therapy. Often they feel as if they have done something wrong and are going to an authority like a school principal who will further blame them for their difficulties. Therefore, it is important to make time for some play activity in which the child feels comfortable in beginning to express himself; he can have the expectation that his wishes, desires, curiosity, and intrinsic motivation will become central to the therapy process.

Initial Play Activities

After the orientation to therapy and initial clinical information concerning the presenting problems, developmental history, and history of the divorce are gathered and goal setting is done, some initial family play activities occur. These activities are directed by the therapist. The goal of such activities is not only to gather some initial information as to the dynamic interactive patterns seen in interactive play, but to help parents and children, specifically, understand some of their problems in concrete play terms. In this particular case, such family activities occurred with Mary and the two children and Mary and Jason together in some sessions, and then with Emilio and Jason and Emilio and the two children together in another series of sessions.

Initial activities for this case were (1) Jason and his mother playing a game of follow-the-leader, with both getting a chance to be leader; (2) Jason and his mother doing a drawing activity on the same piece of large newsprint on which (a) they both drew a house in front of them, (b) they took turns drawing a system of roads and adding any other images such as freeways, lakes, parks, and so forth, and (c) they drew themselves coming out of their house, developing some kind of story; (3) Jason and his mother using the stuffed animals and pillows to enact a story about a family; and (4) free play. Jason and his father completed the same series of directed activities during another session. Jason, his sister, and mother played follow-the-leader and engaged in free play. Emilio and the two children also completed these activities.

As stated previously, one of the central concepts of dynamic play therapy is that the process and content of a family's interactive play is directly related to their basic system of emotional attachments, especially those involving unresolved loss and separation. Therefore, it is assumed that the process by which each of these groupings of family members complete these drawing, movement, and dramatic activities reveals the quality of their emotional relationships with each other. In these activities there are clear episodes of participation leading to a genuine feeling and spirit of spontaneity and creativity, while there are other episodes in which the family shows avoidance, overcontrol, and lack of participation leading to general feelings of emotional tension, frustration, and isolation. The therapist, by observing and reflecting back to the family members when and how such moments occur, can help reframe these deeper emotional family issues into a dramatic game and play context. By observing the general content of the various story lines, images, and dramatic metaphors that are mutually created, the therapist can also gain an understanding of the underlying emotional content. It should be noted that, in these initial expressions, the metaphors likely include a great deal of disguise and distance.

During follow-the-leader, both Jason and his mother attempted to control each other. Jason initially nominated himself as leader and kept introducing physical ideas, while Mary appeared to become more uncomfortable with her body—standing in one place with her arms crossed and offering only verbal directions to her son. This interactive style led to many disagreements, and the initial good feeling of playing together quickly changed into frustration and annoyance. They declared the game over after only a few minutes while Jason was somersaulting over the pillows.

During the drawing activity, Jason made a house that occupied a great amount of space. The walls were thick and protected. He also refused to develop any mutual imagery with his mother. During the story part, Jason drew himself on a separate corner of the paper. During the family story, Jason and his mother were able to produce only one short, superficial story involving stereotyped characters completing simple, predictable daily activities such as watching TV. The enactment was completed without much input or creative, spontaneous expression of feeling. Likewise, free play in which there was far more demand placed on spontaneous engagement produced a very short, nonengaged activity. Jason suggested and engaged in several more physical activities, jumping or somersaulting on the pillows, while his mother observed, showing an angry, withdrawn body posture and facial expression.

In the activities among Jason, Carla, and their mother, Mary became far more involved with Carla, and left Jason somewhat isolated. During the family enactment with his sister present, Jason developed a subscenario in which one of the stuffed animals got hurt, while his mother and sister played out simple scenarios involving the mother and little girl animals talking with each other.

Initial Play with Emilio, Jason, and Carla

In their episodes together, Jason, Carla, and Emilio produced more spirited mutual play. While completing the follow-the-leader activity with his father, Jason immediately became an enthusiastic leader and Emilio followed his son's ideas. When Jason switched roles with his father, the follow-the-leader game spontaneously broke down into simple games of chase and wrestling. While completing the mutual drawing activity of houses and developing a story with turn taking, the drawing between Emilio and Jason produced a similar style of house, covering a large amount of space on the paper. However, in the session, Jason included himself approaching his father and their engaging in far more mutual activities in the common drawing space. Despite this more interactive style, Jason's and Emilio's story was remarkable for the lack of any specific metaphors and narratives relating to families.

When Carla was included in the play, follow-the-leader quickly became a game of wrestling, with the children climbing on their father. These improvisations produced fun and laughter. The quality of the free play was similar to that previously described, with the father and two children enjoying each other, but with little content or imagery emerging.

While the differences between Jason's and Carla's interactions with their mother and father were quite pronounced in the amount of ease and fun shared by adults and children, a common theme emerged. Family play was characterized by a general avoidance and development of imagery that would suggest deeper emotional engagement. This avoidance was more clearly seen in the actual play process between Jason and his mother and sister, with Jason and Mary showing less attunement, sense of spontaneity, and engagement. Such play led to a lack of enjoyment and a general dampening of positive feeling by both mother and son. The play between Emilio, Jason, and Carla was characterized by more positive feeling in its overall emotional tone. However, the avoidance was evident by a lack of development of dramatic scenarios or images that could give reference to more troubling themes involving separation and loss. In this play, the interactions between Jason and his mother had lost their natural spontaneity and creativity, while the play between Jason and his father was not reflective of the stronger, more painful emotional imagery. In general, such interactions served to protect this family from experiencing painful emotional issues they have faced together—at the expense of a more full and deep sense of expressed intimacy.

These initial activities demonstrated how the general emotional/behavioral difficulties presented in the initial interviews were expressed in both the process and content of the play. Through observation, the therapist can begin to understand how the spontaneous play needs to be broadened to address a wider spectrum of emotional exchange. However, the most useful part of these initial activities is to introduce to the family how their play can be expanded in very concrete and child-friendly terms. After viewing these activities, the therapist was able to talk with both parents and Jason about a general direction the play might go in therapy. For example, after the session with Mary and both children, the therapist was able to talk with Jason about how the hurt animal was ignored by the other animals and how that animal might be taken care of, as a means of introducing the general theme of alienation. In this way, the therapist was able to speak through the metaphor, suggesting more positive outcomes. The process of the avoidant style of play between mother and son was addressed through therapist comments such as, "Gee, it looks like you and your mom will need to learn how to do tug-of-wars so you can learn to have fights that are more fun."

The strengths of the father's relationships with his children were commented on to reinforce their general positive nature and ability to improvise with each other. However, the therapist also introduced metaphors of how such play could be used to enact stories to include more family narratives and imagery. In this way, the more psychologically minded language of psychotherapy was translated directly into play terms that both children and parents understood. The advantage of such explanations for Jason was that he was encouraged to participate in an active way in goal setting and developed an understanding of the general direction play sessions would take. For example, Jason enthusiastically added that he would like to play tug-of-war with his mother and have his hurt animal attended to by a family of animals.

Therapy: Initial Stages

After these beginning evaluative sessions were completed, Jason met the therapist with each of his parents separately for several weeks to begin addressing the immediate problems in the home, while at the same time participating in mutual interactive play in the office. During these sessions, Jason came with his mother on one week and with father the next. In the initial part of the sessions, approximately fifteen minutes was spent discussing home behavior and response to homework, and focusing both parent and child on the presenting problems. In this case, the problem involved Jason's moodiness, withdrawn behavior, and more angry outbursts when he came home from school, as well as his mother's frustrations in response.

After having both Jason and Mary describe their interactions after school, the therapist attempted to help mother and son reframe their behavior into their positive communicative intentions. Jason's moodiness was described as an attempt to show his mother how bad he was feeling, and Mary's frustration was described as her helplessness at being unable to help her son. Both Jason and Mary appeared to accept this understanding, and both were eager to develop an alternative and playful way to communicate with each other.

The therapist then suggested that Jason and Mary move into the playroom and have a scribble war. A scribble war is accomplished by having a parent and child each pick a separate colored crayon and begin to try out scribbling each other on a large piece of newsprint, with the general rule that the person who makes the most scribbles is declared the winner. As it is usually impossible to tell who produces the most scribbles, the therapist then includes an enactment of a more playful argument of who the winner is, leading to more scribble arguments to solve that problem, and so forth. The goal of this is to help the parent and child produce an activity, for example, the scribble argument, as a playful metaphor to address the more serious interactive problem of emotional tension and negative interaction that goes with disagreement. Usually these scribble arguments last only a few minutes, and several can be completed in one session.

After several such scribble wars have been completed with some sense of mutual enjoyment, the child and his parent could be asked to find and create an animal by drawing with different colors among the scribbles on the paper used in these art productions. Once these animals are generated, they can be given names, elaborated with further drawings, and then the parents asked to use them to develop more extended stories. Often such stories are drawn out using several pieces of paper. In such stories, animals typically talk with each other and participate together in dramas with several scenes. Sometimes each animal needs its own separate home on separate pieces of paper, and each participant needs several pieces of his or her own paper to produce the next scene of the story. These animal stories proceed within the general framework of each participant adding individual ideas freely without the sense of control from the other person and within the terms of a general interactive pattern of give and take. The therapist often needs to remind each participant that both are free to develop their own ideas and each new action and animal furthers an enactive story. Further, the therapist needs to help these animals engage in a metaphorical expression of feelings toward each other in a playful context.

Timing is important in that verbal interpretations of such metaphors should be made cautiously. During the initial stages, it is important to reinforce a general spirit of enjoyment and active mutual participation rather than to interpret the deeper issues involving intimacy and loss. It is easier to begin addressing emotional issues through the metaphor of the animals than to make direct references. The therapist might talk to the imaginary animal about how angry he or she might be as opposed to talking directly to the parent or child. Also, when working this way in a family situation, it is important not to take sides in introducing this metaphor, but rather to introduce the value of these metaphorical stories to address a wide range of emotional feeling within the context of a mutual narrative.

After Jason and Mary had several scribble wars in the office, the therapist introduced developing animals and a story. Mary initially drew a large fish, while Jason made a small puppy out of the scribble lines from one of their wars. When they were helped in developing a story, Jason immediately identified the fish as a shark, and both he and Mary decided that the puppy needed to get "out of the water." When asked how the two of them would solve this problem, Jason and Mary drew a boat together and another scene in which they rescued the puppy. Rather than interpret the story in any elaborate way, the therapist talked about how the story contained both a threatening figure as well as a puppy who was scared, and how well Jason and Mary worked together to give the story a positive ending. Both Jason and Mary enjoyed the play activity and accepted the discussion freely. Both also readily agreed to try scribble wars and stories when Jason came home from school. Over the next several weeks, as Jason and Mary were able to complete some wars and stories together with some enjoyment, the therapist pointed out how the two of them had successfully interacted with each other during a frustrating time of the day, without resorting to violence or other mean-spirited behavior. Such comments helped reinforce the goal of labeling the times mother and son could actually play together as a partial solution to their difficulty in relating to each other.

During the initial sessions with Emilio, Jason and his father were also asked to complete scribble wars and develop stories. Jason's character in this situation was a large bear, and Emilio also drew a bear. The two then produced a story about the bears wrestling. The final drawing turned into another scribble war. The therapist commented that both Jason and his father enjoyed having fun fights so much that they liked to forget everything. When asked if they could identify a tense time together during which they could use scribble wars at home, Emilio and Jason decided to try this activity during times when Jason would first arrive at his house for visits and just before he was to leave. After trying this, both reported that visit transitions went a little smoother.

Improvisation: The Development of Initial Play

The general goal of the next series of sessions is for the therapist to introduce directed play scenarios to help focus the interactions, to provide a safe structure to ensure successful play between Jason and his parents, and to encourage spontaneous improvisation to extend play. When using such an initial structure, the dynamic play therapist is very observant of the style each parent and child brings to the play and how this contributes to breakdowns in their play together. The general task of the therapist is to notice the various breaks, from the initial structure, in the play, in order to incorporate these into further improvisations. Such breaks are thought to be related to deeper conflicts.

After Jason and his parents had some success with the scribble wars, the therapist introduced a tug-of-war game with Jason and Mary. The therapist presented this game because Jason's and Mary's description of their conflicts had the quality of a continuing power struggle.

The tug-of-war was set up with Jason and Mary using a stretch rope placed around their waists. Before starting the game, the therapist, Mary, and Jason took the time to plan how the game could be played so that they could be "safe" or fall on the pillows. A pit of pillows was made and several pillows placed around the room. Both Mary and Jason were asked to make falls into the pillows with each other and individually. This step helped establish a playful, light atmosphere as well as reassuring everyone that falling could be done without injury. The therapist again reminded Jason and Mary that they could become energetic with each other, be safe, and could enjoy mutual physical activity. This preparation was important, given the history of abuse.

As the game proceeded, Mary became more passive and Jason's mood became more negative, and he refused to continue. Both Jason and Mary exhibited a communicative style similar to the way they had initially completed other expressive play activities. When asked, Jason and Mary reported that the frustration in playing the tug-of-war felt the same way their arguments did at home.

This stop in the game was a clear break, and the dynamic play intervention was to help both Mary and Jason develop play improvisation from their own expressive styles. The intervention further assisted mother and son in extending their development of a playful feeling, nonverbal cues from the players, and creativity from their break in an effort to change their frustration into a positive orientation.

The therapist first reported that tug-of-war was really a game of "pull." Then Jason and his mother were helped to creatively develop and extend a pull game using the stretch rope and pillows. Jason offered to pull in several ways (slowly, fast, blindfolded) while his mother at first offered no resistance, turned away, and even sat down. Their mood changed as each responded with creative ideas. Finally, the two began to improvise more freely and pulled each other into the pillows. The therapist labeled these pillows as the "mood pit."

During the same period of sessions with his father, Jason reported that he had difficulty with visits because he felt he didn't have his own room. After discussing this, the therapist set up a game in which Emilio and Jason made a house with the pillows in which they made sure the stuffed animals had separate rooms. During the construction, Emilio and Jason started wrestling playfully, the stuffed animal characters became lost, and the rooms were kicked over.

The wrestling activity clearly stopped the initial room building and changed the metaphorical intent of "having a room." Further, for both Emilio and Jason this wrestling was the same interactive style they had shown throughout most of their play together. Using these cues, the therapist suggested that Jason and Emilio continue their wrestling under a parachute, calling this "the land where everyone loses his or her room." Emilio and Jason then extended the game creatively by crawling under the parachute to "find the room" in a playful manner.

By noticing and using the breaks or changes from the initial game structure, the therapist was able to help this family develop metaphors that were far richer in their content in second-level interpretation. The goal of this was to help family members use their normal defensive interactive patterns as a springboard to develop expressive metaphorical play with each other. Such metaphors were brief at first, and the family needed to play several times to develop their own in a more intrinsic manner. However, as the therapist helped them use this process of creative play together through coaching them to incorporate their more immediate emotional states and behavior within an ongoing improvisational flow of play, Emilio, Jason, and Mary could extend their periods of natural play improvisation significantly.

Individual Therapy Stages

When therapy reached the point where family members began developing and extending their play, individual sessions for Emilio and Mary occurred. Mary and Emilio were directed to use such treatment to examine their own interpersonal issues surrounding loss. Clearly Mary needed to address the issues surrounding the death of her father, the death of her infant, and the breakup of her marriage. In turn, Emilio needed to address how the alcoholism of his brother and father and the breakup of his marriage impacted on his ability to understand and relate to Jason's feelings.

In general, during this stage of treatment, individual therapy with the parents was seen as important so that both parents could more effectively help their children achieve some sense of trust and security. Without this stage, both Emilio and Mary ran the risk of projecting their difficulties onto their spouse with a significant amount of blame. Clearly, there were very real events that led to this. Mary began to blame Emilio's affair as a source of her unhappiness and thereby failed to gain a deeper emotional appreciation of her feelings of unresolved loss as contributing to her son's difficulties. Emilio pointed to Mary's depression and emotional withdrawal in the marriage as leading to his affair and thereby failed to more fully appreciate his contributions to the situation. Finally, it was important for Jason to have some individual sessions so that he could develop independent play and, ultimately, some verbal expression of his feelings surrounding the breakup of his family.

This series of individual sessions is seen as crucial if a family is ever to accomplish the goal of developing play that both expresses and helps resolve core issues involved with loss and separation. Without such individual resolution, particularly by the parents, it is highly unlikely that interactive play can develop to address the deeper issues involved, and only part of the goals outlined initially will be accomplished.

Generally, as this stage of therapy is initiated, a frank discussion with each parent individually describing the goals needs to occur. It is helpful if the parents seek out their individual treatment with different therapists of their own choosing. While the style of treatment can vary, the individual adult therapist should have some understanding of the goals of family treatment. The child's individual therapy could easily proceed with the same therapist. If either parent feels unable or unwilling to commit to individual treatment, the next phase of family therapy—which addresses the underlying issues of loss, separation, and breakup of the family—should not proceed, as there is some risk of harm to the children. Given this possibility, if either parent cannot agree to such individual treatment, the therapist should consider termination.

However, as both Emilio and Mary agreed to proceed under these conditions, the next phase of treatment involved seeing Jason individually. During these sessions, the therapist told Jason that, while most of what happened would be confidential, they would discuss what portions to share with his parents. The therapist explained to Jason that communicating his strong basic feelings, such as being angry or sad, was important in helping him build a more positive relationship with his parents. As the therapist helped Jason choose what emotional expressions to tell his parents about and how he could show them his inner experience (e.g., with a drawing or play), Jason was able to gain some control and a sense of security and purpose in his play.

During this series of individual sessions, "volcano" became one of Jason's favorite activities. In volcano, Jason lay down on his back under a pile of pillows. After all the pillows were in place, he began to kick them off while the therapist threw them back over him. He was successfully able to win, or kick the pillows off faster than the therapist could throw them back. Jason spontaneously reported that the game was similar to times when he felt angry, and he enjoyed being "mad" in such a fun way.

Interestingly, when he was asked to draw a picture of the mad volcano, he drew a mountain exploding with heavy red flames, while his small figure fell into the larger hole. When asked how this story could continue, he drew his mother and father throwing in ropes to rescue him from the lava source. When the therapist suggested that he could actually play this rescue scene out with his parents one at a time, he readily agreed.

During the next session with his mother and then his father, Jason made a large pile of pillows (lava) and had his parents actively pull him out of the volcano with the stretch ropes. As he was rescued, Jason showed joy in being pulled into his parent's body. Even though everyone clearly was playing, the metaphorical significance was clear to Jason and his parents.

After these scenes in which Jason and both his parents had experienced the success of enjoying playful, creative, and cathartic communication with each other concerning themes of strong emotion, the therapist began to address the question with Jason of how he felt about his parents' divorce. This was accomplished by asking Jason to concretely describe his emotional and physical sensations the moment he realized his parents were separating. As with other children who have experienced a family breakup, Jason reported that he had strong physical and emotional reactions of shock that he felt he could not express to either parent. Jason described the sensations of his chest tightening and his heart breaking the moment his mother and father told him they were going to divorce. Additionally, he was frightened by this moment and had no way to put his feelings into words for his parents.

The therapist had Jason initially just scribble to help him develop a representation of these feelings. Gradually, he was able to choose colors and draw a shape of a heart breaking among the scribbles. By the end of the session, Jason was able to lie down while the therapist traced his body. Jason then filled in the tracing with an elaborate color mural of his feelings. With some coaching, he was able to use this drawing to talk with mother in a later session about his strong hurt concerning the breakup. Mary was also able to listen in a nonjudgmental way to Jason. This session was very cathartic for both.

Jason was initially resistant to showing his picture to his father. The therapist told Jason that, as his feelings were important to Emilio as well, they needed to find some way to communicate it to him. Jason agreed to tell his father that he had strong feelings he could not tell him. He then developed a game whereby the therapist threw "telling scarves" in the air while he ran through the room either avoiding the scarves or allowing them to touch a body part. If a scarf touched him, he then would tell a small part of his feelings and move his touched body part to show how he felt. After several telling games, Jason wanted first to videotape the game to teach his father and later to play the game with Emilio. Though this process took several additional sessions, Jason was able to tell his father about his feelings in much the same way as with his mother. These moments between father and son were cathartic as well.

Working Through: Development of Ritual Play

After Jason had been able to express his feelings related to the divorce, sessions were planned that included all family members together. In this session, the therapist helped the family find a way to say Goodbye to the old "married" family through the use of ritual. This was accomplished by having all family members actively draw a mural in which a positive activity of the family acting together was produced. Even at Carla's young age, her spontaneous art attempts at using scribbles and other mark making was quite important for the mural. This family made a picture of themselves playing together. The family was then encouraged to bury the picture, ritually. This activity consisted of tearing up the mural and burying it with pillows. The intent of the activity was to symbolically let the idealized version of the past family go.

It was important that this activity was well planned out. Emilio and Mary discussed and rehearsed parts of this event with both children separately before the whole family completed it. Both parents were consulted prior to the event to see if each had the emotional maturity to attempt this together with the ex-spouse. This ritual was quite a painful moment for the family to confront.

A similar activity of ritually burying and saying goodbye to the child who had died followed. It was important that Jason and Carla also were involved in this ritual burial, as their emotional development was likely affected by the death of their sibling. Like the ritual Goodbye of the family, this ritual was prepared for through consultation with both parents and performed both individually and in dyads with Jason before the whole family participated. The actual actions of this ritual burial and saying Goodbye needed some symbolic representation of the infant. This included the infant's clothes, pictures, and a drawing in combination. The therapist encouraged Emilio and Mary to talk with their children about their feelings of both sadness at losing the infant and their joy at still having the uniqueness of their living children. This was accomplished by encouraging the parents to tell of their feelings around the birth of their children as well as stories of the memories of their children's early years. This activity preceded and followed the ritual and was done both together as a family and in separate parent-child dyads.

Following these rituals, interactive play with each parent and Jason separately occurred. These play sessions were characterized primarily by more free improvisation and less therapist direction. These activities were far more difficult to predict as they usually developed more unique characteristics between each parent and child. It was the goal for each parent and child to have the opportunity to develop his or her own natural healing play in which the playful process of image, metaphor, and storymaking occurred with some expressed momentum. At this point, the role of the therapist was to reflect the feelings and help incorporate minor breaks for the parent and child in the creative process. Importantly, this play continued to generate positive feeling spontaneously between parent and child. Both parent-child dyads also provided play images and scenarios that reflected the personal and family emotional dynamics of loss, control, alienation, and hope. At this point, Mary, Emilio, and Jason began verbally connecting their play stories and activity to their feelings with little or no intervention.

In the sessions following the ritual, Jason usually asked Mary to play volcano or tug-of-war with him. During one such session, a monster emerged in Jason's creative play that attacked the large bears in a very intense manner. Jason became very involved in the drama and at times was extremely rageful, while maintaining the role of engaged witness and occasionally speaking to the monster identifying feelings, describing actions, and expressing understanding and appreciation of his "life and death struggle." At the end of the session, both Mary and Jason reported how glad they were that they both used the drama to express such strong feelings, that they had not tried to control each other, and that the drama ended before they got into a "for real" fight themselves. Mary particularly became aware of how she could just accept her son's feelings without having to stop or control him, especially in the play activity.

In another scene with Jason and Emilio, the volcano game evolved into a game of chase under and through the pile of pillows. At this point, both Emilio and Jason began building separate houses at some distance from each other out of the loose play props, as well as a "wall" between their respective areas. Jason then became somewhat withdrawn in his house and, after some coaching, was able spontaneously to invite his father into his house to show him his "playthings." His mood lightened markedly during this episode. Both Emilio and Jason commented on how different this play was from their earlier wrestling matches in that both felt sadness in separation, and both felt special and more intimate when they found a way to visit Jason's house; Emilio was particularly struck by how emotionally important he was to his son.

At this point, usually parents and children are able to creatively extend their own play for a significant amount of time, even perhaps the entire session. Such play follows a general pattern of the beginning of a mutual expression of creative activity that naturally extends into more playful metaphor making. Gradually, these metaphors begin to more clearly represent the core emotional issues between the parent and child related to such issues as trust, separation, love, and intimacy. The therapist should not prematurely overinterpret or overintellectualize such play but rather should allow the creative experience to emerge between the parents and children. A general rule is for the therapist to merely observe or gently help extend the playful activity as long as the parent and child are able to keep generating such play intrinsically on their own, incorporating each other's ideas in a natural flow. This experience of natural play between parents and children has a curative power in helping to regenerate a sense of trust. The therapist must also learn to trust this process and allow the parents to transform their imagery and narratives over a period of the entire session. Usually some discussion at the conclusion is important and helps integrate the session. Sometimes it is useful for the therapist to help the family members summarize their session through a mutual storytelling technique that elucidates the main points of the metaphor rather than reducing such play to simple over/intellectualized insights. It is during the ongoing development of such play over several sessions that a core theme between each parent and child will emerge.

Negative Reactions

Negative reactions in dynamic play therapy are usually dealt with quite easily and directly. In general, the process of therapy is to incorporate all the breaks, strong emotional reactions, and emotional resistance into the play itself, changing the activity to help families adjust their play with each other to be more relevant. Also, through the use of emergent expressive homework, children's strong reactions at home are likewise included. However, it is also likely that families may have episodes of very strong anger, especially in the working-through portion of therapy prior to and following the rituals dealing with the breakup of the family or the death of a sibling. During this time, the therapist could deal with such strong emotional reactions by scheduling more sessions, particularly individual sessions. As the parents are resistant to these difficult subjects, they can be referred to their individual therapists for more sessions as well. The planning of the rituals and setting the context to include individual therapy prior to addressing more painful issues—either through improvisational play or family rituals of the later stages of therapy—are particularly important. It is recommended that the family members be well prepared for such activities, as even the more playful expression can elicit quite powerful reactions.

Because expressive activities can elicit such powerful emotions—particularly in Jason's family, in which strong feelings of loss and unresolved separation predominated—it is very important that the therapist establish a thorough understanding of the role of therapy in relation to any legal matters that the family might face. If such steps are not taken, the therapist faces the possibility that the emotional acting out may present itself in legal maneuvers that can be damaging to all the family members involved, particularly the children. This is especially true when matters of divorce, custody, visitation, and allegations of abuse present themselves, as in the case of Jason's family. If such an understanding with the parents, in terms of the role of therapy and the possibility for its eliciting strong feelings, is not dealt with in an honest, forthright manner, there is a likelihood that legal intervention, including testimony and report writing by the therapist, will be counterproductive from a mental health perspective. Unfortunately, the courtroom offers a very fertile ground for irresponsible acting out by the parents and attorneys involved, contributing to a parallel process in which the adults continue to ignore the children's emotional needs in the name of "serving the best interests of the children." Because of this very real and very profound negative influence, when using a family-based intervention the therapist should state (even in writing) that therapy is not a custody evaluation and that he or she will avoid taking sides, offering support of all parent-child relationships. Appropriate referrals to experienced custody evaluators and mental health case managers should be made if legal concerns do arise (Garrity and Baris, 1994).

Termination Procedures

With the development of such natural play between Jason and his parents, the therapist pointed out the positive developments and set a date for termination. The therapist helped Jason and his parents reflect on the growth and expansion in the play relationship, as well as on feelings of intimacy that occurred over the several months of treatment together. At this point, sessions occurred less frequently and were set on a once-per-month basis with follow-up sessions. A final follow-up session was set for two months later. During this time, Jason met with each parent separately and reviewed some of the things that had happened that were important to them.

On one occasion, Mary, Emilio, Jason, and the therapist drew the things that each remembered and gave these drawings to each other as a Goodbye present. This Goodbye session was planned for and homework assignments of the drawing of specific moments in treatment were made. Such drawings were put together in a book that was given to Jason on the last session. As Carla did participate, her drawings were used as well. During the last session with each parent alone, Jason was encouraged to again play some of his favorite games with his parents, such as volcano and the scarf-touch game.

During the final session, the whole family was encouraged to come together to both play and discuss some of the important events with the therapist. The therapist encouraged the family not only to observe what happened in their experience, but also to reflect on their history of several losses together and to define the positive aspects of their current relationships that they discovered through the therapy process. During this last session, the therapist assisted Jason, his mother, and his father to talk about the feelings of hope they experienced with each other during the therapy process, as well as the positive aspects of their relationships that they expected to come in the future. Because this family had experienced so much tragedy together, this verbal recognition of hope for their future was very important to emphasize. As part of the termination, the therapist reminded each family member how they produced the play and positive emotional outcomes themselves. To accomplish this task, the therapist very concretely pointed out several of the more positive, hopeful moments of the family's play together, despite the other difficult moments that occurred within the therapy. By this point, the parents and children had experienced much success in participating in activities over a range of feelings. Supportive reminders of such moments served this family well in the development of hope for a better future together.

EXPECTED OUTCOME OR PROGNOSIS

This chapter has outlined treatment progress for Jason and his family. These parents and children have developed a different, more trusting relationship. While the pain of several separations would not go away, this family was certainly in a position to gain some resolution and distance from it. As described, Jason's angry and moody behavior diminished and he was able to use his above-average intellectual skills more to his advantage in the classroom. He could begin to be more cooperative and less controlling of his relationships with peers. Finally, the family achieved far more capacity to tolerate differences and experience more intimacy in their interactions.

Because of the divorce setting, there will likely be conflicts and problems in the future. However, following such a family-oriented intervention style, it is expected that such problems will be approachable with more flexibility and openness. While future conflicts surrounding visitation may still occur, such conflicts may be addressed far more easily in a straightforward mediation process.

CONCLUSION

Parents and children play together naturally from conception onward. This can be observed in a father and mother talking in imaginative, playful, and creative ways to their unborn child, in the development of face play and other games during infancy, and in the strong sensorimotor games and dancing in which toddlers and parents participate. Imaginative dramatic play of the preschool child in the home setting, more organized play and storytelling of elementary years, and the kind of humorous, joking exchanges that happen through teenage years and into early adulthood offer further ways to observe such playful interactions. One of the most striking characteristics of such interactions is its naturalness and spontaneity. In normal situations in which families have positive relationships, such play occurs easily and naturally throughout the day whenever needed. Such play clearly functions to help family members enjoy each other's presence and produces a creative avenue for the transformation of emotional tensions. In the most positive situations, the outcome of play produces affiliation and trust and helps family members elaborate and extend the quality of their emotional relationship together.

As family members engage in mutual playful exchange, they create an expressive momentum with each other. This allows parents and children to thoroughly engage in a creative mutual reverie or emotional state with each other. Such play allows individual family members to step outside their own sense of control and emotional conflict and give themselves over to the positive co-creation of a mutually developed positive state. In observing these kinds of interchanges, it is clear that both the expressive process and the content of the expressions produced relate to the emotional strains, tensions, and resolutions of issues surrounding closeness, intimacy, and attachments. Such moment-to-moment play functions as a natural curative process to produce and regenerate positive emotional connections in a family setting.

In this way, play is not incidental by any means but can be used therapeutically. This is the main tenet of dynamic play therapy. Through helping family members engage in spontaneous, improvised play using art, movement, drama, and video, families can develop or restart their own natural play with each other. As therapy progresses, play addresses very painful and conflicting issues surrounding unresolved loss and separation. By guiding family members to generate the playful spirit in a naturally creative fashion, feelings of trust, mutuality, and affiliation can be produced. From this development, a therapist can help focus the content of the resulting improvisational play in such a way to help family members restructure their emotional relationships together. The play therapist can be thought of as a choreographer of a healing experience as family members are assisted in incorporating their spontaneous expressions with each other into a more playful whole episode.

This style of play proceeds with the therapist first using directive activities such as having family members play tug-of-war, scarf fights, scribble wars, follow-the-leader, and enactment of family scenarios. By observing how emotional states and the actual process of play produce avoidance, interference, and resistance, such play breaks can be incorporated through helping family members evolve a more elaborate and flexible style of interaction. Gradually, families can be guided into developing their own style of improvisation with the resulting experiential play episodes serving to facilitate emotional change.

While verbal discussion can be used to focus and develop insight, conversation is helpful only to the extent that it can promote the experience of mutual creativity by family members. It is this experience on which dynamic play therapy draws as its most powerful element of change.

Because of the emphasis on the development of trust and the elaboration of a positive and accepting relationship between family members, this intervention can be useful in helping parents and children recover from the experience of divorce. In this particular case, Jason's symptoms reflected his emotional difficulties with his situation. As angry, moody symptoms persisted, his parents became more and more helpless to assist him. By helping his family engage in playful and creative activities, which later addressed more specific issues of loss and separation, they created new emotional experiences for themselves. As the emotional relationship expanded and became more flexible, they opened themselves to the experience of intimacy.

BIBLIOGRAPHY

Bowlby, J. (1972). *Attachment and loss: Vol. I, Attachment*. London: Hogarth Press.

Bowlby, J. (1973). *Attachment and loss: Vol. II, Separation*. New York: Basic Books.

Bowlby, J. (1980). *Attachment and loss: Vol. III, Loss*. New York: Basic Books.

Bowlby, J. (1982). *Attachment and loss: Vol. I. Attachment* (2nd ed.). New York: Basic Books.

Byng-Hall, J. (1991). The use of attachment theory in understanding and treatment in family therapy. In C.M. Parks, J. Stevenson-Hynde, & P. Maris (Eds.), *Attachment across the life cycle*. London: Tavistock-Rutledge.

Garrity, C., and Baris, M. (1994). *Caught in the middle*. New York: Lexington Books.

Getzels, J.W., and Csikszentmihalyi, M. (1976). *The creative version: A longitudinal study of problem finding in art*. New York: Wiley.

Harvey, S.A. (1989). Dance of intimacy: Expressive arts therapy approaches to intimate relationships within the family context. Paper presented at the Tenth Nordic Conference of Expressive Arts Therapies, Copenhagen, Denmark.

Harvey, S.A. (1990). Dynamic play therapy: An integrated expressive arts approach to the family therapy of young children. *The Arts in Psychotherapy, 17*, 239–246.

Harvey, S.A. (1991). Creating a family: An integrated expressive approach to adoption. *The Arts in Psychotherapy, 18*, 213–222.

Harvey, S.A. (1993). Ann: Dynamic play therapy with ritual abuse. In T. Kottman & C. Schaefer (Eds.), *Play therapy in action: A casebook for practitioners*. New York: Jason Aronson Inc.

Harvey, S.A. (1994a). Dynamic play therapy: Creating attachments. In B. James (Ed.), *Handbook for treatment of attachment-trauma problems in children*. New York: Lexington Books.

Harvey, S.A. (1994b). Dynamic play therapy: Expressive play interventions with families. In K.J. O'Conner & C.E. Schaefer (Eds.), *Handbook of play therapy, Vol. II*. New York: Wiley.

Harvey, S.A. (1994c). Dynamic play therapy: An integrated expressive arts approach to the family treatment of infants and toddlers. *Zero to Three, 15*, 11–17.

Harvey, S.A., Kelly, E.C. (1993). The influence of the quality of early interaction in a three-year-old's play narratives: A longitudinal case study. *The Arts in Psychotherapy, 20*, 387–395.

Imber-Black, E., Roberts, J., & Whiting, R. (Eds.). (1988). *Rituals in families and family therapy*. New York: Norton.

Maine, M., & Solomon, J. (1993) Infants as disorganized/disoriented during the Ainsworth strange situation. In M.T. Greenberg, D. Cicolletti, & E.M. Cummins (Eds.), *Attachment in the preschool years*. Chicago: University of Chicago Press.

Satir, V. (1967). *Conjoint family therapy*. Palo Alto: Science and Behavior Books.

Satir, V. (1972). *Peoplemaking*. Palo Alto: Science and Behavior Books.

Schaefer, C.E. (1993). *The therapeutic powers of play*. New Jersey: Jason Aronson Inc.

Stern, D.N. (1985). *The interpersonal world of the infant*. New York: Basic Books.

Tortera, S. (1994). Join my dance: The unique movement style of each infant and toddler can invite communication, expression, and intervention. *Zero to Three, 15*, 1–10.

CHAPTER 13

Strategic Family Play Therapy

SHLOMO ARIEL

INTRODUCTION: THEORY

This is a genre of therapy in which all the family members, together with the therapist, are engaged in free, imaginative, make-believe play, with or without toys, costumes, and props. All the stages of therapy are conducted by means of conjoint play activities. Play is used as a source of diagnostic information, a medium of therapeutic communication, and as a precision instrument for effecting change. Strategic family play therapy (SFPT) is founded on concepts and methods whose origins lie in both play and family studies. These have been integrated in a theoretical framework based on cognitive-scientific (information-processing) and semiotic (theory of signs) models (Coyne, 1994; Morris, 1971; Western, 1994). The main sources of SFPT are family systems theory and therapy in general, and structural, strategic, symbolic-experiential and narrative family therapy in particular (Gurman & Kniskern, 1981), psychoanalytic play therapy (Erikson, 1940; Freud, 1922; Klein, 1960; Sears, 1951), cognitive-scientific, ethological, and anthropological theories of play (Curry & Arnaud, 1974; Fein 1989; Garvey & Kramer, 1989; Klinger, 1971; Piaget, 1962; Singer, 1973; Smilansky, 1968; Sutton-Smith, 1984; Yawkley, 1986).

SFPT has the advantage of making family therapy accessible to young children. It makes it possible for them to participate in the therapeutic process fully, actively and meaningfully. SFPT has other advantages too. Its main vehicle is make-believe play, which constitutes a singularly rich and flexible medium of expression and communication for both family and therapist. Make-believe play also has the advantages of projective and expressive techniques. It exposes covert and unconscious thoughts, emotions, and relationships. Play in SFPT is used as a precision instrument. Therefore interventions are sometimes extremely condensed and produce immediate change. Their power is partly due to the fact that they detour defenses and create a direct, semiconscious, cognitive-emotional experience. SFPT has been practiced successfully with a very wide range of presenting complaints. It has proved applicable to families of various cultural and social backgrounds.

A comprehensive introduction to SFPT is presented in *Strategic Family Play Therapy* (Ariel, 1994). See also Ariel, Carel, and Tyano, 1985.

A Definition of Make-Believe Play

Since make-believe play is the major vehicle of SFPT and many of the concepts introduced below are derived from its peculiar properties, following is a formal definition: Any behavior can become make-believe play if the behavior assumes the following *propositional attitudes* (Hintikka, 1969):

> *Realification*—Treating a purely mental entity as if it is really present in the external environment. (E.g., the player saw the Power Rangers® on TV. He adopts the propositional attitude "Power Rangers are not just in my mind. They are present here now, in the immediate real world.")
>
> *Identication*—Describing the realified entity verbally, or denying the original identity of a tangible element in the external environment and identifying it with the realified mental entity. (The player says: "Here is a Power Ranger." Or, the player plays as if he or she is not himself or herself but a Power Ranger, or as if a paper-cutting knife is a Power Ranger.)
>
> *Playfulness*—Denying the seriousness of the previous two propositional attitudes. (The player does not really believe that Power Ranger is there and that he himself or the paper-cutting knife is Power Ranger. He is making these claims just for the fun of it.)

For a fuller discussion of the definition, see Ariel, 1984 and Ariel, 1994.

Personality Theory

SFPT attends both to the family system as a "social personality" and to each of its individual members. Concentration here is on the latter first.

Emotives

Many theories of cognition and emotion have attributed a major motivational function to cognitive-affective complexes representing central emotional concerns (e.g., Freud's *complex* (1917); Piaget's *affective schema* (1962); Izard's *affective-cognitive structures* (1978); Klinger's *current concerns* (1971). The term the author has been using for such complexes is *emotives*. Examples of emotives in the Jason L. case are Mary's *frustration and anger related to her inability to fulfill her aspirations toward self-realization* and Jason's *separation anxiety.*[*]

The general hypothesis here is that information processing is facilitated if the information to be processed is associated with a person's central emotives. This applies to all the stages of processing—sensation, perception, memory, divergent and convergent thinking, motor activity, among others. However, if the level of arousal around an emotive gets intolerably high, this is reversed; that is, information processing is delayed or blocked. This mechanism of facilitation versus delay may be

---

[*]See "Orientation to the Text: The Case of Jason L." p. 1.

viewed as a homeostatic feedback mechanism for regulating the level of emotional arousal associated with a person's emotives.

An example of the working of this homeostatic mechanism in the case of Jason L. is his responses about going to school. In preschool, he used to cry a great deal when separated from Mary, and was distant for several hours when back home. He sulked and was negativistic when back home from grade school. Apparently, these mood fluctuations were related to his emotive *separation anxiety*. Going to school raised his level of anxiety, making him more alert and active than usual. However, when his anxiety became intolerable, his routes of cognitive-affective information processing were blocked and he became less alert and active than usual.

This homeostatic mechanism is directly manifested in make-believe play. This form of play is primarily a mental activity. It involves retrieving information from memory and creating mental associations. It also involves perceiving entities in the external environment and turning them into representations for these mental associations. It follows from this general hypothesis that information related to the player's central emotives will be overrepresented in make-believe play. However, if the very introduction of emotive-related play and signifiers provokes intolerably intense emotions in the player, she or he will calm down by choosing less threatening themes and means. Then the player will be ready to reintroduce themes and signifiers laden with intense emotions. Subsequently this homeostatic feedback loop will repeat itself.

Reducing the level of arousal can be accomplished by replacing the threatening themes with more benign ones (e.g., introducing a fishing boat into the play instead of a submarine that is in danger of being torpedoed and sunk). Another way to reduce anxiety is by bringing in protective themes (e.g., a doctor's tool box symbolizing a red-cross submarine). In some cases combinations of more and less threatening themes are created (e.g., a boatsy submarine—half a boat, half a submarine). The author developed a technique called *componential analysis,* an adaptation of a method used by anthropological linguists, for revealing the emotives and the structure of the homeostatic cognitive-emotional feedback mechanism underlying the make-believe play of specific players. This may be used as a diagnostic projective technique for learning about the person's emotives and defenses. For a more complete discussion see Ariel, 1986, and Ariel, 1994.

Family Programs

The family may be visualized as a group of intercommunicating "human computers." The family system is explicated as the set of goal-oriented information-processing programs internalized by these "computers." Each program is directed toward the achievement of specific proximity or control goals. The goals involve other family members or external targets. Examples of goals involving members of Jason L.'s family are Jason's goal of getting close to Mary and living up to her expectations without being coerced; his goal of controlling Carla; Mary's goal of controlling and taming Jason; her goal of reaching higher socioeconomic and professional status; as well as Emilio's goal of remaining a part of his current family and social milieu.

A program is an ad hoc or a routine plan for reaching the goal and overcoming obstacles. The formulation of a program includes the family members' presuppositions about the targets of their goals and the alternative courses of action they take to reach their goals. For example, Mary's program for reaching her goal of controlling and taming Jason was based on the presupposition that Jason hated being bothered. Therefore, she demanded that he perform just minimal, basic duties. However, if he did not comply, she would apply increasingly stronger pressure on him until he did.

When family members are engaged in free conjoint make-believe play, their goals and programs are almost invariably reflected in their play, albeit in a symbolic, imaginary disguise. Make-believe play enables family members to conduct their interpersonal transactions and conflicts in a benign, nonthreatening manner. The function of make-believe play as a moderator of interpersonal relations is manifested in children's social interactions from a very early age. Children use fantasy themes in play as a means for disguising manipulative transactions that are designed to detour obstacles to attaining their proximity and control goals. For example, in the following dialogue, two kindergarten girls, Dina and Ruth, used fantasy to disguise their proximity-control conflict:

Ruth: (Pretending to ride a horse) Move! I am going away for a long, long journey.
Dina: Let's pretend you are a mommy-baby. You are a queen but you are my baby queen. And all this (sweeping the yard with her arm) is your nursery.
Ruth: But let's pretend I did not come to the nursery today. Move!

A technique for analyzing play interactions with a view to exposing and formulating underlying interpersonal goals and programs is presented in Ariel, 1992, and Ariel, 1994.

Model of Psychopathology

Psychodynamic Explanations of Symptoms

In this model, psychopathological symptoms in individual family members are partly explained as outward manifestations of disturbances in the cognitive-affective homeostatic feedback mechanism associated with the person's emotives. Such disturbances are the results of inadequate functioning of the regulatory feedback mechanism. This is shown in overtension (uninhibited emotional arousal) or, contrarily, in rigid defenses. Symptoms reflecting the former are for instance panic or terror attacks, hypomania, and deep depression. Symptoms realizing the latter are, among others, dissociation, massive denial, emotional isolation, and apathy.

Family Dysfunction and Symptoms

Another hypothesis partly explaining symptoms is that they are outward manifestations of dysfunctional family programs. The term *bugs* was borrowed from computer jargon to refer to errors in information processing built into family programs.

Programs infested with bugs are dysfunctional. They process too much or too little information, fail to process relevant information, or process irrelevant information. Such programs misinterpret the information, produce ineffective output, and the like. For example, Mary's program for reaching her goal of controlling and taming Jason, briefly described above, was bugged. It included information-processing errors. Her presupposition that Jason hated to be bothered was wrong. It failed to take into account his (admittedly unexpressed) goal of being close to her and living up to her expectations. Her habit of applying more and more powerful pressure on him to comply ignored his resistance to being coerced.

Bugs lie at the source of family dysfunction. They prevent the family members from attaining their goals with respect to each other. The bugs in Mary's programs, for instance, contributed to her inability to control Jason. Proper family functioning requires smooth communication, and the disturbances of communication caused by bugs prevent the family from effectively performing its daily tasks. The conflict between Mary and Jason, rooted in their bugged communication, prevented them from leading a cooperative relationship.

Symptoms in individuals are explained in this theoretical framework as direct or indirect manifestations of family dysfunction. One class of symptoms is the direct output of bugged programs. Mary's loss of self-control, which sometimes led to bouts of violence, can be explained as a direct output of her program, just described.

Another class of symptoms is manifestations of emotional stress caused by bugged information processing. A third class includes indirect results of the family's reduced level of daily functioning. For example, severe cases of child neglect are often the outcome of poor family communication and task performance.

For a more complete discussion of dysfunctional family programs, see Ariel, 1987.

The Interface between the Psychodynamic and the Family Systemic Explanations

The two types of dysfunction discussed above, disturbances in the cognitive-emotional regulation mechanism and bugs in family programs, are closely interrelated. Psychodynamic dysfunction creates bugs in family programs, and vice versa. Thus, Mary's frustration and anger related to her inability to fulfill her aspirations toward self-realization made it difficult for her to empathize with Jason's uncooperative attitude. Her reduced empathy made her blind to the bugs in her own program. Jason's frustration related to Mary's perceived inability to understand him reinforced his separation anxiety and subsequently made his own bugged programs more rigid.

Concept of Curing

It follows from the above discussion that the overall goals of SFPT are: (1) To remove or weaken the bugs in the family's dysfunctional programs, and (2) To recalibrate the family member's disturbed emotive-related cognitive-affective feedback mechanisms. If these goals are reached, family and individual functioning are spontaneously improved and symptoms disappear or become tolerable.

How Is Change Effected in SFPT?

How Are These Goals Reached?

In a SFPT session, the family initiates its own play themes. The therapist observes and attempts to identify dysfunctional interactions. Then the therapist initiates his or her own play moves. The latter intertwine with the family's, but at the same time steer the activity, subtly and gently, in well-chosen directions. The family is induced to play in ways that automatically activate well-defined curative structural and psychosocial properties of play. These properties are nicknamed "bug-busters" because they have the power to remove or weaken bugs in the family's programs and recalibrate cognitive-affective feedback mechanisms that had gone out of tune.

Bug-busters have drawn from the following three major sources:

1. The formal definition of the concept *make-believe play* proposed above;
2. Make-believe play as a version of the general emotive-related cognitive-affective homeostatic mechanism, discussed above; and,
3. Make-believe play as a medium for carrying out interactions governed by family programs. This function of make-believe play has also been mentioned above.

Let me list, define, and illustrate the main bug-busters used in SFPT:

Bug-Busters Derived from the Formal Definition of Make-Believe Play

OWNING AND ALIENATION.   Since the player assumes the attitudes of *realification* and *identification*, he or she *owns* the content of the play; that is, he or she is committed to its being real. However, since the player also makes the claim of *playfulness*, he or she is also *alienated* from this content, is not committed to its being real. The main therapeutic uses of *owning and alienation* are shaking one's deep convictions about oneself or others (from owning to disowning), and making one accept previously rejected truths (from disowning to owning).

For example: In the play therapy session with Jason and Mary described below, Jason, in the make-believe role of a Power Ranger, pretended to kick the therapist's chest. The latter fell on the carpet, groaning, and said, "He is much more powerful than I thought." This was an activation of *owning and alienation,* to introduce the information that Jason's power was not real (from owning to disowning). The purpose of this move was to weaken the impact of Mary's view of Jason as "a macho man," like Emilio.

In the same session a make-believe scene was created in which Jason gave Mary a magical device with which she could make him obey her. Here *owning and alienation* (from disowning to owning) was activated in order to expose Jason's unexpressed wish to live up to his mother's expectations, without forcing him to admit this openly.

BASIC DUALITY.   Due to the attitude of *playfulness,* the player is both inside the play, as a make-believe figure, and outside it as an actor who observes himself or herself playing a role. The main therapeutic uses of this bug-buster are:

1. Increasing awareness of bugs. For example: In a play session Jason played the role of a Mickey Mouse® balloon that could be inflated to enormous proportions and become Mighty Mouse. Mary "inflated" Jason and turned him into Mighty Mouse. The *basic duality* of play enabled her to observe herself playing this role and to become aware of the fact that she herself was the one that made Jason the "powerful man" that he was not.

2. Emphasizing paradoxical or contradictory information. For example: In one of the play sessions Mary told the therapist: I sometimes let Jason dominate me. Then the therapist induced Mary to "persuade Jason to play as if he dominated her." This intervention was designed to expose the paradoxical nature of Mary's complaint. The basic duality of play placed the proposition that Jason dominated Mary inside the make-believe world and the contradictory proposition that Mary let him dominate her outside the make-believe world.

ARBITRARINESS OF THE SIGNIFIER. Since *identication* is not a serious attitude, there should not necessarily be any similarity between the signifier and its signified content. Therapeutic uses are:

1. Softening or intensifying the emotional impact of the signified. For example: In a session Carla asked for a baby doll she used to play with in previous sessions. The therapist could not find the doll. He said: "I'm afraid I lost it." Then he noticed that Mary started and became very agitated. He thought that his answer reminded her of the loss of her own baby. Then he told Carla, "Let's play losing and finding. Let's pretend I've lost this" (he pointed at a piece of Lego®) and you'll find it." Then he hid the piece of Lego under the carpet.

The therapist replaced the baby doll as the lost object by an emotionally neutral toy. He activated *arbitrariness of the signifier* to soften the emotional impact of the theme of loss.

2. Emphasizing paradoxical or contradictory information. For example: In one of the play sessions Jason was represented by an enormous strong man doll. This emphasized for Mary the contradiction between the real Jason and the powerful image she projected on him.

POSSIBLE WORLDS. Due to the arbitrariness of the attitudes of *realification* and *identication,* make-believe play can be used to "realize" unrealizable (potential, unlikely, or unreal) possibilities. The possible world of make-believe can be a bug-free, emotionally tolerable world. For example: Jason played the part of a little dog, and Mary was his owner. Mary threw things away and Jason, as a little dog, fetched them back to her. In this scene, a possible world was created in which Jason's hidden wish to please Mary was materialized.

Bug-Busters Derived from the Psychodynamic Functions of Play

SYMBOLIC CODING. The underlying meaning of a central emotive is signified by a symbol that is privately associated with this underlying meaning in the player's mind, but is less threatening than the underlying meaning itself. The main therapeutic use of this bug-buster is that of facilitating the expression and communication of complex or emotionally difficult messages. Another use is recalibrating the homeostatic cognitive-affective mechanism around a particular emotive. For example: The theme of unfinished mourning related to the death of Mary's baby figured prominently in her make-believe play. However, even just playing about it openly was too much for her. The therapist helped her express her grief indirectly by introducing themes that could be associated in her mind with her major loss, such as the loss of objects with a sentimental value, the loss of pets, and the like.

REGULATION OF EMOTIONS.   This bug-buster regulates the level of emotional arousal associated with the players' emotives. This can be achieved by repeating emotive-related themes in the family's play, and by introducing protective devices. For example: In some of the dog-owner make-believe games, Jason's fear of being abandoned was played in various ways. For example, in one scene the dog's owner, Mary, left her little dog, Jason, alone in the street, tied to a post, while she was doing her shopping in a department store. The dog whimpered pitifully, not knowing whether his owner would come back at all. Then the therapist, in the guise of a nice old lady, reassured him that his owner would never leave him. She had gone shopping and would soon come back for him.

Bug-Busters Derived from the Function of Make-Believe Play as a Moderator of Interpersonal Relations

COVERT COMMUNICATION.   The thematic contents of make-believe play disguise the players' communication intents, facilitating the expression of complex or emotionally difficult interpersonal messages and detouring resistance. For example: Jason wanted to be hugged by Mary, but could not admit this openly. He expressed this wish by playing the part of Batman® and asking Mary, as Wonder Woman®, to help him with his outfit.

Make-Believe Play as a Vehicle of Therapeutic Communication

The *main therapeutic moves* in family play sessions are those in which specific bug-busters are deliberately activated in order to weaken or remove particular bugs or improve emotional regulation around emotives. However, in order to be able to make such moves, the therapist has to make series of *preparatory moves,* designed to secure the family's cooperation, keep up the playful atmosphere, and prepare the ground for the main move. The last move should often be accompanied by *auxiliary moves* controlling undesirable side effects. All the properties of play discussed above can be mobilized for devising such running-of-the-show moves. Furthermore, a repertoire of standard move types has accumulated with experience. Some of these move types have been observed in children's natural play. Others have been borrowed from various schools of psychotherapy and adapted to the needs of this form of therapy. Here is a sample:

MIMICKING.   Imitating family members' play behavior. Purposes: Joining, channelling behavior to chosen routes; reflecting; commenting.

FOCUSING.   Stressing aspects of the play by sound and lighting effects or by verbal and nonverbal comments. Purposes: Turning attention; interpreting.

EXPLICATING.   Making hidden entities explicit, by verbalizing them or acting them out nonverbally. Purposes: Emphasizing; interpreting. For example, in the dog and the old lady scene described above, the therapist, as the nice old lady, explicated Jason's feelings by saying things like "Don't worry little doggie, mommy is going to come back soon."

THE DOUBLE.   Playing the role of a family member directly or through a doll. Purposes: Representing a family member who is unable or unwilling to represent himself or herself. For example, in the first session, Mary and Jason acted out Little Red Riding Hood. Mary was Grandmother, and Jason was the wolf and the hunter. Carla was supposed to be Red Riding Hood, but she was too shy to play. The therapist took a doll representing a little girl and said. "Let's pretend this is Carla who is too shy to play Red Riding Hood and let's pretend I am a not-shy Carla who does play Red Riding Hood."

PROVIDING STIMULI.   Stimulating play by providing behavioral and material stimuli. Purposes: Encouraging certain activities or changing the course of an activity.

ILLUSION OF ALTERNATIVES.   Suggesting two alternatives for play. The more attractive one is the one the therapist wants the player to choose. Purpose: Inducing family members to play in ways that serve specific therapeutic goals. For example: The therapist wanted Mary to play the part of Wonder Woman. She was reluctant to play any role at all. The therapist said, "Do you prefer to play Monster Woman, or Wonder Woman?" Sure enough, Mary chose Wonder Woman.

OBEDIENT ACTOR.   Letting family members dictate the therapist's play. Purpose: To be accepted by the family.

WILLY-NILLY.   The therapist performs a play act that engages a family member in a complementary role. Purpose: To engage family members in play or influence their play. For example: The therapist wanted Jason, who played the part of a helpless puppy, to change into a bold, aggressive dog. He, the therapist, assumed the role of helpless kitten, begging the puppy not to devour him.

Change and Its Generalization and Transfer

Bug-busters serve as change agents because they create a sudden cognitive change indirectly and automatically. They take the defenses by surprise and bypass them, without allowing a conscious process of thinking, which could leave time for the defenses to be erected again. At the same time, the impact of the sudden cognitive-emotional change is softened by the very fact that it is done in a playful atmosphere.

The cognitive-emotional experience created by bug-busters can be easily transferred from the level of make-believe to the level of the family's reality out of the playroom because of the basic duality of make-believe play. Every play experience is also a reality experience. When bugs are removed, dysfunctional programs recover, and the changes are spontaneously generalized to other parts of the system and to other situations, not directly touched on by the therapeutic interventions. The process of change, transfer and generalization, failures in these processes, and ways of overcoming them are discussed in detail in Ariel, 1994, pp. 228–229.

Termination

The termination of therapy is also conducted through the vehicle of make-believe play. The therapist can read in the family's play various signs indicating its wish to terminate, for example, distancing, avoiding sensitive themes, and others. Working through the termination and leave taking can be carried out within the fantasy, make-believe world. Techniques that can be used in this phase are allaying anger and sadness into the play, encouraging make-believe regression, summarizing the therapy in a make-believe story, and staging a make-believe continuation of the therapy.

CASE FORMULATION

The Cross-Cultural Factor

It would be an oversight to disregard the cultural factor in this case. Emilio and Mary's marriage was an intermarriage between a middle-class Anglo-American woman and a working-class Mexican-American man, both Catholic. Apparently, this has crucial implications with respect to many aspects of the case. Although many writers, including the authors, have cautioned against imposing cultural stereotypes on psychotherapy clients (Ariel, in press; McGoldrick, Pearce, & Giordano, 1982), one cannot easily brush aside the apparent predictability of some of the features of this case, given the literature on cultural differences. Many studies have emphasized the importance of the values of machismo, familismo, and gregariousness in Hispanic culture, in contrast to the values of individualism, personal distinction, achievement, and self-control in Anglo-American culture. (See, for instance, McGoldrick, et al., 1982). These clusters of values had unquestionably been espoused by Emilio and Mary, respectively.

The Presenting Complaints

The main problem for which the family was referred to therapy had been Jason's physical abuse by his mother Mary. This was one extreme manifestation of serious difficulties in the parental relationship. Mary found it difficult to manage Jason. He was stubborn, uncooperative, negative, and insubordinate. Apparently these problems were context-dependent, since Jason's father Emilio did not seem to have such difficulties with Jason.

The school was another problematic context. Jason was not regularly able to participate in routine school activities without physical intervention by an adult. When he came home from school he was often in a bad mood, expressing his anger by throwing down his books. Socially, Jason was withdrawn, a lone wolf, and bossy. He was often moody and sulky.

Psychodynamics

It will be recalled that in this model the term *psychodynamics* refers to the family members' feedback mechanisms regulating the level of emotional arousal around central emotives.

Mary's Emotives

1. **Unfinished mourning, anger, disappointment, and guilt associated with her parents' divorce and with her own divorce.**

   Direct or inferred evidence: Apparently, Mary's experience of her own divorce was for her a painful repetition of the shock caused to her by her parents' divorce. Since she and her family were Catholic, the divorce was probably conceived by her as a transgression, giving rise to moral doubts and guilt. She seems to have blamed her father for her parents' divorce, as evidenced by the fact that she did not have much contact with him after the divorce and grieved his death only moderately. She certainly blamed Emilio for their own divorce. Instead of supporting her when she was depressed after their child's death, he had an affair and drifted away from her. She must have been deeply hurt and angry.

   Both as a child and as an adult, Mary's characteristic way of coping with arousal of extreme, acute emotions had been becoming depressed, emotionally isolated, inactive, and withdrawn. This coping style had prevented her from completing the mourning process in relation to these and the other losses in her life (e.g., the loss of her child).

2. **Unfinished mourning, sadness, and perhaps guilt related to her father's death and, later, the death of her baby. Sadness, bitterness, and anger about being lonely and having to struggle alone with life's burdens, with very little support.**

   Direct or inferred evidence: Apparently, Mary's father was never a significant source of support, and he died when she was an adolescent. Her mother's help was mainly instrumental. She was more interested in her own difficulties than in Mary's. Since the baby's death, Emilio almost totally withdrew as a husband and a friend. Furthermore, in contradistinction to Emilio, Mary was not in the habit of asking for or getting help from her children. Finally, Mary did not like her job. There was no source of encouragement there.

3. **Frustration and anger related to her inability to fulfill her aspirations toward self-realization—an interesting job, independence, and high socioeconomic status—due to her meager economical resources, heavy burdens, and lack of external support.**

4. **Suspicion and anger toward men.**

Direct or inferred evidence: The men in Mary's life (her father, her husband) proved disappointing and unreliable. Since Jason seems to have taken after his father in so many ways, she probably classed Jason with "men." Her attitude toward him as a man conflicted with her motherly empathy and worries with respect to his emotional difficulties (see below).

5. **Worries and guilt about Jason's well-being.**

Direct or inferred evidence: When Jason was a baby, Mary worried constantly about his health and was afraid that he might die, although he was healthy. Apparently this was related to the loss of her baby years earlier.

The problems she reported as most serious in the CBCL were that he was lonely, and he felt unloved and persecuted, perhaps partly a projection of her own feelings toward herself. She also denied or tried to conceal the fact that she had abused him.

Mary's Style of Emotional Regulation

To elaborate what has been stated above, Mary used to deal with extreme emotional arousal around her emotives by mobilizing rigid defenses such as denial, withdrawal, and depressive inactivity. These defenses are not effective. They are rigid and fragile, as evidenced by the outburst that led her to abuse Jason. Their output prevented her from mobilizing her strengths to deal successfully with life's challenges.

Emilio's Emotives

1. **Fear of his honor and pride as a man being injured.**

Direct or inferred evidence: Emilio's family of origin is characterized by a strict gender-role separation. When Mary was depressed after the death of the baby, Emilio drifted away and started an affair. One may speculate that he could not tolerate Mary's neglect of her marital and parental duties, which injured his pride as a man. Emilio's main concern about Jason was that he was not as bold as Emilio would like him to be.

Emilio's Style of Emotional Regulation

Apparently Emilio used to deal with extreme emotional arousal related to his emotives by avoiding the distressing issues and becoming active and physical. That is how he dealt with his baby's death and his wife's depression. This was also his way of helping Jason overcome his bad mood when he came back from school.

Jason's Emotives

1. **Unfinished anger and mourning about his parents' divorce.**

Direct or inferred evidence: Apparently, the divorce has never been worked through by any of the family members. Jason's second wish was "Mom and dad to be remarried."

2. **Separation anxiety; fear and anger related to being abandoned.**

Direct or inferred evidence: In preschool, Jason used to cry a great deal when separated from Mary, and he was distant for several hours when back home. Possibly his sulking and negativism when he arrived home from grade school were partly due to being fixated to the above-mentioned earlier emotional response. Jason was partly abandoned and suffered losses several times in his life: His mother's periods of depression and withdrawal, her preference of his sister, his father's having drifted away, the divorce, and so forth.

3. **Worry and frustration related to the family's limited financial means and his mother's general dissatisfaction with her life.**

   Direct or inferred evidence: His first wish was "lots of money." In a TAT story a girl was concerned about getting an okay job when she grew up. He said, "Something is always going wrong." His identification with his mother and his wish to please her are discussed below. It is reasonable to suppose that his mother's unhappiness, to which he had been continuously exposed, had a great impact on him.

4. **Anger, guilt, and frustration related to his inability to live up to his mother's expectations with respect to his level of academic and social functioning at school and at home.**

   Direct or inferred evidence: This comes out clearly in his TAT stories. In the MIM, he complained that the task "drawing our house" was too hard, but he complied.

Jason's Style of Emotional Regulation

Jason used to cope with arousal of extreme emotions related to his emotives by making his inner world duller and more superficial than it really was, and, behaviorally, by sulking, withdrawing, and becoming aloof, negativistic, and passive-aggressive. These defenses were rather fragile.

Direct or inferred evidence: Jason's general intelligence and his expressive abilities were normal and age-appropriate, as shown in his verbal interview, MIM, and test results. However, his verbal and nonverbal products were of much lower quality than expected when directly related to his emotives, or when embedded in problematic interactions. He became virtually nonverbal when the interviewer wanted to focus on his history or current difficulties. He became overly concrete when his experience was discussed. He avoided mentioning any negative affect. His human figure drawing was much duller than expected. His "drawing a picture of our house" with his father was much better than with his mother. His emotional lability comes out from various test results.

Carla's emotives and defenses are not included in this analysis because the case description does not include a great deal of information about her.

Family Programs

Mary's Goals

Move higher in her socioeconomical and professional status; become more independent socially and professionally.

Be close to her mother as long as she gets instrumental assistance from her, but keep her at emotional distance.

Control and tame Jason. Keep him at a comfortable distance and get him close only if he pleases her.

Be close to Carla. Draw emotional support from her.

Direct or inferred evidence: Mary did not like her current job. She would like to return to school and get a business degree.

Mary's major complaint was that she was unable to manage and control Jason. When he came back angry and sulky from school, she used to leave him alone for an hour or so. Mary brought Carla to the parents' interview, apparently to feel supported and protected by her presence. She described Carla as most warm and loving. She was observed seeking Carla's but not Jason's physical proximity. But she did enjoy his physical closeness when he participated with her in the lotion rubbing task.

Mary's Mother's Goal with Respect to Mary

Be close to Mary by giving her help and getting from her emotional support.

Emilio's Goals

Preserve his own socioeconomic status and continue belonging to his current family and social milieu.

Be close to his family of origin, especially the men, and to his friends.

Be close to Jason by turning him into a "man" like himself.

Be close to both children by doing things together with them.

Jason's Goals

Be close to Emilio by following his lead and "clinging."

Be protected by Emilio.

Be close to Mary. Live up to her expectations without being coerced.

Be close to Carla and control her.

Direct or inferred evidence: Although the children at school saw Jason as independent and self-assured, Emilio saw him as clingy and dependent. Jason became affectionate toward Mary on weekends, when she avoided making demands on the children.

Jason's TAT stories seem to allude to his wish to please Mary and win her approval.

Carla's Goals

Be close to both parents and please them. Keep a comfortable distance from Jason, without being dominated by him.

Space limitations prevent formulation of information-processing programs for reaching these goals in detail. One central program is formulated involving Jason and Mary:

Jason's Program

General presuppositions: Mother forces me to do things because she does not trust my willingness and ability to live up to her expectations. Mother wants me to be close to her only if I live up to her expectations.
Therefore

I should comply with mother's demands and get close to her only if she does not coerce me.

Prediction: Mother will understand that she was wrong, that the only way to get what she wants with me is trusting my willingness and ability to live up to her expectations, in accordance with my goals.

Mary's Program:

General presuppositions: Jason prefers being alone and doing what he wants. He does not believe I love him and want what is good for him.
Therefore

I should leave him alone and not bother him.
I should demand that he perform just his minimal basic duties.
If he does not comply, I should force him.
If he still does not comply, I should increase my pressure on him.
If he does comply or does things to please me I should give him affection, in accordance with my goals.

One can see a diluted version of this program in action in the lotion-rubbing task of the MIM.

Bugs and Disturbances in Cognitive-Affective Regulation

Jason's general presupposition does not take into account the fact that his mother does not know or understand his goals, that her general presuppositions run counter to his goals with her. His prediction is wrong; it ignores the fact that his mother's plan includes increasing rather than decreasing pressure in response to his non-compliance.

Mary's general presupposition is wrong. It does not take into account Jason's goals. Her plan does not take into account his plan; it fails to realize that Jason's noncompliance is at least partly a response to her own actions.

Although the other family programs have not been analyzed in detail, it is easy to identify some other major bugs:

It seems that a general norm in this family was to keep one's own inner world to oneself. What the family members could see and understand were mainly the other family members' defenses, not their emotives. Mary felt that her mother used to demand but not give emotional support. However, she preferred to deal with this by interacting with her mother as little as possible rather than by sharing these feelings and thoughts with her.

Both parents were pleased with Carla's being such a sweet little girl but never asked themselves how she felt inside. Apparently, Mary and Emilio never discussed or worked through their emotional difficulties following the baby's death. The differences in cultural norms and values between them had never been explicated. Emilio and Jason seemed to get along with one another quite well, but their relationship appears to be superficial, lacking in sharing of thoughts and feelings. As a result, each of the family members was left to deal with the difficulties in his or her inner world alone, without emotional support or empathic understanding. Furthermore, the thoughts and feelings that lead to misunderstandings and difficulties in the relationships were not clarified and led to further polarization and rift.

These bugged relationship patterns were intimately interrelated with disturbances in family members' cognitive-affective homeostatic feedback mechanisms. As detailed above, the relevant family members, each for his or her own reasons, used to deal with extreme emotional arousal by mobilizing rigid and fragile defenses, which prevented them from owning and sharing their emotive-related inner cognitive-emotional events.

Explaining the Presenting Problems

Mary's use of physical violence toward Jason can be partly explained as a direct output of the bugged program formulated above. Mary's plan includes the clause "If he still does not comply I should increase my pressure on him." Since Jason's plan includes the clause "I should comply only if she does not coerce me," this program constitutes a deviation-amplifying, feedforward mechanism that must lead Mary to use increasingly severe disciplinarian measures.

The same can be explained also as loss of self-control as a result of the fragility of Mary's defenses and the frustration caused by her by the bugged family programs. The latter prevented her from solving her anger for having to struggle alone, for being unable to fulfill her aspirations, and for her bitterness toward men. These burst out in acts of violence.

Jason's negativism and insubordination are also built into the program formulated above. These responses generalized over to the school situation because being good in school was one way of complying with Mary.

The same can also be explained as direct expressions of Jason's rigid defenses. These defenses, together with the bugged family programs, also constitute a deviation-amplifying, feedforward mechanism. Being duller than he can be, withdrawn, and negativistic reduced his general level of functioning at school and home. This caused disappointment and frustration in Mary and perhaps also in his teacher. He got less love, attention, and appreciation and more anger and dissatisfaction. He mobilized more rigid defenses. Since these were fragile, there were intermittent outbursts.

TREATMENT DESCRIPTION

The term *strategy* will be employed for the general treatment plan and *tactic* for the plan of a particular intervention.

A Strategy for the Whole Therapy

A strategy includes the objectives of therapy, broken down into series of subobjectives, that can be reached by small changes. It includes also a decision procedure concerning the focus of intervention. The focus will consist of those subobjectives which, if reached, will bring about, automatically and without any further intervention, the attainment of the greatest number of other subobjectives. An additional consideration for selecting the focus is the minimization of resistance and of undesirable side-effects.

Following is the procedure of breaking down the objectives into a series of subobjectives with the following objectives, derived from Jason and Mary's program:

Objective A

Help Jason realize that Mary's plan includes increasing rather than decreasing her pressure on him in response to his noncompliance.

SUBOBJECTIVE 1.   Reduce the level of arousal associated with Jason's emotives "fear of being abandoned" and "living up to his mother's expectations."

SUBOBJECTIVE 2.   Help Jason develop more flexible styles of emotional regulation with respect to the emotives related to his relationship with his mother.

These two subobjectives are expected to make Jason emotionally more receptive to information related to the main, final objective.

SUBOBJECTIVE 3.   Show Jason, within the make-believe play, that he can control the level of pressure applied by his mother. If he complies with her instructions, she decreases her pressure. If he does not comply, she increases her pressure.

SUBOBJECTIVE 4.   Generalize subobjective 3 to a variety of different situations.

Objective B

Help Mary be aware of Jason's goals of being close to her and living up to her expectations without being coerced.

SUBOBJECTIVE 1.   Reduce the level of emotional arousal associated with Mary's main emotives, especially her worries and guilt about Jason's well-being, her suspicion and anger toward men (including Jason), and her bitterness for having to struggle alone, with little support.

SUBOBJECTIVE 2.   Help Mary develop more flexible defenses, instead of denial, withdrawal, and depressive inactivity.

Again, these subobjectives are designed to prepare Mary for the following ones, by making her emotionally more receptive to corrective information.

SUBOBJECTIVE 3.   Help Jason spell out his goals with respect to Mary and making sure that she listens and understands.

SUBOBJECTIVE 4.   Allay Mary's suspicion and disbelief with respect to Jason's sincerity.

The therapy will be focused on the program described above and the associated emotives and defenses. As has been shown, most of the presenting complaints are related to these. The core of the difficulties for which the family was referred to therapy resides in the psychodynamics of Jason and Mary and their problematic relationship. This program captures some of the major bugs in this relationship. If these bugs are removed and the defenses made more flexible, many other positive changes may be expected to ensue spontaneously.

Expected Sources of Resistance and Negative Side Effects

If the relationship between Mary and Jason is improved, the latter is likely to redirect her bitterness toward Emilio and reawaken the parental conflict, and Mary's frustration for not having fulfilled herself is likely to increase. Carla is likely to feel threatened by the rapprochement between Mary and Jason, and begin to develop symptoms of her own. The first two difficulties can be approached by methods other than family play therapy, for example, individual therapy and consultation for Mary, a number of sessions of couples therapy with Mary and Emilio, or the like. The third can be treated within the family make-believe play sessions.

Logistics for the Strategy

Participants

Different combinations of family members can be invited to different sessions or session-series, according to the development of the therapeutic process. In accordance with the strategy, the first sessions included just Mary and Jason. Carla joined them later. Mary's mother was also included in one or two of these sessions. For balance and working toward additional gains, parallel sessions were held with Jason, Carla, and Emilio.

Setting and Materials

All the sessions took place in a family play therapy room, equipped with toys, puppets, containers, props, dress-up clothes, musical instruments, tools, "junk," sports and movement aids, and creative materials.

Frequency and Duration of Treatment

Fifty-minute sessions were held once a week. Strategic family play therapy is in most cases brief, up to ten sessions. The Jason L. therapy took fifteen sessions.

General Tactics for Treatment Stages

Introducing the Family to Play Therapy

One of the queries very often raised by novices is: How can parents be made to agree to play like little children? How can one persuade an adult to overcome the shyness and inhibitions that make it difficult for him or her to act in a childish manner? Moreover, how can one convince a parent that something so serious as therapy can be carried out by means of something so frivolous as play? Experience has shown that the difficulty is not so great as it may seem. Parents often enjoy the opportunity to play and a legitimate reason to act childish. They might accept the idea of play even more readily if it suggested to them that play is the most suitable method where children are concerned.

Before the family gathered in the room for the first time, the therapist prepared the room and the play items for their arrival. He chose suitable play objects and placed them in various visible locations around the room. The choice of play materials in SFPT is dictated by the diagnostic information available and by the ages of the family members and their interests. In the sessions that included Mary, Jason, and Carla, play objects that were likely to provoke pretend play around issues of gender and control were chosen—for instance puppets, dress-up clothes, and make-up materials representing a royal family and wildlife of all sorts. In the session in which Jason and Emilio participated, objects encouraging physical activities such as balls, boxing gloves, and the like were selected. Subsequently these were replaced by objects encouraging emotionally significant pretend play, for example unstructured "junk" objects and materials.

In the first session, after some moments of shyness and hesitation, exploration of the room and the play objects begins. Often, following this stage, conjoint family make-believe play begins spontaneously. If this does not happen, the therapist can help the family start playing, using various techniques such as inviting the parents to join, modeling, using the children as ushers and inviting the parents to direct the show. Here are two examples:

Inviting the Parent to Join

Jason lay face down on a big soft blue pillow. Carla lay face up on another pillow. Mary sat stiff on a little chair in the corner. The therapist asked Jason, "What are you doing?" He said, "I'm swimming." "And I'm lying on the beach," said Carla. The therapist said, "I am the lifeguard." He pointed to a third pillow and addressed Mary, "There's an easy chair here; you can rest on it."

As may have been noticed by the readers, the therapist's intervention here conveys messages that go beyond just inviting Mary to join the play. His having assumed the role of lifeguard was designed to give all the participants a feeling of safety and confidence. The invitation for Mary to rest offered her a time-out from being overburdened with daily life duties.

Modeling

Jason and Emilio were present in the room. Jason explored the toys, and Emilio sat on the carpet, smiling shyly. Jason picked up boxing gloves and asked Emilio to help him put them on, which Emilio did. Jason began boxing the air, but Emilio did not join him. The therapist put on the other pair of gloves and began "fighting" with Jason. Then he said, "In the second round you are going to fight with the world champion," and handed his pair of gloves over to Emilio.

For a description of the other techniques, and other examples, see Ariel, 1994, pp. 84–87.

Tactics for Specific Interventions

A tactic includes the specific target of the intervention (e.g., a specific bug or a particular emotive), expected change (e.g., making the players aware of the bug; making the defenses associated with the emotive less rigid), bug-busters by which the change can be effected, and expected resistance or undesirable side effects and how to deal with them. Let me illustrate this with two of the subobjectives formulated above.

Tactic A

SUBOBJECTIVE. Reduce the level of emotional arousal related to Mary's main emotives.

SPECIFIC TARGET OF INTERVENTION. Mary's suspicion and anger toward men (including Jason).

EXPECTED CHANGES. Making Mary less suspicious and angry toward men in general; sharpening her realization that Jason is not a man but a little boy; helping her discriminate between Jason and Emilio.

BUG-BUSTERS. Regulation of emotions, by repeating themes representing these emotive and reinforcing homeostatic feedback cycles, Mary's level of emotional arousal associated with this emotive can be reduced.

Owning and alienation; if Mary's anger and suspicion toward men in general and Jason in particular will be placed within make-believe play, she will partly disown these feelings.

Basic duality; Mary can be made aware of the absurdity of identifying Jason with Emilio by looking at her own make-believe play in which she makes this identification.

Arbitrariness of signifier; the contradiction between "Jason the man" and "Jason the little boy" can be emphasized by having Jason play the role of "the big strong, macho man."

EXPECTED RESISTANCE AND UNDESIRABLE SIDE-EFFECTS. The hypotheses on which this intervention is based on meager evidence and may well be wrong. If this is so, Mary is likely to resist the therapist's attribution of such emotions to herself. However, it is quite possible that she resists this intervention for another reason— because it exposes thoughts and feelings she is ashamed of. These possible reactions can be handled in the following two ways: Reinforcing the make-believe aspect of the play and playing down the reality aspect (Ariel, 1994, pp. 208–210). The therapist will turn himself or herself into a figure in the conjoint make-believe play and in this capacity will apologize and facilitate expressions of anger directed toward himself or herself.

Tactic B

SUBOBJECTIVE. Show Jason that he can control the level of pressure applied on him by his mother.

BUG-BUSTERS.   Possible worlds; basic duality—Jason and Mary will observe themselves playing and activating their bugged program.

EXPECTED RESISTANCE AND UNDESIRABLE SIDE-EFFECTS.   Mary and Jason are likely to resist playing a situation in which Jason does not comply and Mary increases her pressure. This can be overcome by reinforcing the make-believe aspect of the activity, removing it from Mary and Jason's daily experience.

Carrying Out the Tactics

A specific intervention includes the following steps:

> *Observation*—The therapist observes the family's free play and attempts to understand it. Sooner or later, themes and actions relevant to the targets specified in the tactic are bound to emerge naturally.
>
> *Planning*—Before the therapist actually joins the play, he or she plans some moves ahead of time.
>
> *Preparatory moves*—The therapist makes some moves that prepare the ground for his or her main move.
>
> *Main and auxiliary moves; observing the results of the intervention*

These steps should never be carried out rigidly. The family's free play can include unexpected materials, which require the therapist to put aside the preplanned tactic and intervene according to another, ad hoc, tactic. After some preparatory moves, the therapist may decide to be cautious and refrain from carrying out the main move. In general, the therapist is advised, when beginning to actually make the moves, to push the tactic and the specific plan to the back of his or her mind, and rely on intuition.

The following is a session with Jason, Carla, and Mary in which Tactics A and B are carried out. Specific types of movements appear in square brackets.

Jason approaches the box of dress-up clothes. He picks up a Batman costume and starts putting it on. He makes an effort to be visible to Mary and Carla, but they ignore him. Mary picks up a make-up mirror and hands it over to Carla. Jason starts walking around, restless without playing any role.

The therapist interprets this sequence as a manifestation of Mary's passive-aggressive expression of her dislike of Jason's wanting to play a macho game. He decides to plan an intervention; he will involve Mary in a make-believe play in which she will openly express these feelings. Then he will help her find make-believe ways of flexibly regulating her level of hostility. The therapist puts on a Power Ranger mask and starts walking around the room restlessly. [Mimicking, focusing, and providing stimuli.] These are preparatory moves. He wants to stimulate Jason to interactive play in which the latter will openly express his aggression and roughness. He also wants to symbolize the male father figure and attract a part of Mary's revulsion of macho men toward himself.

It will be observed that the therapist's actual moves have more facets and purposes than preplanned. This is characteristic of the actual practice of family play therapy.

Mary continues to ignore Jason and the therapist. Carla says, "Mommy! Look!"

and shows Mary her smiling face in the mirror. Mary comes very close to her, looks with her into the mirror and smiles. Mary says:

"Mirror, mirror on the wall,
Who's the most beautiful of them all?"

The therapist kneels down, with his face behind the mirror, and says in a hoarse voice:

"My queen! You are the most beautiful over here,
But Snow White is a thousand times more beautiful than you,
Even Batman, your obedient bodyguard, left you for her,
And now he is ready to fight against you."

These have been preparatory moves, designed to draw Mary and Jason to a make-believe fight. However, they may also be viewed as main moves. The bug-busters of *covert communication* and *symbolic coding* have been activated by these moves, to evoke in Mary and Jason tactic-related themes associated with their emotives and hugged programs for example, Jason's insubordination and men's treachery. [Explicating, focusing, providing stimuli.]

At this point Jason begins playing Batman. He spreads his wings and starts hovering around Mary, making barely audible screeching sounds.

Carla: Mommy, there are two Carlas! One here (pointing to herself) and one here (points to the mirror).
Therapist: Both are beautiful princesses. (An auxiliary move, to compensate Carla for being ignored.) Are there two queens too?
Carla: Yes.
Therapist: Are both of them good?
Carla: Yes.
Therapist: Are both of them strong?
Carla: Yes.
Therapist: And are there two Batmen, too?
Carla: Yes.
Therapist: Are both of them good and strong?
Carla: (Smiling uneasily) I don't know.
Therapist: (Addressing everybody) How can we find out?

Again, these moves have been preparatory, to provoke a make-believe battle, but also main moves. Under covert communication and symbolic coding, the therapist alluded to the mutual ambivalence inherent in Jason and Mary's emotives and interpersonal programs.

Nobody says anything.

Therapist: (Addressing Mary) Is Batman good or bad? Is he strong or weak?
Mary: (Thoughtfully) I don't know either.

Therapist: (Bombastically) Power Ranger will find out! I have a black belt in Karate, a black belt in Bushido, and a black belt in Kung Fu. I dare you to fight me, Batman!

He starts confronting Jason, mocking Karate movements [willy-nilly]. Jason, hesitantly, begins "fighting back." Both warm up. Jason pretends to kick the therapist's chest. The latter falls on the carpet.

Therapist: (Groans) This hurts. He is much more powerful than I thought.

Here the therapist used the bug-buster *owning and alienation* to introduce the information that Jason's power was not real. This was designed to weaken the impact of Mary's view of Jason as "a macho man," like Emilio.

Jason comes close to the therapist and starts hitting and kicking him, laughing. Although he touches the therapist's body, his movements are still controlled, make-believe ones.

Mary: I don't like this. Jason, stop it!
Therapist: (Still on the floor, groaning) Jason? Who is Jason? Thank you, my queen, for coming to my rescue. Listen to me, you can stop him any time you want. (The therapist is getting up, talking to Jason.) "This time you won. Next time I win."

The therapist holds Carla's hand and says, "Come with me." She follows him. He says, "I know a secret place where we can get what we need." He picks up two magicians' hats. He puts on one and put the other on Carla's head, saying, in a different voice. "I am in charge of this magic tricks storehouse and you are my assistant. Where's the queen?"

Mary comes closer to him. He hands over a torchlight to Carla and whispers to her. "Give it to the queen and tell her it's a magic beam which can make Batman stop fighting." Carla hands the torchlight over to Mary and whispers something in her ear.

These have been preparatory moves and auxiliary moves, for engaging Carla.

The therapist takes off the magician's hat and approaches Jason, saying: "Here I am again, Power Ranger. Come on Batman! Make my day! Fight me!" [willy-nilly.] Jason starts fighting him again. The therapist pretends falling on the floor again.

Therapist: Queen! Help me!
Mary: (After some confusion) O yes, the magic beam! (She lights the torch and directs at Jason.) (To Jason) Let's play as if you freeze when the magic beam hits you.

Jason freezes. Mary, Jason, and Carla laugh. The therapist joins them. Here the therapist used the bug-buster *possible worlds* to show Mary that Jason can be willing to be controlled. The property of *owning and alienation* made it possible for

Jason to be controlled, despite the clause in his program that prevents him from being coerced by Mary to control himself.

The therapist puts on the magician's hat and whispers to Carla: "Tell the queen that Batman is hypnotized now. He will repeat mechanically whatever you want him to say."

Mary: What shall I tell him?
Therapist: You can tell him, for instance, "I apologize for having preferred Snow White."
Mary: (To Jason, who still stands frozen) Say, "I apologize for having preferred Snow White."
Therapist: He is hypnotized. He will repeat your words mechanically.

Jason repeats these words mechanically.

Therapist: You are the most beautiful of them all.

Mary says these words and Jason repeats.

Therapist: I'll never leave you for anybody. (The cycle is repeated.)
Therapist: I'll always obey you and be your faithful bodyguard. (Cycle repeats.)
Therapist: You can hit him and kick him and curse him now. He is completely under your control.
Mary: Why, I don't want to do all these things to him; he is a good Batman!
Therapist: Okay! You can switch the magic beam off now.
Jason: (De-freezes; he cries) I did not mean any of the things that I said when I was hypnotized! I just pretended!
Therapist: Of course, this was a make-believe game!
Jason: And now I am going to show you who I really am! (He starts "lighting" the therapist again.)

Later in the session this whole sequence was repeated spontaneously. Some of the play ideas were elaborated on the players' own initiative. For example, Jason approached the magic tricks storehouse and asked the therapist for "an antibeam beam."

Therapist: Sorry, we've run out of them. But you don't need one. You can cause the beam to be switched off by itself, by saying the right words.

Jason ignores him. He searches the pile of toys on the carpet, until he finds a toy traffic light. He says: "When I'm pushing this button it's a red beam. Mommy, what are you waiting for?"

Mary: Waiting for what?
Jason: The magic beam! When the red light is on, the magic beam is turned on too, and when the green light is on, your magic beam is off!

Mary: But what should I do when it's an orange light?
Jason: Be ready to switch the magic beam off!

In this intervention the therapist activated the bug-busters *covert communication, possible worlds, symbolic coding, owning and alienation, basic duality,* and *emotional regulation* to regulate the level of hostility between Jason and Mary and to weaken some of the bugs in the dysfunctional program between them. Covert communication and symbolic coding rendered it possible for Jason to tell Mary, "I love you and I am willing to obey you, but you cannot coerce me." The same property enabled Mary to tell Jason, "If you love me and obey me there's no need for me to coerce you." A make-believe possible world was created in which Mary controlled Jason and he obeyed her willingly. The property of owning and alienation enables Mary and Jason to achieve this without forgoing their habitual communication pattern. Basic duality enabled them to observe both the superficial and deeper levels of their relationship at the same time. Emotional regulation gave them make-believe means for regulating the level of their mutual aggression and hostility.

Termination

Even if the therapy has an happy end, leave-taking is likely to involve some emotional difficulties. Jason's family suffered many losses, in particular the departure of a male figure. Mary, in particular, was likely to feel lonely and helpless again without the support offered by the therapy. These feelings were worked through by means of make-believe play in the termination sessions. Techniques employed were giving vent to these feelings in make-believe play, encouraging make-believe play, regression, and make-believe continuation of the therapy.

The following vignette provides an example of a termination session.

Mary and Jason slump in large pillows in different corners of the room. Carla is running about, restlessly. The therapist puts on the magician's hat. He takes hold of Carla's hand and says, "Help me with the blankets." He takes blankets from the cupboard and, with Carla's help, covers Mary, and then Jason, saying, "Let's tuck them up nicely. They should get a good rest, to gain strength for tomorrow. Tomorrow I'm not going to be here. I am going to other places to help other people with my magic tricks."

Carla: Are you going to take all the tricks with you?
Therapist: I can leave some with you here if you promise to take good care of them and use them properly.
Carla: (Excitedly) I promise.
Therapist: (To Jason) What about you?
Jason: What about me?
Therapist: Shall I leave some of my magic tricks with you?
Jason: I don't need them.
Therapist: You can throw them away and make up your own magic tricks. They will be even better than mine. Mine are quite old.

Therapist: (Addressing Mary) What about you?

Mary: I'm too tired to think.

Therapist: Have a good rest. (He fills a bowl with water and puts it by her side.) After you've rested enough, you can drink some of this magic water. It will give you strength. Now people, I'm going to disappear into thin air. Take good care of yourself. I'm going to be back in five years, to see that everything is all right with you. (Wraps himself with a sheet of cloth and rushes away, out of the room.)

Mary, Jason, and Carla, quite surprised, get up and go out into the corridor to look for him. Within a few seconds, he rushes back into the playroom, still wrapped with his cloth, and says, "I'm back! The five years has passed like wind! Jason, You are twelve years old now. Big boy! Carla, you're eight and a half! Big girl! Mary! You don't look a bit older than five years ago. In fact you look better! You must have had a very good life!"

Mary: (Smiling) Yes, I have a good life! I finished business school and I have my own little business now, and I have two wonderful kids!

Therapist: And what about you, Jason? I would not have recognized you if I met you in the street. You are such a fine young man!

Jason: Yes, I am good at school and I help my mom a lot and I have a black belt in karate!

Therapist: Gee! That's great. Have you used any of my magic tricks?

Jason: No, I've made up my own!

Therapist: Carla! How are you!

Carla: I am still playing with your magic tricks and I told all my friends how to use them, and they never pick at me and always want to play with me!

Therapist: Great! I see that you are all doing very well. I'll come back for another visit in another five years.

He rushes out of the room.

EXPECTED OUTCOME

Interventions such as just described are supposed to be transferred from the make-believe world to the world of the family's reality, and they generalize to many non-play situations. For example, in the previous session Jason went through the play experiences of controlling the magic beam by saying the right words. In all likelihood this was a powerful cognitive-emotive insight experience, which had impact on both his own inner reality and the reality of his relationship with his mother. The cumulative effect of many such experiences, induced in the family members in accordance with the overall general therapeutic strategy, is expected to bring about the removal of the major bugs in the family programs and help the family members develop better emotional regulation mechanisms. If this is achieved, the problems for which the family was referred to therapy are likely to fade away.

CONCLUSION

In strategic family play therapy, the therapist takes the family to a journey in Wonderland. It is a weird place, very different from their own world, and yet strangely familiar. They chance upon the most wonderful places, wild jungles, unexplored planets, dreamlike cities. They meet people of the past and of the future, unknown creatures and supernatural beings. They themselves can be transformed into any of these, whenever they feel like it. They can go through any adventure contrived by their imagination, and their emotions bounce up and down like a rubber ball. Big black bugs crawl among them, but they have only to play to bust them. They come back from this journey better people. And if they want to go back there, they can, on their own. They do not need the therapist to take them there.

REFERENCES

Ariel, S. (1984). Locutions and illocutions in make-believe play. *Journal of Pragmatics, 8,* 221–240.

Ariel, S. (1986). *Componential analysis of children's play.* Jerusalem, Israel: The Hebrew University.

Ariel, S. (1987). An information-processing theory of family dysfunction. *Psychotherapy, 24,* 477–495.

Ariel, S. (1992). Semiotic analysis of children's play: A method for investigating social development. *Merrill-Palmer Quarterly, 38,* 119–138.

Ariel, S. (1994). *Strategic family play therapy* (2nd ed.). Chichester: Wiley.

Ariel, S. (in press). *Culturally competent family therapy.* New York: Wiley.

Ariel, S., Carel, C., & Tyano, Sh. (1984). A formal explication of the concept of family homeostasis. *Journal of Marital and Family Therapy, 4,* 337–349.

Ariel, S., Carel, C., & Tyano, Sh. (1985). Make-believe play techniques in family therapy. *Journal of Marital and Family Therapy, 11,* 47–60.

Coyne, J.C. (1994). Possible contributions of "cognitive science" to the integration of psychotherapy. *Journal of Psychotherapy Integration, 4,* 401–416.

Curry, N., & Arnaud, S. (1974). Cognitive implications in children's spontaneous role play. *Theory into Practice, 13,* 173–277.

Erikson, E. (1940). Studies in the interpretation of play. *Genetic Psychology Monographs, 22,* 557–671.

Fein, G. (1989). Mind, meaning and affect: Proposals for a theory of pretense. *Developmental Review, 9,* 345–363.

Freud, S. (1917). *Introductory lectures on psychoanalysis.* Standard Edition of the Complete Psychological Works of Sigmund Freud. London: Hogarth Press.

Freud, S. (1922). *Beyond the pleasure principle.* London: International Universities Press.

Garvey, C., & Kramer, T.L. (1989). The language of social pretend play. *Developmental Review, 9,* 364–382.

Gurman, A.S., & Kniskern, D.P. (Eds). (1981). *Handbook of family therapy*. New York: Brunner/Mazel.

Hintikka, K.J. (1969). *Models for modalities*. Dordrecht: D. Reidel.

Izard, C.E. (1978). *Human emotions*. New York: Plenum.

Klein, M. (1960). *The psychoanalysis of children*. New York: Grove Press.

Klinger, E. (1971). *Structure and functions of fantasy*. New York: Wiley.

McGoldrick, M., Pearce, J., & Giordano, J. (Eds). (1982). *Ethnicity and family therapy*. New York: Guilford.

Morris, Ch. (1971). *Writings on the general theory of signs*. The Hague: Mouton.

Piaget, J. (1962). *Play, dreams and imitation in childhood*. New York: Norton.

Sears, D.S. (1951). Doll-play aggression in normal young children. *Psychological Monographs, 65*, 6.

Singer, J.L. (1973). *The child's world of make-believe*. New York: Academic Press.

Smilansky, S. (1968). *The effects of sociodramatic play on disadvantaged pre-school children*. New York: Wiley.

Sutton-Smith, B. (1984). *The masks of play*. New York: Leisure Press.

Western, D. (1994). Implications of cognitive science for psychotherapy: Promises and limitations. *Journal of Psychotherapy Integration, 4*, 387–399.

Yawkley, T.D. (1986). Creative dialogue through sociodramatic play and its uses. *Journal of Creative Behavior, 20*, 52–60.

Author Index

Subject Index